Make the Grade.
Your Atomic Dog Online Edition.

The Atomic Dog Online Edition includes proven study tools that expand and enhance key concepts in your text. Reinforce and review the information you absolutely 'need to know' with features like:

- **Review Quizzes**
- Key term Assessments
- Interactive Animations and Simulations
- Notes and Information from Your Instructor
- Pop-up Glossary Terms
- A Full Text Search Engine

Ensure that you 'make the grade'. Follow your lectures, complete assignments, and take advantage of all your available study resources like the Atomic Dog Online Edition.

How to Access Your Online Edition

If you purchased this text directly from Atomic Dog ....
Visit atomicdog.com and enter your email address and password in the login box at the top-right corner of the page.

If you purchased this text NEW from another source....
Visit our Students' Page on atomicdog.com and enter the **activation key located below** to register and access your Online Edition.

If you purchased this text USED from another source....
Using the Book Activation key below you can access the Online Edition at a discounted rate. Visit our Students' Page on atomicdog.com and enter the **Book Activation Key in** the field provided to register and gain access to the Online Edition.

Be sure to download our *How to Use Your Online Edition* guide located on atomicdog.com to learn about additional features!

This key activates your online edition. Visit atomicdog.com to enter your Book Activation Key and start accessing your online resources. For more information, give us a call at (800) 310-5661 or send us an email at support@atomicdog.com

1756TXCX7

*Some online Editions do not contain all features.

Third Edition

Marketing Research

AN AID TO DECISION MAKING

Third Edition

Marketing Research

AN AID TO DECISION MAKING

Alan T. Shao
University of North Carolina, Charlotte

Kevin Zheng Zhou
University of Hong Kong

Australia • Canada • Mexico • Singapore • Spain • United Kingdom • United States

Marketing Research: An Aid to Decision Making, 3e
Alan T. Shao ~ Kevin Zheng Zhou

Executive Editors:
Michele Baird, Maureen Staudt, and Michael Stranz

Marketing Manager:
Mikka Baker

Managing Editor:
Kendra Leonard

Marketing Coordinators:
Lindsay Annett and Sara Mercurio

Production/Manufacturing Manager:
Donna M. Brown

Production Editorial Manager:
Dan Plofchan

Rights and Permissions Specialists:
Kalina Hintz and Bahman Naraghi

Custom Production Editor:
K.A. Espy

Cover Image:
© Getty

The Adaptable Courseware Program consists of products and additions to existing Thomson products that are produced from camera-ready copy. Peer review, class testing, and accuracy are primarily the responsibility of the author(s).

Marketing Research: An Aid to Decision Making / Shao ~ Zhou – Third Edition

Book ISBN
ISBN-13: 978-1-592-60287-2
ISBN-10: 1-592-60287-8
Package ISBN
ISBN-13: 978-1-592-60288-9
ISBN-10: 1-592-60288-6

Library of Congress Control Number:
2006929384

International Divisions List

Asia (Including India):
Thomson Learning
(a division of Thomson Asia Pte Ltd)
5 Shenton Way #01-01
UIC Building
Singapore 068808
Tel: (65) 6410-1200
Fax: (65) 6410-1208

Australia/New Zealand:
Thomson Learning Australia
102 Dodds Street
Southbank, Victoria 3006
Australia

Latin America:
Thomson Learning
Seneca 53
Colonia Polano
11560 Mexico, D.F., Mexico
Tel (525) 281-2906
Fax (525) 281-2656

Canada:
Thomson Nelson
1120 Birchmount Road
Toronto, Ontario
Canada M1K 5G4
Tel (416) 752-9100
Fax (416) 752-8102

UK/Europe/Middle East/Africa:
Thomson Learning
High Holborn House
50-51 Bedford Row
London, WC1R 4L$
United Kingdom
Tel 44 (020) 7067-2500
Fax 44 (020) 7067-2600

Spain (Includes Portugal):
Thomson Paraninfo
Calle Magallanes 25
28015 Madrid
España
Tel 34 (0)91 446-3350
Fax 34 (0)91 445-621

This book is lovingly dedicated to my father, Dr. Stephen P. Shao. His devotion to family and commitment to education helped pave the path for my future.

—Alan T. Shao

This book is dedicated to my lovely wife, Julie and our baby, Erin.

—Kevin Zheng Zhou

Brief Contents

Contents

Part **Three**   Research Implementation   287

Preface

We'd like to express our sincere gratitude for your interest in *Marketing Research: An Aid to Decision Making,* third edition. We are confident that the changes we have made in this edition will dramatically improve students' knowledge of marketing research because practitioners, academicians, and past users of the text recommended many of the changes and new topics that we incorporated into this edition. The fact is, there have been numerous changes in the research industry and global marketplace that warrant special attention. When you consider how research organizations are consolidating, economies are growing worldwide, and competition is intensifying, there is a resounding plea for improved knowledge by decision-makers. Thus, let us review some of the ways we've addressed this request to help users make informed decisions.

Overall Highlights

We will briefly review some of the improvements that have been made in this third edition. First, we decided that two minds are better than one, and so a coauthor was added to our writing team. Professor Kevin Zhou is a highly successful scholar who has taught marketing research for several years, both at the undergraduate and graduate levels. Since obtaining his doctorate from Virginia Polytechnic Institute (Virginia Tech), he has taught at Virginia Tech and The University of Hong Kong and has published in many prestigious journals, including *Journal of Marketing, Journal of International Business Studies, Journal of Business Research,* and *International Journal of Research in Marketing.* His knowledge and fresh ideas have been an integral part of producing this new edition.

A second change is the ordering and numbers of chapters. We decided that nineteen chapters, as appeared in previous editions, was a bit too long, so we consolidated some of the content and agreed on eighteen chapters as the ideal number for either semester or quarter terms. Reviewers recommended that we reorganize and rename some of the chapters to better suit the course content, and we feel the changes

we've made create a better flow of knowledge and ensure that each chapter builds on the content of the previous one. You'll notice that we offer more material about information technology and online research in Chapter 3 to reflect today's technology-equipped students. You'll further notice how we simplified the statistical explanations in the latter chapters. We are confident you'll like the new and improved organization of the chapters. We'll discuss some of these changes in more detail a bit later.

Another notable change in the text is the Cheerwine case study woven throughout the chapters. We feel that this "real world" example of marketing research will permit students to put themselves into the shoes and mindset of consultants. We want to thank Mark Ritchie, president of Carolina Beverage Corporation, for allowing us to use his superb soft drink product as our case study.

A fourth change to the text is that we have updated many of the examples to make the text more relevant in today's global business arena. You'll see examples from all over the world to reflect the reality that today's businesspeople do not limit themselves to their own countries' borders. In the subsequent discussion, we will highlight these and many more changes we've made to develop what we believe is the most user-friendly—to both students and instructors—marketing research book on the market today.

Decision-Making Orientation

The primary reason we conduct market research is to aid decision makers. Think about it . . . the better the research, the less risk there is; the less risk there is, the less uncertainty; and the less uncertainty, the better decisions we can make. We have taken managers' needs into consideration because we want our text users to provide the best possible information to managers. It is important to remember that marketing research is not just about data, but rather about how to use information to aid decision makers.

As a pedagogical tool, we put students in the role of business consultants and guide them to perform market research to aid decision makers. We use numerous real-life examples to illustrate how to define decision-making problems and corresponding research objectives, how to design research to accomplish the research objectives, and how to use research findings to solve decision-making problems.

Logical Topics Covered

We realize that students must be the focus of this text. To keep their attention and address their concerns and questions, we conducted our own survey to find out what students wanted to know, and then we created the text by combining these findings with what we felt they needed to know. Consider these logical questions covered in the first chapter: Why study marketing research? Who does marketing research? Who uses marketing research? Do marketing researchers have an ethical responsibility? What job opportunities exist in marketing research? A similar theme permeates the remaining chapters.

Integrated Real-Life Case

To develop the student's ability to be a consultant, we integrate a real-life consulting project—using a popular southern soft drink, Cheerwine—throughout the entire text. We introduce the case in Chapter 2 to help students identify decision problems and research objectives. The students are then asked to collect qualitative information in Chapter 5 and to revise the questionnaire designed especially for this case in Chapter 8. Chapter 13 provides a dataset for students to run data analysis and draw recommendations for decision making based on research findings.

Extensive Global Coverage

While the world isn't flat, it is much easier than ever before for us to travel and learn about business outside of our domestic boundaries. While the first two editions concentrated heavily on international businesses, we've stepped up our efforts to ensure that even more parts of the world are represented. The fact is, as per capita increases worldwide and industries look to expand their efforts, the need for accurate market research will continue to grow, so you'll see a plethora of examples and references that are relevant to all parts of our universe.

On The Lighter Side

We shouldn't take life too seriously. This is certainly the case with market research. We've highlighted some funny surveys and findings that we know students will enjoy reading. In fact, most students will relate to many of the products and situations mentioned in these stories.

Online Research Coverage

The trend today is for research to be conducted online. It makes sense financially and the reach to respondents is wider. Let's face it: online researchers can survey one, one thousand, or one million people for marginal cost differences. This is not the case with mail surveys, personal interviews, and telephone interviews. Our students need to understand these new trends and know how to utilize online research tools.

Integration of Information Technology

Chapter 3 is devoted to a discussion of integrating information technology. In addition, in each chapter, we integrate salient Internet topics, and the *Net Impact* feature at the end of every chapter tells how the Internet relates to topics covered in that chapter. The *Net Exercises* at the end of each chapter have students perform market research tasks using the Internet.

End-of-Chapter Practice Quizzes

Every chapter has a quiz that challenges students to recall what they have learned about important marketing topics that were covered in that chapter. These quizzes originated because students indicated to us that they like to get into a testing mindset before taking their actual tests.

Research Realities

To ensure that we continue our tradition of incorporating the "real world" into our text, we have included several real facts and figures that demonstrate how market research is applied. These are informative and entertaining bits of information that will help students understand the challenges that are ahead of them after graduation.

Concept Comparisons Using Tables

How many times have you tried to explain something, only to be overshadowed by a simpler presentation of the information? We feel that a highly effective way to present information is in tabular form. This format permits us to make side-by-side comparisons and lay out the data in an organized manner. Students have repeatedly mentioned to us the importance of tables to explain concepts, so we've responded to these requests by creating tables that are user-friendly.

Chapter Vignettes

Each chapter begins with a vignette. These short stories that students can relate to are intended to capture their attention so that they will enter each chapter with interest. You'll read stories relating to golf, shopping, McDonald's, religion, advertising, opinion polls, names, and even branding at a gambling resort.

Reality Screens

It's one thing to describe something; it's another thing to show it. We prefer the latter. That is why we've incorporated numerous real pictures and computer screen dumps to demonstrate particular topics. The less we can leave to the imagination, the better.

Relevant Cases

What good are cases in a text if students can't relate to the situations presented in them? We believe that students will learn more effectively when they can relate to products, services, and situations presented in each case. We have made a concerted effort to write realistic cases with which students can associate.

Guidance for Students Using SPSS Software

For students using SPSS software, we incorporated step-by-step instructions throughout the text on how to apply and analyze output so that students can effectively analyze the information that is gathered.

Decision Time!

The situations described in the Decision Time! features, occurring near the end of each chapter, are designed to put students into managerial situations. Our goal is to challenge students by getting them to share with each other how they would solve specific research problems.

Organization

The organization of the text has been streamlined. It contains the following three parts:

Part 1: An Overview of Marketing Research (Chapters 1 and 2). This section introduces students to some of the most basic concepts in marketing research. It raises some initial questions students often ask the first couple of days in class and explains the marketing research process with a focus on decision problem identification.

Part 2: Research Design (Chapters 3 through 11). The section begins with an entire chapter that addresses the increasing role of information technology and the Internet in marketing research. It progresses by discussing various research designs such as secondary data research and primary data collection, as well as information collection techniques such as measurement, survey design, and sampling. Part 2 concludes with a discussion about the major concerns researchers have when conducting market research in different countries.

Part 3: Research Implementation (Chapters 12 through 18). This part shows students how to prepare data for analysis, run meaningful statistical tests, draw conclusions from the results, and make recommendations to aid decision makers. We provide an easy-to-follow, step-by-step approach for students to run the analysis, and our focus is on how to use the results from the analysis to draw recommendations that help managers make better decisions.

Online and in Print

Marketing Research: An Aid to Decision Making is available online as well as in print. The online version demonstrates how the interactive media components of the text enhance presentation and understand. For example,

- Animated illustrations help clarify concepts and bring them to life.
- Chapter quizzes test students' knowledge of various topics and provide immediate feedback.
- Clickable glossary terms provide immediate definitions of key concepts.
- References and footnotes "pop up" with a click.
- Highlighting capabilities allow students to emphasize main ideas. They can also add personal notes in the margin.
- The search function allows students to quickly locate discussions of specific topics throughout the text.
- An interactive study guide at the end of each chapter provides tools for learning, such interactive keyterm matching and the ability to review customized content in one place.

Students may choose to use just the online version of the text or both the online and print versions together. This gives them the flexibility to choose which combination or resources works best for them. To assist those who use the online and print version together, the primary heads and subheads in each chapter are numbered the same. For example, the first primary head in Chapter 1 is labeled 1-1, the second primary head in this chapter is labeled 1-2, and so on. The subheads build from the designation of their corresponding primary head: 1-1a, 1-1b, etc. This numbering system is designed to make moving between the online and print versions as seamless as possible.

Finally, next to a number of figures and exhibits in the print version of the text, you will see an icon similar to those below. This icon indicates that this figure or exhibit in the Online Edition is interactive in a way that applies, illustrates, or reinforces the concept.

Supplements

Atomic Dog is pleased to offer a robust suite of supplemental materials for instructors using its textbooks. These ancillaries include a Test Bank, PowerPoint slides, and an Instructors' Manual.

The Test Bank for this book includes multiple-choice questions in a wide range of difficulty levels for each chapter. The Test Bank offers not only the correct answer for each question, but also a rationale or explanation for the correct answer and a reference—the location in the chapter where materials addressing the question content can be found. This Test Bank comes with ExamViewPro software for easily creating customized or multiple versions of a test, and includes the option of editing or adding to the existing question bank.

A full set of PowerPoint Slides is available for this text. This is designed to provide instructors with comprehensive visual aids for each chapter in the book. These slides include outlines of each chapter, highlighting important terms, concepts, and discussion points.

The Instructor's Manual for this book offers suggested syllabi for 10 and 14 week terms; lecture outlines and notes; in-class and take-home assignments; recommendations for multi-media resources such as films and websites; and long and short essay questions and their answers, appropriate for use on tests.

About Atomic Dog

Atomic Dog is faithfully dedicated to meeting the needs of today's faculty and students, offering a unique and clear alternative to the traditional textbook. Breaking down textbooks and study tools into their basic 'atomic parts' we were able to recombine them and utilize rich digital media to create a "new breed" of textbook.

This blend of online content, interactive multimedia, and print creates unprecedented adaptability to meet different educational settings and individual learning styles. As part of Thomson Custom Solutions <http://www.thomsoncustom.com/>, we offer even greater flexibility and resources in creating a learning solution tailor-fit to your course.

Atomic Dog is loyally dedicated to our customers and our environment, adhering to three key tenets:

Focus on Essential & Quality Content: We are proud to work with our authors to deliver you a high-quality textbook at a lower cost. We focus on the essential information and resources students need and present them in an efficient but student friendly format.

Value and Choice for Students: Our products are a great value and provide students more choices in 'what and how' they buy-often at a savings of 30–40% versus traditional textbooks. Students who chose the online edition may see even greater savings compared to a print textbook. Faculty play an important and willing roll-working with us to keep costs low for their students by evaluating texts online and supplementary material.

Reducing Our Environmental 'Paw-Print': Atomic Dog is working to reduce its impact on our environment in several ways. Our textbooks and marketing materials are printed on recycled paper and we will continue to explore environmentally friendly methods. We encourage faculty to review text materials online instead of requesting a print review copy. Students who buy the online version do their part by going 'paperless' and eliminating the need for additional packaging or shipping. Atomic Dog will continue to explore new ways that we can reduce our 'paw print' in the environment and hope you will join us in these efforts.

Atomic Dog is dedicated to faithfully serving the needs of faculty and students-providing a learning tool that helps make the connection. We know that after you try our texts that Atomic Dog—like a great dog—becomes your faithful companion.

Acknowledgments

We would like to thank the following reviewers, whose valuable comments have contributed to this text.

Dena Cox
Indiana University

Edward Golden
Central Washington University

Ronald E. Goldsmith
Florida State University

Tim Graeff
Middle Tennessee State University

James E. Hansz
Lehigh University

Timothy P. Hartman
Ohio University

Michael R. Hyman
New Mexico State University

Felicia G. Lassk
Northeastern University

Chris Moberg
Ohio University

Ira Perelle
Mercy College (Dobbs Ferry, NY)

Philip Trocchia
Kansas State University

Robert J. Van Dellen
Baker College of Cadillac

We have developed a textbook that we are extremely proud to offer to faculty in hopes that they will use it to educate students throughout the world. While the process was a lengthy one, it could not have been completed so efficiently without the patience, support, and expertise of several individuals. Alan wishes to thank his wife (Carol) and children (Janine, Victoria, and Alan II) for their patience and support during the development of the text. Kevin is thankful to his wife (Julie Juan Li) and daughter (Erin) for the same reasons.

We would especially like to thank the world-class teams at Atomic Dog and Thomson Custom Solutions. They are experts in the publishing industry and they could not have been more helpful throughout the process. In particular, we would like to thank Steve Scoble, for signing us to this project and making us feel like a member of the Atomic Dog team from the very beginning. We also appreciate the expertise of Christine Abshire, who did a fantastic job in making sure that the project moved along smoothly. Her guidance was invaluable to the success of this text. Mary Monner, Senior Production Coordinator, effectively steered us through the varied stages of production and made it easy for us to ultimately create a product that is full of innovations and easy to understand. Victoria Putman also did an excellent job in helping us throughout the production process. Nikki Herbst, Copy Editor, was remarkable with her vast copy editing knowledge. She was sheer genius with innovative ideas and in improving the wording used throughout the text. The team at Thomson Custom Solutions; Dreis vanLanduyt, Kendra Leonard, Laureen Ranz, Mikka Baker, Dan Plofchan, Tina Espy and Peg Hagar; effectively managed the transition of the title form one company to another—successfully delivering the title on time. There are too many other team members to thank, but we'd like to express our gratitude to everyone at both companies for their professional and knowledgeable assistance.

About the Authors

Alan T. Shao is the North Carolina Ports Professor of Marketing and International Business and serves as the Associate Dean for International Programs at the University of North Carolina at Charlotte. Dr. Shao received his doctorate in marketing, with a minor in statistics, from the University of Alabama (Tuscaloosa) in 1989. He has published more than forty refereed articles in many of the leading marketing and international marketing journals, as well as numerous proceedings at regional, national and international conferences.

Dr. Shao has lectured extensively throughout East Asia and Europe and has served as Executive Research Director at Ashton Brand Group and CEO of Apex Global Group. As an active business consultant, he has conducted marketing research throughout the United States, Asia, and Europe for multinational advertising agencies, financial institutions, sports franchises, technology companies, legal firms, and consumer goods manufacturers. Some of the organizations he has provided marketing research services to include Coca-Cola, Nissan, Wachovia Corporation, Hendrick Motor Sports (NASCAR), Carolina Panthers (NFL), Decision One Mortgage, Wray Ward Laseter Advertising Agency, Tennaro Marketing Communications, Unifi Technology, Aladdin Knowledge Systems, Fuel Pizza, Murata Wiedemann, Physician Network Management, CEM Corporation, Barnhardt Manufacturing Company, Carolina Beverage Corporation, Garfinkel Immigration Law Firm, Foley & Lardner Law Firm, and Holly Ridge Foods.

Dr. Shao is an active member of select organizations, including the *American Marketing Association* and the *Academy of International Business.* He is President of the North Carolina World Trade Association statewide and serves on the Board of Directors of the North Carolina World Trade Association (Charlotte chapter and statewide), NC District Export Council, and other state organizations.

Dr. Shao resides in Charlotte, North Carolina with his wife, Carol, and children, Janine (18), Victoria (16) and Alan II (11). For more detail about his background and scholarly activities, visit http://www.belkcollege.uncc.edu/atshao.

Kevin Zheng Zhou is Assistant Professor of Marketing at the School of Business, the University of Hong Kong. Dr. Zhou received a B.E. (with honors) in Automatic Control and an M.S. in Economics and Management at Tsinghua University, and a Ph.D. specializing in Marketing and Strategy from Virginia Polytechnic Institute and State University.

Dr. Zhou's professional interests include new product development and product entry strategies, market orientation and strategic orientation, relationship marketing, and strategic issues in emerging economies. He has published papers in leading marketing journals, including *Journal of Marketing, Journal of International Business Studies, International Journal of Research in Marketing, Journal of Business Research, Psychology and Marketing*, among others. He has presented his work at prestigious conferences such as American Marketing Association, Association for Consumer Research, Academy of Management, Strategic Management Society, etc.

Dr. Zhou has taught Marketing Research, Principles of Marketing, and International Marketing at Virginia Tech and The University of Hong Kong. He has also taught Business Data Analysis for MBA programs at HKU and Marketing Research for International MBA programs in Shanghai. He has rich consulting experiences working with companies such as Federal Pharmaceutical, 3M, Hennessy, and TCH.

Dr. Zhou lives in Hong Kong with his wife, Julie, and daughter, Erin. For more detail about him, please visit http://www.fbe.hku.hk/people/faculty.asp?doc=kz.zhou.

An Overview of Marketing Research

Marketing Research: Initial Questions

Chapter One

Source: © 2007 JupiterImages Corporation.

Key Terms

applied research   (p. 8)
basic research   (p. 7)
business ethics   (p. 18)
Council of American Survey Research Organizations (CASRO)   (p. 21)
decision-making process   (p. 15)
ethics   (p. 18)
European Society for Opinion and Marketing Research (ESOMAR)   (p. 21)

marketing   (p. 4)
marketing concept   (p. 4)
marketing management   (p. 15)
marketing research   (p. 5)
research   (p. 7)
social responsibility   (p. 18)

Learning Objectives

After studying this chapter, you will be able to:

- Define *marketing research* and speak intelligently about its relevance to marketing management.
- Describe how marketing research relates to the marketing concept.
- Tell why you should study marketing research.
- Explain who conducts marketing research.

- Name two classifications of research and distinguish between them.
- Explain who uses marketing research.
- Discuss the ethical responsibility of marketing researchers to society.
- Talk about job opportunities in marketing research.

GET THIS

Is Radio Advertising Effective?

It's always on in our cars. We listen to it at home. It permeates the places we shop. And it even shows up at the beaches. Our radio is an important part of our culture. The station that we regularly listen to is a reflection of ourselves. Advertisers spend thousands, and in some cases millions, of dollars each year to spread their messages across radio airwaves. One of the best-known groups to radio advertisers is the Arbitron Company. This international media research firm located in Columbia, Maryland, provides information services that are used to develop the local marketing strategies of the electronic media and of their advertisers and agencies. It employs 530 full-time employees; its executive offices are located in New York City. Arbitron has three core businesses: measuring radio audiences in local markets throughout the United States; surveying the retail, media, and product patterns of local market consumers; and providing survey research consulting and methodological services to the cable, telecommunications, direct broadcast satellite, online, and new media industries.

In March 2005, Arbitron conducted telephone interviews with 1,003 radio listeners from its diary keepers, who were drawn to represent a national overview of radio listeners in continuously measured markets. Listeners' responses were compared with data obtained from the Arbitron radio ratings diary, including format preferences and time spent listening to radio overall and by location. The results from this survey were tracked against the previous survey, conducted in June 1999, in which 1,071 Arbitron radio diary keepers were interviewed. The following are some of the most significant findings of the study:

- Most Americans support the basic premise of commercial radio. More than 80% state that listening to commercials is a reasonable price to pay for free programming on the radio.

- The majority of respondents stated that television has more commercials than radio and that the television commercials are more intrusive than are radio commercials. Consumers are also more likely to pay closer attention to radio commercials than to television commercials.

- A majority of listeners responded that they never turn the dial away from radio commercials while listening to the radio at work or at home. Even when they are in their car, where it's much easier to switch stations, only one-third of listeners say they "always" or "usually" change stations during a commercial. Only a few of the radio listeners indicated that they often switch the station immediately after hearing the beginning of a commercial break—6% of those listening at work stated that they switch immediately, 11% said they do so at home, and 28% said they switch when in the car.

- A huge majority of listeners find radio commercials to be informative. Although many so-called experts in the radio industry assume that listeners despise the thought of commercials, the opposite was found to be the case.

- Radio listeners responded that the quality of the commercial is as important a consideration as the quantity of the commercials. Younger listeners appear to be more irritated by numbers of commercials, while older listeners are more bothered by "annoying" ads. A standardized spot load strategy where all listeners hear the same ad is likely not the best strategy for every radio station. Reactions to the quantity and the quality of commercials vary by such concerns as age, gender, and format preference.

- It appears that age is an important criterion when considering the sound of the commercials. Researchers have found that the younger the listener, the louder are the complaints about stations playing too many commercials. Also, 12- to 24-year-olds are much more likely to react positively to stations that minimize the number of commercials they play. Lastly, more than a third of 12- to 24-year-old listeners have noticed radio stations playing fewer commercials and taking shorter breaks.

- Listeners stated that they often want more frequent, shorter commercial breaks instead of long blocks of programming with long blocks of commercials. For example, when asked how to distribute 12 commercials in an hour, either two blocks of six commercials per hour or three blocks of four commercials per hour, they clearly wanted three blocks of four commercials.

Source: Bill Rose and Joe Lenski, "Spot load study 2005: Managing radio commercial inventories for advertisers and listeners," (http://www.arbitron.com/radio_stations/home.htm), May 5, 2005, pp. 2–3.

Now Ask Yourself

- Who is most likely to use the results of this study?

- How could radio advertisers draw managerial implications from these research findings?

- What conclusions could radio stations draw based on these research findings?

The Arbitron study that examined the perceptions of radio listeners illustrates the power of effective marketing research. The company's study revealed some positives and negatives of radio advertising, as perceived by customers. Besides the "Now Ask Yourself" questions posed at the end of the vignette, some questions students of marketing research may have regarding the Arbitron study are: "How could Arbitron interpret these research findings and make recommendations to radio stations and advertisers?" and "How can I get a job at Arbitron or some other marketing research agency?" These types of inquiries will be addressed throughout this text.

It is obvious that for Arbitron to survey the radio market effectively, its knowledge of research techniques had to be exceptional. For students of marketing research, this is exactly our goal. We must possess sufficient knowledge of research techniques so that we can efficiently gather and judiciously use marketing information to solve specific marketing-related, decision-making problems.

We therefore begin with a discussion of some basic questions: (1) Why study marketing research? (2) Who does marketing research? (3) Who uses marketing research? (4) Do marketing researchers have an ethical responsibility? and finally (5) What job opportunities exist in marketing research? In subsequent chapters we will build on these concepts, but for now let's focus on these basics.

1-1 Why Study Marketing Research?

Have you ever wondered how television stations know which programs are the most popular and which ones they should cancel? Have you wondered how radio stations know which deejays are the most listened to during the day? Ever asked yourself how businesses know if they need to change their products' features or perhaps offer something new?

The key to most successful business endeavors is to never lose sight of their customers' needs. It is the customer who makes the ultimate decision about whether to watch a particular television program, listen to a certain radio station, or purchase a specific product, no matter what advertising, sales promotion, personal selling, and public relations gimmicks they encounter. It makes complete business sense, therefore, for companies to stay in close touch with consumers' needs and wants.

Marketing is a tool used by managers to satisfy consumer desires. It is defined by the American Marketing Association as: "An organizational function and a set of processes for creating, communicating, and delivering value to customers and for managing customer relationships in ways that benefit the organization and its stakeholders."[1] Implicit in this definition is the notion that the marketing manager, in order to motivate exchanges between businesses and consumers, must be a very capable manipulator of many variables. The **marketing concept** is a management philosophy holding that companies should first determine the wants and needs of

marketing The process of planning and executing the conception, pricing, promotion, and distribution of ideas, goods, and services to create exchanges that satisfy individual and organizational objectives.

marketing concept Management philosophy in which the wants and needs of target markets are determined before the product is created.

Source: © 2007 JupiterImages Corporation.

their target markets and only afterward create products that satisfy those desires. The extent to which organizations effectively satisfy consumer desires better than their competitors do significantly determines the degree of success in meeting organizational objectives. The marketing concept therefore identifies the ultimate goal of an organization as that of creating customer satisfaction. Although profit generation is an important goal for profit-seeking organizations, it is not the only goal.

Doing the right marketing involves many instances of decision making, such as decisions about product development, the promotional campaign, distributor relationships, and pricing. To make the right decisions, companies must have accurate, relevant, and timely information. One critical information source is marketing research—research performed on markets helps companies make informed decisions to satisfy their customers.

Marketing research is the systematic and objective planning, gathering, recording, and analyzing of information to enhance the decision making of marketing managers. Marketing researchers must carefully collect and analyze information that will aid management decision making.

Many managers attempt to create customer satisfaction by learning as much as they can about their customers. The more managers know about their customers, the better they can satisfy their needs—hence the more important marketing research is to business today. Companies cannot sit idle while their competitors gather rich data on their target markets. For example, teens and students are popular targets of many goods and service providers, so it is important for businesses to understand them. Consider the following examples of research findings about you and your counterparts:

- A survey by JA Worldwide and the Allstate Foundation of 1,065 teens found that 11% of respondents to a non-scientific poll said they have credit cards, down from 13% in 2004. The survey revealed that almost 82% of teens who have credit cards responded that they pay them off monthly. The poll's credit-card ownership rate among teens was similar to that of Neil Prigmore's economics and U.S. government class at the Howard School of Academics and Technology. Only two of the 26 students on the class roll indicated they have credit cards, though most of the respondents indicated that they have debit cards.[2]

marketing research Systematic and objective planning, gathering, recording, and analyzing of information to enhance the decision making of marketing managers.

- A poll of students ages 15 to18, conducted for The Macerich Co. by August Partners, finds 37% were planning to go to their prom in 2005—10% of the girls and 33% of the boys. Those planning to go to the big event expected to spend an average of $379 apiece on prom-related expenses. The survey findings indicated that girls will spend $190 on the prom dress, plus $67 on shoes and accessories and another $59 on their "personal look." The boys plan to allocate most of their prom money to tickets, dinner, and transportation, but they'll still spend an average of $152 on their prom clothing. When the girls were queried about which style they liked the most in a prom dress, "sexy" got the most votes (27%). Also receiving double-digit votes were "glamorous" (19%), "elegant" (18%), and "flirty" (12%). To a much lesser extent were "romantic" (8%), "vintage" (7%), "sophisticated" (6%), "flashy" (2%), and "dramatic" (1%) chosen. As for the most popular color of dresses, the responses were pink (40% of respondents), black (18%), blue (12%), and metallics (10%). Most of the boys plan to wear a traditional tuxedo (44%) or a "vintage-look tuxedo" (14%). When asked to state which celebrity would mainly inspire their prom look, girls most often mentioned such celebrities as Jennifer Garner, Halle Berry, Jennifer Lopez, and Jessica Simpson. The boys' looks were motivated by Usher, Ashton Kutcher, Snoop Dogg, and Johnny Depp.[3]

- Sinomonitor, a Sino-Japanese independent market monitoring company, and China Youth Zeitgeist Cultural Co. Ltd., a domestic media firm specializing in university students, found that contemporary Chinese undergraduates have huge consumption power. The report is based on a sample survey conducted among 10,000 students of 126 colleges and universities in 34 major cities in 2004. The study, titled Consumption and Lifestyle Study on 21st Century Chinese Undergraduates, covers more than thirty kinds of products and services, as well as undergraduates' ideas about brands, fashion, media, and lifestyles. According to the survey, the average disposable income for current undergraduates is $594 per semester. Of students' total earnings, 44% is from family funds, 17.4% is from grants and loans, and 10% the students earn themselves. Tuition fees and expenses for articles related to their study account for a major portion of their expenses. According to the survey, the average amount for tuition and related study expenses throughout China is about $218 per term. The second-largest amount is for food, drinks, and cigarettes. Despite their basic living expenditures and study costs, current undergraduates spend a lot for Internet connections, telecommunications, after-course training, tourism, and some networking activities. Most students appear to be reasonable about their consumption. About 67% of those surveyed could make ends meet, and 22.4% of students have deposits in banks. But as the awareness of credit consumption becomes more widespread, and banks provide convenient services to university students, more and more students are borrowing money for their daily consumption. The study shows 10.5% often have loans from banks.[4]

Of course, consumers from all walks of life, not just college students, are focal points of marketing researchers. Consider these research results:

- Saatchi & Saatchi, a major multinational advertising agency, interviewed kids 8–15 years of age and found that if you want kids to get excited about products and brands, companies should consider an association with animals through events, promotion, sponsorships, curriculum programs, licensing, and spokes-characters. Whether puppies or pandas, the animals kids like the most have one thing in common: they're "cute." Kids also like animals that are curious, intelligent, and beautiful.[5]

- Football fans in Canada revealed in a Gallup poll that they preferred their own Canadian Football League (CFL) over the National Football League (NFL), but many of the fans aged 18 to 29 preferred NFL football games over CFL games.

In Toronto, where the CFL is headquartered, football fans also would rather watch the NFL.[6]

- McDonald's effort to take some of competitor Subway's business in Australia included offering a selection of low-fat sandwiches. Consumer surveys conducted there found that 80% considered it a positive move for McDonald's and approximately 70% of them felt the move was in line with the company's image. McDonald's spokesmen said the move was in line with the company's attempts to stay relevant and respond to changing customer tastes.[7]

- J.D. Power and Associates, the leading automotive consumer research group, found some interesting information in its first customer satisfaction survey of new-car buyers in the United Kingdom. The study measured car owners' attitudes toward both the quality of their vehicles and the service and care they receive from their dealers. The survey revealed that Toyota, the Japanese carmaker, achieved the highest level of overall customer satisfaction. Japanese producers dominated the top half of the rankings, with Mazda and Honda in second and third places, respectively. Daihatsu tied with European producer Mercedes-Benz for fourth place. Subaru placed seventh; Mitsubishi, tenth; and Nissan, thirteenth. The highest-ranked European producer was Mercedes-Benz at fourth, with Saab eighth, Skoda ninth, and BMW eleventh. The performance of the leading volume carmakers in the United Kingdom—Ford, Vauxhall (General Motors), and Rover—was below average, as was the performance of Peugeot, Citroen, Volkswagen, Renault, Audi, Fiat, Lada, Volvo, Seat, and Suzuki.[8]

The preceding examples show that marketing research is all about information—providing accurate, relevant, and timely (ART) information to aid decision making. Companies use research to help them improve their decision making, and most of the time, marketing research does increase a company's chances of making good choices.

1-2 Who Does Marketing Research?

All kinds of companies do marketing research. Any company that needs information about its markets may perform marketing research. But before we discuss the kinds of companies that perform marketing research, it is necessary to distinguish between two kinds of research: applied and basic.

1-2a Applied Research versus Basic Research

Broadly speaking, **research** is a systematic and objective investigation of a subject or problem to discover relevant information or principles. It may be classified as either basic or applied. **Basic research** is research that provides information about a phenomenon or tests a theory or hypothesis. It does not attempt to solve a specific marketing problem. Studies performed to increase understanding of a topic are basic research; thus its usefulness to the marketing manager is somewhat limited. For example, a study published in the *Journal of Marketing* noted that delivering consistently good service is difficult, as organizations have realized. Attempting to explain *why* this is so difficult, the authors collected data via personal and group interviews with managers and employees in various service organizations. They identified an extensive group of factors that potentially affect service quality, including the communication and control processes that organizations use to manage employees and the consequences of these processes (for example, problems with role ambiguity and role conflict). The intent of this study was not to solve a specific practical problem—that is, to design a consistently good service delivery system. Rather, the intent, in the words of the researchers, was to seek "insights by collecting observations about service quality from managers and employees."[9]

research Systematic and objective investigation of a subject or problem to discover relevant information or principles.

basic research Research undertaken to provide information about a phenomenon or to test a theory or hypothesis; it is not intended to solve a specific marketing problem.

Can We Pray . . . for Marketing Research?

Businesses like Starbucks wouldn't dream of opening a new store without first considering how many people in the neighborhood would be willing to pay $3.50 for a Grande half-caf latte. And the Gap wouldn't consider a new location by ignoring where the khaki-wearers are. So why shouldn't churches—which usually represent a larger capital investment than Starbucks or GAP—use marketing research? The fact is that some of them do. For example, Percept, a firm in Costa Mesa, California, offers demographic marketing to churches. They performed a study in a Washington, D.C., suburb and found that roughly 21% of families want their worship to be emotionally uplifting. Only 17% to 18% would rather hear electric guitars than a pipe organ on Sunday morning. And about 35% of the families in the area have no involvement with church.

In Hungary, a survey was implemented to examine how an individual's happiness is affected by religion and economic transition. It was revealed that religious involvement contributes positively to one's self-reported well-being. Taking into account respondents' personal characteristics, money is a less important source of happiness for the religious.

Another uplifting study was done in the south. Certainly there is no shortage of churches in North Carolina, part of the famed Bible Belt. In Charlotte, the Mecklenburg Community Church wanted to find out what the public wanted from a church before they opened their doors. After deciding to focus their recruiting efforts on people who had no connections to any religious institution, the church was unsure what it would take to attract lost souls to a new church, so they hired a research firm. The researchers uncovered several common complaints of people without religious affiliations. The respondents perceived church to be boring, to always ask for money, and to conduct services not relevant to their daily lives.

Based on these findings, the Mecklenburg Community Church decided to take a new approach in their recruiting. They added modern music and skits, loosened the dress code, and had sermons that covered daily-life topics such as parenting and money management. They also sent out direct mail that said: "Given up on the church? We don't blame you. Lots of people have. They're fed up with boring sermons, ritual that doesn't mean anything, music that nobody you know likes, and preachers who seem to be more interested in your wallet than you. Church can be different. Give us a shot." The marketing-concept approach to saving souls has apparently worked. Sixteen months after the church first opened its doors, it had attracted nearly 400 members, 80% of whom did not have a church home before they attended this house of worship.

Sources: Orsolya Lelkes, "Tasting Freedom: Happiness, Religion and Economic Transition," *Journal of Economic Behavior & Organization* (February 2006), vol. 59, issue 2, pp. 173–194; Eric Felton, "Houses of worship: Data divining," *Wall Street Journal* (April 28, 2000): W17; Cyndee Miller, "Churches turn to research for help in saving new souls," *Marketing News* 28, no. 8 (April 11, 1994): 1–2.

---

applied research Research undertaken to provide information about specific problems to help managers improve their decision making.

Applied research, on the other hand, is problem-specific research, focused on helping managers resolve specific problems. Companies use applied research to address questions such as these:

- Should we increase the price of our laundry detergent from $3.00 to $3.50?
- Should we package our product in glass or in plastic containers?
- Should we standardize our product in global markets, or should we adapt it to cultural differences?
- Should we offer coupons to stimulate consumer demand for our product?
- Will our customers purchase chicken wings at our restaurant, where we have traditionally sold only hamburgers?

One example of applied research was undertaken by Coca-Cola to determine whether convenience store shoppers prefer fountain Cokes to bottled or canned Coke. The researchers found that thirst satisfaction is a priority among consumers visiting convenience stores with self-service gasoline pumps. These consumers buy a large-size fountain soda 85% of the time.[10]

Applied research can be conducted by almost any business, including nonprofit institutions such as churches, as illustrated in Research Realities 1-1.

1-2b Marketing Research Companies: A Brief History

The 50 largest U.S.-based research firms in 2004 generated $6.3 billion in revenue in the United States and nearly $13.3 billion worldwide. The annual revenue growth rate for

EXHIBIT 1-1	Top 25 U.S. Research Organizations, 2004–2005

U.S. rank 2005	2004	Organization	Headquarters	Web Site: WWW.	U.S. research revenue[1] ($, in millions)	Percent change from 2004[2]	Worldwide research revenue[1] ($, in millions)	Non-U.S. research revenue[1] ($, in millions)	Percent non-U.S. revenue	U.S. full-time employees
1	1	VNU NV	New York	vnu.com	$1,864.0	3.8%	$3,537.9	$1673.9	47.3%	11,211
2	2	IMS Health Inc.	Fairfield, Conn.	imshealth.com	634.3	7.1	1,754.8	1120.5	63.9	1,700
3	6	The Kantar Group	Fairfield, Conn.	kantargroup.com	439.2*	6.7*	1,237.2*	798*	64.5*	2,300*
4	3	Westat Inc.	Rockville, Md.	westat.com	420.4	5.7	420.4	—	—	1,835
5	5	Information Resources Inc.	Chicago	infores.com	409.0	2.9	625.0	216.0	34.6	1,596
6	4	TNS U.S.	New York	tns-global.com	379.5	−4.2	1,818.6	1439.1	79.1	2,252
7	—	GfK AG USA	Nuremberg, Germany	gfk.com	316.3	3.9	1,313.5	1009.2	76.8	1,028
-	15	*GfK Group USA*	*Nuremberg, Germany*	*gfk.com*	*109.0*	*6.6*	*—*	*—*	*—*	*—*
-	8	*NOP World US*	*New York*	*gfk.com*	*207.3*	*2.6*	*—*	*—*	*—*	*—*
8	7	Arbitron Inc.	New York	arbitron.com	297.6	3.8	310.0	12.4	4.0	919
9	9	Ipsos	New York	ipsos-na.com	226.2	11.2	893.7	667.5	74.6	679
10	10	Synovate	Chicago	synovate.com	216.5	11.0	601.5	385.0	64.0	838
11	13	Maritz Research	Fenton, Mo.	maritzresearch.com	164.2	22.5	207.1	42.9	20.7	415
12	11	Harris Interactive Inc.	Rochester, N.Y.	harrisinteractive.com	162.2	4.8	208.8	46.6	22.3	733
13	12	J.D. Power and Associates	Westlake Village, Calif.	jdpower.com	152.2*	14.0*	198.2*	46.0*	23.2*	630
14	14	The NPD Group Inc.	Port Washington, N.Y.	npd.com	128.3	14.6	161.1	32.6	20.2	700
15	16	Opinion Research Corp.	Princeton, N.J.	opinionresearch.com	94.2	3.0	150.6	56.4	37.5	550
16	17	Lieberman Research Worldwide	Los Angeles	lrwonline.com	65.8	−2.1	75.7	9.9	13.1	318
17	18	Abt Associates Inc.	Cambridge, Mass.	abtassociates.com	52.2	25.8	52.2	—	—	200
18	21	comScore Networks Inc.	Reston, Va.	comscore.com	44.9	19.7	50.5	5.6	11.1	277
19	19	Market Strategies Inc.	Livonia, Mich.	marketstrategies.com	43.0	13.5	44.5	1.5	3.4	175
20	—	MVL Group Inc.	Jupiter, Fla.	mvlgroup.com	38.7	10.6	38.7	—	—	106
21	20	Burke Inc.	Cincinnati	burke.com	37.1	NC	42.8	5.7	13.3	198
22	23	OTX	Los Angeles	otxresearch.com	33.2	11.4	33.2	—	—	134
23	26	Directions Research Inc.	Cincinnati	directionsresearch.com	33.1	21.3	33.1	—	—	115
24	23	Knowledge Networks Inc.	Menlo Park, Calif.	knowledgenetworks.com	31.4	5.4	31.4	—	—	180
25	22	MORPACE International Inc.	Farmington Hills, Mich.	morpace.com	29.3	−5.8	34.3	5.0	14.6	142

*Total revenues that include nonresearch activities for some companies are significantly higher. See individual company profiles for details.

Source: Jack Honomichl, ''Honomichl Top 50'', http://www.marketingpower.com/content/HONO50.pdf (June 15, 2006).

the 50 largest U.S.-based research organizations was 10.0% in 2004, compared with 5.9% the year before. The upward trend in annual revenue can be attributed to a rebounding economy, an uptick in advertising, and pent-up demand due to strong research initiatives (see Exhibit 1-1 for a list of the top 25 U.S. research organizations.)

Marketing research has been around for a long time, but marketing research companies have not. In its rawest form, research has been practiced since biblical times (see Research Realities 1-2). Of course, some businesses—and these can range from small mom-and-pop operations to huge consumer goods manufacturers and enormous multinational conglomerates—will conduct their own research, doing without the services of any specialized agency. For example, Procter & Gamble has satisfied the needs of millions of consumers partly because of its savvy marketing research over the past eight decades (see Research Realities 1-3).

While various organizations conduct marketing research—advertising agencies, financial institutions, and retail stores, to name a few—only three types of agencies conduct marketing research as their core business. These agencies can be grouped by the services they provide as (1) syndicated services, (2) standardized research services, and (3) custom houses. All of these agencies tend to offer various means of data collection, including use of the Internet.

- *Syndicated services.* These full-service agencies routinely collect information and report their findings to the clients or companies that subscribe to their service.

Studying a subject without an appreciation of its antecedents is like seeing a picture in two dimensions—there is no depth. The study of history gives us this depth, helping us to understand why things are as they are.

Early Days

Research has an extensive history. "Even the children of Israel sent interviewers out to sample the market and the produce of Canaan. [Before that], young women tried to foresee their matrimonial prospects by repeating 'He loves me, he loves me not'" (Lockley, 1974) while plucking the petals from a daisy. But these early efforts to provide inklings about the future were crude and unscientific. Many hundreds of years would pass before the science of forecasting was developed.

1800s

The first formal practice of marketing research can be traced back to the 1824 presidential race. As Andrew Jackson, John Quincy Adams, Henry Clay, and William Crawford faced off, a straw poll was taken by the *Harrisburg Pennsylvanian* to forecast the winner, with the following results: Jackson won 335 votes, Adams 169, Clay 19, and Crawford 9. In the actual election, Jackson won 99 electoral votes, Adams 84, Clay 37, and Crawford 41. None of the candidates received a majority of electoral votes, so the House of Representatives was called upon to decide the election. There, Henry Clay threw his support to Adams, who became the sixth president of the United States.

In 1879, the pioneering agency N.W. Ayer & Son used market research to solve marketing and advertising problems. In their effort to establish a national advertising schedule for the Nichols-Shepard Company, the agency contacted both state officials and publishers and gathered information on expected grain production—the first formal market survey by state and county in the United States.

Early 1900s

Marketing research techniques improved considerably between 1910 and 1920. In 1911, J. George Frederick set up his marketing research firm, the *Business Bourse*, the first organization in the United States to establish groups of interviewers around the country. Frederick's firm provided annual marketing data maps, consultation services, and specific marketing research. The Texas Company and General Electric were two of Frederick's early clients. He estimated that in 1910, no more than $50,000 was spent nationwide in gathering marketing information. Frederick wrote *Business Research and Statistics* in 1920; it was used for many years both by colleges and by practitioners. Groups using research techniques before 1920 included DuPont, General Electric, Kellogg, N.W. Ayer & Son, the *Chicago Tribune*, and *Curtis Publishing*, to name a few.

An important breakthrough in market research occurred with the early gathering and sorting of business and marketing data by the U.S. Department of Commerce. In 1926, two major surveys laid the groundwork for the 1929 Census of Distribution and inspired a number of studies on distribution cost analysis. With the growth of large-scale government data collection, market research began to garner national attention.

Mid-1900s

Several associations contributed to the development of marketing research, among them the American Management Association, the American Association of Public Opinion Research, and the Advertising Research Foundation. The American Marketing Association was not formed until 1937; at that time it had 400 members. (Today there are more than 45,000 members—some 27,000 professionals and 17,000 students—from 92 countries and 500 local chapters.)

It was not until the end of World War II, however, that marketing research really took off. A 1963 study by the American Marketing Association found that more than half of the 860 firms surveyed were organized after 1947, with two-thirds of the advertising agencies, publishing agencies, and broadcasting firms established after that year. And, of course, during this time the computer, with its ability to analyze vast quantities of data, began to revolutionize marketing research.

Early 2000s

The personal computer as we know it today was introduced in the early 1980s. Because its speed and memory constantly increase, so do its research capabilities. There seems to be no end in sight to what the computer can do for marketing researchers. A few of its present capabilities include:

- Computer-aided personal interviewing
- Automated fieldwork administration
- Integrated survey packaging
- Online coding/data entry
- Adaptive survey packages
- Online surveying
- Fast tabulations
- Friendly analysis software
- Online panels/databases
- Improved presentation of results
- Data mining/filtering and storage of massive amounts of data (Sowa, 2006)

Sources: V. P. Norris, "Advertising history—according to the textbooks," *Journal of Advertising* 9, no. 3 (1980): 3–11; L. C. Lockley, "History and development of marketing research," in R. Ferber, ed., *Handbook of Marketing Research* (New York: McGraw-Hill, 1974), 1–3; Jeffrey L. Pope, *Practical Marketing Research* (New York: Library of Congress, 1981), 5; L. C. Lockley, "Notes on the history of marketing research," *Journal of Marketing* XIV, no. 5 (April 1950): 733–734; R. Ferber, D. F. Blankertz, and S. Hollander, Jr., *Marketing Research* (New York: Ronald Press, 1964), 14–15; H. Neffendorf, "Survey computing in the 1990s: A technology update," *Journal of the Market Research Society* 35, no. 3 (November 1994): 205–209; Lauri Sowa, "Computer Cache: Data mining digs into our personal lives, secrets," (http://www.theadobepress.com/articles/2006/08/04/news/news11.txt), August 3, 2006, p. 1.

The Man Who Built Market Research

Procter & Gamble credits D. Paul Smelser for developing its market research department. After obtaining his doctoral degree in economics from Johns Hopkins University in 1923, Smelser was hired on at P&G as a commodity market analyst. However, his interest was in consumer research. He began examining consumer-purchasing and product-usage behavior and often asked questions such as, "What percentage of Ivory soap is used for face and hands and what percentage for dishwashing?" No one at P&G had any answers. In exasperation, a corporate officer finally told him, "Go out and find the answers to those damn questions yourself." And so he did—his market research department was formally established at P&G in 1925.

By 1934, Smelser's staff had grown to 34 people. He strongly believed in field research and carefully coached his interviewers (whom he called "investigators") in this strange new endeavor that was part art and part science. His investigators were mostly recent female college graduates, and he made sure that they memorized the instructions, questions, and answers that were to be used in each interview so that conversations would have a natural, uninterrupted flow. Dr. Smelser's contributions helped shape P&G's scientific and quantitative approach to research, its commitment to heavy advertising-media usage, and its continual search for improvements in ways to collect data.

Source: "The man who built market research," *Advertising Age* (August 20, 1987): 117–119.

EXHIBIT 1-2	Media Measurement

Media measurement services provide information on international television and radio audience ratings, and advertising expenditure and print readership measurement. This information serves as the essential currency for negotiating advertising placement and rates. TV ratings are available in 18 countries; radio ratings in 12 markets; and advertising expenditure measurement in 31 markets.

Clients	Principal Brands	Recent Highlights
Television and radio broadcasters, cable and satellite TV providers, publishers, advertisers and their agencies, media planners, and government agencies	• Peoplemeter television audience measurement services • ACNielsen CABSAT Asia cable and satellite television audience measurement services • AdEx International advertising expenditure measurement services • Nielsen//NetRatings, NetWatch, WebAudit, and WebAdEx Internet monitoring services	• Expanded television audience measurement services in China • Launched television audience measurement services in India • Formed a media measurement joint venture in Latin America • Harmonized global production and analytical services for AdEx International

Source: ACNielsen web page, "Media Measurement," http://www.nielsenmedia.com, May 15, 2005.

Usually this data will not be problem-specific; that is, data will not relate to a particular problem of one organization. Data is often provided to subscribers in a standardized format. Some well-known syndicated service providers include ACNielsen television ratings, Nielsen//NetRatings, Arbitron radio ratings, and J.D. Power and Associates customer satisfaction ratings of automobiles. (See Exhibit 1-2 for a description of Nielsen's media measurement.)

- *Standardized research services.* These companies examine a particular aspect of a market in a unique way, though they typically use a standardized method of research for different clients to allow comparisons of results to be made between studies and across other evaluative standards. This also allows clients to receive information at a lower cost than that of information collected by agencies performing customized research. For example, Roper Starch uses a standardized method to evaluate the effectiveness of print advertisements through its Starch Readership Survey.

- *Custom houses.* These agencies are often referred to as offering "ad hoc services" because they tailor (that is, customize) their studies to the needs of their clients. Their one-on-one approach means that they can provide highly specialized and focused services. Their clients determine what to study and take the lead regarding other concerns associated with the research problem. Custom houses, such as Burke Marketing Research, Market Facts, Inc., Custom Research Interactive, Pragmatic Research, Research International, and Data Development, typically gather and analyze the data, concluding their efforts with a research report. These agencies are in high demand, since a variety of businesses may seek their services, particularly companies without their own research departments. However, large companies with their own research arms also call on custom houses to work with them when their own research departments are overloaded or when a specific research expertise void needs to be filled.

Besides the broad-service research agencies, there are also companies that specialize in facilitating various aspects of research. These limited-service suppliers include independent consultants, field services, coding and data entry services, and tabulation houses.

- *Independent consultants.* These individuals offer expert knowledge and skills in specialized subjects and can thus provide information that might not be revealed by the broad-service providers. They are typically hired independent of a marketing research agency. Examples include university professors and other scholars who conduct independent research.

- *Field services.* To understand this type of agency, you need to know the meaning of "field." To a marketing researcher, a field is a place where new information can be collected, such as in front of a retail store, in a bank, over the telephone, through the mail, on a college campus, and so on. Field-service agencies fulfill the need for data collected via interviews—regardless of whether the research involves individuals or groups. Usually these agencies work in a local geographic area, such as a city, county, or state, since they tend to specialize in a particular market. Most companies and even research organizations cannot justify supporting a full-time field research staff, so they use the services of field agencies. Some examples of field-service organizations include Field Surveys and Audits of Milwaukee, Crimmins & Forman Market Research, and Delaware Research Company.

- *Coding and data entry services.* These companies are useful after data collection is completed. They edit surveys that have been received from respondents, as well as code the responses so that analysts can evaluate the information. Some of these companies, such as Data Entry Services, Inc., offer more than basic data entry services. This company, for example, offers services in database design, implementation, and management, as well as data processing, scanning, online services, statistical tabulation, and form design.

- *Tabulation houses.* These agencies offer data analysis services and are thus quantitative specialists. Their sole purpose is to perform statistical analyses and turn raw data into information that managers can use. When raw data is in the form of completed surveys, transcribed interviews, or written descriptions of consumer behaviors, the tab house reformats (codes) the information so that it can be analyzed. The agency then performs the analyses and provides its client with understandable results. These analyses range from basic cross-tabulations of the data to examinations using highly sophisticated multivariate statistics. Several statistical techniques that are used to examine raw data will be covered in subsequent chapters.

1-2c Marketing Research Companies Worldwide

There is a strong need for marketing research companies to exist throughout the world. The reality of the situation is that while there are many research techniques that can be used in multiple markets, there are also quite a few market differences that warrant changes in strategy (see Research Realities 1-4).

Research Realities 1-4 — *Global Research Is Similar and Different from U.S. Research*

Brad Frevert, senior vice president at Custom Research, Inc., in Minneapolis, points out some key differences and concerns between research performed in the United States and that done in foreign markets. He offers a four-stage research process to explain the differences and concerns. The first stage is "planning." He says that this is what is most different in global marketing research from research done in the United States. In this stage, global research requires formalizing a number of components that is usually handled as a matter of course in domestic research. Some key concerns include:

- What are the major objectives?
- Who is the key client(s)?
- Who has input on what?
- Who will get/interpret/use the findings?

Frevert warns that during the planning process, global research can be expensive when compared to research restricted to the United States. Some costs of global research include higher fees for telephone calls, multiple translations, international coordination, multiple client coordination, and long distance project management.

The second stage of the research process is "design." Things to think about in this stage include:

- What cannot be standardized? Is it affordable?

- Will it be actionable, and at what level?
- Will it be comparable?
- Should it be executed locally or centrally?

The third stage of the research process is "execution." When considering this stage, Frevert notes that it's important to be aware of the local differences and nuances in survey design, respondent availability, field execution, and data quality. Furthermore, he recommends that managers should think about the areas of the study that need to be comparable, as the actual data collection methodology might need to differ from country to country. For example, interviewing services with facilities in shopping malls don't exist in most countries.

The last stage is "interpretation." Frevert wonders whether a coherent story can be told from the information collected. He recommends that conclusions and recommendations should be "globalized." That is, compare countries and regions and draw conclusions. He warns that managers must understand each country's procedural uniqueness such as scaling differences, general skepticism, and "yea—saying" countries.

Source: Brad Frevert, "Is global research different?" *Marketing Research,* Spring 2000, pp. 49–54.

| EXHIBIT 1-3 | Top 25 Global Research Organizations, 2003 |

Rank in 2003	Organization	Headquarters	Parent Company	Number of Countries with Subsidiaries or Branch Offices*	Global Research Revenue[†] (in millions of U.S. dollars)	Revenues from Outside Home Country (in millions of U.S. dollars)	Percent of Global Revenues from Outside Home Country
1	VNU NV	Haarlem, Netherlands	Netherlands	81	$3,429.2	$3,394.7[‡]	99.0%[‡]
2	Taylor Nelson Sofres plc	London	U.K.	70	1,720.6	1,430.6	83.2
3	IMS Health, Inc.	Fairfield, Conn.	U.S.	76	1,569.0	998.0	63.6
4	The Kantar Group	Fairfield, Conn.	U.S.	61	1,136.3[‡]	776.0[‡]	68.3[‡]
5	GfK Group	Nuremberg	Germany	59	835.5	541.5	64.8
6	Ipsos Group SA	Paris	France	41	753.2	633.8	84.2
7	Information Resources, Inc.	Chicago, Ill.	U.S.	18	572.8	193.2	33.7
8	Synovate	London	U.K.	46	499.3	407.7	81.7
9	Nop World	London	U.K.	8	407.1	297.3	73.0
10	Westat, Inc.	Rockville, Md.	U.S.	1	397.8	NA	NA
11	Arbitron, Inc.	New York, N.Y.	U.S.	3	296.6	11.9	4.0
12	INTAGE, Inc.[§]	Tokyo	Japan	2	246.2	1.6	0.7
13	Harris Interactive	Rochester, N.Y.	U.S.	6	208.9	54.1	25.9
—	Harris Interactive Inc.	Rochester, N.Y.	U.S.	—	155.4	38.7	24.9
—	Wirthlin Worldwide	McLean, Va.	U.S.	—	53.5	15.4	28.8
14	Maritz Research	Fenton, Mo.	U.S.	4	185.3	48.7	26.3
15	Video Research Ltd.[§]	Tokyo	Japan	3	177.2	2.3	1.3
16	J.D. Power and Associates	Westlake Village, Calif.	U.S.	8	167.6	34.1	20.3
17	Opinion Research Corp.	Princeton, N.J.	U.S.	6	147.5	56.5	38.3
18	The NPD Group Inc.	Port Washington, N.Y.	U.S.	11	139.2	28.7	20.6
19	Market & Opinion Research International	London	U.K.	2	81.0	2.4	3.0
20	Lieberman Research Worldwide	Los Angeles, Calif.	U.S.	2	77.7	10.5	13.5
21	Dentsu Research Inc.	Tokyo	Japan	1	69.9	0.2	0.3
22	IBOPE Group	Sao Paulo	Brazil	15	64.5	14.3	22.1
23	Nikkei Research Inc.	Tokyo	Japan	5	53.0	—	—
24	Burke Inc.	Cincinnati, Ohio	U.S.	1	43.4	6.3	14.5
25	ABT Associates Inc.	Cambridge, Mass.	U.S.	1	41.5	—	—
TOTAL					**$13,320.3**	**$8,944.4**	**67.2%**

Notes:

*Includes countries that have subsidiaries with an equity interest or branch offices, or both.

[†]Total revenue that include nonresearch activities for some companies are significantly higher. This information is given in the individual company profiles.

[‡]Estimated by Top 25 global research companies.

[§]For fiscal year ending March 2005.

Source: Jack Honomichl, "Top 50 U.S. Research Firms," *Marketing News,* (August 15, 2005). Reprinted with permission from the American Marketing Association.

Thousands of marketing research organizations around the world conduct research and shape market strategies, but only a handful of these control the bulk of revenues for marketing, advertising, and public opinion research. The top 25 firms had revenues of $13.3 billion in 2004, with 67% of the revenues from operations outside their home country. Their corporate parents were in Brazil, France, Germany, Japan, Netherlands, the United Kingdom, and the United States. The United States continues to be a popular home for top 25 agencies, with 14 agencies' parent companies based there. The largest conglomerate, VNU N.V., has revenues exceeding $3 billion and subsidiaries or branch offices in 81 countries. (See Exhibit 1-3 for a list of the top 25 global research organizations.)

1-3 Who Uses Marketing Research?

Any company that lacks key information about its markets can benefit from marketing research. Research can reduce uncertainties and improve decision making. A variety of companies use marketing research on a regular basis, and many companies have their own formal marketing research departments. In general, larger companies are more likely to have formal research departments, and smaller companies are more likely to have only one person or no one assigned to research. On average, consumer and industrial manufacturers, advertising agencies, and retailers/wholesalers spend approximately 1.2% of sales on marketing research, while financial services, publishers/broadcasters, health services, and utilities spend about 0.6%.[11]

Within each company, it is the marketing manager who uses the information supplied from the marketing researcher to enhance his or her decision making. That is, marketing managers are the customers of marketing researchers.

1-3a The Marketing Manager

Marketing managers are responsible for making the decisions that will help their company achieve its objectives in its target markets. Numerous environmental variables—cultural and social differences, economic factors, and so on—affect the performance of marketing managers, yet managers have little control over most of these variables. However, they do control their firm's marketing mix—product, price, promotion, and distribution. They must coordinate this mix carefully to achieve their company's objectives.

Marketing management is the analysis, planning, implementation, and control of programs designed to create, build, and maintain beneficial exchanges with target buyers for the purpose of achieving organizational objectives.[12] The four critical functions of marketing managers are also functions of marketing research, as shown in the American Marketing Association definition of marketing research in Exhibit 1-4. Analysis is an essential part of marketing research, as it involves using information to identify and define marketing problems and opportunities. Planning is embedded in the research process because planning helps to create, clarify, and evaluate the actions of marketing. Implementation and control are likewise functions of marketing research through the data collection process and the monitoring of marketing performance. Marketing managers often follow a sequence of steps when making important decisions.

marketing management The analysis, planning, implementation, and control of programs designed to create, build, and maintain beneficial exchanges with target buyers for the purpose of achieving organizational objectives.

EXHIBIT 1-4	Marketing Management Functions in the American Marketing Association Definition of Marketing Research

Marketing research: The function that links the consumer, customer, and public to the marketer through information

Analysis: The identification and definition of marketing opportunities and problems

Planning: The generation, refinement, and evaluation of marketing actions

Control: The monitoring of marketing performance and improvement of understanding of marketing as a process

Planning: The specification of the information required to address these issues, the designing of the method for collecting information, and the management of implementation

Implementation: Putting into effect the data collection process, analysis of the results, and communication of the findings and their implications

The Decision-Making Process
The **decision-making process** is a series of steps that leads to a final judgment (see Exhibit 1-5). Let's see how marketing research is involved in each of these steps.

decision-making process A series of steps that leads to a final judgment.

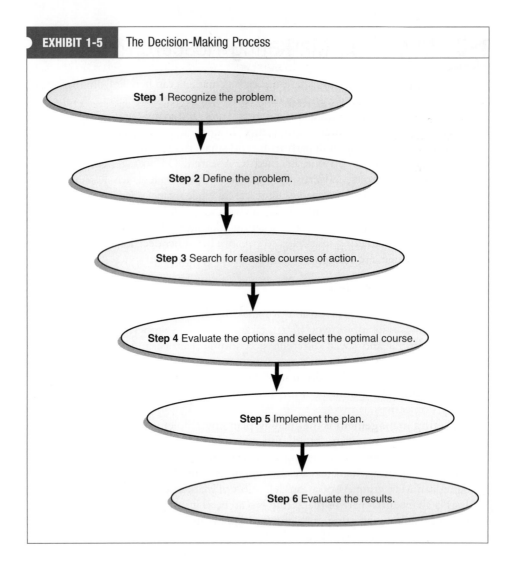

EXHIBIT 1-5 The Decision-Making Process

Step 1 Recognize the problem.

Step 2 Define the problem.

Step 3 Search for feasible courses of action.

Step 4 Evaluate the options and select the optimal course.

Step 5 Implement the plan.

Step 6 Evaluate the results.

Recognize the Problem The first step in making a decision is usually stated as defining the problem or opportunity. However, before it can be defined, marketing managers must sense that a problem or opportunity exists. Therefore, we define the first step as recognizing the problem or opportunity. The dynamic nature of today's markets continually causes problems and continually creates opportunities. In Latin America, Mexico's peso devaluation in the early 1990s hurt companies exporting to Mexico but benefited businesses producing there because of severe reductions in workers' hourly wages. A target market, if not understood in sharp detail, can easily be misdiagnosed and underserved. It is therefore the responsibility of marketing researchers to provide managers with clear pictures of their target markets, even as those markets undergo vigorous changes.

Define the Problem Marketing managers must next correctly define the problem or opportunity. They must perform this step carefully because defining a problem incorrectly can cause precious resources to be frittered away on unimportant concerns. Poorly defined problems or opportunities severely strain finances, since the actions taken to address them are misguided from the outset. Therefore, marketing researchers must provide adequate information to marketing managers so that a problem or opportunity present in a particular market can be accurately identified. Misdefined problems create more problems. Consider Example 1-1.

Example 1-1

Coca-Cola's market share was eroding in the late 1970s and early 1980s. Blind taste tests suggested that people preferred Pepsi over Coke. Managers at Coca-Cola believed that Coke's lack of sweetness was the culprit. So after several nationwide taste tests, a sweeter New Coke was introduced. Managers thought they had fixed the problem. But from the start, sales of New Coke were flat. A few months later, a new poll found that 60% of consumers who had tried New Coke thought that the original Coke tasted better. So the company reintroduced the original beverage as "Classic Coke," and its sales went on to far outperform those of New Coke. Had their marketing research been done properly, they would have known that lack of sweetness was not the problem and that many consumers viewed the original Coke as American as apple pie and the American flag. Furthermore, they would have found that many of these tradition-bound consumers wanted a choice of Coke beverages; they did not want the decision imposed on them. Their lack of choice seemed to affect the acceptance of New Coke and the perceived taste of New versus Classic Coke.

Search for Feasible Courses of Action   The third step in the decision-making process is to search for feasible courses of action to resolve a problem or take advantage of an opportunity. Marketing managers must identify every potential way of addressing the situation so that the most feasible approach can be identified. Once again, the marketing researcher bears the burden of supplying marketing managers with sufficient information. Consider Example 1-2.

Example 1-2

Triangle Products, an international trading company specializing in food items, recognized that its sales were leveling off. To prevent a decline, the company looked at emerging markets in East Asia. Since Triangle Products is small in terms of number of employees and annual sales, it decided to focus its marketing efforts on one country. With pertinent data from Triangle's marketing researcher, management was able to narrow its consideration to four markets: South Korea, Taiwan, Hong Kong, and Vietnam.

Evaluate the Options and Select the Optimal Course   The fourth step is to evaluate all feasible options and select the optimal course of action. Using information supplied by the marketing researcher, marketing managers carefully evaluate each course of action and select one that appears to provide the greatest payoff. This payoff may not necessarily translate into immediate financial gain. Instead, it may involve achieving long-term cost savings, minimizing losses, preserving company resources, or perhaps overcoming some strict governmental regulations. Triangle Products selected South Korea as its target market and limited its product offerings to American-made food products because research indicated that Western goods are quite popular in Asian nations.

Implement the Plan   The fifth step of the decision-making process is to implement the plan. The marketing manager's choice of plan is based on information provided earlier by the marketing researcher, but even the best plans can fail. Proper implementation ensures that the plan fulfills its potential. Effective implementation requires marketing managers to clarify what needs to be done, who will be responsible for each task, and when, where, and how the tasks will be carried out. Consider Example 1-3.

Example 1-3

In the summer of 2005, Captain D's, a seafood restaurant, planned to radically alter its marketing efforts and branding after making significant investments in marketing research. The general focus of the campaign was under the direction of the chief marketing officer, Bob Kendzior. Captain D's was spending $15 million to $20 million per year in advertising and felt they could improve the efficiency of their ad dollars. The firm Sullivan Higdon and Sink of Kansas City, MO, was charged with developing the print, radio and TV ads to begin the push in the fall of 2005. Matt Wegerer, an art director at the firm was charged with developing a campaign with 'attitude' to appeal to a younger clientele. Targeting advertising dollars was a key goal for Kendzior who said, "If we're targeting a 35 year old male, we'll look at what he's watching."[13]

Evaluate the Results After implementation, marketing managers must periodically evaluate the results. If the results are not similar to the plan's objectives, marketing managers closely examine why the deviation exists and what can be done to remedy the problem. Questions are asked. Were the objectives unrealistic? Was the problem erroneously defined? Was the wrong course of action chosen? Any number of factors can cause deviation. Therefore, marketing managers monitor the plan's progress and make changes if situations warrant. Nielsen Media Research's Grabix.com allows users to monitor television ratings of programs on a minute-by-minute basis. The system delivers streaming video of programs and simultaneous ratings information on a two day delay and allows for the comparison of different TV stations in a single market or across markets. Station executives can then make more timely programming decisions.[14]

1-4 Do Marketing Researchers Have an Ethical Responsibility?

A few years ago, consumers were in an uproar over the cartoon character Joe Camel because many believed that R.J. Reynolds Tobacco Company designed the popular advertising campaign to entice young children to smoke. Much of the debate centered on whether the company's actions were ethical. **Ethics** is defined by *The American Heritage Dictionary* as "the study of the general nature of morals and of specific moral choices; moral philosophy; and the rules or standards governing the conduct of the members of a profession."[15] But this definition is too general for our purposes, and it does not deal directly with the business arena. Ferrell and Fraedrich, in their book *Business Ethics,* define **business ethics** as comprising "moral principles and standards that guide behavior in the world of business."[16] The authors go on to say that the public determines whether a particular behavior is ethical or unethical, and these value judgments are manifested in the mass media, interest groups, and the legal system, as well as in individuals' personal morals and values. Furthermore, they state that although the terms ethics and social responsibility are often used interchangeably, their meanings are quite distinct.

Social responsibility refers to the obligation of a business toward society that attempts to maximize positive effects and minimize negative effects on society. As shown in Exhibit 1-6, social responsibility includes economic, legal, ethical, and

ethics The study of the general nature of morals and of specific moral choices; the rules or standards governing the conduct of the members of a profession.

business ethics Moral principles and standards that guide behavior in business.

social responsibility Business's obligation to maximize positive effects and minimize negative effects of its operations on society.

EXHIBIT 1-6	Components of Social Responsibility
Economic responsibilities	To produce goods and services that society needs and wants at a price that can perpetuate the business and satisfy its obligations to investors
Legal responsibilities	The laws that businesses must obey
Ethical responsibilities	Behaviors or activities that are expected of businesses by society but not codified in law
Voluntary responsibilities	Those behaviors and activities that society desires and business values dictate

Source: O. C. Ferrell and John Fraedrich, *Business Ethics: Ethical Decision Making and Cases*, 3rd ed. (New York: Houghton Mifflin, 1997), 6. Copyright © 1997 by Houghton Mifflin Company. Used with permission.

voluntary responsibilities. Interestingly, a recent study conducted by the Gallup Organization found that only about one in four Americans living in households with money invested in the stock market have heard of "socially responsible" investing, but of these, 27% claim to have money in such investments.[17]

To understand the relationship between ethics and the practice of marketing research, we can view marketing research as a chain of requesters and providers of information. This chain includes requesters such as final clients, and providers such as advertising agencies, researcher suppliers, group moderators, and data collection services. Whether a researcher is perceived as ethical depends on the degree to which the public perceives all members of the research chain as ethical and also on the degree to which the members perceive each other as being ethical. Thus not only must researchers build a relationship of trust with the public, they must also adhere to commonly held standards of behavior so that they have a basis for trusting each other.[18]

Since companies use marketing research to support many of their claims, faulty application of marketing research techniques can contribute to unethical behavior. Nonscientific or nonobjective studies damage a researcher's reputation for ethical conduct. Consider the following anecdote from the author of an article appearing in *Discover:*

> You can imagine my surprise when I discovered that despite all the studies linking smoking to disease, "eminent doctors and research scientists have questioned the claimed significance of these experiments." Better still, some cigarettes, it turns out, can even "protect the delicate tissues in your throat"!
>
> Cigarettes aren't the only products whose reputations have been unexpectedly redeemed. According to recent studies, chocolate can actually inhibit the formation of cavities; high-fat nuts can lower the level of fat in the blood; and Wonder Bread, the only known bakery product able to double as a study throw pillow, is really a diet food.
>
> All of this is good news for the health conscious—long as you're willing to overlook a few teensy problems. The smoking study, for instance, was sponsored by the Tobacco Industry Research Committee. The chocolate study was sponsored by a chocolate manufacturer. The nut research was sponsored by the California walnut and almond boards. And the Wonder Bread study was sponsored by, yes, Wonder Bread.
>
> The worlds of commerce and science are rife with this scarcely objective research— and not surprisingly. How many Snickers would the folks at M&M/Mars sell if their advertising relied on government nutrition standards alone?[19]

Certainly, many companies claim that their products are good for individuals, and in fact they are. But unfortunately, some marketing research studies sound positive yet are suspect, at best, when their research methodologies are examined. Consider the following examples:[20]

- The pesticide manufacturer Black Flag claimed that approximately 80% of all Americans believed that using a roach disk would be an effective way to control roaches, and they had the study results to back up this amazing finding. However, it eventually became apparent that when the respondents were initially approached, many of them had never heard of a roach disk—the pollsters had to describe it to them. The pollsters' descriptions were far from objective, for example: "A roach disk is a type of product that poisons a roach slowly. The dying roach returns to the nest, and after it dies, it is eaten by other roaches. In turn, these roaches become poisoned and die. How effective do you think this product would be in killing roaches?"

- The cloth diaper industry sponsored a study that claimed that disposable diapers were nonbiodegradable and overwhelmed landfills. Procter & Gamble, producer of Pampers and Luvs, then conducted its own study and concluded—not surprisingly—that once the compostability of paper, the waste generated by manufacturing, and the repeated cleaning of a single cloth diaper were taken into consideration, the disposable brands were actually the more environmentally friendly of the two. Unfortunately, both studies were faulty because the conclusions they wanted to reach led them to the conclusions they eventually reached.

- A study partially funded by the Quaker Oats Company reported in the *Journal of the American Diabetic Association* that products containing oat bran can dramatically lower cholesterol. The market was soon inundated with all kinds of bran items—cereals, cookies, muffins, and even toothpaste. Later, however, a Harvard University study found that to gain even minimal benefits from bran, individuals would have to consume large quantities (for example, five large bran muffins) each day.

Marketing researchers in many parts of the world have their own codes of ethics. The intent of these codes is to provide frameworks for ethical practice. The American Marketing Association, for example, has more than 45,000 members worldwide in every area of marketing. Members are obligated to abide by its code of ethics, which is shown in Exhibit 1-7. This code addresses the responsibilities of the marketers, the

---

> **EXHIBIT 1-7**   American Marketing Association Code of Ethics

Ethical Norms and Values for Marketers

The American Marketing Association commits itself to promoting the highest standard of professional ethical norms and values for its members. Norms are established standards of conduct that are expected and maintained by society and/or professional organizations. Values represent the collective conception of what people find desirable, important, and morally proper. Values serve as the criteria for evaluating the actions of others. Marketing practitioners must recognize that they not only serve their enterprises but also act as stewards of society in creating, facilitating, and executing the efficient and effective transactions that are part of the greater economy. In this role, marketers should embrace the highest ethical norms of practicing professionals and the ethical values implied by their responsibility toward stakeholders (e.g., customers, employees, investors, channel members, regulators, and the host community).

General Norms

1. Marketers must do no harm.
2. Marketers must foster trust in the marketing system.
3. Marketers must embrace, communicate, and practice the fundamental ethical values that will improve consumer confidence in the integrity of the marketing exchange system.

Ethical Values

Honesty—to be truthful and forthright in our dealings with customers and stakeholders.
Responsibility—to accept the consequences of our marketing decisions and strategies.
Fairness—to try to balance justly the needs of the buyer with the interests of the seller.
Respect—to acknowledge the basic human dignity of all stakeholders.
Openness—to create transparency in our marketing operations.
Citizenship—to fulfill the economic, legal, philanthropic, and societal responsibilities that serve stakeholders in a strategic manner.

Note: For a complete description of the AMA's Code of Ethics, visit the organization's Web site at http://www.marketingpower.com/content435.php.
Source: Ethical Norms and Values for Marketers on http://www.marketingpower.com/content435.php. Reprinted with permission from the American Marketing Association.

guidelines they must adhere to, and the rights and duties of parties in the marketing-exchange process.

The **Council of American Survey Research Organizations (CASRO)**, based in the United States, is the national trade association for commercial research firms. It has over 250 companies and research operations in the United States and abroad that abide by CASRO's "Code of Standards and Ethics." This code, which is mandatory for all CASRO members, is organized into four groups: responsibilities to respondents, responsibilities to clients, responsibilities in reporting to clients and the public, and responsibilities to outside contractors and interviewers. The **European Society for Opinion and Marketing Research (ESOMAR)**, based in Amsterdam, Netherlands, is a society of over 4,000 individual members in 100 countries. All members and their management have entered into an agreement with ESOMAR to act in full compliance with the organization's "International Code of Marketing and Social Research Practice." This code states the rights of respondents, the professional responsibilities of researchers, and the mutual rights and responsibilities of researchers and clients.

Unfortunately, many nations do not have established groups that regulate ethical behavior in business. In the newly emerging democracies of Eastern Europe, the newly industrializing countries of Asia, and many of the less-developed countries of Africa, consumers and organizations are at the mercy of businesses to act ethically and responsibly, since there is no commonly accepted global code of business ethics.[21]

Council of American Survey Research Organizations (CASRO) National trade association for commercial research firms in the United States.

European Society for Opinion and Marketing Research (ESOMAR) International trade association based in Europe and composed of more than 4,000 individual members.

1-5 What Job Opportunities Exist in Marketing Research?

Marketing research is an exciting and challenging field that will offer many career opportunities to qualified individuals in the coming years. According to the U.S. Department of Labor, the employment opportunity of market and survey researchers is expected to be *much higher*—to increase 36% or more—than the average for all occupations through 2012. In particular,

> Demand for market research analysts should be strong because of an increasingly competitive economy. Marketing research provides organizations valuable feedback from purchasers, allowing companies to evaluate consumer satisfaction and more effectively plan for the future. As companies seek to expand their market and as consumers become better informed, the need for marketing professionals will increase. As globalization of the marketplace continues, market researchers will also be increasingly utilized to analyze foreign markets and competition for goods and services.[22]

Many marketing research jobs require little prior training. There are numerous job openings for telephone and shopping mall interviewers—essential tasks in this field. Many of the jobs, though, require good analytical skills, the ability to condense large amounts of data, and a genuine interest in why people do things.[23] If you are interested in this field, you are not limited to working in a marketing research organization. Financial institutions, retailers, wholesalers, manufacturers of consumer and industrial goods, and government agencies are all seeking qualified people to measure such dimensions as customer satisfaction, market demand, and consumer attitude toward product offerings. And the demand for specialists is growing in marketing departments within large companies and in marketing research firms. To be employed as a researcher, you must have adequate training in statistical analysis and experiment design. This training may come from a variety of sources, such as:

- marketing research courses at universities, colleges, and training institutes
- internships with research organizations

- cooperative education with research organizations
- working in some capacity with marketing departments within businesses

A variety of positions are available in marketing research firms, including directors, assistant directors, senior analysts, statisticians, and fieldwork directors. In the following brief descriptions of typical positions, salaries are not discussed, since a company's geographic location, the availability of qualified individuals in various research areas, and an applicant's industry experience and academic degrees all affect salary. But for the most part, salaries for marketing researchers have been steadily increasing over the past five years, with the exception of fieldwork directors, junior analysts, and full-time interviewers. Some of the activities performed by marketing research firms are listed in Exhibit 1-8. The following are the positions available in most marketing research firms:

- *Vice president.* This is the senior position in the research organization. This individual is responsible for all marketing research activities and establishes the goals of the research group.

- *Director.* Following the vice president of the company, this is the senior position within the research organization. The director has the overall responsibility for the creation and implementation of all marketing research projects. He or she often communicates with other executives within the company and with clients to determine what type of research needs to be undertaken.

- *Assistant director.* As the name indicates, this person is right behind the director in the chain of command within the research organization. He or she supervises specific research projects.

- *Senior analyst.* This person works closely with others in planning and executing research projects. He or she also writes the final report covering the research effort.

- *Statistician.* This person is an expert in statistical procedures and works on questionnaire design, sampling, and statistical analyses. His or her services are requested on an "as needed" basis.

- *Analyst.* This person is closely supervised by the senior analyst and often does much of the work associated with designing and supervising the research studies. He or she is also asked to do much of the legwork, including gathering pertinent background information from libraries and inside the company.

EXHIBIT 1-8	Activities Performed by Marketing Research Firms

Business/Economic and Corporate Research
Industry/market characteristics and trends studies
    or surveys
Acquisition/diversification studies
Market share analyses
Internal employee studies (morale, communication, etc.)

Pricing
Cost analysis
Profit analysis
Price sensitivity
Demand analysis (market potential, sales potential,
    sales forecasts)
Competitive pricing analyses

Product
Concept development and testing
Brand name generation and testing
Market testing
Product testing of existing products
Packaging design studies
Competitive product studies

Distribution
Plant/warehouse location studies
Channel performance studies
Channel coverage studies
Export and international studies

Promotion
Motivation research
Media research
Copy research
Advertising effectiveness testing
Competitive advertising studies
Public image studies
Sales force compensation studies
Sales force quota studies
Sales force territory structure
Studies of premiums, coupons, deals, etc.

Buying Behavior
Brand preference
Brand attitudes
Product satisfaction
Purchase behavior
Purchase intentions
Brand awareness
Segmentation studies

Source: Thomas C. Kinnear and Ann R. Root, *1994 Survey of Marketing Research* (Chicago: American Marketing Association, 1995), 49–68. Reprinted with permission from 1994 Survey of Marketing Research, published by the American Marketing Association, 1994.

- *Junior analyst.* This person usually works closely with analysts, doing routine tasks such as editing and coding questionnaires, running simple statistical calculations, and performing basic library research.

- *Fieldwork director.* This individual is responsible for training, supervising, and hiring interviewers "in the field." *Fieldwork* directors usually work in large research departments.

- *Librarian.* This person is responsible for building and maintaining a reference library for use by research department staff.

- *Clerical supervisor.* This supervisor oversees the handling and processing of statistical information and prepares work schedules.

- *Full-time interviewers.* Although very few companies employ them, full-time interviewers tend to spend the bulk of their time conducting personal interviews.

- *Tabulating and clerical help.* These people keep the office running by handling the daily routine work of the department, such as tabulating, filing, and keying.[24]

There are numerous organizations that are constantly searching for qualified individuals to work for them in the research field. The Internet allows this search to be widely publicized. Those people looking for a career in marketing research can go to their favorite search engine and type in "marketing research." Some of the job opportunities will be associated with large research agencies. For example, if you go to ACNielsen's home page (http://www.acnielsen.com) and click on "Careers," you can apply online for jobs in more than 100 countries, including the Americas, Europe, Asia Pacific, and various emerging markets. Some of these jobs are in client services, communications, finance, marketing, operations, and systems. Positions can be applied for by either emailing a text-only resume to the contact person or pasting a text-only resume into the online application form. Arbitron's home page (http://www.arbitron.com) also offers employment opportunities in marketing research. By clicking on "Job Bank," you can access numerous jobs listed by location, category, and position. Once again, resumes are accepted via email.

Decision Time!

Now that you have investigated the importance of marketing research and the various services that marketing research firms provide to their clients, it's time to do some critical thinking. How vital do you think business ethics and social responsibility are to companies today? As a marketing manager, what responsibility do you believe marketing research providers have to be ethical and socially responsible? What if such behavior hurts company profits?

Net Impact

The Internet is already changing the way marketing researchers gather data to aid decision makers. For this reason, the impact of the Internet on each stage of the marketing research process will be discussed in each chapter, examining, for example, issues such as online secondary data, online qualitative research, online survey, etc. A "Net Impact" section will then summarize how the Internet affects the marketing research topics discussed at the end of each chapter. The Internet is advancing in several important areas, including time savings and increased information, security, accuracy, and organization. All of these benefits will aid the marketing research effort and therefore the abilities of managers to satisfy their customers and to make better decisions.

On the Lighter Side—Rate and Research Yourself

There are all kinds of Web sites. There are those that will help you with your golf game, improve your self image, give you advice on losing weight, and now...there is a site that will help you help yourself. As the site states, "Welcome to Rate Yourself—the only site focused solely on the world's most important person: YOU!" They invite visitors to the site to "Take our self-probing surveys, and learn what makes you who you are...at work, at play and in love. Rate Yourself and get the answers." They have surveys on a variety of topics, including careers, love and sex, personality, knowledge, hot topics, and one just for fun. Most of the surveys have 11 questions for respondents to answer. Once all questions are answered, an overall evaluation is provided along with a rating scale where your score is compared to those of the average respondent.

Source: Rate Yourself Web site, http://www.rateyourself.com. Retrieved October 8, 2005.

Chapter Summary

Marketing is a tool that helps managers effectively plan and implement the variables that motivate exchanges between businesses and consumers. The marketing concept is a management philosophy that focuses on customer satisfaction by first learning customers' needs and then creating products that meet those needs. To better understand consumers, companies often use marketing research.

There are two general types of research. Basic research pushes the "frontiers of knowledge" forward by providing information about a phenomenon or by testing a theory or hypothesis. It does not attempt to solve a particular problem. Applied research is much more problem-specific and focuses on helping managers improve their decision making. Therefore, marketing managers usually want applied research to help them solve specific problems or make certain decisions.

Types of agencies that practice marketing research include syndicated services, standardized research services, and custom houses. Facilitators of marketing research services include independent consultants, field services, coding and data entry services, and tabulation houses. Also, several types of companies conduct marketing research, including manufacturers of consumer products, manufacturers of industrial products, financial service firms, publishers and broadcasters, advertising agencies, health services, retailers, wholesalers, nonprofit companies, and utility firms. Most of these companies have formal marketing research departments.

Marketing managers often follow a series of steps when making important decisions. These decision-making steps are (1) recognize the problem, (2) define the problem, (3) search for feasible courses of action, (4) evaluate the options and select the optimal course, (5) implement the plan, and (6) evaluate the results.

Today ethical marketing practices are becoming increasingly necessary for businesses to effectively compete. While many firms follow ethical practices, some do not. The practice of marketing research can be viewed as a chain of requesters and providers. Members of this chain include clients, advertising agencies, research suppliers, group moderators, and data collection services. A researcher's reputation for ethical practice depends on the degree to which members of the chain behave ethically. Marketing researchers and their professional associations often have codes of ethics to serve as a framework for ethical practice.

Marketing research is an exciting and challenging field offering many career opportunities. Finding employment in marketing research organizations usually requires specific skills. Typical positions include vice presidents, directors, assistant directors, senior analysts, analysts, junior analysts, statisticians, fieldwork directors, librarians, clerical supervisors, full-time interviewers, and tabulating and clerical help. Salaries are dependent on a company's geographic location, the availability of qualified individuals in various research areas, and an applicant's industry experience and academic degrees. The potential for employment in the research field can be enhanced by searching for information about the needs of organizations using the Internet.

Review Questions

1. Why should you study marketing research regardless of whether you are a marketing major?

2. What is marketing research? How does it relate to the marketing concept?

3. What is the difference between basic and applied research? Give an example of each type.

4. What are three types of marketing research agencies?

5. Which type of organization uses marketing research most often? Why?

6. What is business ethics? How can you tell if a company is marketing ethically?

7. Must an individual have in-depth marketing research training to work in the field of marketing research? Why or why not?

8. Who is typically in charge of the marketing research department?

9. How can you look for employment in the research field?

Practice Quiz

Note: You can find the correct answers to these questions by taking the quiz and then submitting your answers in the Online Edition. The program will automatically score your submission. If you miss a question, the program will provide the correct answer, a rationale for the answer, and the section number in the chapter where the topic is discussed.

1. Basic research provides information about a phenomenon or tests a theory or hypothesis but does not solve a specific problem.
   a. True
   b. False

2. A researcher would perform applied research if he or she wants to know whether the company should change the color of its product's package from red to blue.
   a. True
   b. False

3. Tabulation houses perform statistical analyses and transform raw data into information that managers can use.
   a. True
   b. False

4. The initial step in the decision-making process is to define the problem.
   a. True
   b. False

5. The Council of American Survey Research Organizations (CASRO) is a Latin American trade association for commercial research firms.
   a. True
   b. False

6. Which of the following types of research is typically done without solving a specific problem?
   a. Normal research
   b. Basic research

c. Applied research
d. All of the above
e. None of the above

7. Which service agencies routinely collect information and report their findings to the clients or companies that subscribe to their service?
   a. Standardized services
   b. Syndicated services
   c. Custom houses
   d. Field services
   e. Independent consultants

8. Which marketing research position oversees the handling and processing of statistical information and prepares work schedules?
   a. Fieldwork director
   b. Junior director
   c. Tabulator

d. Senior analyst
e. Clerical supervisor

9. Which type of research agency is Roper Starch, which evaluates print advertisements through its Starch Readership Survey?
   a. Custom house
   b. Field services
   c. Tabulation house
   d. Standardized services
   e. Syndicated services

10. Which organization from the following list does not use marketing research?
    a. Retailers
    b. Advertising agencies
    c. Financial service providers
    d. Health service providers
    e. All of the above use marketing research.

Thinking Critically

1. Reread the "Get This!" feature at the beginning of the chapter. Is Arbitron conducting basic or applied research? Why?

2. In this chapter you were introduced to different types of marketing research organizations such as those offering syndicated, standardized, and field services. Review each type of organization that conducts marketing research, and then list the courses you feel an individual should take in college to prepare for a career in each position.

3. It was noted in the chapter that there are several types of limited service suppliers including independent consultants, field services, coding and data entry services, and tabulation houses. There are certainly many more of these types of research suppliers. Through secondary research, find four other types of research suppliers besides those listed.

4. List the six steps of the decision-making process.

5. Let's say you are presently employed with a major marketing research firm based in New York City. You were assigned to perform a taste test comparing your client's beverage with the beverages of three major competitors. Before you conducted the test, however, you read a journal article claiming that most people have a preference for the letter A over all other letters of the alphabet. You figured that since it was a blind taste test, you would label your client's beverage A and the competitors' beverages B, C, and D. Do you believe that this was an ethical way to conduct the taste test? Do you feel that you have an ethical responsibility to disclose the information about individuals' preference for the letter A, since this preference might have biased respondents toward choosing your client's beverage? Discuss your answers.

6. Is ethical marketing an oxymoron? Give support for your answer.

Net Exercises

1. The Council of American Survey Research Organizations (CASRO) is an important trade organization for commercial, full-service survey research companies based in the United States. Visit its web page (http://www.casro.org) and read about its "Code of Standards and Ethics for Survey Research." Which two standards do you believe are the most difficult for marketing researchers to adhere to? Why?

2. The Gallup Organization is the world leader in public opinion polling. It is also the world's premier man-

agement research firm. It collects information about employees, workplaces, and customers around the world for 100 of the best-managed *Fortune* 500 corporations. Several employment opportunities exist for new college graduates. Visit its Web site (http://www.gallup.com/) to see whether a position is available for you. Did you find anything that you would be interested in pursuing after graduation?

3. An excellent source for marketing research information is Quirk's Marketing Research Review. You can

read about its 6,200 research providers and search each company by name, geographic area, or area of marketing specialization. You can also read its "Job Mart," which posts and reviews marketing research employment opportunities. Visit its Web site (http://www.quirks.com) and use the "Search by Company or Contact Name" feature to find ACNielsen Co. and Maritz Marketing Research, Inc.

Which research functions can these companies perform for their clients? Are they members of CASRO?

4. In the chapter, it was explained that many organizations are constantly searching for qualified individuals to work for them in the research field. Using the Internet, search for employment opportunities in the marketing research field. What did you find? Do any of these opportunities appeal to you? Why or why not?

Experiencing Marketing Research

Locate the "Employment Opportunities" section in your local newspaper. If some businesses are searching for marketing researchers, write down the job descriptions and then indicate which of the job titles given in the chapter they most closely resemble. If there are no businesses searching for marketing researchers, write down the job opportunities that appear to be related to marketing research.

Case 1-1

Teenagers Are Growing into Major Markets

When children are young, they're cute, cuddly, and the apple of our eyes. But during the teenage years, many parents find their relationships with their teenagers to be much more of a challenge because communicating with them can be quite daunting. They are at a not-so-tender age, and they thrive on being head-strong and independent. A Roper Starch survey recently found that 64% of teens cited friends, not parents, as the top influence in their choice of clothes. And less than half of all respondents stated that their parents are the main influence as they figure out what they want to be when they grow up. They are a complex group, but get used to them. While society has long focused on the aging Baby Boomers, the ranks of teenagers are growing again.

In 1992, the U.S. population of teenagers increased to 24.08 million, ending the 15-year drop produced by the Baby Bust. In 1994, the teen population hit nearly 25 million. In the current decade this group will grow at about twice the rate of the overall population. It will crest about 2010 at 30.8 million—almost a million more than the Boomers' high mark of 1976. But these teens are far different from the post–World War II generations. Today's teenagers have been brought up with dual-income households, personal computers, CD players, portable telephones, VCRs, video games, and microwave ovens, and in a world beset by AIDS. Multiculturalism is also a normal part of their world. In fact, one in three belongs to a minority, compared to one in four in the total population.

Since teens are such a dynamic and growing market, how do you find out about their lifestyles and desires?

Procter & Gamble Co. simply hired a group of teens for eight weeks and paid them $1,000 and a trip to a rock concert. The teens watched television commercials and discussed why they liked or disliked them, took their managers to the mall to identify retail displays that appealed to them, discussed what packaged-goods products they often buy and why they buy them, handled new snack-food shapes and tasted the new flavors, and brainstormed for names of new snack products.

Greenfield Consulting Group and *Adweek Magazine* took a slightly different approach. They separated groups by creating all-girl and all-boy panels. These kids offered insights into how they respond to the constant bombardment of marketing campaigns aimed at them. For example, Levi Strauss & Co. found out that what teens liked and disliked about their jeans.

Mitchell Fox, publisher of *Details*, encourages market researchers to go the unconventional route. When *Details* tried to survey teens using traditional focus groups, they failed miserably because the teens perceived them as "big brother" and as having a "we want something from you" attitude. To get teens to talk, the staff created a relaxing environment that encourages respondents to open up. Sessions are no longer held in rooms with two-way mirrors—they are held in living rooms.

Another research group, Collegiate Marketing Co., located in Chicago, also doesn't believe that standard research techniques work with teens, so they survey them in bathrooms, at school, in lines of people waiting for concert tickets, and in bars. As one researcher says, "It's a strange place to be, doing market research in a club on a Friday night, but it works."

Of course, as Jim Kaufman, CEO of SchoolSports Magazine, notes, "Teens are distracted by a lot of mediums.... They're on the Internet, playing video games, and watching TV all at the same time. As noted in the Packaged Facts teen report, the Pew Internet & American Life Project found that 92 percent of online teens send or read e-mail. Moreover, 74 percent of online teens use instant messaging." The Strategic Group estimates that 17.4 percent of 13 to 17-year olds in the U.S. have a wireless phone, and another 26.3 percent share a phone with another family member. To reach this sacred market, the Packaged Facts teen report notes in the soft drink industry the introduction of Pepsi-Cola North America's new flavor Mountain Dew Code Red with marketing activities such as product launch parties, street team sporting events, sampling in 12 to 14 metro markets with trucks blasting loud music at hip teen hangouts, and radio ads featuring rapper Busta Rhymes.

Sources: "Teens/Tweens," *License!* Vol. 8, issue 5 (June 2005), pp. 70–72; Jack Neff, "P&G enlists 13-year-olds in summer intern jobs," *Advertising Age*, vol. 70, no. 27 (June 28, 1999): 20–25; Ann Smith, "Global teens," *Progressive Grocer,* vol. 78, no. 3 (March 1999): 10; Adam Feuerstein, "Teens weigh in on Levi's ads, and they, like, like 'em," *San Francisco Business Times,* vol. 13, no. 29 (February 19, 1999): 11; Cyndee Miller, "Sometimes a researcher has no choice but to hang out in a bar," *Marketing News,* vol. 28, no. 1 (January 3, 1994): 16, 26; Laura Zinn, Jonathan Berry, Kate Murphy, Sandra Jones, Marti Benedetti, and Alice Cuneo, "Teens," *Business Week* (April 11, 1994): 76–86.

Case Questions

1. Which type of research, basic or applied, was each of the research companies using to learn more about the teenage market? Explain your answers.

2. Which method do you feel allows the researcher to most effectively learn about teenagers' buying habits? Explain your answer.

3. Some people might say that Bugle Boy went too far in gathering data by providing video cameras to students and asking them to document their activities. Is this an invasion of privacy? Do you consider this an ethical way of gathering information? If so, why? If not, why not?

Case 1-2

Too Much Research in New Zealand?

How much research is enough? Thousands of people are being interviewed and surveyed every day throughout the world. So when do we hit the point of diminishing returns? According to the Market Research Society of New Zealand (MRSNZ), they may already be there. James Reilly, statistics director at ACNielsen put it this way: "There is an abundance of research being done in New Zealand, and concern that New Zealand is becoming over-researched. Respondent burden is becoming a widely recognized problem for the whole market research industry." While New Zealand has a population of only 3.8 million people, there are between 500,000 and one million interviews each year.

Ed Simperingham, the MRSNZ immediate past president and Homescan operations manager at ACNielsen believes that New Zealand presently spends about $17 per capita on market research compared with only $12–$14 in other advanced countries such as the United States and in Western Europe. The vast amount of data gathering by marketing researchers is causing some major problems. First, response rates are dramatically falling. That is, more targeted respondents are turning down requests for vital information for companies. One source said that while door-to-door researchers used to expect to obtain one interview for every two and a half households approached, they are now getting one in five.

Second, targeted respondents are becoming increasingly aggravated by marketing researchers and in some cases are providing frivolous and intentionally wrong responses. This, of course, will lead to biased or erroneous results. Third, more researchers are selling under the guise of "research." Colin Ingram, director at Focus Research, believes that people can tell the difference between market research and telemarketing, but many people would disagree. Fourth, some respondents are becoming participants in studies far too often just to make some money. This can bias results if respondents are not carefully screened.

Both MRSNZ and the Association of Market Research Organizations (AMRO) realize that they have a major marketing research problem in New Zealand that will not likely go away without doing something about it. But should they simply stop conducting marketing research? If not, what else can they do?

Sources: Ruth Le Pla, "Is New Zealand being over-researched?" *New Zealand Marketing Magazine,* vol. 19, no. 3 (April 2000): 18+; Ruth Le Pla, "Unmasking the truth," *New Zealand Marketing Magazine,* vol. 18, no. 11 (December 1999/January 2000): 24+.

Case Questions

1. What should MRSNZ and AMRO do about the problem of too much marketing research in New Zealand?

2. Would you say that marketing researchers in New Zealand are not practicing the marketing concept? Why or why not?

3. Do you consider any of the marketing practices in New Zealand unethical? If so, why?

Notes

1. Lisa M. Keefe, "What is the meaning of marketing?" *Marketing News*, vol. 38, issue 15 (Sept. 15, 2004): 17.

2. Bob Gary, Jr., "Fewer American teens have credit cards than last year, poll says," *Knight Ridder Tribune Business News*, Washington (May 11, 2005), 1.

3. Mark Dolliver, "What's a prom without an orgy of spending?" *Adweek*, vol. 46, issue 15 (April 11, 2005), 48.

4. Yu Lu, "Students prove a large market force," *China Daily* (North American ed.), New York (Jan. 4, 2005), 11.

5. Anonymous, "Puppy love," *Restaurant Hospitality* (February 2000), vol. 84, no. 2: 18.

6. Don Muret, "CFL continues to score," *Amusement Business*, vol. 111, no. 29 (July 19, 1999): 25; R. Gary Edwards, and Jon Hughes, "CFL favoured over NFL," *The Gallup Poll*, vol. 56, no. 17 (March 7, 1996): 1–2.

7. Alarcon, Camille, "Maccas targets lunchtime crowd," *B&T Weekly*, vol. 54, Issue 2493 (10/15/2004): p. 6–6.

8. Kevin Done, "Japanese ahead in first new-car customer survey," *Financial Times* (April 16–17, 1994): 4.

9. Valerie Zeithaml, Leonard L. Berry, and A. Parasuraman, "Communication and control processes in the delivery of service quality," *Journal of Marketing*, vol. 52 (April 1988): 35–48.

10. "64 ways to leave your thirst," *Beverage World* (May 1995): 8.

11. Thomas C. Kinnear and Ann R. Root, *1994 Survey of Marketing Research* (Chicago: American Marketing Association, 1994), 7–8, 38.

12. Philip Kotler, *Marketing Management*, 11th ed. (Upper Saddle River, NJ: Prentice Hall, 2003), 9.

13. Gregg Cebrzynski, "Captain D's readies major marketing changes," *Nation's Restaurant News*, vol. 39, Issue 34, (August 22, 2005), 8.

14. Jon Lafayette, "New System Syncs Ratings Data," *Television Week*, vol. 25, Issue 5, 1/30/2006.

15. The American Heritage Dictionary of the English Language (Boston: Houghton Mifflin Co., 2000).

16. O. C. Ferrell and John Fraedrich, *Business Ethics* (New York: Houghton Mifflin, 1997), 5–6.

17. David W. Moore, "One in nine investor households have 'socially responsible' investments," *Gallup News Service*, May 16, 2000: 1–3.

18. Stephen B. Castleberry, Warren French, and Barbara A. Carlin, "The ethical framework of advertising and marketing research practitioners: A moral development perspective," *Journal of Advertising*, vol. XXII, no. 2 (June 1993): 39–46.

19. Jeffrey Kluger, "Poll vaulting: You can trust figures—but can you trust who's doing the figuring?" *Discover*, vol. 16, no. 5 (May 1995): 46–49. Jeffrey Kluger © 1995. Reprinted with permission of *Discover Magazine*.

20. This information was taken from Cynthia Crossen, an editor and writer at the *Wall Street Journal* and author of *Tainted Truth: The Manipulation of Fact in America*, as reported by Jeffrey Kluger, "Poll vaulting: You can trust figures—but can you trust who's doing the figuring?" *Discover*, vol. 16, no. 5 (May 1995): 46–49.

21. Lyn S. Amine, "The need for moral champions in global marketing," *European Journal of Marketing*, vol. 30, no. 5 (May 1996): 81–94.

22. U.S. Department of Labor web page, "Market and survey researchers: job outlook," *http://bls.gov/oco/ocos013.htm#outlook*, June 8, 2005.

23. Alex Benady, "Answers in the question," *The Guardian* (May 18, 1996): S2(2).

24. Thomas C. Kinnear, and Ann R. Root, *1988 Survey of Marketing Research* (Chicago: American Marketing Association, 1989), 53–74.

Marketing Research Process and Problem Identification

Chapter Two

Source: © 2007 JupiterImages Corporation.

Key Terms

causal research (p. 41)
coding (p. 48)
conclusive research (p. 39)
concomitant variation (p. 42)
cross-sectional study (p. 43)
dependent variable (p. 41)
descriptive research (p. 39)
editing (p. 48)
exploratory research (p. 38)
external data (p. 46)
independent variable (p. 41)
internal data (p. 46)

longitudinal study (p. 44)
nonprobability sample (p. 46)
population (p. 45)
primary data (p. 45)
probability sample (p. 46)
problem definition (p. 33)
qualitative data (p. 46)
quantitative data (p. 47)
research design (p. 37)
research objectives (p. 36)
sample (p. 45)
secondary data (p. 45)

Learning Objectives

After studying this chapter, you will be able to:

- Describe the steps in the marketing research process.
- Identify the decision problem or opportunity and specify research objectives.
- Distinguish among three types of research design.

Well-Planned Gallup Research Paves the Road to China

The Gallup Organization is one of the world's largest management consulting firms. Its main expertise is in measuring and understanding human attitudes and behaviors. The company employs more than 2,000 research, consulting, and training professionals and has subsidiary offices in 25 countries. The largest country it operates in is China. Obtaining a clear understanding of consumer attitudes in this elusive market could only be performed by an organization well versed in marketing research. The company's initial study of this market was in 1994 when researchers from the Gallup Organization traveled on foot, by bicycle, by motorbike, and even by camel to painstakingly gather vital marketing information for U.S. businesses. Prior to this time, no nationwide consumer survey had ever been conducted in China because the prospect was daunting and the political climate did not allow it. But Gallup took up the challenge and visited 3,400 households throughout the communist nation to collect the data that Madison Avenue craves.

While the 1994 study provided some unsettling revelations for U.S. businesses—namely that brand name recognition of U.S. products lagged far behind that of Japanese brands—Gallup felt that a more comprehensive and in-depth study was necessary to truly understand Chinese consumers, so three years later they carefully designed and followed a marketing research process. They carefully laid out their research objectives, developed a research design, and prepared and gathered all kinds of consumer data pertaining to attitudes, lifestyles, marketing, finances, and demographics. In May and June of 1997, Gallup conducted more than 3,700 hour-long in-home interviews across China, each comprising more than 400 questions. The entire effort was painstaking but informative. Every province, municipality, and autonomous region of China was covered, using seven primary tongues, including Wie, Tibetan, and Zhang, as well as numerous local dialects. In all, the interviewers surveyed 22 provinces, 3 municipalities, and 5 autonomous regions—from the subtropical island province of Hainan to Inner Mongolia, from Tibet to Heilongjiang, and from coastal Shanghai to Xinjiang in the far northwest.

Gallup's later research revealed that Japanese firms continue to perform well in the Chinese market, although their dominance appears to be waning. Similar to the results of the earlier study, of the 20 most widely recognized foreign brands in China, more than half were Japanese, seven were American, two were German, and one was Dutch. Among non-Chinese brands, the five leaders consisted of three U.S. brands (Coca-Cola, Jeep, and Head and Shoulders), one German brand (Volkswagen's Santana), and one Japanese brand (Panasonic). Each was recognized by at least two-thirds of all Chinese adults nationwide (Coca-Cola, 81%; Jeep, 77%; Santana, 76%; Head and Shoulders, 72%; Panasonic, 70%).

Gallup continues its efforts to understand Chinese consumers in the 21st century. For example, the 2004 Gallup Poll of China showed the emerging "Generation Y" segment (aged 18 to 24), known as "little emperors" as a result of China's one-child policy, are bucking the imperialist and collectivist traditions of China's past and defining themselves as individuals. Interestingly, while Gen Y Chinese may have brand preferences, nobody actually "owns" them: Only 19% believe there is one best soft drink brand, only a third (34%) feel there is one beer for them, and less than a third (30%) say a single brand of athletic shoes is the best. Thus, there are diverse opportunities for companies to satisfy the burgeoning needs for consumer and household goods of Gen Yers.

Sources: Gallup Organization Home Page, http://www.gallup.com, accessed June 9, 2005; Kevin Goldman, "U.S. brands trail Japanese in China study," *Wall Street Journal* (February 16, 1995): B8; "1997 Survey: The People's Republic of China Consumer Attitudes & Lifestyle Trends," William J. McEwen, "Marketing to China's 'Generation Y'—Generation represents a challenging new world for brand marketers," *Business and Economy, Gallup Poll Tuesday Briefing*, March 15, 2005.

Source: © 2007 JupiterImages Corporation.

Now Ask Yourself

- In such a complex market, how did Gallup researchers organize their efforts to conduct a reliable consumer study?

- How did Gallup prepare for its data collection effort?

- Was it really necessary for Gallup researchers to visit over 3,000 homes and conduct personal interviews nationwide?

- Why should managers be interested in understanding Chinese consumers?

When Gallup entered China to perform its marketing study, little was known about Chinese consumer attitudes and lifestyles. No comprehensive study had ever been done until Gallup came in with a well laid out marketing research process. Its 70 years of experience were proven to pay off. To assist students with their future marketing research projects, this chapter will provide an overview of the entire marketing research process. A seven-step process is offered in this chapter. Some other marketers may recommend a four-, five-, or six-step process. The seven-step process offered here ensures that each step of marketing research is covered. In subsequent chapters you will study each step of this important process in greater detail.

2-1 Steps of the Marketing Research Process

Is it really necessary to *know* a step-by-step procedure to effectively conduct marketing research? Yes. Then is it necessary to *follow* each step every time you conduct marketing research? Probably not, but you could be leaving out some very important steps along the way if you do not follow a proven procedure. Academicians tend to believe that offering a step-by-step method will significantly aid students so that no steps are omitted from the entire process. Think about it this way. Say that you were going to cook a pot of seafood gumbo. If you follow the steps in a cookbook, you will likely have a satisfying meal. But if you omit a few steps and thus leave out some

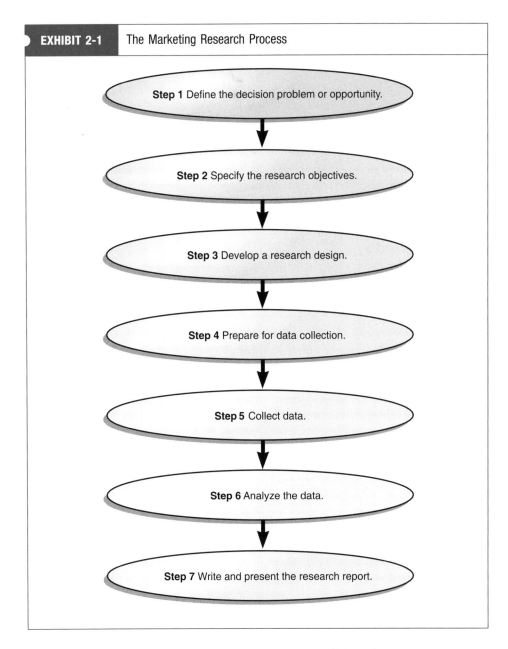

EXHIBIT 2-1 | The Marketing Research Process

Step 1 Define the decision problem or opportunity.

Step 2 Specify the research objectives.

Step 3 Develop a research design.

Step 4 Prepare for data collection.

Step 5 Collect data.

Step 6 Analyze the data.

Step 7 Write and present the research report.

ingredients, the concoction may be less than tasty. So follow the seven-step process outlined in Exhibit 2-1. This systematic approach to research helps ensure that the results will be accurate and relevant.

2-1a Step 1: Define the Decision Problem or Opportunity

The first step to accomplishing anything is the most important. This is especially true in marketing research because it sets the stage for the entire process. The initial step in the marketing research process is to correctly define the problem or opportunity. **Problem definition** is a statement of the specific decision problems for the marketing research project. If the definition is not carefully thought through and precisely formulated, resources will be wasted trying to solve the wrong problem. Poorly defined problems or opportunities severely strain finances, since the actions taken to address them are misguided from the outset. Therefore, marketing researchers must provide adequate information to marketing managers so that a problem or opportunity present in a particular market can be accurately identified. Ill-defined problems create more problems.

problem definition A statement of the specific decision problems for the marketing research project.

Research Realities 2-1   *Microwave Mix-up at Duncan Hines*

It seemed like a perfect opportunity. In the 1970s, managers at Procter & Gamble's Duncan Hines division decided the new craze in the kitchen—microwave ovens—offered them golden profits. This new technology could enable households with limited time—in other words, every household—to cook full-course meals, so Duncan Hines introduced its Microwave Cake Mix. Hot cake fresh out of the microwave oven seemed like a great entry into this new niche, and the company advertised its new products heavily. In its rush to enter the market, however, the company had overlooked the fact that their products were priced higher than conventional mixes and that their microwave cakes had a tendency to fall apart. Needless to say, the product was a miserable failure. This is a problem that could have been avoided by sound marketing research. Consumers should have been queried about these issues during the test-marketing phase of product development.

Years later, microwave technology has improved, as have Duncan Hines' cake mixes. Today even young children make cakes in microwaves with minimum supervision. In fact, microwave delights such as Duncan Hines Moist Deluxe Cake mixes are recommended for vegetarians, by PAWS—Kids Who Care.

Source: PAWS—people helping animals, http://www.pawskids.org/veggiekids/recipes.html, retrieved August 21, 2006); Robert M. McMath, "Copycat cupcakes don't cut it," *American Demographics* 19, no. 1 (January 1997): 60.

Problem definitions are not simple to formulate, so researchers must be thorough in their efforts. Procter & Gamble's Duncan Hines division found this to be the case when it tried to take advantage of the microwave oven craze in the 1970s. Its early microwave products were—well—flops. (See Research Realities 2-1.)

Consider the following examples of how marketing research aids decision making, which we will use later to illustrate how to define decision problems:

- Eastpak, a major manufacturer of backpacks for students, is urging teens to "Get it on" and make their backpacks a part of their everyday lives in a back-to-school campaign that tries more to create an "aura" for the product than list specific attributes. The upbeat ads target 12- to 17-year-olds, 90% of whom own a backpack and use it daily. The commercials were created after marketing research found a problem with Eastpak's previous ad campaign of "Guaranteed for life ... maybe longer." That campaign was designed to demonstrate the longevity and durability of the backpacks, but careful research revealed that students were tired of ads in which they saw beautiful people or celebrities when they most wanted to see real kids who looked like the students themselves. To enhance the emphasis on "real kids," Eastpak used college students to act as brand ambassadors in eight major U.S. cities. These students manage in-store merchandising, conduct product demonstrations, and gather market trend information.[1]

- A credit union in an economically depressed area of Pennsylvania had 3,900 members and $8 million in assets, but there had been no growth in membership for years, so it surveyed its members, made a few changes based on the survey findings, and increased membership by 1,100 and doubled assets in just four years. Another credit union, reluctant to charge member fees for automated teller machines (ATMs), conducted a marketing study and revealed counterintuitive results: Members are willing to pay to retain ATM convenience.[2]

- A survey of IBM customers revealed that the majority were satisfied with their current IBM products and services, but when asked about their plans to replace their equipment, most said that they would go with other suppliers. IBM has to address the problem that customer satisfaction, while important, does not necessarily translate into repeat sales. A Juran Institute study substantiated this concern when it found that fewer than 30% of top managers of America's largest corporations felt that customer satisfaction efforts had contributed economic value to their companies.[3]

To define a problem or opportunity effectively, researchers must consider several concerns, including (1) the decision maker's purposes, (2) what is already known about the issue, (3) the risks associated with the problem or opportunity, and (4) resources available for the research activity.

The Decision Maker's Purposes

The first question that should be addressed when defining the problem or opportunity is "*Why* should we conduct the research?" Because marketing research projects are ultimately undertaken to aid the decision making of the manager, it is vital that the researcher communicates with the manager to accurately understand his or her decision problems, which establish the necessity of a marketing research project.

Managers' decision problems are action-oriented, emphasizing "what should the management do?" Marketing managers must make a variety of decisions, including the following examples:

- How can we position our products in the marketplace?
- How can we introduce a new product to compete successfully against our competitors?
- How can we launch an advertising campaign to effectively reach more customers?
- Shall we consider an alternative marketing channel to deliver our products?
- Shall we revise our pricing strategy to lower/increase our prices?
- How can we build customer loyalty?
- How can we retain customers?

Managers' decision problems set forth the tone of the research project and define the research objectives established by the marketing researcher (i.e., step 2 of the research process). It is a good idea for marketing managers to consult with their researchers when establishing their purposes and clarify the decision problems. Far too often struggling companies invite researchers too late, after research purposes have been established.

What Is Already Known about the Issue?

Why reinvent the wheel? When defining an issue, businesses must consider what they already know and what else they need to know. There is a vast amount of information available that companies often store and can access from their databases to aid in decision-making. There is also a lot of information external to the company, such as on the Internet, that can be used to help define problems and opportunities. In addition, researchers can talk with industry experts and conduct some exploratory studies such as in-depth interviews and observations to further understand the issue.

Risks Associated with the Problem or Opportunity

Resolving problems and cashing in on opportunities entail risks. These risks must be considered, since company constraints set limits on objectives. For example, if a company sees an opportunity to sell its apparel line in Japan but observes that trade relations between its home market and Japan are strained, the company had better reflect this situation in its opportunity definition.

Resources Available for the Research Activity

When defining a problem or opportunity, researchers must consider what resources are available to conduct the study. One company hired a research firm in Mexico to conduct 1,500 interviews within a five-day period. After completion of the study, the client noticed that the firm had only three telephones. When asked how so many calls could have been made in such a short period of time, the research firm replied that calls were made from private residences! The client was disturbed that no in-house central phone bank or monitoring system was available for their study; this made the reliability of the data suspect.[4] Companies have resource limitations, and these must always be considered.

research objectives A statement of what information is needed to solve the decision problems.

2-1b Step 2: Specify the Research Objectives

After defining the problem or opportunity, researchers must state the research objectives clearly. Whereas decision problems ask what the management should do, **research objectives** specify what *information* is needed to solve the decision problems. That is, decision problems are action-oriented, whereas research objectives are information-oriented.

Research objectives should flow from, and be totally consistent with, the decision problem definition. Research objectives must focus on what information can help management to solve the problem. For example, several men's clothing retailers were facing a declining sales figure. The decision problem can be defined as "What must we do to increase store sales?" To answer this question, research objectives were stated in two questions: "What makes men buy apparel?" and "Why don't they buy our merchandise?" After more than 1,000 interviews, the company found that men seek retailers who provide product information and sales assistance because men do not know much about apparel. Based on these findings, the implications for "what to do to increase store sales" are straightforward—these retailers should offer sales assistance to their male customers.[5]

Transferring Decision Problems to Research Objectives

Far too often marketers collect data without a clear understanding of what they are seeking. Bank management may ask the marketing department to gather information regarding customer satisfaction. Their request seems clear-cut, but about which product or service does management want to make decisions? Are they interested in the level of customer satisfaction associated with their credit card offerings, tellers, automatic teller machines, banking hours, or loan programs? Marketing research is undertaken to help decision makers solve specific problems. Therefore, whether the problem is to curtail deteriorating customer satisfaction or increase market share by exploring business opportunities abroad, the information must satisfy the needs of the individuals in a position to use it.

The research objectives should be stated as clearly as possible to allow the marketing manager or client to aid decision making. There is usually a one-to-one corresponding relationship between decision problems and research objectives. Exhibit 2-2 describes this corresponding relationship.

Now let us consider the three examples described in section 2-1a to illustrate how to define decision problems and research objectives and how research projects provide information to aid decision making.

Example 1: Eastpak

- *Decision problem:* How do we launch a new promotional campaign to create an "aura" for Eastpak backpacks?

EXHIBIT 2-2	Translating Decision Problems to Research Objectives
Decision Problems (What do the decision makers need to do?)	**Research Objectives (What information is needed to solve the decision problem?)**
• Should we introduce a particular new product?	• To understand customer preferences and evaluations of the new product.
• Should we launch a new advertising campaign?	• To understand the effectiveness of the current advertising campaign.
• Should we use the Internet as an additional means of distribution channel?	• (1) To understand customer interest in purchasing our product online, and (2) to understand our retailer reactions regarding our online distribution.
• Should we increase our product price?	• To understand customer acceptance of different levels of price increase.

- *Research objective:* To understand the effectiveness of the existing advertising campaign in creating brand attitude.
- *Research findings:* Students were tired of ads in which they saw beautiful people or celebrities when they most wanted to see real kids who looked like the students themselves.
- *Decisions:* Launch a "real kids" campaign with college students acting as brand ambassadors to manage in-store merchandising, conduct product demonstrations, and gather market trend information in eight major U.S. cities.

Example 2: Credit union

- *Decision problem:* Should member fees be charged for ATM use?
- *Research objective:* To understand customer acceptance of charging fees for ATM use.
- *Research findings:* Members are willing to pay to retain ATM convenience.
- *Decisions:* Charge fees for ATM use.

Example 3: IBM

What are the decision problem and research objective for this case?

2-1c Step 3: Develop a Research Design

Sometimes companies get lucky. Consider Sony, Chrysler, and Compaq, which basically ignored the customer to create the Walkman trademark, minivan, and PC network servers, respectively. And sometimes companies are unlucky. Coca-Cola and McDonald's conducted in-depth research, listened to the customer, and created flops like New Coke and McLean burgers.[6] But for the majority of companies, it is vital that they conduct marketing research and create a plan for their studies.

Research design is the framework that directs marketing research efforts. An effective research design does two things: (1) it provides answers to questions as objectively, accurately, and economically as possible; and (2) it controls possible sources of errors, such as collecting data from respondents who are not representative of the population of interest.[7] Of course, another problem can occur when data is not collected from respondents who are part of the population of interest. This problem occurred in a study of credit union members. One credit union's supervisor of member surveys noted, "I recall one credit union that didn't send out any surveys to people who had been members for less than a year. Those omissions badly skewed the results."[8] Developing a research design begins with the research objectives, and then it should briefly cover the following questions:

research design Framework that directs the marketing research efforts.

- What type of information should be gathered?
- How should the research effort be conducted?
- From whom should the information be gathered?
- How will the data be analyzed?
- What findings might be anticipated?

A sound research design is one that is likely to achieve the research objectives. As shown in Exhibit 2-3, research designs may be classified as either exploratory or conclusive. An arrow is drawn from exploratory to conclusive research to indicate that exploratory research is sometimes the first step in doing conclusive research. Exhibit 2-4 presents a brief comparison of these types of research, which we will now discuss in detail.

Exploratory Research

Often the word "explore" conjures up the thought of a dark cave. If we set out to go exploring in a dark cave, we usually do not know what's ahead of us. It could be a large

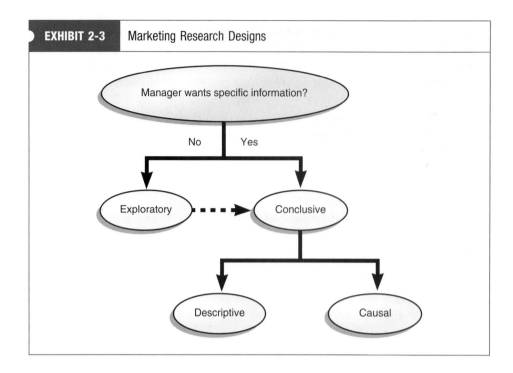

EXHIBIT 2-3	Marketing Research Designs

EXHIBIT 2-4	Comparison of Exploratory and Conclusive Research

Issue	Exploratory	Conclusive
Purpose	Identify problems, generate hypotheses, gain insights	Solve problems, test hypotheses, examine insights for relationships
Study structure	Loose	Rigid
Sample size	Small, nonrepresentative	Large, representative
Cost to implement	Low	High
Data analysis	Qualitative	Quantitative
Findings	Preliminary, tentative	Final, conclusive
Subsequent action	More exploratory research or conclusive research	Used to make decisions

bear ready to take a swipe at us. It could be a bunch of spider webs or bats waiting to entangle us. It could be ancient writings on the wall. It could be any number of things. The fact is, when we explore, we are facing an uncertain future. But as we explore the cave, we gain a better understanding of its contents, and the same goes for marketing research. When we conduct exploratory research, we are searching to provide a better understanding about a particular topic of interest.

exploratory research Research that identifies problems, generates hypotheses, and gains insights into particular subjects.

By definition, **exploratory research** identifies problems, generates hypotheses, and gains insights into particular subjects. Whenever a manager needs information about a topic that he or she knows very little about or has limited experience with, exploratory research is a logical step toward improving knowledge about the topic. A more rigorous, and thus costly, conclusive study may follow, so it is important that the exploratory research project is well done. In the next section we will learn about conclusive research, but for now let's continue to explore a simpler, less expensive research design.

Although exploratory research can satisfy different objectives, such as problem identification or hypotheses generation, all such research shares certain common elements:

- *Small-scale in nature.* Since this research is usually undertaken to provide preliminary information, in-depth and conclusive results are not the goal. Therefore, exploratory studies can be small-scale compared to those seeking definitive results.

- *Costs are relatively low.* Compared to other available research designs, exploratory research is relatively inexpensive to perform. Although experts may be needed to investigate particular concerns, the costs can be kept relatively low because preliminary findings don't require as much detail and are therefore less expensive to obtain.

- *Tends to be flexible.* Exploratory research has fewer rules because unexpected events often occur, requiring adjustments to plans from time to time. In fact, this type of research is usually unscientific. The idea is to redirect the focus as necessary to explore a range of insights, ideas, and feelings. The cutoff point occurs when sufficient information has been gathered or when budget constraints preclude further examination.

- *May be carried out in many ways.* Exploratory research uses a variety of techniques, including previously collected information (or "secondary data"), group interviewing (or "focus groups"), personal interviews (or "in-depth interviews"), various psychological techniques, observation, experiments, surveys, and case studies. (Many of these topics will be discussed in subsequent chapters.)

- *Findings tend to be inconclusive.* Exploratory studies are often performed in industries where little prior knowledge exists. Therefore, sometimes less-than-scientific methods are used in the research process, and this can lead to less-than-conclusive findings. The goal is to explore, not conclude.

An interesting exploratory study examined customer switching in service industries. The researcher stated her intentions this way:

> The goal of this research is to help managers and researchers understand service switching from the customer's perspective. Because the topic has not been examined in prior research, exploratory research was conducted among service customers to investigate the following questions. . . . [9]

The findings of exploratory studies are preliminary and are typically followed up by either *descriptive* or *causal* investigations. Both provide conclusive results, but as you will learn in the following discussion, conclusive research is much more structured and costly than exploratory research.

Conclusive Research

Conclusive research techniques provide specific information that aids the decision maker in evaluating different courses of action. Researchers use sound statistical methods and formal research methodologies to increase the reliability of the information. What clearly differentiates exploratory from conclusive research is the information sought by researchers. When exploratory research is undertaken, little is known about the subject under investigation. Therefore, the information desired tends to be obscure and imprecise. The data sought through conclusive research, on the other hand, tends to be specific and decisive, since much is already known about the topic being studied. It also tends to be more structured and formal than exploratory research. The research approaches differ according to purpose, flexibility, costs, and data collection methods. Descriptive and causal research are two types of conclusive research. A comparison of research designs is offered in Exhibit 2-5.

conclusive research Research that provides specific information that aids the decision maker in evaluating different courses of action.

Descriptive Research

Descriptive research describes attitudes, perceptions, characteristics, activities, and situations. It differs from exploratory research because the researcher already knows which research questions will be addressed. These studies may describe the behavior of targeted consumers, characteristics of customers, or the market potential for specific products. Simply stated, descriptive research examines who, what, when, where, why, and how questions. It is performed after information needs have been entirely specified, the problem has been well defined, and tentative hypotheses have been generated.

descriptive research Research that describes attitudes, perceptions, characteristics, activities, and situations.

EXHIBIT 2-5	Comparison of Research Designs		
Issue	**Exploratory**	**Descriptive**	**Causal**
Purpose	Identify problems, generate hypotheses, gain insights	Describe things	Determine cause-and-effect relationship
Assumed Background Knowledge	None/minimal	Considerable	Considerable
Degree of Structure	Little	A lot	A lot
Flexibility	A lot	Little	Little
Sample	Usually nonrepresentative	Representative	Representative
Research Environment	Relaxed	Formal	Highly controlled
Expected Expenditures	Low	High	High
Findings	Preliminary	Conclusive	Conclusive

The following studies demonstrate the type of information that can be revealed through descriptive research. In each study, prior knowledge existed on the topics under investigation—that is, these are not new topics, but the findings are new. For these findings to be conclusive, the respondents must be representative of the target population.

- Surveys conducted in April of 2006 show that 73% of adults, approximately 147 million adults, use the Internet. High speed internet connections are becoming more prevalent with 42% of home users having broadband service. That's up from 29% as recently as January 2005. Income levels reflect significant differences in internet use with 91% of adults online in households with incomes greater than $75,000. Where household incomes are between $50,000 and $75,000, 86% adults are online. The percentage of users decreases as incomes decrease. Between $30,000 and $50,000 the number drops to 80%. At the lowest levels, those households with less than $30,000 yearly income, only 53% of adults use the Internet. Education is a key indicator for internet use. Of adults with a college degree, the percentage of users is 91%. Those with some college, 84%, with a high school education, 64% and only 40% of adults with less than a high school education are online.[10]

- Increasingly, churches find themselves competing for America's souls, so many denominations are looking to better understand the faith of Americans. A recent descriptive study found that while the percentage of Americans who believe in God has remained relatively constant at close to 90%, an increasing number of Americans also believe in the existence of heaven, hell, angels, and the devil. According to Gallup's Tuesday Briefing report, 81% of Americans believe in heaven and 70% believe in hell. Those proportions are up from 72% and 56%, respectively, in 1997. More than 75% of Americans believe in angels, which is up 3% from 1994. The belief that a devil exists has increased from 65% to 75% from 1994 to 2004.[11]

- As more firms export their products, managers constantly look for new ways to improve their firms' performance. One descriptive study found that marketing strategy, firms' international competence, and managerial commitment are salient success factors in export marketing. Poor performance in export markets was attributed to such factors as lack of strategic planning, failure to adapt products to the changing marketplace, poor choice of distributors, and mistakes in pricing.[12]

Descriptive research can generate a variety of information. However, this type of research shares the following common characteristics:

- *Builds on previous information*. Descriptive studies assume that the researcher has considerable background knowledge relating to the problem or concern. This research builds on the previously generated information.

- *Shows a relationship between variables.* Descriptive research simply shows that there is a relationship or association between two variables. It does not demonstrate that one variable caused another variable to occur.

- *Representative samples are required.* To describe things properly, the data collection process must be sound. A key ingredient is selecting a sample large enough to be representative of the target population.

- *Research plan is structured.* Unlike exploratory research, which is informal and highly flexible, descriptive studies detail why and what will be examined, how the research will be carried out, who will be responsible for it, and when and where it will be administered. Thus, to ensure that these objectives are met, the research plan is highly structured.

- *Requires substantial resources.* Properly implemented descriptive research requires a substantial amount of company resources. For example, if IBM managers want to describe their customers, their researchers may decide to perform interviews, mail surveys to past purchasers, and statistically analyze the results. Such an effort requires several employees and will likely cost thousands of dollars.

- *Findings are conclusive.* Unlike exploratory research, results obtained from descriptive studies are conclusive—not preliminary. These results can be used to help marketing managers make decisions.

Causal Research

The term "causal" refers to cause-and-effect relationships. **Causal research** provides evidence that a cause-and-effect relationship exists or does not exist. The basic premise is that something (an independent variable) directly influences the behavior of something else (the dependent variable). Suppose managers at Procter & Gamble want to know the extent to which advertising creates (or causes) sales for Tide laundry detergent. This information will then aid them in deciding how much money to allocate to advertising for this product.

In studies of causality, dependent and independent variables come into play. A **dependent variable** is affected or predicted through the research. Its value is unknown until the research is completed. In our example, the dependent variable is the sales of Tide laundry detergent. An **independent variable** causes or explains variations in the dependent variable. This quantity is known before the test is started. In our example, the independent variable is the amount spent on advertising Tide detergent during a specified time period.

To help you distinguish between causal and descriptive studies, here is a summary of how they differ:

- Descriptive studies determine the extent to which two or more variables are associated. Causal studies go one step further by inferring whether one or more variables influence (or cause) another variable to act in a particular manner.

- The environments in which descriptive studies take place tend to be much less controlled than the environments for causal studies. Control involves the degree to which independent variables that may influence the dependent variable are contained (that is, ruled out of consideration). Thus a highly controlled environment is one in which all other influences—besides those hypothesized to influence the dependent variable—are contained as much as possible: Laboratories are examples of highly controlled environments.

- In descriptive studies, variables are not logically ordered; that is, it doesn't matter how they are ordered. In causal research, however, the (independent) variable presumed to be the cause must precede the (dependent) variable hypothesized to be the effect.

causal research Research that provides evidence that a cause-and-effect relationship exists or does not exist.

dependent variable Variable to be affected or predicted through marketing research.

independent variable Variable believed to cause or explain variations in the dependent variable.

While causal research differs considerably from exploratory research and has some characteristics in common with descriptive research (that is, structured, statistically sound, costly, conclusive), it also has conditions that distinguish it from the other research designs.

Logical Time Sequence For causality to exist, the cause must either precede or occur simultaneously with the effect—it cannot occur later. For an independent variable (for example, advertising expenditures for Tide detergent) to predict a dependent variable (sales level of the detergent), there must be a logical order of events. To determine how sales levels of Tide detergent would change if advertising expenditures are increased by 50% during December, researchers would first need to implement the advertising effort (the "cause") and then measure the sales level (the "effect"—increase, no change, or decrease) after the month is ended.

concomitant variation Extent to which the cause (independent variable) and effect (dependent variable) vary together as hypothesized.

Concomitant Variation **Concomitant variation** is the extent to which the cause and effect vary together as hypothesized. That is, do the independent (cause) and dependent (effect) variables change together in the hypothesized direction? If it is hypothesized that increased advertising of Tide laundry detergent generates more sales of the product, then when advertising expenditures increase from $100,000 per month to $200,000 per month, sales should increase. Similarly, if advertising expenditures are cut from $100,000 to $50,000, sales reductions should result. The more the independent and dependent variables react together, the more the researcher can infer that concomitant variation exists between the variables. This does not mean, however, that the researcher has proved that advertising causes sales. It simply means the claim that a relationship exists between the variables is defensible.

Control for Other Possible Causal Factors To definitively determine that one variable (advertising) causes another variable (sales) to occur, all outside factors that could influence the association between the two variables need to be eliminated. This ideal state of research never exists. Causality can never be guaranteed because other variables always influence the relationship—the point is to minimize their influence as much as possible. This is where the highly controlled environment is critical: It can increase the amount of confidence a researcher has in the relationship, even though the causality can never be absolute. Scientists often attempt to conduct their experiments in controlled environments to reduce or eliminate outside influences, but it is difficult to do (see Research Realities 2-2).

For example, if researchers wish to examine the relationship between advertising expenditures for Tide detergent and sales, they may carefully monitor sales over several different expenditure levels. They may conclude that increased advertising does indeed cause proportional sales growth. However, since the test was conducted outside of a laboratory (that is, a highly controlled environment) other events may have influenced sales levels during the testing period. Did the researchers consider the following possibilities?

- *Economic situations of target markets.* Perhaps consumers' purchasing power increased, so they were more inclined to purchase national-brand detergents.
- *Sales promotion efforts.* Did Procter & Gamble send consumers coupons or rebate offers during the testing period to entice consumers to buy its products?
- *Spillover effects.* Perhaps the University of Alabama football team won a national championship during the testing period. Does the fact that they are commonly referred to as the Tide (their nickname is the "Crimson Tide") have any influence on the sales of the detergent?

The point is that there are always other possible explanations. Think about the U.S. surgeon general's findings that smoking causes cancer. Tobacco companies and

Research Realities 2-2   *Control Is Elusive in Research Design*

Can we ever be sure that something causes something else to occur? For example, do we really know that spending $2.5 million for a thirty-second commercial during the National Football League's Super Bowl will generate enough sales to be worth the cost? Sure, sales might go up after the advertising takes place, but the increase could have been caused by a number of other factors, such as sales promotion, withdrawal from the market of a competitor's product, or a booming economy. The fact is that in the "real world" of marketing research, nothing is certain. One reason for this reality is that most research environments are not controlled. Margaret Roller, president of Roller Marketing

Re-search in Urbana, Virginia, advocates the need for controls:

"Back in college, there was a lot of talk about controlled environments. Indeed, a primary lesson in the lab was that only by integrating controls into research design could you be assured of the reliability, interpretative value, and projectability of the research results. But in the real world of marketing research, control is elusive. It's difficult, if not impossible, to build in the kinds of controls we want. That's why even the most traditional research designs continue to be debated and refined."

Source: Margaret R. Roller, "Control is elusive in research design," *Marketing News* 31, no. 19 (September 15, 1997): 17.

lobbyists have argued that those studies were erroneous in coming to this conclusion. They asserted that the millions of smokers who died of cancer contracted the disease in other ways—perhaps by living in polluted cities or working in unhealthy conditions. Some people believe that before causal studies can be considered truly conclusive, exhaustive historical research related to the variables under investigation must be carefully performed.[13]

Research Frequency
The researcher deciding to conduct a conclusive study must determine how often it will be performed. The two major choices are the cross-sectional (one-time) study and the longitudinal study.

Cross-Sectional Study   The most common form of study, the **cross-sectional study** is a look at what is occurring at one moment in time. Imagine taking a picture of your family. The picture would be representative of what your family looked like when the picture was taken. When researchers use this form of study, respondents are either observed or questioned and then conclusions are drawn from the results of the one-time study. The following are a few examples of cross-sectional studies:

> **cross-sectional study** A sample that looks at what is occurring at one moment in time; can be thought of as a still photograph, since it is a one-time study.

- A study examined the work-related differences and similarities of 241 Generation X (those born between 1965 and 1980) and Baby Boomer (those born between 1946 and 1964) employees in the public sector. Contrary to the literature and stereotypes on generational differences, the researchers were surprised to find that a more homogeneous pattern of what employees want across age cohorts emerged.[14]

- A study looked at how sports celebrity influences the behavioral intentions of Generation Y (those born between 1981 and 1995). It discovered that celebrity athletes positively affect adolescents' favorable word-of-mouth and brand loyalty. In addition, females tend to spread more positive word-of-mouth about a product or brand endorsed by their favorite celebrity athlete than do males.[15]

- A study assessed the Internet's potential for helping firms directly communicate with consumers using media-rich emails. It found that women are different from men in evaluating information content and the visual presentation used in emails. Women are also more concerned about privacy than are men in email use.[16]

There are several advantages and disadvantages to the cross-sectional method.

Advantages:

- It can generate a realistic picture of what was going on at a particular point in time.
- It may be performed at a relatively low cost.
- It may not take much of the respondents' time.
- Data may be gathered in a relatively short period of time.

Disadvantages:

- It may draw an artificial picture of what was going on at a particular point in time. It is possible that respondents were observed or questioned on a "bad day"—for example, there may have been a staff meeting that day at which several employees learned about possible job cutbacks in the coming months. This kind of problem may be remedied by a sound research design (e.g., do not collect all the data at the same time, in the same place, etc.).
- The data obtained may soon be outdated. In several high-technology industries, such as computer software and hardware, items can be considered obsolete after only a few months.

longitudinal study A sample in which the same respondents are questioned or observed during predetermined time intervals over a span of time; can be thought of as a videotape of a market, since information is accumulated from a series of pictures taken at different time periods.

Longitudinal Study Where one-time cross-sectional studies suffer from attempting to generalize about respondents from information obtained at one point in time, longitudinal studies do not have this shortcoming. The **longitudinal study** is continuous, whereby the same respondents are questioned or observed during predetermined time intervals over a span of time. Instead of a still photograph, it is best thought of as a videotape, since information is accumulated from a series of pictures taken at different time periods.[17] The following examples demonstrate the usage of longitudinal studies:

- A local newspaper contacts 1,000 subscribers by telephone and obtains permission from them to contact each of them every six months over a five-year period to inquire about their level of satisfaction with the newspaper.
- A group of researchers attempts to determine why clients switched from one advertising agency to another. A total of 151 decision makers are interviewed by telephone over a two-year period to determine their perceptions of advertising agencies in general and why they changed from their previous agency.[18]
- Procter & Gamble introduces a new pain reliever and contacts the same group of 500 users each month over a six-month period to determine their level of satisfaction with the product.
- A study examines the relative importance of school, family, personal/psychological, race, and sex variables in predicting educational and vocational aspirations. The nationally representative sample of 10th grade students is followed through two years beyond their graduation from high school.[19]

Just as one-time studies have their strengths and weaknesses, so too do longitudinal studies.

Advantages:

- The information obtained over time will usually be more reliable than that gathered at one point in time.
- It takes changes related to time into consideration.

Disadvantages:

- It can be relatively expensive to carry out, since several studies will be conducted.
- The information takes a considerable period of time to collect.
- It requires a lot of cooperation on the part of respondents.

- It requires a fairly sophisticated research design to control potential biasing factors.

Steps 4–7 of the marketing research process will be covered extensively in later chapters. Therefore, we provide a brief overview of these steps in the following sections.

2-1d Step 4: Prepare for Data Collection

Before data is gathered, researchers must make preparations so that the collection effort is as smooth running and as error-free as possible. The research team should ask, "Where will we get the information?" The data may already exist as **secondary data**—that is, data that has already been collected for a purpose other than the current study—or it may have to be **primary data**—original data gathered to satisfy the purpose of the current study. Secondary data is used whenever possible because it tends to be much less expensive to gather than primary data, and such data is also available in a timely manner. However, businesses are sometimes forced to gather new information if available data is outdated or in an unusable form, or if no data is available. Secondary and primary data will be presented in more detail beginning in Chapter 4.

When marketers gather primary information, they need to understand the essence of sampling as well as how the data will be gathered and how to design the measuring instrument.

secondary data Data that has already been collected for a purpose other than the current study.

primary data Original (new) data gathered to satisfy the purpose of the current study.

Essence of Sampling

Although sampling will be discussed in detail in Chapter 10, we provide an overview here to show how it fits in the marketing research process. A **sample** is a group of individuals or objects from a target population that is chosen to represent the target population. A **population** is the entire group of people, markets, companies, or products that is being investigated by the researcher. Any time data is gathered from a sample rather than from the target population, there is a risk that the results may not truly reflect the whole population. However, gathering data from an entire population is normally prohibitively expensive. If done properly, sampling can represent a population within an acceptable degree of possible error, thus making data gathering much less expensive.

sample Individuals or objects from a target population that are selected to represent the population of interest.

population The entire group of people, markets, companies, or products that is being investigated.

Source: © 2007 JupiterImages Corporation.

For a sample to be useful, it must approximate the characteristics of the target population. The procedure for selecting a representative sample depends on numerous factors, including time, budget, personnel skills available for drawing a sample, and the nature of the individual elements of the population. Furthermore, the researcher must be concerned with determining the correct size of the sample and who should be considered for selection in the study. One research group was interested in the demographics and lifestyles of young men who enjoy certain types of movies, so they sampled young men in their late teens to early 20s who were buying tickets to movies like *Hellraiser* and *Dumb and Dumber.* Going to hotels, college campuses, clubs, bars, and other places where young people tend to congregate, the researchers obtained important demographic and lifestyle data by offering respondents bags of goodies including T-shirts, bumper stickers, compact discs, audiocassettes, coupons for discounts on items at concession stands, and temporary tattoos.[20]

probability sample Subset of a population in which the probability of obtaining the sample can be computed and that is non-zero for every sampling unit in the population.

nonprobability sample Any subset of a population in which the probability of obtaining the sample cannot be computed.

There are two types of samples: probability and nonprobability. A **probability sample** is a subset of a population in which the probability of obtaining each sample can be computed and is nonzero for every unit in the population. What this means is that we can use statistics to determine the degree of sampling error—that is, the extent to which our sample is not representative of the population. This is not possible with a **nonprobability sample,** where this probability cannot be computed. Therefore, nonprobability samples are not considered statistically representative of the population. For example, in one country, some local research firms collect data without much regard for accuracy. One client asked for 1,000 completed interviews for their project; the research firms selected anyone from anywhere to interview and hired untrained and inexperienced people to do the tasks as quickly as possible. With such a nonprobability sample, sampling error will be enormous.

So why should a firm ever use nonprobability samples? The answer is simple. Probability sampling is not always possible. It is not even always necessary. A company may simply be looking for inexpensive information that provides managers with some direction about a particular issue. The various types of nonprobability and probability sampling techniques will be covered in detail in Chapter 10.

How Will the Data Be Gathered?

internal data Information obtained from within the organization for which the research is conducted.

Secondary marketing data can be classified as one of two types: internal or external. When the information is obtained from within the organization for which the research is conducted, the information is called **internal data.** Businesses often maintain many kinds of information in various departments for long periods. The sales department keeps sales invoices. The human resources department keeps the individual records of employees. The production department keeps daily records concerning the amount of raw material, direct labor, and manufacturing expenses used and the units of finished product produced. All such data can be useful in a research study.

external data Information obtained from outside the organization for which the research is conducted.

When the information is obtained from outside the organization for which the research is conducted, it is referred to as **external data.** External data is usually classified by the method of obtaining it, whether it is published data or original data. The most convenient and economical way of obtaining external data is to find the information from material published by outsiders, such as federal, state, and city governments; corporations; trade and professional associations; banks; newspapers; magazines; research institutions; colleges; and other private publishers.

When published data is not available, collecting original data, or primary data, may become necessary. Collecting external data by survey is usually costly, tedious, and time-consuming. However, effective survey methods have been developed to save money, energy, and time.

qualitative data Information gathered from a small sample of the target population that is used to understand a group's feelings and insights but cannot predict with absolute certainty and is not projectable to the target population.

Data may be either qualitative or quantitative. **Qualitative data** is information gathered from a small sample of the target population that is used to understand a group's feelings and insights. It does not involve numbers; thus qualitative data cannot predict with absolute certainty and is not projectable to the target population. People are asked to talk about a general topic—for example, what sorts of features they would like in a new car—but it is what the respondents have to say, rather than a pre-determined questionnaire, that determines the content of the discussion. As a result, the data does not include quantitative information, such as rating the importance of various features on a seven-point scale.

Qualitative studies are quite popular because they are often inexpensive and can be performed in a relatively short amount of time. They can be performed through personal interviews, group interviews, or projective techniques with individuals. Projective techniques, aimed at eliciting the deeper, hidden aspects of personality, use vague or ambiguous stimuli that respondents are asked to describe.

For certain groups, qualitative inquiry is the best way to collect data. One researcher interested in understanding the lifestyles and attitudes of Generation Xers—people between the ages of 21 and 29 at the time of the study—conducted group interviews in a variety of settings—trendy hotel suites, pizzerias, college campuses, clubs, bars, rollerblade rental stands, volleyball games, and malls. He found that to get honest answers from this age group, researchers must interview them informally in an environment in which they are comfortable.[21] Qualitative techniques will be discussed in Chapter 5.

Qualitative research is not as popular as it once was because many marketing research executives want to focus on fact rather than "speculation." They feel that qualitative research is an art, not a science.[22] **Quantitative data** is information gathered from many members of the target population that can be quantified and projected to represent the target population. Since this information involves numbers, statistical procedures are usually required to analyze the data. To handle this type of information effectively, a clear understanding of primary data collection, measurement error, and statistical techniques is necessary. These topics are discussed in subsequent chapters, beginning in Chapter 5.

quantitative data Information gathered from many members of the target population that can be quantified and projected to represent the entire target population.

How Will the Questionnaire Be Designed?

When using survey approaches, researchers must construct a well-designed questionnaire. It is vital that researchers refer to the previous steps to ensure that the questionnaire addresses the problem or opportunity definition adequately and is compatible with the research design. Deviations from these concerns will cause the data-gathering effort to stray from its original goals. When creating questionnaires, novice researchers tend to tag on questions that are intended to reveal data beyond the studies' goals. It is not unusual, for example, for a bank survey intended to find out about its customers' satisfaction with its credit cards to add a few questions about customer usage of automatic teller machines. Tag-on questions should be avoided whenever possible. An in-depth discussion of questionnaire design is provided in Chapter 8.

2-1e Step 5: Collect the Data

Information is gathered in a variety of ways, including personal interviews, telephone surveys, mail surveys, and computer-assisted surveys. Choosing the technique appropriate for a particular study depends on such factors as budget; time frame; demographics of respondents; transportation needs; product demonstration needs; survey content, length, and structure; desired response rate; desired sampling precision; and the percentage of people in the general population who have the characteristics being studied. No matter which survey technique is used, researchers must be aware of, and make adjustments for, problems or errors that could exist throughout the data-gathering efforts. In our opening vignette, primary data was collected in China by the Gallup Organization. The details associated with each data collection technique and related problems are discussed in Chapter 4.

2-1f Step 6: Analyze the Data

Once data collection is complete, the next step is to analyze the information. Analysis makes sense of the data so that marketing decision makers can draw conclusions about the variables being studied. When questionnaires are used to gather information, ideally the return rate by respondents is high, and the questionnaires are legible, completely filled out, and answered honestly. However, seldom does this ideal occur. Thus researchers must edit and code the information. **Editing** means carefully checking survey data for completeness, legibility, consistency, and accuracy. **Coding** is the process of systematically and consistently assigning each survey response a numerical score or code.[23] Responses are coded to facilitate identification and analysis.

editing Carefully checking survey data for completeness, legibility, consistency, and accuracy.

coding The process of systematically and consistently assigning each survey response a numbered score or code.

Once the data has been edited and coded, it is ready to be analyzed. Various methods are used in the analysis—from frequency distributions that simply indicate the number of respondents in each category, along with a few simple statistics, to complex techniques that involve highly mathematical investigations. The complexity of the analysis depends on how the information was gathered, the subtlety of the desired results, and the expertise of the marketing researcher. No matter which analytical procedure is used, the results must provide, in a timely manner, the information that the decision maker seeks.

It is no longer necessary to analyze data using manual methods; high-speed computers use statistical software to perform all sorts of calculations, and software packages like SPSS and SAS lessen the burden of statistical analyses. Microsoft Excel also performs numerous statistical calculations. Data analysis is discussed in Chapters 12 through 17.

2-1g Step 7: Write and Present the Research Report

After the data has been collected and properly analyzed, a written report covering the entire research project is usually prepared. The research team may also be requested to

Source: © 2007 JupiterImages Corporation.

EXHIBIT 2-6	Factors Affecting Marketing Research in Developed and Developing Markets

Developed Country	Developing Country
√ Research focuses on operational issues.	√ Research focuses on strategic issues.
√ Data is widely available, easy to gather, and reliable.	√ Data gathering is difficult, expensive, and time-consuming.
√ Research infrastructure is sophisticated.	√ Research infrastructure is unsophisticated.
√ Media is advanced and available.	√ Media is undeveloped and poor in quality.
√ There is no government interference.	√ Government is involved in business decisions.
√ The language and nationality are homogeneous.	√ Population is multilingual and multicultural.
√ Communication systems are advanced.	√ Communication systems are inefficient.

Sources: Adapted from A. C. Samli, R. C. Still, and John S. Hill, *International Marketing* (New York: Macmillan, 1993): 388; Erdener Kaynak, "Marketing research needs of less-developed countries: Standardization versus localization," in *Developments in Marketing Science* VII, Jay D. Lindquist, ed. (Kalamazoo, MI.: Academy of Marketing Science, 1984): 161.

present their findings orally. The report should summarize all of the steps in the study. A carefully written report permits the reader to understand the research problem or opportunity, the design of the study, and the conclusions drawn from the research effort. The marketing manager must clearly understand the entire report, since he or she is typically not involved in each step of the research process but must make decisions based on this process.

It is important not to overwhelm management with details in the report, unless they specifically request them. The report should begin with a succinct statement of the research objectives. The research design is then briefly described. Once management understands how the study was conducted, the findings can be presented and the implication of the findings explored. Finally, the report presents recommendations based on the results of the study.

2-2 The Marketing Research Process in Global Markets

When analysts conduct research in familiar environments, they deal with numerous issues to generate reliable results, but these issues are at least known to them. When research is conducted in a less familiar environment such as a foreign country, there are many additional concerns—cultural, political, legal, and social factors that can be subtle and complex. The problem is compounded when researchers accustomed to examining developed markets are faced with problems or opportunities in developing markets.[24] (See Exhibit 2-6 for a comparison of developed and developing markets.) While the research process itself does not change, there are additional considerations when global markets are studied. These concerns are discussed in Chapter 11.

2-3 Optimal Results from the Marketing Research Process

The marketing research process is a recommended plan to follow to effectively conduct marketing research. While there is no guarantee that it will produce useful findings, it should enhance the probability that the results will be useful. Listed below are results that are aimed for by effectively developing and following the marketing research process. All of the topics below were either addressed in this chapter or will be covered in subsequent chapters.

- Clear problem (or opportunity) definition
- Clearly stated and accurate research objectives
- Well laid out research design
- Efficient and effective data collection method
- Utilization of proper data analysis techniques
- Accurate, reliable, and defensible findings
- High ethical standards applied
- Limitations explicitly stated
- Decision maker's information needs satisfied
- Research report well written and accurately presented
- Study measured what it intended to measure

Decision Time!

By now you are familiar with the marketing research process. Does it seem cumber-some and perhaps too detailed? If so, how would you design the research process? Do you really need to perform all seven steps each time you research a topic? If so, why? Do you think the order in which the steps are followed is important? If not, how would you reorder them, and why?

Net Impact

The Internet is radically changing the way the marketing research process is performed. Research design and data collection, in particular, are beginning to feel the impact of the Net. As the Internet becomes increasingly organized and user-friendly, researchers will gather the bulk of their data on the Net—through surveys or chat rooms, or simply by accessing preexisting data. Substantial cost savings can be realized as marketing researchers shift from the postal service and personal interviews to using the information superhighway.

On the Lighter Side—Students Need Incentives to Take Tests Seriously

In March 2005, 553 foreign language students were surveyed so administrators could learn what would motivate them to take the High School Assessment (HSA) exam. The 15-question survey attempted to find out what students knew about the importance of standardized tests as well as what would motivate them to attend school on test days and give their best effort on exams. The findings showed that 31% of all respondents believe that standardized tests are not important to their success in high school, so administrators concluded that students needed to be told that the tests are important. They knew that if students didn't feel that a test was important then they wouldn't try to do well on it. They also wanted to create incentives to motivate them to take the test. The strongest incentive was the hypothetical chance to win a free car on test day. Students also could recommend their own incentive. The most outlandish suggestion was to threaten the children with cattle prods. Other popular replies included serving test takers free pizza and letting students leave school as soon as they finished the test.

Source: Michael Bushnell, "HAS survey results shed light on what Blazers want," Montgomery High School's Online Student Newspaper, *Silver Chips Online,* http://silverchips.mbhs.edu/inside.php?sid=5240. Retrieved on October 8, 2005.

Chapter Summary

To ensure that research results are relevant, reliable, and usable, follow a systematic process. While there is more than one way to execute proper research, the following seven-step process consistently yields sound results:

1. Define the decision problem or opportunity.
2. State the research objectives.
3. Develop a research design.
4. Prepare for data collection.
5. Collect the data.
6. Analyze the data.
7. Write and present the research report.

When defining problems or opportunities, researchers need to consider why the study is being conducted, what the decision maker's purposes are, what they already know about the issue, what risks are associated with the concern, and what company resources are available. These answers lead to the research objective, which specify what information is needed to aid the decision maker. Decision problems and research objectives set the tone for subsequent research steps.

The research design is the framework for how the research will be conducted. There are different types of designs. They may be classified as either exploratory or conclusive. Exploratory research identifies problems, generates hypotheses, and gains insights into particular subjects. It has the following characteristics: small scale, low cost, flexibility, can be implemented in many ways, and produces inconclusive findings. Conclusive research can be further broken down into descriptive and causal studies. Descriptive research describes attitudes, perceptions, characteristics, activities, and situations. Causal research provides evidence that a cause-and-effect relationship exists or does not exist. Conditions for causal research include logical time sequence, concomitant variation, and control for other possible causal factors. Research frequency can be either cross-sectional (one-time study) or longitudinal (series of studies over time).

The sampling procedure is designed to ensure that the sample selected approximates the characteristics of the population of interest. In this step, researchers must determine whether probability or nonprobability sampling is appropriate. Probability samples are subsets of the population for which the probability of selecting the sample can be computed and is nonzero. Nonprobability samples are all samples for which this probability cannot be computed. When collecting data, researchers may draw from both internal and external sources.

Review Questions

1. What are the seven steps of the marketing research process?
2. When defining either a problem or an opportunity, what factors should researchers consider?
3. Do the marketing research objectives have to be consistent with the problem or opportunity definition? Why or why not?
4. What is concomitant variation?
5. What is the difference between probability and non-probability sampling?
6. What is the difference between descriptive and causal research?
7. How do exploratory research and descriptive research differ?
8. What is a research design?
9. What results should a researcher aim for by following the marketing research process?

Practice Quiz

Note: You can find the correct answers to these questions by taking the quiz and then submitting your answers in the Online Edition. The program will automatically score your submission. If you miss a question, the program will provide the correct answer, a rationale for the answer, and the section number in the chapter where the topic is discussed.

1. Decision problems are defined by research objectives.
   a. True
   b. False

2. Descriptive research is a type of conclusive research that describes attitudes, perceptions, characteristics, activities, and situations.
   a. True
   b. False

3. For causality to exist, the cause must either precede or occur simultaneously with the effect—it cannot occur later.
   a. True
   b. False

4. Concomitant variation is defined as the extent to which the cause and effect vary together as hypothesized.
   a. True
   b. False

5. Qualitative studies are not popular to marketing researchers since they are typically costly to implement and tend to take a long time to perform.
   a. True
   b. False

6. Which of the following is *not* a common element of exploratory research?
   a. Findings tend to be inconclusive.
   b. Expenditures are relatively low.
   c. The research tends to be flexible.
   d. The research environment is relaxed.
   e. The sample is representative of the target population.

7. Which of the following is *not* a common element of descriptive research?
   a. It requires minimal background knowledge.
   b. It builds on previous information.
   c. Samples are representative.
   d. Expected expenditures are high.
   e. Findings are conclusive.

8. A subset of a population in which the probability of obtaining each sample can be computed and is non-zero for every unit of the population is called a:
   a. nonzero sample.
   b. nonprobability sample.
   c. probability sample.
   d. minimal sample.
   e. none of the above

9. Which of the following exists when a researcher carefully examines survey data for completeness, legibility, consistency, and accuracy?
   a. Checking
   b. Marking
   c. Editing
   d. Coding
   e. Reviewing

10. Which of the following is *not* true regarding qualitative studies?
    a. They are often expensive and take a long time to perform.
    b. They can be implemented via projective techniques.
    c. They can be implemented via personal interviews.
    d. They are not as popular as they used to be.
    e. Some experts feel that this type of research is more an art than a science.

Thinking Critically

1. Reread the chapter-opening vignette entitled "Well-Planned Gallup Research Paves the Road to China." Based on your knowledge of research design, what type of design was used in each study performed by the Gallup Organization? Support your answer.

2. Your college athletic administration wants you to outline a research process to examine the student body's attitudes and perception of its women's basketball team. Recommend a research design. Why did you choose this particular one?

3. Scott Boss manages a small business in Charlotte, North Carolina. He is keenly interested in marketing research and has decided to learn more about the process. At the local university where he is enrolled, his instructor talks about "problem or opportunity definition" and "research design" during the first lecture. Scott approaches you and says, "Can you help me clarify something? I can't understand how the problem definition and research design are related." What would you say to him?

Net Exercises

1. Many organizations worldwide perform qualitative research for their clients. Several of these providers can be found on the Internet at the following location: http://www.imriresearch.com/. This site allows you to locate agencies that perform qualitative research by world regions or individual countries. One of the agencies you can visit is Research International Qualitatif, which is among the world's largest custom marketing research agencies. Click on its Web site and read about its operations. What kinds of research problems does it solve, and which services does it offer its clients?

2. SPSS (Statistical Product and Service Solutions), headquartered in Chicago, provides information

about what customers want and what they will do. Its marketing research division, SPSS MR, is the world leader in software solutions and supporting services for market research. Its software is adapted to suit regional markets, making it the ideal global partner for anyone looking at the bigger picture. SPSS MR claims to invest 10 times more resources than any competitor, so whatever an organization's needs may be, whether small or large, local or global, SPSS MR may be the ideal technologies partner. Visit its Web site (http://www.spss.com) and read about its services. While you're there, try the demo that will take you through an easy-to-understand data analysis exercise.

Experiencing Marketing Research

In this chapter, you learned about the marketing research process. It was presented as a sequence of steps that should be followed to effectively conduct marketing research, though some experts believe that it is unnecessary to conduct all of the steps to be successful in research. Visit a local business and inquire about its mode of marketing research. Is the process as systematic as it is presented in this chapter? If not, how does the business satisfy its research needs?

Case 2-1

This H.O.G. Is in Heaven

In the late 1970s, motorcycle manufacturer Harley-Davidson's parent company, sporting goods conglomerate AMF, was losing money because of a "more is better" philosophy. It cranked out Harleys so quickly that it could not ensure quality would be along for the ride. As a result, in 1981 Harley-Davidson left AMF and nearly went bankrupt as an independent company. But by 1989, the company had made substantial improvements to its motorcycles, and it introduced guaranteed trade-in allowances. Its reputation has improved dramatically, and sales have grown rapidly. In recent years, Harley-Davidson has been living the good life. It has two-year-long waiting lists all over the United States. In spite of its enviable position, Harley's managers were not sure whether it should continue producing at the current rate and maintain its admirable reputation in the heavyweight bike industry, or increase production to meet demand and risk a market downturn should product quality decline. "Dealers were begging us to build more motorcycles. But you have to understand our history. One of the things that caused past problems was a lack of quality, and that was the result of a too-rapid expansion. We did not want to relive that situation," stated Frank Cimermancic, Harley's director of business planning.

While Harley was doing just fine, the industry as a whole was shrinking. Harley's managers needed to know whether the company's growth could continue. They had observed that a new type of customer was evolving—one that could lead to significant market growth: Many white-collar motorcycle enthusiasts, known as "Rubbies" (Rich Urban Bikers), had begun buying Harley bikes, which led to an increase in both sales and image. But no one at the company really knew whether this market was dependable and whether the new customers would be long-term Harley loyalists. Graham Sanderson, marketing manager of Three Cross Motorcycles, portrayed the Harley market this way: "Bikers represent a broad church. Bikers can be Dukes or dustmen—and everything in between—but once they've put their leathers on, they are all part of the same club." Management wondered whether it should market its products differently to different audiences. The company needed answers that only marketing research could give them.

Researchers conducted group interviews and sent out more than 16,000 surveys to past, present, and potential customers. All types of psychological, sociological, and demographic questions were on the surveys. There were also subjective questions, such as, "Is Harley typified more by a brown bear or a lion?" On the basis of the responses, researchers identified seven core-customer types: the Adventure-Loving Traditionalist, the Sensitive Pragmatist, the Stylish Status-Seeker, the Laid-Back Camper, the Classy Capitalist, the Cool-Headed Loner, and the Cocky Misfit. They further found that customers universally associate Harley motorcycles with independence, freedom, and power. The majority of owners are also extremely loyal to Harley. "No one tattoos Honda on their arm," stated Ronald Seidner, owner of a Harley dealership. Such loyalty meant that Harley could build and sell its bikes without having to overextend itself. In 1990, the company increased production to 62,000, and in 2000, it sold 204,592 bikes. None of them were built at the expense of quality. The marketing manager had this to say about the marketing effort: "I'm not going to tell you that research was the only reason for the investment, but I like to think it did help answer the question.... We have plans to continue on that slope for the next few years."

Today Harley is the only major U.S. maker of motorcycles and the nation's top seller of heavyweight motorcycles. In 2004, the company shipped 317,289 Harley-Davidson motorcycle units, 9% more than in 2003. Harley-Davidson offers 24 models of touring and custom cycles through a worldwide network of more than 1,300 dealers. Many of its biking brethren are members of the Harley Owners Group (H.O.G.), cruising along with more than 500,000 devotees.

Sources: Ian P. Murphy, "Aided by research, Harley goes whole hog," *Marketing News* 30, no. 25 (December 2, 1996):

16–17; Matthew Carter, "On yer bike, fat boy," *Director* 543, no. 8 (March 2000): 69; Kelly Barron, "Hog wild," *Forbes* 165, no. 11 (May 15, 2000): 68+; Harley-Davidson: *Harley-Davidson 2004 Annual Financial Report.*

Case Questions

1. Define Harley-Davidson's decision problem(s).

2. What was Harley's research objective(s)?

3. Which type of research design did the research group use to understand Harley's market?

4. Did the marketing researcher gather qualitative or quantitative data? Explain your answer.

Case 2-2

Give Credit to BAIGlobal's International Expansion

Companies seem to collect data on just about anything. Credit card companies in particular know where we eat, where we shop, where we go for vacation, how often we travel on airplanes, how often we fill up our gasoline tanks ... just about all of our expenses are documented from our credit card transactions. The fact is, we can't escape it because credit cards are convenient to us.

One company is capitalizing on the credit card explosion worldwide by focusing on the needs of companies through marketing research. BAIGlobal, Inc., has gone international with its direct-mail tracking products. BAIGlobal has had an effective direct-mail research methodology in place for the past five years, but its efforts were concentrated in the United States. No longer. Its product, called "Inside Track," provides information on credit card direct-mail customer retention and activation. This research tool for direct marketers measures which recipients received the mailing, opened the envelope, read the components, and understood the message. Kathy Knight, president of BAIGlobal, explained that expansion into international markets involves new challenges for direct marketers and for measuring their effectiveness. She stated, "In these other places, direct mail is not as trusted ... (and) the cultures are profoundly different."

Christopher Batenhorst, vice president of the Competitive Tracking Services division, leads the expansion of Inside Track as well as Mail Monitor, a product that analyzes the

performance of credit card direct-mail acquisition programs, into Canada and the United Kingdom. BAIGlobal is part of Market Facts, a multinational marketing research agency that provides the company with access to large research panels, or groups of consumers who have agreed to be studied. Some of BAIGlobal's clients include AT&T, Chase Manhattan Corp., Citibank, IBM, Bausch & Lomb, Lucent Technologies, Inc., and Pfizer Inc.

Business has not been entirely successful for BAIGlobal. One project that failed was its Catalog Monitor, which measured sales behavior of catalog shoppers. It was intended to assist retailers by finding out who receives what catalog, who purchases what catalog merchandise, and how much money they spend on purchases. After the project's development, the catalog industry was not interested in the kind of data BAIGlobal thought they would be interested in.

Source: Loren Brody, "BAIGlobal plans strategy for international markets," *Westchester County Business Journal* 38, no. 16 (April 19, 1999): 5–6.

Case Questions

1. Does BAIGlobal seem to perform cross-sectional or longitudinal studies? Explain.

2. Before BAIGlobal ventured outside of the U.S., what do you believe were their objectives? State them as you believe BAIGlobal did.

3. What type of research design does BAIGlobal seem to use in its studies? Support your answer.

Case 2-3

The Integrated Case—Part 1

Cheerwine—In Need of Unique Research

It all started back in the early days of the 20th century when L. D. Peeler, owner of a small grocery store, and other investors bought stock in a regional branch of a Kentucky company that made a popular soft drink called MintCola. As fate had it, shortly after the purchase a "flavor salesman from St. Louis" sold Peeler and the others on a unique cherry flavor to blend with other flavorings that would later become Cheerwine—a popular soft drink beverage in the southern United States, particularly North and South Carolina. Their company, Carolina Beverage Corporation (CBC), developed the name Cheerwine because back then soft drinks were often named for their appearance, as with the names root beer and ginger ale. Therefore, it made sense to name a burgundy-red, bubbly, cherry beverage "Cheerwine."

The beverage's popularity grew in parts of North and South Carolina and soon developed a loyal following. When L. D. died in 1931, the momentum of Cheerwine's popularity became the responsibility of his son, Clifford Peeler, who served as CBC's president until 1992 and as its chairman until his death in 2000 at the age of 96. Thanks to him and some of the company's old-style marketing (see photo), the brand grew stronger in its heartland.

By 1981 a radical marketing plan for expansion was unveiled by L. D. Peeler's great grandsons, Mark Ritchie and Cliff Ritchie. Their efforts continued to pay off, and by the start of 1986 sales had doubled, spurring a continued expansion of Cheerwine. In 1992, Mark Ritchie, former vice president of sales and marketing at CBC, was promoted to president and CEO. His marketing acumen spurred recognition of two concerns that required immediate attention. First, there was the rapid rise in popularity of noncarbonated drink beverages—particularly sports drinks such as Powerade and Gatorade, along with purified water. While CBC was still financially sound, Ritchie knew something had to be done to offset this sales growth of alternative beverages. Second, CBC's advertising campaigns were outdated. While young adults throughout the Carolinas were their core market, the company had sights beyond the Carolinas—thus highlighting the urgency to replace their current advertising slogan "It's a Carolina Thing!"

Ritchie contacted CBC's local advertising agency in Charlotte—Wray Ward Laseter—to explain his concerns. The result was a new promotional program that would highlight less their southern roots and more their product's unique qualities (i.e., flavor, color, and name). This "unique" campaign was motivated from the findings of a market research study that had been performed a few

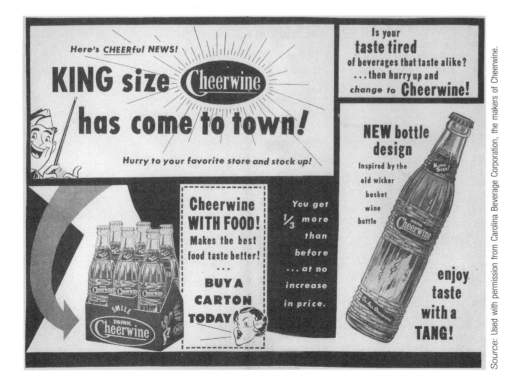

Source: Used with permission from Carolina Beverage Corporation, the makers of Cheerwine.

years earlier. But the findings were suspect, since they were based on a small sample of telephone interviews with an alarmingly low response rate (2%). Although management did have some concerns about the reliability of the findings, they always believed that their product was unique and wanted to trust the results.

After lengthy deliberations between Ritchie and representatives at the WWL agency, the new theme "Now That Would Be Something Different!" was born. However, the shortcomings of the initial research study lingered, so Ritchie wanted more solid consumer information about Cheerwine's market. He knew that to be an effective decision maker he would need reliable information to understand the market's attitudes and perceptions about Cheerwine. This concern was obvious during a meeting with Greg Campana, Executive Vice President and Director of Client Services at Wray Ward Laseter:

Ritchie: Greg, you know my concerns about the changing consumer preferences for beverages and our company's longstanding concentration on the Carolinas. Do you agree with my concerns?

Campana: Yes. I've always felt that Cheerwine could dramatically improve its sales numbers by expanding into many more markets beyond the Carolinas. I say let's begin this expansion with a new ad campaign that highlights the findings of the research that was performed two years ago—you remember, the perceived uniqueness of the product.

Ritchie: We're certainly in agreement on this. I'm sure my great grandfather Peeler would have approved of this market expansion. But are you sure that the market perceives Cheerwine as a unique product, or do consumers simply believe that consumption of Cheerwine will make them seem unique to others?

Campana: Well, I'm not exactly sure. As I recall, the sample size on that research study was really small. This can

call into question the reliability of its findings. I recommend that we move forward with a new, highly reliable market research study before we roll out our new advertising campaign this summer.

Ritchie: That's a great idea. Although it will increase our costs in the short-run it should permit us to establish a clear position in the market if, in fact, the results confirm our previous "uniqueness" finding.

Sources: For historical information, see the Web site of Cheerwine (www.Cheerwine.com), June 22, 2005. The dialogue in this case is fictitious but is based on conversations between the market researcher (Alan Shao) and Mark Ritchie. Used with permission from Carolina Beverage Corporation, the makers of Cheerwine. Please do not contact Caroline Beverage Corporation for marketing data.

Chapter 1 Questions Related to the Case

1. What type of marketing research needs to be performed? Applied or basic? Why?

2. Which steps of the decision-making process did Ritchie seem to use throughout the case?

Chapter 2 Questions Related to the Case

1. What are the management decision problems? (i.e., What should CBC do to solve the problems?

2. What are the research objectives? (i.e., What information is needed to solve the decision problems?)

3. What type of research design should be used to gather the needed information?

4. Should a cross-sectional or longitudinal study be performed on consumers of Cheerwine? Why?

5. Should qualitative or quantitative data be gathered from consumers of Cheerwine? Why?

Notes

1. Barbara Brody, "Backpack marketer to create 'aura,'" *Advertising Age* 69, no. 31 (August 3, 1998): 43.

2. Patrick Totty, "Getting to know your customers," *Credit Union Magazine* 66, no. 3 (March 2000): 54.

3. Robert Passikoff, "The limits of customer satisfaction," *Brandweek* 38, no. 9 (March 3, 1997): 17.

4. Naghi Namakforoosh, "Data collection methods hold key to research in Mexico," *Marketing News* 28, no. 18 (August 29, 1994): 28.

5. Ira P. Schneiderman, "Why men buy," *Daily News Record* 25, no. 147 (August 2, 1995): S2–S10.

6. Vijay Mahajan and Jerry Wind, "Rx for marketing research," *Marketing Research* 11, no. 3 (Fall 1999): 6+.

7. Fred N. Kerlinger, *Foundations of Behavioral Research*, 3rd ed. (New York: Harcourt Brace Jovanovich, 1986), 280.

8. Patrick Totty, "Getting to know your members," *Credit Union Magazine* 66, no. 3 (March 2000): 54.

9. Susan M. Keaveney, "Customer switching behavior in service industries: An exploratory study," *Journal of Marketing* 59 (April 1995): 71–82.

10. Mary Madden, "Internet penetration and impact", *Pew/Internet and American Life Project*, (April 2006), http://www.pewinternet.org/pdfs/PIP_Internet_Impact.pdf

11. Anonymous, "Rising belief in hell, angels, heaven, devil," *The Christian Century* 121, no. 12 (June 15, 2004).

12. S. T. Cavusgil and Shaoming Zou, "Marketing strategy-performance relationship: An investigation of the empirical link in export market ventures," *Journal of Marketing* 58 (January 1994): 1–21.

13. Ruth Ann Smith and David S. Lux, "Historical method in consumer behavior: Developing causal explanations of change,"

Journal of Consumer Research 19, no. 4 (March 1993): 595–610.

14. Carole L. Jurkiewicz, "Generation X and the public employee," *Public Personnel Management* 29, no. 1 (Spring 2000): 55–74.

15. Alan J. Bush, "Sports celebrity influence on the behavioral intentions of Generation Y," *Journal of Advertising Research* 44, no. 1 (March 2004).

16. Marissa V. Phillip, "Impact of gender differences on the evaluation of promotional emails," *Journal of Advertising Research* 44, no. 4 (December 2004).

17. A. B. Blankenship and George E. Breen, *State of the Art Marketing Research* (Chicago: American Marketing Association, 1993), 47.

18. Lucy L. Henke, "A longitudinal analysis of the ad agency-client relationship: Predictors of an agency switch," *Journal of Advertising Research* 35, no. 2 (March–April 1995): 24(7).

19. Wei-Cheng Mau and Lynette Heim Bikos, "Educational and vocational aspirations of minority and female students: A longitudinal study," *Journal of Counseling & Development* 78, no. 2 (Spring 2000): 186–195.

20. Cyndee Miller, "Sampling program strikes out at moviegoers," *Marketing News* 29, no. 8 (April 10, 1995): 1–2.

21. Cyndee Miller, "Research reaches Xers with her focus groups on the road," *Marketing News* 29, no. 1 (January 2, 1995): 10.

22. Robert Barash, "The dying art of qualitative research," *Marketing News* 31, no. 12 (June 9, 1997): 17.

23. A. B. Blankenship and G. E. Breen, *State of the Art Marketing Research* (Lincolnwood, IL: NTC Publishing Group, 1993), 252–253.

24. Erdener Kaynak, "Marketing research needs of less-developed countries: Standardization versus localization," in *Developments in Marketing Science* VII, Jay D. Lindquist, ed. (Kalamazoo, MI: Academy of Marketing Science, 1984), 161.

Research Design

Part Two

Marketing Research and Information Technology

Chapter Three

© 2007 JupiterImages Corporation.

Chapter Outline

Key Terms

Learning Objectives

After studying this chapter, you will be able to:

- Explain how information becomes knowledge.
- Describe a marketing information system and a decision-support system.
- Describe how information systems and marketing managers relate to marketing research.

- Explain the concepts of databases, data warehousing, and data mining.
- Understand the advantages and disadvantages of collecting data on the Internet.

GET THIS

Let's Go Shopping . . . Online!

Today we go surfing on the web to learn more than we probably want to know about all kinds of products. According to a survey conducted by ComScore Networks, consumers spent $143.2 billion online in 2005, up 22% from the previous year. Shoppers spent more than $82 billion online on nontravel items, up 24% from the previous year. Spending on travel increased by 20% to $60.9 billion. Apparel and accessories tied with computer software as one of the fastest-growing product categories, with consumers spending 36% more than in 2004. Other rapidly increasing categories included home and garden and toys and hobbies; each increased by 32% from the previous year. Jewelry and watches grew by 27%; event tickets by 26%; furniture by 24%; and flowers, greetings, and gifts by 23%.

While some of this huge growth can be attributed to the Internet, over one-third of apparel manufacturers do not have a web presence at all. Of those manufacturers who do have sites, 56% are pursuing strategies from providing basic company information to providing a full-scale site that offers users the opportunity to learn about the company, review product information, order items, check availability, and track orders.

Several online surveys by Cybershopper, shop.org, and Greenfield Online show that consumers are becoming increasingly comfortable using the web as a shopping and purchasing medium. The barriers in the apparel industry—returns, security, cost, and the inability to "experience" clothing (that is, you can't physically touch, feel, or try on anything)—are coming down, becoming less important to consumers. DELiA●s, Liz Claiborne, and Nike are three companies that have used the web in a variety of ways to motivate sales.

- *dELiA●s* (http://www.delias.com). This multichannel retailer markets apparel, accessories, and home furnishings to teenage girls and young women. The company reaches its customers through its catalog, Web site, and retail stores. The Web site is designed for and incorporates features to address its target market. In addition to shopping, visitors may participate in fashion polls to drive future product offerings, take quizzes to determine styles for their personality, keep a wish list of their favorite items of clothing, enter contests, and much more. It even allows girls to email items to friends to get their opinions before buying.

- *Liz Claiborne* (http://www.lizclaiborne.com). This site has a full-featured promotion of its products. The advertising campaigns are prominently displayed, and the site allows visitors to create the looks that they might have seen in the campaigns by providing detailed product and store locator information. It creates a sense of community by hosting live chat events, promotes goodwill by giving information on what the company is doing to help women, and creates excitement through a variety of contests.

- *Nike* (http://www.nike.com). This site encourages online shopping, with a powerful search engine that allows visitors to search products by gender and sports activity as well as special size considerations. It is linked to inventory information that permits visitors to know whether the product of interest is available. The site also contains customer service information, live chats with sports stars, and the ability to create and send a customized sports clip.

Sources: Antone Gonsalves, "Online spending reaches 6% of total retail sales," *Information Week* (January 5, 2006); Kathryn Kelly and Arthur Andersen, "Apparel e-commerce: Online and kicking," *Apparel Industry Magazine* 61, no. 3 (March 2000): 48–50; Anonymous, "Online survey tells what sells," *Home Textiles Today* 21, no. 26 (March 6, 2000): 1; Anonymous, "Online retail sales, profitability continue climb," *PR Newswire US*, May 24, 2005.

Now Ask Yourself

- Apparel items are very personal products to most people, but it was noted in the case that, "The barriers in the apparel industry—returns, security, cost, and the inability to "experience" clothing—are coming down." Why are these barriers coming down?

- What are the reasons for the fact that "over one-third of apparel manufacturers do not have a web presence at all"?

- Besides the examples given from the company profiles, what other ways can apparel companies use the Internet to promote sales of their products?

- Do you believe all apparel manufacturers and retailers should use the Internet to promote sales of their products? If so, why? If not, why not?

- How do online databases help apparel companies to boost their sales?

The "Get This" feature demonstrates how the apparel industry is changing to meet the surge of Internet technology. The more important issue is to understand how the information system supports online sales. This chapter will provide an in-depth discussion about databases and will go much further into how they are used by marketing researchers. Furthermore, hot topics like information systems, decision-support systems, data mining, data warehousing, data marts, and online data collection will be discussed so that you will be up-to-date on some of the latest technology marketing researchers have at their disposal. First, though, we will discuss the importance of information, the creator of knowledge.

3-1 Changing Information into Knowledge

The main goal of marketers is to satisfy their customers' needs. One way to ensure this occurs is to develop procedures that will enhance the manager's decision-making abilities. This can be achieved through either labor-intensive efforts or technological tools. Technology is becoming an increasingly important aspect of business—today it is not enough for managers to simply make decisions; these decisions usually must be made in a timely manner. That is, the timing of a decision may be as critical to the outcome as the decision itself.

There is a lot of information in the world. What is needed is organized information, information that has a purpose and can be readily accessed regardless of its location. Organized information leads to knowledge. Knowledge leads individuals to look for more information about the topic in order to understand it. The absence of organized information leaves people knowing something about the topic, but usually very little about it. When someone has knowledge, he or she knows how to make sense of information, knows how to relate the information, and knows when information is or is not useful.[1] Computers have helped create organized information. By using directories and subdirectories, people can organize their documents into more homogeneous groups. Computers also make our data searches increasingly efficient. Users can search for information about virtually any topic from almost anywhere in the world in a matter of seconds. This chapter will concentrate on some of the major topics in computer technology and how they enhance marketing research efforts.

3-2 Information Systems

information system A system that collects, processes, stores, analyzes, and disseminates information for a specific purpose.

An **information system** allows its users to collect, process, store, analyze, and disseminate information for a specific purpose.[2] Computerized information systems store information about people, places, and trends within the organization or within the business environment.[3] The main components of most information systems are as follows:[4]

- *Hardware* to accept data and information, then process and display the information
- *Software* to enable the hardware to process data

- A *database* to store data and the associations among them
- A *network* (a connecting system) to permit the sharing of resources by different computers
- *Procedures* to provide instructions that combine the above components in order to process information and generate the desired output
- *People* to work with the system or use its output

Consider Example 3-1.

Example 3-1

Amazon.com is an example of a company using an information system to increase sales and satisfy customers' needs. Amazon.com, the first Internet-based bookstore, offers more than 4 million books online. It can deliver almost any book in a short time and offers a discount of up to 40%. Furthermore, the company provides comprehensive reviews of books, the possibility of electronic communication with some authors, bibliographies of any topic desired with a table of contents, and other information on other books. Another example is Nu Skin International, a producer of additive-free skin care products for aging Baby Boomers. The company has a global network of distributors and uses information systems to track orders, make deliveries, make payments, communicate with distributors and suppliers, and service international management reporting needs.[5]

Savvy marketing managers make it their business to know what kind of information they need. If a situation is recurrent, marketing managers often request that a database be designed, complete with automatic updating. Suppose a marketing manager needs to decide whether the ingredients of a product should be changed. Other marketing managers in the company have most likely faced such decisions before and are routinely collecting data in the information system that will help with this decision. The marketing manager can thus request the following from the information system:

- In terms of sales, how has the product performed in the past 12 months?
- In terms of sales, how has the product performed in the past 5 years?
- In test markets, how have consumers reacted to the new ingredients?
- How will the price of the product change if the new ingredients are used?
- How sensitive is the market to a small price increase?
- How will competition react to a change in the product's ingredients?

An information system performs three functions with data that can be used by managers as they make decisions, control operations, analyze problems, and create new products or services. These functions are input, processing, and output. **Input** is raw data captured from inside or outside the organization. Marketing researchers gather this raw data, which is entered into a database. **Processing** transforms the raw data into usable form. Marketing researchers, many with strong statistical backgrounds, may also be active in the processing operations. **Output** transfers the processed data to the people who need it.

How the information system evolves in a particular organization is dependent on the business environment. This environment is composed of individuals and groups surrounding the organization, including the organization's customers, suppliers, competitors, and stockholders, as well as industry regulators. Customer and stockholder satisfaction are paramount, and the actions of competitors, suppliers, and regulatory agencies can significantly affect company performance. Exhibit 3-1 depicts the functions of an information system within its environment.

The main function of marketing is to link the company and its customers, and the task of the marketing information system is to bring about this connection as

input Raw data captured from inside or outside the organization.

processing The transformation of raw data into usable form.

output Processed data that is transferred to the people who need it.

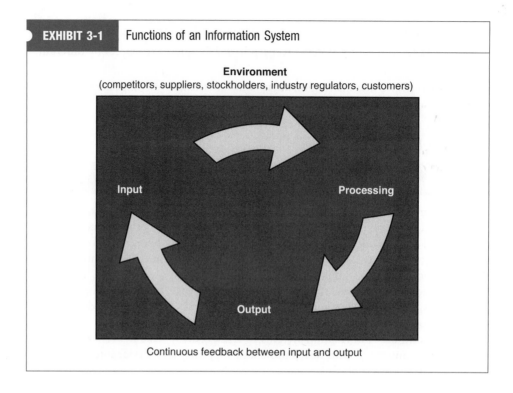

EXHIBIT 3-1 | Functions of an Information System

Environment
(competitors, suppliers, stockholders, industry regulators, customers)

Input

Processing

Output

Continuous feedback between input and output

marketing information system (MkIS) A system that facilitates information collection, storage, manipulation, and dissemination in marketing, including customer service and contacts.

efficiently as possible. The **marketing information system (MkIS)** facilitates information collection, storage, manipulation, and dissemination in marketing, including customer service and contacts.[6] Input for the MkIS comes from all parts of the organization. MkISs gather, organize, and report data to help marketing managers meet such objectives as

- Managing the overall marketing process
- Directing support of sales activities and sales personnel
- Identifying new product or service opportunities early on
- Establishing competitive prices without sacrificing profit
- Controlling costs related to marketing activities
- Analyzing marketing effectiveness

decision-support system (DSS) Any system that supports the decision-making process; it is an interactive, user-controlled information system that helps managers predict the results of various alternatives before making a decision.

In the 1970s, a new concept in information systems began to pique management interest, mainly because it aims at information needs of specific managers rather than entire organizational units.[7] This is the **decision-support system (DSS),** which can be loosely defined as any system that supports the decision-making process. More specifically, it is an interactive, user-controlled information system that helps managers predict the results of various alternatives before making a decision. When a DSS is used to support marketing decisions, it is referred to as a marketing decision-support system (MDSS). (See Research Realities 3-1 to learn how BankBoston's DSS was used to understand its customers' banking habits.) An MDSS can provide answers to "what if" questions and model future environments.[8] Suppose a marketing manager wants to know, "How many units are we likely to sell if we lower the price by $1?" An MDSS statistical model will help the manager make this prediction. One expert recently stated that 75% to 90% of the value in technology is in decision-support systems because these systems decide how to deploy resources based on the business's needs.[9]

A key difference between an MkIS and an MDSS involves the frequency with which particular decisions recur. While an MkIS usually helps in similar situations that occur

Research Realities 3-1

BankBoston Uses DSS to Understand Customers' Banking Habits

BankBoston has created a decision-support system that provides a clear picture of how its customers access its bank. With 440 branches and 700 automated teller machines plus the Internet and telephone banking, BankBoston wanted to optimize its delivery network using raw data on how its two million customers interact with the bank. Jon Voorhees, director of distribution planning, put it this way: "We wanted to understand, on a day-to-day basis, how a customer accesses us, in everything from routine transactions like making a deposit or cashing a check to the things that are more complex, like arranging for financing or opening a new account."

What BankBoston created was a system that can do many things. At the heart of the system is a database that stores customer data and draws from many of the bank's source systems. These source systems might come from either internal records or external sources, but they all contribute to the bank's understanding of their customers.

Data is extracted each month and eventually merged with similar information after being cleaned so that it can be loaded into the database. The data is stored according to geographic region and can be directly accessed by researchers, and some of the data is ultimately analyzed using powerful statistical methods like multidimensional scaling. (We'll discuss this statistical technique in Chapter 17.)

DSS systems can have a variety of purposes besides direct marketing but yet related in terms such as delivery. For example, a well-known bank uses a DSS system to examine delivery routes so as to minimize the probability of robbery. (Tarantilis, 2004.)

Source: Jeanne O'Brien, "Channel tracking," *Bank Systems & Technology* 36, no. 10 (October 1999): 22; C.D. Tarantilis, C. T. Kiranoudis, "An adaptive memory programming method for risk logistics operations" *International Journal of Systems Science,* vol. 35 Issue 10, (August 15, 2004), p. 579.

several times, an MDSS benefits the marketing manager when an unstructured and unique situation arises. If marketing managers want to stay up-to-date on product sales, they request monthly sales reports from the MkIS. However, if they want to make a specific decision, such as whether to divest a certain product line, an MDSS will help them predict the effects on the bottom line. So, once again, an MDSS deals with analyzing unique decisions that concern *specific* problems and "what if" scenarios. Exhibit 3-2 shows how MkISs and MDSSs differ.

> **EXHIBIT 3-2**   Differences between an MkIS and an MDSS

Topic	MkIS	MDSS
Data focus	Retrieval	Analysis
Decisions	Structured, semi-structured	Unstructured, unique
Analytical ability	Little	A lot
Flexibility	Little	A lot
Orientation	Data-oriented	Action-oriented

Source: Laudon, Kenneth C.; Laudon, Jane P., *Management Information Systems,* 8th, © 2004. Electronically reproduced by permission of Pearson Education, Inc., Upper Saddle River, New Jersey.

Marketing researchers often use decision-support systems because they are interactive and, as we earlier noted, allow "what if" analyses. For example, ACNielsen uses a decision-support system to determine how much to spend on trade promotion. Manufacturers use decision-support systems to forecast, implement, and evaluate promotional spending. The system places years of field observations, marketing acumen, and advanced statistical models at the fingertips of management; this allows corporate headquarters to institute the organization-wide promotion tactics that have proved to be most successful. Manufacturers use the system to increase sales by promoting the right product in the right store at the right time; by creating, communicating, and tracking volume objectives and expense reports; by improving production and inventory management; and by making sure that the sales force understands and abides by trade spending guidelines.[10]

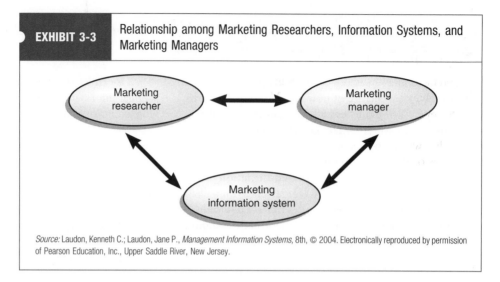

| EXHIBIT 3-3 | Relationship among Marketing Researchers, Information Systems, and Marketing Managers |

Source: Laudon, Kenneth C.; Laudon, Jane P., *Management Information Systems*, 8th, © 2004. Electronically reproduced by permission of Pearson Education, Inc., Upper Saddle River, New Jersey.

The association of marketing researchers, marketing information systems, and marketing managers tends to be a close one. As shown in Exhibit 3-3, marketing managers routinely communicate with researchers regarding their informational needs. Researchers gather the necessary data from entities inside or outside the organization—including the marketing information system. After collecting the data, the marketing researchers may share it directly with the marketing managers, or they may store it in an information system, where it is instantly retrievable. Marketing managers also input data into the information system, market knowledge they want to store for later use. Marketing managers typically retrieve weekly, monthly, and yearly marketing reports from MkISs—not day-to-day activities.[11] For example, an MkIS allows the previous year's sales to be compared with the advertising expenditures to determine next year's advertising budget.

3-3 Databases

database A large collection of related data, organized for rapid search and retrieval.

Before the advent of computer technology, when people wanted secondary data, they would go to their local library and thumb through a card catalogue to find what was available on a specific topic. But times have changed. Today, information can be more easily found and retrieved from electronic databases. A **database** is a large collection of related data, organized for rapid search and retrieval. Databases have been called the core of an information system because they establish limits for the information that is available from the system.[12] Consider Example 3-2.

Example 3-2

Bureau van Dijk, a leader in financial information publishing, has its own database called "ISIS," a global insurance company database. ISIS (Insurance Information and Statistics) has detailed reports on 7,000 insurance companies around the world. ISIS users can screen the 7,000 insurance companies using over one hundred search criteria to obtain up to four years' worth of information. The software on ISIS helps users perform financial analyses, design and analyze peer groups, and create customized graphics for individual or groups of companies.[13]

database marketing The process of gathering relevant information about potential and existing customers to learn about their needs and to use this information to provide the right product, at the right price, at the right time.

Database marketing is the process of gathering relevant information about potential and existing customers to learn about their needs and to use this information to provide the right product, at the right price, at the right time. The talent necessary to perform database marketing is unique. These individuals need to have more than

---

Research Realities 3-2   *You Can't Run, and You Can't Hide*

"You have zero privacy anyway," Sun Microsystems' CEO Scott McNealy said. "Get over it." McNealy backs his claim by pointing out that there are huge databases on just about everything from our medical histories to whether we like beef jerky, thanks to the power and abilities of computers to manipulate information in every possible way. Unfortunately, these databases can be sold to third parties. This has raised concerns from consumer privacy advocates and regulators. They are debating whether the practice of consumer information sharing should be banned, regulated, or left alone.

Stephen Manes, a writer for *PC World*, advocates that we should not "get over it." Instead, he believes that citizens need to demand clear rules on privacy, security, and confidentiality. He writes: "We won't get real privacy or security until we demand it as a matter of law.... We probably won't see much change in electronic privacy law until some poor Supreme Court nominee gets caught downloading files from psychic-friends.net."

Source: Liu Qihong and Konstantinos Serfes, "Customer Information Sharing Among Rival Firms," *European Economic Review* (August 2006), vol. 50, no. 6, pp. 1571–1600; Stephen Manes, "Private lives? Not ours!" *PC World* 18, no. 6 (June 2000): 312.

---

analytical skills; they need to be skilled strategic thinkers, program developers, and creative practitioners.[14] A more advanced strategy of database marketing is customer relationship management (CRM), which promises to seamlessly connect a company's Web site, email, call center, and other customer-facing operations. The payoff is a transparent and consistent interface providing a clear understanding of the company's customers.[15] (Case 3-1 at the end of the chapter gives more description of CRM and how companies are using the technique.)

According to Donnelley Marketing's annual survey of promotional practices, 56% of manufacturers and retailers had built databases, an additional 10% plan to do so, and 85% believe they will need database marketing capabilities in the near future to be competitive. The Associated Press reported that worldwide relational database software sales totaled $7.79 billion in 2004.[16] Marketers use databases to focus on market niches. They identify a segment of customers with similar buying habits and then tailor a promotional message to appeal specifically to that segment. CEOs of major companies warn consumers to get used to the fact that databases will continue to store vast amounts of data on them. (See Research Realities 3-2.)

Here are some examples of database marketing in action:

- Condé Nast, a publisher of more than a dozen upscale magazines, offers its advertisers access to its 18 million-name subscriber database. The database is used for research, telemarketing, and driving subscribers to an advertiser's point of purchase or Web site. Users also use it for profiling, customer cloning (finding new prospects with a similar profile), list selection (mailing and emailing according to a composite of demographic, lifestyle, or behavioral selections), and geo-demographic mapping (targeting at the zip code or household level for retailing or customer relationship marketing activities).[17]

- A school in Fairfax County, Virginia, plans to spend $11 million for a computer database that would hold personal and academic information on some 150,000 school children. So far, school systems in more than a dozen states have linked their new databases to a nationwide data exchange program being organized by the Department of Education. The program would make student information available to other schools, universities, government agencies, and possibly employers.[18]

- To help newspapers boost their circulations, Larry Sackett, president and CEO of the Barry Group, created custom-built software designed to pull hard-to-access information out of a newspaper's databases about its subscribers and combine the information with market research to create profiles of desirable subscribers.[19]

Research Realities 3-3   *Major Database Providers*

- The *Educational Resources and Information Center* (ERIC) database, sponsored by the U.S. Department of Education, is the premier U.S. national bibliographic database of education literature. The database contains more than 1.1 million abstracts of documents and journal articles on education research and practice. It also contains over 1,800 records that feature the full text of the original document. It is a network of 16 clearinghouses that specialize in separate subject areas. It consists of the Resources in Education (RIE) file of document citations and the Current Index to Journals in Education (CIJE) file of journal article citations from over 775 professional journals.

- *ProQuest* is a collection of electronic databases serving the library and educational communities. Its archive includes more than 5.5 billion pages of information, spanning 500 years of scholarship. It is available to almost two-thirds of the 15 million college students in the United States, attracting nearly two million page views per day via the Internet.

- *Hoover's Online* features a database of information on more than 12 million corporations and organizations, with in-depth coverage of 40,000 of the world's top business enterprises. The information on companies includes the following sections: overview, stock information, officers, contact information, business information, key competitors, and financial portrait.

- *Hoover's Company Capsules* provide brief background and financial information for over 120,000 public and private companies in more than three dozen countries.

- *ABI/INFORM Global* allows users to search 2,000 premier worldwide business periodicals for information on advertising, marketing, economics, human resources, finance, taxation, computers, and more. Also, it provides information on more than 60,000 companies.

- *Business Source Elite* provides abstracts and indexing for more than 7,600 periodicals, plus searchable full text for more than 1,100 active periodicals. Subjects covered include general reference, business, health, social science, education, science, humanities, and news and current events.

- *Dow Jones Interactive* includes databases for current business news, business-related articles, full-text company reports, and company financial data.

- *Thomson Research* (formerly *Global Access*) provides access to business and financial information of U.S. publicly owned companies and foreign companies whose stocks are traded on major U.S. exchanges. It has a database of more than 3.4 million research reports, with an average of 3,000 new reports added each business day.

- *Simmons Survey of Media and Markets* is an electronic database of statistical information on buying habits for consumer products and services and for media usage. It is based on a sampling of the American population and is used for marketing research to identify consumer buying habits and media preferences. It is useful for determining:
  1. Which population groups use specific consumer products/services
  2. Market share for selected product brands
  3. Spending habits
  4. Types of media useful to reach consumers of particular products

- *National Trade Data Bank* is a compilation of full-text reports of trade statistics, market research reports, country background information, trade practices and policies, and much more—in all, over 190,000 publications from various federal agencies that are compiled by the U.S. Department of Commerce.

Database providers supply databases to online publishers who make the information available through online systems. IBM and Oracle Corporation had 67.8% of the total database software market in 2004, with IBM having 34.1% and Oracle 33.7%, followed by Microsoft with 20% of the market.[20] While many of the databases are free of charge, some providers charge a fee. For example, *Polling the Nations* gives the polling results from over 700 organizations including Gallup, Roper, and Market Resource Group for a fee of $450. *The Corporate Technology Directory* is a database of 4,500 technology companies and developers and costs $1.50 per record. (See Research Realities 3-3 for a list of some of the major database providers with a brief description of their services.)

Databases may be classified as online or offline. **Online databases** are collections of information, stored and managed electronically, that can be searched using the

online databases Collections of information, stored and managed electronically, that can be searched using the Internet.

Source: © 2007 JupiterImages Corporation.

Internet. Accessing online databases requires a device (usually a modem) that can facilitate communication between a computer user and an external database. **Offline databases** are collections of information, too, and they are usually electronically stored and managed. However, offline databases are not accessible using the Internet. Instead, the information may be available on CD-ROMs.

Thousands of different databases can be retrieved either online or offline. They may be classified as bibliographic, directory, full-text, or numeric. **Bibliographic databases** are collections of complete citation information from published sources, such as marketing research studies, newspaper articles, magazine articles, journal articles, government reports, store audit reports, dissertations, and books. The citations in bibliographic databases contain the authors' names, titles of the works, publishers' names, publication dates, and sometime brief abstracts of what the works contain. We have already discussed *ERIC, ABI/INFORM,* and *Business Source Elite.* Another excellent source is the *Columbia Encyclopedia,* the largest one-volume general encyclopedia available, with over 40,000 bibliographic citations. Predicasts' *PROMPT* is another popular service that produces a bibliography of abstracts. Its database holds over 2 million records, and hundreds of thousands more are added every year.

Directory databases are directories and indexes that offer information on people, organizations, and services. Among the most often used business-related indexes is the *Social Sciences Citation Index,* which covers more than 1,500 journals in the social and behavioral sciences, including management and economics. Other directory databases include *Directory of Corporate Affiliations, Yellow Pages, Dun & Bradstreet, World Directory of Marketing Information, infoUSA,* and *Directory of Polish Companies.* The *World Directory of Marketing Information Sources* contains over 6,000 entries, including leading marketing research companies, trade associations, trade journals, online sources, and international business contacts.

Full-text databases contain the entire text of the source documents that comprise the database. Users of a full-text database can request a complete magazine article, newspaper story, or trade journal report. The "full text" of a publication may,

offline databases Collections of information that are electronically stored and managed but are not accessible from the Internet.

bibliographic databases Collections of complete citation information from published sources, such as marketing research studies, newspaper articles, magazine articles, journal articles, government reports, store audit reports, dissertations, and books.

directory databases Directories and indexes that offer information on people, organizations, and services.

full-text databases Databases that contain the entire text of the source documents.

however, exclude photographs and other graphics accompanying an article. The advantage of full text over bibliographic databases is their accessibility. There is no need to go to another source, since the entire article is available in the database, often at no cost but sometimes for a nominal fee. We have already discussed some full-text databases, including *ERIC, Business Source Elite, Dow Jones Interactive,* and *National Trade Data Bank.* Other popular full-text databases are *LexisNexis* and *Dialog.*

LexisNexis contains a vast array of news and business information from around the worldwide, including databases in German, Dutch, French, Italian, and Spanish. These databases and documents are constantly updated from thousands of sources of information. *LexisNexis* offers business, news, legal, and reference information. The LexisNexis service is a useful source for legal information. It covers all major fields of practice, including tax, securities, banking, environment, energy, and international affairs. LexisNexis is a comprehensive news and business information service that contains more than 36,000 full-text sources, including the *New York Times, Business Week,* the *Washington Post,* and the *Economist.* It also carries both national network and regional television broadcast transcripts, along with Cable News Network and National Public Radio news and features.[21]

The Dialog Corporation offers the most comprehensive, robust collection of information databases in the world. Its brands include *Dialog, DataStar,* and *Profound,* providing access to over nine terabytes, or more than six billion pages, of essential information. It serves over 20,000 corporate customers in 120 countries. The "classic" *Dialog* contains several hundred databases from a broad array of disciplines. It contains millions of documents drawn from more sources than any other online service—ranging from trade journals to news wires. *DataStar,* Europe's leading online database service, provides access to over 350 databases with worldwide coverage. It offers a comprehensive collection of business information. *Profound* is a premier source for in-depth market research reports. It encompasses more than 250,000 reports produced by more than 170 of the world's top publishers.

Numeric databases contain numeric and statistical information from original surveys. Some vendors providing these types of databases include Donnelley Marketing Information Services, Metropolitan Area Forecasts, CACI Marketing Systems, and the United States Bureau of the Census. Many of the census data reports are available through *CENDATA*—which may be accessed through *Dialog* and CompuServe. This service provides immediate access to news releases from the U.S. Bureau of the Census, new product announcements and ordering information, and a broad scope of census data.

3-4 Data Warehousing

Companies that compile and store multiple databases often use data warehousing systems. The purpose of a data warehouse is to assist decision making. A **data warehouse** is a repository for an organization's existing and ongoing data. It collects data from multiple sources and stores it in a way that allows end users to have fast, easy, and flexible access to important information.[22] According to the SAS Institute, **data warehousing** involves the entire information delivery process—from access and transformation of data from different operational stores, through the organization process that makes it available for decision making, to surfacing the data for exploitation via a range of decision-support tools. A successful data warehousing solution provides organizations with the ability to bring together data from any source, manage it, and turn it into consistent information that users need. Here are two examples of how data warehouses are helping companies:[23]

numeric databases Databases that contain numeric and statistical information from original surveys.

data warehouse A repository for an organization's existing and ongoing data; it collects data from multiple sources and stores it in a way that allows end users to have fast, easy, and flexible access to important information.

data warehousing A system that involves the entire information delivery process—from access and transformation of data from different operational stores, through the organization process that makes it available for decision making, to surfacing the data for exploitation via a range of decision support tools.

- A pharmaceutical company increases its revenues by 20% by both analyzing competitive behavior and cross-selling products to its existing customer base.
- A major long-distance company reduces its product development cycle time by 40% by understanding which specific features it should combine to create new and innovative products.

Many companies are using data warehousing information to profile customers. It helps marketers understand the characteristics and behavior of their target groups. Customer profiling allows marketers to understand who is purchasing particular products and how they are reacting to promotions and price changes. After a data warehousing system is designed, it should be able to answer three questions:

- What happened (reporting)
- Why did it happen (analyzing)
- What will happen (predicting)

The data warehouse can be described as a collection of smaller "data marts." A **data mart** is a subject-specific data warehouse. One department or group of users in a company often uses data marts for a defined set of tasks. For example, a telephone company might have a data mart specific to network planning. This data mart helps the company's networking staff determine its technology assets, optimal network routing, and capacities. It gets the data from a larger "enterprise data warehouse" that the company maintains in a separate location. There are dependent and independent data marts. The previous example was a **dependent data mart,** since it receives data from a data warehouse. An **independent data mart** gets its data directly from transaction systems that don't rely on other data warehouses.

3-5 Data Mining

Data warehouses and data mining are complementary. Data warehouses are for storing data; data mining turns stored data into knowledge. Data warehousing is not a product but rather an architecture, a system made up of processes, products, data, human resources, and services. On the other hand, **data mining** involves extracting hidden predictive information in large databases through statistical analysis.[24] It uses a variety of analytical tools to find patterns and relationships. It fully uses information about customers' buying patterns and behavior, analyzes the variables in the data from the last campaign, and creates a mathematical model of those who did and did not respond based on known customer information such as age, income, and buying history. This information helps the user determine, for example, which customers are most likely to respond to a direct mail campaign.

Data mining can also help the user predict a customer's lifetime value. It can enable a business to mail to only 40% of its original list and obtain 80% of the responses, dramatically improving the return on investment. The major shortcoming, though, of data mining is that it requires historical data to determine how the variables relate to each other when it creates models.[25] Data mining is a powerful tool because it fully uses behavioral data about customers and gains a greater understanding of customer motivations to help reduce fraud, anticipate resource demand, increase acquisition, and curb customer attrition. SAS Institute is the leading player in data mining, capturing about 35% of the $500 million market for 2003.[26]

Data mining is being used in a variety of industries. For example, online brokerages are using it to track the type of investment, research, and information a particular customer is viewing and, based on this data, prompt the system to offer additional investment advice. Both data warehousing and mining are often performed in the information technology department of corporations, though many companies are finding it easier to concentrate on developing, manufacturing, and selling their core products and services if they leave the data analysis to the experts. (See Research Realities 3-4.)

data mart A subject-specific data warehouse.

dependent data mart A data mart that receives its data from a data warehouse.

independent data mart A data mart that gets its data directly from transaction systems that don't rely on other data warehouses.

data mining Involves extracting hidden predictive information in large databases through statistical analysis.

Research Realities 3-4   *Pros and Cons of Outsourcing Data Warehousing and Mining*

Elizabeth Koehler, manager of financial planning and analysis at CBS MarketWatch.com Inc., says that for a long time, her business was confronted with a need to upgrade its software to a stronger version of its data analytics package and the increased hardware and support costs needed that went with it. To steady costs and stay up with its ever-expanding data, the firm outsourced its data warehouse operations from Accrue Software Inc. in Fremont, Calif., to outsourcer digiMine Inc. in Bellevue, Wash. Koehler maintains that had she not done so, it's likely her analysts would not have received their daily reports when, one year later, the financial Web site experienced all-time high traffic loads after the Sept. 11 attacks in New York sent stock markets falling.

There are benefits and drawbacks to outsourcing data warehouse and data mining efforts. Some of the benefits are:

- Outsourcing can lower the initial cost of implementing a data warehouse.
- Outsourcing advanced data management initiatives leaves the job to the experts.

- Outsourcing lets a business focus on its core products and services.
- Web-based data analysis lets companies analyze what's happening on their Web sites and makes other online information easily available to analytical services providers.

Some drawbacks are:

- Offloading core business-intelligence applications requires attention to an array of confidentiality, competition, and security issues.
- Traditional data warehouses are poorly suited for outsourcing.
- Distancing users from the data warehouse process can be problematic; most successful data warehouse implementations rely on close relations between users and warehouse developers.

Source: Mark Hall, "Seeding for Data Growth," *Computerworld* (April 15, 2002), vol. 36, no. 16; Barbara Depompa, "Companies see gold in outside data analysis," *Information Week, vol. 778* (March 20, 2000): 86–88.

3-6 Collecting Data via the Internet

The Internet offers a wealth of resources and services that can help marketing researchers in their work. Here are some of the Internet services that are most useful for marketing researchers:

- Access to library catalogs worldwide
- Transfer of data and files between computers
- Communication between individuals and groups
- Access to discussion groups and bulletin boards

Source: © 2007 JupiterImages Corporation.

- Access to community information
- Access to electronic books, journals, and databases
- Access to statistical data and document files

The Internet can aid marketing researchers in two fundamental ways: (1) by making secondary information widely accessible, and (2) by serving as a vehicle for collecting primary research data that cannot be found elsewhere. In this section, we will explore primary and secondary research through the Internet.

The Internet helps researchers gather information in a more effective and efficient manner than ever before. Although it has not entirely replaced the need for researchers to physically travel to other locations—such as to libraries, businesses, associations, and other institutions—to gather information, it has made data collection significantly easier. The Internet offers the following advantages over other forms of data collection:

- *It allows researchers to collect data fast and is cost-effective.* Since data collection is performed online, it can be done quickly and at less cost than traditional data-gathering methods like mail surveys, personal interviews, and telephone interviews.

- *It has no physical form and fast turnaround.* This allows information to be transferred across the country or around the world in a matter of seconds.

- *It has a global reach.* It can visit all parts of the world; this allows a wide audience from which to sample.

- *It is interactive.* It permits users to control their own information search by selecting hyperlinks or web addresses for information they want to access. Hyperlinks on web pages can lead researchers to related or supporting web pages at the current site or at other sites around the world.

- *It is dynamic.* Information can be continuously updated and expanded at minimal cost and with little effort. Not much lead time is required, and virtually all changes can be done in-house.

- *It simplifies navigation through very large documents.* By permitting instant access to topics and key words, users travel effortlessly through documents at their own pace.

- *It is multimedia-friendly.* Options include not only text and pictures but also sound and video. A product can therefore not only be seen and explained; it can also be heard and demonstrated.

Although the Internet is an amazing research tool, it does have some important limitations. Some of these shortcomings are as follows:

- *Lack of security features.* This problem makes businesses wary of trusting the Net with confidential data, such as credit-card numbers. However, advanced data encryption/decryption techniques are fast becoming available that will secure data transmissions.

- *Unreliability of information collected through personal interviews and surveys.* As with telephone interviews and mail surveys, researchers don't know for sure who is actually completing the interview or questionnaire they are administering over the Internet.

- *Although voice and visual technologies are making it easier to talk to and see others through the Internet, these technologies are still in their infancy.* Also, research has shown that people report only about 40% of what they actually spend in a sensitive product category like alcohol and cigarette consumption. However, research based on scanners and credit-card purchases allows marketers to build databases based on respondents' actual, not their personally reported, behavior.

- *Absence of the human element.* Once again, although voice and visual technologies are becoming available on the Internet, they cannot completely replace the human interaction that occurs when respondents are in the same room. Companies may, however, be tempted to ignore this reality in face of the substantial time and cost savings the Internet offers.

- *Potential overflow of customers on any particular Internet provider.* As new users flood the Internet, the Internet is becoming crowded. Flat-rate pricing, now common among Internet service providers, allows subscribers unlimited use, encouraging users to stay online for longer periods. All this extra usage is overloading Internet access lines, causing long delays getting online and slow surfing.

- *Lack of organization.* Although search engine providers like Yahoo!, Webcrawler, Lycos, and Excite allow users to search for information in a hurry, typically the information is not arranged in any particular user-friendly order.

- *Too much information to handle.* The Internet often provides so much information that it is difficult to know when to end a search. For example, typing in a key word in Yahoo! can provide thousands of sources to visit.

- *Lack of representativeness.* Companies have begun to offer online data collection and opinion research. However, the results are not representative of many populations because online users tend to be better educated, more affluent, and younger than the average consumer, and are typically male.

- *Uncertainty about information quality.* While there is a lot of excellent information on the Internet, there is also a vast amount of useless and unreliable data. This is because anyone can publish on the web. There is no formal group that reviews the published content before it goes online, so users should be cautious when taking information from the Internet. To examine the quality of online information, consider the following suggestions:

  1. Use your common sense to evaluate its legitimacy.
  2. Check the author's credibility with regard to the information.
  3. Be sure the date of publication is acceptable.
  4. Compare the data with other available data that is similar.

Decision Time!

You are the new marketing manager of a small consumer-packaged goods company. Your first day on the job you realize that all of the historical documents within the company are unorganized and unusable in their current form. You decide to hire someone to help you straighten out all of the data and ultimately turn the data into a usable form. Are you going to hire a marketing researcher, a marketing information systems specialist, or an individual proficient with decision-support systems? Or is there someone else you should consider?

Net Impact

The Internet has transformed the way individuals and businesses use many of the tools discussed in this chapter. Databases in particular have become readily accessible via the Internet. Certainly much of the information that is used for competitive intelligence, data mining, data warehousing, information systems, and electronic data interchange comes from various sources on the Internet.

On the Lighter Side—An Alien Experience

You can browse through the Internet and find all kinds of information. The problem is, you can't always be sure it is reliable—or believable. Take, for example, the Alien Abduction Survey.

Most of the questions on the survey require yes/no responses. Check its Web site (http://www.abduct.com/survey.htm) to see if the questions are alien to you.

Source: Alien abduction experience and research, "Alien Abduction Survey," http://www.abduct.com/survey.htm, accessed October 9, 2005.

Chapter Summary

Most companies need organized information—information that has a purpose and can be readily accessed regardless of its location. Organized information is sought, since it leads to knowledge. Computers have helped create organized information. Information systems in particular help to gather, process, store, analyze, and disseminate information for a specific purpose. They tend to comprise hardware, software, a database, a network, procedures, and people. An information system performs three functions for managers: input, processing, and output. The decision-support system is an interactive, user-controlled information system that helps managers evaluate alternatives before making a decision. A marketing decision-support system provides solutions to "what if" questions and allows companies to model future environments. It is important that the marketing researcher, marketing information system, and marketing manager work closely together.

Since a vast amount of information is necessary for decision makers, databases are often used to organize, search, and retrieve information. Database marketing provides information to help marketing managers offer the right product, at the right price, at the right time. There are all kinds of online and offline databases available to marketing researchers, including bibliographic databases, directory databases, full-text databases, and numeric databases. Companies that compile and store multiple databases often use data warehousing systems. These systems are meant to enhance decision making by storing data until it is needed. A data mart is a subject-specific data warehouse. Data mining turns stored data that comes from a data warehouse into knowledge. Use of the Internet makes data collection much easier. However, there are both advantages and disadvantages to using the Internet for data collection.

Review Questions

1. How are information systems and decision-support systems related? How are they different?

2. What is a database, and what is it used for? Whose responsibility is it to maintain a specific database? Why?

3. Name the different types of databases. Give an example of each.

4. Is it possible for a company to offer both bibliographic databases and full-text databases? If so, how? If not, why not?

5. How are data warehouses, data marts, and data mining related? How are they different?

6. What are the advantages and disadvantages of data collection via the Internet?

Practice Quiz

Note: You can find the correct answers to these questions by taking the quiz and then submitting your answers in the Online Edition. The program will automatically score your submission. If you miss a question, the program will provide the correct answer, a rationale for the answer, and the section number in the chapter where the topic is discussed.

1. Marketing decision-support systems are designed to allow "what if" questions and model future environments.
   a. True
   b. False

2. A marketing information system's focus is on data analysis; a marketing decision-support system's focus is on data collection.
   a. True
   b. False

3. A marketing manager would use a marketing decision-support system if he or she wanted to know, "If we raise the price of our product by five dollars, how many units are we likely to sell?"
   a. True
   b. False

4. A large collection of unrelated data is called a database; it is basically unorganized and it takes some time to search through and retrieve specific information from it.
   a. True
   b. False

5. Data extracting involves removing hidden predictive information from large databases through statistical analysis.
   a. True
   b. False

6. Which of the following is true about a marketing information system?
   a. It facilitates information collection, storage, manipulation, and dissemination in marketing.
   b. It is data-entry oriented.
   c. Its focus is on retrieval.
   d. It has little analytical ability.

7. Which of the following descriptions is *not* true regarding data warehousing?
   a. It involves the entire information delivery process.
   b. If successful, it provides organizations with the ability to bring together data from any source.
   c. It collects data from multiple sources and stores it in a way that allows end users to have quick access to important information.
   d. It assists decision making.
   e. All of the above are true.

8. Which of the following descriptions is *not* true about a data mart?
   a. It is subject specific.
   b. It is a data warehouse, but larger.

   c. One department or a group of users in a company often uses it for a defined set of tasks.
   d. It helps the company's networking staff determine the company's technology assets, optimal network routing, and capacities.
   e. All of the above are true.

9. One of the following individuals or groups facilitates information collection, storage, manipulation, and dissemination in marketing, including customer service and contacts. Which one is it?
   a. Marketing researcher
   b. Data mart
   c. Marketing decision-support system
   d. Data warehouse
   e. Marketing information system

10. Which of the following has been described as "a more advanced strategy of database marketing"?
   a. Data warehousing
   b. Customer relationship management
   c. Electronic data interchange
   d. Competitive intelligence
   e. The eXtensible Markup Language

Thinking Critically

1. Visit your local library or search the Internet and make a list of the five best databases you can find to learn about MBA programs throughout the world. What did you find?

2. Hundreds of companies are using data warehouses to improve their operations. Search for five articles that discuss how companies are using them. What did you find?

3. Hundreds of companies are mining their data to improve their decision making. Search for five articles that discuss how data mining has benefited their companies. What did you find?

4. You are a young entrepreneur who wants to start an apparel business. While you have extensive knowledge and experience in designing athletic apparel, you are not sure whether the market is large enough to warrant your attention. Since your research budget is small, you don't have enough financial resources to do your own mail survey of consumer demand. How would you go about researching this market to help you make your decision?

Net Exercises

1. SPSS and SAS are two of the most famous companies that help firms mine their data to turn stored data into knowledge. Visit http://www.spss.com and http://www.sas.com and learn how they do this. What do they have to offer? How similar or different are their descriptions?

2. Visit Nielsen//NetRatings online (http://www.nielsen-netratings.com) and find which countries the company is presently gathering data in.

Experiencing Marketing Research

Universe Technology has created an integrated software solution that its developers claim can dramatically improve most manufacturing systems of automobile suppliers. You have been hired as a consultant to locate 200 companies for it to target to sell its software solution. You are not expected to find the companies, but simply describe how you will determine which companies to target. Which sources would you use, and why?

Case 3-1

Automakers Mine Customers through Databases

The wheels are turning once again in the automotive industry. The industry is embracing a highly evolved form of database marketing called "customer relationship management" (CRM). It tantalizes businesses with the promise of seamlessly connecting their web, email, call center, and other customer-facing operations. The result is a transparent and consistent interface with customers and a "360-degree view" of them. CRM can take advantage of advances in software technology to use information accumulated about a consumer to create a more effective direct-marketing effort, according to Jeff Bickerstaff, business director of SilverCube, an e-commerce consultancy group.

Although CRM has been around for five years, the auto industry is late in grasping it when compared with marketers such as banks, telecommunications, and catalog retailers. The basic idea behind CRM is to keep in touch with your owners and prospects; understand their life styles and hobbies; and know their vehicle needs. The marketer will benefit by generating consumer brand loyalty. Auto manufacturers are scuffling to unify their customer information from different parts of their organizations into a single database.

Mary Doris-Smith, executive vice president of CRM business development at InterOne Marketing Group, claims that it is about five times more expensive to attract buyers to a brand than it is to keep the ones a company already has. Bickerstaff claims, "Everyone in the industry is saying it makes sense, but there's no model yet to say it works." Mercedes-Benz USA was a CRM pioneer. Ken Enders, vice-president of marketing, said that in the early 1990s, the company realized that owner data was "the brain trust of the company," so the database was moved inside the company, providing the seed for a structure to manage customer details.

The initial CRM-related effort at Mercedes was its Client Assistance Center, a 24-hour-a-day toll-free customer service operation. In 1999, the company opened "Personal Information Centers," a service that offers owners individual Web sites to communicate with the company. In 2002, the Assistance Center updated its system to obtain network management tools, contact centers, and connectivity solutions. The company that advertises DaimlerChrysler's products produces 1,300 different product brochures across all models. If a prospect expresses interest in, say, performance and handling of the Chrysler Concorde sedan, four spaces in the car's mailing can be customized with that data. Enders realizes that his competitors are jumping on the CRM bandwagon: "CRM is a buzz word and you see everyone using it, but I'm not sure everyone is living it." Enders admits that CRM is easier to implement for a small volume company like Mercedes, which has about 1.5 million consumers who have expressed interest in the brand on its database.

Advertising agencies are skeptical about CRM, since they stand to lose some direct mail billings. An ad agency will usually send 3 million to 4 million direct mail units to launch a particular vehicle, but with CRM's better customer data, the list can be reduced to 1 million to get the same number of respondents. Ad agencies also could be threatened by the web aspect of CRM, says Geoff Smyth, CEO of Ford Motor Company's Ford/Teletech customer relationship management joint venture in Denver. But according to Smyth, ad agencies "can morph" to provide CRM services and execute strategies that result in closer relationships with clients. And that seems to be what they are doing. Ross Roy Communications changed its name to InterOne to stress its main CRM thrust. Wunderman Cato Johnson, whose clients include Ford's Lincoln and Mercury brands, changed its name to Impiric to reposition itself as a CRM business.

After 18 months of setting up the infrastructure, InterOne launched a major program—mailings are sent to customers after they ask for information about the marketer's products or services. It also produces a Dodge owner's magazine that dealers can order. The publication, which includes stories about its products, is customized with dealership information and specials on service deals. It also contains a business reply card to update owner data. "We added the ability to capture information letting us tailor after-market messages to make them germane to our owners," said Phil Bienert, manager of CRM and future products at the Irvine, Calif., unit of Ford. He added that it allows their customers "to do more than just tell the company what (identification) number is on his windshield. He or she gets to say what their preferences are: how they want to be contacted, what services and accessories they may be interested in." Don Sparkman, vice president of Ford's marketing and sales, summed CRM up this way, "We want to make millions of customers feel special."

Sources: Jean Halliday, "Carmakers learn to mine databases," *Advertising Age* 71, no. 17 (April 17, 2000): S6; David Drucker, "Online customer support doesn't come in a wrapper—Eddie Bauer, USA Group and others find truly integrated CRM to be a technical and organizational challenge," *Internetweek* 816 (June 5, 2000): PG14; Anonymous, "Avaya drives away with euro 1.3 million Mercedes-Benz deal," *CRM Today* (February 1, 2002); Karl Greenberg, "Looking for Mr. Goodwrench," *Brandweek* 44, no. 13 (March 31, 2003): 24.

Case Questions

1. How is CRM really different from database marketing? Or is it?

2. What is meant by saying that CRM can create a "360-degree view" of customers?

3. The title of one of the sources to this case is "Car-makers learn to mine databases." Are the authors referring to data mining, the concept introduced in the chapter? If so, how are companies using it, according to the case?

4. Does data warehousing have a role to play at Mercedes and Ford? If so, what is it?

5. It was noted in the case that "Advertising agencies are skeptical about CRM, since they stand to lose some direct mail billings." Should they be skeptical? How might they lose direct mail billings?

Case 3-2

Avon's Dilemma: The Internet or Sales Representatives?

Analyst Mary Meeker warned that there would soon be a story about traditional companies missing the Internet revolution. The result would be CEOs falling by the wayside. But how can a 115-year-old direct-sales company grasp the Internet when the foundation of its company rests on its salespeople? Whether or not Avon's dramatic drop in sales was caused by its failure to grasp the superhighway is debatable, but the fact is that Avon's board replaced CEO Charlie Perrin with Andrea Jung, who pledged to expand Avon more aggressively. She was careful to downplay the role of the Internet and stand by the sales force, saying Internet sales will be incremental—some 5% of the total in the next few years. Avon's ace in the hole has always been its personalized attention provided by its sales representatives, which often develops into long-term friendships with customers.

Avon Products, Inc., is a manufacturer and marketer of beauty and related products, which include cosmetics, fragrances and toiletries, jewelry, accessories, apparel, and gift, decorative, and home entertainment products. Avon's business is comprised of one industry segment, direct selling, which is conducted in North America, Latin America, the Pacific, and Europe. Avon's products are sold worldwide by three million representatives that Avon refers to as "Leadership," 445,000 of whom are in the United States. Almost all representatives are women who sell on a part-time basis.

"The direct sales industry in general is having a hard time" reaching its audience, said Brian Hume, president of retail consulting firm Martec International, Inc., in Atlanta. In response, Avon has created additional channels, including more catalog offerings, a Web site, and 40 new retail stores

nationwide. Avon Products' new chief information officer, Sateesh Lele, said he plans to develop a worldwide intranet for sharing information among countries and an extranet to tie in with suppliers, and to allow sales representatives to place orders quickly and directly, check product availability in real time, and track order delivery.

Not only does Avon have its own Web site, it offers to assist sales representatives with creating their own sites to generate sales. Avonway Web Design claims that the Web sites "... will give you that edge. The edge which will set you apart from all others and display your products and services for your clients to evaluate, in the best possible manner. Don't be left trailing your competitors in the Internet revolution."

Sources: Patricia Sellers, "Big, hairy, audacious goals don't work—just ask P&G," *Fortune* 141, no. 7 (April 3, 2000): 39–44; Stacy Collett, "Avon calls for revamp of its Worldwide IT," *Computerworld* 33, no. 28 (July 12, 1999): 38; Christine Bittar, "Revlon, Avon need touch-up, but not complete makeover," *Brandweek* 40, no. 39 (October 18, 1999): 30–32; Nanette Byrnes, "Avon—lots of new reps: A sales-force makeover helps the company's U.S. turnaround," *Business Week* 3835 (June 2, 2003): 53.

Case Questions

1. Does it seem like Avon missed the Internet revolution and is attempting to play catch-up? If so, why? If not, why not?

2. What do you think of Avon's technology plan? Be sure to mention its web page, intranet, and extranet plans.

3. What else can Avon do to improve its sales in the United States?

4. What else can Avon do to improve its sales worldwide? What technology problems might Avon run into in markets abroad?

Notes

1. Neil Postman, "Who, what, where, when, and wise," *Editor & Publisher*, vol. 133, no. 19 (May 8, 2000): 34.

2. Efraim Turban, Ephraim McLean, and James Wetherbe, *Information Technology for Management* (New York: John Wiley & Sons, 1999), 17.

3. Kenneth C. Laudon and Jane P. Laudon, *Essentials of Management Information Systems* (Upper Saddle River, NJ: Prentice Hall, 1995), 6.

4. Efraim Turban, Ephraim McLean, and James Wetherbe, *Information Technology for Management* (New York: John Wiley & Sons, 1999), 18.

5. Kenneth C. Laudon and Jane P. Laudon, *Management Information Systems,* 8th ed. (Upper Saddle River, NJ: Prentice Hall, 2003).

6. Ritva Toivonen, "Planning the use of information technology in marketing: The case of Finnish forest industries," *Forest Products Journal* 49, no. 10 (October 1999): 25–31.

7. Y. L. Raymond, Raymond McLeod Jr., and John C. Rogers, "Marketing information systems in the Fortune 500 companies: Past, present, and future," *Journal of Management Information Systems* 10, no. 1 (Summer 1993): 165–192.

8. John Quinn, "DSS software can help predict effects of changes," *Computing Canada* 25, no. 24 (June 18, 1999): 31.

9. Suzette Hill, "Picking signals out of noise," *Apparel Industry* 61, no. 3 (March 2000), 30.

10. A. C. Nielsen Insights, "A. C. Nielsen trade manager enables clients to re-engineer promotional practices," *Progressive Grocer* 75, no. 9 (September 1996): A1(2).

11. Kenneth C. Laudon and Jane P. Laudon, *Management Information Systems,* 8th ed. (Upper Saddle River, NJ: Prentice Hall, 2003).

12. Ritva Toivonen, "Planning the use of information technology in marketing: The case of Finnish forest industries," *Forest Products Journal* 49, no. 10 (October 1999): 25–31.

13. Bureau van DIJI web page, http://www.bvdep.com/ISIS.html, accessed June 12, 2005.

14. Keith Fletcher and Linda Peters, "Issues in customer information management," *Journal of Marketing Research Society* 38, no. 2 (April 1996): 145 (16).

15. David Drucker, "Online customer support doesn't come in a wrapper—Eddie Bauer, USA Group and others find truly integrated CRM to be a technical and organizational challenge" *Internetweek* 816 (June 5, 2000): PG14.

16. Mark Boslet, "Database sales up 10 percent; IBM, Oracle tied for lead," *Financial News* (May 24, 2005).

17. Robert McKim, "Build your database to boost the bottom line," Folio: Sourcebook 2000: 138–139.

18. Marcia Stepanek, "Invasion of the databases," *Business Week.* 3679 (May 1, 2000): 138.

19. Joe Nicholson, "Two old newspaper hands suggest some new tricks to boost circulation," *Editor & Publisher* 133, no. 17 (April 24, 2000): 48.

20. Mark Boslet, "Database sales up 10 percent; IBM, Oracle tied for lead," *Financial News* (May 24, 2005).

21. Anonymous, "LexisNexis at nexis.com," http://www.lexisnexis.com/businessonline/features.asp, accessed June 12, 2005.

22. Lei-da Chen and Mark N. Frolick, "Web-based data warehousing," *Information Systems Management* 17, no. 2 (Spring 2000): 80–87.

23. Jill Dyche, *e-Data* (Reading, MA: Addison-Wesley, 2000), 14.

24. Judy Strauss and Raymond Frost, *E-Marketing* (Upper Saddle River, NJ: Prentice Hall, 2000), 116.

25. Katie Haegele, "Nuts & bolts," *Target Marketing* 23, no. 2 (February 2000): 26(7).

26. Anonymous, "Report shows SAS dominates data mining market," *Triangle Business Journal* (August 9, 2004).

Integrated Software Solutions

Appendix

So far in this chapter we have discussed ways to retrieve and analyze vital information to enhance decision making. This section will introduce you to an excellent software tool that will simplify your analysis tasks: SPSS. There are, however, other companies that offer software solutions such as SAS and Excel. Since SPSS and SAS tend to perform similar operations, we will discuss only SPSS in some detail as it relates to marketing research. In Chapters 12 through 17 we will discuss SPSS operations in more detail to solve specific problems. While Excel will typically be part of the basic Microsoft Office package, SPSS and SAS are more powerful but are quite expensive if purchased individually. However, most colleges and universities have either SPSS or SAS in their computer labs. Earlier in this chapter we discussed many of the analyses that SPSS and SAS can perform, such as data warehousing, data mining, and competitive intelligence. You will learn that their analytical abilities go far beyond these tools.

Statistical Product and Service Solutions (SPSS)

Headquartered in Chicago, SPSS has over 1,400 employees, more than 100 offices and authorized partners around the world, and 2004 revenues of over $220 million. The company claims to make marketing research easier by providing solutions that discover what customers want and predict what they will do. Their products integrate and analyze marketing, customer, and operational data. SPSS has developed its own marketing research line of products called SPSS MR, which provides users with a complete complement of integrated software solutions that covers the entire research process. Its major segments of marketing research expertise are survey design, data collection, analysis, and publishing.

- *Survey design*. SPSS creates questionnaires using a graphical interface and drag-and-drop techniques. Using two design packages—In2form Designer and Quanquest—users can input analysis specifications so that once data is gathered the results will be available almost instantaneously.

- *Data collection*. SPSS can help gather data through the web, computer-assisted telephone interviews, or computer-assisted personal interviews. After data collection is completed, SPSS has software to allow the user to input the data into the computer.

- *Analysis*. SPSS can turn data into information. It has software packages that tabulate and manipulate data, create tables, analyze and create statistical models, and mine data.

- *Publishing.* SPSS software will turn traditional papers into multimedia presentations. It will create electronic presentations and allow others to access and customize the reports to fit their individual needs.

Some of the companies that have used SPSS to help with their research needs include ACNielsen, Fox Kids, and British Airways. ACNielsen wanted to spend less money and time conducting surveys without compromising quality. It used SPSS's Quancept web page to create an electronic panel of respondents whose demographics resembled respondent samples taken from proven mall-intercept studies. It resulted in a 15,000-member web survey panel, increased survey capacity by 35%, lowered study prices by an average of 20%, and reduced the time to actually conduct the study by 10%.

Fox Kids, a leading pan-European media network targeting kids in each major market, recorded the reported thoughts, attitudes, and lives of children in the United Kingdom to find what was important to kids entering the new millennium. Its findings showed that the kids have a real social conscience, as well as retain the usual fascination for music, TV, and computer games; they are also aware of world issues, such as homelessness, starvation, and war.

British Airways wanted to gauge the effectiveness of using online auctions to create sales. The survey was hosted on one of SPSS MR's servers and showed that 78% of those who actively bid hadn't planned to travel. This means auctions actually create incremental revenue by encouraging people who don't normally use British Airways to try it.

Secondary Data and Information Online

Chapter Four

Source: © 2007 JupiterImages Corporation.

Key Terms

copyright   (p. 93)

infringement   (p. 93)

licensing   (p. 93)

North American Industry Classification System (NAICS)   (p. 91)

plagiarism   (p. 92)

secondary data   (p. 84)

Learning Objectives

After studying this chapter, you will be able to:

- Discuss the role of secondary data in marketing research and identify the shortcomings of secondary data.

- Understand how to evaluate the appropriateness of secondary data.

- Locate sources of secondary data and describe the kinds of data available from internal and external sources.

- Identify and describe different venues through which data is available to researchers.

- Discuss plagiarism and copyright laws, and explain how to properly cite sources.

GET THIS

Hong Kong Professors Clarify Media Decisions in China

It's certainly no secret that more businesses than ever before are focusing their efforts on selling their goods and services in the world's largest market. China has a huge population of 1.3 billion people, and its economy has grown faster than any other economy in the world over the past 20 years. As a result, their advertising industry is as healthy as it has ever been. The country's advertising ad expenditures have increased more than 108-fold in 16 years, ballooning to $14.5 billion in 2003. The industry is employing more than 870,000 people in 102,000 firms and agencies.

Three researchers at the University of Hong Kong sought to better understand an important sector of the industry—its upper crust, status-seeking Chinese consumers. (This information is necessary, since advertisers are demanding more in-depth information on media audiences beyond sociodemographic profiling.) More specifically, the researchers examined the targeting effectiveness and cost efficiency of the major media of television, newspapers, and magazines in China. They looked closely at a variety of secondary data sources. First, they examined the China National Readership Survey, which contains 48,000 responses in 15 cities in China; these are the most extensive media behavior survey results in China. This survey is implemented annually by China Central Television (CCTV), a national television station that telecasts sports, business, and international topics. Second, to understand the audience profile of each media type, they chose representative vehicles in each medium using datasets from Zenith Media, the largest media research firm in China. The television dataset contained responses from viewers of the largest three television channels in China—CCTV-1, CCTV-6, and CCTV-5. The newspaper readership dataset was comprised of responses from readers of at least one of eight regional newspapers. For magazine readers, they chose data about the top magazine vehicles in terms of adult readership in each of eight categories of magazines (business, in-flight, auto, travel, women's interests, entertainment, and fashion).

Their findings confirmed that relative to television and newspapers, magazines are effective vehicles for reaching upscale and status-seeking target markets. Among magazines, targeting effectiveness is particularly powerful for the fashion magazines that they used as prototypes of special interest magazines. Their study further revealed that in-flight, business, and travel magazines attract upscale consumers, whereas in-flight and fashion magazines attract status-seeking consumers. These findings suggest that it is important for advertisers in China as it is for advertisers in developed economies to use multiple indicators to profile media audiences, as demographic or psychographic information alone provides only partial information.

Source: Kineta Hung, Flora Fang, and David K. Tse, "Improving media decisions in China," *Journal of Advertising* 34, no. 1 (Spring 2005): 49–53.

Now Ask Yourself

- Why didn't the researchers simply gather the data themselves rather than purchasing it from the China National Readership Survey and Zenith Media?

- How is this secondary data in China any different from similar data in the United States?

- How did the researchers evaluate the appropriateness of secondary data?

- Were there likely any other internal or external sources that could have provided similar types of data to that obtained from the China National Readership Survey and Zenith Media?

As noted in the "Get This" feature, secondary data is critical for researchers to gain an understanding about media decisions in China. A lot of insight can be obtained from data collected by others—provided you feel confident in the data that you're planning to use. One thing is for sure—conducting secondary research is a fast and cost-effective way to become knowledgeable about a topic. You need to clearly understand what secondary data is, where to find it, and how to evaluate it. You learned in Chapter 3 how to retrieve all kinds of secondary data from databases. In this chapter, we discuss the role of secondary data in marketing research, the sources of this information, legal and ethical obligations when using the information, alternative formats for citing secondary data sources, and the availability of secondary data in global markets.

4-1 The Role of Secondary Data in Marketing Research

secondary data Data previously collected for a purpose other than the current study.

Marketing researchers can use secondary or primary data, or both, to satisfy their information-gathering needs. In this chapter, we focus on secondary data. Primary data will be discussed beginning in the next chapter. As you learned in Chapter 2, **secondary data** is data that has been previously collected for a purpose other than the current study.

For example, the National Trade Data Bank compiles full-text reports of trade statistics, marketing research reports, country background information, trade policies, and much more. In fact, most of the information online users find on the Internet is secondary data, but this type of data has not always enjoyed such popularity among marketing researchers.

Secondary data support the majority of marketing research activities due to the giant expansion in databases and other computerized informational sources that has occurred in recent years. Marketing managers often use secondary data because previously collected information can benefit marketing managers and researchers in a number of ways:

- *Availability.* Data from a wide variety of sources is readily available to solve many different marketing concerns. Secondary data is available from journals, from the company's own database, or from the Internet.

- *Time saving.* Not only is it available, but secondary data can be obtained fairly quickly in most cases. Whether the researcher needs economic data from Kuala Lumpur or consumer data from Poland, if the data is available, it can be retrieved in a short period of time.

- *Low cost.* Since there is no need to formulate an extensive research design and sample individuals, costs of using secondary data tend to be minimal. Sometimes companies charge a fee for certain information, but many times the data is free as long as it is not confidential.

- *Accessibility.* Computers can rapidly retrieve pertinent information, especially through the Internet, so data is becoming increasing accessible.

- *Complements primary data.* Secondary data can be used to help generate hypotheses for data collection, or it can be used to confirm information that has already been gathered. Sometimes primary and secondary data research is presented as exclusive events. But for most researchers, they often work hand in hand.

While secondary information provides numerous benefits to organizations, it also has some serious shortcomings. First, secondary data may be *inaccurate*. Since researchers were not involved in the initial collection of the information, they should always question the reliability of the data. Potential problems with secondary data may not be immediately apparent. For example, if interviewing was used to gather the information, were the interviewers qualified, and, if so, was the data accurately reported? Was the information correctly analyzed? Was the final report representative of the findings?

A second shortcoming of secondary data is that it may be *inconsistent*. When the question was asked, "how many people visited Gay.com," Nielsen//NetRatings said 196,000 at work, 287,000 at home; Media Metrix said it was 446,000; and Gay.com CEO Lowell Selvin reported it to be 1.8 million. Naturally everyone can't be correct. The actual number of visits is an important number, since millions of advertising dollars are at stake.[1]

Third, secondary data may be *inconvenient to compare*. Data from one country may not be in units that are easily comparable with those of other nations. When nations report their exports and imports for a given year, they typically do so in their own currencies. Due to fluctuating exchange levels, comparing data can be difficult.

Fourth, secondary data may be *inaccessible*. It is highly possible for researchers to find out that they need certain existing information but cannot gain access to it. Libraries may not carry pertinent publications, some data may be confidential, or costs for the information may be unaffordable. Companies experiencing the most problems with existing information are often involved in cross-border data comparisons. Globalization is a reality in today's business environment, and many companies are having trouble getting comparable data. Consider these facts:

- In countries with widely fluctuating currencies, there are likely to be discrepancies in company data reported by different sources. If the information is available, pay close attention to the date the data was reported.

- Some countries, like Denmark, do not want to divulge financial data beyond their borders.

- Different publications may provide different figures for the "fact." For example, the U.S. Department of Commerce reported that China's trade surplus with the U.S. hit a new high ($162 billion) in 2004, a 30.6% increase since 2003.[2] However, according to the Chinese Ministry of Commerce, China's trade surplus with the U.S. was $58.6 billion in 2004.[3]

- Some countries report their gross national product, while others provide their gross domestic product (which excludes net factor income received from abroad).

4-2 Assessing Secondary Data

Have you ever had someone say to you, "Don't believe everything you hear"? Well, when using secondary data, don't believe everything you read. While there is a lot of reliable and valid information to use, there is also quite a bit of erroneous data gathered from imprecise research efforts. So how do you decide what and what not to believe? If you consider the following questions, your chances of knowing what information to use and what to ignore will be significantly better:

1. *Who collected the data?* This question deals with the source of the data. That is, what qualifications does the researcher have to give you confidence in the information? Did it originate from a well-known marketing research firm, or did it come from a researcher with little research training in a developing country? The more information you can gather about the source of the data, the more or less confidence you should have in the secondary data.

2. *For whom was the data collected?* Data may be gathered for anyone throughout an organization, but most of the time it will be collected for managers. Then again, there are several different levels of management. A manager of a department will usually require much more specific data than will senior vice presidents of the entire company. Furthermore, certain trade languages will be used in different industries. Recognizing whom the data was initially intended for will give an indication about the usefulness of the information for your specific purposes.

3. *What was the purpose of the research?* The purpose of the research will indicate why the data was collected in the first place. Was it exploratory, descriptive, or

causal research? As we noted in Chapter 2, exploratory research tends to use smaller samples than the other types of research and is inconclusive. Therefore, the results should be treated as directional, not conclusive.

4. *When was the data collected?* Just like most other things in life, data can become outdated. Does it make sense to compare 1980 information with data gathered in 2005? In most cases, the answer is clearly "no." So if you are comparing information, make sure that you are using comparable data in terms of when the data was collected.

5. *How was the data collected?* This is a question of research methodology. The information should be reliable and valid and relate to your specific problem. In terms of sampling, the sample size and sampling frame have a lot to do with how useful the data will be to most researchers.

6. *How was the data analyzed?* We will discuss data preparation and analysis in Part 4, beginning with Chapter 12. At that time, you will learn that there are specific statistical tests that should be used on certain types of scaled data.

7. *How does the data compare with similar information from different sources?* To determine the quality of the data, it is always a good idea to consider how the data compares with similar data from other sources. For example, per capita income in France is reported in various publications and online sources, including *The World Fact Book*, *The National Trade Data Bank*, and *The World Bank*. Check to see if the figures are similar in each publication. The more similar they are, the more confidence you should have in the data.

4-3 Sources of Secondary Data

Exhibit 4-1 lists a few of the many places where previously gathered information is readily available. Many of these sources make the information available through the Internet, printed publications, and electronic databases on CD-ROM.

EXHIBIT 4-1	Secondary Data Sources
Internal Sources	**External Sources**
Accounting records	Government agencies
Marketing records	Libraries
Production records	Trade associations and other nonprofit organizations
Information systems personnel	Private companies
Sales force personnel	
Other individuals within the organization	

Let's say that you are doing a study on the automotive supplier industry. An excellent source to go to is Hoover's Online (http://www.hoovers.com), which provides profiles (available only to members) and company capsules of thousands of suppliers. Exhibit 4-2 shows the homepage of Hoover's Online.

Accessibility of information varies by organization. Many online sources and companies charge fees for access to their privileged information. However, some publishers, such as the U.S. government, cannot legally charge fees. Still other organizations will not permit access to parts of the gathered information for confidentiality reasons.

4-3a Internal Sources

The logical place to begin a search is to contact sources within your own company, since that data is accessible and free. *Accounting records* are valuable sources of information because they contain a lot of sales-related information, such as customer

EXHIBIT 4-2	Hoover's Online

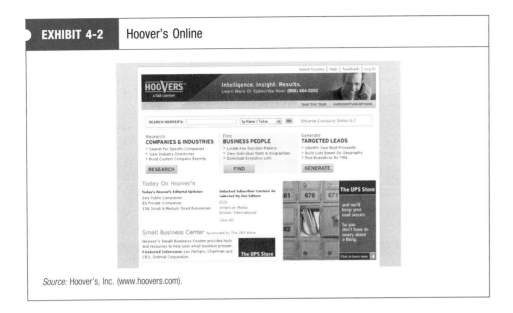

Source: Hoover's, Inc. (www.hoovers.com).

names, quantities ordered, and sales totals. *Marketing records* may yield specific information on product-line sales, purchasing terms, size of purchases, and geographic locations of customers. Other possible sources include your company's production personnel, information systems personnel, the sales force, and any employee with expertise in an area relevant to the research problem.

Suppose you work for High-Tech Appliance Store and you have been assigned the task of determining why company sales have been falling over the past two years. You first examine accounting records, such as monthly sales reports and the number of client accounts receivable. Then you examine the company's marketing records to find the number of holiday orders, the sales performance of each salesperson, and the regions of the country where the sales slump is worst. Finally, you talk to salespeople to determine their motivation levels. Based on the data collected, you might discover that overall sales are actually stable and the slump is centered in the Northeast, where a major competitor arrived two years ago.

4-3b External Sources

Many sources outside your company can provide useful secondary data. Government agencies, libraries, trade associations and other nonprofit organizations, and private companies are all good places to look for information. The Internet, another important external source for secondary data, is getting more popular due to the expansion of Web sites. (See the Appendix at the end of this chapter for some excellent sites for marketing researchers.)

Government Agencies

In some cases, marketing researchers rely on government data. For example, if a company is considering whether to build a large shopping mall in a certain city, it may examine population growth, average income, age structure, and number of houses being built in an area to determine potential consumer demand. This information can be found at local chambers of commerce, at courthouses, and from county clerks.

Local, state, and federal governments offer reliable and extensive collections of data. Local agencies are dispersed among counties, cities, and other judicial classifications, so information is usually more difficult to obtain than from state and federal levels. Some of the more accessible government groups to contact for local information include county clerks' offices, tax departments, economic development agencies, and courthouses. Local information is also available at nongovernment locations, including chambers of commerce, public libraries, newspaper offices, and public utility companies. State government sources include the state commerce department, attorney general's office, department of state, and banking and insurance commissions.

The most prolific government information sources are federal publications. The U.S. Government Printing Office (GPO) is the largest publisher in the world, with information widely available through the mail, telephone, Internet, and bookstores. Over 1,500 libraries across the United States regularly subscribe to federal publications. Exhibit 4-3 demonstrates the richness of data from the GPO. The Web site provides all kinds of links associated with the GPO, including business and contracting opportunities, employment opportunities, government information products, and services available to federal agencies.

EXHIBIT 4-3 U.S. Government Printing Office

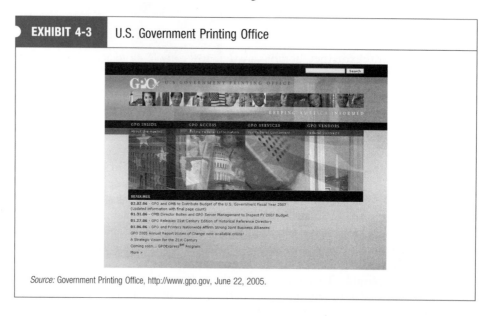

Source: Government Printing Office, http://www.gpo.gov, June 22, 2005.

Some of the best federal agencies to contact for information include the U.S. Bureau of the Census, U.S. Department of Commerce, U.S. Department of Labor, U.S. Department of Agriculture, U.S. and Foreign Commercial Service, U.S. Customs, and U.S. Small Business Administration. Exhibit 4-4 shows some information available from the U.S. Customs Service. In this case, online users can access travel data that pertains to general travel information, pets and animals, mailing goods to the United States, and so on. The Customs Service Web site also provides

EXHIBIT 4-4 U.S. Customs Service

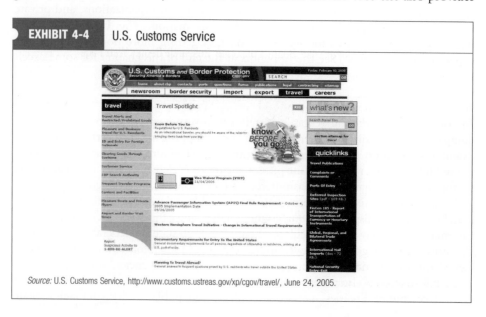

Source: U.S. Customs Service, http://www.customs.ustreas.gov/xp/cgov/travel/, June 24, 2005.

data on restricted and prohibited merchandise, medications and drugs, and general business travel information. Marketing researchers in the travel and tourism industry would likely be interested in this information.

The U.S. Department of Commerce is another rich source of secondary data. It publishes much of the statistical, economic, and demographic information collected by the U.S. federal government, making the information available to the general public through its bureaus and offices, which are known collectively as the Economics and Statistics Administration. Useful information can also come from other non-U.S. government agencies, such as the Canada Customs Assessment Division, the Embassy of Mexico Trade Office, the Canadian Embassy in Mexico, foreign embassies, foreign consulate offices, and international government-related trade associations.

Libraries

Except possibly for the Internet, libraries are the most complete and accessible sources of secondary data. Libraries can be either public or private. Public libraries are, of course, open to the general public, and their information is free of charge. Local libraries and university libraries are common stops for marketing researchers. Private libraries are closed to the general public but may allow researchers access to their information by appointment. Large private companies with their own libraries include Coca-Cola, PricewaterhouseCoopers, and Bank of America. Coca-Cola, for example, offers an abundance of information about the soft-drink industry and general data about markets throughout the world.

Trade Associations and Other Nonprofit Organizations

Trade associations are voluntary organizations whose members are individuals and companies involved in the same type of business or industry. The purpose of these associations is to provide industry information to their members. They do not always share their information with the general public, but they will sometimes accommodate requests for specific information free of charge or for a nominal fee. The American Association of Advertising Agencies (AAAA), American Marketing Association (AMA), and American Advertising Federation (AAF) are a few trade groups in the advertising industry. Other nonprofit organizations available for a wide range of research purposes include university libraries, the RAND Corporation, the National Bureau of Economic Research, and the Conference Board. The Conference Board, for example, is the world's leading business membership and research organization, connecting executives from nearly 2,000 companies in 60 countries worldwide.[4] Exhibit 4-5 shows the web page of its Consumer Research Center. It claims that it is the one-stop source for

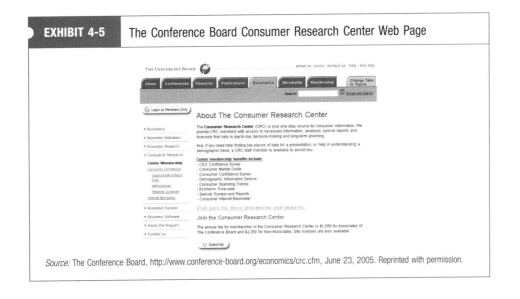

EXHIBIT 4-5	The Conference Board Consumer Research Center Web Page

Source: The Conference Board, http://www.conference-board.org/economics/crc.cfm, June 23, 2005. Reprinted with permission.

consumer information that provides members "with access to necessary information, analyses, special reports and forecasts that help in day-to-day decision-making and long-term planning."[5] Marketing researchers should also be interested in its publication *Consumer Affluence: The Next Wave*, which discusses where the changing U.S. marketplace is taking the American consumer. Other publications and services of interest to marketers are Business Cycle Indicators and the Consumer Confidence Index.

Private Companies

Researchers often contact private companies for information. (Many of the best sources of marketing information are shown in the Appendix at the end of this chapter.) Companies in accounting, advertising, or insurance are the most often contacted. According to a study of small-business owners and accountants, the majority of business owners said they rely on their accountant for business information and for help finding ways to save time and money. The findings also showed that business owners working with an accountant tend to perceive their business growth as more significant than those who did not.[6] Many accounting offices can aid marketing researchers by providing them with information on the economic, cultural-social, demographic, political-legal, competitive, and technological aspects of their target markets. A few of the large accounting firms with rich marketing data include Arthur Andersen, Ernst & Young, PricewaterhouseCoopers, Deloitte & Touche, and Haskin and Sells. As an example, Ernst & Young has offices worldwide and gathers marketing data that it makes available online.

Some companies are information specialists (also called information brokers, information intermediaries, or information consultants). These companies have expertise in retrieving all kinds of data. Often, they are independent businesses, but many libraries also fall into this category. In either case, they have access to important online databases and frequently have expertise in specific areas of business and industry. John F. Lescher points out in *Online Market Research* some marketing research projects performed by information specialists,[7] including:

- Describing opportunities created by government outsourcing
- Helping a garden supply company enter new consumer markets
- Developing the market strategy for a company selling corporate 800 telephone accounts
- Defining markets, insurance issues, and competitors for a company importing auto security systems
- Researching business failures and personnel injuries caused by faulty computer software
- Determining the patents held by a competitor

To learn about other free or low-cost external sources, you could contact:

- The editorial staff of trade publications
- Local barter organizations and clubs like the Chamber of Commerce, Lions Club, and Rotary Club
- Colleges and universities for departments/experts working in the field
- International clubs
- Industry-specific advertising, promotion, and public relations agencies
- Local and national broker, distributor, and private label manufacturers
- Buyer targets

You can also search computerized databases such as America Online, Compuserve, and the like.

Census Data

The U.S. Bureau of the Census has been counting the population every ten years since 1790. Before 1940, everyone in the United States had to respond to questions presented to them by census takers. Beginning in 1940, only a sample of households was asked to complete the questions on the survey. In 2000, one in six households was asked to complete the 53 questions on the so-called "long form" survey, which sought a detailed profile of a family's income, living habits, and racial composition. The national 67% Final Response Rate for Census 2000 exceeded the 65% response rate from the 1990 census and far exceeded the 61% response rate expected for the census.[8] But even with its success, Census 2000 still had some problems.

The major problem of Census 2000 is that the data can easily become obsolete. The survey results were released two years after the data was collected, and the data will not be updated until 2010. For companies that use census data—precise down to the zip code—to target sales pitches and decide the best sites for plants and other businesses, such dated information is not satisfactory, especially in locations where populations change rapidly.

Although it has its faults, the Census Bureau remains the best source that describes the people living in the United States. Consider the insight it provides for us to better understand Americans. According to a recent report, the U.S. population is rapidly growing more ethnically and culturally diverse:

- By 2020 the overall population in the United States should increase by 20% and by 50% by 2050. By 2050, the proportion of minorities in the U.S. will significantly increase. Asians will increase from 3% to 8%; the Hispanic population from 10% to 25%; African-Americans from 13% to 14%. During the same time, the proportion of Caucasians in the U.S. will decrease from 74% to approximately 50%. Caucasians will account for less than half of those under the age of 18 and 75% of people over the age of 65.

- While ethnic diversity is occurring in large numbers, it is unequally distributed throughout the country. Immigration is rapidly increasing the diversity of urban regions, while "native flight" to the suburbs and rural areas is also going up. Cities are becoming increasingly diverse, while many rural areas are becoming not nearly as diverse.[9]

The North American Industry Classification System (NAICS)

In 1930, the U.S. government created the Standard Industrial Classification (SIC) system to classify businesses by the industries in which they participated. It was updated in 1987, but today the codes are no longer current because the United States is more services-oriented, international, and technological. The SIC system was not compatible with the Mexican and Canadian classification schemes. To establish comparability among the three nations, representatives from the North American Free Trade Agreement joined efforts to create the **North American Industry Classification System (NAICS)**. In 1997, the U.S. Office of Management, and Budget (OMB) announced that the new NAICS (often referred to as "nakes") system would replace the SIC system. There are 1,170 industries, grouped in 20 economic sectors. The six-digit NAICS codes are relatively easy to understand:

- The first two digits represent the general economic sector in which the industry is classified.

- The third digit designates the subsector.

- The fourth digit is the industry group.

- The fifth digit is the NAICS industry.

- The sixth digit is the national industry.

Each country can designate detailed industries in order to meet national needs. For example, NAICS 311811, "Retail Bakeries," is used only for Canadian bakeries, while

North American Industry Classification System (NAICS) A six-digit code used to perform industry searches; improves on the Standard Industrial Classification (SIC) code by using a production-based framework.

NAICS 311812, "Commercial Bakeries," is used only for U.S. bakeries. To better understand the NAICS numbering system, consider the 513322 code:

- 51: represents "information"
- 513: represents "broadcasting and information"
- 5133: represents "telecommunications"
- 51332: represents "wireless telecommunications carriers" (except Satellite)
- 513321: represents "paging"
- 513322: represents "cellular and other wireless telecommunications"[10]

4-4 Citing Secondary Data Sources

A tremendous amount of work goes into creating new information to help decision makers. This effort should not go unappreciated—nor should it go uncited. Failure to give credit where credit is due is both unethical and illegal. Most students realize the importance of citing authors of printed matter, but it is just as necessary to cite authors of information available online. The format used to cite files available on the Internet can differ by discipline, but the content of the citations will not differ dramatically. In general, you must provide the author's name (last name first, then initials if known) and the date of publication in parentheses. Next, list the full title of the work, capitalizing only the first word and any proper nouns; the title of the complete work or site (if applicable) in italics, again capitalizing only the first word and any proper nouns; any version or file numbers, enclosed in parentheses; the protocol (e.g., "http") and the full URL, including the path or directories necessary to access the document; and finally the date accessed, enclosed in parentheses.[11] For example, if an article was written by Piyush Kumar and the work is published in the *Journal of Marketing Research*, it should be cited this way:

Piyush Kumar, "Brand counter extensions: The impact of brand extension success versus failure," *Journal of Marketing Research* 42, no. 2 (May 2005): 183–194.

Information obtained from the Internet should be cited using this format:

U.S. Customs Service, "Travel spotlight," http://www.customs.ustreas.gov/xp/cgov/travel/ (June 24, 2005).

4-4a Plagiarism and Copyright Laws

plagiarism Using someone's work without giving credit or without obtaining permission when it is necessary.

Using someone's work without giving credit or without obtaining permission, where necessary, is **plagiarism.** While in some cases individuals intentionally attempt to take credit for someone else's work, often the problem is that the rules for "fair use" of others' work are unclear. Many publications either have no written policies on plagiarism, or their codes of ethics are incomplete. For example, the *Society of Professional Journalists* simply states that "plagiarism is dishonest and unacceptable." The new *Statement of Ethical Principles for the Associated Press Managing Editors* reads, "The newspaper should not plagiarize words or images."[12]

Based on the ethical codes of a number of organizations, author William Strong offers the following suggestions for avoiding plagiarism:

- The researcher should not use someone else's research and fail to cite the individual.
- The researcher should not copy information from a source text without proper acknowledgment.
- The researcher should not leave out quotation marks when reproducing material from a source text and must use proper documentation.

- The researcher should not paraphrase material from a source text without appropriate documentation.
- The researcher should not buy completed research from a research service and fail to cite the service.[13]

Copyright issues go hand in hand with plagiarism because they determine what and how much can be safely used from a person's work. Works of art and literature are protected under copyright laws. A **copyright** is a right granted by statute to the authors or originators of literary works, artistic productions, and computer programs.[14] Some important changes were made recently to the copyright laws, as follows:

- Works created on or after January 1, 1978, automatically receive statutory copyright protection for the life of the author plus seventy years (instead of the life plus 50 years as it used to be).
- For works for hire (and works published anonymously and pseudonymously), protection is extended from 75 to 95 years.
- For unpublished works and works in their renewal terms, protection is extended for an additional 20 years.
- No expired copyrights will enter the public domain until 2019.[15]

Research Realities 4-1 lists what steps should be followed to obtain copyrighted information legally. Obtaining copyright permission is the process of getting consent from a copyright owner to use the owner's creative material. Obtaining permission is called **licensing;** when you have permission, you have a license to use the work. If you use a copyrighted work without the appropriate permission, you may be violating the owner's rights to that work, which is called **infringement**. Infringement may be subject to legal action, including being forced to cease using the work or paying financial damages.

The three key terms in copyright protection are *fixed, original,* and *expression.* The work must be "fixed," which means that it exists in a tangible form in which other people can perceive it. A story, for example, can be perceived when it is either written down or read aloud. Fixation is important because it designates the moment the work is federally copyrighted and differentiates between federal copyright protection and common law copyright. Under federal law, copyright is obtained at the time an individual's work is in tangible form. The work must be "original" in order to be copyrightable. That is, the work must originate from

copyright A right granted by statute to the authors or originators of literary works, artistic productions, and computer programs.

licensing Obtaining permission to use creative material by getting consent from a copyright owner.

infringement When a copyrighted work is used without the appropriate permission.

Research Realities 4-1   *Steps to Getting Copyright Permission*

There are some basic steps to follow to obtain copyright permission. Attorney Richard Stim offers a six-step procedure:

1. *Determine whether permission is needed.* Ask two important questions: "Is the material protected under law?" And "Would your use of the material violate the law?"

2. *Identify the owner.* Finding the owner of the work is crucial to obtaining permission.

3. *Identify the rights you need.* Each copyright owner controls all of the rights related to the work, including reproduction, distribution, and modification of the work. Be sure to specify the rights you need.

4. *Plan ahead for permissions.* Permissions often take one to three months to obtain.

5. *Negotiate whether payment is required.* In general, the less amount of work that is used, the lesser chance payment will be required.

6. *Get permission in writing.* An oral permission may be legally enforceable if it qualifies as a contract under general contract law principles. But if the agreement is explicitly stated, there is less chance for a successful suit against you.

Source: Adapted from Richard Stim, *Getting Permission,* Nolo.com (2000), 1–6.

the individual's own mind. Originality is not sufficient by itself, however; works must be an "expression" in order to be copyrightable. That is, individuals cannot copyright an idea but only the expression of it. Ideas cannot be copyrighted—they are public domain.[16]

The following works can be copyrighted:

- Literary works
- Musical works, including any accompanying words
- Dramatic works, including any accompanying music
- Pantomimes and choreographic works
- Pictorial, graphic, and sculptural works
- Motion pictures and other audiovisual works
- Sound recordings[17]

The following works cannot be copyrighted:

- Ideas
- Procedures
- Processes
- Systems
- Methods of operation
- Concepts
- Principles
- Discoveries

4-4b International Copyright Laws

Copyright laws are territorial, which means that they apply only to actions and individuals within the borders of the country in which they are enacted. Thus, U.S. copyright law applies in the United States, and English copyright laws prevail in England. Today, much effort is focused on curbing copyright violations in foreign countries, and some of the most blatant offenders of copyright protection laws have attempted to reduce these violations. The presence of copyright laws does not guarantee that violations will not occur. (See Research Realities 4-2.)

Businesses can protect their intellectual properties, such as copyrights and patents, at the international level. Over the last five decades, countries have formed treaty arrangements for the international protection of copyrights. The

Research Realities 4-2   *China's New Intellectual Property Rules to Take Effect*

At the end of November 2004 a new set of rules clarifying the criteria for punishing intellectual property rights violators went into effect in China. Diplomats continue to study the new rules to ensure that they genuinely provide better protection of intellectual property rights.

Cao Jianming, vice president of the Supreme People's Court, said in a news conference that the rules primarily focus on general principles, lack applicability, and don't provide enough specific criteria regarding conviction and sentencing. For example, the rules indicate that sales of

more than $6,000 of commodities bearing counterfeited registered trademarks will fall under "relatively large" sales of such goods, and those engaged in it could face imprisonment of three years or less.

China has come under increasing pressure from the United States, Europe, and Japan to strengthen the protection of intellectual property rights in the country.

Source: Anonymous, "China's new intellectual property rules to take effect," *Japan Economic Newswire* (December 21, 2004).

United States signed the Universal Copyright Convention (UCC) in 1952 and the Berne Convention of the Protection of Literacy and Artistic Works in 1988. The United States was a founding member of the UCC in the early 1950s but did not join Berne until the late 1980s. The UCC gives an author copyright protection in every country that has signed when he or she first publishes a work in one of the countries with the prescribed notice. Each country is bound to protect the work according to its laws. The Berne Convention likewise grants citizens of any other member country the same copyright protections that it provides its own citizens.[18] Consider the case of a photograph created by a Parisian photographer that appeared on the Web site of a Seattle company that sells posters. The photographer had authorized the photograph for use only in a promotional portfolio and for cards sold in Paris. Although he took the photograph in Paris and it never legally left France (because it didn't do so with his permission), U.S. copyright law protects the work when it's on U.S. soil. Thus, the photographer could prevent the Seattle company and its Web site from using the image on the Internet and from selling the photo as a poster.[19]

4-4c Alternative Formats for Citing Secondary Data Sources

Original works must be cited fully, both to meet legal requirements and to allow readers the opportunity to read the original works if desired. Proper credit can be given in various ways. Four often-used style sources are the *Publication Manual of the American Psychological Association*, the *Chicago Manual of Style*, the Modern Language Association's *MLA Style Manual*, and the *Government Printing Office Style Manual*. The chosen style should be followed consistently through the entire document.

4-5 Availability of Secondary Data in Global Markets

Using secondary data is a cost-effective means of evaluating foreign markets. Insufficient knowledge is the main reason companies fail in the international marketplace.[20] The availability of data in global markets depends heavily on the level of development of the country being researched. In general, the more developed a nation, the more likely it is that reliable information is available. Researchers have little trouble obtaining a variety of information in the United States, Canada, Western Europe, Japan, Australia, and other well-established markets. In emerging markets like China, Poland, Mexico, and Brazil, however, reliable and useful information occurs only sporadically—although this situation is improving. Today most countries and organizations around the world realize the importance of data collection and storage. Secondary data in global markets will be further discussed in Chapter 11.

Decision Time!

As a marketing manager, you now know that preexisting data is readily available both online and offline. You also know that there are benefits and problems associated with secondary data. What would you do if you asked your marketing researcher to gather some industry data and when she presented you with the information, you were not comfortable with her findings? How would you deal with it? Would you ignore the feeling and accept the data, ask the researcher to recheck the information, ask for primary data, or perhaps choose a different course of action?

Net Impact

The Internet makes a researcher's quest for secondary data a relatively quick and cost-effective activity. With the exception of a few proprietary pieces of information, sources discussed in this chapter are all retrievable from the Internet. As information technology continues to improve, more secondary data will be available to marketing researchers through online sources. The Appendix of this chapter, "Web sites for Marketing Researchers," summarizes the most relevant Web sites in each major area of marketing.

On the Lighter Side—Publications in Medical Journals Often Need Treatment

The *Journal of the American Medical Association* looked at research findings published in three medical journals between 1990 and 2003. The sample encompassed 45 popular studies of drugs that claimed to be an effective treatment or drug. The findings revealed that in nearly one-third of the cases, research results were potentially exaggerated or were totally contradicted by later studies. Dr. John Ioannidis, the study author and researcher at the University of Ioannina in Greece, added, "There's no proof that the subsequent studies . . . were necessarily correct."

Source: Lucy Sherriff, "One in three medical studies is dodgy," *The Register* (July 14, 2005); http://www.theregister.co.uk/2005/07/14/medical_studies_wrong/print.html, accessed October 7, 2005.

Chapter Summary

Secondary data is data that has been previously collected for a purpose other than the current study. There are numerous reasons to use it, including availability, time savings, low cost, and accessibility, and it usually complements primary data. There are also a few reasons that may motivate researchers not to use it, including possible inaccuracies, inconsistencies, inconvenience for making comparisons, and inaccessibility.

When deciding whether to use certain secondary information, researchers should inquire into the source of the data; who the information was gathered for; the purpose of the research; when the data was collected; how it was collected and analyzed; and how comparable it is to similar data.

Secondary data may come from either internal sources or external sources. The external sources include government agencies, libraries, trade associations and other nonprofit organizations, and private companies. Some other excellent sources of secondary data are books, journals, and the Internet. The U.S. Bureau of the Census collects demographic information on households that is shared with individuals and businesses. Because of the North American Free Trade Agreement and other international considerations, the U.S. government created the North American Industry Classification System to replace the shortcomings of the Standard Industrial Classification code.

Since a tremendous amount of work goes into creating new information to help decision makers, plagiarism must be avoided and copyright laws upheld—regardless of where the violation occurs.

Review Questions

1. What is the purpose of secondary research? Why not simply collect your own data?

2. What are the shortcomings of secondary data? Can you think of any additional shortcomings that were not mentioned in this chapter?

3. Why did the NAICS replace the SIC code?

4. How should secondary data be evaluated?

5. How are U.S. companies' copyrights protected in markets abroad?

Practice Quiz

Note: You can find the correct answers to these questions by taking the quiz and then submitting your answers in the Online Edition. The program will automatically score your submission. If you miss a question, the program will provide the correct answer, a rationale for the answer, and the section number in the chapter where the topic is discussed.

1. One major shortcoming of secondary data is high cost.
   a. True
   b. False

2. One important factor when assessing secondary data is the source of the data.
   a. True
   b. False

3. One important source of external secondary data is accounting records.
   a. True
   b. False

4. NAICS is replacing the Standard Industrial Classification (SIC) system because Asian and European trading partners found the SIC system confusing.
   a. True
   b. False

5. Using someone's work without giving credit or without obtaining permission is plagiarism.
   a. True
   b. False

6. Asking which of the following is *not* a way to assess secondary data?
   a. What was the purpose of the research?
   b. When was the data collected?
   c. How was the data collected?
   d. How was the data analyzed?
   e. How does the data compare with primary data?

7. Which of the following is *not* a way to avoid plagiarism, according to William Strong?
   a. Don't fail to cite someone else's research.
   b. Don't leave out quotation marks when reproducing material from a source text.
   c. Don't paraphrase material from a source without appropriate documentation.
   d. Don't buy completed research from a research service because it cannot be legally cited.
   e. Don't copy information from a source text without proper acknowledgment.

8. Which of the following involves obtaining permission to use copyrighted material from its owner?
   a. Expression
   b. Licensing
   c. Grazing
   d. Pushing
   e. Copyrighting

9. The correct order of elements when citing an article from the Internet includes listing the
   a. source, title of the work, web address, and date you accessed the site.
   b. title of the work, source, date you accessed the site, and web address.
   c. source, web address, title of the work, and date you accessed the site.
   d. title of the work, source, web address, and date you accessed the site.
   e. None of the above is correct.

10. The _____ gives an author copyright protection in every country that has signed when he or she first publishes a work in one of the countries with the prescribed notice.
    a. United States Copyright Committee
    b. Universal Copyright Convention
    c. United Copyright Committee
    d. Universal Copyright Committee
    e. Union Copyright Convention

Thinking Critically

1. You are planning to start a new business that sells men's facial care products, but you don't know much about the competition. If your research budget is almost exhausted, where would you go to find the information?

2. You are a marketing researcher, and your marketing manager says, "Why do you keep giving me this information that others have collected? I'm not even sure it's worth anything. If I were in your position, I wouldn't trust any information someone else had collected. Why don't you go out and collect some data yourself?" Begin your defense by informing your manager about the advantages of using secondary data over primary data.

Net Exercises

1. For up-to-date information about patent, copyright, and trademark laws, visit http://www.nolo.com. It also has extensive information about Internet law.

2. The World Intellectual Property Organization provides basic international copyright information. Visit

its Web site at http://www.wipo.org to learn about international copyright laws.

3. Hoover's Online is an excellent source for company and industry information. Visit http://www.hoovers.com and write down the types of information that are available at the General Motors site.

 ## Experiencing Marketing Research

Most colleges and universities have nicknames or mascots to express something about the institution. What does your institution's nickname or mascot convey? Why was it

chosen? When was it adopted? Use some secondary sources to find the answers. Which sources did you use?

 ## Case 4-1

Census Data: Needless or Necessary?

The intentions of the U.S. Census Bureau seem honorable. After all, census information is meant to help communities get financial assistance for hospitals and free health clinics; obtain more federal funding for planning schools, hospitals, and roads; help determine where to build more roads, add lanes, install stoplights, or adjust speed limits; and help decision makers understand which neighborhoods need new schools and which ones need services for the elderly, as well as childcare centers. Businesses use the census data to determine if the market for a new product is large enough or if the product will be accessible to consumers. And the information helps to determine how many seats your state will have in the U.S. House of Representatives and the number of seats in your state legislature.

The U.S. Bureau of the Census used to send a "long form" every 10 years to 1 in 6 households. This amount was approximately 20 million households in 2000. Each time the census was taken, the findings of this 53-question survey would be released two years later, and users of the data would then have to wait another 10 years for updates. In locations where rapid population growth occurs, the census findings become obsolete in a hurry. For example, in Tucson, Arizona, approximately 6,000 people are added to the population annually. And its county, Pima, is increasing by more than 14,000 people each year.

The long form for the official census is not used anymore, but citizens are asked to respond to the same questions in a new monthly survey. Each year, about 3 million households—approximately 1 in 40—will get a 67-question survey. It will go to a sample of households in each of the nation's 3,142 counties. Beginning in 2005, annual data

was released on communities with 65,000 or more people and, by 2008, on communities of 20,000 or more. By 2010, specific data will be available on individual neighborhoods.

Marketers and planners are ecstatic about the availability of fresh market information. "A lot of our clients are very interested in data on income, identifying patterns of income distribution for small areas," says Ken Hodges, chief demographer at Claritas, a San Diego-based marketing research company. The company uses census data to assist retailers, ski resorts, automakers, newspapers, cities' economic development officials, and others to reach the people they target. Joan Naymark, director of research and planning for Target, says the retail chain uses census data to make informed merchandising and marketing decisions and select locations for new stores.

The Census Bureau hopes that the monthly survey, which goes to fewer people and lacks the national fanfare of the decennial count, will quiet the critics. "Let's call it the stealth census," says Taylor, the Tucson planner. "Your average citizen is totally clueless about its existence."

Source: Frank Wilmot, "The Census Bureau: Aren't they on vacation until 2010?" *IN Context* 5, issue 5 (Sept./Oct. 2004): 10.

Case Questions

1. Do you have enough faith in the Census Bureau data that you would be willing to base your company's strategic planning on it?

2. When does the Census Bureau's new plan to do the census take effect?

3. If you were the manager of a Target store located near your university, how could you use census data to devise your marketing strategic plans?

Case 4-2

Secondary Data Improving in China

China has 1.3 billion citizens. That's one-fifth of the world's population. It has low unemployment and a rich pool of people ready to work hard at their jobs. China has been described as an emerging market for most multinational firms. It was over twenty years ago that the Economic Open Door policy was adopted, inviting foreign businesses to enter the previously closed doors. International marketers are eager to learn more about the characteristics of this market and of the people there. This is often done in foreign markets from primary research. But before the adoption of the Economic Open Door policy, China did not permit foreign researchers to conduct primary research. Foreign firms were forced to rely on secondary data released by the Chinese government to become more educated about the goings-on behind the curtain. Today, the control over market information has been relaxed, allowing foreign marketers to conduct their own research, but it is necessary to examine secondary data before primary data collection is undertaken.

A good source of sociopolitical and economic aspects of the country comes from the State Statistics Bureau (SSB). It has branches at different administrative levels and implements four major types of national surveys: the Census survey, the Urban Household survey, the Rural Household survey, and the Children Census survey. Another source of secondary data comes from the State Council, which has research organizations that can be classified into six categories:

- Research units under the State Council
- Research units under the State Council's Development Research Center
- Research centers affiliated with various ministerial systems
- Research organizations affiliated with industry or trade associations

- Industry-specific intelligence units at different administration levels
- Economic research units within local government

One must be cautious when using the data from the SSB, as the current situation with statistics in China is not satisfactory. Li Deshui, director of the National Bureau of Statistics, has put pressure on local officials for artificially inflating their growth in gross domestic product (GDP). He explained that GDP figures he received from a variety of provincial governments were $320 billion more than the amount his bureau derived. There are three major causes for these erroneous figures: technical issues like unscientific statistical methods. improper accounting systems, and issues other than statistics, usually intervention from local authorities. The first two problems are simple to correct, but intervention from local officials is much more challenging to deal with, as statistics are still the primary measurement of performance evaluation and promotion of officials. A lengthy time frame is needed to build an unbiased system that will accurately evaluate the performance of officials.

Sources: Sherriff T. K. Luk, "The use of secondary information published by the PRC government," *Journal of the Market Research Society* 41, no. 3 (July 1999): 355–365; Anonymous, "Data accuracy requires independent collecting system," *Business Daily Update* (March 16, 2005): 16.

Case Questions

1. Based on what you've read in the case, would you feel comfortable using secondary data from the Chinese government? Why or why not?

2. What can be done to solve the problem of manipulating statistical data due to the intervention from local authorities? (This is a major issue in many developing countries.)

3. How do you believe foreign businesses currently conducting marketing research in China will affect the quality of information coming out of China?

Notes

1. Jon Swartz, "Net rankings vex dot-coms," *USA Today* (June 20, 2000): B1.
2. U.S. Census Bureau, "Trade with China: 2004," http://www.census.gov/foreign-trade/balance/c5700.html#2004 (June 24, 2005).
3. Ministry of Commerce of China Web Page, "Sino-US Bilateral Trade 2004," http://www.mofcom.gov.cn/guobie/guobie.shtml (June 24, 2005).
4. The Conference Board Membership, http://www.conference-board.org/memberservices/ (June 24, 2005).
5. The Conference Board Membership, http://www.conference-board.org/memberservices/ (June 23, 2005).
6. Anonymous, "Intuit survey of accountants and clients," *The Practical Accountant* 37, no. 11 (November 2004): 12
7. John F. Lescher, *Online Market Research* (Reading, MA: Addison-Wesley, 1995), 27–28.

8. U.S. Census Bureau, "United State Census 2000," http://www.census.gov/main/www/cen2000.html (June 24, 2005).

9. Angela Peterson and Georgia Aquarium, "2004 diversity trends report," http://www.aza.org/AboutAZA/Diversity/Documents/DiversityTrendsReport.pdf (June 24, 2005): 1.

10. North American Industry Classification System, http://www.census.gov/epcd/www/naics.html (June 24, 2005).

11. The Columbia Guide to Online Style, "The World Wide Web," http://www.columbia.edu/cu/cup/cgos/basic.html (July 26, 2005).

12. Trudy Lieberman, "Plagiarize, plagiarize, plagiarize, only be sure to always call it research," *Columbia Journalism Review* 34, no. 2 (July–August 1995): 21–25.

13. William S. Strong, *The Copyright Book: A Practical Guide* (London: MIT Press, 1993), 1.

14. Herbert M. Bohlman, and Mary Jane Dundas, *The Legal, Ethical and International Environment of Business* (Cincinnati, OH: West Educational Publishing Company:, 1999), 212.

15. Nolo.com, "Copyright law changes that may affect you," http://www.nolo.com (June 25, 2005).

16. William S. Strong, *The Copyright Book: A Practical Guide* (London: MIT Press, 1993), 1.

17. Esther R. Sinofsky, *A Copyright Primer for Educational and Industrial Media Producers* (Friday Harbor, WA: Copyright Information Service, 1988), 12–13.

18. Herbert M. Bohlman, and Mary Jane Dundas, *The Legal, Ethical and International Environment of Business* (Cincinnati, OH: West Educational Publishing Company, 1999), 212.

19. Susan P. Butler, "Put your work under lock and key," *Macworld* 17, no. 7 (July 2000): 113–115.

20. Michael R. Czinkota, and Ilkka A. Ronkainen, "Using secondary sources of research," *International Trade Forum* 3 (July–September, 1994): 22(13).

Web sites for Marketing Researchers

To identify opportunities and potential problems, businesses must perpetually monitor trends and other movements in the market environment. This continuous monitoring of the external environment is called *environmental scanning*. Likewise, marketers must constantly research markets to clearly understand the arena in which they operate. In industrialized nations, for example, rules and regulations are often strict, due to the existence of such regulatory agencies as the Federal Trade Commission and the Food and Drug Administration. In developing countries, however, where dealing with starvation, developing infrastructure, and maintaining law and order are immediate concerns, forming regulatory agencies to protect consumer rights is usually not given high priority.

Businesses' knowledge of the environment enables them to better serve the needs of their customers. To aid in the research process, Exhibit 4-A1 provides some of the most important web addresses, along with brief descriptions of each of them, to aid your research efforts. The major topics covered are:

- marketing research/advertising
- country information
- international trade
- banking and finance
- statistics/economics
- political and legal concerns
- competition
- technology
- news/periodicals
- academic resource links

EXHIBIT 4-A1	Web sites for Marketing Researchers

Marketing Research/Advertising

ACNielsen (http://www.acnielsen.com)

ACNielsen is the world's largest marketing research firm. This page will explain what services it can deliver in individual countries. You also can visit some past surveys conducted in various markets.

The American Marketing Association Home Page (http://www.ama.org)

The American Marketing Association (AMA) is the world's largest and most comprehensive professional society of marketers. The AMA is the only organization that provides direct benefits to marketing professionals in both business and education and serves all levels of marketing practitioners, educators, and students.

Council of American Survey Research Organizations (CASRO) (http://www.casro.com)

CASRO is based in the United States and is the national trade association for commercial research firms.

ESOMAR (http://www.esomar.nl/directory_internat.html)

ESOMAR, The World Association of Research Professionals, founded in 1948 as the European Society for Opinion and Marketing Research, unites 3,800 members in 96 countries, both users and providers of opinion and marketing research. Provides country list and links to companies offering international marketing research.

Market Research and Data on the Internet and WWW (http://www.isoc.org/links/webstats.html)

Lists and describes international marketing research companies accessible online.

Country Information and International Trade

Background Notes (http://www.state.gov/www/background_notes)

Provided by the U.S. Department of State. Background Notes provide information on geographic regions and international organizations and are updated periodically.

Governments on the WWW (http://www.gksoft.com/govt)

Comprehensive database of governmental institutions on the World Wide Web: parliaments, ministries, offices, law courts, embassies, city councils, public broadcasting corporations, central banks, and multinational organizations.

SmallShop—Import-Export (http://www.smallshop.com/import-export.htm)

Offers trade leads and information about general import-export trade, global trade, and trade in specific regions.

U.S. Dept. of Commerce, U.S. Commercial Service http://www.export.gov/comm_svc/index.html

The International Trade Administration lists companies that do all kinds of marketing research such as customized marketing research, country commercial guides, and search trade leads. It also has an excellent Basic Guide to Exporting and gives a lot of export trade information.

Export-Import Bank of the United States (http://www.exim.gov)

Export-Import Bank is the official export credit agency of the U.S .government. This site provides an abundance of information on Export-Import Bank's export/import credit insurance and pre-export/import financing.

Banking and Finance

Banking and Finance (http://www.qualisteam.com)

Access to essentials of banking and finance. It provides 95% of bank Web sites, stock exchanges from 105 countries, and a directory of 10,000 financial servers.

Foreign Central Banks (http://www.federalreserve.gov/centralbanks.htm)

Allows immediate access to the central banks of the major countries. Provided by the U.S. Federal Reserve and offered in multiple languages.

Global Investor (http://www.global-investor.com)

Directory of financial resources. It compares the performance of the world's major markets and provides a complete listing of international American Depositary Receipts issued in the United States.

Small Business Administration's Office of International Trade Home Page (http://www.sbaonline.sba.gov/oit/)

Provides information about the financial assistance program for qualified small businesses.

Overseas Private Investment Corporation (http://www.opic.gov)

The Overseas Private Investment Corporation is an independent U.S. government agency that sells investment services to assist U.S. companies investing in some 140 emerging economies around the world. Provides information about medium- to long-term financing for sound overseas projects.

EXHIBIT 4-A1   Continued

Statistics /Economics

STAT-USA (http://www.stat-usa.gov)

Provided by the U.S. Department of Commerce.

Site for the U.S. business, economic, and trade community, providing authoritative information from the federal government. Includes the National Trade Data Bank.

U.S. Bureau of the Census (http://www.census.gov)

Patent agency is the U.S. Department of Commerce. Provides statistics from United States and foreign statistical agencies. Conducts demographics and economic surveys.

CIA World Factbook (http://www.theodora.com/wfb/)

Prepared by the Central Intelligence Agency

for the use of U.S. government officials. Best feature is country profiles that describe geography, people, government, economy, communications, transportation, military, and transnational issues.

International Monetary Fund (http://www.imf.org)

Besides supervising the international monetary system and providing financial support to member countries, the IMF assists its membership by making technical assistance available to member. Provides all kinds of financial information on such topics as debt initiatives, economic policies, and banking system soundness of member nations.

Background Notes (http://www.state.gov/www/background_notes)

Excellent source from the U.S. State Department that provides information on geographic entities and international organizations.

Political and Legal Concerns

Library of Congress (http://www.loc.gov)

Resources for researchers and information professionals. These include the catalogs of the Library of Congress and other libraries, databases on special topics, and other Library of Congress Internet resources.

LEXIS-NEXIS (http://www.lexis-nexis.com)

This is an online service for legal, news, and business information.

ACNielsen (http://www.acnielsen.com)

A global leader in delivering market research, information, and analysis to the consumer products and service industries. Provides legal, political, and marketing information from over 90 nations.

United Nations (http://www.un.org)

Provides political and legal data with links to peace and security, international law, human rights, humanitarian affairs, and economic and social developments. Can access numerous online databases related to these topics.

Office of Foreign Assets Control (OFAC) (http://www.ustreas.gov/ofac/ofactxt.html)

Provided by U.S. Department of Treasury. OFAC administers and enforces economic and trade sanctions against targeted foreign countries, terrorism-sponsoring organizations, and international narcotics traffickers based on U.S. foreign policy and national security goals.

It publishes an extensive list of "Specially Designated Nationals and Blocked Persons" with whom U.S. persons may not deal.

Competition

The Fuld Competitive Intelligence Center (http://www.factiva.com)

Provides executives and business managers at all levels with powerful company, industry, and trend analysis tools that help them efficiently compile, evaluate, and act on competitive intelligence.

The World Competitiveness Yearbook (http://www02.imd.ch/wcc/yearbook/)

Analyzes and ranks the ability of a nation to provide an environment that sustains the competitiveness of enterprises. Features 46 industrialized and emerging economies.

Provides 259 different criteria, grouped into eight Competitiveness Input Factors.

SEC EDGAR database (http://www.sec.gov/edgarhp.htm)

Provides all kinds of information about companies, such as annual reports, press releases, senior executive speeches, distribution networks, and product launch information.

Dialog (http://www.dialog.com)

These online research services provide a huge amount of information about products and companies.

Hoover's Online (http://www.hoovers.com)

This site allows users to search most companies by name or SIC code (or NAICS). It provides excellent profiles of companies.

Thomas Register of American Manufacturers (http://www.thomasnet.com/)

This source allows users to buy and specify from manufacturers of millions of industrial products and services. A huge online source that provides product, service, or company information.

EXHIBIT 4-A1   Continued

Technology

SEC EDGAR database (http://www.sec.gov/edgar.shtml)

EDGAR, the Electronic Data Gathering, Analysis, and Retrieval system, performs automated collection, validation, indexing, acceptance, and forwarding of submissions by companies and others who are required by law to file forms with the U.S. Securities and Exchange Commission (SEC).

BusinessWire (http://www.businesswire.com)

Provides online searches of the latest business headlines for all states in the U.S. Can also perform searches by topic and gives useful Web sites in various business areas.

International Energy Agency (http://www.iea.org)

Based in Paris, this site provides linkages to technology publications from the Organization of Economic Co-operation and Development (OECD) and energy groups, as well as oil and gas data and other statistics.

A Business Researcher's Interests (http://www.brint.com)

An online network for contemporary business, technology, and knowledge management issues. It provides full text articles on a wide range of business and technology topics.

News/Periodicals

The Wall Street Journal (http://www.wsj.com)

The home page of the *Wall Street Journal*. Offers links to WSJ's web offerings as well as its services. The complete newspaper can be found online. Subscription is for a fee.

The Economist (http://www.economist.com)

The Economist Web site features a selection of articles from the current issue for free. Subscription is required to access the complete edition as well as to retrieve articles from the archives. Searching the archives is free with registration.

Bloomberg Business News (http://www.bloomberg.com)

The online edition of *Bloomberg Business News*. Extremely detailed, including news from world markets and headlines from many newspapers around the world.

International Herald Tribune (http://www.iht.com)

The *International Herald Tribune* is a global newspaper, with features and news stories from around the world. Also of interest are special reports that take an industry or country and investigate it in detail.

Advertising Age International (http://www.adageglobal.com/)

A preeminent source of marketing, advertising, and media news, information, and analysis. The site provides daily international news as well as event listings, agency reports, and ranked listings of global marketers.

Academic Resource Links

Georgia Tech University Center for International Business (CIBER) (http://www.ciber.gatech.edu/)

This is one of the 27 centers for international business that is funded by the U.S. Department of Education. It provides all kinds of information about international business in markets abroad.

Michigan State University International Business Resource on the WWW (http://ciber.bus.msu.edu/busres.htm)

Excellent resource of international business provided by Michigan State University Center for International Business (CIBER).

University of Connecticut CIBER Hope Page (http://www.ucc.uconn.edu/~cibadm01/)

Located at the UConn School of Business Administration (SBA), the UConn CIBER is one of 26 national centers of excellence in international business.

University of Hawaii CIBER Home Page (http://www.cba.hawaii.edu/CIBER)

UH CIBER serves as a national resource for improved business techniques, strategies, and methodologies that emphasize the international context in which business is transacted. It also serves as a regional resource to businesses in the Pacific Rim by offering programs and providing research designed to meet their international training needs.

University of Illinois at Urbana-Champaign (http://www.ciber.uiuc.edu/)

The International Trade Center at the University of Illinois provides current and potential exporters with the information and expertise needed to increase international sales.

Primary Data Collection: Qualitative and Observational Research

Chapter Five

Source: © 2007 JupiterImages Corporation.

Chapter Outline

Key Terms

Learning Objectives

After studying this chapter, you will be able to:

- Explain the importance of primary data and qualitative research.
- Describe the different types of qualitative research techniques.

- Explain the uses and methods of observational research.
- Introduce a combination approach to capture customer information.

GET THIS

Focus Group Concentrates on New Product Development

For a long time qualitative research has offered to companies first-hand knowledge of customers' product preferences. What is increasingly taking place today is that businesses can concentrate their efforts and make changes to their products in a short period of time based on input from focus group participants. "There is a genuine need to compress time, especially (in) new product development," says Sharon Seidler, senior vice president of C&R Research Services, Inc., a full-service custom marketing research and consulting company based in Chicago. "The idea is to conduct a series of qualitative focus groups and treat everyone as if they are in an underwater submarine: Turn off the cell phones and do nothing else for two days."

To address specific problems on the spot, though, businesses must ensure that certain employees are at every focus group session. Experts state that salient personnel include market researchers, product engineers, graphic artists, and product managers—those that they have specific roles in a product's development.

Espoo, Finland-based Nokia Corp., the world's largest mobile phone maker, has saved important resources in development by having specific employees attend qualitative research sessions. For example, in 2003, Nokia set up focus group sessions with a series of individual end-user respondents in the United States to get feedback on a new messaging product they were planning to introduce to the market later on.

"We had the (respondent) interact with the product in order to figure out if we needed to make changes," says Bernard Brenner, senior manager of the American market research for Nokia. In one session, the respondent experienced problems with the emailing product command, which was buried within two submenus. They altered the menu at the session and moved it to the forefront of the system for easier access, and made the email system a menu of its own.

The adjustment, based on input from Nokia's product engineers, product managers, and marketing employees, allowed the user to bring up the email system without having to search through a bunch of menus. The product managers and marketers decided to simplify the menu system, while the product engineers were primarily responsible for modifying the system.

Brenner stated that after the change was made, they showed it once again to the respondent without revealing what specific feature was changed. The respondent then tried to interact with the product once again and found it was much more user-friendly.

The adjustment will ultimately save Nokia a lot of time and money allocated to customer service resources that would have been spent addressing queries on that particular feature. Brenner notes: "We were able to save what I call 'soft money' to (future) customer service requests. It changed opportunity costs going forward."

Researchers indicate that executives need to be careful about how and when they use all that extra information. Terry Grapentine, president of Grapentine Company, Inc., an Ankeny, Iowa-based market research firm, noted, "Changes can be made on the spot at focus group sessions, depending on what the change is. But the (important thing is) the problem has to be identified or consistently mentioned across a series of focus groups."

Pat Sabena, president of Westport, Conn.-based Sabena Qualitative Research Services, a market research consultancy, added: "Because of the speed to market these days, time lines have collapsed. We need to be able to make changes to concepts, and (make sure) somebody is (at focus group sessions) who has all of the files.... We all want the same things from the brands we work on, and if we can achieve that making on-site changes, why would we want to (do it) any other way?"

Source: Deborah L. Vence, "Turned on a dime: Fixes made on the spot change focus groups' role," *Marketing News* 38 no. 5 (March 15, 2004): 51.

Now Ask Yourself

- Why does Nokia use the focus group technique to improve its new product development instead of interviewing individual customers?

- How could a focus group improve new product development on the spot?

- What are the important things we should pay attention to when using this technique for new product development?

In Chapter 4 we introduced secondary research and presented the advantages and disadvantages of secondary data collection. We also noted that secondary and primary data sometimes work hand in hand. Secondary data is information that already exists and was collected by someone else for some other purpose. **Primary data,** on the other hand, is original data, gathered fresh from the source for the current study. Why use valuable resources to gather data if information already exists? The answer is simple. Primary data gives the researcher information on the particular question or problem that needs to be answered, not data that merely applies to an industry or specific type of business. That is, existing information may not be relevant to the matter at hand or may be out of date. As illustrated in the "Get This!" feature, primary information must be collected for Nokia to better understand consumer needs and preferences of its new products.

Consider Example 5-1.

primary data Original data gathered fresh from the source for the current study.

Example 5-1

First Bank wanted to investigate customers' degree of satisfaction with its bankcards, Visa and MasterCard. Certainly, generic information was readily available in the trade publications, but First Bank didn't want to know what customers from all over the country using all manner of bankcards thought. They wanted to know what their own customers thought about First Bank's cards. Only primary data would give them this information.

In this chapter we will introduce the techniques researchers use to better understand their target markets. Asking consumers what they think is just one approach. Sometimes consumers don't always know why they do or do not like something. To get an accurate picture, researchers use methods such as psychological techniques and direct observation of behavior. We will explore both direct and indirect methods of obtaining information, including focus groups, depth interviews, projective techniques, and observation.

5-1 Primary Data Collection Techniques

Primary research can be classified into two categories: qualitative and quantitative. The difference between qualitative and quantitative research closely parallels the difference between exploratory and conclusive research (see Chapter 2, Exhibit 2-2). In this chapter we will concentrate on qualitative research. Subsequent chapters will cover other methods to gather primary data.

Qualitative research is exploratory in nature and involves a small sample, with aims to provide insights and understanding of the question being researched. Typical qualitative techniques include depth interviews and focus groups. Qualitative research is less structured than quantitative research. Because of the small sample sizes and the subjective nature of the responses, qualitative data is not necessarily representative of the target population. The data gathered using qualitative techniques is subjective and nonquantifiable. Therefore, qualitative research is often used at the initial stage of a research project to provide information that deepens understanding of the problem on hand.

qualitative research Research that is exploratory in nature and involves a small sample with aims to provide insights and understanding of the question being researched.

quantitative research Research that is conclusive in nature and uses mathematical measures and statistical techniques to determine relationships and differences among large samples of target populations.

experimental research Primary research conducted when the researcher controls and manipulates elements of the research environment to measure the impact of each variable.

laboratory studies Studies performed in a highly controlled environment.

field studies Studies performed in select "real-world" locations.

survey research Research that obtains information through a structured questionnaire from a large, usually representative sample. It describes the characteristics, attitudes, and/or behaviors of the target population and intends to identify their relationships.

In contrast, **quantitative research** is conclusive in nature and uses mathematical measures and statistical techniques to determine relationships and differences among large samples of target populations. Highly structured, quantitative research (e.g., a mail survey) involves designing questions with a choice of specific responses so that the responses can be measured and analyzed mathematically.

Quantitative research can be further classified into survey (i.e., descriptive) and experimental (causal) research. **Experimental research** is conducted when the researcher controls and manipulates elements of the research environment to measure the impact of each variable. For example, a group of test subjects (perhaps consumers with specific demographic and psychographic compositions) is shown a few television commercials, and afterward the group members are queried about their intentions to purchase the product advertised. Experimental research is further divided into two groups: laboratory studies and field studies. **Laboratory studies** are performed in a highly controlled environment. Several variables are controlled (that is, not manipulated), and one variable of interest is manipulated to determine its behavior in a particular situation. **Field studies** are performed in the "real world," usually by test marketing a product in select locations to determine whether consumers are willing to purchase the product.

Survey research obtains information through a structured questionnaire from a large, usually representative sample. It describes the characteristics, attitudes, and/or behaviors of the target population and intends to identify their relationships. Because in reality the environment cannot be as closely controlled as in experimental research, taking a survey is the most popular primary data collection method performed in the normal course of business.

Quantitative and qualitative research often complement each other. Qualitative research usually precedes quantitative research, and quantitative research often substantiates qualitative findings. Recently, there has been an emerging trend to integrate qualitative and quantitative research. Sometimes, quantitative research is conducted before qualitative research, and this hybrid qualitative/quantitative approach tends to yield more insights for marketers. As authors Carol Phillips and Andlinda Stegeman note, the hybrid approach "solves many of the all-too-familiar problems associated with qualitative research. Qualitative studies are often used to conduct preliminary or exploratory research, but marketers often jump into qualitative projects without enough background information. The hybrid approach solves this problem by using a quantitative survey to better identify and understand the target market prior to a costly qualitative exploration."[1]

Researchers also conduct qualitative research after quantitative research to explain or reinforces quantitative findings—and even reveal new information. Consider Example 5-2.

Example 5-2

Managers in the credit card industry want to continuously attract new customers while retaining already acquired customers. To determine the extent the needs of new and loyal customers are different, researchers studied the data on 573 credit card holders from an existing satisfaction study for a credit card company. They did a cross-sectional study and followed it up with qualitative research. The initial study found that the format of the statement and performance of the customer service representative are more important for new, rather than loyal, customers. Conversely, the promotional benefits related with the card and adequacy of the credit limit were more important to loyal customers than to new ones. The qualitative research showed that new customers felt it important to be able to understand their statement. Further, because they were most likely to face problems understanding the "system," they also called the customer service representatives more often, which resulted in the higher importance placed on these two attributes.[2]

Even though qualitative research provides information that is not necessarily representative of the target population, it is still useful. Qualitative techniques are particularly effective when phenomena that have not been previously addressed or topics that are not easily quantified are being explored. These techniques are quite popular because researchers get a feel for the nuances of the topic as responses are detailed, in depth, and more specific. Remember, nuances are often pivotal in the solution phase of marketing research. Three common types of qualitative techniques are focus groups, depth interviews, and projective techniques.

5-2 Focus Groups

A **focus group** is a qualitative research technique in which a skilled moderator leads a small group of participants in an unstructured discussion about a particular topic. Recently, there has been increasing use of online focus groups, in which respondents are recruited either by telephone or email and must log onto a Web site at a specific time to participate in the study. Although online focus groups have some merits, offline focus groups are still popular now and serve an important role in marketing research. Consider the following benefits of traditional focus groups over online focus groups:

1. It is extremely difficult to be an effective moderator and establish authority from behind a computer screen.
2. Much of the group interaction is lost behind a computer screen.
3. It is impossible to address nonverbal reactions in an online focus group.
4. There is much more security in a traditional focus group than in the online version. Participants are asked to show photo identification cards at the traditional focus group. This is not the case online.
5. It is much more effective to show stimuli to the participants in a live setting than in an online focus group.[3]

Typically, people are more willing to speak their minds in small groups and comfortable settings. This makes traditional focus groups quite popular with researchers. In fact, they are the most often used research technique in the United States, and global use of them is rapidly growing. Virtually every company that sells goods and services to retail consumers uses focus groups in its efforts to create more desirable products, better advertising, or more exciting promotions.[4]

The leader of the focus group sessions, referred to as a **moderator,** should be a highly skilled interviewer, capable of making group members feel comfortable enough to freely express their thoughts and opinions. Moderators must be careful to stimulate and direct group conversation yet not force their particular beliefs on participants. (See Research Realities 5-1 for seven good habits of effective moderators.)

5-2a Requirements for Effective Focus Groups

To make focus group sessions as effective as possible, researchers typically adhere to the following guidelines:

1. *Six to twelve participants.* An international network of focus group research centers found that groups of six to eight participants are popular in the United States, but groups of five or six people are preferred in Canada.[5] Westat, an employee-owned research company, has designed and conducted hundreds of focus groups typically involving 8 to 10 participants. While the ideal number is debatable (as many as twelve are used), researchers try to recruit enough participants to generate lively discussions but not so many as will lessen the focus of the discussion or prevent participants from adequately voicing their thoughts. Focus groups with more than twelve participants limit participants' opportunities to share insights and observations. Furthermore, group dynamics change when participants wish to speak but are unable to because there are too many participants. One indication that a group may be too large is when people who

focus group A qualitative research technique in which a skilled moderator leads a small group of participants in an unstructured discussion about a topic.

moderator A skilled focus group leader.

Research Realities 5-1   *Ten Good Habits of Effective Moderators*

1. Establish personal contact with each respondent early in the session. Look at all participants during the introductory remarks, refer to them by name, and thank them for participating after they introduce themselves.

2. Help respondents feel relaxed early on. Humor works. Simple humor can go a long way in relaxing the participants.

3. Win respondents to your side. Let respondents know that you are dependent on them and that their honest opinions will help you do your job. Then try to find some area of commonality with each respondent to form bridges with group members that will help you keep the conversation going.

4. Deal with loud respondents, but don't intimidate other respondents. Don't criticize or put down the too-frequent talkers because this risks making others afraid to speak. Body language works well. For loud respondents: Don't look at them when you ask questions; don't acknowledge their raised hands; use hand gestures to indicate "stay back."

5. Deal with inconsistent, unclear answers by mobilizing the group to help. If there are ambiguities, simply ask participants to clarify their positions.

6. Create an environment where anything a respondent wants to say is acceptable. This way you hear those surprising tidbits that give you key insights. By being nonjudgmental, you put respondents at ease and encourage them to "open up."

7. Don't assume you know what a respondent means by an ambiguous answer. Ask and probe for clear answers. Voicing your assumptions may lead the respondent to stating what you think you know instead of what the respondent actually meant.

8. Be supportive but constructive. Don't cut off respondents—this will only discourage opinions. But don't permit tangential discussions meander. If people express the same opinion, state that it's been recorded but it's time to move on.

9. Be a neutral party. Don't be affiliated with any one individual or group. This will open up respondents' willingness to express their opinions.

10. Form focused, easily understood questions that elicit thoughtful answers. For example, a restaurant owner may want to know, "If there was one item on our menu you would add, what would it be?"

Source: Robert Schnee, "Seven habits of highly effective moderators," *Marketing News,* vol. 28, no. 18 (August 29, 1994): 16–17. Reprinted with permission from the American Marketing Association; Betsy Cummings, "DIY Consumer Research," *Restaurant Business* (June 2006), vol. 105, no. 6, pp. 18–29.

are not getting a chance to share their experiences in the total group start talking with the person next to them.[6]

2. *Careful screening of participants.* Screening is an important task in focus group research. To collect relevant information, focus groups must contain people who have knowledge about the topics at hand or who are important as a target group. Without carefully selected respondents, the session results may not be useful.

3. *Homogeneous participants in terms of some characteristic under study.* Each session should be composed of participants who are relatively similar in terms of a characteristic being examined. For example, if McDonald's wants to conduct focus groups to better understand children's perception of McDonald's dining room atmosphere, they need to use children who have recently visited their restaurants.

4. *Relaxed atmosphere.* The surroundings should not stifle the participants' desire to speak their minds and should encourage free-flowing discussions. Therefore, make sure the room is comfortable and arranged to encourage discussion. Typically, large meeting rooms equipped with comfortable chairs surrounding a large table are used, but settings don't have to be this bland. For example, unconventional sites—trendy hotel suites, parks, pizzerias, roller blade rental stands, and volleyball games—may be just the ticket. A study conducted in Atlanta, Portland, San Francisco, Kansas City, and New York to ascertain the lifestyles and attitudes of 21- to 29-year-olds (a group notoriously resistant to

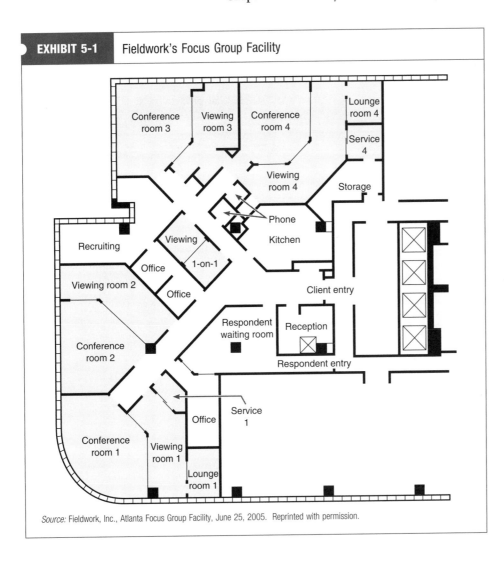

| **EXHIBIT 5-1** | Fieldwork's Focus Group Facility |

Source: Fieldwork, Inc., Atlanta Focus Group Facility, June 25, 2005. Reprinted with permission.

surveys) chose just such sites for their focus group sessions. These environments made interviewees more comfortable and more inclined to be truthful and open.[7] See Exhibit 5-1 for a look at Fieldwork's focus group facility in Atlanta, Georgia.

5. *Room with one-way mirror and audio- and video-recording capabilities.* Although rooms with one-way mirrors are not always available for focus group sessions, they are preferred, since such observation can reveal key insights. Each session should be audio- and video-recorded, so that researchers and decision makers can carefully examine each discussion later. See Exhibit 5-2 for a view of Group Dynamics' focus group meeting room.

Expenses and time can be issues if participants must travel to the session, and videoconferencing solves these problems admirably. Videoconferencing enables clients and other interested observers to tune in and participate in a timely and inexpensive manner.

6. *Session duration between one and three hours.* Sessions should last long enough to cover the topics but be short enough to prevent interviewee fatigue from setting in. It is the moderator's responsibility to keep the discussion moving and to make sure the topics of interest have been covered within a reasonable period of time.

7. *Trained moderator.* To guide discussions effectively, the moderator must be knowledgeable about the issues, tactful, tolerant, and capable of controlling

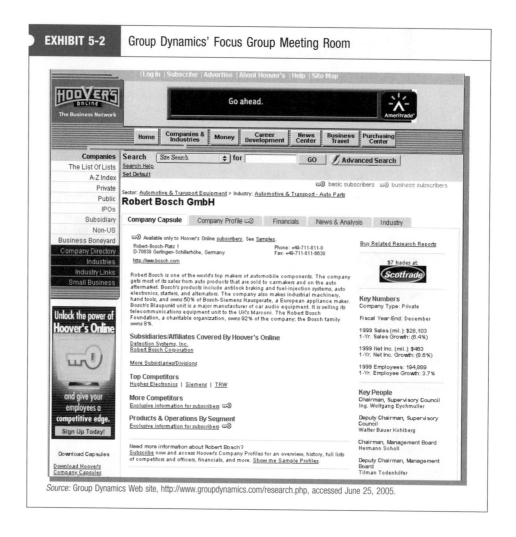

EXHIBIT 5-2   Group Dynamics' Focus Group Meeting Room

Source: Group Dynamics Web site, http://www.groupdynamics.com/research.php, accessed June 25, 2005.

group dynamics. A good rapport with group members helps create a comfortable atmosphere for all group participants. The moderator must be able to keep the discussion moving, while gently and skillfully keeping the group focused on the test topics. (Review Research Realities 5-1.) Dr. Walter Kendall, founder and CEO of The Greeley Institute, a well-known research and career education center, feels that inexperienced moderators yield not just inadequate but dangerously misleading information. He warned, "Stop using amateurs to moderate so-called focus groups, which are little more than casual gatherings; instead, pay the going rate ($4,000–$6,000) for experienced, well-trained professionals, or pay to have your own people trained as Focus Group Directors—and thus turn those sessions into profit centers."[8]

8. *Compensation for participation.* Participants should be paid, but there is no set amount. Payments may range from a few dollars to several hundred dollars, depending on the amount of time and effort involved. For example, college students may be offered $50 per session, whereas medical doctors may require as much as $200 to $400 per session. If participants are employees of the organization running the study, however, they are not usually compensated.

5-2b Uses of Focus Groups

Focus groups can be used for a variety of reasons. They *generate information for questionnaires.* They provide vital information that can improve any measurement instrument. Consider Example 5-3.

Example 5-3

The Minnesota Extension Service commissioned an evaluation of a farm-credit mediation program, and the research group planned a large-scale mail survey to farmers, creditors, volunteer mediators, and county extension agents. Some of the farmers in the survey were on the verge of bankruptcy or foreclosure and were attempting to reach mediated settlements so they could keep their farms—a very sensitive situation. The researchers conducted focus group interviews in advance of the mail survey to develop tactful questions that these respondents could answer without losing face that would still collect the needed data. The focus group sessions also helped the researchers develop successful survey procedures.

Focus groups *assess needs*. Procter & Gamble created a Multicultural Market Development Organization to create programs targeted to specific groups. One of its first efforts was Avanzando con tu Familia ("Advancing with your family"), which uses focus groups to research what is important to Hispanic women, such as family and education. Based on findings from the focus groups, P&G launched a bilingual magazine that was distributed door-to-door to some 4.5 million households.[9]

Focus groups can be used to *clarify promotional wording*. In discussions of a project to inform drivers of hazardous intersections, State Farm Insurance Company's Claims, Research, and Public Affairs departments identified intersections described as "crash-prone," "hazardous," "accident prone," and "deadly." But a focus group moderator from the research department found that focus group participants felt the word "dangerous" captured the essence of these intersections. Thus the project was named the "10 Most Dangerous Intersections."[10]

Need to *find out what your customers consider when they make decisions*? Use a focus group, which is what MCI did when it first entered the long-distance market. MCI wanted to know how customers make telephone-related decisions. The findings convinced management to change policies on minimum rates, pursue the business market more effectively, and create a new advertising campaign. A key insight? MCI found that customers don't blame the telephone company for high long-distance rates; they blame themselves for talking too long. Hence the company's advertising slogan: "You're not talking too much, just spending too much."

Findings from focus groups can be used to *recruit new members for the organization*. For example, a church in a metropolitan area conducted focus groups with people who were not at the time attending religious services. It found that its target "market," Baby Boomers, were not loyal to specific denominations—they would make decisions on church attendance based on the quality of the church programs. In response, the church leaders dropped the denominational designation from the name of the church and concentrated on developing programs to appeal to this group.

Focus groups are good forums for *testing existing programs*. A group that was promoting locally grown specialty vegetables found through focus groups that its campaign in supermarkets using recipes and display posters was not affecting consumer purchases of vegetables. It concluded that food samples and in-store demonstrations were better avenues to expand its customer base.

Focus groups are effective *follow-ups to mail surveys*. After conducting a mail survey of farmers in northwestern Minnesota, researchers invited a group of 27 farmers to share their interpretations of the data in three focus group sessions. These meetings led to ways of improving marketing, farm decision making, and stress management—issues identified in the surveys and expanded in the sessions.

Mirror, mirror on the wall—just what is our *organization's image?* Focus groups mirror society's perceptions. A city zoo discovered through focus groups that its public viewed it as "stodgy." The zoo's focus on education was not what the public wanted. Entertainment was. The zoo found ways to make education entertaining.

Use focus groups to *assess products*. Often marketers conduct focus group sessions to gain preliminary information about a product's effectiveness, shape, and color. Since the invention of microwave ovens, consumers have disliked the fact that they take up so much kitchen counter space. General Electric used focus groups to assess its answer to this problem—the "Spacesaver," a microwave that does not rest on the kitchen counter but rather hangs under a cabinet. It was an instant success.

5-2c Advantages and Disadvantages of Focus Group Research

Focus group research has four major distinct advantages: it can generate fresh ideas, it is flexible, it allows clients to observe respondents, and it is controllable. We discuss each in turn.

1. *Generate fresh ideas.* This is one of the most important benefits. People often need the stimulation of other ideas being bandied about before they can voice their own thoughts. And lively exchanges spark new insights.

2. *Able to observe respondents.* One-way mirrors and video-recording mechanisms allow clients and researchers to view and listen to respondents. Respondents' behavior, facial expressions, and tone of voice give insights not possible with surveys.

3. *Flexible.* In focus group research, virtually all types of research topics and issues can be discussed. If researchers need additional information, the moderator can lead discussions toward that topic of interest. The comfortable surroundings relax inhibitions and encourage more telling responses.

4. *Controllable.* Capable moderators can control the group and move discussions in any direction they desire. However, moderators must take care not to overpower participants, who must feel comfortable enough to speak their minds. Focus group research affords the *opportunity for quick execution*. In today's business environment, information is needed fast. Focus groups can be formed and the results evaluated quickly.

Although focus group research offers researchers and marketing managers many benefits, there are three major disadvantages: it lacks scientific validity, it is prone to bias, and the interpretation is subjective.

1. *Lack scientific validity.* This is probably the greatest shortcoming of focus group research. The results may be valid, but are they *scientifically* valid? Like all qualitative techniques, focus groups involve small samples that may not be representative of the target population. Therefore, the findings are not conclusive in a statistical sense. As noted earlier, focus group research should be supplemented with quantitative research; we will discuss quantitative techniques in subsequent chapters.

2. *Prone to bias.* Since each session is conducted by a moderator, the performance of the group is heavily subject to the biases of the moderator. Group members may also influence each other. Because groups are composed of 6–12 individuals, one individual can inadvertently bias results by dominating the conversation. Such dominating behavior can be controlled, but sometimes this is easier said than done.

3. *Subjective interpretation.* Because the qualitative information from a focus group is difficult to measure, the interpretation is subjective to researchers and managers. It is not uncommon that managers tend to selectively interpret the results: they can always find something to support their preconceived notions, but ignore the information that does not support their views. As a result, a focus group can give marketing managers a false sense of security. Since focus groups do provide information—often valuable information—it is easy to forget that the results are inconclusive. Marketing managers may be tempted to accept the results as fact rather than as preliminary findings that typically need a rigorous follow-up study.

Source: © 2007 JupiterImages Corporation.

5-3 Depth Interviews

Sometimes the best way to uncover beliefs and attitudes about particular topics is to interview individuals. **Depth interviews** are typically unstructured, one-on-one conversations between a highly skilled interviewer and a member of a target population. While depth interviews and focus group discussions are the two most widely used qualitative research methods, in certain cases depth interviews have proven to be better at assessing beliefs and attitudes. Focus group participants are often subject to peer pressure, and moderators can't always follow up on responses. Depth interviews, however, give researchers ample opportunity to explore individuals' responses.[11]

Interviewing is a two-way interchange, and the interviewer is key to successfully eliciting information. Therefore, he or she must be skilled in methods clinical psychologists use to uncover hidden motivations and feelings. The Burke Institute explains why they often use depth interviews:

> One-on-one depth interviews are often used to avoid the influence of group dynamics or when there is a substantial need to probe deeply into the underlying logic or motivations behind individual attitudes or behaviors.[12]

Depth interviews are used in various contexts and for many purposes. In research contexts, they are used for polling, for surveys, and to obtain substantial information on personality and behavior to test some hypothesis or theoretical proposition.[13] Consider the following examples:

1. Depth interviews were conducted with 18 CMOs and/or CEOs from global companies to gain a deeper understanding of what drives success and failure among chief marketers.[14]

2. Depth interviews with managers and professionals from nine enterprises based in Taiwan were conducted to explore the critical success factors of enterprises currently implementing market segmentation for Internet marketing.[15]

An important dimension of depth interviews is the degree to which they are structured or unstructured. Interviewing is not a science in which a step-by-step procedure must always be followed to solicit information. Rather, the process varies

depth interviews
Unstructured, one-on-one conversations between a highly skilled interviewer and a member of a target population.

unstructured interviews
Interviews in which the subjects discussed are free-floating from one issue to the next.

structured interviews
Interviews that follow checklists to cover narrowly focused topics.

with the purpose and context of the interview. Most interviews are highly **unstructured interviews,** allowing participants to freely float from one issue to the next. Other interviews are highly **structured interviews,** in that the interviewer uses checklists to cover narrowly focused topics. There is no ideal way to interview people. The degree of structure interviewers choose to use should significantly contribute to accomplish their specific goals.

5-3a Requirements for Effective Depth Interviews

Effective depth interviews require some planning. Here are a few guidelines for setting up the interview situation:

1. *Allow between a half hour and two hours for each session.* Due to the unstructured nature of one-on-one interviews, there is no set amount of time that works for every interview. However, a session should run for no more than two hours, so that fatigue does not impact the respondent's answers.

2. *Screen each respondent carefully.* Since the researcher is interested in revealing underlying motivations and feelings about specific topics from a target population member, it's important that the respondent be a worthy representative both of the target group and the topic of interest. All potential participants should fill out a brief survey that describes their backgrounds, purchasing habits, and associations with the topic.

3. *Make sure the interviewer is capable.* While a certified psychologist is not necessary, the interviewer should have knowledge of techniques that psychologists use to reveal hidden motivations. Many times, it is the covert information that aids researchers in understanding respondents' true motivations. The interviewer should also be warm, open, and nonjudgmental.

4. *Use a tape or video recorder.* Typically, either a tape or video recorder is used to document the interview. Following each session, the information must be transcribed by a qualified researcher who endeavors to be entirely objective. Transcription is one step in the research process where results can be tainted by personal biases.

5. *Make the interview setting comfortable.* For respondents to "open up," they must feel relaxed with both the interviewer and the surroundings where the interview takes place. Therefore, make sure a comfortable chair, adequate lighting, and refreshments are available during the interview.

6. *Provide rewards for participation.* A study conducted in Ontario, Canada, assessed the impact of cash incentives on personal interview participation. Besides cash rewards, other incentives may be offered to recruit participants. For example, hand out movie tickets or product samples to participants in shopping mall interviews. Giving participants some type of reward should not be construed as unethical behavior, since participation is voluntary and the outcome is a win-win situation. The research firm wins, since it obtains information important to strategic planning, and participants win, since they receive a reward for providing useful data. Research has found that prepayment of $1 to participants yields significantly higher responses and less sociodemographic bias than either $1 or $10 promised at the conclusion of the interviews.[16]

5-3b Advantages and Disadvantages of Depth Interviews

Depth interviews have certain advantages over other research techniques. First, one-on-one conversations are often much more *detailed and revealing* than group discussions. Typically, the interviewer can probe more deeply in a personal interview than in a group session, and one-on-one situations allow interviewers to investigate feelings that may come up during the interview. Second, depth interviews *can handle more complex topics* than other techniques. For example, interviewing financial experts on investment strategies may work better in personal interviews because they can expound at length and in great detail. Third, personal interviews are much *easier to schedule* than group interviews. It's often difficult to find a convenient time so that all members can be in attendance; this is especially true when dealing with professionals, whose schedules are not flexible. Fourth, when the topic is embarrassing or highly sensitive, respondents may feel *more comfortable* discussing the issues with just one person. Responses may be more frank because interviewees aren't concerned about group reaction.

Depth interviews also have shortcomings. One problem is the *inability of the participant to interact with others* and bounce ideas off them. Sometimes respondents feel trapped and alone. Their comfort level may actually go down, and they may hedge on their answers. The lack of group dynamics is an argument in support of focus groups. Another problem with depth interviews is the *cost of implementation*. Interviewing enough individuals to collect sufficient data can be quite expensive. A third problem is that *interviewers may not be reliable*. Reliability demands consistency, but interviewers differ in their appearance, approach, and style, and therefore in the impressions they make on subjects. Such variations can cause respondents to differ in behavior. Also, interviewers' perceptions of respondents may be distorted by their own experiences and personality. A fourth problem is that *interviewers' energy levels tend to deplete rapidly*. Because it's difficult to sit for hours and talk to individuals about only a few topics, interviews have to be spread out over several days. Fifth, interpretational errors may be introduced in transcription. Hence, depth interviews can *lack consistency and thus reliability because* taped conversations are interpreted differently by different people. Finally, since depth interviews are fairly unstructured, they are unscientific, so they *lack statistical validity*. Therefore, statistically verifiable tests need to be administered after the depth interview.

5-4 Projective Techniques

In a marketer's ideal world, respondents would be accurate, thoughtful, and honest in their answers. But this world does not exist. People don't always want to say what's on their minds. Indeed, they themselves may not be aware of their innermost attitudes. Projective test theory assumes that people have thoughts and feelings they may be unaware of or do not wish to express, so clinical psychology techniques may be needed to aid in exposing their thoughts. **Projective techniques** provide verbal or visual stimuli that encourage respondents to reveal unconscious feelings and attitudes. These techniques "get below the surface and overcome several barriers to communication.... Because subjects are allowed to project their perceptions and feelings on to some other person or object—or in some other way are allowed to 'depersonalize' their responses—they feel freer to express their thoughts and feelings."[17]

Marketing researchers routinely use projective techniques to tap the subconscious minds of consumers. Consider Example 5-4.

projective techniques
Research techniques that use verbal or visual stimuli to reveal respondents' unconscious feelings and attitudes.

Example 5-4

- A study funded by the Marketing Science Institute in Cambridge, Massachusetts, attempted to identify consumers' latent needs for products through word association. Researchers asked mothers to look through a list of 279 verb-object combinations, each relating to food, and to rate them. The combination of "travel and food" scored among the high-interest combinations. In follow-up interviews, respondents said they wanted better ways to keep food fresh and easy to use while traveling with their children in the car.[18]

- A marketing study by Norma Larkin, director of consumer research for the Nabisco Biscuit Co., used projective techniques to help the company discover that consumers see something "magical" in the Oreo cookie. This perception led to the slogan "Unlocking the Magic of Oreo."[19]

- A major urban arts organization was facing multiple problems. Its image was conservative and dull, and its audience had been steadily aging over the last decade. To improve its image and audience base, the organization used projective techniques to generate fresh ideas on various aspects of qualities and image. This provided insights for the organization to develop new ground to broaden its appeal.[20]

Most projective tests consist of vague or ambiguous stimuli that respondents are required to describe. The descriptions reveal respondents' underlying (true) thoughts and feelings. While there are numerous projective tests available, the ones most popular with marketing researchers are word association, sentence completion, picture interpretation, the third-person technique, role-playing, and cartoons.

5-4a Word Association

word association A projective technique in which respondents are given a word and they respond with the first word that comes to mind.

Word association is a projective technique in which the researcher says a word and the participant responds with the first word that comes to mind. The associations reveal participants' feelings about the stimulus word. This test is normally used in conjunction with other projective techniques. It requires paper and pencil, a timing device, and an appropriate list of words. The researcher begins each session by stating, "I am going to read you a list of words, one at a time. Please answer with the first word that comes into your mind." The word response and the time that elapses between the stimulus word and the client's response are recorded.

Through word association tests, marketers learn about consumers' feelings toward certain products. For example, in a study of women's attitudes towards soaps and detergents, respondents were instructed to state their first thoughts on hearing a series of words read one at a time. The stimulus response words and responses from two women are given in Exhibit 5-3. These two women, of similar age and family status, responded quite differently, indicating differences in personality and in their attitudes toward housekeeping. Respondent A's associations suggest that she is resigned to dirt, seeing it as inevitable, and is unlikely to do anything about it. Respondent B is more energetic, fact-oriented, and less emotional and ready to fight the dirt with her weapons of soap and water.[21] Marketers must consider this information when they design promotional strategies for these cleaning products.

EXHIBIT 5-3	Word Association to Determine Attitudes toward Soaps and Detergents	
Stimulus Words	**Respondent A**	**Respondent B**
Washday	Everyday	Ironing
Fresh	And sweet	Clean
Pure	Air	Soiled
Scrub	Don't; Ray (husband) does	Clean
Filth	This neighborhood	Dirt
Bubbles	Bath	Soap and water
Family	Squabbles	Children
Towels	Dirty	Wash

Source: Sidney J. Levy, "Interpretation is the essence of projective research techniques," *Marketing News* (September 28, 1984) Reprinted with permission from the American Marketing Association.

5-4b Sentence Completion

In **sentence completion,** researchers present a series of incomplete sentences and ask respondents to complete them. How respondents complete the sentences reveals their feelings. Marketers often use this technique to better understand individuals' feelings and motivations toward particular consumer products. For example, a large consumer goods manufacturer wanted to know what mothers think about their toothpaste, so they asked participants to complete the following sentence: "Mothers always say toothpaste _____."[22] Participants are usually asked to complete a series of sentences. Other potential sentence fragments for the toothpaste study could be:

1. "I brush my teeth because _____."
2. "I use my particular brand of toothpaste because _____."
3. "I feel my toothpaste tastes like _____."
4. "When I brush my teeth, I _____."

Responses give manufacturers important data relating to taste, why people brush their teeth, and why they choose a particular brand. Advertisers will use this information to design effective promotional campaigns.

> **sentence completion** A projective technique in which respondents complete a series of incomplete sentences.

5-4c Picture Interpretation

Picture interpretation is based on procedures used in psychological research depicting abstract visual stimuli to help respondents describe thoughts and feelings that would not emerge otherwise. One picture interpretation method, the **thematic apperception test (TAT),** has respondents describe what is going on in pictures and what will happen as a result of the situation. Marketers have used picture interpretation in interesting ways. For example, one study showed two women in a supermarket setting. Respondents were told that one woman was purchasing a dry soup mix and that the other one had never tried a dry soup mix. Respondents were asked to invent a story. Responses revealed four main profiles of the woman buying the soup mix: She was seen as a creative woman; a practical, modern woman; a lazy or indifferent woman; or a deprived woman. Marketers used this information to understand what respondents felt other people might think about them for using the product, what their attitudes were toward serving their families this product, and how they viewed the pros and cons of using this product.

Picture interpretation tests are also useful in evaluating print advertisements. Advertising agencies and company promotion departments often ask respondents to explain what they see in pictures that were developed for clients. They want to ensure that the pictures evoke their intended message. Picture interpretation has proved to be invaluable to marketers because as participants describe what is going on in the picture, they often provide embellishments—thoughts and feelings of the characters, events that led up to the situation, and the outcome of the story, nuances that are difficult to obtain. Such detailed stories enable researchers to investigate aspects of their target markets that cannot be effectively investigated using other methods of research.

> **picture interpretation** A projective technique depicting abstract visual stimuli to help respondents describe thoughts and feelings that would not emerge otherwise.

> **thematic apperception test (TAT)** A picture interpretation technique that has respondents describe what is going on in pictures and predict what will happen as a result of the situation.

5-4d Third-Person Technique and Role-Playing

Some research topics require questions that could be uncomfortable for participants to answer. For example, a personal hygiene product may entail questions about personal hygiene habits, a topic most people would hesitate to discuss with a stranger. To make such questions less embarrassing, researchers frame questions in the third person. In the **third-person technique,** researchers ask participants to answer questions for a third person, such as a neighbor or an acquaintance, instead of for themselves. Using "someone else" as the focus makes the questions less personal for respondents and therefore less uncomfortable to answer. For example, smoking is becoming less socially

> **third-person technique** A projective technique in which respondents answer questions for a third person, such as a neighbor or an acquaintance, instead of for themselves.

acceptable in U.S. society, so if asked directly about smoking, respondents may feel social pressure to respond negatively, even if they enjoy smoking. However, if the question is couched in the third person, such as "How does your friend feel about cigarette smoking?" respondents are more likely to reveal their true feelings.

role-playing A projective technique in which participants play the role of someone else in a particular scenario; this allows participants to reveal their feelings in a less personal way.

Role-playing is similar to the third-person technique in that "another person" is also used in the scenario. However, instead of asking participants to respond to a list of questions, researchers ask them to play the role of someone else in a particular situation. These responses may be verbal or nonverbal. Research shows that respondents are more likely to reveal their true feelings if they assume the role of a person other than themselves. For example, a little boy may be asked to show how his father (the role model in this case) acts as he (his father) eats Pizza Hut's new thick-crust pepperoni pizza. The little boy begins to eat the pizza from the crust end rather than the conventional point end of the pizza.

5-4e Cartoons

cartoon technique A projective technique similar to third-person projection in which cartoon characters are the third party. Characters are shown in a particular situation, and respondents are asked to describe what the characters are doing and explain the situation depicted.

The **cartoon technique** uses cartoon characters as the third party. Researchers show characters in a particular situation and ask respondents to describe what the characters are doing and explain the situation depicted. Blank "bubbles" appear above the cartoon characters, and respondents write what the characters would say in the bubbles. Like the third-person technique, cartoons make respondents feel more comfortable revealing personal information because the responses are "not about themselves."

Consider Example 5-5.

Example 5-5

Consider a study that sought to understand how people anticipated the coming of the millennium. They explored brands in the new millennium using bubble pictures in which informants projected what a brand might speak aloud about itself as opposed to what it privately thinks in the new millennium.

A traditional U.S. car brand speaks aloud: "I have a new design and new advertising. I'm really good for up-and-coming newly marrieds." But privately it thinks: "My God. Will I really make it into the new millennium? I keep trying, but it's hard to be really modern."

Again, using bubbles, brands are projected by respondents as talking to one another in the new millennium. This way, consumers project their beliefs about the likely futures of brands. In a projected dialogue between two brands of soup, one new and the other old, a respondent wrote that the new soup says out loud to the old: "You look as good as ever, but I haven't seen you for a while," to which the old brand replies, "You're new around here. Nice to see you." But privately thinks: "She thinks she's so healthy. I'm healthy too, and all I have to do is add some more vitamins for the health." Then the new brand politely thinks to herself: "She's never changed her look. Same as her grandmother. She'll be sitting on the porch in the new millennium, while I'll have the energy for all the excitement."[23]

5-4f Disadvantages of Projective Techniques

The most glaring problem with projective techniques is the *low reliability* that arises from the subjectivity of the scoring. None of the techniques can be considered highly reliable, so all findings must be cautiously accepted. A related problem is the validity issue. Studies have shown that most of these techniques suffer from *low validity*. The close relationship between reliability and validity will be discussed in Chapter 7. Another problem is the *lack of substantiating evidence* to support the theory that individuals project their own feelings onto ambiguous stimuli. Also, these tests *require considerable training* to administer, score, and interpret. Furthermore, scoring stories, such as those used in picture interpretation, is *time-consuming and complex.*

5-5 Shortcomings of Qualitative Research

The qualitative techniques discussed in this chapter all have shortcomings in common. Probably the greatest problem is a tendency for marketing managers to use results generated by these techniques without fully recognizing their limitations. All traditional qualitative methods use small sample sizes and unstructured formats, which limit the degree to which the findings can be generalized over the entire target population. For the most part, these findings are not statistically supportable and thus cannot be viewed as representative of the target population. But the user-friendly nature of these techniques for gathering information, along with the knowledge that "real people" have been a major part of the data-gathering process, lead many marketing managers to believe that they have captured what they are looking for. Users of qualitative research results need to recognize that these findings are simply exploratory and should only be used in defining problems or in suggesting hypotheses to be tested in subsequent studies, such as a quantitative survey.

Another limitation of qualitative research methods is the critical role of the moderator/interviewer. This individual is instrumental in the group dynamics and information generation, and it is vital that his or her performance in the project be considered in the evaluation of the study's results.

5-6 Observation Research

The old adage "Seeing is believing" seems to be quite apt for market researchers because observation techniques are quite popular. **Observation** is a method for gathering data that involves watching test subjects without interacting with them. Researchers who do the observing do not communicate verbally or in any other way with the respondents. They take great pains to be neutral observers. Researchers record their observations using such devices as a pencil and paper, a video camera, or a cassette recorder. Recently, observation methods used in product development have received a great deal of attention.

observation Data-collection methods in which researchers watch test subjects without interacting with them.

Companies such as Motorola, Gillette, Steelcase, and Xerox have used observation research to identify opportunities for entirely new products. This occurs by researchers going to customers' environments to watch people in context. Hewlett-Packard is a frequent user of observational research. In one case, the company's medical products division sent researchers to hospitals to watch surgeons operate. During the operations, surgeons would watch their scalpel movements on a television monitor, but other staff members repeatedly walked past the monitor while conducting their duties, blocking the doctors' view. The doctors didn't complain about the problem, but it would have been difficult to identify the inconvenience without direct observation. As a result of the observations, H-P developed a surgical helmet with goggles that cast images right in front of a surgeon's eyes.[24]

5-6a Types of Observation Methods

Observation research can be categorized as direct or indirect; disguised or undisguised; structured or unstructured; and human or mechanical.

Direct and Indirect Observation
Direct observation simply means that the researchers actually watch a behavior as it occurs and report what they see. For example, researchers may pose as shoppers in supermarkets to observe how consumers purchase cereals. They observe particular

direct observation A data-collection method in which researchers watch a behavior as it occurs and report what they see.

Basic Guidelines for Direct Observation Research

Bob Becker, founder and principal of Jump Associates, a San Mateo, California–based design planning consulting firm, recommends that firms looking to better understand customers in the process of product development would do well to employ direct observation techniques. He provides basic guidelines to follow:

1. *Watch first, then ask.* Begin with quiet observation. Once the activities are completed, follow up with questions to understand why the person acted in a certain way and what he or she felt during the observed situation.

2. *Look for needs, not solutions.* This is best handled by stating the need independently of how the need might be served.

3. *Avoid intrusions to keep behavior natural.* People tend to act differently when they know they are being observed.

4. *Look for nonverbal clues.* Watch for facial expressions and body language that may convey people's attitudes and feelings.

5. *Record even the obvious or the seemingly unimportant.* In other words, document everything.

6. *Beware of leading questions.* Use open-ended questions that allow the customer to speak his or her own words.

7. *Record information in the customer's terms.* When documenting a customer's comments, use the person's words as much as possible.

8. *Look beyond the immediately solvable problem.* Recognizing and dissecting deeper problems permits the company to plan for the issues that should be dealt with later on, even when they are not currently solvable.

Source: Bob Becker, "Take direct route when data-gathering," *Marketing News,* vol. 33, no. 20 (September 27, 1999): 29, 31. Reprinted with permission from the American Marketing Association.

---

obtrusive observation Observation research in which the subjects realize they are being observed.

undisguised observation The same as obtrusive observation; observation that exists when subjects realize they are being observed.

unobtrusive observation Observation research in which the subjects do not realize they are being observed.

disguised observation The same as unobtrusive observation; it exists when subjects do not realize they are being observed.

indirect observation Observation made by researchers who observe the results of a behavior rather than the behavior itself.

structured observation Observation research in which observers record only certain well-defined behaviors, typically on a checklist or standardized form.

behaviors, such as whether the shoppers look at the ingredients and nutritional facts, whether they spend time examining other cereals, and whether others accompanying them influence the buying decision. If the shoppers realize they are being observed, then the technique is referred to as **obtrusive observation** or **undisguised observation.** If the shoppers don't know they are being observed—perhaps through cameras or one-way mirrors—then the technique is **unobtrusive observation** or **disguised observation.** (See Research Realities 5-2 for some basic guidelines for direct observation research.)

Indirect observation occurs when researchers observe the results of a behavior rather than the behavior itself. It isn't always necessary to see a behavior when it occurs to understand what behavior actually occurred. For example, some researchers search through individuals' garbage cans to determine their food preferences. Today, many retailers use scanning devices to read Universal Product Codes (UPC), not only to determine the total cost of the merchandise but also to record what consumers purchase at a particular point in time.

Structured and Unstructured Observation

Structured and unstructured observation refers to the amount of discretion given the observer in deciding what behaviors to record or not to record. **Structured observation** techniques require observers to record only certain well-defined behaviors, typically on a checklist or standardized form. Behaviors not listed on the form are not part of the study and are not recorded. On the other hand, **unstructured observation** techniques require observers to judge whether or not observed behaviors are important enough to record. Unstructured techniques do not typically use checklists or standardized forms. Theoretically, all sorts of behaviors could be documented because observers have not been given limits or specific guidelines.

Human and Mechanical Observation

As the term implies, **human observation** involves a person observing a behavior as it happens. The observer is a neutral bystander, not involved in altering behavior but simply recording it. Subjects may or may not be aware they are being observed. This form of data collection is highly effective in research on children. The observations constitute first-hand knowledge and do not inadvertently direct responses as questions can do when asked from an adult perspective. A researcher watching the behaviors of a little boy playing with a toy train to see whether design changes are needed is an example of personal observation.

Mechanical observation uses a nonhuman device to record observations. Such devices include cameras, Nielsen's people-meters, eye movement recorders, voice-pitch analyzers, and scanners. Mechanical observation methods are becoming more popular because they are highly reliable and don't experience the fatigue to which their human counterparts are prone.

In mechanical observation, there is no direct interaction with respondents, and sometimes they do not realize they are being observed. This is the case with one-way mirrors and hidden cameras in retail stores. This mode of data collection may be highly structured (where specific behaviors are being investigated) or unstructured (where all behaviors are of interest). Examples include a U.K. research team using small, hand-held cameras to observe behaviors in homes, pubs, and clubs; retailers using optical scanners to record customers' shopping behavior; and television meters placed in some homes to record television-viewing behavior.[25] The television "people meters" measure who is watching television and what they are viewing. Numerous other mechanisms that we take for granted routinely record our behavior every day:

1. Store video recorders and cameras
2. Turnstiles used at athletic events, zoos, and libraries
3. Counters on the Internet that record the number of "hits" at a particular address
4. Credit cards that record consumer purchasing habits
5. Laser beams at the entrances of stores that record the number of visitors during a given period
6. Heart monitors that record changes in the subject's heartbeat
7. Voice pitch monitors that record changes in the subject's tone of voice

5-6b Observational Techniques

There are three types of observational techniques: audit, content analysis, and physical-trace analysis.

An **audit** is an information-gathering technique in which researchers examine pertinent records or conduct inventory analyses of items under investigation. This technique is highly structured and is carried out through indirect observation. Note that the behavior of interest has already occurred. Audits are performed by individuals or teams with or without the assistance of mechanical devices. Those being audited are aware that the audit is taking place. Several marketing research firms conduct audits, including Audits & Surveys Worldwide and IMS Health. Audits & Surveys Worldwide provides clients with a variety of services that track retail sales, product inventory, and factors relating to distribution. IMS Health provides global insights to companies marketing around the world. They perform the following services:

1. Pharmacy audits
2. Hospital audits
3. Prescription audits
4. Medical audits
5. Promotion audits

A popular audit for understanding consumer behavior is a **pantry audit,** in which the researcher inventories items in a participant's household—typically in the kitchen pantry. This technique gets to the heart of purchasing behavior—there is no truer indication of an individual's interest in products than the items that have actually been

unstructured observation Observation research in which the observers judge whether or not observed behaviors are important enough to record.

human observation Observation performed by an individual designated to observe behavior.

mechanical observation Studies that use mechanical devices, such as scanners or television meters, to record observations.

audit A method in which information is gathered by examining pertinent records or inventorying items under investigation.

pantry audit An inventory of items in an individual's household.

content analysis A research technique in which the content of a communication vehicle is examined to determine whether a study inference is valid.

purchased. However, the presence of an item in the pantry is no guarantee that members of the household presently desire it. Canned foods, for example, can stay in a pantry for several months without spoiling.

Content analysis examines the content of a "communications vehicle" to determine whether a study inference is valid. The communication vehicle may be television, radio, the Internet, newspapers, or billboards. Content analysis is highly structured and is carried out through indirect observation. The data is often collected through a mechanical device such as a computerized coding system. Examining information in advertisements is a common form of content analysis. For example, many parents and social groups have protested that apparel designer Calvin Klein portrays young teenage girls in print advertisements in an overtly sexual manner. A content analysis of Calvin Klein advertisements proved this to be the case. Another content analysis, conducted by *Life* and *Ebony*, examined 9,314 advertisements and found that fewer elderly figures appeared in the magazines now than during the previous decade. The figures that appeared in the magazines more often were associated with aging products and services.[26]

While content analysis frequently involves advertisements, the target of analysis can also be words, slogans, or specific topics. For example, one study analyzed the portrayal of smoking in Hollywood films starring 10 popular actresses. It was found that leading female actors were as likely to smoke in movies aimed at juvenile audiences as in R-rated movies, whereas male actors were 2.5 times more likely to smoke in R-rated movies.[27]

Content analysis is performed both manually and by computers. A study comparing human-coded analysis with computerized analysis of the same text communications found that differences could be attributed to two sources of errors. The first source of error is in the instructions and training given to the human coders. Vague phrases for concepts and unclear directions for coding created inconsistent coding by humans. The second source of error is in the computer coding instructions. When the list of key words and phrases used in the computerized coding rules is insufficient, the content analysis does not provide accurate results.[28] It is extremely difficult to generate an exhaustive list of key words and phrases.

physical-trace analysis A research technique that examines evidence or "traces" of individuals that were left behind to understand their past behaviors.

Physical-trace analysis places the researcher in the role of detective. This technique uses evidence or "traces" of individuals that were left behind to understand their past behaviors. In a movie theater, for example, the number of popcorn containers on the floor gives an indication of the amount of popcorn sold during a movie. The wear-and-tear on theater seats indicates where most people prefer to sit. Receipts in the garbage cans of supermarkets give researchers an idea of what items were purchased during a given time period. It is an indirect method because the results of a behavior are observed, not the behavior itself. Physical-trace analysis is disguised because respondents are unaware they are being observed. Both humans and mechanical devices are used to collect physical-trace data. The analysis is highly structured in instances where researchers know what they are searching for, or unstructured when they are simply "fishing" for behavioral data.

5-6c Advantages and Disadvantages of Observational Research

The most obvious advantage of observational research is that the researcher collects *observed information* rather than directed or response data relating to intentions or preferences. Because of this, clients tend to believe the data. Another advantage is the *reduction or elimination of recall error*. The researcher gathers and records data as it is observed. Whether the respondent's recollection of past experiences is accurate is not an issue. Observation methods *allow researchers to obtain information from subjects who are unable to communicate in written or oral form*. For example, data can be collected on young children. Finally, there may be no better way to gather information than through observation. The ability of scanning systems to create accurate profiles of shoppers' preferences and behaviors is *well documented*.

An obvious disadvantage of observational research is that the researcher's findings are *limited to those observed*. Also, these techniques usually *do not examine motives* for, or feelings toward, particular behaviors. Another shortcoming is the *subjectivity of the observer*. The observations are usually accepted as accurate and objective, but they may not be. Also, sample sizes are usually small, so they *cannot be considered representative of the target population*. A final problem with the non-mechanical approaches in particular is that the time and energy researchers expend observing behaviors can lead to fatigue, and *observer fatigue* potentially means less-than-accurate data.

5-7 Ethnographic Research

Ethnographic research involves a mixture of techniques already discussed in this chapter to capture better customer information. It involves observation techniques, depth interviewing, and using videotape to record people in their natural settings. The ethnographic method has been used extensively in anthropology to study cultures. Now it's showing companies how people live with products—how they purchase and use them in their everyday lives.[29] It is helping businesses closely examine a host of problems, including developing new products, learning the relevance of brands, and positioning products and services in new and existing markets. It is widely becoming an acceptable alternative to other qualitative research techniques. Consider Example 5-6.

ethnographic research A research method that involves observation techniques, depth interviewing, and using videotape to record people in their natural settings.

Example 5-6

General Mills, Inc., used ethnographic research to gather data to develop a new breakfast food product. The manufacturer of such brands as Cheerios cereals, Yoplait yogurts, and Betty Crocker baking goods hired anthropologists to interview, observe, and videotape consumers in their homes, studying how they ate their breakfast. In one household, the researchers saw that the two children there didn't eat the name-brand cereal and waffles served to them. One child left the room and didn't eat any breakfast, while the other went to the kitchen cupboard and retrieved a box of unhealthy cereal to eat. These findings were important because their mother had reported in a focus group that her family only ate healthy foods for breakfast.[30]

Another example of ethnographic research can be found in the beef industry. The National Cattlemen's Beef Association (NCBA) wanted to better understand what consumers were thinking when they shopped at the meat counter. Consumers' purchasing behaviors and their preparation habits at home were videotaped. The consumers were interviewed each step of the way: what they thought about beef, why they did or did not select particular cuts, and how they prepared the family meal—whether it was cooked in the kitchen or on the backyard grill. In addition to these depth interviews, random shoppers were interviewed around the meat counter and asked for their thoughts on beef, the meat department's layout, and the availability of recipes and cooking information. The study cost $60,000 but was well worth the investment. The NCBA found that consumers were comfortable with their own meat experience because they would typically purchase the same cuts—ground beef, boneless chicken breast, and maybe a steak—each time. But when other's meat selections were brought up, most consumers had no idea what the researchers were talking about.[31]

5-8 Online Qualitative Research

The online environment is not an ideal setting for traditional qualitative research methods. However, with the development of technology, online qualitative research has gained its popularity in recent years, especially in global marketing research. Online

Source: © 2007 JupiterImages Corporation.

qualitative research can be conducted across time zones in different countries and therefore greatly save time and resources for global marketing research.[32]

5-8a Online Focus Groups

For online focus groups, respondents are recruited either by email or online discussion groups and must log into a Web site at a specific time to participate in the study. Once in the "chat room," the respondent's screen typically is divided into two parts: One side has the motion pictures of the discussants, and the other can be used by the moderator; for example, the moderator might show images for the respondents to comment on. Clients watch from their own computers and can send messages to the moderator without disrupting the focus group. Online focus groups or "chat sessions" have proven effective in getting elusive teen, single, affluent, and well-educated audiences to participate. In online focus groups, respondents participate from their own house or office and at their own convenience. The two major advantages to this form of data collection are its *speed* and *cost effectiveness*. Although online focus groups require some advance scheduling, responses are instantaneous, as they can be captured the moment participants key them in. And since there are no travel, lodging, and facility costs, online chat sessions are much less expensive than traditional focus groups.

However, online focus groups lose the advantage of group *dynamics*. Important nonverbal input, such as hand gestures, facial expressions, eye contact, and body language, is lost as well. And it is obvious that watching the computer screen is not the same as watching respondents.

5-8b Online Depth Interviews

For online depth interviews, respondents may be recruited by email or through discussion groups. If there is a discussion group that fully or partially matches the research topic, a message can be placed in the group, asking whether any individuals are interested in participating in further research. Online interviews allow a high degree of confidentiality and closeness between the interviewer and respondent. They can provide a similar confidential advantage, as well as similar significant time and cost savings, as online focus groups. A major shortcoming of online depth interviews is the lack of opportunity to view body gestures and eye contact between the interviewer and respondent.

5-8c Online Observation

There are a number of ways to observe people's online behaviors. The simplest technique is to monitor the number of visits or "hits" to a Web site. This will provide an indication of the popularity of a particular Web site. However, if there are 1,000 hits, no one knows for sure if the site was visited by 1,000 different people or the same person 1,000 times. Another way is to install Web site log software, like Sane Solutions' NetTracker, which gives Web site traffic analysis. This software creates reports on the number of users who view each page, the location of the site visited prior to the company's site, and what users purchase at a site. The data can be arranged by date, time, and user's geographic location. It can be further broken down to create ratios such as pages viewed per sale or number of impressions for a banner ad. [An "impression" is the gross sum of all media exposures (number of people or homes) without regard to duplication.][33] Another way to watch what people are doing on the Internet is to monitor consumer chatting and email posting through chat rooms, bulletin boards, or mailing lists.

Decision Time!

As a marketing manager, you will have to decide when—or whether—to use qualitative research techniques. You know these techniques may have low reliability and low validity and that considerable training is necessary to administer, score, and interpret the results. While you will not likely be involved in implementing the research, you will use the results. Do you have enough faith in these methods to use them to make strategic decisions? If so, which one do you feel has the most merit in marketing research? Why?

Net Impact

The major advantages of using the Internet to conduct qualitative research are that it saves time and is cost effective. As technology improves and both audio and video communication become available, the shortcomings of online focus groups and depth interviews will decline. However, projective techniques are not good candidates for online research because of the "personal touch" they require. As for observational research, physical trace analysis is used quite extensively.

On the Lighter Side—NBA Faces Challenges

In the 2005 regular season, although the National Basketball Association (NBA) saw a record attendance of 21.3 million, it lost about half of its network television audience in the seven years leading to 2005, according to Nielsen Media Research. The dramatic fall partially is attributable to the loss of viewers in big cities such as Los Angeles and New York, the teams from neither of which made the playoffs. Additionally, sales of licensed NBA apparel decreased substantially during the regular season. To better understand what should be done to remedy the problem, qualitative research such as depth interviews and focus groups must be conducted to find out what the fans are thinking about.

Source: Kortney Stringer, "On the rebound, NBA seeking a lift," *Knight Ridder Tribune Business News* (June 10, 2005): 1.

Chapter Summary

Researchers face important decisions when they collect information on specific issues. They must decide whether secondary data will provide adequate information. If not, primary data—original data, gathered fresh from the source for the current study—may need to be gathered. If primary data is necessary, researchers must then decide whether to collect qualitative or quantitative information.

Qualitative research techniques tend to be unstructured and encompass small samples of individuals who provide information that is not necessarily representative of the target population but is still useful in describing a group's feelings and insights. Three common types of these methods include focus groups, depth interviews, and projective techniques.

Focus groups involve interviewing a small group of individuals in an unstructured setting to reveal their innermost thoughts about a particular topic of interest. This technique can be used to generate information for questionnaires, assess needs, test new programs, find what customers consider when making decisions, recruit new members, test existing programs, follow up mail surveys, identify the image that an organization presents, and assess products.

Depth interviews are typically unstructured one-on-one conversations between a highly skilled interviewer and a member of a target population. Since there is no ideal way to interview people, the degree of structure an interviewer chooses to use depends on the goals.

Projective techniques reveal the deeper, hidden aspects of personality, the conflicts and anxieties that are peculiar to the individual being tested. Projective tests consist of vague and ambiguous stimuli that respondents are required to describe. These tests include word association, picture interpretation, sentence completion, third-person responses, role-playing, and cartoons.

While qualitative research techniques are useful in gathering primary data, shortcomings exist. One of the most common pitfalls involves managers using study results without fully understanding their limitations. The small sample sizes and unstructured formats limit the usefulness of the findings considerably.

Observing behavior is an effective way to gather data. Observational research is carried out in a number of ways: direct or indirect, disguised or undisguised, structured or unstructured, and by humans or by mechanical devices. The three specific types of observational techniques include audit, content analysis, and physical-trace analysis. The most obvious advantage of this research is that the data being gathered is of actual behaviors, not of respondents' intentions or preferences. However, the shortcoming is that the findings are limited to those observed and that motives for, or feelings toward, the observed behaviors are not measured.

A relatively new qualitative data collection method that is becoming popular among practitioners is ethnographic research. This method involves a mixture of techniques, including observation, depth interviewing, and using videotape to record people in their natural settings. Ethnographic research helps businesses examine a host of problems, including developing new products, learning the relevance of brands, and positioning products and services in new and existing markets.

Review Questions

1. What is the difference between survey and experimental research?

2. What is qualitative information, and why do researchers use it? When does quantitative data become necessary?

3. When should depth interviews be used instead of focus group interviews?

4. Briefly describe a focus group session. How many participants should there be? What is the atmosphere like in a typical session? What talents should the moderator possess to conduct sessions successfully?

5. What are five uses of focus groups?

6. What are projective techniques? Critique each of the tests described in the chapter. Would you have confidence in the results retrieved from each method? If so, why? If no, why not?

7. When should personal observation be used instead of mechanical observation? Which one do you prefer? Why?

8. What are some important shortcomings associated with qualitative research? Explain your answer.

9. What is ethnographic research? Why is it becoming an increasingly popular research approach today?

Practice Quiz

Note: You can find the correct answers to these questions by taking the quiz and then submitting your answers in the Online Edition. The program will automatically score your submission. If you miss a question, the program will provide the correct answer, a rationale for the answer, and the section number in the chapter where the topic is discussed.

1. Qualitative research uses mathematical measures and statistical techniques to determine relationships and differences among large samples of target populations.
   a. True
   b. False

2. A focus group is a qualitative research technique in which a skilled moderator leads a small group of participants in an unstructured discussion about a particular topic.
   a. True
   b. False

3. Depth interviews are unstructured, one-on-one conversations between a highly skilled interviewer and a member of a target population.
   a. True
   b. False

4. Depth interviews are conducted to help in the generation of surveys and polling and to obtain in-depth information on personality and behavior to test some hypothesis or theoretical proposition.
   a. True
   b. False

5. Projective techniques provide verbal or visual stimuli that encourage respondents to admit their true, conscious feelings and attitudes.
   a. True
   b. False

6. Focus groups can be used for each of the following reasons *except*
   a. to generate information for questionnaires.
   b. to conduct scientific tests.
   c. to recruit new members for the organization.
   d. to assess needs.
   e. to test existing programs.

7. When shoppers know that a researcher is observing them, then _____ observation is taking place.
   a. disguised
   b. undisguised
   c. unobtrusive
   d. realized
   e. None of the above

8. Which of the following methods is *not* a type of qualitative research?
   a. Focus group
   b. Depth interview
   c. Experiment
   d. Projective technique
   e. Third-person technique

9. The _____ observation technique could have researchers come into your pantry and examine your household products.
   a. content analysis
   b. physical-trace
   c. audit
   d. mechanical observation
   e. action evaluation

10. Which of the following is *not* a characteristic of ethnographic research?
    a. Used in anthropology to study cultures
    b. Involves observation techniques
    c. Involves depth interviewing
    d. Uses videotape to record people in their natural settings
    e. All of the above are characteristics of ethnographic research.

Thinking Critically

1. Assume that Procter & Gamble is redesigning its Tide laundry detergent box. It has hired you to serve as a moderator for focus group sessions. Who will you include in the focus group sessions? Which qualitative technique will you use? Why? What questions will you ask?

2. Shelton Park Elementary School is interested in finding out what its students' attitudes are toward school lunches. Which research technique would you use? Why?

3. You have just graduated from your academic institution and have been hired by Quaker to increase sales of its Cap'n Crunch, Life, and Quisp breakfast cereals. You are in charge of package design as well as product content. Because of budget constraints, you have been told to use only qualitative and observation research methods to gather market data. Write a brief plan describing how you would do it.

Net Exercises

1. MarketSearch offers a wide array of marketing services. One area of expertise is its focus group research. Visit its web page at http://www.msearch.com and read about its service offerings. You can also visit its facilities in Columbia, South Carolina (http://www.msearch.com/FGfacility.html) and see the floor plans of its focus group areas, as well as read about its focus group program, services, on-site catering, accommodations, and directions to the facility.

2. The Burke Institute is a huge market research organization. Visit its Web site (http://www.burke.com/qualitative/prac_ProjectiveTech.htm) and read about the different types of projective techniques it uses such as personification, category sculpting, modified TAT, collages, fantasy excursions, and sensory immersion.

3. IMS Health, Inc., one of the largest marketing research organizations in the United States, had revenues in 2004 of $1.569 billion. The company is the largest global provider of market information, sales management, and decision-support services to the pharmaceutical and health care industries. It actively performs audits in the pharmaceutical, hospital, prescription, medical, and promotion industries. Visit its Web site (http://www.imshealth.com) to read about these audits.

Experiencing Marketing Research

1. You and your best friend have a disagreement regarding the target market of Budweiser ("Bud") Light. One of you believes it is targeted toward female consumers who enjoy beer but want to watch their weight, and one of you thinks that it targets young males who enjoy sports. Conduct a content analysis of popular magazines to determine who is right. What did you find?

2. Conduct depth interviews with six students from your college or university to determine their satisfaction/

dissatisfaction with their education thus far. Describe your experiences as interviewer. What are your findings? Do you feel they are representative of your entire college or university population? Why or why not?

3. You are a manager at an amusement park and want to know which ride is the most popular and why. Which observation method will give you the best information? Why? Does it help you answer your question about the ride? Why or why not?

Case 5-1

Dilemma for Mutual Fund Advisors: How to Treat New vs. Loyal Customers

You make your money and look for places to make it grow. Some experts say the stock market is a sure bet to continue to go up. Others say the bond market is strong. And others will encourage you to invest in mutual funds. Mutual funds have become one of the hottest topics of discussion on Wall Street, and potential investors are lining up with their brokers for investment advice. Many mutual fund companies help these households by offering consultation with a mutual fund advisor, but mutual fund advisors aren't sure how to treat their customers: Should they treat all customers the same, irrespective of the duration of their relationship with them? That is, are the needs of new and loyal customers different? A satisfaction study was conducted to answer this query. Both quantitative and qualitative research techniques were used to locate the key drivers of customer satisfaction with mutual funds.

Over 1,200 telephone interviews were conducted among customers of a mutual fund company. Among these customers, 37% were considered "new," since they had been with the company for five years or less. The remaining 63% were considered "loyal," since they had been with the company for more than five years. The five-year cutoff was used because the company had taken on new initiatives to reward customers who had been with the firm for five or more years, and it would be beneficial to blend the insights from this study to improve the existing initiative. To understand the attribute importance among new and loyal customers, a series of depth interviews with managers was conducted with customers who had been with the firm for one year, two years, and five or more years. They found from the qualitative study that:

1. Attributes such as "courteous," "makes me feel comfortable," and "spends a lot of time with me" are important among customers who have been with the company for fewer than five years.

2. Attributes such as "can solve problems in one visit," "does not waste my time," and "provides just the right amount of information" are more important for loyal customers.

3. The advisor's ability to instill confidence in the customer is slightly more important to customers who have been with the firm for more than five years.

Based on the findings, the managers built a "dynamic relationship model" between the firm and its clients. The cornerstone of the model was the insight that new customers were looking to build trust and rapport with a mutual fund advisor. After that was developed, along with a high level of confidence in the advisor, their concern shifted toward efficiency issues. The main concern involved conducting transactions with a high degree of speed and efficiency, so the "touchy feely" side of mutual fund advising—establishing trust, confidence, and courtesy—was found to be a necessary precondition to cultivating a long-term relationship. Once accomplished, the advisors need to concentrate on efficiency by concluding the transaction quickly and efficiently.

Source: Vikas Mittal and Jerome M. Katrichis, "Distinctions between new and loyal customers," *Marketing Research*, vol. 12, no. 1 (Spring 2000): 26–32.

Case Questions

1. Assume you are the interviewer of one of the depth interviews conducted to understand the attribute importance among new and loyal customers. What questions would you use to lead the discussions? List

three of them. Where would you conduct the interviews? Why?

2. Is depth interviewing the best qualitative research method available to cover such a personal topic as investments? If so, why? If not, why not?

3. Is it possible to use any of the observational approaches to understand the attribute importance among new and loyal customers? If so, which approach(es)? If not, why not?

Case 5-2

Time to Improve the Image of U.S. Clients Abroad

There are two major parts to the research equation: client needs and researcher performance. Clients have information gaps that need to be filled by research findings. But which group should be the leader of the research process? Should it be the client, since they are paying for the research to be performed? Or should it be the research agency, since it holds the research expertise? Who is "in charge" is debatable. However, their images are clear-cut. International qualitative researchers worldwide paint an unattractive portrait of the U.S. client as overbearing, arrogant, and insensitive to cultural differences when conducting research overseas. These researchers complain that they feel like "hired lips" for U.S. clients that insist that they follow verbatim the 12-page discussion guides given to them 30 minutes prior to the first focus group start. The image is depressing to say the least. This overbearing behavior by U.S. clients has increased the assertion that there are two models of qualitative research: the superior "European" model and the inferior "U.S." model. Non-U.S. researchers wrongly assume that U.S. clients act the same way with their qualitative research suppliers in the United States.

These perceptions may be erroneous; after all, international researchers are used to Asian, European, or South American clients who rarely participate in the qualitative research process. Rather, they wait for their researchers to prepare a lengthy written analysis of the findings. The U.S. client is used to attending the majority of focus group sessions. Qualitative research is ingrained so much in the United States psyche that controlling the style and flow of the research becomes second nature, particularly when it is being conducted in a different setting in a different language.

U.S. clients want two things from qualitative research: to obtain rich and enlightening data, and for nothing to go wrong to embarrass or delay them in their data quest. It is possible that the latter insecurity makes clients seem rude and rigid when dealing with non-U.S. qualitative researchers. Here are 10 tips for U.S. clients to improve their image and outcomes when conducting qualitative research abroad:

- Treat qualitative researchers in other countries as partners rather than as performers, since they are highly skilled professionals.

- Share the study's objectives with local researchers so they understand why specific questions are so important.

- Even in today's busy turnaround time, send the discussion guide in advance to generate comfort, ownership, and feedback.

- Ask qualitative-researcher partners how they would have designed this study differently if left to them.

- Respect local cultural differences that may affect group recruiting, scheduling, composition, dynamics, and respondents' candor.

- Ask local research partners how they interpret what respondents said in the context of their experience.

- Read about culture and history of the countries being visited to become informed about their unique perspectives and lifestyles.

- Be flexible and polite about any differences between U.S. and foreign amenities and accommodations.

- Recognize that the purpose of multicountry research is not only to find common ground, but also to catch the nuances of difference.

- Avoid the tight scheduling that renders you too tired to appreciate the new environment and makes you crankier toward those with whom you come in contact.

Instead of the ugly American, the best U.S. qualitative researchers find the U.S. client loyal and grateful when qualitative research proves to be useful. International researchers should clearly state to U.S. clients that the best findings are those that come from understanding local cultural differences. More respect for qualitative researchers abroad will create better information—the goal of both parties.

Source: Patricia Sabena, "Ten tips for the U.S. client abroad," *Marketing News,* vol. 34, no. 5 (February 28, 2000): 16–17.

Case Questions

1. Some skeptics believe that the 10 tips for U.S. clients to improve their image when conducting qualitative research abroad are going too far. What do you think?

2. What would you say to someone who says that it is more important to understand how to correctly conduct qualitative research than it is to understand foreign cultures?

3. What is meant in the case by the statement, "These researchers complain that they feel like 'hired lips' for U.S. clients that insist that they follow verbatim the 12-page discussion guides given to them 30 minutes prior to the first focus group start"?

Case 5-3

The Integrated Case—Part 2

Cheerwine—In Need of Unique Research

After the meeting with Greg Campana, Mark Ritchie called Alan Young, an independent consultant with rich experience in marketing research, for advice. Young confirmed Ritchie's concern about the validity of the previous research. He explained, "With a response rate of 2%, there is no way to guarantee the sample is representative of the target market. Therefore, the findings can be biased and even misleading." He added, "To obtain accurate information about consumer perceptions and attitudes toward Cheerwine, well-designed research must be conducted."

Ritchie decided to commission Young to conduct the research project. Young started with secondary data analysis, from which he found that the target market of Cheerwine is kids in middle schools and high schools. The school-goers certainly have some unique characteristics: they have money to spend and they enjoy spending it;

they are prone to following trends yet want to be independent.

From his experience in marketing consulting, Young knew that the most important issue is to understand how the school-goers perceive Cheerwine. To acquire insights and gain an understanding of this issue, an exploratory, qualitative research study is necessary.

Case Questions

Based on the case information, and the decision problems/research objectives you have identified in Part 1 (see Case 2-3), answer the questions that follow.

1. Which qualitative research method are you going to use? Why?

2. For the method suggested, list the questions you will use to lead the discussions.

3. Explain in detail how you will conduct the research.

Notes

1. Carol Phillips and Andlinda Stegeman, "Hybrid approach tends to yield more insight," *Marketing News* 39, no. 2 (April 1, 2005): 22.

2. Vikas Mittal and Jerome M. Katrichis, "Distinctions between new and loyal customers," *Marketing Research* 12, no. 1 (Spring 2000): 26–32.

3. Thomas L. Greenbaum, "Focus groups vs. online," *Advertising Age* 71, no. 7 (February 14, 2000): 34.

4. Thomas L. Greenbaum, "Using focus groups effectively in packaging research," *Marketing News* 29, no. 12 (June 5, 1996): H34.

5. Leslie M. Harris, "Technology, techniques drive focus group trends," *Marketing News* 29, no. 5 (February 27, 1995): 8.

6. Richard A. Krueger, *Focus Groups* (Thousand Oaks, CA: Sage, 1994), 78–79.

7. Cyndee Miller, "Researcher reaches Xers with her focus groups on the road," *Marketing News* 29, no. 1 (January 2, 1995): 10.

8. Anonymous, "Focus group warning," *Marketing News* 34, no. 6 (March 13, 2000): 6.

9. Roberta Bernstein, "Food for thought," *American Demographics* 22, no. 5 (May 2000): 39–42.

10. Faith Russell, "Dangerous intersections," *Marketing News* 34, no. 5 (February 28, 2000): 18.

11. Richard A. Feder, "Depth interviews avoid turmoil of focus groups," *Advertising Age* 68, no. 16 (April 21, 1997): 33.

12. Burke Web site, "The Burke approach to qualitative research," http://www.burke.com/qualitative_capabilities.htm, June 25, 2005.

13. Lewis R. Aiken, *Psychological Testing and Assessment* (Boston: Allyn & Bacon, 1994), 264–271.

14. Gail McGovern, and John A Quelch, "The lamentable law of marketing management," *Advertising Age* (Midwest region edition), (Feb. 2005): 7.

15. Tom M Y Lin, Pin Luarn, and Peter K. Y. Lo, "Internet market segmentation: An exploratory study of critical success factors," *Marketing Intelligence & Planning* 22, no. 6/7 (2004): 601.

16. John Goyder, "An experiment with cash incentives on a personal interview survey," *Journal of the Market Research Society* 36, no. 4 (October 1994): 360–366.

17. E. Day, "Share of heart: What is it and how can it be measured?" *Journal of Consumer Marketing* (Winter 1989).

18. Pamela Sebastian, "Really new products are the aim of a word-association quiz for consumers," *Wall Street Journal* (June 26, 1997): A1.

19. Chad Rubel, "Three firms show that good research makes good ads," *Marketing News* 29, no. 6 (March 13, 1995): 18.

20. Burke Web site, "The Burke approach to qualitative research," http://www.burke.com/qualitative_capabilities.htm, June 25, 2005.

21. Sidney Levy, "Interpretation is the essence of projective research techniques," *Marketing News* 20 (September 28, 1984): 1, 20.

22. Sharon L. Hollander, "Projective technique uncovers *real* consumer attitudes," *Marketing News* (January 4, 1988): 34.

23. Gene Shorter and Peter Cooper, "Projecting the future," *Journal of the Market Research Society* 41, no. 1 (January 1999): 33–45.

24. Bob Becker, "Take direct route when data-gathering," *Marketing News* 33, no. 20 (September 27, 1999): 29, 31.

25. Karen Fletcher, "Not just a room with a view," *Marketing* (March 23, 1995): 27.

26. Sharon Bramlett-Solomon, "Nowhere near picture perfect: images of the elderly in Life and Ebony magazine ads, 1990– 1997," *Journalism and Mass Communication Quarterly* 76, no. 3 (Autumn 1999): 565–572.

27. Gina Escamilla, Angie L. Cradock, and Ichiro Kawachi, "Women and smoking in Hollywood movies: A content analysis," *American Journal of Public Health* 90, no. 3 (March 2000): 412–414.

28. Rebecca Morris, "Computerized content analysis in management research: A demonstration of advantages and limitations," *Journal of Management* 20, no. 4 (Winter 1994): 903(29).

29. Kendra Parker, "How do you like your beef?" *American Demographics* 22, no. 1 (January 2000): 35–37.

30. Michelle Wirth Fellman, "Breaking tradition," *Marketing Research* 11, no. 3 (Fall 1999): 20–24.

31. Kendra Parker, "How do you like your beef?" *American Demographics* 22, no. 1 (January 2000): 35–37.

32. Decision Analyst Inc., Web site, "Qualitative research," http://www.decisionanalyst.com/Services/qualitat.asp, October 7, 2005.

33. Sane Solutions, Web site, http://www.sane.com/, October 7, 2005.

Primary Data Collection: Survey Research

Chapter Six

Source: © 2007 JupiterImages Corporation.

Key Terms

computer-assisted personal interview (CAPI)   (p. 140)

computer-assisted self-interview (CASI)   (p. 140)

computer-assisted telephone interview (CATI)   (p. 144)

door-to-door interview   (p. 138)

electronic white pages (EWP)   (p. 143)

fully automated telephone interview (FATI)   (p. 145)

mail panel   (p. 147)

mall-intercept ("man-on-the-street") interview   (p. 139)

office interview   (p. 139)

omnibus survey   (p. 140)

one-time mail survey   (p. 147)

online survey   (p. 148)

personal interview   (p. 136)

random-digit dialing (RDD)   (p. 142)

survey research   (p. 136)

systematic random-digit dialing (SRDD)   (p. 143)

telephone survey   (p. 141)

Learning Objectives

After studying this chapter, you will be able to:

- Understand the different types of survey methods.
- Discuss the advantages and disadvantage of each major survey method.

- Know how to select a particular data collection method based on the resources available and the constraints.

GET THIS

Atlantic City Brand Survey—A Gamble Worth Taking

There are waves crashing on the shore, beautiful beaches, amusement parks and motels, casinos, and tons of entertainment. It's also positioned close to New York, Newark, and other dynamic U.S. cities. So what's wrong with Atlantic City's gambling mecca? New Jersey tourism officials want to know what beachgoers like and what they don't like about visiting seashore resorts as they look to restore the way the region is marketed.

In August 2004, marketing researchers hit the resort in droves, surveying 10,000 visitors at New Jersey beaches, amusement parks, and motels. They asked things like how friendly the locals are, what other destinations the visitors considered before choosing the Jersey shore, and how the shore experience could be better.

"We want honest feedback," said Gov. James E. McGreevey in announcing the survey. "The first step in any planning is to know what the customer wants. . . . The Jersey Shore is certainly a household name. But the tourism marketplace is increasingly competitive. We need a marketing strategy." State officials hope to develop the Jersey Shore as a brand as familiar to visitors as Las Vegas. They feel that it will make them more competitive with other locales such as Cape Cod, the Hamptons, and the Outer Banks.

A variety of ideas evolved from the research efforts. For example, Troy Roberts, 52, of Queens, N.Y., who visits the gaming town twice a year, stated that the resort area can stand to be a little cleaner and that they need to rid it of bums. While he enjoys shows and concerts, he was disappointed there weren't more entertainment options. "I just came from Las Vegas and there is tons of entertainment there," Roberts says.

New Yorkers John and Gail Porter could visit the casinos in nearby Connecticut, but the state lacks the beaches that Atlantic City can offer. The couple makes the drive down the Garden State Parkway about twice a year to gamble and walk the boardwalk. But they would like to see better shopping options and more family entertainment. "It's come a long way from where it was and it has a ways to go," says John Porter.

Source: Kathy Hennessy, "Survey helps branding project down the Jersey Shore," *Marketing News,* vol. 38, issue 14 (Sept. 1, 2004): 34.

Now Ask Yourself

- Why would tourism officials in New Jersey use a survey rather than some type of qualitative method such as focus group and depth interview for the development of the Jersey Shore?

- How would the survey results substantiate the findings from depth interviews such as the comments from visitors like Troy Roberts and John and Gail Porter?

- Why wasn't an Internet survey used in this project?

The "Get This" feature focuses on how tourism officials in New Jersey used survey research for the development of the Jersey Shore. Survey research clearly has its unique advantages, but the technique also has its limitations. In this chapter, we'll discuss different types of survey methods and the strengths and weaknesses associated with each type of survey method. We begin this chapter with a discussion of the pros and cons of survey research, the types of survey methods, and factors to consider when selecting a survey method.

6-1 Advantages and Disadvantages of Survey Research

survey research A descriptive research method that obtains information with a highly structured questionnaire from a large number of respondents.

As a descriptive research method, **survey research** obtains information with a highly structured questionnaire from a large number of respondents. A survey can cover a variety of topics, ranging from consumption behavior, brand perceptions, and attitudes, to demographics and psychological factors. The major advantages of survey research are that surveys are easy to administer and suitable for statistical analysis. A survey with structured, closed-ended (multiple-choice) questions can be easily answered by potential respondents. The results of survey research can be coded into numerical information that is suitable for analysis. As a result, the interpretation of the results is objective and conclusive.

Some challenges of survey research are how to motivate potential respondents to participate and how to obtain their candid answers. Due to the increasing number of surveys conducted each year, it has become more difficult for researchers to get enough qualified respondents to participate. Moreover, respondents may be unable to provide the needed information or unwilling to provide an honest answer. Therefore, a well-designed questionnaire and appropriate survey techniques are extremely important to obtain accurate information. Despite its limitations, survey research is still the most popular primary data collection method in marketing research.

6-2 Types of Survey Methods

Survey data collection can be costly, tedious, and time-consuming. Companies must be familiar with the market's communication infrastructure before they gather data. Consider the following concerns associated with survey research worldwide:

- A large percentage of U.S. businesses and households have communication vehicles such as telephones, fax machines, and computers.
- Latin American business-to-business research interviews need to be performed face-to-face because businesspeople will not open up to strangers on the telephone.
- The Italian postal system is so poorly run that research by mail is almost impossible.
- In developing countries telephone ownership is low.
- The Japanese language does not lend itself to long sessions on the telephone.[1]

It's apparent from these considerations that companies must pay close attention to which method will maximize their resources. Companies usually choose from these primary data collection methods: personal interviews, telephone surveys, mail surveys, and online surveys. Some of these techniques require an interviewer, while others can be self-administered. Exhibit 6-1 summarizes the major survey methods.

6-2a Personal Interview

personal interview Data collection through face-to-face communication between an interviewer and a respondent.

A **personal interview** involves face-to-face communication between an interviewer and a respondent. Westat, an employee-owned research corporation serving agencies of the U.S. government, samples from 1,500 to more than 30,000 households through personal interviews. Personal interviews can be performed almost anywhere, from shopping malls, offices, restaurants, universities, and homes to any location where meetings are possible. Similar to the depth interview discussed in Chapter 5, one-on-one conversations occur between an interviewer and a member of the target population. Unlike depth interviews, however, personal interviews are usually not

| EXHIBIT 6-1 | Major Survey Methods |

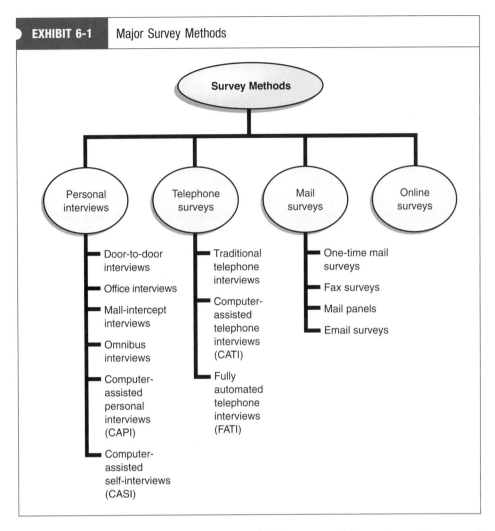

recorded and tend to be more structured. The personal interview offers several advantages over other data collection methods:

- *A lot of flexibility.* A personal interview allows the interviewer considerable flexibility during the interview. If a respondent is confused by a question, the interviewer can clarify it. The interviewer must be careful, however, not to alter the original content of the question.

- *Abundance of information.* It is possible to collect a lot of information during a personal interview because the interaction tends to generate more interest and less fatigue on the part of respondents than do written, telephone, or computer-assisted surveys. For example, personal interviews were conducted with top offcials of five venture capital companies, including the president of the Indian Venture Capital Association, and revealed a lot of information about the growth of the industry and how it has been restricted by several factors like conservative government policies, limitations on availability of funds, and lack of an adequate equity market infrastructure to facilitate the exit process.[2]

- *Exceed original questions.* Personal interviews permit the interviewer to go beyond original questions. If appropriate, the interviewer can delve into related topics. A marketing study on horseracing used personal interviewing that permitted the researchers to go beyond their original study intentions and learn about aspects they didn't consider prior to the study, such as betting exchanges, an online phenomenon where people can bet against one another rather than through a book maker.[3]

Source: © 2007 JupiterImages Corporation.

- *Data control is high.* The researcher has control over the interview questions. This is contingent on the researcher being the same person who conducts the interview. If, however, someone other than the researcher is performing the interviews and that someone doesn't adhere to interview procedure, responses may be biased. The interviewer must not change the intent of the question.

- *Relatively higher response rates.* Response rates tend to be considerably higher in personal interviews than the 10–20% researchers typically expect from mail surveys. (Mail survey response rates will be discussed later in the chapter.)

Collecting data by personal interview also has disadvantages:

- *Expensive.* Personal interviews tend to be expensive, particularly when they are spread over a large geographic region. A global study using this method is usually out of the question due to potentially high travel costs and extensive time commitment.

- *Slow data collection.* Because travel is usually involved and personal interviews take time to complete, data collection is slow.

- *Narrow geographical coverage.* Personal interviews often cover a narrow geographical area to keep travel costs reasonable.

- *Lack of respondent anonymity.* Because data collection takes place face to face, respondents may feel uncomfortable responding to some questions and may answer with less sincerity than when responding to mail, computer-assisted, or telephone interviews.

- *Interviewer bias.* Personal interviews expose data collection to the possibility of interviewer bias.

The most common personal interviews are door-to-door interviews, office interviews, mall-intercept interviews, omnibus surveys, computer-assisted personal interviews, and computer-assisted self-interviews.

door-to-door interview A personal interview that takes place at respondents' homes.

Door-to-door interviews take place at respondents' homes. This interviewing strategy is the most aggressive of all survey techniques because it not only taps the minds of respondents, it also requires that they allow the interviewer into their homes. This can work to the advantage of the interviewer because the respondents are in a familiar, safe, and comfortable environment. Familiar environments encourage respondents to give honest and thorough answers. The problem is getting into the home. Today, fewer people are willing to allow strangers into their homes. Increased crime is one reason, but there are others. With the increase in two-income families, more people than ever work outside their homes. Their time at home is precious and limited, and they are less willing to share it with others. Also, people don't often allow "somebody off the street who just shows up" into their homes. By arriving unannounced, interviewers may be interrupting some activity, such as dinner, household chores, or family time.

Office interviews take place at respondents' places of business. The objective of office interviews is different from that of door-to-door interviews. While door-to-door interviews inquire about attitudes and habits regarding consumer products, office interviews concentrate on information about industrial products or services. Telephoning ahead of time to find out who in the organization should be interviewed is important. In most organizations, various employees can provide useful information, including the following:

- *Gatekeepers.* These individuals control the flow of information to others within the organization. For example, administrative assistants and secretaries often screen information intended for their bosses. Before an interview can take place between a manager and a researcher, gatekeepers must usually be convinced of the importance of the interview before they will approach their managers, since they are responsible for filtering out unnecessary interruptions in the office.

- *Product users.* These individuals use the product or service and therefore possess hands-on knowledge that others are not likely to have.

- *Product buyers.* These employees negotiate with and choose suppliers, so they can provide information about many aspects of their products or services, particularly the distribution part of the business.

- *Influencers.* Certain people affect key decisions in organizations. They may be difficult to locate because they aren't directly involved with the product or service, but they are important sources of information.

- *Final decision makers.* These people have the final say. They are usually easy to locate.

Mall-intercept ("man-on-the-street") interviews take place at large shopping malls, as the considerable traffic flow of malls should facilitate capturing a large sample. Marketing research firms typically position young and energetic individuals in high-traffic locations of malls to gather marketing data. As the term indicates, in mall-intercept interviews shoppers are intercepted or stopped to answer a series of questions. These questions may be asked at the location where the shopper was stopped or at an interview facility located somewhere else close by. In concept, the mall-intercept method makes a lot of sense. However, in practice, there are major shortcomings to this method:

- *Low response rates.* People typically come to malls to shop, not to answer questions that they view as time-consuming or as an intrusion on their privacy.

- *Data is suspect.* Malls tend to draw from a relatively small area and thus may not be representative of the target population. The stores immediately surrounding the location of the interviewer also influence the sample. Upscale stores typically draw high-income people, and discount stores draw a higher percentage of lower-income and more cost-conscious people, both of which can bias the sample. Thus, if the intention is to sample a wide variety of income levels, interviewers need to roam the mall to increase their likelihood of obtaining a more representative mix of consumers. Of course, if the mall is considered an outlet mall, where discount prices are the theme of each resident store, then the majority of shoppers will likely be cost-conscious consumers.

office interview A personal interview that takes place at the respondent's place of business.

mall-intercept ("man-on-the-street") interview A personal interview that takes place at a shopping mall or similar shopping location.

- *Possible respondent selection bias.* Respondents are chosen by the interviewer, who may be less than qualified to make this important decision.
- *Crowded, loud place.* The inherent noise of a mall makes it less than conducive to perform serious marketing research.

omnibus survey Regularly scheduled face-to-face interviews with a consistent set of respondents, using questions from multiple clients.

Omnibus surveys are a quick and cost-effective way to obtain consumer or market information. They involve face-to-face interviews that are conducted on a regularly scheduled basis. The survey questions used each period, which may be weekly, monthly, quarterly, or semiannually, are supplied by several clients, so they are not always of a consistent thought pattern. Each client company has its own questions and survey objectives, and interviewers must cover every client's material. An important advantage of omnibus surveys over other interview methods is that clients share the costs; the amount charged is based on the number of questions asked. Also, since the interviews are conducted on a regularly scheduled basis, clients can keep abreast of respondents' evolving attitudes. NOP Research Group, a marketing research company in the United Kingdom, regularly uses omnibus surveys to conduct 2,000 face-to-face interviews with 15-year-olds (1000 male and 1000 female) through a national sample.[4]

computer-assisted personal interview (CAPI) A personal interview in which the interviewer inputs responses directly into a computer terminal during the interview.

Computer-assisted personal interviews (CAPI) are becoming more popular because of the advancements in technology. In this technique, the interviewer uses a keyboard to input responses directly into a computer terminal, desktop, or laptop during the interview. The popularity of CAPI has been increasing dramatically in recent years. Since 1990, RSL became the first U.K. research company to establish a national computer-assisted personal interview operation in Europe. Today, most leading companies have CAPI technology.

There are several advantages associated with this method of data collection:

- Respondents don't have to be computer literate. This is particularly important in impoverished areas.
- Follow-up questions can be incorporated into the survey.
- Words generated by respondents can be used to make the survey-completion effort user-friendly.
- The amount of time it takes a respondent to complete certain questions can be accurately measured. This is important because it gives an indication of the complexity of the question.
- Graphic displays that relate to specific questions help respondents answer particular questions.
- Data need not be manually coded from paper surveys, since the responses are fed directly into the computer.
- The chance of making data entry errors is low compared to that when manual methods are used, since the computer accepts only an established set of numbers.
- Data collection and coding are quicker.

The major shortcoming of this method is that it doesn't allow respondents to choose their own schedule for completing the survey.

computer-assisted self-interview (CASI) An interview in which a researcher locates potential respondents and leads them to nearby computer terminals, where the respondents read and respond to questions directly on the computer.

In **computer-assisted self-interviews (CASI),** researchers locate potential respondents and lead them to nearby computer terminals. Respondents then read and respond to each question directly on the computer. This method has the same advantages as computer-assisted personal interviewing, but it also allows respondents to complete the surveys at their convenience. However, this method requires that respondents have some computer skills.

Consider the usage of CAPI and CASI at Westat:

On most studies, data collectors use laptop personal computers for computer-assisted personal interviewing (CAPI) and audio computer-assisted self-interviewing (CASI).

These technologies enable interviewers to collect more complex information than was practical with hard-copy methods and to deliver it more accurately and more quickly. To meet the needs of complex government surveys, Westat has developed and maintains a software system called Cheshire and is also a leading user of the Blaise survey system. Both the Cheshire system and the Blaise system are integrated with our computerized Field Operations and Management Systems, which handle the assignment of cases to interviewers, provide reliable and secure transmission of confidential survey data, and yield timely information for monitoring interviewer performance and directing the overall survey effort.[5]

6-2b Telephone Surveys

In **telephone surveys,** researchers communicate by telephone with respondents either directly, by voice, or indirectly, by fax, voice mail, or computer assistance. One study found that the use of telephone surveys for marketing and opinion research is replacing personal surveys in several countries with a high telephone penetration.[6] Westat has its own Telephone Research Center (TRC) that operates major facilities in Rockville and Frederick, Maryland, as well as four smaller facilities in other locations. Its interviewing capacity of approximately 400 stations enables it to deliver 25,000 to 35,000 hours of interviewing each week. Each interviewing station, regardless of geographic location, operates as part of a single "virtual TRC" managed from the Rockville home office, allowing it to supervise interviewers to meet project requirements.[7] This survey method has certain advantages:

- The area of potential coverage is *extensive because* telephone ownership is common worldwide. Most households and businesses in industrialized nations and many of those in developing areas of the world either own or have access to telephones. An ACNielsen Canada telephone survey of 2,000 Canadians that spanned across the country found that the majority of respondents preferred cash as the preferred retail payment method. Six out of their past 10 retail transactions were made in cash.[8]

- Data collection is *fast.* There is little or no delay between the time when the telephone number is dialed and the targeted respondent can respond to the inquiries.

- The interviewer has *control* over the survey content, although to a lesser extent than in personal interviews because the lack of face-to-face interaction slightly diminishes the interviewer's ability to exchange and clarify information.

- Administration *costs* tend to be lower than for personal interviews but higher than for mail surveys. The cost is, of course, dependent on interview length and respondents' locations.

- Respondents have some *anonymity* compared to personal interviews. While respondents are not entirely anonymous, they may derive some comfort in knowing that they are not in plain view of the interviewer.

Like all research techniques, collecting data by telephone has some disadvantages:

- As with personal interviews, there is a potential for *interviewer bias.* Telephone interviewers can influence respondents by changing the content of the original question or offering their own points of view. To ensure that queries are properly administered, companies have been known to secretly listen in on interviews and reprimand interviewers who bias responses in any way.

- *Response rate* is another concern. The extent to which subjects are willing to respond to interviews depends on several factors. One factor is the time of day calls are placed. For example, early morning hours are generally not a good time to conduct telephone surveys. The degree of cooperation depends on the subject

telephone survey A form of data collection in which the researcher communicates by telephone with respondents either directly, by voice, or indirectly, by fax, voice mail, or computer assistance.

RSVP Telephone Interviewing

RSVP Research Services, located in northeast Philadelphia, claims, "We provide extensive experience in all aspects of data collection and data processing; highly proactive project management; stringent quality control and production standards; wide scope of services; and unparalleled service and responsiveness." Their facilities include: 120 computer-assisted telephone interviewing (CATI) stations, a staff of over 200 trained interviewers, computerized least-cost call routing, on-site and off-site (remote) monitoring control, and the latest in telecommunications and data transfer technology. Interviewer training is extensive. It includes:

- General orientation on the purpose and importance of marketing research company policies and quality standards,

- Intensive training on the "basics" of interviewing itself—overcoming refusals, the handling of skip patterns, probing techniques, sample administration, CATI interviewing, etc.,

- Observing and listening to experienced interviewers conducting actual interviews, and

- Practice interviews during which each trainee's performance is closely monitored and evaluated under actual interviewing conditions.

After completing eight hours of training (two sessions of four hours each), interviewers are assigned to an actual project under close supervision. New interviewers are monitored at a 100% rate until their performance is established.

Source: RSVP Research Services, "Interviewer training," http://www.rsvpresearch.com, June 23, 2005.

matter under investigation. People don't feel comfortable sharing with strangers their views on sensitive topics like sexual activity, alcohol consumption, and religious preference. The capabilities of the interviewers are a crucial factor. Well-trained interviewers can sometimes make respondents feel comfortable with a sensitive topic through their tact and demeanor. Finally, the number of survey questions influences the success or failure of an interview. People become impatient answering numerous questions over the phone. There is no ideal survey length, but well-trained interviewers can usually sense when respondents are losing patience.

There are three major ways to gather information via telephone lines: (1) traditional telephone interviews, (2) computer-assisted telephone interviews, and (3) fully automated telephone interviews.

Traditional Telephone Interviews

Telephone interviewers may be positioned at either a central research location or at their homes. The vast majority of telephone surveys initiate from a central location where telephone lines have been set up specifically for interviewing. (See Research Realities 6-1 for a description of RSVP Research Services' resources and training program.) Telephone interviewing virtually eliminates the transportation expenses associated with personal interviews.

Central locations allow management to monitor conversations. Conducting all interviews from a central telephone facility is one of the most important elements of quality control because there is no way to verify whether the interviewers are doing the work properly when letting them work at home. In addition, when questions arise, operating centrally ensures immediate attention to problems and consistency of data.

As noted earlier, from a separate room managers can listen randomly to the interviews. This enables them to evaluate the work of each interviewer and to make recommendations whenever they detect problems.

random-digit dialing (RDD)
A telephone dialing system that randomly generates telephone numbers of sample respondents.

Telephone interviews increase the probability of obtaining a representative sample of the targeted population. **Random-digit dialing (RDD)** is a telephone dialing system that randomly generates telephone numbers of sample respondents. Using RDD, researchers can approximate a random sample for the survey. RDD does not use

Source: Comstock.com.

telephone books or other lists of telephone numbers. It randomly generates numbers, thus giving all numbers, including unlisted numbers, an equal chance of being in the sample. This is important because, of the 99 million U.S. households with telephones, about 35 million are unlisted.

Most polling organizations outside the United States and Canada do not use RDD in many of their public opinion surveys because it tends to be expensive and often dials nonworking numbers and businesses. However, researchers who use nonrandom samples may be biasing their results because the responses come from preselected groups. Although RDD has its shortcomings, many researchers in the United States and Canada feel the biases introduced by not using it are unacceptable.[9]

One type of RDD is **systematic random-digit dialing (SRDD)**; this allows researchers to specify particular geographic regions or area codes to sample. SRDD enables researchers to limit geographic coverage of the survey to targeted areas.

An alternative to RDD and SRDD is **electronic white pages (EWP)**. This method permits a researcher to draw a random sample from the directory listing in the white pages of the telephone book, which is available on compact disk. Random-digit dialing has been found to be more costly than EWP—which translates into being able to conduct more EWP surveys each year from limited budgets. Studies using EWP have also produced higher response rates than RDD studies. However, EWP suffers from the omission of unlisted telephone numbers and incomplete population coverage of telephones.[10]

Conducting personal interviews by telephone also has disadvantages:

- *They are impersonal.* Talking to a stranger over the telephone doesn't allow interviewers to cultivate relationships with respondents as talking face-to-face does. Even though technology will soon make telephones with video screens commonplace, personal interviews by telephone will still lack the direct and intimate communication possible with face-to-face interviews.

- *Low participation.* This is inevitable because of telephone answering machines and caller ID, and because people don't want to be bothered at home by strangers.

- *No product demonstrations.* Telephone surveys are limited to studies that do not require product demonstrations.

systematic random-digit dialing (SRDD) A telephone dialing system that allows the researcher to specify particular geographic regions or area codes from which to randomly contact individuals.

electronic white pages (EWP) A telephone dialing system that permits a researcher to draw a random sample from the directory listing in the white pages of the telephone book, which is available on compact disk.

When surveying some global markets, telephone availability should be considered. According to a recent study on telecommunication market, while over 95% of households in the U.S. have fixed-line telephones, the penetration rate of fixed-line telephones in Latin America is only 17%, primarily owing to a general shift from fixed-line to mobile phones. The study notes:

> In early 2005, there were around 176 million mobile phones in Latin America compared with approximately 92 million fixed-line phones. Paraguay leads the trend, with four times more mobile than fixed-line subscribers. Regional mobile penetration stood at around 32% in early 2005; however it varies greatly from country to country, with Chile, Jamaica and Puerto Rico recording the highest rates at around 61%, 59% and 48% respectively, while Haiti and Honduras languish at 2% and 8%, respectively.[11]

Computer-Assisted Telephone Interview (CATI)

The **computer-assisted telephone interview (CATI)** simplifies the tasks of data collection and tabulation. The survey is displayed on interviewers' computer screens, allowing the interviewer to directly input responses during the interview. This not only eliminates the need to create hard copy but also allows the researcher immediate access to all entered data. The benefits of CATI are similar to those of computer-assisted personal interviewing, except that graphics and product demonstrations cannot be done by telephone. Many companies use CATI extensively for data collection. Consider a few of the following examples:

- Humanvoice, Inc., used CATI to ask attitudinal questions about various Brigham Young University (BYU) publications conducted among BYU alumni.[12]

- Gallup Poll conducts most interviews from regional interviewing centers around the country using CATI, which displays the survey questions on a computer monitor and allows questionnaires to be tailored to specific responses given by the individual being interviewed.[13]

- At Nielsen Media Research, CATI is operated on a 24 hour, seven-day schedule in order to provide clients with fast, dependable service.[14]

- Venture Data bases its entire business on CATI, since it conducts all of its data collection by using CATI technology. The company claims that its data is of high quality since:[15]

  1. Every interviewer is monitored and evaluated during every shift.
  2. All interviewers have formal two-day training.
  3. There is a 1 to 5 supervisor-to-interviewer ratio.
  4. A supervision staff member validates 15% of all work.

While CATI is often effective for collecting survey data, one of its major shortcomings involves the requirements made of the respondent group and the study's fielding requirements. One marketing research company described these problems as follows:

> The respondents in this particular sample travel frequently and are usually away from their office location and 'assigned' a telephone number. Because of the constant travel, evening/weekend interviewing is not possible with this audience. Our field service must place an average of 16 calls before actually reaching each of these respondents. Not only do these additional attempts significantly add to the field time and cost of the study, they also detract from the overall response rate. When the respondents are at least contacted during the workday, gaining participation is extremely challenging due to their hectic and busy schedules. This negatively impacts data quality. Because of their mobility, this respondent group relies heavily on email and web-based information. They are extremely comfortable using the Internet and prefer email in lieu of the telephone as a primary method of communication.

computer-assisted telephone interview (CATI) A telephone interview in which the questions are displayed in front of the interviewer on the computer screen and the interviewer inputs responses into the computer during the interview.

Surveys on Cell Phones

The immense popularity of cell phones has given rise to a new data collection technique that allows researchers to study consumer behaviors in the shopping and consumption environment. A text-based wireless survey can be retrieved on an Internet-enabled cell phone screen by the respondent while she is actually in the shopping location. She then text-messages her answers via the cell phone dial pad. A voice-based wireless survey allows the respondent to listen to the questions and speak her answers into the cell phone. The speed with which the questions and answers are processed and analyzed gives market researchers access to something heretofore impossible to attain—instant feedback on what, when, where and why consumers buy.

Source: Ju Long, Andrew B. Whinston, Kerem Tomak, "Calling All Customers", *Marketing Research* 14, no. 3, (Fall 2002): 28–34.

Consequently, interviewers encounter even more resistance when attempting a telephone survey.[16]

Fully Automated Telephone Interview (FATI)

In a **fully automated telephone interview (FATI),** an automated voice asks respondents questions over the telephone. Respondents enter their replies using keys on their touch-tone telephones. The advantages and disadvantages are similar to those associated with computer-assisted telephone interviewing, except the computer does not use respondent-generated words in questions throughout the survey. FATI is best suited for short, simple surveys that can be completed in ten minutes or less, use structured questions for the most part, and do not include any open-ended questions. FATI has been employed in several contexts, including:

> **fully automated telephone interview (FATI)** An interview in which an automated voice asks questions over the telephone and respondents enter their replies using keys on their touch-tone telephones.

- *Customer satisfaction measurement.* A national survey organization used a FATI system to measure customer satisfaction.
- *Service quality monitoring and troubleshooting.* A service company, such as a repair shop, can give recent customers a toll-free number to call to rate their experiences with the service and personnel and to describe problems they experienced.
- *Election-day polls.* FATI polls have consistently predicted the outcomes of political elections.
- *Product/warranty registration.* Computer hardware and software manufacturers give customers the option of registering their products by making a toll-free telephone call. During the registration, a FATI system collects warranty data, purchaser demographics, reasons for selecting the brand, and other strategic information for marketing databases.
- *In-home product tests.* After consumers try the prototype of a new product, they call a toll-free number to be interviewed by the FATI system.[17]

See Research Realities 6-2 for a description of text-based wireless surveys conducted on Internet-enabled cell phones.

6-2c Mail Surveys

Mail surveys are used extensively to gather research data. Walker Research, Inc., estimates that 10% of the 90 million telephone-owning households in the United States have participated in mail surveys.[18] Westat alone has conducted mail surveys of up to 90,000 respondents (e.g., private and public sector employees, nurses, teachers, military personnel) as well as smaller, complex surveys of businesses (e.g., manufacturers and utilities).[19] It is important to take necessary steps to improve response rates. Consider the following:

- The day of the week mail surveys are received by respondents doesn't affect response rate.

- Short questionnaires are preferred over long ones.
- The content of the survey is the most important factor in responding to them, followed by the sponsorship of the study and postage paid reply envelopes.[20]

The many advantages of mail surveys make this method popular. Some of the advantages are as follows:

- Although many might argue the point, when the enormous number of letters and packages distributed worldwide are considered, mail services are cost-efficient and effective. This is a powerful advantage over the traditional data collection methods we have discussed thus far. Of course, advancements in technology have made many computer-assisted survey techniques even less expensive than mail surveys.
- Mail surveys have no interviewer bias, a concern with personal interviews and personal interviews by telephone.
- Respondents remain anonymous, if they choose to do so, freeing them to be candid in their responses.
- Mail surveys can cover an extensive geographic area. Mail surveys can be sent anywhere in the world with little effort from the researcher—assuming, of course, no language barriers.

Mail surveys also have some disadvantages compared to other data collection methods:

- They often have inadequate response rates, rates that are lower than both telephone and face-to-face modes.[21]
- They take a considerable amount of time in generating the necessary information from respondents. Months may pass before the surveys are returned, and many don't come back at all. Therefore, researchers may have to send the surveys to respondents a second or third time.
- Mail surveys are inflexible; they cannot be changed once they are mailed.
- Researchers have little or no chance to ask follow-up questions. Thus researchers have little control over the data. It is important to note that mail surveys should be short because targeted respondents often ignore extensive surveys, unless they are offered some sort of compensation to make it worth their while. This issue will be discussed in the response-rate section of this chapter.

Mail surveys targeting either consumers or businesses can be implemented through one-time surveys, fax surveys, mail panels, and email surveys.

One-Time Mail Surveys

When marketing researchers have no need to continuously gather information about a particular issue, they send out **one-time mail surveys**—mail surveys that respondents will answer only once. While this type of study tends to be cost-efficient because it entails no transportation costs of people, the problem is getting recipients to respond. However, researchers can increase response rates considerably by following these guidelines:

1. *Create a survey that can be completed within a reasonable time.* What a "reasonable time" is can be determined by pretesting the survey. Pretesting of questionnaires will be discussed in Chapter 8.

2. *Provide a benefit to respondents.* People by nature want to know "What's in it for me?" Offering some financial incentives or supplying a summary of the results can motivate people to complete and return the survey. Some researchers place a dollar bill along with the survey in an envelope. The dollar incentive generates a response rate averaging 31% over the nonincentive response rate.[22]

3. *Send repeated follow-up mailings* to nonrespondents to improve response rates.

4. If the survey is targeted at businesses, it's a good idea to *send a copy of the survey to upper-level executives* who will not be completing the surveys so that they can "look it over." Once executives become vested in the survey development process, then they will often encourage their employees to fill out the survey. Also, if their approval of the survey can be gotten, then their names should be included in the cover letter to targeted respondents (i.e., employees) who will be expected to complete the survey. This often raises response rates.

one-time mail survey Mail surveys sent to respondents only once because the research issue doesn't require continuous information gathering.

Fax Surveys

Most businesses have facsimile machines or access to one. Some marketing researchers gather data by simply faxing businesses short surveys and requesting a prompt response. Computer-generated fax surveys are becoming common because a researcher's computer can automatically dial the telephone numbers of potential respondents' fax machines and electronically send a survey. Respondents simply provide written responses on the paper copies and fax or mail the completed survey back to the researcher.

The major advantages of fax surveys are their ease of implementation, quick response time, high response rate, and low cost. It does not take many resources to fax surveys to numerous companies. Furthermore, a study has found that fax surveys obtained information similar to that of mail surveys, but the faxed responses were returned more quickly and in greater numbers than the mail surveys.[23]

Similar to mail surveys, the major disadvantages of fax surveys are the impersonal nature of faxes and the inability to control who completes the survey. To motivate individuals to complete faxed surveys, researchers often offer some type of benefit, such as a summary of the study results, or a nominal financial compensation.

Mail Panels

While most mail surveys are administered only once, mail panels are often used to gather information continuously from the same respondents. **Mail panels** are composed of a consistent set of respondents who are questioned from time to time about marketing-related issues. For example, Nielsen Marketing Research has a panel of 40,000 households from which it collects demographic and buying-habits data.[24] Nielsen and other research firms often use an omnibus survey through the mail instead of conducting personal interviews.

mail panel A consistent set of respondents who are questioned from time to time about marketing-related issues.

Like the interview version, an *omnibus mail survey* uses a consistent panel of respondents and different questions for each survey. Typically, the research methodology is the same each time the surveys are sent to each panel member. Only the question content changes.

Before determining who will be on the panel, researchers gather a variety of demographic information from each potential panel member to ensure that their characteristics match the needs of the company. Selected panelists are usually modestly compensated for their ongoing participation in the studies. A manager of a consulting firm stated, "They pay these people something like $100 a year, and they go to them with ideas, new products, new fabrics, and get their opinions. They use these consumers as a sounding board, and essentially treat them like part of the staff."[25]

Email Surveys

Researchers can send email surveys to individuals who use email—which is the majority of the population. Respondents key in their answers and send an email back. Another way to use this survey method is to use interactive email, in which researchers send potential respondents email asking them to access an address that contains an interactive survey. Respondents access the survey—either via a hot link or by "cutting and pasting" the web address—and enter their answers.

Email surveys are significantly faster to administer and cost less than traditional mail surveys. The popularity of email surveys is partially due to people's heavy reliance on emails in daily life. According to a recent survey of 4,012 respondents at least 18 years old in the 20 largest U.S. cities, Americans are so hooked on email that 41% of survey respondents check their email inbox right after getting out of bed in the morning; some check for messages in the bathroom, in church, and while driving. On average, an email user in the U.S. has two or three email accounts and spends about an hour every day reading, sending, and replying to messages.[26]

Unfortunately, the usefulness of email survey research is waning. First, the increasing use of "junk email" (i.e., abundance of email messages soliciting sales of products and services) makes the response rate of email surveys extremely low. Second, the growing popularity of online surveys makes email surveys less attractive. Third, not everybody has a computer or uses email—especially in developing countries—limiting its application as a survey tool.

6-2d Online Surveys

online survey A survey placed directly on a Web site; respondents are invited to complete the entire form online.

Online surveys are administered by placing a survey directly on a Web site and inviting respondents to complete the entire form. Often times there are incentives to complete a survey. For example, Greenfield Online offers cash prizes ranging from $5 to $2,000 to fill out marketing research surveys online.[27] Once the survey is filled out, it goes directly to an analysis package, and results are typically immediately generated.

The benefits of online surveys are obvious. First, the process is very fast. Normally respondents complete the surveys by simply clicking the mouse. Second, it is cost-effective. Cost is minimal since stamps, envelopes, letterhead, and return postage are not required. Also, costs are not much different between sending 1,000 questionnaires and sending 100,000.

Third, online surveying eliminates coding errors and interviewer bias because there is no need for data entry or interviews, and responses are collected automatically. Fourth, respondents may feel more comfortable in answering sensitive questions with their anonymity ensured.[28]

One of the greatest challenges to all researchers conducting online surveys is to obtain an acceptable response rate. Many factors can influence response rates, including incentives, topic of the study, who is conducting the study, and respondent characteristics. Companies must carefully consider these factors when conducting online surveys.

6-3 Selecting a Data Collection Method

The key characteristics of survey methods are summarized in Exhibit 6-2. Researchers must choose from the major primary data collection methods to learn more about their target markets. In many cases, companies use a combination of these methods. For example, some researchers initially interview individuals and then ask them to complete and return a mail survey.

EXHIBIT 6-2	Key Characteristics of Major Survey Methods			
Characteristics	Personal Interview	Telephone	Mail	Online
Cost	High	Moderate	Low	Low
Speed of collection	Slow to moderate	Fast	Very slow	Fast
Response rate	High	Moderate	Low	Low
Flexibility	High	Moderate	Low	Moderate
Area coverage	Narrow	Wide	Wide	Wide
Potential interviewer bias	High	Moderate to high	None	None
Data control	High	Moderate	Low	Low
Anonymity of respondent	Low	Moderate	High	High
Amount of possible data	A lot	Moderate	Moderate	Moderate

Every survey project has constraints. These constraints arise from available resources, characteristics of the target market, characteristics of the survey, and the desired quality of the data. Researchers must select a data collection method that can be implemented within these constraints. Common constraints that researchers must consider in choosing a data collection method are presented here.

6-3a Available Resources

Budget

Companies do not have unlimited funds. They must make choices about how to allocate their resources. When companies conduct marketing research, they routinely set limits on the amount of money that can be spent gathering data. Researchers, then, must select a collection method that can be implemented within the budget. For example, small companies that want to sell their products abroad may not be able to afford the expense of conducting personal interviews in several foreign markets. They will choose less expensive methods, like mail surveys or computer-assisted surveys.

Time Availability

Typically, companies want information in a hurry. In these cases, mail surveys are not fast enough. Researchers thus select more immediate methods, such as telephone surveys or computer-assisted surveys. As communication technology continues to advance, computer-assisted surveys will become increasingly popular.

Communication Vehicle Availability

While telephones and computers are widely available in developed countries, they are not so common in developing countries. Therefore, personal interviews or perhaps mail surveys may be more appropriate choices. As a general rule, the more developed a country, the more technology available in households and businesses for marketing researchers to use to gather information.

6-3b Characteristics of the Target Market

The demographic composition of the target market significantly impacts the choice of data collection method. Important concerns such as literacy level and rate, age, income, language proficiency, and writing skills all play vital roles in the selection. If the target population has low literacy rates, personal interviews or telephone surveys will be more successful than written surveys.

6-3c Characteristics of the Survey

Need for Demonstration

When information needs to be gathered on products that are new, technologically complex, or unknown to target groups, product demonstrations may be necessary. Describing the product alone may not suffice. However, computers can display product images, so computer-assisted methods may be used, and, of course, personal interviews in which the interviewer can demonstrate the product will meet this need.

Topic Sensitivity

When researchers ask respondents to reveal information about themselves or their company, researchers must consider the sensitivity of the questions. For example, potentially embarrassing or confidential survey information should be collected with a method that allows respondents to hide their identity. Mail surveys and, to a lesser extent, telephone surveys can guarantee anonymity.

Survey Length

As a general rule, the longer the survey, the less likely it is to be completed and returned. Likewise, the more input asked from respondents, the less likely they are to participate. Researchers must consider respondents' tolerance toward completing long versus short surveys before deciding on which data collection method to use. For example, most people don't want to be disturbed at home to respond to lengthy questionnaires. This forces most survey efforts directed at respondents' homes to be succinct, especially if they are telephone surveys.

Question Format

The type of questions asked also impacts the choice of method. Open-ended questions are usually best administered through some form of personal interview because researchers can ask additional questions if necessary. If certain questions require elaboration, mail surveys are not the desirable vehicle.

6-3d Desired Quality of the Data

Desired Sampling Precision

The desired level of sampling accuracy is an important consideration when choosing a data collection method. A client or researcher might require that a certain degree of accuracy be achieved. While all research efforts should strive for a totally accurate sample, reality dictates that a compromise must be reached between sampling accuracy and cost. For example, while door-to-door and office interviews can provide highly accurate results, they may not be the most feasible collection method if they require researchers to travel thousands of miles to sample targeted individuals.

Desired Response Rate

While clients don't always indicate what response rate they want to see achieved, response rate is an important consideration. For example, a statistically significant response rate increases the likelihood that a sample is representative of its population. And different data collection methods give very different response rates; for example, personal interviews have higher response rates than mail and telephone surveys. Generalizations on the response rates for the different collection methods are difficult, since researchers can do various things to improve response rate. Consider Example 6-1.

Example 6-1

A study of 15 representative mail surveys looked into the issue of response rate. Respondents ranged from consumers at home to managers at Fortune 500 companies. The study revealed five major influences on response rates: contact, incentives, reward, length, and prose. The results of the study were summarized as follows:

> The hypothetical response rate for mail surveys is 36%; that is, if you were able to
> send out a zero-length survey to a named respondent with first-class postage, etc.,

you could anticipate a response rate of 36%. Getting back to the real world, we can note that this 36% will be reduced by 0.85% for every minute it takes a respondent to fill out the survey. Thus, a 10-minute survey should result in a 27.5% response rate.

If you can identify respondents before sending the survey, the rates should increase to 33.7%, and if you can secure their cooperation it should rise to nearly 40%. However, if you have to include a page of descriptive prose along with the survey, your anticipated response rate plummets from 40% to around 21%.

Including a small gift with this survey should bring the response rate back to 34.5%, and if your client insists on a 50% response rate, you would have to enclose (or promise) a $10 bill, assuming now that the survey is proprietary and that you cannot send respondents a summary of results.[29]

Consider a few more studies regarding ways to improve response rates:

- In India, 600 randomly selected companies were systematically assigned to one of four groups, with a mailing size of 150 for each group. The four groups were the dollar-incentive group, the prize-giveaway group, the joint-effects group, and a control group. The results demonstrate that the prize-giveaway type of incentive yields a response rate of 25%, which is significantly higher than the 7% rate for the joint-effects and the control groups.[30]

- A study found that most shopping malls are plagued by noise and confusion, and the refusal rate can be as high as 70%.[31]

- A two-stage telephone interview approach was used to gather data about a "no hassles" buying approach at automobile dealerships. The first step was to contact potential respondents and ask their permission to be interviewed. The second step was the actual interview by telephone. Of 209 subjects, 189 agreed to participate (80%) and 151 completed interviews (72%).[32]

- Based on 1,300 direct mail campaigns, Direct Mail Information Service reported that consumer direct mail posts an average response of 8%, which is twice that of the average response to business mail. The low business-mailing response rates were attributed to poor-quality lists and information.

- A recent study of automobile dealerships using mail surveys found that respondent anonymity and survey sponsorship make a difference in response rates. When respondents were guaranteed anonymity, 73% of surveys were returned. In a university-sponsored study, 84% of the surveys were returned, and 67% of commercial research firm-sponsored surveys were returned.[33]

The problem is that there are many strategies for obtaining high response rates, but each strategy has associated costs. The client and researcher must decide what level of response rate is desired for the cost and what level of confidence in the results can be expected from the response rate.[34]

Decision Time!

As a marketing manager, you want to accomplish tasks as efficiently and effectively as possible. Several computer-assisted data collection methods exist to help you do so. New techniques are continuously being invented to speed up the accuracy and timeliness of data collection. In many cases, the human "collector" is replaced by a mechanical "collector." How important do you believe the human collector is in terms of data collection? Do you believe it is possible for humans to eventually be totally replaced by high-tech devices?

Net Impact

Researchers are realizing the enormous possibilities for collecting data on the Internet. Traditionally, companies devoted considerable resources to conducting personal interviews, telephone interviews, and mail surveys. More recently, online surveys have continued to increase in popularity because of their low cost, wide reach, and timeliness. But in many countries, especially developing countries, Internet surveys tend to obtain biased information when consumer surveys are conducted because there are still so many people who do not have computers at home. Bias is less of a problem in business-to-business surveys.

On the Lighter Side—A Frightening Study

A Gallup poll found that 32% of all adult Americans believe in ghosts. Nineteen percent aren't so sure of their existence, while 48% stated that there is no such thing as ghosts. The same poll revealed that 37% of Americans believe houses can be haunted, 16% weren't sure, and 46% said that it's not possible for houses to be haunted. This suggests that 5% of those polled believe that other worldly domestic activity can occur, even though ghosts aren't the culprits. A political perspective confirms party allegiance. 42% of liberals say that ghosts exist, while only 25% of conservatives believe in their existence. Moderates rest in between, as expected, at 35%.

Source: Lester, Haines, "One third of Americans believe in ghosts," *The Register* (July 14, 2005); http://www.theregister.co.uk/2005/07/14/us_ghost_survey/, accessed October 7, 2005.

Chapter Summary

Gathering data by survey can be both time-consuming and costly. Therefore, care must be taken in deciding which method maximizes the use of resources, given the requirements of the survey. The three primary data collection methods are personal interviews, telephone surveys, and mail surveys. Personal interviews involve face-to-face communication between an interviewer and a respondent. They may be carried out through door-to-door interviews, office interviews, mall-intercept surveys, or computer-assisted methods.

Telephone surveys involve either direct or indirect communication between researcher and respondent. The major methods of gathering information by telephone include telephone interviews, computer-assisted telephone interviewing, and fully automated telephone interviewing. Mail surveys have reasonable costs but suffer from low response rates. They can be implemented through one-time surveys, fax surveys, mail panels, and electronic mail.

The data collection method chosen must conform to a number of constraints, including budget allocation, time availability, communication vehicle availability, characteristics of the target market, the need for demonstration, topic sensitivity, survey length, question format, desired sampling precision, and desired response rate.

Review Questions

1. What is the difference between CATI, CASI, and FASI?

2. How do computers facilitate the task of data collection?

3. What is an omnibus survey?

4. What is random-digit dialing (RDD) used for? Is it effective in helping to gather data? What problems are associated with RDD? What alternatives exist to RDD?

5. What are the major advantages and disadvantages associated with personal, telephone, and mail surveys?

6. What can be done to improve a survey's response rate?

Practice Quiz

Note: You can find the correct answers to these questions by taking the quiz and then submitting your answers in the Online Edition. The program will automatically score your submission. If you miss a question, the program will provide the correct answer, a rationale for the answer, and the section number in the chapter where the topic is discussed.

1. Questions on an omnibus survey are supplied by several clients so the questions may not be consistent in content or format.
   a. True
   b. False

2. Systematic random-digit dialing does not allow researchers to limit geographic coverage of the survey to targeted areas.
   a. True
   b. False

3. Interactive voice response technology enables information to be collected by a human interviewer and respondents to use their touch-tone telephones to record their responses.
   a. True
   b. False

4. The major limitation of a mail survey is low response rate.
   a. True
   b. False

5. Mail panels can be used to gather information continuously from different respondents.
   a. True
   b. False

6. Which of the following choices is *not* an advantage of personal interviews?
   a. Data control is high.
   b. Personal interviews tend to be inexpensive.
   c. The interviewer can go beyond the original interview questions.
   d. The interviewer has considerable flexibility during the interview.
   e. It is possible to collect a lot of information.

7. Which of the following is *not* a way to increase the response rate of a mail survey?
   a. Make the survey short.
   b. Offer incentives.
   c. Send follow-up mailings.
   d. Use a mail panel.
   e. Send a detailed cover letter to ask for participation.

8. Which of the following is *not* a personal interview data collection method?
   a. Door-to-door
   b. Mall intercept
   c. Office interview
   d. Omnibus
   e. None of the above

9. If we want to survey consumers' evaluations of a new fragrance, what is the best survey method?
   a. Personal interview
   b. Telephone interview
   c. Mail survey
   d. Online survey
   e. Fax survey

10. _____ are *not* a major way to gather information via telephone lines.
    a. Computer-assisted telephone interviews
    b. Fully automated telephone interviews
    c. Traditional telephone interviews
    d. Fax surveys
    e. All of the above are major ways to gather information via telephone lines.

Thinking Critically

1. The only shortcoming cited in the text when using CAPI is that it doesn't allow respondents to choose their own schedule for completing the survey. What do you believe may be some other problems associated with this research method?

2. You are hired by a bank to gather data about its consumers' level of satisfaction with their new online banking system. How will you obtain this data?

3. The greatest problem marketing researchers have when conducting mail surveys is to get respondents to return the completed surveys. Several methods were discussed to improve response rates. Which one do you feel is the most effective? Why? What does it depend on?

4. Would you be willing to participate on a mail panel? Why or why not?

5. Several reasons were given in the chapter for selecting a data collection method, such as budget allocation, time availability, demographic composition of targeted respondents, and so on. Reread section 6-3 and try to come up with two more reasons why you might use a particular data collection method.

Net Exercises

1. Synthesis Technology, Assessment & Research (STAR) has a rare combination of leading technology and human resource expertise. It can administer telephone, web, and fax surveys using its automated survey process. It claims to be among the first companies to offer automated surveys via the phone. Furthermore, it claims to be the first to integrate telephone technology and email. Visit STAR's Web site at http://rapidsurvey.com/ and try its sample survey. The site will give you a telephone number to dial for a web address to visit to take the sample survey. They'll also send you sample reports.

2. WebSurveyor provides online survey services that enable people to easily design their own online surveys and collect real-time data. Visit its Web site at http://www.websurveyor.com/ and try to design your own online survey, get some responses, and check out the result you immediately get!

Experiencing Marketing Research

1. Visit as many restaurants as necessary to obtain five different surveys or "comment cards" that management provides customers in order to determine customer satisfaction with service and food selections. List for each of the surveys any possible problems caused by improper questionnaire design.

2. A marketing research company needs to conduct a study of consumer preferences of popular soft drinks. The questionnaire has 98 questions. The survey is to be completed in 3 weeks. Which survey method would you recommend for this project?

Case 6-1

Cool Teenagers Are a Hot Market

Adults often think teenagers must come from Jupiter. They wear clothes with holes in them, their pants hang on by a miracle, they dye their hair blue and green, and they talk funny—"Funky diva to the max." Now what does that mean? Indeed, many parents fantasize about skipping these teenage years. Retailers, on the other hand, like teenagers. There are six major reasons why the teen market is so attractive:

1. Teens have real spending power. Their spending is mind-boggling—nearly $100 billion a year. When these figures include the family money that teens dispense, teens spend an amount equal to about half of the U.S. defense budget. Teenage boys spend an average of $68 a week, and girls an average of $65.

2. Teens spend family money. Most teens live in families with two working parents or a single parent, so they have assumed a greater responsibility for household shopping than did teens in the past. More than half of teenage girls and more than one-third of teenage boys do some food shopping each week for their families.

3. Teens influence household spending. Whenever teens accompany their parents to the store, their parents usually let them add something to the cart. Also, teens influence their parents even when they are not with them by encouraging them to buy preferred brands. Furthermore, their parents purchase birthday and holiday gifts for them based on the teens' preferences.

4. Teens set trends. They influence trends both for their peers and for the general population. Blue jeans and rock music are classic examples.

5. Teens are future spenders. Forward-thinking companies actively market adult brands to teens. For example, condom manufacturer Trojan advertises on national television promoting safe sex.

6. Finally, teens are a growing market. In 2002, there were more than 32 million teenagers in the United States, and this number will swell to 35 million by the year 2010. To appeal to this growing market, marketers must understand it. A market study group asked teens the following question: "Thinking about brands of products, what makes a brand a cool brand?" Two-thirds of respondents cited quality as being cool. After quality, they felt that products must be "for people my age." To identify the brands teens believe are coolest, the study group asked: "Thinking about brand names of clothes, foods, drinks, shoes, cosmetics, video games, cars, audio/video products, etc., which are the three coolest brands?" Over 200 brands were mentioned, but the top five were Nike, Guess, Levi's, Gap, and Sega.

Since teens are tomorrow's adults, companies are trying to develop a long-lasting relationship with this group. But teen brand loyalty appears to be product-specific. Respondents were given a list of 20 categories and asked: "Thinking about the last three times you bought (or your parents bought for you) this product, how many times was it the same brand?" With the exception of camera film, the top ten categories were all health-and-beauty aids. It seems that the more intimate the category, the less teens are willing to risk trying a new brand, if they are satisfied with the brand they are using.

A tremendous amount of marketing research about the teen market has already been done, but there is still a lot to learn. Older teens, for example, dislike being called "teenagers." Younger teens embrace the term—12- to 15-year-olds have waited years to be teenagers. Now they want somebody to notice. In contrast, older teens feel the 'teen' label refers to somebody much younger than themselves.

Sources: Lee Clifford, "Sells like teen spirit (not)," *Fortune* 142, no. 2 (July 10, 2000): 242; Peter Zollo, "Talking to teens," *American Demographics* 17, no. 11 (November, 1995): 22–28; Susie Stephenson, "Tackling teens," *Restaurant & Institutions* 107, no. 4 (February 15, 1997): 57(3); DataMonitor, "Tween & teen trends," http://www.mindbranch.com/products/R313-8104.html, January 2005; Packaged Facts, "U.S. teens market," http://www.mindbranch.com/products/R567-0063.html, August 2002.

Case Questions

1. You are a marketing researcher at a large apparel company that manufactures many different types of garments. Your management has decided to enter the teenage market and begin manufacturing blue jeans. You have been assigned to determine what teenagers look for when they purchase blue jeans. Which primary data collection technique will you use? Why?

2. Do you feel that the questions that were used to inquire about "what makes a brand a cool brand" and "which are the three coolest brands" are good questions for the teen market? If yes, why? If not, what alternative questions might you ask?

Case 6-2

Delta's Mileage Plan—Sky High or Free Fall in Customer Satisfaction?

The U.S. airline industry is in a tailspin these days. Most major airlines are, in fact, in financial turmoil, protected only by Chapter 11. The industry has lost $30 billion since 2000, and fuel costs are soaring.

While airline experts tout the importance of customer satisfaction and retention, it is their interiors and service improvements that have often been promoted to targeted consumers—even as they reduce wages and personnel.

Atlanta-based Delta Airlines is hoping its SkyMiles frequent flier program will boost customer satisfaction without spending too much. "The streamlining of the SkyMiles elite qualification process and the consolidation or reduction of travel service fees are part of Delta's commitment to improve the travel experience, and also to produce significant savings through simpler, more efficient ways of doing business," says Jeff Robertson, director of SkyMiles—a part of Delta's marketing department. SkyMiles, launched in 1981 as Frequent Flyer Program (the name was changed to SkyMiles in 1995), is one of the airline industry's revered frequent flier programs. These early loyalty programs have been duplicated throughout the hospitality industry.

Delta's SkyMiles program is part of an overall initiative the company started in September 2004 to restructure the airline and realize $5 billion in annual cash savings by 2006.

The major carrier has made additional changes to improve their bottom line, including shifting its hub cities, simplifying and reducing air fares, adding service to its discount carrier Song, and eliminating 6,000 to 7,000 jobs.

In December 2004, Delta made the process to qualify for its elite status in the program much easier. The number of tiered categories of membership were reduced to three—Platinum, Gold, or Silver Medallion—and Delta now awards a full Medallion (or elite-qualification) mile for discounted economy fares and one and a half Medallion miles for full-price economy, business-class, and first-class fares. This is a 50% improvement over the past benefit levels, and it helps members of its SkyMiles program, especially those who take economy flights, achieve Medallion status quicker and puts Platinum Medallion status within reach of more customers. (United Air Lines, Continental Airlines, and American Airlines also offer 150% of miles for various price classes of tickets, although Continental and American, for example, also offer 50% awards on deeply discounted trips.)

Delta made another significant change to boost its loyalty program. Frequent fliers may apply unused travel credits to flights purchased for friends or family members. Its previous policy did not permit this kind of generosity; travel credits could only be traded for tickets for the originally ticketed passenger.

Source: Kelly Shermach, "Delta uses mileage plan to boost customer satisfaction," *Marketing News,* Vol. 39 Issue 8 (May 1, 2005): 21.

Case Questions

1. With the intense competition from United, Continental, and American Airlines, do you believe Delta's changes in its mileage plan to boost sales are going to be successful? Why or why not?

2. What research method would you recommend that Delta use to monitor the effects of its changes?

3. How would you conduct the research?

Notes

1. Research International, "Some things we've learned about global research," *Marketing News* 30, no. 7 (March 25, 1996): 7.

2. Devashis Mitra, "The venture capital industry in India," *Journal of Small Business Management* 38, no. 2 (April 2000): 67–79.

3. Richard Parker, "Problems in the marketing of spectator sports," *The Mid-Atlantic Journal of Business* 36, no. 1 (March 2000): 37–46.

4. NOP World Omnibus Surveys, "Random location omnibus," http://www.nopworld.com/products.asp?go=product& key=86, June 26, 2005.

5. Westat web page, "Survey data collection," http://www. westat.com/CAPABILITIES/survey_data_collection.cfm, June 23, 2005.

6. Humphrey Taylor, "The very different methods used to conduct telephone surveys of the public," *Journal of the Market Research Society* 39, no. 3 (July 1997): 421 (12).

7. Westat web page, "Telephone survey," http://www.westat.com/ CAPABILITIES/survey_data_collection.cfm, June 16, 2005.

8. Anonymous, "Canadians prefer paying by cash over credit," *Computer Dealer News* 16, no. 4 (February 25, 2000): 22.

9. Humphrey Taylor, "Horses for courses: how survey firms in different countries measure public opinion with very different methods," *Journal of the Market Research Society* 37, no. 3 (July 1995): 211–219.

10. David H. Wilson, Gary J. Starr, Anne W. Taylor, and Eleonora Dal Grande, "Random digit dialing and electronic white pages samples compared: Demographic profiles and health estimates," *Australian and New Zealand Journal of Public Health* 23, no. 6 (December 1999): 627–633; Anne W. Taylor, David H. Wilson, and Melanie Wakefield, "Differences in health estimates using telephone and door-to-door survey methods— a hypothetical exercise," *Australian and New Zealand Journal of Public Health* 22, no. 2 (April 1998): 223–226.

11. Okokok Web site, "2005 Latin America telecoms, mobile and broadband overviews," http://www.okokok.com.cn/ pdayres/Agency_show.asp?ArticleID=4870, June 26, 2005.

12. Karl G. Feld, "Using E-Interviewers with online surveys," *2000 EXPLOR Forum,* American Marketing Association and University of Wisconsin-Madison, November 16–17, 2000.

13. Gallup Web site, http://www.gallup.com/, June 27, 2005.

14. Nielsen Media Research, "Company History, Dunedin—The Nerve Center," http://www.nielsenmedia.com/history.html, June 19, 2005.

15. Venture Data web page, "Quality," http://www.venturedata. com/pages/brochure1.html, June 26, 2005.

16. Bill Stone, "The conversion from telephone to web e-interviewing: a case history," *2000 EXPLOR Forum,* American Marketing Association and University of Wisconsin-Madison, November 16–17, 2000.

17. Peter J. DePaulo and Rick Weitzer, "Interactive phone technology delivers survey data quickly," *Marketing News* 28, no. 12 (June 6, 1994): H33–H34.

18. Henry C. K. Chen, "Direction, magnitude and implications of non-response bias in mail surveys," *Journal of the Market Research Society* 38, no. 3 (July, 1996): 267(10).

19. Westat web Page, "Telephone survey," http://www.westat.com/ CAPABILITIES/survey_data_collection.cfm, June 16, 2005.

20. Thomas V. Greer, Nuchai Chuchinprakam, and Sudhindra Seshadri, "Likelihood of participating in mail survey research: Business respondents' perspective," *Industrial Marketing Management* 29, no. 2 (March 2000): 97–119.

21. Paul D. Larson, "A Note on Mail Surveys and Response Rates in Logistics Research," *Journal of Business Logistics* 26, no. 2, (2005): 211–222.

22. Wesley J. Erwin, Lori A. Wheelwright, "Improving Mail Survey Response Rates Through the Use of a Monetary Incentive," *Journal of Mental Health Counseling* 24, no. 3 (2002): 247–255.

23. Shawn R. McMahon, Martha Iwamoto, Mehran S. Massoudi, Hussain R. Yusuf, John M. Stevenson, Felicita David, Susan Y. Chu, Larry K. Pickering, "Comparison of E-Mail, Fax, and Postal Surveys of Pediatricians," *Pediatrics* 3, no. 4 (2003): 299–303.

24. Laura Klepacki, "Stores urged to use consumer panels," *Supermarket News* 44, no. 19 (May 9, 1994): 38.

25. Dianne M. Pogoda, "Consumer rapport: That 'critical' link," *WWD* 173, no. 63 (April 2, 1997): 11.

26. Juan Carlos Perez, "US residents addicted to e-mail," http:// www.infoworld.com/article/05/05/27/HNsurveyemail_1. html, IDG News Service, May 27, 2005.

27. Libby Estell, "Corporate spotlight: Greenfield online," *Incentive* 174, no. 2 (February 2000): 26–27.

28. Richard Kottler, "Eight tips offer best practices for online MR," *Marketing News* 39, no. 6 (April 1, 2004): 24–25.

29. Bill Farrell and Tom Elken, "Adjust five variables for better mail surveys,"*Marketing News* 28, no. 18 (August 29, 1994): 20. Reprinted with permission from *Marketing News,* published by the American Marketing Association, August 29, 1994 (vol. 28).

30. Madhukar G. Angur and Rajan Nataraajan, "Do source of mailing and monetary incentives matter in international industrial mail surveys?" *Industrial Marketing Management* 24, no. 5 (October 1995): 351(7).

31. P. H. Bloch, N. M. Ridgway, and S. A. Dawson, "The shopping mall as consumer habit," *Journal of Retailing* 70 (Spring 1994): 23–42.

32. Sukgoo Pak and Louis G. Pol, "Two-stage data collection for retail stores," *International Journal of Retail & Distribution Management* 23, no. 7 (July 1995): 24(7).

33. A. J. Faria and John R. Dickinson, "The effect of reassured anonymity and sponsor on mail survey response rate and speed with a business population," *Journal of Business & Industrial Marketing* 11, no. 1 (Winter 1996): 66(11).

34. Wilson Research Group, "Response rates," http://www. wilsonresearch.com/main/process.html, June 23, 2005.

Measurement and Scaling

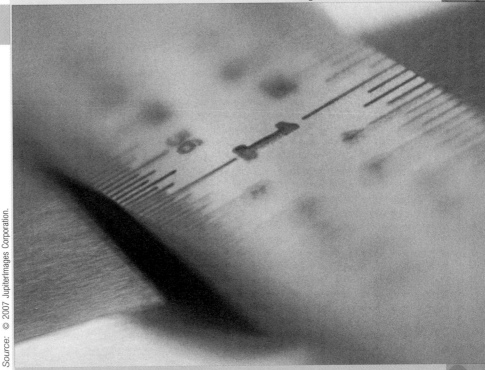

Chapter Seven

Source: © 2007 JupiterImages Corporation.

Key Terms

alternative-forms reliability (p. 174)

attitude (p. 164)

balanced scale (p. 172)

coefficient alpha (p. 175)

comparative rating scale (p. 164)

constant-sum scale (p. 166)

content or face validity (p. 175)

criterion-related validity (p. 176)

funny-faces scale (p. 173)

graphic rating scale (p. 168)

halo effect (p. 170)

internal-consistency reliability (p. 175)

interval scale (p. 161)

itemized rating scale (p. 168)

Likert scale (p. 168)

measurement (p. 159)

measurement error (p. 173)

nominal scale (p. 160)

noncomparative rating scale (p. 164)

ordinal scale (p. 160)

paired comparison scale (p. 164)

Q-sort scale (p. 167)

random error (p. 174)

rank-order scale (p. 165)

ratio scale (p. 162)

reliability (p. 174)

scale (p. 160)

semantic differential scale (p. 170)

split-half technique (p. 175)

Stapel scale (p. 171)

systematic error (p. 173)

test-retest reliability (p. 174)

unbalanced scale (p. 172)

validity (p. 175)

Learning Objectives

After studying this chapter, you will be able to:

- Identify and discuss the four measurement scales.
- Identify and discuss two basic classifications of attitude measurement scales.
- Describe and compare several comparative and noncomparative rating scales.
- Discuss the factors to consider in scale development.

- Explain reliability and validity and distinguish between them.
- Discuss the major approaches to reliability and validity assessment.
- Explain the relationship between reliability and validity.

GET THIS

What's in a Name: It's Time to Change Your Attitude about Private Brands

What do you think of when you hear the names Lexus, Mercedes Benz, Rolex, Ralph Lauren, Gucci, Armani, and Rolls-Royce? High quality, expensive, and prestigious, right? Now consider the more commonplace products made by Johnson & Johnson, Procter & Gamble, Kellogg's, Ralston-Purina, and Nestle. Are your attitudes as favorable toward instant coffees that lack the familiar Nescafe, Folgers, and Maxwell House brand names? For the past 50 years, manufacturers have been the principal builders of branded consumer products. They have done this through carefully constructed strategies that build brand equity. The fortunes of manufacturers increased and decreased based on their ability to compete with other manufacturers by differentiating their brands in the minds of consumers. Over the past 5 to 10 years, however, a new brand-building process has emerged. Retailers like CVS, Eckerd, RiteAid, Kroger, Albertsons, and Safeway are increasingly viewing their own portfolios of brands as viable engines designed to differentiate themselves from other chains, build a sustainable equity that they own, and create proprietary category volume and profit.

The supermarket industry has been particularly dependent on the appeal of national labels. But times are changing. Many supermarkets now recognize the benefits of carrying lesser-known yet sensibly priced goods. Private-label brands, store brands, no-names, and generics are increasingly popular in certain consumer-goods categories such as milk, cheese, paper napkins, canned vegetables, juices, cereal, and pet food.

Store brands appeal because they offer consumers a lower price and another choice. It hasn't been easy for these less-heralded brands to compete with national brands because they don't use much promotion to sway consumers' attitudes.

To increase market share, private-label manufacturers are using the same strategies that brand manufacturers have used for decades. They are studying the shopping patterns of their loyal customers and using this information to appeal to consumers who aren't yet convinced of the benefits of their labels. The private-label people have come around to the idea that attitudes are learned and can therefore be changed. But how do they do this?

Store brands fill gaps in the marketplace. These are price niches—the quality and the look of national brands are matched, but the price is lower. Generic products—which occupy even lower price niches—don't attempt to match either the look of national brands or their quality, but instead offer consumers acceptable quality at extremely low prices. So where do store brands fit in? Apparently it's simple: you like the store, you'll buy their brand. Greg Starzynski, vice president of retail consumer services for ACNielsen North America, believes, "There are retailers who have a lot of equity with their customers. These retailers can build on their equity and transfer it to their products. It's almost a Good Housekeeping Seal of Approval. If customers support and trust their supermarket, they may be more likely to support and trust their supermarket's private labels." David Stewart, professor of marketing at the University of Southern California, Los Angeles, adds, "There are a number of things a retailer can do to build up his private-label brand. One of them is translating store loyalty into brand loyalty. In essence, the store becomes the product. But a retailer can also stress high quality by guaranteeing customer satisfaction through such things as buy-back programs, in which a customer will be refunded if the store brand does not live up to expectations."

Today, consumers can find just about every supermarket item in a store brand. In fact, national brands that have traditionally seemed unassailable, such as Coca-Cola, Pampers, and many ready-to-eat cereals, find themselves strongly challenged by private labels. In some categories, private labels outsell national brands. According to ACNielsen's latest International Private Label Yearbook, sales of private label across Europe in 2004 increased to record levels, with the biggest gains made by retail in Spain (29%) and Germany (35%). The market share of private label products in the United Kingdom hit a record high (41%), the highest in Europe.

Still, retailers have a lot of work to do—private labels are not consumers' first choices. According to the Food Marketing Institute of Washington, D.C., most consumers are willing to buy private labels some of the time but not all of the time.

Sources: Debby Garbato Stankevich, ''Sowing its wild oats,'' *Discount Merchandiser* 40, no. 1 (January 2000): 42; Private Label Manufacturers Association, ''Growth and success,'' http://www.plmainternational.com, June 19, 2005.

Now Ask Yourself

- What factors influence consumers' attitudes toward supermarket products?

- If you were going to measure consumers' attitudes toward supermarket products, how would you do it? What questions would you ask?

- How can the Internet be used to measure consumers' attitudes toward supermarket products?

The ''Get This'' feature suggests that retailers are changing consumers' attitudes about private brands. Attitudes are learned, so the retailers have a good chance of success if marketing efforts are carefully planned. But before marketers can change attitudes, they must understand them. In this chapter, you will learn what an attitude is and how to measure it. You will also learn how to determine whether the measurement is reliable and valid.

7-1 What Is ''Measurement''?

You are strolling through the middle aisle of your favorite supermarket, and a researcher asks you to taste a new pizza. You sample it, and the researcher asks you to complete a short survey. You are to rate the pizza using the following scale: (5) strongly agree, (4) agree, (3) neither agree nor disagree, (2) disagree, or (1) strongly disagree. Here are some sample statements from the survey:

1. The pizza tasted good.

2. The pizza was seasoned just right for me.

3. The size of the pizza was just right for me.

4. The crust of the product was too thick.

5. I intend to purchase this brand the next time I shop for pizza.

In this example, although a scale of ''strongly agree'' to ''strongly disagree'' is used to rate the pizza, the responses can be effectively analyzed only by assigning numbers to them. These numbers aid in *measuring* the responses. **Measurement** means assigning numbers to characteristics according to specified rules to reflect the quantity of the characteristics that test products possess. In our pizza survey, a ''5'' represents *strongly agree*, a ''4'' represents *agree*, and so on.

Let's say your friend asks you, ''How's the weather?'' How would you reply? Would you say, ''good'' or ''bad''? You might, but that response is not going to help your friend's knowledge about the weather, because how you define ''good'' and ''bad'' weather may be dramatically different from your friend's interpretation of how she defines weather. A more helpful reply to your friend would be to use characteristics of the weather as descriptors such as ''rainy,'' ''sunny,'' ''hot,'' ''cold,'' and so on. Marketing researchers use this same principle. They generally want to measure characteristics of test products, not the products themselves. In our earlier example, the researcher was measuring characteristics of the pizza—its size, taste, and crust quality. These elements are associated with or contained in the product—they are not the product itself.

Furthermore, although we can measure people's behaviors through direct observation and actual purchase behavior, we often measure their perceptions of their behaviors, not the behavior itself. For example, one survey asked 659 professional employees of an organization how much of their working day they spent

measurement Assigning numbers to characteristics according to specified rules to reflect the quantity of the characteristics that test products possess.

doing business over the telephone. One hundred stated that they spent more than half of their time talking on the telephone, and 23 replied that they spent more than 75% of their time on the telephone. However, company phone records revealed that phones were in use only about 30% of the time, and few were in use that much. This is a common pitfall of measurement: Actual behavior and perceptions of behavior can differ considerably.[1]

7-2 Measurement Scales

scale A measuring instrument designed to quantify and record the extent to which test products possess a characteristic.

Our goal in measurement is to accurately describe the extent to which the test product possesses a characteristic or attribute. To accomplish this, we need to use an appropriate scale. A **scale** is a measuring instrument designed to quantify and record the extent to which test products possess a characteristic. Numerous types of scales have been used to rate test subjects. However, there are only four basic scales: *nominal, ordinal, interval,* and *ratio.*

7-2a Nominal Scales

nominal scale A scale that uses names or numbers to label test topics or characteristics for identification, with no rank ordering implied.

A **nominal scale** uses names and numbers to label test topics or characteristics so they can be properly identified. Jerseys used on basketball, baseball, football, and hockey teams have numbers—that is, a nominal scale—simply to identify an athlete. Racecar drivers have numbers on their hoods and doors to identify them and their sponsors. Businesses place numbers on their offices to identify and differentiate one person's office from another. Nominal scales are used throughout the world. But the numbers assigned to products have no intrinsic meaning. NASCAR's Jeff Gordon (number 24) is not three times better than Dale Earnhardt, Jr. (number 8)—although Gordon fans may argue the point. Only two basic rules apply to nominal scales:

1. Different test responses must be assigned different numbers.
2. The same test responses should be assigned the same number.

Marketing researchers use nominal scales to identify characteristics of their test subjects—their target consumers—which could include gender, social class, race, religion, habits, traits, and physical location. The categories created by nominal scales must be mutually exclusive and collectively exhaustive. In other words, the scale must include every test subject or product in one and only one category for a particular characteristic. For example, if Procter & Gamble wants to examine whether laundry detergent purchasing habits differ by gender, all males could be assigned the number "1" and all females could be assigned number "2." Each test subject would fall into one of these categories (exhaustive) but never into more than one category (mutually exclusive).

7-2b Ordinal Scales

ordinal scale A scale with an implicit rank ordering, such as greater or smaller, higher or lower.

An **ordinal scale** is a scale that *orders* or ranks the test characteristic. Each ranking may be greater or smaller, higher or lower. That is, the numbers are arranged to indicate a "greater than" or "less than" position. Two college students who were asked to rank their activities at a shopping mall from favorite to least favorite (using an ordinal scale of 1 to 5) responded as shown in Exhibit 7-1.

EXHIBIT 7-1	An Example of an Ordinal Scale	
Activity	**Jack**	**Victoria**
Shopping	4	1
Socializing	5	3
Walking	1	2
Eating	2	4
Watching other people	3	5

According to Jack's responses, his favorite mall activity is walking (1); his least favorite activity is socializing (5). Victoria's favorite activity is shopping (1); her least favorite is watching other people (5). Ordinal-scale data also shows intermediate preferences. For Jack, this is watching other people (3); Victoria's is socializing (3).

Although ordinal-scale data can be valuable, ordinal scales have some shortcomings:

- *The distance between the rankings cannot be assumed to be equal.* In other words, Jack's scores indicate that he dislikes socializing more than shopping and Victoria's scores indicate that she dislikes watching other people more than eating. But we do not know whether the difference between Jack's dislikes (his 4 and 5) and Victoria's dislikes (her 4 and 5) is the same. The intensity may be quite different. Just because the difference between the numbers is the same does not mean that the degree of dislike is the same.

- *Median responses may not be compared between respondents.* While Jack's intermediate response (3) was watching other people and Victoria's was socializing (3), we cannot conclude that Jack enjoys watching other people to the same extent that Victoria enjoys socializing.

Marketers use ordinal scales to gather a variety of information, such as consumer taste preferences and comparisons involving pricing, packaging, promotion, quality, and performance rankings. Consider Example 7-1.

Example 7-1

A recent survey revealed the grocery shopping characteristics most important to customers. The top eight factors are, in order from the top: a clean, neat store; high-quality fruits and vegetables; high-quality meat; use-before/sell-by dates; money-saving specials; convenient store layout; fast checkout; and personal safety outside the store.[2]

7-2c Interval Scales

Interval scales rank characteristics using equal increments between ranking points to show relative amounts. They have no fixed zero point. Interval scales have the same characteristics as ordinal scales except that they can show relative differences in rankings. For example, ordinal scales do not assume that the distance between 1 and 2 is equal to the distance between 3 and 4. With interval scales, these distances are assumed to be the same. Furthermore, in interval scales, the distance between 1 and 3 is assumed to be equal to the distance between 2 and 4.

To understand the care that researchers take when drawing conclusions from interval scale data, consider Example 7-2.

interval scale A scale that ranks characteristics using equal increments between ranking points to show relative amounts and has no fixed zero point.

Example 7-2

We want to know how Jack, Victoria, Lawrence, and Alan perceive the advertisements for condoms on television. We ask them to respond to the statement "Advertising condoms on television is fine with me," using the following scale: 1 = strongly agree, 2 = agree, 3 = neither agree nor disagree, 4 = disagree, and 5 = strongly disagree. Their responses are shown in Exhibit 7-2.

EXHIBIT 7-2	An Example of an Interval Scale
Respondent	**Scores**
Jack	2
Victoria	1
Lawrence	4
Alan	5

| EXHIBIT 7-3 | Blockbuster Survey Using Interval Scales |

BLOCKBUSTER

HOW ARE WE DOING?

Each of us here at **BLOCKBUSTER®** is empowered, authorized and expected to take care of you. Please take a few moments and let us know how you were treated today.

	Very Dissatisfied			**Very Satisfied**	
	1	2	3	4	5
Overall, how would you rate your experience at BLOCKBUSTER® during your last visit?	❑	❑	❑	❑	❑
How satisfied were you with the service you received from the customer service representative?	❑	❑	❑	❑	❑
How satisfied were you with the time it took to checkout?	❑	❑	❑	❑	❑
How appealing was the store environment to you?	❑	❑	❑	❑	❑
How satisfied were you with the availability of the product you were looking for?	❑	❑	❑	❑	❑

Comments: _____   Date of Store Visit: _____

_____

_____

_____

_____

If you would like a response to your comments, please fill out the following:

Name: _____ Phone: (_____) _____

*Drop this postage paid card in the mail and your feedback
will go directly to the Regional Director of Operations for your area.*
BLOCKBUSTER name, design and related marks are trademarks of Blockbuster Inc. ©2000 Blockbuster Inc. All Rights Reserved.

92515

Source: BLOCKBUSTER name, design, and related marks are trademarks of Blockbuster, Inc. © 2001 Blockbuster, Inc. All rights reserved.

Although Jack's "2" response is "twice" that of Victoria's "1," we cannot conclude that Jack agrees with the statement twice as much as Victoria. Nor can we say that Alan disagrees five times as much as Victoria. What we can say is that the difference between Jack's and Victoria's scores is the same as the difference between Alan's and Lawrence's scores. This is because the numbers used in interval scales represent equal increments between ranking points. Understandably, such a scale has no meaningful zero points. Exhibit 7-3 shows a survey conducted by Blockbuster, Inc., which offers consumers the opportunity to rent their favorite videos. The "very dissatisfied–very satisfied" interval scaled questions are used for renters to provide feedback to the company about their rental experiences.

7-2d Ratio Scales

ratio scale An interval scale that has a true zero point and assumes equal intervals throughout.

Ratio scales resemble interval scales, except that they have meaningful zero points. The shortcoming created by the arbitrary zero points in interval scales does not exist with ratio scales. The zero point using a ratio scale is absolute. Therefore, we can state how much greater or smaller something is than something else. Because there is an absolute zero point, we can confidently use all arithmetic functions—addition, subtraction, multiplication, and division—to compare numbers. For example, if Alisa

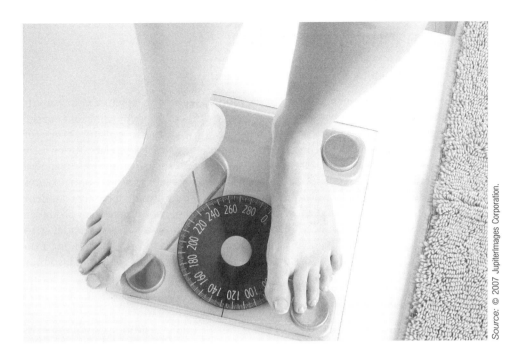

Source: © 2007 JupiterImages Corporation.

weighs 100 pounds, Bob weighs 200 pounds, and Carl weighs 300 pounds, we can draw the following conclusions:

• Bob weighs twice as much as Alisa.
• Carl weighs three times as much as Alisa.
• Carl weighs 100 pounds more than Bob.
• The difference between Alisa's and Bob's weights is equal to the difference between Bob's and Carl's weights.
• The weight of three Alisas would equal the weight of one Carl.

Marketers use ratio scales to describe company sales, profits, market share, advertising costs, number of competitors and customers, and so on. For example, if a firm's sales were $1 million in 2005 and $2 million in 2006, we can confidently conclude that sales doubled in one year. Without an absolute zero point, we cannot draw this conclusion. Ratio scales are the most commonly used scales in all aspects of business. Exhibit 7-4 summarizes the characteristics of ratio scales, as well as nominal, ordinal, and interval scales.

EXHIBIT 7-4	Characteristics of Measurement Scales			
	Categorical Scales		**Continuous Scales**	
Characteristic	**Nominal**	**Ordinal**	**Interval**	**Ratio**
Used for	Identity	Order	Equal increments	Comparing absolute magnitudes
Order	No	Yes	Yes	Yes
Equal Distance between Successive Numbers	No	No	Yes	Yes
Zero Point	No	Arbitrary	Arbitrary	Natural, absolute
Application Examples	Gender, social class	Preferences, comparisons	Attitudes, knowledge	Sales, market share, profit

7-3 Measuring Attitudes

7-3a What Is an "Attitude"?

attitude A learned tendency to respond in a consistently favorable or unfavorable manner toward something.

What do you think of when you see a Pontiac Bonneville? Do you picture your parents driving the family car, or do you imagine someone a bit younger enjoying some of the finer things in life? Well, D'Arcy Masius Benton & Bowles, the advertising agency for Pontiac, prefers that you think the latter. It is targeting males in their late 30s or early 40s who have maintained a "youthful" attitude. The advertising campaign's tagline is "Luxury with attitude." Today, "attitude" is used in a variety of ways. Pontiac seems to use it to describe both an individual's young outlook on life and a highly confident personality. But marketers want consumers to respond a specific way to their products, that is, to purchase their products. By definition, an **attitude** is a learned tendency to respond in a consistently favorable or unfavorable manner toward something. Two key words in this definition are *learned* and *consistently*. Attitudes are learned, so they can be changed; when responses are consistent, behavior is predictable.

7-3b Comparative and Noncomparative Scales

comparative rating scale A scale on which respondents compare one characteristic or attribute against a specified standard, according to some predetermined criterion.

Researchers use several methods to measure people's attitudes, comprised of *comparative* and *noncomparative rating scales.* In **comparative rating scales,** respondents compare one characteristic or attribute against a specified standard, according to some predetermined criterion. Since the standard of comparison is specified, researchers have a reference point. For example, if researchers want to know how Americans perceive the quality of Mercedes-Benz automobiles, they may ask respondents to compare Mercedes' quality to that of the auto they currently drive. Because direct comparisons are made, the data can be interpreted in relative terms. Furthermore, the findings should be considered to have ordinal-scaled properties.

noncomparative rating scale A scale on which respondents compare one characteristic or attribute against a standard of their own choosing, according to some predetermined criterion.

Noncomparative rating scales differ from comparative scales in that respondents do not judge a characteristic or attribute against a specified standard. That is, respondents create their own standards or reference points. For example, the researchers may ask a sample group of Americans to rate the quality of Mercedes-Benz cars using a five-point scale (5 = excellent quality, 1 = lowest quality). Here the researchers don't know whether the respondents are comparing Mercedes to their own car, their neighbor's car, or a car they owned in the past. Despite this shortcoming, marketing researchers often use noncomparative rating scales because they are easy to create and administer. The major types of scales within each category are shown in Exhibit 7-5 and summarized in Exhibit 7-15.

Comparative Rating Scales

As stated earlier, comparative rating scales allow respondents to make comparisons according to some predetermined criterion, such as importance of or preference for something. Four common comparative scales are *paired comparisons, rank ordering, constant-sum,* and *Q-sort.*

paired comparison scale A scale that asks respondents to select their preferences from among sets of two items, according to a predetermined criterion.

Paired Comparisons   The highly popular **paired-comparison scales** technique is implemented by having respondents note their preference between items in paired sets. Respondents are asked to choose which item rates higher, according to a predetermined criterion. Suppose we want to find out which brand of jeans from a choice of four brands (Levi's, Wrangler, Calvin Klein, and Lee's) a particular group of consumers prefers. In a hypothetical test, we set up six comparisons: Levi's vs. Wrangler; Levi's vs. Calvin Klein; Levi's vs. Lee's; Wrangler vs. Calvin Klein; Wrangler vs. Lee's; and Calvin Klein vs. Lee's. The number of required comparisons is determined by applying the following formula:

$$\text{Number of required comparisons} = \frac{n(n-1)}{2} = \frac{4(4-1)}{2} = \frac{4(3)}{2} = 6$$

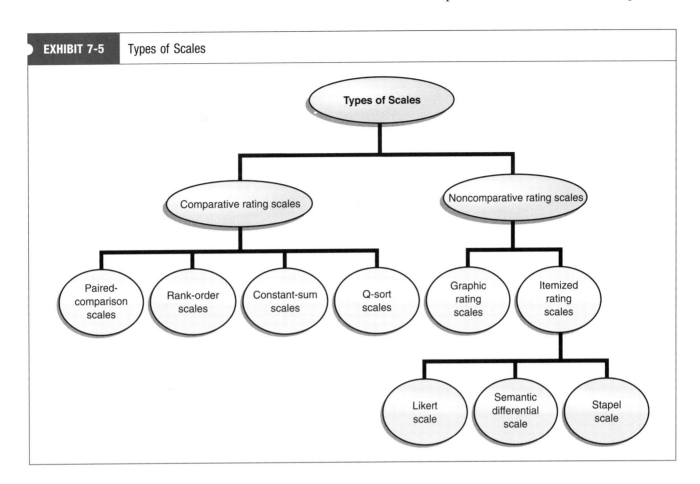

EXHIBIT 7-5 Types of Scales

EXHIBIT 7-6 Respondents' Preferences (%)

	Levi's	Wrangler	Calvin Klein	Lee's
Levi's	—	30	35	15
Wrangler	70	—	42	68
Calvin Klein	65	58	—	62
Lee's	85	32	38	—

---

where *n* indicates the number of individual items being compared. This requisite number demonstrates a shortcoming of the paired-comparison technique. When several comparisons are required, the technique becomes less effective and less accurate due to respondent fatigue. For example, with seven brands, 21 comparisons are necessary. Another concern among researchers is that when comparisons are made, the order of the items or questions can bias the outcome.

Exhibit 7-6 shows that our respondents preferred Levi's brand to all other brands. That is, 70% of the respondents preferred Levi's to Wrangler, 65% preferred Levi's to Calvin Klein, and 85% preferred Levi's to Lee's. Responses could also have been shown by assigning a "1" to the pairing that receives more than half of the preferences and a "0" to the pairing that receives 50% or less of the preferences. This scoring method uses an ordinal scale. As shown in Exhibit 7-7, Levi's received the highest score (3), followed by Lee's (2), Wrangler (1), and Calvin Klein (0).

Rank Order **Rank-order scales** are easy to implement and popular with marketing researchers. Respondents rank products according to some predetermined criterion,

rank-order scale A scale on which respondents rank items, according to a predetermined criterion.

EXHIBIT 7-7	Paired-Comparison Using Exhibit 7-6 Data			
	Levi's	**Wrangler**	**Calvin Klein**	**Lee's**
Levi's	—	0	0	0
Wrangler	1	—	0	1
Calvin Klein	1	1	—	1
Lee's	1	0	0	—
Total Score	3	1	0	2

EXHIBIT 7-8	Respondents' Rankings			
	Frequency of Ranking			
Brand	**First**	**Second**	**Third**	**Fourth**
Levi's	6	3	1	2
Wrangler	2	2	6	2
Calvin Klein	1	2	4	5
Lee's	3	5	1	3

Brand	Computation	Score
Levi's	$(6 \times 1) + (3 \times 2) + (1 \times 3) + (2 \times 4)$	23
Wrangler	$(2 \times 1) + (2 \times 2) + (6 \times 3) + (2 \times 4)$	32
Calvin Klein	$(1 \times 1) + (2 \times 2) + (4 \times 3) + (5 \times 4)$	37
Lee's	$(3 \times 1) + (5 \times 2) + (1 \times 3) + (3 \times 4)$	28

such as quality, taste, style, or attractiveness. For example, we could ask 12 respondents to rank the four brands of jeans according to their preference for each brand. The results are summarized in Exhibit 7-8. We determine the overall preference score by multiplying each ranking by the frequency in each category. The lower the score, the higher the ranking. In this comparative rating scale, Levi's again emerged as the most preferred.

There are two major shortcomings with rank ordering. First, it gives only ordinal-scale data. While ordinal data provides the researcher with an appreciation for respondents' preferences, only a limited number of statistical techniques can be used to analyze the results. Indeed, even simple means cannot be calculated using ordinal data. Second, it is less useful when numerous items must be ranked. If respondents must rank, say, 40 items, the results may be inaccurate due to respondent fatigue and difficulty in differentiating rankings toward the bottom. Can you really determine which brand should be ranked 37th instead of 38th?

Constant-Sum Scales In **constant-sum scales** respondents allocate a predetermined number of rating points (typically 100) among several items, according to some criterion, to indicate the relative preference or importance of each item compared to all others on the list. Rating points may be allocated a few different ways. In a personal interview, 100 pennies or tokens may be used. In a telephone interview, verbal distribution of 100 points will be the likely choice. Whichever technique is used, the proportion of points must reflect preferences for the item. That is, if Brand A is given 20 points and is preferred twice as much as Brand B, then Brand B must be given 10 points.

constant-sum scale A scale on which respondents allocate a predetermined number of rating points among several items, according to a predetermined criterion, to indicate relative preference or importance of each item compared to all others.

Let's say we want to determine the relative preference of college students for different fast-food restaurants. We randomly sample 100 students and ask them to do the following:

Divide 100 points among the following fast-food establishments to indicate your relative preference for each:

Restaurant	Points
McDonald's	—
Burger King	—
Hardees	—
Taco Bell	—
Arby's	—
KFC	—
Total	100

The advantages of this scaling technique are that it does not require a large number of individual comparisons, as paired comparisons can, and the point system indicates strengths of preferences. However, constant-sum scales also have a few problems.

As with the previous techniques, the alternatives should be limited to a manageable number. The total points must add to 100 (or any other predetermined amount), so too many choices may cause problems because some respondents will invariably assign points that add to more or less than 100.

Another problem with this technique is the requirement that respondents allocate points in a way that indicates their relative preference among items. This requires that respondents understand proportion, and this is not always a realistic expectation.

A final shortcoming is that it has not been definitively established that the data produced uses an interval scale. This form of scaling has not been thoroughly tested, so most marketers use it with caution.

Q-Sort Scales   Unlike the other scaling approaches we have studied thus far, the **Q-sort scale** discriminates among a large group of items in a relatively short time. Respondents rank a group of items into sets, according to some criterion, such as preference, attitude, or behavioral intent. Cards are the most popular and simplest items to use in the sorting process. Each card notes an item to be ranked. To increase statistical reliability, at least 60 cards should be used, but no more than 140.[3] If cards are used, respondents are usually instructed to sort a specific number of cards into separate piles according to the specified criterion, with the count in each pile ultimately resembling a normal or quasi-normal distribution. Consider Example 7-3.

Q-sort scale A scale on which respondents rank a group of items into sets, according to some criterion.

Example 7-3

A hamburger fast-food restaurant wants to adopt a new advertising jingle. A sample of individuals is asked to indicate their preferences from a list of 80 slogans printed on several cards. Each respondent is given the following instructions:

We are interested in finding your preferences for 80 advertising slogans. Each card in the pile has a slogan. Please follow these steps.

Step 1: Using the 5-point "Slogan Score Cards" (most prefer, somewhat like, neutral, somewhat dislike, least prefer), please choose the 10 slogans you most prefer and stack those cards under the "most prefer" category.

Step 2: From the remaining 70 cards (80 − 10), please choose the 10 slogans you least prefer and stack those cards under the "least prefer" category.

Step 3: From the remaining 60 cards (70 − 10), please choose the 15 slogans you most prefer and stack them under the "somewhat like" category.

Step 4: From the remaining 45 cards (60 − 15), please choose the 15 slogans you least prefer and stack them under the "somewhat dislike" category.

Step 5: Please list the remaining 30 cards (45 − 15) under the "neutral" category.

The major advantages of the Q-sorting approach are the short amount of time the process takes to complete, the systematic manner in which preferences are categorized, and the ease of implementation. The downside of this approach is the vast number of choices requested from the respondent in a relatively short period of time and the uncertain reliability as the number of cards used in the process increases.

Noncomparative Rating Scales

While noncomparative rating scales are relatively easy to create and administer, they do *not* allow respondents to compare items according to some predetermined criterion, such as preference or importance. Rather, respondents choose their own standards or reference points against which to compare. Therefore, researchers don't usually know what standards respondents are using. Two types of noncomparative rating scales are graphic and itemized.

graphic rating scale A scale in which respondents indicate their responses to questions on a continuum with two extreme points.

Graphic Rating Scales   In **graphic rating scales** (also referred to as *continuous ratings*), respondents indicate their responses on a continuum. Between the continuum's extreme points are responses that represent a gradual progression toward the extremes. Respondents place a mark at a location on the continuum that reflects their response to the question. A performance appraisal study used for employee development surveyed 96 police officers. It contained 16 performance dimensions, and its endpoints were "unsatisfactory" and "excellent."[4]

There are several possible variations of presentation—horizontal or vertical, qualitative or quantitative. There may be designated points (for example, 1, 2, 3, and so on) between the two extreme choices or simply a blank straight line (see Exhibit 7-9). If a blank line is used, the researcher applies a numerical scale after respondents complete the survey. Either way, the researcher segments all responses into a usable number of groups and then analyzes the information as interval data. Although graphic rating scales are easy to apply, marketing researchers seldom use them because they are not very reliable. This is because there are usually no standard responses.

These scales also cause problems for international researchers. Less-educated respondents have difficulty conceptualizing a continuous scale with equally divided intervals. Hence, the researcher must allow considerable time to explain the scale.[5]

Some people theorize that unnumbered slider scales can be more effective in providing dependable results. Web based surveys can greatly simplify the administration and evaluation of graphic rating scales by eliminating tiresome hand scoring.[6]

itemized rating scale A scale on which respondents answer questions by selecting from a finite number of choices.

Itemized Rating Scales   **Itemized rating scales** resemble graphic ratings, except that respondents select from a finite number of choices rather than from the theoretically infinite number on a continuum. Each choice has a number or descriptor associated with it. For example, respondents may be asked to respond to the statement "When I visit Wal-Mart, it is a pleasant experience" by selecting from the following choices: "strongly agree," "agree," "neutral," "disagree," and "strongly disagree." The strengths of these scales are that respondents can complete each question in a relatively short time and researchers can easily analyze the responses because quantitative scores can be assigned to each response. (The task of assigning quantitative scores to responses is discussed in Chapter 13.) Three popular itemized rating scales are the Likert, semantic differential, and Stapel scales.

Likert scale An itemized rating scale on which respondents select from choices ranging from "strongly agree" to "strongly disagree" to indicate their attitudes toward the statements presented to them.

Likert Scale   The **Likert scale** (also known as the *summated ratings scale*) is an itemized rating in which respondents select from choices ranging from "strongly agree" to "strongly disagree." The choices are assumed to have equal distances between them and may be numbered, such as 5 (strongly agree), 4 (agree), 3 (neither

---

EXHIBIT 7-9 | Four Examples of Graphic Rating Scales

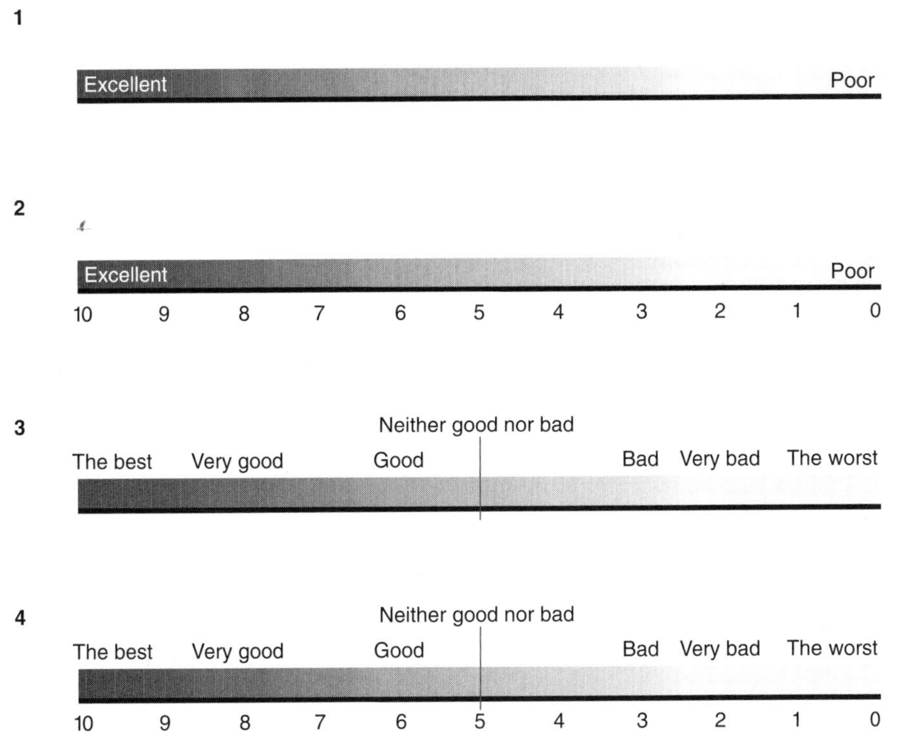

1

Excellent   Poor

2

Excellent   Poor

10   9   8   7   6   5   4   3   2   1   0

3

                 Neither good nor bad

The best   Very good   Good   Bad   Very bad   The worst

4

                 Neither good nor bad

The best   Very good   Good   Bad   Very bad   The worst

10   9   8   7   6   5   4   3   2   1   0

EXHIBIT 7-10 | Survey Using a Five-Point Likert Scale

1. Nation's Bank provides excellent customer service.

Strongly agree	Agree	Neither agree nor disagree	Disagree	Strongly disagree
5	4	3	2	1

2. Nation's Bank has convenient locations.

Strongly agree	Agree	Neither agree nor disagree	Disagree	Strongly disagree
5	4	3	2	1

3. The automated teller machines at Nation's Bank are easy to operate.

Strongly agree	Agree	Neither agree nor disagree	Disagree	Strongly disagree
5	4	3	2	1

4. The atmosphere at Nation's Bank is pleasant.

Strongly agree	Agree	Neither agree nor disagree	Disagree	Strongly disagree
5	4	3	2	1

---

agree nor disagree), 2 (disagree), and 1 (strongly disagree) (see Exhibit 7-10). They can also be numbered 1 through 5, 2 through –2, or –2 through 2. In other words, minus signs could have just as effectively been used, where "–2" indicates "strongly disagree," "0" indicates "neutrality," and "2" indicates "strongly agree."

When using Likert scales, a series of statements that relate to the topic of interest are developed and administered using the "strongly agree" to "strongly disagree" choices. Then responses may be analyzed either individually or on a total ("summated") basis by adding across items. Likert scales are meant to be user-friendly. Therefore, the survey

EXHIBIT 7-11	Likert-Scale Survey without Numeric Scores					
		Strongly agree	Agree	Neither agree nor disagree	Disagree	Strongly disagree
1. Nation's Bank provides excellent customer service.		____	____	____	____	____
2. Nation's Bank has convenient locations.		____	____	____	____	____
3. The automated teller machines at Nation's Bank are easy to operate.		____	____	____	____	____
4. The atmosphere at Nation's Bank is pleasant.		____	____	____	____	____

EXHIBIT 7-12	A Semantic Differential Scale for Pepsi-Cola							
Sweet	____	____	____	____	____	____	____	Sour
Tasty	____	____	____	____	____	____	____	Tasteless
Satisfying	____	____	____	____	____	____	____	Unsatisfying
Expensive	____	____	____	____	____	____	____	Inexpensive

EXHIBIT 7-13	How to Avoid the Halo Effect					
Effective	____	____	____	____	____	Ineffective
Hard to swallow	____	____	____	____	____	Easy to swallow
Work quickly	____	____	____	____	____	Does not work quickly
Low quality	____	____	____	____	____	High quality
Safe	____	____	____	____	____	Unsafe

in Exhibit 7-10 may be written without numbers, as shown in Exhibit 7-11, to reduce the clutter. The researcher assigns scores after the surveys are completed.

Semantic Differential Scale The **semantic differential scale** is a five- or seven-point itemized ordinal scale with dichotomous (opposite) pairs of descriptive words or phrases representing the two extremes and a neutral midpoint. The extreme points are meant to be interpreted as "strongly" or "extremely," with the next rating being somewhat less extreme, such as "very," and the next being even less extreme, and so forth.

semantic differential scale A five- or seven-point itemized ordinal scale with dichotomous pairs of descriptive words or phrases representing the two extremes and a neutral midpoint.

Suppose PepsiCo wants to find out what consumers think about Pepsi-Cola. Exhibit 7-12 is a sample of pairs that respondents could use to evaluate Pepsi-Cola. The first pair is "sweet-sour," which can be ranked as "extremely sweet," "very sweet," "sweet," "neither sweet nor sour," "sour," "very sour," and "extremely sour." Respondents place a mark in the space that most appropriately reflects their rating of the attribute.

Researchers often place favorable adjectives and phrases randomly on either the left or the right ends of the scale to avoid the **halo effect,** which means an overall evaluation of an object biases a respondent's answers on its specifics.[7] A study that examined consumer preference toward three solid oral dosage forms (capsules, caplets, and tablets) in nonprescription pharmaceutical products used the format shown in Exhibit 7-13.

halo effect An overall evaluation of an object biases a respondent's answers on its specifics.

While the semantic differential scale is a reliable technique that marketing decision makers often use, it also has a few shortcomings.[8] First, developing dichotomous descriptive words and phrases is not always possible. Second, neutral responses (ratings at the midpoint of the scale) are difficult to interpret. Does a neutral response mean that the respondent is confused about the word choices or simply indifferent toward the test item? When several pairs of words are used in the rating, a "central tendency"—several noncommittal responses (say, represented by several 4's)—can render suspect results.

EXHIBIT 7-14	Stapel Scale for Pepsi-Cola		
+3	+3	+3	+3
+2	+2	+2	+2
+1	+1	+1	+1
Sweet	Tasty	Satisfying	Expensive
−1	−1	−1	−1
−2	−2	−2	−2
−3	−3	−3	−3

Stapel Scale The **Stapel scale** mirrors the semantic differential scale, with a few exceptions. Instead of using two dichotomous descriptive words or phrases as choices, only one word or phrase is used. This makes the task easier for both the rating developer and the respondent to use. Furthermore, although points are not assigned numbers in semantic differential scale, they are assigned numbers in a Stapel scale—typically using a ten-point scale. Categories may be assigned a range of +5 to –5 or even +3 to –3. The Pepsi-Cola example in Exhibit 7-12 can be recast using a Stapel scale, as shown in Exhibit 7-14. The higher the positive number, the more accurately the respondent believes the word or phrase describes the test item. The downside of the Stapel scale is the potential to bias the respondent by the word choice of the categories. Exhibit 7-15 summarizes comparative and noncomparative scales.

Stapel scale A scale that resembles a semantic differential scale but uses an even number of positive and negative points, usually +3 and –3, with a single descriptive word or phrase positioned in the middle of the ordinal scale to indicate the direction and intensity of attitudes.

7-4 Designing Itemized Rating Scales

When designing itemized rating scales, researchers must answer some important questions:

1. *How many choices should be included?* There is no correct number of choices. When making this decision, researchers' main concern is the extent to which respondents can discriminate among choices. In general, the fewer choices, the easier it is for respondents to discriminate between them. Five- to nine-point scales are quite popular with marketing researchers, but if respondents are very knowledgeable about the test topic, then more choices may be used.[9] Also, the survey method must be considered when selecting the number of choices. If oral interviews will be used, such as telephone or in-depth interviews, no more than a five-point scale is recommended because respondents may have difficulty remembering what each point on the scale represents.

2. *Should the scale have an even or odd number of choices?* This question really concerns whether a midpoint or neutral position should be included. If a neutral position is included, then there will be an odd number of choices with the same number of positive as negative choices. Proponents for an odd number of choices argue that

   - Respondents may be neither for nor against a particular product or service and should be given the opportunity to remain neutral.
   - To avoid biasing respondents, there should be an equal number of favorable and unfavorable choices.

Proponents for an even number of choices argue that

   - Respondents' attitudes cannot be neutral, so they should be encouraged to take either a favorable or unfavorable stance.
   - If there is a neutral position on a scale, respondents may want to "sit on the fence" because it is the easy way out, particularly if they don't have strong feelings about the test topic.

EXHIBIT 7-15	Summary of Comparative and Noncomparative Scales		
Scale	**Implementation**	**Major Advantage(s)**	**Major Disadvantages(s)**
Comparative	Respondents make comparisons according to some predetermined criterion, such as preference or importance.	Since standard is specified in the test, researchers know respondents' reference point.	Since data is considered ordinal, generalizability of data is limited.
• Paired comparisons	Items are presented two at a time, and respondents are asked to choose the item that rates higher according to a predetermined criterion.	Direct comparisons are made; respondents have little difficulty following directions.	When several comparisons are required, respondent fatigue can cause inaccuracy.
• Rank order	Respondents rank items according to some predetermined criterion (quality, style, attractiveness).	Easy to implement and understand.	The available list of selections may not be exhaustive; produces only ordinal data.
• Constant-sum	Respondents allocate a predetermined number of rating points among several items according to some criterion to indicate relative preference or importance of each item.	Easy for respondent to perform; distances between preferences are consistent.	Number of alternatives should be limited to a manageable amount; question whether tokens or points accurately represent an individual's relative preference.
• Q-sort	Respondents rank groups of items into sets, according to some criterion.	Discriminates among a large group of items in a short time; easy implementation.	Vast number of choices can be requested from the respondent in a relatively short time; reliability less certain as number of cards increases.
Noncomparative	Standard for comparison not specified in test, so respondents must choose their own preference points.	Generally easy to create and administer.	Researchers typically don't know respondents' standard or reference point.
• Graphic rating	Respondents indicate responses on a continuum with two extreme points; respondents can mark responses anywhere between extreme points, wherever best reflects their responses to the questions.	Easy to implement; respondents may graphically visualize selections.	Question regarding reliability, since respondents may have difficulty using a continuum as an interval scale.
• Itemized rating	Respondents are asked to select from a finite number of categories.	Respondents can complete each question in a relatively short amount of time, and researchers tend to have little problem.	Each type of itemized rating scale (Likert, semantic differential, Stapel) has its own disadvantages.
• Likert	Respondents select from among itemized choices ranging from "strongly agree" to "strongly disagree" to indicate attitudes toward presented statements.	Easy for respondents to understand scale; respondents must consider only one phrase or statement at a time.	If implemented orally, respondents may have difficulty remembering choices.
• Semantic differential	Five- or seven-point itemized scale with dichotomous descriptive words or phrases as extreme points and a neutral midpoint.	Highly reliable results if implemented correctly.	Difficult to write truly dichotomous descriptive words and phrases; neutral responses are difficult to interpret.
• Stapel	Resembles semantic differential, except only one descriptive word or phrase is used, and it appears in the middle of a ten-point ordinal scale ranging from +5 to −5.	Easier for both scale developer and respondent, since only one descriptive word or phrase at a time must be considered.	Descriptive words may bias respondent if phrased in a positive or negative manner.

balanced scale A scale with the same number of favorable and unfavorable choices.

unbalanced scale A scale with an uneven number of favorable and unfavorable choices and thus skewed in one direction.

3. *Should the scale have the same number of favorable and unfavorable choices?* Scales with the same number of favorable and unfavorable choices are referred to as **balanced scales.** Scales with an uneven number of favorable and unfavorable choices, making them skewed toward one direction or the other, are **unbalanced scales.** When deciding which scale to use, researchers must consider the type of information they are seeking and whether the target population's attitudes will likely be skewed in either a favorable or unfavorable direction. For example, if the intention of a particular survey is to reveal the attitudes of young mothers toward abusive fathers, the scales should be skewed in a negative direction, since most respondents' attitudes are likely to be negative.

4. *Should the scale have a "no response" or "don't know" choice?* In some cases, respondents may be confused or lack sufficient knowledge to adequately answer a particular question on a survey. A "no response" or "don't know" choice allows them to convey their confusion or lack of knowledge. However,

opponents of uncommitted response choices argue that, much like the neutral position discussed earlier, permitting noncommittal choices gives respondents an easy way out and discourages them from answering the question. Researchers must decide whether they want to force respondents to answer all of the survey questions. Sometimes even forcing them into answering questions is not effective. Respondents may skip questions they are not in a position to answer.

5. *In what form should the scale be presented?* When surveying an industrialized country's mainstream population, traditional written surveys with multiple-choice responses are acceptable. But what do you do in underdeveloped nations where the illiteracy rate is high? And what about young children who cannot yet read? Should researchers simply avoid them? Of course not. These situations force marketing researchers to become creative in their surveying techniques. One way to get around illiteracy is to read the questionnaire aloud and collect oral responses. Another technique that is often used is to replace written choices such as "very happy" and "very unhappy" with pictures of faces with expressions ranging from wide smiles to deep frowns. This **funny-faces scale** is especially useful when surveying young children and less-educated respondents in developing countries. It has also been used in the medical profession to elicit children's self-reports of pain. In these cases, smiles were used to indicate less pain; frowns would indicate more pain.[10]

funny-faces scale An ordinal scale in which the choices are smiling and frowning faces ranging from wide smiles to deep frowns.

7-5 Measurement Accuracy

Whenever items or individuals are measured, there is likely to be some sort of error, whether intentional or unintentional. Intentional mistakes may be seen in sports team programs, for example, when a player is listed as 6 feet, 7 inches tall when he is actually 6 feet, 5 inches tall—perhaps done to intimidate opponents. Unintentional mistakes may occur when something under investigation is measured and the true response is sought but not revealed. This is extremely common in research. Since virtually all research efforts are flawed, marketing researchers must routinely measure the accuracy of their information. That is, researchers must determine **measurement error,** which is the difference between the information sought and the information actually obtained in the measurement process. Every measurement includes true, accurate information plus some degree of error. We can summarize this idea as follows:

measurement error The difference between the information sought and the information obtained through the research process.

Measurement results = true measurement + measurement error

Two potential sources of error exist in the measurement process: *systematic error* and *random error*. **Systematic error** is caused by a constant bias in the design or implementation of the measurement situation. This type of error occurs in samples where the findings are either consistently higher or consistently lower than the actual value of the population parameter being measured. It can be a problem associated with a person (unqualified interviewer), a situation (constant distractions during interviews), poorly printed surveys (the same few words illegible on all surveys), poorly designed surveys (leading questions), or any other problems that can constantly (consistently) disrupt the measurement situation. Systematic error is often called *constant error* because it is a constant problem in the entire measurement situation. For those that it biases, it does so in the same direction (either always positive or always negative).

systematic error Error caused by a constant bias in the design or implementation of the measurement situation.

Each of the following examples of systematic error demonstrates the potential for consistent misdiagnosis or mismeasurement:

- A hotel survey biases respondents by asking them, "How well did you enjoy your visit at our beautiful hotel?" *Systematic error:* The word "beautiful" will likely constantly bias respondents by creating a favorable image of the hotel.

- During a three-hour span, an interviewer at a shopping mall was instructed to interview all adult shoppers wearing some sort of athletic apparel. However, she decided on her own to interview only those shoppers wearing athletic apparel who were looking directly at her and who appeared to be receptive to an interview. *Systematic error:* The interviewer decided on her own whom she would interview. Since she deviated from the initial plan, she consistently biased the sample.

- On a customer comment card in a family-style restaurant, customers are asked "How often do you eat at other restaurants that have lower cleanliness ratings than our "A" rating? *Systematic error:* Anyone who responds to the question is likely being negatively influenced about the cleanliness of competitors' restaurants.

random error Error that results from randomly occurring differences in respondents or circumstances.

In contrast, **random error** does not occur in a consistent fashion and instead results from randomly occurring differences in respondents or circumstances. To determine whether or not random error exists, researchers may measure an individual or group of individuals twice. Random error is present if the two measurements are not identical. Consider the following examples of random error:

- A college student incorrectly recalls the service she received during her most recent experience at McDonald's because she was exhausted from a party the previous night.

- A respondent unusually forgets to bring his reading glasses and places marks in unintended boxes on a survey.

- Following an argument with her spouse, a woman is overly critical of a local bakery on a customer service survey.

The only way to reduce random error is to increase the number of people in the sample. That is, as sample size increases, random error should decrease.

As noted earlier, measurement results may be described as "true measurement + measurement error." Therefore, we can extend the equation as follows:

$$\text{Measurement results} = \text{True measurement} + \underbrace{\text{Systematic error} + \text{Random error}}_{\text{Measurement error}}$$

In the remainder of this chapter, you will learn about reliability and validity. These terms describe the degree to which a scale produces accurate and consistent results.

7-5a Reliability

reliability The ability of a scale to produce consistent results if repeated measurements are taken; the extent to which scales are free of random error and thus produce consistent results.

Reliability refers to the ability of a scale to produce consistent results if repeated measurements are taken. If a professor gives a group of students two different (independent) tests to measure their knowledge of marketing research, and the students' scores from the two measures are highly similar, then the measures can be said to be reliable since they replicated each others' scores. So reliability is the extent to which scales are free of random error and thus produce consistent results. In general, the less random error detected, the more reliable the data will be. In most marketing situations, reliability is not absolute. There are three major ways to assess reliability: *test-retest, alternative forms,* and *internal consistency.*

Test-Retest Reliability

test-retest reliability The ability of the same scale to produce consistent results when used more than once under similar conditions.

Test-retest reliability is conducted by measuring the same subjects at two different times and under similar conditions to determine the similarity of the scores. The results, or scores, indicate the extent to which the scales are reliable. In general, the greater the difference in scores, the more random error is present. The more random error is present, the lower the reliability. Likewise, the smaller the difference between scores, the higher the reliability.

Alternative-Forms Reliability

alternative-forms reliability Ability of two equivalent scales (scales that respondents perceive to be different but that measure the same content) to obtain consistent results.

Alternative-forms reliability (sometimes called "equivalent-form reliability") is the ability of two "equivalent" scales to obtain consistent results. This test first involves developing two equivalent scales—scales that respondents perceive to be different but that actually measure the same content. Consider these examples:

- An item in an arithmetic test is "46 + 84 = __"; the equivalent item is "28 + 72 = __." Both items measure respondents' mathematical knowledge.

- An item in an inventory designed to measure emotional stability is "Do you sleep well at night?"; an equivalent item is "Do you have bad dreams at night?"[11]

To carry out the alternative-forms reliability test, researchers administer one scale to respondents and, approximately two weeks later, administer the second equivalent scale to the same respondents. In theory, there should be no carryover effect because the items are different, so scores from the first scale should not affect the scores on the second scale. There should be approximately the same number of questions used on each scale to measure the topic under investigation. After the respondents have completed the two scales, researchers compare the measurement instruments item-by-item to determine how similar they actually are.

Internal-Consistency Reliability

In **internal-consistency reliability,** two or more measurements of the same concept are taken at the same time and then compared to see whether they agree. Suppose the following four statements using a Likert scale (choices range from "strongly agree" to "strongly disagree") are used to determine consumers' attitudes toward First Bank's customer service: "I always enjoy visiting First Bank," "I like the people who work at First Bank," "First Bank satisfies my banking needs," "The services I receive at First Bank are excellent." The extent to which the four measures correlate across a sample of respondents indicates the reliability of the measures. As the correlation increases, the reliability of the measures increases.

The easiest way to test for internal consistency is to use the **split-half technique**. To administer this test, the test items are randomly split into two equal groups and their degree of correlation is examined. The higher the correlation, the more reliable the measure because high correlation indicates that the items are associated in some way.

Although the split-half technique is easy to administer, the results are highly dependent on how the halves are split. Therefore, to remedy this shortcoming, researchers use a second approach, **coefficient alpha** (or *Cronbach's alpha*), which averages all possible ways of splitting the test items. The final score can range from 0 to 1. A score of 0.60 or less indicates that the items measure different characteristics.[12]

7-5b Validity

Validity is the degree to which a test measures what it is supposed to measure. Just because a measurement scale produces consistent results doesn't mean that it measures the right concept. Take, for example, the scales used at supermarket checkout counters to weigh fresh fruits and vegetables. A reliable scale *consistently* indicates that a specific bag of apples weighs the same amount each time it is weighed. If a bag of apples was found to weigh 454 grams, for the scale to be reliable, it should indicate 454 grams each time the bag is weighed. Let's say that our bag of apples actually weighs 500 grams. If the scale *repeatedly* indicates that the bag weighs 454 grams, the scale is still reliable. Therefore, a scale can be reliable but not valid. Because measurement validity assessment is a complicated process that largely pertains to academic researchers, here we briefly introduce two popular techniques to assess the validity of measurement instruments: *content validity* and *criterion-related validity*.

Content Validity

Content (or face) validity involves a subjective assessment of how well a scale measure the construct or variable. This test for validity is highly subjective because the personal experiences and beliefs of the experts inevitably come into play. Suppose

internal-consistency reliability Assesses reliability by taking two or more measurements of the same theoretical concept at the same time and determining the extent to which the measurements agree.

split-half technique A method of judging internal consistency of a measurement instrument by randomly splitting the total test items into two equal groups and examining their degree of correlation; the greater the correlation, the higher the internal consistency.

coefficient alpha A technique for judging internal consistency of a measurement instrument by averaging all possible ways of splitting test items and examining their degree of correlation; the greater the correlation is to a score of 1, the higher the internal consistency.

validity The degree to which a test measures what it is supposed to measure.

content or face validity The ability of test scale items to measure the topic of interest, as judged subjectively by professionals or experts on the topic.

Research Realities 7-1

What Are We Really Measuring?

Car dealers go to great pains to stay in contact with their customers. They mail out surveys and telephone customers to measure their satisfaction levels. Dealers believe that customer satisfaction equals customer loyalty—that is, that high customer satisfaction ratings mean that customers will likely be repeat purchasers.

However, a study of car owners found that although 90% claim to be either satisfied or very satisfied with their purchase, only 35–40% come back for another purchase at the same dealership. Furthermore, research has repeatedly shown that 60–80% of customers who defected had said on a survey immediately prior to defecting that they were satisfied or very satisfied. As a result, customer satisfaction does not necessarily mean repeat business.

Source: Peter Gilbert, "Can't get no customer satisfaction?" *Business Day,* January 17, 2005: 4.

---

researchers want to determine how satisfied customers are with a banking institution. After they develop an exhaustive listing about services offered, location, attitudes of tellers, cleanliness of branches, ATM availability, and hours of operation, they have a panel of banking experts judge whether the list adequately covers the relevant concerns associated with customer satisfaction. If a concern is missing or the panel decides certain items are improperly phrased, then the content validity of the scale could be challenged. Content validity is the most often used validation technique because it is not time-consuming and it's easy to implement.

Criterion-Related Validity

criterion-related validity The ability of a scale to perform as predicted in relation to a specified criterion.

Criterion-related validity is the ability of a scale to perform as predicted in relation to a specified criterion. The criterion is the attribute of interest. The predictor is the respondent's score. Suppose that USA University's graduate business school, in order to determine the applicants' potential for success in the program, requires all applicants to take the Graduate Management Admissions Test (GMAT). The criterion is each applicant's potential success in the business school program. The predictor is the applicant's GMAT score. What is important is how well the predictor determines the applicant's potential for success in the program.

Consider the relationship between whether a consumer buys a product and his or her *attitude* toward the product. Attitude theory maintains that one way to predict whether consumers will buy a product is to measure their attitudes toward the product.[13] The question is, if consumers like Ivory soap, will they buy it? Or, is liking this product a valid predictor of consumer purchases? This is what researchers at Procter & Gamble would test. In Research Realities 7-1, read how researchers found that customer satisfaction does not predict repeat business.

7-5c Relationship between Reliability and Validity

There is a one-way relationship between reliability and validity: a scale must be reliable to be valid; it does not have to be valid to be reliable. In other words, reliability is a necessary but not sufficient condition for validity:

Reliability $\Rightarrow$ Validity Reliability is a necessary but not a sufficient condition for validity

Validity $\Rightarrow$ Reliability Validity is a sufficient condition for reliability

To demonstrate the difference, let's draw an analogy. At a carnival, you play a game that requires you to throw ten balls through a tire. Let's break your efforts into two parts: hitting an area consistently—this we will call reliability—and accuracy at getting the balls through the center of the tire—this we will call validity. You play the game three times, and your attempts are shown in Exhibit 7-16.

In the first game, you missed the center of the tire on all ten attempts. Your attempts were neither consistent nor accurate, thus they were neither reliable nor valid. In the second game, you again missed all ten attempts, but the majority of your misses were in the same general area of the tire. That is, your attempts were consistent (reliable) but not accurate (not valid). But you finally get the hang of the game, and your throws are both consistent (reliable) and accurate (valid).

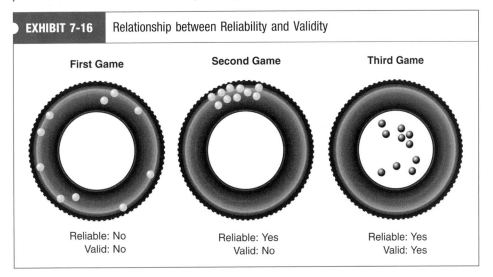

| EXHIBIT 7-16 | Relationship between Reliability and Validity |

First Game

Second Game

Third Game

Reliable: No
Valid: No

Reliable: Yes
Valid: No

Reliable: Yes
Valid: Yes

Decision Time!

As a marketing manager, you need reliable data that tells you how satisfied your customers are with your company's overall service. You tell your researcher what you need, and he informs you that he has already surveyed customer satisfaction levels. When you review the data, you notice that the scale he used to gather the data had the following choices: "high," "medium," and "low." What kind of measurement scale is this? Can it be improved? If so, how? Can the data be used? What other types of scales could have been used to measure customer satisfaction?

Net Impact

As noted earlier, marketing researchers routinely use the Internet to gather data via surveys and online chat sessions. These online methods lend themselves well to attitude research. When companies want to learn about consumers who use the Internet, the Internet is a logical vehicle to gather this data. A company can send questionnaires to consumers by email or post a survey on the company Web site. Collecting attitude data online has several advantages:

- It is fast and inexpensive. Questionnaires are delivered instantaneously worldwide over the Internet, and there is no postage charge or interviewer salary to pay.
- The potential respondent group is large, diverse, and in 200 countries.
- Some researchers believe that web surveys reduce errors.
- Consumers will often answer more directly, since they have a computer between them and the researchers.

The disadvantages of online research include the following:

- It is not possible to draw a probability sample of Internet users.
- Respondents may not answer truthfully or can pose as different people.
- People may interpret email surveys as "junk mail."
- Researchers have little control over which people or how many people fill out the questionnaire.

On the Lighter Side—I Agree with Whatever You Ask

 Arthur Sterngold warns people about surveys that overstate their attitudes, activities, and future behavior. Consider his warning about affirmation bias. He advocates that it is more sinister and subtle than people may realize. He told a story about his colleagues and him at Pennsylvania State University who conducted a national study to determine how concerned people were about several food safety issues. They noticed that most respondents indicated that they were concerned about every issue they mentioned. So to test affirmation bias they included a question that asked about a fictitious issue—IMS in seafood. More than half of the participants said they were concerned about this imaginary hazard. Sterngold asked one respondent why he was very concerned about IMS in seafood. He said that although he had never heard of it, he thought that it must be a serious problem if it was included in a survey by Penn State, and so he gave what he felt was the right response.

Source: Arthur Sterngold, "Battling Bias," *Planning,* vol. 71 Issue 7 (July 2005), pp. 42–44.

Chapter Summary

Researchers measure responses by assigning numbers according to specified rules to reflect the quantity of the characteristic that test products possess. Nominal, ordinal, interval, and ratio scales help the measurement process by quantifying and recording the extent to which test topics possess a characteristic.

Several methods are used to assess attitudes. These methods can be classified as comparative or noncomparative. Comparative scales specify a standard of comparison and ask respondents to compare the test stimulus against this standard. The most popular types of comparative scales are paired comparisons, rank-ordering, constant-sum, and Q-sort scales. In noncomparative scales, a standard of comparison is not specified, so researchers do not know the standard against which respondents are comparing the test stimulus. Common noncomparative scales include graphic rating, itemized rating, Likert, semantic differential, and Stapel.

Mistakes are an unavoidable part of life. In marketing research, mistakes can cost a company millions of dollars, so researchers must measure the extent to which error exists in their measuring instruments, including both systematic and random error. Systematic error occurs when there is a consistent bias in the measurement because of a problem with the measurement instrument or process. Random error does not occur in a consistent fashion. It is present when there are random differences in respondents or circumstances. When a measure is free of random error, it is said to be reliable. Reliability is the extent a scale produces consistent results if repeated measurements are taken; it is the extent to which scales are free of random error and thus produce consistent results. It may be assessed by using any of the following methods: test-retest, alternative forms, and internal consistency. The fact that a measurement instrument produces consistent results does not guarantee that it is measuring the right thing. Validity is the degree to which a test measures what it is supposed to measure. Reliability is a necessary but not sufficient condition for validity. However, reliability can exist without validity.

Review Questions

1. What is "measurement"?

2. What is the difference between ordinal and interval scales? How are they similar?

3. What is the difference between interval and ratio scales? How are they similar?

4. If attitudes are learned, then they can change, so why measure them?

5. What is the difference between a semantic differential scale and a Stapel scale? How are they similar?

6. What factors do researchers consider when deciding whether to use an even or an odd number of choices on a measurement scale?

7. Do you believe that respondents should be forced to take either a favorable or an unfavorable stance toward the test item? What arguments can be made for including "neutral," "no response," or "don't know" choices on surveys?

8. Can random error be avoided? If so, how? If not, why not?

9. When using the test-retest method, can researchers realistically expect their respondents to have no "carryover effect" to the second testing period?"

10. When measuring reliability, how is a coefficient alpha any better than the split-half technique?

11. How is reliability related to validity?

Practice Quiz

Note: You can find the correct answers to these questions by taking the quiz and then submitting your answers in the Online Edition. The program will automatically score your submission. If you miss a question, the program will provide the correct answer, a rationale for the answer, and the section number in the chapter where the topic is discussed.

1. Marketing researchers use nominal scales to identify and rank the test characteristics.
   a. True
   b. False

2. An interval scale ranks characteristics using equal increments between ranks to show relative amounts.
   a. True
   b. False

3. Interval scales are like ratio scales, but interval scales have meaningful zero points.
   a. True
   b. False

4. The semantic differential scale has respondents select from choices ranging from "strongly agree" to "strongly disagree."
   a. True
   b. False

5. When using a nominal scale, the numbers assigned to test objects have no intrinsic meaning.
   a. True
   b. False

6. The following is an example of which type of scale: "What is your race? African American ____, White ____, Latino____, Other ____"?
   a. Ordinal
   b. Nominal
   c. Ratio
   d. Interval
   e. None of the above

7. _____ scales are used when respondents rank products according to some predetermined criterion. The overall preference score is determined by multiplying each ranking by the frequency in each category. The lower the score, the higher the ranking.
   a. Constant-sum
   b. Rank-order
   c. Q-sort
   d. Paired-comparison
   e. Semantic-differential

8. _____ scales use dichotomous (opposite) pairs of descriptive words or phrases to represent the two extremes and a neutral point.
   a. Likert
   b. Stapel
   c. Graphic rating
   d. Semantic differential
   e. Itemized

9. _____ averages all the possible ways of splitting the test items and determines their degree of correlation.
   a. Test-retest
   b. Internal-consistency
   c. Split-half technique
   d. Coefficient alpha
   e. Alternative-forms

10. Which of the following statements is *not* true?
    a. Reliability is a necessary condition for validity to occur.
    b. Validity is a necessary condition for reliability to occur.
    c. Reliability can occur without validity.
    d. Convergent and discriminant validity are two parts of construct validity.
    e. Coefficient alpha is a type of reliability test.

 ## Thinking Critically

1. A marketing researcher wants to know which brand of shoe female consumers prefer from a choice of 18 brands. Using a paired-comparison scale, how many comparisons are necessary?

2. A manager of a new clothing store wants a random group of consumers to help him select a name for his business by choosing from among 120 names he has already developed. Which comparative scale would you recommend? Why?

3. You are a marketing researcher and want to understand the attitudes of college students toward illegal drugs. Develop five semantic differential scales for this inquiry. Then develop ten Stapel scales using similar descriptive words. Which scale do you prefer? Why?

4. Using the situation in Question 3, develop five questions using the Likert scale.

5. If a man weighs 200 pounds and he steps on his bathroom scale 20 times within a four-hour period, assuming his actual weight does not fluctuate between measurements, does the scale have to display "200 pounds" every time he steps on it to be reliable? If it indicates that he weighs exactly 200 pounds only 17 of

the 20 times, what could have caused the three measurements to be off? What type of error, systematic or random, could have caused these differences? Explain.

6. Create a measurement instrument that measures college students' degree of satisfaction with the computers they use. Then create a second "equivalent" instrument. Are they really "equivalent"? Do they appear different? Why or why not?

7. To demonstrate the relationship between reliability and validity, describe two real-world examples that clearly explain the following concepts:
   a. Reliability
   b. Validity
   c. Validity's dependence on reliability
   d. Reliability's lack of dependence on validity

Net Exercises

Hispanic & Asian Marketing Communication Research, Inc., is a full-service multicultural marketing research firm offering attitudinal measurement in Spanish, Portuguese, and most Asian languages. Read about some of its recent attitudinal studies at http://www.hamcr.com.

Experiencing Marketing Research

1. Make a list of six fast-food restaurants and ask five friends to rank them in order from "best" to "worst" in terms of their perception of food quality. Using rank ordering, which restaurant received the best overall score? What problems are associated with this technique?

2. Get together with five other students and generate a ten-question survey that can be used to evaluate the services that the reference desk of your campus library offers. Which type of scale did you use for your questions? Why is your group's scale the best one for this task? Explain.

3. Refer to the preceding exercise and create an alternative-forms test to assess the reliability of your scale.

4. Using the scale you created in exercise 2 (in this section), examine its content validity. Write up your analysis in a two-paragraph report.

Case 7-1

Give Generation Y Some Credit

New generations of people offer tremendous marketing opportunities for businesses. Generation X—those born between 1965 and 1981—comprise 25% of the adult population. Generation Y, sometimes referred to as "Millennials," is made up of many high-schoolers, but only 7% of them are old enough to be classified as being part of the adult population. There are 53 million of them, or about the same size as the Boomer generation. According to Shannon Ingram, a marketing and communications consultant from Costa Mesa, Calif., "They are confident and upbeat, education-minded, tolerant and accepting of diversity. They are more conservative than Generation X, but not as skeptical. Family really matters to them because parents stay together more often than Boomers."

Some of the marketing techniques that have been successful in recent years with Generation X also apply to Generation Y, Ingram said. Technology is a huge part of the lives of members of both groups.

According to Ingram, credit unions should aim their efforts toward Generation Yers and begin preparing for their arrival into adulthood. She recently led an educational session at the CUES Nexus conference, where she said, "Generation X is online all the time. The Internet is a way of life. They read the newspaper online. Their buying behaviors are immediacy, independence, and innovation. They have no brand loyalty, which is a very important piece of information for those in the credit union industry." She continued, "For credit unions to market to Millennials, technology really is the way. They will respond better to an email or an interactive Web site than other forms of advertising."

Advertising campaigns targeted at Generation X have followed a similar theme: use visuals, make it educational, offer value, and use their language. "Remember that hype 'sucks' and creativity 'rules,'" said Ingram.

However, Millennials grew up in a zero-tolerance environment. They watched President Bill Clinton squirm through a televised sex scandal, braced for the arrival of a new century, viewed peers killed at Columbine High School and other schools, and saw the September 11th terrorist attacks.

On the positive side, Ingram points out that unlike Generation X, which included the "latch-key" kids of the 1980s who developed a sense of alienation, members of Generation Y embrace community service. They feel they have a rendezvous with destiny.

Marketing campaigns aimed at Generation Y should stress simplicity and resist commercialism, she advocates. Yers are significantly less edgy than Xers, and they want to connect on an emotional level. Millennials want empowerment, positive messages, a respect for diversity, and distinctive product and service benefits.

While Generation X is typified by the popularity of Backpackers Express Airline, Generation Y's hallmark appears to be the World Dodgeball Association, Ingram said. "Dodgeball has become a really cool thing for the older members of Generation Y, from high school up to 22 years old. If credit unions want to target Generation Y, they are going to have to make it fun. Even goofy."

Source: Michael Bartlett, "Generation X? So old school. The emphasis now is on the "Millennials'" *Credit Union Journal,* vol. 9, issue 18 (May 9, 2005), 14.

Case Questions

1. If you were asked to measure the attitudes of Generation Y, which type of scale would you use and why? Please provide some examples of the scales you propose.

2. If you were asked to compare members of Generation Y to Generation Xers, which type of scale would you use and why? Please provide some examples of the scales you propose.

Case 7-2

The Tide Is Right to Surf the Korean Wave

Korea is hot. We're not referring so much to the weather as we are the society as a whole. Consider the popular television drama series *Daejanggeum,* bands like H.O.T., and movies like *Old Boy*—which have won huge audiences across Asia. An international brokerage firm says the so-called "Korean wave" of pop-culture exports is not only sharpening South Korea's national brand but coincides with an improvement in the country's perennially underrated stock market. But some experts believe that the Asian-centric nature of the wave, macroeconomic conditions, and broader problems facing the national image undermine this belief.

"Basically, we think the wave is a broader phenomenon that will help accelerate a recovery in domestic self-confidence," said CLSA Korea research head James Paterson, while visiting Hong Kong with a assembly of Korean film and record producers on a five-city investment road show that also took them to London, New York, Boston, and Singapore. "We think the spin-off will be increased consumption, capital investment, and equity fund inflows."

In a report and accompanying video documentary, CLSA, the Hong Kong-headquartered unit of France's Credit Agricole, argued that while Korea's image was formerly associated with war, military tension, violent demonstrations, and political corruption, it is presently viewed by Asian peers as a cool, hip, happening, and modern society.

The report also notes that while the actual economic effect of pop culture exports is insignificant compared to industries such as semiconductors, ships, and auto manufacturing, the wave is boosting confidence in Korea and things Korean-made both domestically and internationally.

CLSA noted that the Korean wave—a term coined by Chinese media to describe a deluge of Korean pop culture entrancing the nation's youth—coincided with two substantial changes in the Korean economic landscape. First, due to carefully developed government policies in the early 1990s, leading-edge infrastructure, such as broadband Internet and CDMA-standard mobile telecommunications networks, was coming online towards the end of the millennium, converting Korea into a test-bed for hi-tech products and services. Second, after the economic crisis of 1997, the country's conglomerates had to restructure and concentrate on core industries—for Samsung, electronics; for Hyundai, cars; and for LG, consumer electronics. This led to the establishment of Korea's first world-class brands: Samsung mobiles, Hyundai cars, and LG air conditioners. The wave grants these companies an Asia-wide marketing platform.

"Korean products were historically not at the top of the global spectrum, and Koreans were skeptical of the success of their own companies," said David Cotterchio, CLSA Korea's country head. He added that Koreans have not traditionally invested in their own stocks. "That is the main reason for the low stock valuations here: the so-called 'Korea discount.'"

According to the report, Korean markets have climbed 22% since the last quarter of 2004 against a backdrop of net foreign selling. And in an Asia-wide survey, it found that South Korean brands scored 4.47 out of a possible 5.5 points—following closely behind Britain's products, with 4.59, and far ahead of China's, which were rated just 3.37.

Mr. Cotterchio is firm about his claims: "The unprecedented confidence being shown in Korea by the outside world will lead Koreans to an increased awareness and confidence in their own companies and brands."

Source: Andrew Salmon, "Investors getting ready to surf the Korean wave; an explosion of pop culture and rising confidence both at home and abroad may herald boom times ahead," *South China Morning Post* (July 13, 2005): 7.

Case Questions

1. If you were in charge of a company's attempt to "surf the Korea wave," how would you measure consumers' attitudes toward the Korea wave?

2. How would you address the concern regarding the reliability and validity of the measurement scales you propose?

Notes

1. Pierre Chandon, Vicki G. Morwitz, and Werner J. Reinartz, "Do intentions really predict behavior? Self-generated validity effects in survey research," *Journal of Marketing* 69, no. 2 (April 2005): 1–14.

2. Food Marketing Institute, "Consumers cite value and nutrition as primary drivers for shopping decisions," *FMI Trends 2002*, http://www.fmi.org/media/mediatext.cfm?id=416, July 16, 2005.

3. F. N. Kerlinger, *Foundations of Behavioral Research*, 3rd ed. (New York: Harcourt Brace Jovanovich, 1986).

4. Aharon Tziner, Christine Joanis, and Kevin R. Murphy, "A comparison of three methods of performance appraisal with regard to goal properties, goal perception, and rate satisfaction," *Group & Organization Management* 25, no. 2 (June 2000): 175–190.

5. S. P. Douglas and C. S. Craig, *International Marketing Research* (Upper Saddle River, NJ: Prentice Hall, 1983), 200.

6. C. Cook, F. Heath, R. Thompson, B. Thompson, "Score Reliability in Web or Internet-Based Surveys: Unnumbered Graphic Rating Scales versus Likert-Type Scales", *Educational and Psychological Measurement*, vol. 61, No. 4, (2001), 697–706, © 2001 SAGE Publications, http://epm.sagepub.com/cgi/content/abstract/61/4/697.

7. H. H. Friedman, L. W. Friedman, and B. Gluck, "The effects of scale-checking styles on responses to a semantic differential scale," *Journal of the Market Research Society* (October 1988): 477–481.

8. W. D. Barclay, "The semantic differential as an index of brand attitude," *Journal of Advertising Research* 4 (March, 1964): 30–33.

9. E. P. Cox, "The optimal number of response alternatives for a scale: A review," *Journal of Marketing Research* (November 1980): 407–422; A. M. Givon and Z. Shapira, "Response to rating scales: A theoretical model and its application to the number of categories problem," *Journal of Marketing Research* (November 1984): 410–419.

10. C. T. Chambers, K. Giesbrecht, K. D. Craig, S. M. Bennett, and E. Huntsman, "A comparison of faces scales for the measurement of pediatric pain: children's and parents' ratings," Pain, October 1999, vol. 83, no. 1, pp. 25–35.

11. E. E. Ghiselli, J. P. Campbell, and S. Zedeck, *Measurement Theory for the Behavioral Sciences* (San Francisco: W. H. Freeman, 1981), 249.

12. G. A. Churchill and J. P. Peter, "Research design effects on the reliability of rating scales," *Journal of Marketing Research* (November 1984): 360–375.

13. Richard P. Bagozzi, *Measurement in Marketing Research* (Cambridge, MA: Blackwell, 1994), 20.

Questionnaire Design

Source: © 2007 JupiterImages Corporation.

Key Terms

Learning Objectives

After studying this chapter, you will be able to:

- Discuss the attributes of an effective questionnaire.
- Describe the questionnaire design process and discuss the major considerations in each phase.
- Identify common problems in questionnaires.
- Discuss key considerations in questionnaire organization and layout.
- Explain the process of pretesting a questionnaire domestically and globally.

GET THIS

Survey Says...Why Shoppers Abandon Online Shopping Experiences

Consumers often visit Web sites to browse product offerings of online retailers. A tremendous amount of time and effort goes into building these sites so that consumers are attracted enough to shop there and buy their products. Once consumers stroll down the virtual aisles, though, they oftentimes don't complete their shopping experience. They may have had products registered in their shopping carts, but for one reason or another they never checked out.

Understanding why prospective customers abandon shopping carts and registration pages is crucial to online businesses. They should make every effort possible to understand and address consumers' concerns to increase conversion rates and improve sales.

The shopping cart abandonment rate is a huge problem for businesses. Take a look at the variety of reasons for shopping abandonment, as reported from a recent study by Global Millennia Marketing (the percentage of respondents giving particular reason is provided in parentheses):

- Cost of shipping too high and not shown until checkout (69%)
- Changed mind and discarded cart contents (61%)
- Comparison shopping or browsing (57%)
- Total cost of items is too high (49%)
- Saving items for later purchase (47%)
- Checkout process is too long (44%)
- Out-of-stock products at checkout time (39%)
- Checkout requires too much personal information (35%)
- Poor site navigation and long download times (31%)
- Lack of sufficient product or contact information (31%)

While these statistics reflect the plethora of reasons visitors abandon Web sites in general, they do not indicate why visitors abandon specific Web sites. To improve their site conversion rate, companies are encouraged to administer online shopping cart abandonment surveys to understand where concerns exist so that they can address them and hopefully increase their sales.

Many marketers agree that online shopping cart abandonment surveys are easy to implement. The ideal time to learn why a shopping cart was abandoned is when a visitor leaves the purchase page without pressing the "Purchase Now" or "Submit" buttons. A short pop-up survey can be done quickly and go a long way in gathering this important feedback. Some online survey tools allow marketers to insert information from the visitors' online activity into the survey as a hidden field so that the number of questions asked is minimized and the data is richer.

Since most sites do not gather contact information from visitors who haven't completed the purchase or registration process, marketers cannot send an email invitation to take the survey. Even if the company has that contact information, the visitor may have forgotten exactly why he or she abandoned the purchase.

Source: Tom Lueker, "Abandonment surveys help boost sales," *Marketing News* 37, no. 24 (November 24, 2003): 16–17.

Now Ask Yourself

- What are the two major questions you should answer through your abandonment survey?
- How many questions should be included in the abandonment survey?
- How would you lay out the questionnaire items in the survey?

The "Get This" feature says that we need to understand how to design a good questionnaire to collect valid information. A well-designed survey not only is necessary to generate reliable responses, but also is a critical way to gain cooperation from potential respondents. We discussed measurement scales in Chapter 7. In this chapter, you will learn how to plan and construct effective questionnaires. But first we will introduce you to the necessary attributes of an effective questionnaire.

8-1 Attributes of an Effective Questionnaire

A **questionnaire** is a formal set of questions or statements designed to gather information from respondents that will accomplish the goals of the research project. Questionnaires measure people's attitudes, behavior, and feelings toward just about everything—products and services, new product features, advertising slogans, new product concepts—the list is endless. Consider, for example, in Pennsylvania where an organization of 2,300 real estate professionals wanted to learn if it was on the right track before implementing its strategic plan. So it surveyed both agents and brokers about the association's educational programs, benefits, communications, and social events. The results helped the Montgomery County Association of Realtors fine tune its ideas for change. Questionnaires provide a uniform structure that allows responses to be analyzed and compared.[1]

Suppose we want to understand why people eat donuts. There are lots of questions we could ask. Here are some possibilities:

- Why do you eat donuts?
- Do you like the taste of donuts?
- Does eating donuts make you feel good?
- Are you concerned about the calories in donuts?
- You are grossly overweight, so why do you allow yourself to eat donuts with all that sugar?

Needless to say, how we phrase questions has a lot to do with what kinds of responses we get. Think about the answers we might get from the questions about donuts. Some of them lean toward certain responses, don't they? Can you see what problems we might have when we analyze our results? As you can see, questionnaires must be carefully designed so that the questions don't influence respondents toward answering in particular ways and so that the data accomplishes the purpose of the study.

When creating a questionnaire, keep several goals in mind:

1. *Questionnaires should be user-friendly.* The instrument must be culturally sensitive and clearly understandable for all respondents. The easier the questionnaire is to understand, the more likely it is that respondents will complete it.

2. *The questionnaire should look professional.* All questionnaires should be clean, typed, and carefully designed.

3. *It should be valid.* In Chapter 7, we described validity as "the degree to which a test measures what it is supposed to measure." The questions in the questionnaire should be reliable and measure what you intended to measure. Designing a questionnaire that provides the information that you need to collect can be a daunting task.

4. *It should be attractive and motivational in nature.* For respondents to want to complete questionnaires, the topic must be interesting or intriguing, and respondents must feel they are "getting something out of it." Marketers use

questionnaire A formal set of questions or statements designed to gather information from respondents that will accomplish the goals of the research project.

various incentives to motivate respondents to complete questionnaires, such as a summary of the results, rewards, and the backing of top management.[2]

5. *The questionnaire should encourage respondents to answer honestly and accurately.* Respondents are sometimes intimidated by questions, and their reasons can vary—job insecurity, desire for confidentiality, or lack of knowledge, for example. Whatever the reason, respondents must be assured that the results they provide will not come back to haunt them. Typically, researchers note on the questionnaires that respondent confidentiality is guaranteed and that the responses will only be used as part of the study findings and not for any other purpose.

See Research Realities 8-1 for a description of the global Internet as a prime tool for conducting surveys.

Research Realities 8-1

The Global Internet Enhances Survey Implementation

The global Internet is a prime tool for conducting surveys. Web pages can be designed that allow for interactivity with the user and a direct connection to databases that can hold responses. Analytical engines can be programmed to summarize the data as it's recorded. This technique is much faster than traditional methods and makes sense in a global marketing world. The advantages of speed, relative low cost and quicker reporting can help managers make prompt decisions in an increasingly competitive international marketplace.

Source: Robert J. Bonometti, Jun Tang, "A Dynamic Technique for Conducting Online Survey Based Research," *Competitiveness Review,* vol. 16 Issue 2, (2006): p. 97.

Results from questionnaires often guide a company's strategic planning. This is a critical purpose, so questionnaires must be carefully constructed to gather accurate, relevant information. There are no cookbook formulas for creating the ideal questionnaire. In fact, questionnaire design is really more art than science.

Examine the questionnaire in Exhibit 8-1. This questionnaire solicits information about customers' shopping experiences at The Home Depot. The questionnaire is short and simple, so that customers will take the time to fill it out and so that processing the results will be facilitated. As you study this chapter, refer to this questionnaire and decide whether it followed sound design principles. What does it do well? What problems does it pose? What changes could make it better?

Questionnaires are constructed in three phases, as shown in Exhibit 8-2. Each phase presents issues that must be resolved before researchers proceed to the next phase. Let's examine these phases and see what issues researchers consider as they design and construct effective questionnaires.

8-2 Preconstruction

Before researchers can construct an effective questionnaire, they must address several issues. Consider what architects look at when they design houses. If they don't examine the goals, the method of construction, the intended number of inhabitants, and the resources available, construction may not go well. Similarly, researchers give careful thought to questionnaire objectives, target respondent characteristics, resource constraints, and data collection methods. These considerations are summarized in Exhibit 8-3.

8-2a Revisit Research Objectives

At this point in the research process, management has already identified a specific information need and clearly defined the problem or opportunity. The information

EXHIBIT 8-1	Home Depot Comment Card

Your Total Satisfaction Means Everything. Your Comments Make A Difference

	Excellent	Above Average	Average	Below Average	Poor
The Store					
Overall shopping experience	○	○	○	○	○
The Merchandise					
Selection	○	○	○	○	○
In stock	○	○	○	○	○
Value	○	○	○	○	○
The Sales Personnel					
Sales people available	○	○	○	○	○
Sales people knowledgeable	○	○	○	○	○
The Checkout Area					
Speed	○	○	○	○	○
Friendliness	○	○	○	○	○
The Service Desk					
Courtesy	○	○	○	○	○
Helpfulness	○	○	○	○	○

Customer Type   Do-It-Yourselfer ○   Contractor / Commercial Customer ○

Additional Comments: _____

_____

_____

_____

_____

3607

Optional, but appreciated:
Name _____
Address _____
Phone ( ) _____

Source: © 2006 Homer TLC, Inc. ("Homer TLC"). Reproduced with permission.

need must now be translated into clear questionnaire items so that the questionnaire can be designed to obtain the needed information. This step in questionnaire construction has the researcher asking, "What information should be obtained from the data-gathering effort?" Key people in the organization must determine what needs to occur in the data-gathering effort.

The formulation of objectives should be a team effort. Employees who will be directly affected by the study should have input. When objectives are clearly understood, the researcher can design questionnaires that accomplish them. Establishing goals provides direction and a standard against which to measure success.

8-2b Target Respondent Characteristics

When planning a questionnaire, researchers must clearly understand the attitudes, attributes, and past actions of the target respondents; the questions must be written specifically for these respondents. If researchers want to gather information about the purchasing habits of homemakers, they will design different questionnaires for homemakers in the United States and in Nigeria because the habits, disposable

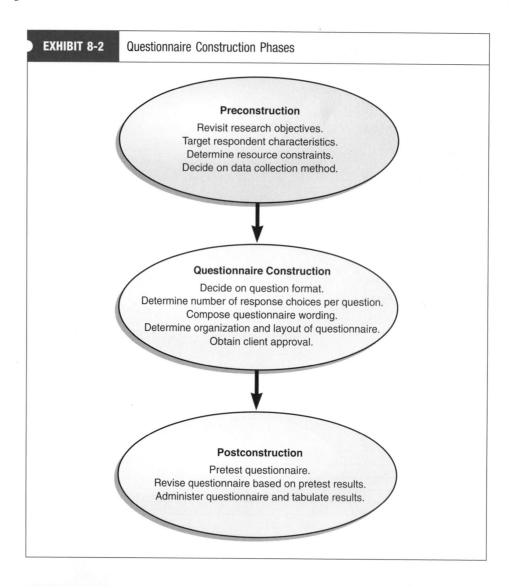

EXHIBIT 8-2   Questionnaire Construction Phases

Preconstruction

Revisit research objectives.
Target respondent characteristics.
Determine resource constraints.
Decide on data collection method.

Questionnaire Construction

Decide on question format.
Determine number of response choices per question.
Compose questionnaire wording.
Determine organization and layout of questionnaire.
Obtain client approval.

Postconstruction

Pretest questionnaire.
Revise questionnaire based on pretest results.
Administer questionnaire and tabulate results.

EXHIBIT 8-3   Considerations in the Preconstruction Phase

Revisit Research Objectives
• What information should be obtained from our data-gathering effort?

Target Respondent Characteristics
• What characteristics of our target respondents affect questionnaire design?

Resource Constraints
• What are the limits of our company resources?

Decide on Data Collection Method
• Should the information be obtained through telephone interviews, mail surveys, personal interviews, or perhaps online surveys?
• Should the research efforts be structured or unstructured, human or mechanical, and should they be conducted directly or indirectly?

income, and social norms of these two target populations are quite different. Therefore, before developing questions, the researcher should write a clear description of the target respondents and refer to it periodically. This will ensure that the respondents are kept in mind as questions are developed.

Source: © 2007 JupiterImages Corporation.

8-2c Resource Constraints

It would be wonderful if researchers could spend whatever they need to in order to accomplish their research objectives. But this, of course, is unrealistic. All research projects are constrained by company resources. Therefore, prior to constructing a questionnaire, researchers must state project requirements—costs, employee time, and physical space—and obtain management approval. Running out of resources in the middle of a project causes a helpless feeling that should be avoided. It can be, with a full accounting of resource requirements prior to starting the study.

8-2d Decide on a Data Collection Method

Prior to creating the questionnaire, it is important for the researcher to decide how the information sought will be gathered. That is, should it be obtained through telephone interviews, mail surveys, personal interviews, or perhaps online surveys? Additionally, should the research efforts be structured or unstructured, human or mechanical, and conducted directly or indirectly? You may recall that each issue has its advantages and disadvantages, so the questionnaire's content must reflect those concerns.

For example, Unifi Technology, which offers web-enabled solutions connecting manufacturing, supply chain, and e-business, wanted to interview 200 managers at electronic companies about their manufacturing systems. To accomplish this, the researcher created a questionnaire that was user-friendly for telephone interviewers. However, some of the targeted respondents didn't want to take the time on the telephone to complete the survey but indicated that they would fill it out if it were faxed to them. The researcher then had to revise the questionnaire to make it suitable for this less-personal data collection mode.[3]

8-3 Questionnaire Construction

Once the objectives, target respondent characteristics, resource constraints, and data collection method have been determined, the process of constructing the questionnaire begins. This task is complex and requires great attention to detail— mistakes in format, content, wording, clarity, organization, or layout can jeopardize

---

> **EXHIBIT 8-4** Considerations in the Construction Phase
>
> **Question Format**
> - Should we use open- or closed-ended questions (dichotomous, multiple-choice)?
>
> **Number of Response Choices per Question**
> - What type of information are we seeking from the respondent?
> - To what extent are respondents able to discriminate among the choices?
> - What is our cut-off point for the number of response choices?
> - What survey method will we use to deliver the questions?
>
> **Questionnaire Wording**
> - Are the instructions easy to understand?
> - Are the questions easy to understand?
> - Use unambiguous wording.
> - Use appropriate wordings for the target respondents.
> - State questions succinctly.
> - State alternatives in questions explicitly.
> - Avoid using over-demanding recalls.
> - Avoid using double-barreled questions.
> - Avoiding using leading questions.
>
> **Organization and Layout of Questionnaire**
> - Introduction
> - Main Body
>
> **Obtain Client Approval**
> - Has our client approved the survey that we plan to use?

---

the questionnaire's usefulness. As shown in Exhibit 8-4, question format is a key issue because it affects the entire questionnaire design.

8-3a Question Format

Two question formats are used in survey research: *open-ended* and *closed-ended*. The closed-ended format can be divided into *dichotomous* and *multiple-choice questions*. Each format has its strengths and weaknesses. Although they will be presented as independent formats, they are often used together. For example, a recent study of U.S.-based executives of large multinational advertising agencies used open-ended and closed-ended questions. Open-ended questions were used to examine the agencies' globalization process, while closed-ended questions were used to determine the relative importance of various aspects of interoffice coordination and use of information technology.[4] Sales managers are sometimes encouraged to use both types of questions to learn about their customers.[5]

Open-Ended Questions

open-ended questions
Questions that do not supply response choices, that respondents can answer any way they want.

Open-ended questions do not provide response choices; respondents can respond however they want. While researchers hope that respondents will answer the questions as clearly and succinctly as possible, the wording of the question really dictates the extent of responses. That is, straightforward questions such as "What is your favorite television program?" don't require as long a response as "What do you like and dislike about your favorite television program?" Examine Exhibit 8-1 and decide which are the open-ended questions?

Open-ended questions have several advantages. They allow respondents *freedom of response*. Respondents aren't limited to choosing from a finite set of responses;

they can answer in whatever way seems right to them. When not provided with choices, respondents are less likely to be influenced into responding a particular way.

Open-ended questions are *sensitive to respondents' desire for expression*. Most respondents like to state their feelings in their own words. While the researcher must be careful not to overburden the respondents with questions that require extensive writing, a few open-ended questions toward the end of the survey can provide some interesting insights.

Open-ended questions are *well suited for exploratory* studies. If little previous research has been done, open-ended questions are convenient because they don't require in-depth knowledge on the part of the researcher. Researchers can educate themselves about a topic by paying close attention to responses to open-ended questions.

Finally, an open-ended format is *suitable for certain types of questions*. If respondents are asked, "What is your favorite television program?" the blank provided for the answer should be short to discourage lengthy responses.

There are disadvantages to open-ended questions. *Interpretation of the responses can bias the findings.* Answers to open-ended questions require interpretation. When interpretation is necessary, the perceptive filters of the interpreters come into play, and this can bias the results.

Researchers must form *representative categories that encompass all responses*. This is not an easy task when it is done "after the fact." Since there are no preestablished responses, which are carefully controlled, answers may be "all over the map," so to speak, and condensing and categorizing such responses can be difficult. The categories must be based on a thorough understanding of the responses. To simplify the coding effort, researchers sometimes form tentative response categories before the survey results are coded. After the responses are examined, slight revisions are made; the responses are then coded by placing a check mark next to the appropriate category or marking "other" if the response doesn't match any of the categories.

Open-ended questions *may discourage respondents from completing the questionnaire*. People often look for reasons not to fill out surveys. If they believe that completing it will require too much time and effort, they may not answer all of the questions, or they may refuse to take the survey at all, so researchers must be careful not to have too many open-ended questions on their surveys. How many is "too many" open-ended questions should be determined during the pretest stage of survey development—an issue that we will get to later in this chapter.

Finally, *coding open-ended questionnaires can be expensive and time-consuming*. Coding hundreds of surveys with numerous questions can take a long time, and time is money.

Closed-Ended Questions

Closed-ended questions supply a certain number of responses from which respondents are expected to choose. The choices can take the form of a rating system or a set of alternatives. Respondents are asked to choose the most appropriate answer. Exhibit 8-1 includes closed-ended questions in The Home Depot questionnaire. For example, "Overall shopping experience", "Selection", "In stock", "Value", "Sales people available", "Sales people knowledgeable", "Speed", "Friendliness", "Courtesy", and "Helpfulness" uses five-point scales ranging from "Excellent" to "Poor".

Closed-ended questions have several advantages. First of all, *they are easy to administer*. Typically closed-ended questions do not require much, if any, explanation, so surveys with these questions can be carried out with relative ease. *They reduce interpreter bias.* Researchers don't interpret the responses in the coding process because they are already in a form that can be coded. *Closed-ended questions tend to motivate respondents to complete surveys.* Providing choices that require only a checkmark simplifies the task, thus reducing the time and energy needed to complete the survey. Closed-ended questions *simplify coding and tabulating efforts* because

closed-ended questions
Questions that provide response choices from which respondents are expected to choose.

interpreters don't have to create categories from a wide range of narratives, as is the case with open-ended questions. Finally, *providing choices prompts respondents to ponder alternatives that they might not otherwise consider.* If a study is interested in finding out why people attend sporting events, the choices might be "fan of the team," "enjoy getting out of the house," "relieves stress," "to socialize," "to spend time with the kids," and "to watch the half-time entertainment." Perhaps an individual would not have thought of "relieves stress" and "to watch the half-time entertainment" if the choices were not provided in the questionnaire.

There are also disadvantages to closed-ended questions. The most prominent shortcoming is *the extensive effort required in questionnaire construction to create either an exhaustive list of choices or a short list of the most likely choices.* For the choices to be exhaustive, all possible answers should be included, and this is usually not practical. Therefore, researchers usually list the most likely choices and include a choice stated as "Other; please specify: _____." To ensure that the lists of choices are exhaustive or include the most likely choices, the researcher must gain a thorough understanding of the subject by reading extensively and communicating with experts in the field.

Another problem with closed-ended questions is *their inhibiting effect on respondents.* When choices are provided, respondents are limited to the selections listed, unless the "Other; please specify" choice is offered. This can channel their thoughts and thus prevent them from providing responses that most accurately reflect their feelings. A third problem with closed-ended questions is *relying on the respondent to know whether to "select one" or "check all that apply."* Savvy marketing researchers will create closed-ended questions that clearly inform the respondent to provide only one answer or as many as are appropriate to each question. However, sometimes respondents will ignore the instructions and respond how they feel like responding. When this violation occurs, it is in the best interest of the study to either disregard the responses to these questions or report the findings along with an explanation of what occurred.

dichotomous questions
Closed-ended questions that provide two response choices.

Dichotomous Questions   **Dichotomous questions** are closed-ended questions that offer only two response choices. Dichotomies can be formed by simply breaking a category into two parts—for example, gender (male/female), age (young/old), religion (Christian/non-Christian), body type (fat/thin), and athletic ability (athletic/nonathletic). Researchers often use dichotomous questions to understand the respondent's demographic composition or behavioral inclination. For example, if researchers are interested in understanding why teenagers patronize fast-food restaurants, they could use the following dichotomous questions:

1. Please specify your gender.
   Male   1   Female   2
2. Have you eaten at a fast-food restaurant during the past seven days?
   Yes   1   No   2
3. How would you describe your most recent visit to a fast-food establishment?
   Pleasant   1   Unpleasant   2
4. Are you concerned about the nutritional content of fast food?
   Yes   1   No   2
5. The prices at most fast-food restaurants are too high.
   Agree   1   Disagree   2
6. The environment at most fast-food restaurants is pleasant.
   Agree   1   Disagree   2

The main strength of dichotomies is that they *do not require much time or thought* on the part of respondents. Other strengths include *minimal interpreter bias* and *simplified coding and analysis.* The main shortcoming is the *omission of intermediate points.* Since the questions are polarized, respondents are forced to choose between extremes, rather than give some intermediate response.

A word of caution for people designing dichotomous questions: Because there are only two response choices, questions must be carefully phrased so as not to bias respondents toward a particular response. Directional or "leading" sentences such as "Do you enjoy shopping at XYZ supermarket, which usually has a lousy produce section?" obviously influence respondents' answers. "A lousy produce section" leads respondents to the negative response. Sometimes, researchers include a third choice such as "no response" or "don't know" for those respondents either unable or unwilling to choose one of the extreme selections listed.

Multiple-Choice Questions **Multiple-choice questions** (sometimes called "multichotomous questions") are closed-ended questions that give respondents several choices. Respondents are expected to select the alternative that most closely relates to their position on the topic. These types of questions are relatively simple to complete, and easy to code and analyze. Multiple-choice questions can give a complete listing of responses or a shortened listing of the most likely responses, like those designed to collect data about why teenagers patronize fast-food restaurants:

multiple-choice questions
Closed-ended questions that provide more than two response choices.

1. How would you rate the food quality at the fast-food restaurant you last visited?
   ____ Excellent   ____ Fair   ____ Very good   ____ Poor   ____ Good

2. When do you plan to visit another fast-food restaurant?
   ____Within five days ____16–20 days ____5–10 days____ More than 20 days
   ____11–15 days

3. How much did you spend during your last visit to a fast-food establishment?
   ____$1.00 or less   ____$3.01–$4.00   ____$1.01–$2.00   ____$4.01–$5.00
   ____$2.01–$3.00   ____More than $5.00

As with other question formats, multiple-choice questions have strengths and weaknesses. Their strengths are similar to those of dichotomous questions: They reduce *interpreter bias,* they are *easy to complete,* and they are *simple to code and analyze*—especially if responses are marked on a bubble form that can be electronically scanned. Furthermore, multiple-choice questions are *free of bias in grading* and are believed to be *more valid and reliable than open-ended questions.*[6] Multiple-choice questions are often preferred to dichotomous questions because they *allow respondents to indicate their feelings more precisely.* The main problem with multiple-choice questions is that *researchers must create carefully worded questions and exhaustive lists of choices to ensure that responses are representative.* Therefore, it is important for researchers to provide respondents the option of "Other; please specify: ____".

8-3b Number of Response Choices per Question

Once researchers decide to use closed-ended questions, they must consider the number of response choices to provide. Too many choices overwhelm and confuse; too few don't give representative answers. To decide on the number, marketing researchers consider several factors:

- *What type of information are we seeking from the respondent?* Some questions require only two choices. If researchers want to know whether respondents eat at fast-food restaurants, a simple "yes" or "no" suffices. However, if they want to know how often the respondents eat fast food each year, more choices are necessary.

- *To what extent are respondents able to discriminate among the choices?* Often five or seven choices are provided, particularly when gathering attitudinal and behavioral information. Five choices are easier for respondents to discriminate among, but seven choices give more detail. The exact number of choices should be finalized after the questionnaire is pretested. We will discuss this step later in the chapter.

- *What is the cut-off point for the number of response choices?* Researchers must decide what is most efficient and effective for the data they wish to collect. The question "Which of the following is your favorite fast-food establishment?" could list as potential responses all possible fast-food restaurants, but the question is, which restaurants do the researchers wish to examine and which do they think are the most likely choices? An "Other; please specify" category, of course, can be used to cover the remaining possible answers.

- *What survey method will we use to deliver the questions?* If telephone or personal interviews are the survey vehicle, then a maximum of five responses to each question should be used because respondents have trouble remembering more than five. More than five choices confuses respondents. If a written questionnaire or online survey is used, more choices can be provided because respondents can reread them.

8-3c Questionnaire Wording

Deciding on the wording of a questionnaire is a crucial step for researchers because of **item nonresponse**—when a respondent who agrees to participate in a study refuses to respond to certain questions. Obviously questions are placed on surveys to gather important information on topics. The more respondents refuse to answer questions, the less successful will be the study, so researchers must try to generate questionnaires that will be completed as fully as possible by targeted respondents. To this end, the researcher must ask good questions—which are dependent on how questions are phrased. Question phrasing depends on such factors as the information being sought, the characteristics of target respondents, and where the survey is administered. Good questionnaire writing requires that researchers follow nine key guidelines:

- *Are the instructions easy to understand?* Instructions should always be easy to read or hear and easy to follow, since clear instructions ensure that respondents all follow the same procedures; this is important in obtaining valid results. Ambiguous instructions result in misinterpretation and flawed conclusions. Oral instructions should not deviate from the script because this can bias results. Avoid using confusing or uncommon words in instructions, and avoid jargon.

- *Are the questions easy to understand?* As with instructions, questionnaire administrators' attempts to clarify unclear questions can bias the results. Therefore, use simple words and phrases whenever possible, and test each question for wording, clarity, and completeness. Have others answer the questions to check for ambiguity and unintended meanings. Testing the questions on a focus group is an excellent way to do this. Have the group offer suggestions for improvement.

    The **Delphi technique,** in which a panel of experts determines survey content, is also helpful. Each group member makes a concealed judgment about an issue. These judgments are then compiled and shared with others. Group members then have the option of changing their judgment. Conclusions are attained after multiple iterations of revising judgments.

- *Use unambiguous wording.* To ensure that the information sought is obtained, questions must have only one possible interpretation. Questions subject to differing interpretations cloud the results. Consider the following question:
    In a typical month, how often do you shop at department stores?
    ___ Never ___ Occasionally ___ Sometimes ___ Often ___ Regularly
    The answer options can be interpreted very differently for different respondents. For those who shop at department stores once a month, some may choose "regularly" while others may select "sometimes." A much clearer question is as follows:

item nonresponse When a respondent who agrees to participate in a study refuses to respond to certain questions.

Delphi technique A technique that uses a group of experts to determine the appropriate content of the survey. Group members first make concealed individual judgments. Then they are exposed to other members' judgments and can revise their judgments if they wish. After multiple iterations of revising judgments, the group reaches a conclusion.

In a typical month, how often do you shop at department stores?
___less than once ___ 1 or 2 times ___ 3 or 4 times ___ more than 4 times

- *Use appropriate wordings for the target respondents.* Questionnaires should be customer-oriented, just like businesses. The "customers" of the questionnaire are the respondents, so the questions must fit the respondent demographics, including education level, knowledge of the subject, language, ethnic background, age, and many other characteristics. For example, the question "With what frequency have you experienced this of late?" sounds awkward. A better wording is "How many times have you had this happen recently?"

- *State questions succinctly.* Wordy questions confuse and fatigue respondents. Conciseness is the goal. How many words are enough? Use only as many words as are necessary. Elaborate only when necessary. Do not overexplain—just get to the point.

- *State alternatives in questions explicitly.* Use questions that give alternatives sparingly because they cannot be answered yes or no. When alternatives are given, they should be explicitly stated to avoid misinterpretations. For example, if researchers want to know about the preferences of consumers for eating at home versus restaurants, they could phrase the question in these two ways:
  1. Do you enjoy eating in restaurants?
  2. Which do you prefer—eating in restaurants or eating at home?

Both questions address consumers' attitudes toward restaurant dining. However, the latter question is preferred because it compares restaurant and home dining, which is the information the researchers are looking for.

- *Avoid using over-demanding recalls.* People do not have perfect memory and cannot recall everything, especially the details of certain purchase behavior. For example, "How much did you spend on each item you bought during your last trip to a supermarket" obviously is beyond respondents' ability to remember what happened.

- *Avoid using double-barreled questions.* A **double-barreled question** is a single question that asks for two responses. The results cannot be effectively interpreted because the researcher does not know which part of the question is being answered. The question "Do you believe most Japanese automobiles are comfortable and worth their price?" is a double-barreled question. You can see that although one question is asked, it actually asks for two responses—about comfort and price. We wouldn't know if the respondent is answering yes or no to both questions or to only one of them. Not knowing this makes the results inconclusive. To remedy this problem, two separate questions should be generated:
  1. Do you believe most Japanese automobiles are comfortable?
  2. Do you believe most Japanese automobiles are worth their price?

double-barreled questions A single question that asks for two responses.

- *Avoiding using leading questions.* Leading or biasing questions should carefully be weeded out. A **leading question** is a question that influences respondents toward a particular response. Leading questions take numerous forms. They can suggest answers that reflect the researcher's attitudes or opinions. Simply adding, "I'm sure you agree" or "Don't you think" to a statement can significantly bias responses. If the question is, "Don't you think that fast food is bad for you?" respondents are likely to respond differently than if it is, "Do you believe fast food is good for you?" And respondents who are asked, "Do you enjoy eating greasy hamburgers more than healthy salads?" are likely to be influenced by the words "greasy" and "healthy."
Researchers have also found that respondents tend to agree with plausible propositions unless they have a strong opinion or alternatives are provided. Even when alternatives are offered, respondents tend to agree rather than disagree with plausible statements.[7] Given this tendency, questions should be neutrally worded.

leading questions A question that influences respondents toward a particular answer.

Source: Comstock.com.

8-3d Organization and Layout of Questionnaire

Question sequencing and the physical layout of the questionnaire significantly impact responses. A survey is usually organized in the following ways:

Introduction

The introduction explains the purpose of the questionnaire to the respondent and the value of returning the questionnaire.[8] It should be short, inviting, easy to read, and unambiguous. The introduction should also explicitly state what the incentives are to motivate respondents to participate.

Main Body

- *Screen and warm-up questions.* The first question is usually a screening question to determine whether the potential respondents are qualified to participate in the survey. For example, if we want to obtain consumers feedback on mobile phone service, the first question could be "Do you have a mobile phone?"

  After the screen question, a few simple and easy-to-answer warm-up questions can be asked to further motivate respondents to participate. For example, "How long have you owned a mobile phone?" and "Which company's service are you using now?" serve nicely as warm-up questions.

- *Middle part.* Place the majority of questions that relate to the research objectives in the middle of the survey. All questions on a particular topic should be grouped together and in a logical fashion before the questionnaire moves on to another topic. Usually, place the more complicated, difficult-to-answer, embarrassing, or emotionally charged questions toward the end of the survey.

  Don't make the questionnaire too long. This overwhelms respondents. Long questionnaires are tiring and tend to have high nonresponse rates. One way to alleviate the length problem is to split the questionnaire into several components and administer only one component to any sampled individual. The answers taken together will generate the information sought.[9]

- *Ending.* Place demographic or lifestyle questions at the end of the survey. Then, conclude the survey by thanking respondents for their time. You may also want to inform respondents how they can obtain results of the survey.

8-3e Obtain Client Approval

Many times researchers will conduct studies for an individual or organization that is external from their company. If this is the case, it is extremely important to share a draft of the questionnaire with the client to allow feedback prior to implementing it. If questions on the questionnaire are either inappropriate or perhaps can be improved, it is necessary for the client to convey these changes to the researcher. This may cause multiple iterations, but it is important for the client to "bless" the final questionnaire that will ultimately be used.

8-4 Postconstruction

The questionnaire is created; now it should be scrutinized to determine whether it is as good as you think it is. At this point, researchers usually feel fairly confident that the instrument will serve its purpose. Still, some changes may be necessary. The questionnaire should not be used until its developers are confident that it will effectively measure what it is intended to measure. This confidence should be supported through objective testing. Exhibit 8-5 summarizes the considerations in the postconstruction phase.

8-4a Pretest the Questionnaire

Regardless of the experience and expertise of the questionnaire's designer, individuals who were not involved in its design should test it to ensure that it communicates clearly and correctly. The designers can become too familiar with the questionnaire—they may not see the forest for the trees.[10] **Pretesting** involves a trial run of the questionnaire using a small sample from the target population to detect any problems. The goal is to affirm that the questionnaire will capture the information sought by the researcher. The pretest helps refine the instrument and identifies errors that may be apparent only to the targeted population. More specifically, its value comes from determining whether questions make sense, are in logical order, contain bias wording, or will provide the researcher with the desired information.[11] Sometimes pretesting can be a humbling experience because weak-nesses previously overlooked become glaringly apparent. Unfortunately, though, while the pretest stage often identifies fundamental problems in a questionnaire, it is the stage most likely to be squeezed out because of cost and time constraints.[12]

While there is no magic number that should be sampled during a pretest, most experts would agree that the sample size should be relatively small—

pretesting A trial run of a questionnaire using a small sample from the target population to detect problems with the questionnaire.

> **EXHIBIT 8-5**   Considerations in the Postconstruction Phase

Pretest the Questionnaire
- What is pretesting?
- Should we always pretest our questionnaire?
- How do we effectively pretest our questionnaire?

Revise Questionnaire Based on Pretest Results
- Have we adequately pretested our questionnaire?

Administer Questionnaire and Tabulate Results
- Did we effectively implement the survey, tabulate, and code the responses so that statistical tests can be run and relationships be determined?

20–40 respondents knowledgeable about the test topic. Keeping the sample small minimizes time and costs. Most companies want to reserve the bulk of their resources for the actual administration of the questionnaire. Some experts stress that while the sample size may be small, it should cover all subgroups of the target respondents.[13]

Pretesting is usually implemented in two stages. The first stage is personal interviews, regardless of the way the questionnaire will later be administered, because researchers need to observe the behaviors of both the interviewers and the respondents. Respondents' reactions to the questions are of primary interest. The interviews can be carried out through protocol analysis or debriefing. **Protocol analysis** is an interviewing technique in which respondents think aloud while responding to each question. This technique affords the researcher the luxury of "getting into the mind" of each respondent. **Debriefing** is an interview conducted after respondents have completed the questionnaire. The respondents are then informed that the exercise was a pretest and are asked to share with the researcher their thoughts about the questions, their answers, and any shortcomings of the survey.

The second pretest stage involves administering the survey to a small sample in an environment as similar as possible to the one in which the questionnaire will ultimately be administered. This stage of the pretest often reveals problems undetectable through personal interviews. In either phase of pretesting, researchers should attempt to eliminate any of the following questionnaire problems:

protocol analysis An interviewing technique in which respondents think aloud while responding to each question.

debriefing An interview conducted after respondents have completed a questionnaire, in which they are informed that the exercise was a pretest and are asked to share with the researcher their thoughts about the questions, their answers, and any shortcomings of the survey.

- Double-barreled questions
- Ambiguous questions
- Ambiguous word meanings
- Leading questions or phrases
- Improper level of question difficulty
- Unbalanced response categories
- Missing response categories
- Missing questions
- Questions with incomplete instruction
- Questions that bias responses
- Nonresponse questions

8-4b Revise Questionnaire Based on Pretest Results

Undoubtedly it will be necessary for the researcher to make changes to the questionnaire based on the findings during the pretest. There is no such thing as minor changes because all changes are important, since they will likely clarify wording and meaning. If several changes are made during the initial pretest, it may be necessary to pretest the questionnaire a second time. The bottom line is that the researcher should not implement the survey to its intended audience until it is entirely ready to be used. After pretesting is complete, researchers should tabulate the data and run some simple statistical tests to get a preliminary indication of what to expect from administering the full-scale test.

8-4c Administer Questionnaire and Tabulate Results

At this point, researchers should administer the questionnaire to targeted respondents, code the information, tabulate the data, and run appropriate statistical tests to look for relationships and differences among variables. These topics will be discussed in subsequent chapters.

Decision Time!

As a marketing manager, you make important decisions using data provided by marketing researchers. Who should take charge of the questionnaire design task—you, the ultimate user of the information, or the marketing researcher? How closely do you think you should work with the researcher to ensure that the right type of data is collected? If you prefer open-ended instead of closed-ended questions, should you let this be known?

Net Impact

The Internet can enhance questionnaire design in a number of ways. First, it can assist the researcher in better understanding the characteristics of the target market, since it provides access to so much information. Second, it can help in pretesting the final questions because email enables the researcher to send pretest questions to a variety of individuals at various locations. Finally, the Internet provides an additional alternative in data collection. As we stated earlier, it is an increasingly accepted vehicle for gathering primary information.

On the Lighter Side—Worst Neighbors in Taiwan

In Taipei, Taiwan, Sinyi Realty conducted an online survey that asked home buyers who they considered to be the worst neighbors. Sex-related businesses and gangsters were cited to be the worst possible neighbors and those to avoid the most. The second-worst neighbors are couples who often argue, followed by those who ignore complaints about water leaks from their apartments. The fourth- and fifth-worst neighbors were home-based factories that are noisy or emit odors and those who stack garbage in and around their homes, respectively. The final group of worst neighbors include those who play mah-jong all night, those who sing to karaoke or play loud music at night, those who steal, those who place their shoe shelves or other articles in the stairways, and those who allow their dogs to bark continuously and do not clean up the excrement left by their pets.

Source: Anonymous, "Bad neighbors," *Taiwan News* (July 3, 2005): 2.

Chapter Summary

Questionnaires are an effective way to gather information. When creating a questionnaire, the researcher should make sure that it is user-friendly, looks professional, attracts respondents to the topic so that they will complete the questionnaire, reveals the desired information, and encourages respondents to provide honest and accurate answers. The design process can be broken down into three phases: preconstruction, questionnaire construction, and postconstruction.

The preconstruction phase involves revisiting research objectives. The question "What information should be obtained from the data-gathering effort?" must be addressed first because it provides direction for the entire design process. To create an effective questionnaire, researchers must keep in mind the characteristics of the target respondents. The question of cost should be addressed early

in the development process. Finally, the mode of data collection should be considered, since there are advantages and disadvantages to each method.

During the questionnaire construction phase, researchers decide on the question format, number of response choices for each question, wording of instructions and questions, and organization and layout issues. If the questionnaire is being designed for a client, then the client should be given the opportunity to provide feedback prior to it being implemented.

The most important facet of the postconstruction phase is pretesting the questionnaire. A pretest is a trial run of the questionnaire using a small sample from the target market. The first stage of the pretest is personal interviews, so that researchers can observe the behaviors of both interviewers and respondents. Interviews can be done using protocol analysis or debriefing. The second stage of pretesting involves testing the questionnaire in an environment as similar as possible to the one in which the questionnaire will be administered. Following the initial pretesting, the questionnaire should be revised to reflect the pretest comments. Once the questionnaire has made it through pretesting, it should be administered to target respondents, the information should be coded and tabulated, and then appropriate statistical tests should be run to look for relationships and differences among variables.

Review Questions

1. What should be considered when creating a questionnaire?

2. What questions should be addressed during the pre-construction phase?

3. What questions should be addressed during the questionnaire construction phase?

4. What is the difference between open- and closed-ended questions?

5. What are the advantages and disadvantages of open-ended questions? Of closed-ended questions?

6. How is the Delphi technique used? What is a leading question? What is a double-barreled question?

7. What part of the questionnaire should be pretested?

8. When are protocol analysis and debriefing used?

Practice Quiz

Note: You can find the correct answers to these questions by taking the quiz and then submitting your answers in the Online Edition. The program will automatically score your submission. If you miss a question, the program will provide the correct answer, a rationale for the answer, and the section number in the chapter where the topic is discussed.

1. Multichotomous questions are closed-ended questions that offer only two response choices.
   a. True
   b. False

2. A double-barreled question is two questions that ask for one response.
   a. True
   b. False

3. The first step in survey design is to determine how to ask questions.
   a. True
   b. False

4. Debriefing is an interviewing technique in which respondents think aloud while responding to each question.
   a. True
   b. False

5. "Isn't our beautiful restaurant the best in the area?" is an example of a leading question.
   a. True
   b. False

6. Which of the following is a double-barreled question?
   a. What is your annual income?

   b. Do you plan to visit our restaurant again and order our delicious steak?
   c. What is your gender?
   d. Do you plan to eat our delicious food next month?
   e. None of the above is a double-barreled question.

7. _____ is not a concern during the construction phase of a questionnaire.
   a. Pretesting
   b. Questionnaire wording
   c. Number of response categories per question
   d. Question format
   e. All of the above are concerns during the construction phase.

8. The _____ technique involves a panel of experts who determine survey content by first making concealed judgments about an issue, and then each judgment is critiqued, followed by multiple iterations of revising judgments.
   a. Delta
   b. Epsilon
   c. Omega
   d. Alpha
   e. Delphi

9. What should be the final concern when constructing a questionnaire?
   a. Pretest the questionnaire.
   b. Revise the questionnaire based on pretest results.
   c. Obtain client approval.
   d. Administer the questionnaire and tabulate the results.
   e. Examine target respondent characteristics.

10. Which of the following goals states "the degree to which a test measures what it is supposed to measure"?
    a. The questionnaire should look professional.
    b. The questionnaire should be user-friendly.
    c. The questionnaire should encourage respondents to answer honestly and accurately.
    d. The questionnaire should be valid.
    e. None of the above

Thinking Critically

1. Critique Exhibit 8-1 and indicate whether any loaded questions or other problems exist. What are the strengths and weaknesses of this questionnaire?

2. You are designing a questionnaire to test customer satisfaction with automobile repair shops. Write five leading questions for this questionnaire. Now write five questions that are similar but don't lead the respondent.

3. A research organization asks you to critique the following statements about German automobiles. Indicate whether the question is good or bad, and explain why. Assume that the responses are "agree" or "disagree."
    a. Mercedes-Benz manufactures superior automobiles.
    b. German automobiles are dependable and reliable.
    c. German automobiles will last a lifetime.
    d. The Mercedes-Benz 190E automobile is fairly priced.
    e. The quality of BMW cars is better than that of Mercedes-Benz cars.
    f. German cars are not as good as Japanese cars.

4. In the banking industry, customer service is often all that separates one institution from another. Safe Bank realizes this and has developed a survey to rate the service its customers most recently received by telephone in the card products division—the most profitable division for most banks. You are asked to critique the following questions and recommend improvements.
    a. With which product(s) did we most recently assist you?
    - Visa/MasterCard
    - Visa Gold/Gold MasterCard
    - Visa Business
    - Prime Equity Line
    - Other (please specify)
    b. Availability of our representative to assist you
    Poor Fair Good Very good Excellent N/A
    c. Representative's attitude when assisting you
    Poor Fair Good Very good Excellent N/A
    d. Representative's product knowledge
    Poor Fair Good Very good Excellent N/A
    e. Concern for your banking needs
    Poor Fair Good Very good Excellent N/A
    f. Promptness in addressing your request
    Poor Fair Good Very good Excellent N/A
    g. Completion of your request
    Poor Fair Good Very good Excellent N/A
    h. Overall performance of representative
    Poor Fair Good Very good Excellent N/A
    i. Was your request satisfied in one call?
    No Yes N/A
    j. As a result of the service we provided, how do you feel?
    Very dissatisfied Somewhat dissatisfied Neither dissatisfied nor satisfied Somewhat satisfied Very satisfied N/A
    k. How did we perform relative to your expectations? Did not meet expectations Met expectations Exceeded expectations

Net Exercise

Visit the Web site http://www.websurveyor.com/ to learn how to design an online survey. Download a trial version of the software WebSurveyor and design your own online survey. What benefits and limitations of online survey design do you see from this exercise?

Experiencing Marketing Research

Create a questionnaire with at least ten questions that investigate consumers' satisfaction level with their personal computers. Have a classmate do the same. Critique your classmate's questionnaire, and have him or her critique your questionnaire. What's wrong with them? What's right with them? How can they be improved?

Case 8-1

Many Americans Are Fat—But What Can Be Done about It?

Let's face it ... too many Americans are far beyond their ideal weights. The federal government reports that almost two-thirds of Americans are overweight or obese, and more than half get too little physical activity. The battle of the bulge is obvious when you see people in shopping malls, restaurants, at work ... even at health clubs. But they don't have to depend on Atkins, Dr. Phil, Beverly Hills, Jenny Craig, or any of the other diet gurus to tell them how to shed the excess weight.

The U.S. Department of Health and Human Services (HHS) and the U.S. Department of Agriculture (USDA) recognize the problem and recently released the federal government's Dietary Guidelines for Americans 2005. By law, the dietary guidelines must be reviewed every five years, and this latest edition contains up-to-date recommendations to encourage people of all ages to adopt good eating habits and to participate in regular exercise. Experts advise that eating right and being physically active are the keys to a healthy lifestyle. Living and eating healthfully will likely reduce one's risk of developing many chronic diseases, such as heart disease, diabetes, osteoporosis, and certain cancers, and increase one's chances of living longer.

To help Americans improve their level of health, the new dietary guidelines emphasize reducing calorie consumption and increasing physical activity. Eating a healthy balance of nutritious foods is very important, but balancing nutrients is not enough for health.

To find out how healthy Americans perceive their eating habits to be, a questionnaire was administered outside retail food stores on the East and West coasts that asked consumers, "Are you eating more 'healthy' or 'natural' foods? What are the main reasons driving these purchases, and what products in particular do you seek out?" Many shoppers say they are redirecting their purchases toward healthier products. The most frequent reasons cited for switching to healthier diets are the addition of children into a household and the onset of a health problem. Furthermore, shoppers say they practice preventive medicine through healthy eating and regular exercise.

Health-food items most frequently included on shopping lists are products for low-fat and low-cholesterol diets, preservative-free items, and fresh fruits and vegetables. Nabisco's SnackWell's fat-free cookies and crackers capitalized on the healthy trend. But some consumers cite the poor taste of healthy foods and frustration over conflicting media reports of the benefits of natural foods as reasons why they are not buying healthier items. Although some people may find it difficult to classify snack foods as healthy, SnackWell's products are not doing so well due to their taste. "People are sick of biscuits that taste like cardboard," says Goldman Sachs food analyst Romitha Mally. As a result, Nabisco had to boost the fat content to improve the taste, but so far that hasn't helped SnackWell sales. Nabisco's sugary and salty lineup is selling briskly. Could it be that the health fad has run its course?

A second questionnaire administered by *Supermarket News* asked supermarket bakery executives about their customers' purchasing patterns. The majority stated that while shoppers talk healthy eating, they still eat their donuts. At the bakery counter, customers think about taste, not health. Although Americans know they should eat more grains and breads as part of a healthy diet, most fall far short of the U.S. Department of Agriculture's Food Guide Pyramid, which recommends six to ten servings daily. Jim Finnerty, bakery-deli director for the 70-unit Abco Foods, sums up our eating habits this way: "People are buying donuts and drinking a diet pop and thinking that balances out, somehow."

Sources: Keith Naughton, "Bring on the junk food," *Newsweek,* vol. 136, no. 2 (July 10, 2000): 44; Lisa Tibbitts and Elliot Zwiebach, "Consumers are buying 'healthy,'" *Supermarket News* (May 22, 1995): 14–17; Congressional Report, "New dietary guidelines promote healthy lifestyles," *Congressional Press Releases,* (January 27, 2005).

Case Questions

1. Evaluate the following questions that were posed to consumers outside retail food stores on the East and West coasts: "Are you eating more 'healthy' or 'natural' foods?" "What are the main reasons driving these purchases, and what products in particular do you seek out?" How would you have stated the questions to find out about eating habits?

2. While there is clearly a movement by the U.S. government to get its residents to eat healthier foods, there is still much confusion about whether Americans are eating better. Design a questionnaire that could solve the misunderstanding.

3. Which types of questions (open-ended, closed-ended, dichotomous, multiple-choice) did you use in the questionnaire that you designed? Why?

Case 8-2

The Integrated Case—Part 3

Cheerwine—In Need of Unique Research

From the second data analysis and qualitative research, Mr. Alan Young gained a better understanding of how high-schoolers perceive Cheerwine. Mr. Young further proposed to conduct a quantitative research such as survey to obtain the accurate information from the target market. Visitations to area high schools in the Charleston and Greensboro regions were deemed to be the optimal data collection method. Therefore, principals (or head masters in private schools) at different high schools in the regions were contacted to solicit participation. To encourage high school principals to allow their institutions to participate in the study, they were informed that a $250.00 donation would be given to each cooperating school. This incentive was considered to be crucial, since most secondary schools lack appropriate state funding and must seek alternative ways to generate working capital.

With the aid of secondary and primary data, Young drafted the questionnaire as follows.

A Survey of the Soft-Drink Industry

The purpose of this survey is to develop a better understanding of the carbonated soft-drink consumption habits of high school students in your region. It should take you less than 15 minutes to complete. Your responses will remain confidential—only broad averages will be compiled. Please respond to the following questions by circling the most appropriate answer. Thank you very much for your cooperation.

1. During a typical day, how many soft drinks do you consume?
   a. None
   b. 1–2
   c. 3–4
   d. 5–6
   e. More than 6

2. Who decides which type of soft drink you consume when you *are* at home?
   a. Yourself
   b. Parents
   c. Friends
   d. Other (please specify) _____

3. Who decides which type of soft drink you consume when you *are not* at home?
   a. Yourself
   b. Parents
   c. Friends
   d. Other (please specify) _____

4. Which type of soft drink do you most prefer?
   a. Diet
   b. Sugar sweetened
   c. I don't consume soft drinks.
   d. Other _____

5. Please indicate your preference for the following brands of soft drinks:

	Excellent	Good	Fair	Poor	Never Tried It
a. Cheerwine	E	G	F	P	N
b. Coca Cola	E	G	F	P	N
c. Dr. Pepper	E	G	F	P	N
d. Mountain Dew	E	G	F	P	N
e. Pepsi	E	G	F	P	N
f. RC Cola	E	G	F	P	N
g. Seven Up	E	G	F	P	N
h. Sprite	E	G	F	P	N
i. Mr. Pibb	E	G	F	P	N
j. Other _____	E	G	F	P	N

6. Please indicate the availability of each of the following soft drinks according to the following scale.

	Extremely Available	Somewhat Available	Rarely Available	Never Available	Don't Know
a. Cheerwine	E	S	R	N	DK
b. Coca Cola	E	S	R	N	DK
c. Dr. Pepper	E	S	R	N	DK
d. Mountain Dew	E	S	R	N	DK
e. Pepsi	E	S	R	N	DK
f. RC Cola	E	S	R	N	DK
g. Seven Up	E	S	R	N	DK
h. Sprite	E	S	R	N	DK
i. Mr. Pibb	E	S	R	N	DK
j. Other_____	E	S	R	N	DK

7. Using the choices in Question 6, which soft drink first comes to mind when reading each statement? Please indicate in each space provided either a, b, c, d, e, f, g, h, i, or j.

Rebellious	_____
Funny	_____
Tasty	_____
Refreshing	_____
Fun to drink	_____
Thirst quencher	_____
Good with a meal	_____
Good drink to give to a friend	_____
Good party drink	_____
Trendy	_____

For active people   _____
Relaxing drink   _____
Makes me unique   _____
Tastes terrible   _____
An extreme drink   _____
Other _____   _____

8. Can you recall a soft-drink advertisement in the past 3 months that you particularly *liked*?

    Yes   No

    If you responded "yes," what was it about the advertisement that you particularly *liked*? Please explain.

    _____

    _____

    If you responded "yes," were any promotional give-aways involved? If so, which of the following were used?
    a. Cash
    b. Products with company logo
    c. Movie tickets
    d. Discounts on company products
    e. Sweepstakes
    f. Other _____

9. Can you recall a soft-drink advertisement in the past 3 months that you particularly *disliked*?

    Yes   No

    If you responded "yes," what was it about the advertisement that you particularly *disliked*? Please explain.

    _____

    _____

10. Use the following scale to respond to each of the statements about Cheerwine.

	Strongly Agree	Agree	Neither Agree nor Disagree	Disagree	Strongly Disagree	Don't Know
a. I like its taste.	SA	A	N	D	SD	DK
b. It's hard to find in stores.	SA	A	N	D	SD	DK
c. It's hard to find in restaurants.	SA	A	N	D	SD	DK
d. It's got an unusual taste.	SA	A	N	D	SD	DK
e. It is not a soft drink.	SA	A	N	D	SD	DK
f. It's too expensive.	SA	A	N	D	SD	DK

11. At which type of store(s) do *you* purchase soft drinks on a regular basis? (Check all that apply.)
    a. Convenience store (e.g., Circle K, 7-Eleven, etc.)
    b. Drugstore (e.g., Kerr Drugs, Walgreens, etc.)
    c. Gasoline stations (e.g., BP, Exxon, etc.)
    d. Vending machines
    e. Restaurants
    f. Other _____

12. At which type of store(s) does *your mother* purchase soft drinks on a regular basis? (Check all that apply.)
    a. Convenience store (e.g., Circle K, 7-Eleven, etc.)
    b. Drugstore (e.g., Kerr Drugs, Walgreens, etc.)
    c. Gasoline stations (e.g., BP, Exxon, etc.)
    d. Vending machines
    e. Restaurants
    f. Other _____

13. Which of the following beverages is your favorite?
    a. Carbonated soft drinks
    b. Sports drinks (e.g., Gatorade)
    c. Water
    d. Tea
    e. Coffee
    f. Other _____

14. What is your age category?
    a. 12–13
    b. 14–15
    c. 16–17
    d. 18 and over

15. What is your gender?
    Male   Female

16. What is your ethnic background?
    a. White/Caucasian
    b. Latin American/Hispanic
    c. Asian
    d. African American
    e. American Indian
    f. Other _____

17. How many years have you lived in the Carolinas?
    a. less than 2
    b. 2–4
    c. 5–7
    d. 8–10
    e. More than 10 years

18. How many hours do you work at a paying job during a typical week?
    a. None
    b. 1–10
    c. 11–20
    d. 21–30
    e. 31–40
    f. more than 40 hours

19. How much allowance do you get from your parents on a weekly basis?
    a. None

b. $1–10

c. $11–20

d. $21–30

e. More than $30 each week

20. In which of the following categories do you spend the *greatest* percentage of your money each week?

a. Recreation (e.g., movies, games, etc.)

b. Food

c. Clothes

d. Automobile expenses

e. Other _____

Thank you very much for participating in this study!

Case Questions

1. Is the visitation to high schools the best data collection method in this case? If not, what alternative methods (e.g., telephone interview, online survey) would you recommend and why?

2. Explain the procedures through which you will collect the data.

3. Referring to the decision problems and research objectives identified in Case 2-3, examine the questionnaire very carefully to (a) point out which questionnaire items provide information to fulfill the specified research objectives, and (b) find out as many problems as you can and suggest how to fix them.

Notes

1. Jessica Tetrault, "Surveys Provide Crucial Feedback," *Nonprofit World,* vol. 22, no. 5 (Sept/Oct 2004), pp. 22–23.

2. Bill Farrell and Tom Elken, "Adjust five variables for better mail surveys," *Marketing News* 28, no. 18 (August 20, 1994): 20.

3. This example was based on the author's experience during a consulting job with Unifi Technology, August 2000.

4. Stephen J. Gould, Dawn B. Lerman, and Andreas F. Grein, "Agency perceptions and practices on Global IMC," *Journal of Advertising Research* 39, no. 1 (January/February 1999): 7–20.

5. Tom McCarthy, "Time to hone your questioning skills," *Lodging Hospitality* 55, no. 13 (November 1999): 18.

6. William E. Becker and Carol Johnston, "The relationship between multiple-choice and essay response questions in assessing economics understanding," *Economic Record* 75, no. 231 (December 1999): 348–357.

7. J. C. Sherblom, C. F. Sullivan, and E. C. Sherblom, "The what, the whom, and the hows of survey research," *The Bulletin* (December 1993): 58–64.

8. Tim Prunk, "The value of questionnaires: Surveys allow you to get to know your customers and build your database," *Target Marketing* 17, no. 10 (October 1994): 37(2).

9. Trivellore E. Raghunathan and James E. Grizzle, "A split questionnaire survey design," *Journal of the American Statistical Association* 90, no. 429 (March 1995): 54(10).

10. Adamantios Diamantopoulos, Nina Reynolds, and Bodo Schlegelmilch, "Pretesting in questionnaire design: The impact of respondent characteristics on error detection," *Journal of the Market Research Society* 36, no. 4 (October 1994): 295–314.

11. Susanne E. Gaddis, "How to design online surveys," *Training & Development* 52, no. 6 (June 1998): 67–71.

12. S. D. Hunt, R. D. Sparkman, and J. B. Wilcox, "The pretest in survey research: Issues and preliminary findings," *Journal of Marketing Research* 19 (May 1982): 269–273.

13. D. S. Tull and D. I. Hawkins, *Marketing Research,* 6th ed. (New York: Macmillan, 1993), 361.

Experimentation and Test Marketing

Chapter Nine

Source: © 2007 JupiterImages Corporation.

Key Terms

Learning Objectives

After studying this chapter, you will be able to:

- Discuss experimentation.
- Describe the three conditions of causality.
- Explain internal and external validity.
- Describe the various types of experimental designs.
- Explain the purpose of test marketing.
- Explicate how to run a successful test market.

Test Market Products: Yeah or Nay?

Think about it . . . before you get into the bathtub, you feel the water to be sure it is the right temperature. Before you purchase a car, you drive it to make sure that it runs the way you expect it to run. And before you purchase new clothes, you try them on to make sure they look and feel right. Well, marketers are no different. Before we put products on the market to sell, we try them out in the marketplace to get consumer reaction. After all, a recent study by Datamonitor found that 80% of newly introduced products fail to establish a market presence after two years. This means marketers can't be too careful. Consider the following examples of companies that are making sure their products are accepted in the market *before* they are introduced on a wide-scale:

- McDonald's Corp. in Oak Brook, Illinois, tested a new concept in better-for-you-food—Fruit 'n Yogurt Parfait. This was a "generous portion of sliced strawberries and whole blueberries packed between two layers of low-fat vanilla yogurt," topped with a layer of crunchy granola.

- Arby's tested a trio of adult-focused appetizers called "Sidekickers" and a new deli-style sandwich line. To differentiate itself from other fast-food restaurants, Arby's offered mozzarella sticks, fried jalapeno bites, and onion petals at $1.79 to $3.89.

- Anheuser-Busch tested the "keggy," a scaled-down version of the beer keg, at the Ice Palace in Tampa, Florida. The miniature keg was equipped with a self-serve dispensing system and held thirty-five 12-ounce servings of beer.

- Hellenic Milk Industries SA's Evga ice cream, a well-known brand throughout Greece and most of Europe, test-marketed its ice cream in New York before the large-scale launch.

- Miller Brewing Company has test marketed a plastic beer bottle.

It all makes sense, right? Not to everybody. Procter & Gamble launches many new brands each year and does not rely on test marketing for them to succeed. And P&G is not alone. Other companies may downplay the importance of test marketing their products for a variety of reasons:

- Marketers need to get their products to the marketplace faster and faster. In today's markets, products often have short lives and delays in getting them to the consumer can mean lost profits.

- Marketers are concerned that test marketing will reveal too much about their products and competitors will soon follow with copycat products.

- Marketers claim that consumer research techniques are now so sophisticated that full-blown tests are no longer necessary. Companies spend countless hours communicating with potential consumers during product development. They feel there's little need to communicate with consumers once the product design is finished.

- Companies invest huge sums of money in research and development, so they are already committed to going commercially with the items. Mark Sherrington, a market consultant at Added Value states, "The fixed costs are so high that you might as well get on with it."

- Product development is so expensive that brand managers are favoring more line-extension products, which are simply low-risk, low-investment reformulations of already successful items.

- Test marketing is expensive, costing millions of dollars in many cases, so companies like Fisher-Price usually test only larger products or items it anticipates will be big sellers.

- When test marketing is done, it is not always performed well. When RJ Reynolds tested its smokeless cigarette, it failed to discover that smokers wanted to see and smell their smoke.

Although most companies do test marketing, many believe they have legitimate reasons to bypass this stage.

Sources: Donna Berry, "McYogurt to go," *Dairy Foods* 101, no. 3 (March 2000): 31; Kate MacArthur, "Arby's adds adult-focused foods," *Advertising Age* 71, no. 22 (May 22, 2000): 76; Jack Neff, "P&G's Jager vows new, faster ways to sell its products," *Advertising Age* 70, no. 25 (July 14, 1999): 10; Anonymous, "Plastic beer bottle may be headache for recyclers," *BioCycle* 40, no. 2 (February 1999): 6; Anonymous, "Good things come in new packaging: A-B bows its PET beer bottle and a compact keg," *Beverage World* 118, no. 1674 (April 15, 1999): 24; Anonymous, "Why new products are bypassing the market test" *Management Today* (October 1995): 12; Patrick Barrett, "The good (and bad) die young," *Marketing* (July 11, 1996): 16; Allison Lucas, "When every penny counts: How creativity allows Fisher-Price to stretch its market research dollars," *Sales & Marketing Management* 148, no. 2 (February 1996): 74(2).

Now Ask Yourself

- Both the positive and negative sides of test marketing were described. What do you think? Should a company test market its products or not?

- How do you feel about Mark Sherrington's comment, "The fixed costs [of developing the products] are so high that you might as well get on with it"?

- Doesn't McDonald's Fruit 'n Yogurt Parfait sound good? If you agree, then why test it?

While most companies commit resources to thoroughly test market their products, the "Get This" box explains why some companies choose to bypass this important step. It is clear though that when test marketing is done right, the results can save companies millions of dollars. This chapter will show you how to test market correctly. Before we do this, we will introduce you to experimentation, so that you will be able to plan and run experiments.

9-1 Experimentation

experiment A research process designed to determine what factors influence a particular behavior, and the extent and direction of the influence.

experimental research Research in which the researcher controls and manipulates elements of the research environment to measure the impact of each variable and to test a hypothesis.

The word *experiment* has the same root as the word *experience:* both derive from Latin for try or test.[1] An **experiment** is a research process designed to determine what factors influence a particular behavior, and the extent and direction of the influence.[2] **Experimental research** occurs when the researcher controls and manipulates elements of the research environment to measure the impact of each variable and to test a hypothesis. If marketers want to find out what causes sales, they might test the influence of certain variables such as advertising, store location, company image, and product selection on sales. As you learned in Chapter 2, the *dependent variable* is the variable to be affected or predicted through marketing research. The *independent variables* are the factors believed to cause or explain variations in the dependent variable. In an experiment, researchers manipulate the independent variables and then measure the effects on the dependent variable. In our example, sales is the dependent variable, and advertising, store location, company image, and product selection are the independent variables.

Large consumer goods companies often use experimental research to test:

- The effectiveness of new advertising, or competitors' advertising
- The effect of various prices on sales of a product
- Consumer acceptance of new products at trial and repeat-purchase levels
- The effect of different package designs on sales

If researchers want to examine whether event A causes event B—that is, to determine whether a cause-and-effect relationship exists—they will measure changes in a single variable by manipulating one or two other variables under controlled conditions. By controlling conditions, researchers aim to eliminate outside influences from the study.

9-1a Causality

Philosophers have said that causality refers to the "way of knowing" that one thing causes another. They will refer to Aristotle, Galileo, and Hume and inform us that these early philosophers and scientists concentrated on conceptual issues and questions while later philosophers concentrated on concrete issues and questions. Today scientists define causality in limited contexts, for example, in a controlled experiment. You may recall from Chapter 2 that *causal research* is research that provides evidence that a cause-and-effect relationship does or does not exist. Experiments are a type of causal research, since their goal is to demonstrate cause-and-effect relationships. That is, experiments are used to determine whether or not a change in one variable causes a change (or effect) in another variable. In our example, marketers hypothesized that advertising (independent variable) leads to increased sales (dependent variable).

While it is easy to claim that this relationship exists, it is much more difficult to prove it. Consider Example 9-1.

Example 9-1

Consider the relationship between advertising and sales of Pepsi-Cola. It seems reasonable to believe that PepsiCo's advertising campaigns cause it to sell more Pepsi. But astute researchers will notice that other events also contribute to sales. Sales promotions such as coupons and price reductions contribute significantly.

PepsiCo's marketers need to prove causality. Three conditions must be met for causality to exist:

1. *Logical time sequence.* The cause must either precede or occur simultaneously with the effect—it cannot occur later. For an independent variable (Pepsi's advertising expenditures) to predict a dependent variable (sales of Pepsi-Cola), the independent variable must occur before or at the same time as the dependent variable.

2. *Concomitant variation.* **Concomitant variation** concerns the extent to which the independent variable (cause) and dependent variable (effect) vary together as hypothesized. If it is hypothesized that increased advertising of Pepsi generates more sales, then sales should increase as advertising expenditures increase. Similarly, if advertising costs were reduced, sales should decrease. The stronger the relationship between independent and dependent variables, the more confident a researcher can be that concomitant variation exists between the variables. This does not mean, however, that the researcher has proven that advertising causes sales. It simply means that the relationship is defensible.

   > **concomitant variation** The extent to which the independent variable(s) and dependent variable vary together as hypothesized.

3. *Control for other possible causal factors.* To determine whether one variable causes the hypothesized change in another variable, all other factors that can influence the relationship between the two variables have to be eliminated as much as possible. Of course, this condition can never be met completely. This is why marketers measure random error. Causality can never be absolute because random error can never be controlled absolutely. However, highly controlled environments can minimize the error and increase our confidence in the relationship.

9-1b Validity

As a student, you've taken many tests designed to measure your characteristics. An IQ test is supposed to measure your intelligence. Your SAT score is supposed to measure your aptitude or likelihood for success in college. Your principles of marketing exams are supposed to measure your knowledge of marketing concepts. Whether these tests actually measure what they are intended to measure relates to validity. As you learned in Chapter 7, validity asks the question: Are we measuring what we think we are measuring?

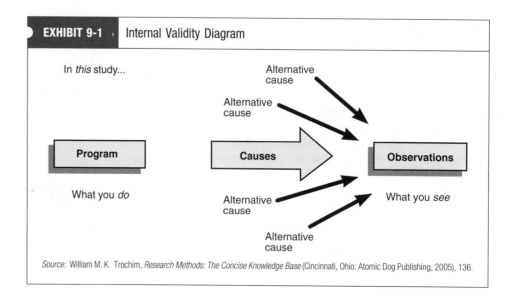

EXHIBIT 9-1 ▸ Internal Validity Diagram

In *this* study...

Alternative cause

Alternative cause

Program

What you *do*

Causes

Alternative cause

Observations

What you *see*

Alternative cause

Source: William M. K. Trochim, *Research Methods: The Concise Knowledge Base* (Cincinnati, Ohio: Atomic Dog Publishing, 2005), 136.

In experimental research, there are two forms of validity: internal validity and external validity. These forms help the researcher understand the extent to which a causal relationship exists between variables.

Internal Validity

Internal validity is the degree to which an experiment shows that the change in the dependent variable is caused by changes in the independent variable. Internal validity is only relevant in studies that attempt to establish a causal relationship. An experiment is internally valid if the independent variables are the only cause of the change in the dependent variable. If other explanations can be given for changes in the dependent variable, then the experiment lacks internal validity; the major concern in internal validity is whether observed changes can be attributed to a specific program (i.e., the cause) and not to other possible causes (that is, alternative explanations). This reasoning is diagramed in Exhibit 9-1. Also, consider Example 9-2.

internal validity The degree to which an experiment can clearly show that the change in the dependent variable is caused by changes in the independent variables rather than by other outside factors.

Example 9-2

If the sales of Pepsi increased dramatically during the period when advertising increased by 50%, but supermarkets also ran coupons, Coca-Cola happened to be in short supply because of a truckers' strike, and the summer was especially hot, researchers would have trouble concluding that the increased advertising caused the increase in sales.

There are seven major threats to internal validity. These are also known as "extraneous factors."

history External incidents that occur between the beginning and end of an experiment that are beyond the researcher's control but may influence results.

History Internal validity can be compromised by **history**—external incidents that occur between the time the experiment starts and when it is completed. These outside events may influence subjects during the experiment or between repeated measures of the dependent variable. These incidents are beyond the control of the researcher but may nevertheless influence the experimental results. Suppose PepsiCo wants to find out how a 50% increase in advertising between January 1, 2009, and June 30, 2009, impacts sales. What if on March 1, 2009, a U.S. government study reports that Pepsi drinks have extraordinarily high sugar content? This incident will obviously have a considerable impact on the results of the experiment. Notice that the history effect does not deal with an event that occurs before the experiment, but rather it refers to an incident that occurs during the experiment.

Maturation   There is a chance that test subjects will "mature" during the testing period. **Maturation** in this context means unintended changes in test subjects occurring during an experiment that are unrelated to the experiment but that may influence the results. Such changes include fatigue, boredom, and irritation. Subjects will also likely become older and more experienced, which may impact the way they respond in an experiment. Therefore, researchers must be careful not to conclude that the individuals have changed because of manipulations in the experiment. To reduce the maturation effect, researchers can shorten the testing time period and keep their experiments interesting for the individuals involved.

Testing Effect   The **testing effect** or "pretesting effect" is concerned with the extent an initial test sensitizes respondents to the process of experimentation, causing respondents to react differently to a second test than they would if no initial test had been conducted. For example, if we measure a person's intelligence, and we give the person a test on March 1, 2007, and then again a month later, the individual will likely score higher the second time around since he has been sensitized to the test.

Instrumentation Effect   The **instrumentation effect** occurs when the outcome of an experiment is influenced by a change of any of the following: how questions are asked, who asks the questions, problems with the surveys, and other procedures used to assess the dependent variable. Inherent inconsistencies within the instrument itself or those that occur in the process of administering it can cause variations in experimental results. For example, this effect can occur if:

- The same measurement instrument is used at the beginning and end of an experiment. Respondents can become familiar with the terminology used on a questionnaire and respond differently the second time they encounter the same questions.

- A different measurement instrument is used at different stages of an experiment. Even if the instrument is intended to measure the same characteristics, different questions can result in different interpretations by respondents.

- The same interviewers are used at different stages of an experiment. Both respondents and interviewers may change during the process. They may become fatigued or bored, or act differently because of familiarity with the interviewing process.

- A different interviewer is used at different stages of an experiment. Using a different interviewer can change experiments due to their different methods of interviewing.

Mortality Effect   The **mortality effect** occurs when test subjects drop out of an experiment while it is taking place. Subjects drop out for numerous reasons— time constraints, loss of interest in the study, and so on. And when they do, the study results may be biased in some way. When subjects leave a group being observed and the characteristics of those leaving the group differ significantly from those remaining, the experiment will be biased.

Selection Effect   The **selection effect** is the bias that results when the experimental group differs significantly from the target population or from the control group. Typically, it is important that the experimental group and the control group be as similar as possible so that any differences in results can be attributed to the variable and not to differences in group composition. To make the groups as similar as possible, researchers assign participants to groups randomly, or they match

---

maturation Changes in test subjects that occur during an experiment that are unrelated to the experiment but may influence the results.

testing effect The effect that occurs depending on the extent an initial test sensitizes respondents to the process of experimentation, causing respondents to react differently to a second test than they would if no initial test had been conducted.

instrumentation effect What occurs when the outcome of an experiment is influenced by a change of any of the following: how questions are asked, who asks the questions, problems with the surveys, and other procedures used to assess the dependent variable.

mortality effect The effect on experimental results of the loss of test subjects while the experiment is taking place. Significant differences between subjects that leave and those that stay can bias results.

selection effect The bias that results when the experimental group differs significantly from the target population or from the control group.

participants in the test and control groups, using certain characteristics (age, income, sex, and so on).

regression toward the mean The tendency of participant responses to migrate (or regress) toward the average score as the experiment progresses.

Regression toward the Mean **Regression toward the mean** means that a participant's responses tend to migrate (or regress) toward the average score as the experiment progresses. If a participant's responses start out on the extreme ends of the measurement scale at the beginning of the experiment, their responses usually become less extreme as the experiment goes on. As the extreme scores migrate toward the middle, the overall experimental results for that test variable will move toward the average score as well. Consider Example 9-3.

Example 9-3

An experienced bowler bowls an average of 215 points per game. Owing to a stretch of good luck, the bowler bowls a series of games with scores in the range of 250 to 260. Eventually, however, the bowler's luck changes, and her scores regress back toward the true mean of 215 points per game. Were we to measure her scores during the run of good luck and then again after the run had ended, we would conclude that her scores had decreased. However, the regression of the scores back to the true mean explains the decrease in scores, not the effect of some causal independent variable.

External Validity

external validity The degree to which the results of an experiment can be generalized beyond the experimental situation to other populations.

While internal validity refers to the extent to which an experiment shows relationships between variables, **external validity** refers to the ability to generalize the study results to other populations (see Exhibit 9-2). The usefulness of any experiment depends upon the degree to which the results can be "generalized" or applied to other populations. Let's say a researcher uses 50 undergraduate college students majoring in

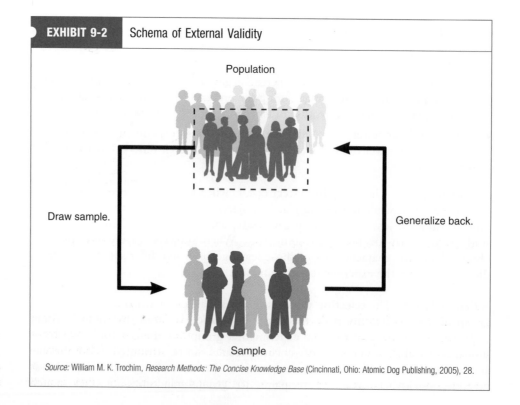

EXHIBIT 9-2   Schema of External Validity

Population

Draw sample.

Generalize back.

Sample

Source: William M. K. Trochim, *Research Methods: The Concise Knowledge Base* (Cincinnati, Ohio: Atomic Dog Publishing, 2005), 28.

marketing to test attitudes toward a new sandwich made of ostrich meat. This sample was composed of individuals aged 19–22, so it is sensible to believe that the results can be generalized over young college students majoring in marketing—assuming the sampling design was sound. But can the results be generalized to other groups of people in the general population, such as working adults, senior citizens, children, and nonmarketing majors? As a rule, the more generalizable or representative the results of an experiment, the more externally valid it is.

Threats to external validity arise when the experiment is conducted in an *unrealistic* setting. As shown in Exhibit 9-3, these are three threats specific to external validity. First, a study can be invalid when its *test subjects (people) are unusual.* Suppose a study examining consumer purchasing habits in fast-food restaurants samples only vegetarians or people with a history of heart attacks. These are not typical consumers of fast food. Second, a study might succeed only because of the *unusual place* it was performed. A study of fast-food consumption performed in a small town where most people are employees of fast-foot restaurants will likely be overly positive. Third, study results may be invalidated if the study is performed at an *unusual time*. Had a study been performed during an *E. coli* scare that occurred at Jack in the Box restaurants, study results on fast-food consumption might have been invalid because people could have been avoiding fast-food restaurants at the time.

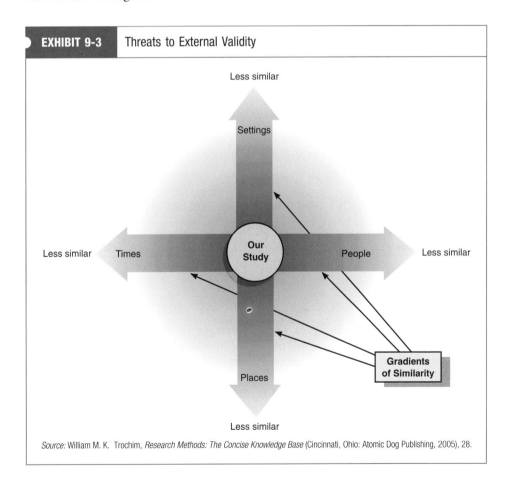

EXHIBIT 9-3 | Threats to External Validity

Source: William M. K. Trochim, *Research Methods: The Concise Knowledge Base* (Cincinnati, Ohio: Atomic Dog Publishing, 2005), 28.

9-1c Trade-offs between Internal and External Validity

There are trade-offs between the internal and external validity in every study. These trade-offs deal with two major concerns: cost and control. Consider the two areas where most studies are undertaken, in laboratories and field settings. A **laboratory** is an unrealistic setting where researchers can run experiments at a reasonable cost and have considerable control over the research environment. Although costs can be

laboratory An artificial setting where researchers can run experiments and have considerable control over the research environment.

kept low, many large consumer products companies often allocate anywhere from $50,000 to over $100,000 per test leg. The upside to laboratory experiments is the high degree of reliability and correlation with actual market performance when the test conditions (product, pricing, and advertising) are like those actually used in the real market. In a typical lab study, potential test respondents are approached at a shopping mall and prescreened for type of products used and brand preference. Then they are exposed to some advertising that is being tested and are given the opportunity to purchase the brand among a group of competitors' products. Then the consumers are given some of the product to take home and use. The researcher then follows up with the test respondents to find out whether they used the product, how they felt about it, and whether they would purchase it again.[3]

field setting A real-world or natural setting where numerous uncontrollable variables may exist.

A **field setting,** on the other hand, is a real-world setting where numerous uncontrollable variables exist. In general, the costs of experiments in field settings are considerably higher than in laboratories. Cost can range from a small city test market study of $10,000 to a large company spending over $1 million in a single test market. There are considerable opportunities for bias in local or regional market sites, consumer behavior and habits, and local competitive products.[4] The major advantage of running field experiments is that respondents often don't realize they are being examined and so they tend to act naturally. This is not the case in laboratories, where respondents know they are being observed and may alter their natural tendencies.

As summarized in Exhibit 9-4, internal validity tends to be higher in controlled environments such as laboratory settings because it is possible to eliminate many of the other explanations (that is, "extraneous variables") from the study results. Internal validity tends to be considerably lower in less-controlled environments like field settings because it is difficult to minimize measurement error in the real-world environment. External validity, on the other hand, tends to be much higher with field experiments because the results can be generalized to the target population. External validity tends to be much lower in laboratory settings due to the artificial environment.

EXHIBIT 9-4	Trade-offs between Laboratory and Field Setting Research	
Type of Research	**Internal Validity**	**External Validity (Generalizability)**
Laboratory (controlled)	Higher	Lower
Field setting (real world)	Lower	Higher

Maximizing internal validity at the early stages of research ensures that the independent variable(s) are causal factors of the dependent variable. However, marketers work in an applied environment, so marketers should verify these relationships in the real world before they base marketing decisions on test results. In other words, external validity should be maximized at later stages of research.

9-2 Experimental Design

experimental design A plan for running an experiment, in which the researcher has control over and will manipulate at least one independent variable.

An **experimental design** is a plan for running an experiment, in which the researcher has control over and will manipulate at least one independent variable. Referring to our earlier example, there are numerous ways researchers can design an experiment to test undergraduates' attitudes toward ostrich meat sandwiches. The researchers can describe the new sandwich and ask students their attitudes toward the product, or they can have the students taste the sandwich and describe their reactions. They can videotape students eating these sandwiches, and so on.

When creating experimental designs, researchers must identify the following experimental elements:

- *Independent variable*—the **treatment variable** or manipulated variable(s) that will be in the experiment. Researchers manipulate the independent variable to determine whether it has a causal relationship with the dependent variable.

- *Dependent variable*—the variable that is examined to determine whether it has been affected by the manipulated independent variable.

- *Assumptions*—the set of assumptions made about the data. Violating assumptions may jeopardize the inferences made about the effects of the independent variable. When choosing an experimental design, the researcher must consider which assumptions are implied, whether they are likely to be satisfied, and how failing to meet them will affect the usefulness of the study inferences.

- *Subjects*—individuals who are treated—that is, they participate in the experiment.

- *Control group*—subjects who receive no treatment. Because a **control group** is not treated, it can be used for comparison purposes. A control group helps minimize the effects of extraneous variables—variables other than the independent variable that affect the study and hence can potentially invalidate its results. The characteristics of the people, places, and times—the **extraneous variables**—used in an experiment determine whether the results can be generalized to the target population.

- *Plan*—the steps that ensure that correct procedures are used throughout the experiment.

Experimental designs are classified as preexperimental, true experimental, quasi-experimental, and statistical experimental designs and are summarized in Exhibit 9-5. To describe experimental designs, we will use the following notation:

$X =$ Independent variable—an occurrence or treatment that may or may not have an influence on the dependent variable

$O =$ Dependent variable that is observed or measured either before or after the treatment takes place (subscripts such as O_1 and O_2 provide organization in the measurements and delineate one treatment condition from another)

$R =$ Random assignment of experiment participants to experimental and control groups

9-2a Preexperimental Designs

Preexperimental designs are designs in which participants are not assigned to groups randomly. Strictly speaking, they are not really experimental research because they don't establish causal relationships. They are exploratory in nature and have minimal control over extraneous factors present during an experiment.

treatment variable An independent or manipulated variable in an experiment.

control group A group that has no treatments imposed on it so that it can be used for comparison against the experimental group.

extraneous variables Variables other than the manipulated independent variable that affect the study and hence confound its results.

preexperimental designs Experimental designs that do not randomly assign test units to experimental and control groups.

EXHIBIT 9-5	Summary of Types of Experimental Designs
Preexperimental Designs • One-shot case study • One-group pretest/posttest design • Static-group comparison **True Experimental Designs** • Pretest/posttest control group design • Solomon four-group design • Posttest-only control group design	**Quasi-Experimental Designs** • Time-series design **Statistical Experimental Designs** • Completely randomized design • Randomized block design • Latin square design • Factorial design

experimental group A group
of respondents that is exposed
to the experimental treatment.

One-Shot Case Study

The one-shot case study uses the most basic of all experimental designs. An **experimental group** is a group of respondents that is exposed to the experimental treatment. The one-shot case study involves exposing one experimental group to a treatment (independent variable) one time and then observing whether a change occurred in the dependent variable. It is diagrammed as follows:

Experimental group: X O

Consider Example 9-4.

Example 9-4

A group of 30 volunteer workers at University Hospital performs many different tasks throughout the hospital for one year. At the end of the year, the hospital asks each of them, "Would you like to work full-time as a paid employee of University Hospital?" Of the 30 volunteers, 20 say yes. The purpose of the experiment is to determine how many hospital volunteer workers want to work as full-time paid employees at the hospital after having volunteered.

X = Treatment: worked as a volunteer at University Hospital
O = Observation: 20 out of 30 workers would like to work full-time as an employee of University Hospital

The problem with the one-shot case study is that it does not allow the researcher to compare the observation with what would have occurred had there been no treatment. Also, extraneous factors like history, mortality, and maturation may influence the observation, since they are not controlled in this simple design.

One-Group Pretest/Posttest Design

This design involves testing the test subjects twice. The first time involves testing the subjects before any treatment has taken place. The second time involves exposing the subjects to the treatments and then testing them after the treatment has taken place. We can determine the treatment effect by subtracting O_1 from O_2. This design is symbolized as follows:

Experimental group: O_1 X O_2

Consider Example 9-5.

Example 9-5

A company wants to determine the attitudes of teenagers toward alcohol consumption. The teenagers involved in the experiment are first interviewed about their attitudes toward alcohol consumption. They are then exposed to a video put together by Mothers Against Drunken Driving (MADD), showing graphic pictures of traffic deaths caused by drunk drivers. This is the treatment. The students are then interviewed again about their attitudes toward alcohol consumption.

O_1 = Pretreatment measure: interview about attitudes toward alcohol consumption
X = Treatment: teenagers view film by MADD
O_2 = Posttreatment observation: interviewed again shortly after the MADD film about attitudes toward alcohol consumption

Static-Group Comparison

The third preexperimental design is the static-group comparison. Unlike the previous designs, this one uses two groups—an experimental group and a control group. The experimental group is exposed to the treatment and the control group is not. A control group—a group that has no treatments imposed on it—is used so that it can be compared against the experimental group. Researchers determine the effect of the treatment on the dependent variable by comparing the experimental group after treatment against the control group, which received no treatment. The dashes between the two groups indicate that the groups are separate and that the control group does not come into contact with the treatment. The experiment is symbolized as follows:

Experimental group: $\quad X \quad O_1$
Control group: $\qquad\qquad O_2$

Consider Example 9-6.

Example 9-6

Sociologists want to examine the impact of television on college students' overall grades. They divide students into two groups. During the experiment, the experimental group watches at least ten hours of television each week and the control group does not watch any television. The sociologists measure the difference between the control group's grades (O_2) and the experimental group's grades (O_1) to determine whether watching at least ten hours of television each week impacts college students' overall grades.

X = Treatment: exposure to at least ten hours of television each week
O_1 = Posttreatment measure: grades of group that watched at least ten hours of television each week
O_2 = Posttreatment measure: grades of group that did not watch television

---

A few problems exist with this type of design. First, there is no guarantee that the two groups were alike before the experiment began. That is, how can we be sure that the control group of students really never watched television prior to the experiment? Since the study's purpose was to determine whether watching at least ten hours of television each week impacts students' grades, then those respondents in the control group who have watched television at least ten hours a week prior to the experiment will likely confound the results. Another problem is associated with the way students involved in the experiment were selected. Nonrandom recruitment practices could cause differences in the experimental and control groups. Finally, any differences between the groups could have been caused by differential mortality—that is, more students may have dropped out of one group. Mortality can be a problem for any experimental design.

9-2b True Experimental Designs

True experimental designs differ from preexperimental designs in that they *randomly* assign test units to experimental and control groups. The pretest/posttest control group design, the posttest-only control group design, and the Solomon four-group design are true experimental designs.

true experimental designs Experimental designs that randomly assign test units to experimental and control groups.

PreTest/Posttest Control Group Design

This design adds a control group to the one-group pretest/posttest design. It also uses equal groups, since all test subjects are chosen at random.

Experimental group: R O_1 X O_2 _____

Control group: R O_3 O_4

By using equal groups, we find the difference between O_1 and O_2 and compare it to the difference between O_3 and O_4 to determine the effect of the treatment on the observation:

$$(O_2 - O_1) - (O_4 - O_3) = \text{Estimated impact of } X$$

Consider Example 9-7.

Example 9-7

A company measures the reaction of college students to a new beer commercial. First, a sample of college students is randomly selected. Then half are randomly assigned to the experimental group, and half are assigned to the control group. The students in both groups are given a questionnaire, so that researchers can record their pretest attitudes toward alcohol consumption. The experimental group is then shown the beer advertisement. After this treatment, they are once again asked to complete a questionnaire, to measure any changes in their attitudes toward alcohol consumption. This is the posttest measure. Therefore,

X = Treatment: beer advertisement

$O_2 - O_1$ = Difference between before and after treatment of experimental group, with treatment

$O_4 - O_3$ = Difference between before and after measurement of control group, without treatment

---

This design controls for all the major threats to validity except for *mortality* and *history*. As discussed earlier, mortality becomes a problem when individuals in either group begin to drop out, and the characteristics of the dropouts differ significantly from those of subjects who remain. History becomes a problem when occurrences other than the treatment affect one group but not the other. In our example, suppose that following exposure to the ad, a common friend of the experimental group—whom the control group did not know—was killed in a traffic accident by a drunk driver. Changes in the group members' attitude toward alcohol consumption may not be due to their exposure to the beer ad (the treatment), but to the loss of their common friend.

Posttest-Only Control Group Design

This design is similar to the static-group comparison design, except in this case the group members are randomly selected. Assuming the sample size is relatively large, this randomness creates groups that are about equal regarding the dependent variable before the independent variable is tested.

Experimental group: R X O_1

Control group: R O_2

This design is susceptible to a few extraneous factors, particularly mortality and selection bias. Mortality is always a concern because we don't know whether those who leave the experimental group are similar to those who leave the control group. There are no pretreatment measurements, so selection bias is a problem because we can never be totally confident that the two groups are similar regarding the dependent variable. The random selection of test units should ensure that the two groups are similar. Unfortunately, though, we cannot be entirely sure.

Solomon Four-Group Design

This design is similar to the pretest/posttest control group design, except for the addition of another set of experimental and control groups. The key difference between the two sets of groups is that the second experimental group is not pretested. This design allows the researcher to control for the pretest measure effect in the first experimental group. The second set of groups inherently controls for the interactive testing effect, as well as for other extraneous variables. However, this design is prohibitively expensive and takes considerable time to implement, so it's rarely used. This design can be symbolized as follows:

$$\text{First experimental group:} \quad R \quad O_1 \quad X \quad O_2$$
$$\text{First control group:} \quad R \quad O_3 \quad \quad O_4$$
$$\text{Second experimental group:} \quad R \quad \quad X \quad O_5$$
$$\text{Second control group:} \quad R \quad \quad \quad O_6$$

The second experimental/control group allows the following comparisons to be made:

$$(O_2 - O_1) - (O_4 - O_3)$$
$$(O_5 - O_6)$$
$$(O_2 - O_4)$$

Each of the comparisons measures the experimental treatment *(X)* effect. Whenever there is agreement in these comparisons, the strength of the inferences made about the treatment is considerably increased.

9-2c Quasi-Experimental Designs

Quasi-experimental designs are more realistic than true experimental designs, since the researcher lacks full control over the *when* and *to whom* parts of the experiment and will often *nonrandomly* select group members. When the researcher lacks control over these experimental stimuli, the design is regarded as quasi-experimental. Every experiment is imperfect, no matter what design is used. Therefore, researchers should design the best experiment that the situation makes possible. One of the most popular quasi-experimental designs is the time-series design.

quasi-experimental designs Experimental designs in which the researcher controls the *when* and *to whom* aspects of data collection but does not totally control the scheduling of treatments and cannot subject test units to treatments randomly.

Time-Series Design

This design is like the one-group pretest/posttest design, except repeated measurements of an effect are taken both before and after the experimental treatment. The strong point of this design is the presence of a periodic measurement process on group members and the introduction of a treatment into this time series of measurements. The results are shown by discontinuous measurements recorded in the time series. This type of study may be symbolized as follows:

$$\text{Experimental group:} \quad O_1 \quad O_2 \quad O_3 \quad O_4 \quad X \quad O_5 \quad O_6 \quad O_7 \quad O_8$$

This design is often used when data is collected through consumer panels. In these cases, consumers may be asked to provide information about their purchasing habits for a particular product. At some time, a treatment may occur, such as an advertising campaign. The same consumer panel's purchasing behavior would then be tested for their reactions to the advertising campaign.

One problem associated with this type of design is that group members are not selected at random. Also, since the panel members are initially asked questions about a topic at the beginning of the study, they may respond differently during the study, since they have been sensitized to certain issues and know that they will be asked additional related questions throughout the study. Another problem is not knowing the historical effects group members bring to the study. Finally, any changes in interviewers or measurement instrument can impact the results of the study.

9-2d Statistical Experimental Designs

statistical experimental designs Experimental designs that are conducted simultaneously and allow the researcher to measure the effects of multiple independent variables.

Statistical experimental designs do not use pretreatment measures, so they are "after-only" designs. They allow the researcher to measure the effects of multiple independent variables. They can also aid the researcher by isolating the effects of extraneous variables. The completely randomized design, randomized block design, Latin square design, and factorial design will be discussed subsequently.

Completely Randomized Design

This design involves randomly assigning treatments to group members. Randomly assigning treatments to group members is the researcher's effort to control all extraneous variables while manipulating the treatment variable. This type of experiment is simple to administer but should not be used unless the test members are generally similar and also alike regarding a particular extraneous variable. The Xs (X_1, X_2, and X_3) can be considered different treatment levels. The term "levels" refers to the different forms of the same independent variable. The design may be symbolically represented as follows:

Experimental group:	R	X_1	O_1
Experimental group:	R	X_2	O_2
Experimental group:	R	X_3	O_3

Consider Example 9-8.

Example 9-8

A grocery store chain is trying to motivate consumers to shop their stores. They create three possible sales promotional efforts to encourage individuals to visit their stores (the three levels are X_1, X_2, and X_3):

X_1 = Offer a discount of 5% off customer's total grocery shopping bill.
X_2 = Offer taste samples of selected foods.
X_3 = Control group; no sales promotion effort is applied.

Using the completely randomized design, management at the grocery store chain may choose nine grocery stores to offer their promotional efforts for a week, and randomly assign them to groups of three stores. This design would look like Exhibit 9-6.

EXHIBIT 9-6	Promotional Technique		
Levels	5% Discount	Taste Samples	No Sales Promotion
Stores	Sales total, store 3	Sales total, store 5	Sales total, store 9
	Sales total, store 1	Sales total, store 8	Sales total, store 7
	Sales total, store 6	Sales total, store 4	Sales total, store 2
	Average sales	*Average sales*	*Average sales*

The grocery stores are randomly assigned to the three sales promotion (treatment) groups. The promotional technique that results in the highest average sales during the test week would likely be the type of promotion used by the other grocery store chain members, since it proved to be the most effective.

Randomized Block Design

This design is particularly useful when small sample sizes are necessary, perhaps motivated by limited company resources. As the name indicates, this design randomly assigns treatments to experimental and control groups. Researchers identify an extraneous variable that they believe confounds the study's results. Therefore, this design is used to control one important extraneous variable that could affect respondents' responses. Using a randomized block design, the researcher breaks the test units into similar "blocks," or groups, according to an extraneous variable such as location, age, gender, income, education, or any other variable believed to impact the test units and the dependent variable. A block must be controlled because it can cause changes in the dependent variable. It should be noted that it is conceptually different from an independent variable. That is, independent variables represent decision variables that can be manipulated by decision makers to achieve desired results in the dependent variable. Blocking factors, however, are characteristics beyond the control of managers (e.g., age or gender of consumers). They are used in a statistical analysis, out of technical necessity, so that their influence on the dependent variable is not confounded with the influence of the independent variable. Blocking works the same way as stratified samples—where a population is divided into natural subgroups that are more homogeneous than the population as a whole—since we are interested in establishing a similarity between test units. We discuss stratified samples in Chapter 10. Consider Example 9-9.

Example 9-9

Assume that our chain store management believes that the length of time a store has been in operation is an extraneous variable that is used to determine a store's sales level. They reason that a store's experience impacts its total sales. Nine stores are selected according to the length of time they have been in operation. The nine stores are then grouped into three blocks, as follows:

- *Block 1:* Three stores that have been in operation for less than five years
- *Block 2:* Three stores that have been in operation for five to ten years
- *Block 3:* Three stores that have been in operation for more than ten years

After the blocks are formed, one block is assigned each treatment (5% discount, taste samples, no sales promotion). When determining our sample size, since we have three treatments and three types of stores according to their length of time in operation, our sample must be divisible by 9 (that is, 3×3). So we could use a sample of $9 \times 1 = 9, 9 \times 2 = 18, 9 \times 3 = 27, 9 \times 4 = 36$, and so on. The design for our example would look like Exhibit 9-7.

EXHIBIT 9-7 Randomized Block Design

Blocks	Treatment								
	5% Discount			Taste Samples			No Promotion		
Less than 5 years	R	X_1	O_1	R	X_2	O_2	R	X_3	O_3
5 to 10 years	R	X_1	O_4	R	X_2	O_5	R	X_3	O_6
More than 10 years	R	X_1	O_3	R	X_2	O_8	R	X_3	O_9

Latin Square Design

In the randomized block design discussion, we noted that we wanted to control only one extraneous variable that could create problems in our results. The goal of the Latin square design, however, is to control or eliminate the effect of two extraneous sources of variability that can cause problematic results. This design attempts to systematically block in two directions by grouping experimental units according to two extraneous variables. It is used for comparing t treatment levels in t rows and t columns, where rows and columns represent the two blocking variables. In other words, if we have three treatment levels, we must also have three rows and three columns. This is why it is called a Latin square design. It is important to note that the treatments are randomly assigned to each cell in the design. Mathematically, the Latin square of order t is an arrangement of t Latin letters in a square of t rows and t columns, such that every Latin letter occurs once in each row and once in each column. Think of the Latin letters as treatments.[5] Consider the 3×3 matrix shown in Exhibit 9-8.

EXHIBIT 9-8 Latin Square Design

Extraneous Variable 2		
A	B	C
B	C	A
C	A	B

where *A*, *B*, and *C* are all treatments (i.e., X_1, X_2, X_3, in our example)

| EXHIBIT 9-9 | Latin Square Design—Store Sales |

Time in Operation	Per Capita Income		
	High	Medium	Low
Less than 5 years	X_1	X_2	X_3
5–10 years	X_2	X_3	X_1
More than 10 years	X_3	X_1	X_2

where: X_1 = 5% discount
  X_2 = Taste samples
  X_3 = No sales promotion
Extraneous variable 1 = Store's time in operation
Extraneous variable 2 = Store's immediate vicinity's average per capita income

In the randomized block design example, our extraneous variable was a store's length of time in operation. Let's say that we believe another extraneous variable that can confound our study results is the average per capita income in the store's immediate vicinity. Therefore, our design would look like that shown in Exhibit 9-9.

Factorial Design

In the preceding designs, the effects of only one independent variable on a dependent variable were studied, although it was possible to have multiple levels. Using a factorial design, we look at the effects that the manipulation of at least two independent variables simultaneously at different levels has on the dependent variable. Consider Example 9-10.

Example 9-10

A grocery store chain wants to use 12 of its stores to examine whether the stores' sales would change at three different hours of operation and two different types of sales promotions. The dependent variable would be the change in sales, and the independent (treatment) variables would be:

- Hours of operation: Store open between 6 A.M. and 6 P.M.
- Hours of operation: Store open between 5 A.M. and midnight (12 A.M.)
- Hours of operation: Store never closes (open 24 hours per day)
- Sales promotion: Stamps that can be applied toward a free gift
- Sales promotion: Food samples given to shoppers

This would be a 3×2 factorial design, since there were three different levels of hours of operation and two levels of sales promotion. This type of design will have the following six (that is, 3×2) experimental groups:

- X_1: 6 A.M. to 6 P.M.; gift stamps
- X_2: 6 A.M. to 6 P.M.; food samples
- X_3: 5 A.M. to midnight; gift stamps
- X_4: 5 A.M. to midnight; food samples
- X_5: 24 hours a day; gift stamps
- X_6: 24 hours a day; food samples

Therefore, the following factorial design would be used:

Experimental group 1:	R	X_1	O_1	$n = 2$
Experimental group 2:	R	X_2	O_2	$n = 2$
Experimental group 3:	R	X_3	O_3	$n = 2$
Experimental group 4:	R	X_4	O_4	$n = 2$
Experimental group 5:	R	X_5	O_5	$n = 2$
Experimental group 6:	R	X_6	O_6	$n = 2$

main effect The impact that each independent variable has on the dependent variable.

The researchers want to know the effects that the different hours of operation and different sales promotions have on a store's sales. The impact that each independent variable has on the dependent variable is referred to as a **main effect.** In this case, both the influence the hours of operation has on a store's sales level and the impact that sales promotion has on sales are the main effects. But using a factorial design, it is possible to determine how the interaction of independent variables influences the dependent variable. This is referred to as the **interaction effect.** Based on the results shown in Exhibit 9-10, it appears that those stores open for 24 hours a day and offering food samples have the greatest increase in sales.

interaction effect The extent to which the combination or interaction of independent variables influences the dependent variable.

EXHIBIT 9-10	Results of a Factorial Design

Experimental Group	Change in Sales Levels (%)
1	+5
2	+3
3	+8
4	+1
5	+10
6	+12

9-3 Test Marketing

Just as a reminder, the "Get This!" feature at the beginning of this chapter discussed the test marketing tendencies of companies like McDonald's, Anheuser-Busch, and Miller Brewing Company. It noted that other companies chose not to test market their products, offering a variety of reasons for this decision. But most marketers would agree that before a company spends vast resources on a full-scale launching of a new or altered existing product, it should carefully examine—on a limited basis—how receptive the market is to the product. That is, it should test market the product. **Test marketing** can reveal market-acceptance problems before the company has invested in full-market rollout.

test marketing Testing market acceptance of a new or altered existing product on a small scale before investing in a full-scale product launch.

Test marketing is a controlled experiment conducted on a small segment of the target market. Companies not only test new products, they also test new features on existing products and changes to a product's marketing mix. There are two major objectives of test marketing. First, companies want to know *how well their products will be accepted* in the marketplace. Oftentimes this is determined by the amount of sales the product generates during a limited testing period. Second, they want to know *how changes in their marketing mix (product, price, promotion, and distribution) efforts will likely affect product success.* Consider Example 9-11.

Example 9-11

CompUSA wants to replace the bottom 30% of its product assortment with better-selling items. As an industry-leader, it wants to be the first to bring new technology to the marketplace, so CompUSA searches for new products and technology with strong potential and tests these new products right on its shelves in several stores. To ensure that the products being tested are given a fair chance to succeed, CompUSA chooses stores with high sales in the client company's product category and optimum traffic flow past its product. Since CompUSA wants to determine how well a product performs relative to the competition, the test product is merchandised among similar products in its category. If the test market is successful, CompUSA will add the products as part of its standard product line in all of its stores.

The major reason for test marketing is risk reduction. It makes much more sense to lose $1 million in the test-market phase than to lose $50 million on a product that fails when it is introduced nationwide. However, test marketing has shortcomings as well. One problem is that the price of a test market can be rather steep. It was noted earlier in our discussion on laboratory and field setting testing that costs tend to range from $50,000 to well over $1 million. Another problem is that test marketing often takes considerable time to implement. It is not unusual for the effort to take one year to complete, which allows ample time for competitors to respond to a company's new product. A final shortcoming is that competitors can disrupt test markets. If competitors believe another company's product will be successful, they may reduce their prices and increase their promotion efforts in the test-market area to disrupt the test.

9-3a Types of Test Markets

There are four major types of test markets: standard, controlled, electronic, and simulated. Each type has strengths and weaknesses.

Standard Test Market

This is a rather straightforward approach to test marketing. In **standard test marketing,** companies use their regular distribution channels to sell their products to a small segment of the market. Companies try to choose locations that are representative of the target market. The strong point of this form of test marketing is that it allows the marketing manager an opportunity to evaluate the product under normal and actual market conditions. However, the value of this test market is based on a number of factors:

> **standard test marketing** A test marketing method in which the company uses its normal distribution channels to distribute a product to a small segment of the market.

- Number of locations used for the experiment
- Representativeness of the locations selected for the experiment (although random sampling is rarely used)
- Duration of the experiment
- Existing market conditions remain "normal"
- Cost of the experiment versus the quality of information gathered from it

Controlled Test Market

This type of testing procedure is typically much less expensive than the standard test market. In **controlled test marketing,** an outside research firm collects the data by having the product warehoused, shelved, stocked, distributed, and priced by retailers that are representative of the target market. Many times, data collection is done through electronic scanning devices, so that repeat purchase rates can be tracked, as well as household penetration, consumer demographics, and other buyer-related information. Occasion Based Marketing (OBM) implemented a controlled store test for Coca Cola in Augusta, Georgia, and not only grew consumer soft drink sales but also increased growth for the overall beverage category. The findings also showed that impulse purchases in the test stores doubled.[6] Sometimes companies alter their controlled test marketing procedures to better suit their clients. Read about Information Resources, Inc. (IRI) in Research Realities 9-1.

> **controlled test marketing** A test-marketing method in which the company hires an outside research firm to conduct the study.

Source: © 2007 JupiterImages Corporation.

Electronic Test Market

electronic test marketing A method that uses scanner-based systems in supermarkets and highly sophisticated broadcasting systems to examine the relationship between what consumers purchase and different advertising messages they watch on television.

Electronic test marketing uses scanner-based systems in supermarkets and highly sophisticated broadcasting systems to examine the relationship between what consumers purchase and different advertising messages they watch on television. This test market technique allows researchers to measure the extent to which different television ads shown within the same market impact their sales levels. This is done by hooking up a device on television sets in panel households and the researcher cutting into regularly scheduled ads to substitute its own ads that are of interest to its clients. These tests are typically conducted in a few small cities where local retailers have agreed to participate. This type of testing involves a panel of consumers who agree to carry an identification card with them that they must present at the register when purchasing goods and services at supermarkets. The major advantage of the card is that it registers demographic and other salient data as products are being bought. The upside of electronic test marketing compared with the other methods is the low cost and confidentiality. The downside of this type of market test is that people who have agreed to serve as members of the shopping panel may not be typical shoppers, so the generalizability of the results comes into question.

Simulated Test Market

simulated test marketing Test marketing done in a laboratory by exposing prospective customers to new products, competitive products, and marketing stimuli, and giving them money to make purchase decisions.

As the name indicates, the market conditions using this method are highly artificial. **Simulated test marketing** is done in a laboratory, where prospective customers are exposed to a new product, competitive products, and marketing stimuli (for example, advertisements, sales promotion). Using the money supplied by the research organization, prospects shop in this artificial setting. All product prices reflect actual market prices. Then the prospects are asked a series of questions such as, "How likely is it that you would buy this product?" and "What do you like best about this product?" It is the responsibility of the researcher to figure out how each one of the possible feature alternatives affects demand. Using an experimental product design, every reasonable feature and price is evaluated.[7] Laboratory tests are usually based on a minimum of 100 to 300 respondents per location, with the tests completed in a few days at a mall or other location where target respondents tend to cluster.[8]

Although the simulated market environment detracts from the reality of the normal shopping situation, it can benefit companies, since it is simple to implement, it is easy

Information Resources, Inc.'s Controlled Test Marketing Procedures

Product Overview

A controlled store test (CST) may be the ideal way to evaluate the sales impact of changing one or more in-store variables before risking national expansion of such changes. IRI handles all aspects of the test, from obtaining retailer participation to controlling the in-store conditions to analyzing the final results.

While computer simulations can be helpful in estimating price and promotion elasticity, models have limited ability to accurately predict the impact of changes outside the range of historical experience. In contrast, a CST measures actual consumer response under today's-world, yet controlled, conditions.

One variation on a CST is a matched store test: IRI selects matched test and control stores, collects data, and analyzes the results, while the client (typically, a major manufacturer with a direct-store-delivery system) handles the retail sell-in and in-store execution. Another variation is a targeted store test: test and control stores are selected from neighborhoods matching the desired geodemographic criteria (e.g., high percentage of Hispanic households), and the test treatment is executed and evaluated in these target stores.

Methodology

Over twenty-five years of in-market testing experience combined with InfoScan Census data enables IRI to provide controlled store tests of the highest quality, including:

- Highly accurate retail scanner data from all stores in a chain, with unsurpassed quality control

- Complete and immediate back data, allowing selection of matched test and control stores prior to test start and accurate analysis of pre vs. post, test group vs. control group changes

- Key facts about each store (e.g., number of checkouts, format) plus geodemographics of the store's trading area (e.g., income, age, ethnicity)

- Experienced in-market staff recording weekly merchandising activity and executing test conditions

- Test start-up with just 4–8 weeks lead-time

- Statistically sound methodology

Matched groups of test and control stores are typically selected from within one chain within one market to minimize extraneous differences and increase IRI's ability to isolate the impact of the test treatment on sales. If geographic diversity is desired, several markets/retailers may be used. Marketers can select from a wide variety of retailers and markets for testing.

IRI begins by running a sensitivity analysis to estimate the number of test stores that will be needed to read the expected percentage change in sales. After obtaining authorization from the desired retailer, a statistical matching procedure is used to select balanced groups of test and control stores. IRI ensures on-time implementation of the test conditions and visits each participating retailer several times per week to monitor in-store conditions, enabling a fast, accurate read of the test's impact on sales. At the end of the test, IRI uses a statistical technique called analysis of covariance to (1) identify and adjust for any nontest-related factors that could have affected sales, (2) compare the adjusted sales pre- to post- and test vs. control to quantify the effect of the test treatment, and (3) estimate the statistical level of confidence that can be placed on the reported test effect.

Because sales of any product will vary week-to-week and store-to-store (and some products more than others), this scientific approach ensures that the reported change in sales is truly due to the test treatment and not to normal, random variability in sales.

Key Applications

- Determine the optimal stocking location for a product.

- Estimate the profitability of alternative pricing/package size scenarios.

- Measure the impact of a package design change.

- Evaluate the effectiveness of various in-store promotion tactics: off-shelf display, shelf talkers, in-store sampling or couponing.

- Validate category management strategies, such as category store location, shelf arrangement, and SKU assortment.

Features

- Preferred markets/retailers: 17 grocery, 1 mass merchandise, and 5 drug chains across 19 InfoScan markets. Additional markets and retailers available on demand.

- Controllable variables: Virtually any in-store condition.

- Outlets: Grocery, drug, mass merchandising, convenience stores.

- Type of data: Scanner sales and in-store merchandising. Custom audits are usually required to capture in-store display activity.

- Analytic services: Statistical matching procedure to select test and control stores. Analysis of covariance to accurately isolate and quantify the percentage change in sales due to the test variable.

Source: Information Resources, Inc. web page, http://www.infores.com, "Controlled Store Testing," June 29, 2005.

to control market conditions, and the process does not usually leak much information to competitors. Consider Example 9-12.

One company that could have benefited from a simulated test market was IBM. The company was struggling as retailers returned more than $600 million worth of unsold products in the early 1990s. When it introduced the Aptiva line of personal computers, the company decided to be conservative in its sales estimates. This lack of understanding of its market cost the company $100 million in fourth-quarter revenue because it did not have enough products to sell. Experts believe that a simulated test-market study could have told IBM what to expect, so that it could have better planned production to meet heavy demand.[9]

9-3b Steps in Test Marketing

As shown in Exhibit 9-11, researchers follow certain steps in running a test market:

1. *Determine the objectives.* In this step the researcher asks the question, "What do I want to accomplish from my market test?" The objectives may be to

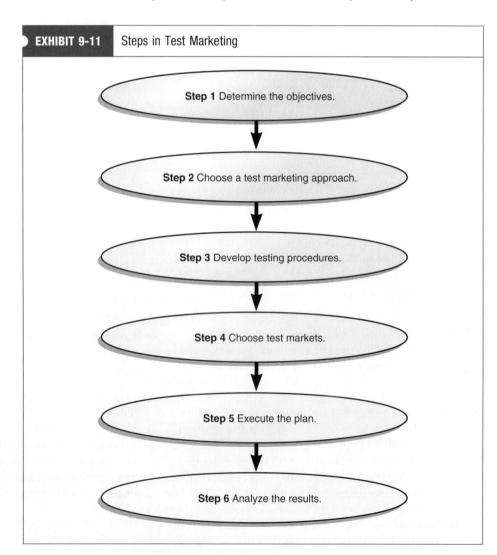

EXHIBIT 9-11   Steps in Test Marketing

Step 1 Determine the objectives.

Step 2 Choose a test marketing approach.

Step 3 Develop testing procedures.

Step 4 Choose test markets.

Step 5 Execute the plan.

Step 6 Analyze the results.

determine how acceptable a product will be in the marketplace as measured by sales, consumer product acceptance, or changes in customer attitudes caused by a change in price.

2. *Choose a test marketing approach.* After determining the study objectives, researchers decide which test marketing approach would best achieve the desired objectives. As noted earlier, the choices are to use a simulated test market, standard test market, or controlled test market approach.

3. *Develop testing procedures.* This task involves carefully developing a "game plan" to guide the test-marketing effort. A detailed description of the role of each element of the marketing mix should be included in this plan.

4. *Choose test markets.* This is a critical part of test marketing. The chosen test markets must be representative of the larger target market, or the results will be useless.

5. *Execute the plan.* Once the testing procedures are clear and the test markets are chosen, it is then time to put the plan into action. A test market typically takes 9–12 months or more.[10] The longer a test is conducted, the more expensive it becomes. Additionally, an extended test market duration allows competitors an opportunity to design and introduce similar products of their own.[11]

6. *Analyze the results.* This final analysis of the data collected should address our established objectives. It may also provide insight into secondary areas of interest that were not originally stated as objectives. While test marketing should provide useful information regarding a company's products, it may also indicate that further testing is necessary or perhaps that testing efforts that were used were faulty, necessitating changes in the test-market design.

Decision Time!

Many people who hear the term *experiment* often think of scientists with thick glasses and test tubes. They do not usually think of marketing researchers running tests in a highly controlled environment. If you recently developed a new shampoo and wanted to conduct a controlled experiment to test its effectiveness, how would you do it? Would you use one of the experimental designs discussed in the chapter? How would you test market the product?

Net Impact

The purpose of experiments is to determine which factors influence a particular behavior, and the extent and direction of the influence. The Internet can provide specific data to understand those behaviors. However, experiments usually require control for as many extraneous variables as possible, so the Internet is not the best medium for experimentation. But the Internet does allow the researcher to better understand certain behaviors, since a wide range of information can be received in a relatively timely and efficient manner. For example, if an apparel company wants to examine how its target market will react to its new advertising campaign, it can use a pretest/posttest control group design. Before and after the experiment is run, though, the Internet allows the company to gather a lot of information related to both the characteristics of its target market and its products such as the market's income, education, and recreational activities.

By taking advantage of such technological advances as virtual product displays and chat sessions, market researchers can use the Internet to test market products. For example, Product Testing Services (PTS) has tested hundreds of products online since 1985. It maintains a database of reliable Internet users to whom it offers product-testing opportunities as they arise.

On the Lighter Side—Dishonest Joe

People are often inundated with offers to participate in surveys—and they repetitively shun away from them. However, there are some people who embrace the opportunity to complete surveys. These "research groupies" turn up time and time again to respond to all sorts of market data gathering efforts. They can be spotted a mile away in focus groups—where they arrive early and enjoy the freebie snacks—and as survey respondents. Their eagerness to participate is not the problem, it's their changing identity. While they don't usually attempt to camouflage their identity by wearing masks and wigs, the same person will in one interview pose as being married with no children; six months later in a different interview he/she will be divorced with teenage children.

The incentive for these groupies is that more and more people are declining opportunities to participate in surveys and focus groups. The Market Research Society (MRS) has cited certain problems for this slide in response rates. One concern is poorly designed questionnaires. Questions on surveys that are irrelevant are especially problematic. Another shortcoming is an increasingly cynical public, who erroneously view genuine market research for sales pitches. So how do you remedy the predicament. The MRS advocates a three-pronged attack. First, improve the quality of interviewers. (There is now an accredited interviewer training scheme offered by MRS.) Second, deal with the fact that market research is viewed by many as a sales gimmick. Interviewer ID cards can help to legitimize researchers. Lastly, since questionnaires tend to be too long and too complicated, the MRS is devising guidelines on how to produce simple and effective surveys.

Source: Jo-Anne Flack, "Not-So Honest Joe," *Marketing Week* (UK), vol. 25, no. 39, p. 43.

Chapter Summary

Experiments are undertaken to determine which factors influence a particular behavior, and the extent and direction of the influence. The factors whose effects are to be studied and manipulated are referred to as independent variables; the measures of the behavior that will be investigated are the dependent variables. Experiments are often called "causal research," since they have the ability to demonstrate cause-and-effect relationships. To show that causation exists, three conditions must be met: logical time sequence, concomitant variation, and control of other possible causal factors.

Testing the validity of an experiment is essential to sound research. Validity is the test's ability to measure what it is intended to measure. Internal validity refers to the degree to which the independent variable(s) is the only cause of the observed change in the dependent variable. Simply put, if other reasons can be given for changes to occur in the dependent variable, then the experiment lacks internal validity. External validity, on the other hand, concerns the extent to which test results can be generalized to the larger population.

To run an experiment effectively, researchers must have a plan—the experimental design. The major types of experimental designs include preexperimental designs, true experimental designs, quasi-experimental designs, and statistical experimental designs.

Before a company spends much time and effort on a full-scale launching of a new or altered product, it should test market the product, on a limited basis, to determine how receptive the marketplace is to the product. Test marketing is a controlled experiment used not only for testing market acceptance of a new product, but also for testing new features of existing products and the effects of changes in the marketing mix. There are four major test markets: standard, controlled, electronic, and simulated. Test marketing has two major objectives: to determine how well products will be accepted in the marketplace and to determine how changes to the marketing mix variables will likely affect product success.

Review Questions

1. What is an experiment, and what is it used for in marketing?

2. What is meant by "causality"? What conditions must be met for it to exist?

3. How do internal and external validity differ? How are they related?

4. What are the major types of experimental design? Draw two types of designs, using the *X, O,* and *R* notation.

5. What are statistical experimental designs, and how do they differ from quasi-experimental designs?

6. In which types of experimental design do study designers randomly select their test participants?

7. Why do companies bother with test marketing their products?

8. Briefly discuss the different types of test markets.

9. List the six steps in test marketing.

Practice Quiz

Note: You can find the correct answers to these questions by taking the quiz and then submitting your answers in the Online Edition. The program will automatically score your submission. If you miss a question, the program will provide the correct answer, a rationale for the answer, and the section number in the chapter where the topic is discussed.

1. Testing effect is the extent an initial test sensitizes respondents to the process of experimentation, causing respondents to react differently to a second test than they would if no initial test had been conducted.
   a. True   b. False

2. The mortality effect is the bias that results when the experimental group differs significantly from the target population or from the control group.
   a. True   b. False

3. "Regression toward the mean" is the tendency of a respondent's responses to move toward the average score as the experiment progresses.
   a. True   b. False

4. Internal validity refers to the degree to which an experiment can clearly show that the change in the dependent variable is caused by changes in the independent variables rather than by other outside factors.
   a. True   b. False

5. External validity tends to be higher in controlled environments such as laboratory settings but lower in less-controlled environments such as field settings.
   a. True   b. False

6. _____ designs are the most basic of all experimental designs.
   a. One-group pretest/posttest
   b. Time-series
   c. One-shot case study
   d. Completely randomized
   e. Latin square

7. _____ designs have the experimental group exposed to the treatment and the control group not exposed.
   a. One-group pretest/posttest
   b. Static group comparison
   c. One-shot case study
   d. Time-series
   e. None of the above

8. Which of the following designs differs from pre-experimental designs in that it allows study designers to randomly assign test units to experimental and control groups?
   a. Quasi-experimental
   b. Statistical experimental
   c. Artificial experimental
   d. True experimental
   e. None of the above

9. Which of the following is the fifth step in test marketing?
   a. Execute the plan.
   b. Choose test markets.
   c. Analyze results.
   d. Determine the objectives.
   e. Develop testing procedures.

10. _____ design has this type of study: O_1 O_2 O_3 O_4 X O_5 O_6 O_7 O_8.
   a. Latin square   d. Completely randomized
   b. Time-series   e. Factorial
   c. Randomized block

Thinking Critically

1. McDonald's wants to determine how the presence of a Ronald McDonald clown in its restaurants affects sales. In one McDonald's franchise restaurant, the clown is present during all hours of operations. In another McDonald's franchise restaurant, no clown is ever present during the testing period. What type of experimental design is being used? What is the treatment? Which group is the control group?

2. Assume that 50 college students participated in internships with a local furniture manufacturer for one year. At the end of the year, the company wanted to know whether any of the students would like to become full-time employees of the company. Five of the 50 students indicated that they would like to work for the furniture company. Which type of experimental design was used? Was there any type of treatment involved? If so, what was it?

3. Describe a real-life experiment that used a simulated test market. Do you believe the usefulness of the experiment results suffered from the artificial market conditions? Why or why not?

Net Exercise

In 1985, long before the World Wide Web came along, Product Testing Services (PTS) already worked with the emerging online community, in the market research sense of surveying people who could send in their feedback via a modem. Today, PTS maintains an ever-growing member-ship of many thousands of Internet users who volunteer to evaluate products. Visit the PTS Web site at http://www.product-testing.com/ to see how the company tests new products with online experiments.

Experiencing Marketing Research

Visit a local retail store and interview, if possible, the store manager or assistant manager. Ask him or her to describe the advertising efforts the store or its parent company has done in the past 12 months. Then ask whether he or she feels that the advertising has directly impacted store sales during the same time period. Following the interview, decide whether you believe that the advertising caused sales to increase. Be sure to discuss the three conditions for causation to occur.

Case 9-1

Listen to Your Customers— Yeah . . . Right!

The battle cry of most marketers is, "Know your customers!" Today, customers are being described as "king," "first," "number 1," and "always right." They are so revered that most companies are scared to move without first conferring with them. Some experts, however, believe that this devotion has gone a bit too far. More and more companies have achieved staggering successes by periodically ignoring their customers. Consider just a few of them:

- Chrysler moved ahead with the original minivan despite research showing that people did not like their strange-looking vehicle. The minivan went on to be the automobile success story of the 1980s. Interestingly, when the company began work on its 1996 model, its designers knew significant changes were called for, such as making the minivan more rounded and aerodynamic in appearance. But when the company first tested the designs, consumers were upset that it had been changed.

- In the early 1990s, Compaq put millions of dollars into personal computer network servers, even though customers said they would not abandon their mainframes.

- Barry Diller forged ahead with Fox Broadcasting, even though surveys said there was no room for another network.

- Rawlings, Spalding, and Mizuno each attempted to market pump baseball gloves in the early 1990s. They operated like pump shoes, where the gloves contained inflatable bladders designed to provide a better, tighter fit. They tested well in markets, but consumers would not purchase them.

- Other products that met with initial consumer naysaying include fax machines, videocassette recorders, Federal Express, and CNN.

So how do you know how customers will respond to new products if you don't ask them? Larry Keeley, president of a Chicago consulting firm, says, "The best way to understand customers is to study them under normal, natural conditions." Steelcase, an office-furniture manufacturer, used such a method when it designed a new product especially for work teams. During the important early design stage, the company set up video cameras at various companies and exhaustively analyzed the tapes, looking for the patterns of behavior and motion that customers themselves do not notice. The main observation was that people in teams function best if they can do some work collaboratively and some privately.

Sources: Rajesh Sethi, Daniel C. Smith, and C. Whan Park, "How to kill a team's creativity," *Harvard Business Review* 80 (August 2002): 2–3. Kevin Zhou, Bennett Yim, and David Tse, "The effects of strategic orientations on technology- and market-based breakthrough innovations," *Journal of Marketing* 69, no. 2 (April 2005): 42–60.

Case Questions

1. Do you agree with the notion of ignoring what consumers have to say about products in test markets? If so, why? If not, why not?

2. Does it appear that Steelcase used some type of experimental design? If so, which kind? If not, why do you believe they did not use one?

3. Why do you think companies test market their products, only to ignore the results?

 ## Case 9-2

The Body Shop Changes Its Complexion

In 1976 Anita Roddick started a company that literally changed the scent of the human body using homemade naturally inspired products with little packaging. The Body Shop rapidly grew from just 25 hand-mixed products to a mega-company with a worldwide network of shops. Her mode of market growth was through franchising. It permitted her company to expand globally as hundreds of entrepreneurs from around the world sold her products. Today, The Body Shop operates in 50 countries with more than 1,900 outlets and annual sales of $1.52 billion worldwide.

Unfortunately, company growth has stalled due to intense competition in the cosmetic market. An increasing number of retailers, such as Shoppers Drug Mart and Loblaw, are expanding their beauty assortments, which makes it crucial for The Body Shop to grow.

A successful strategy the company has used is to test a new store concept in an effort to liven up its brand image and revive decreasing sales. Traditionally The Body Shop format uses dark green store fixtures and bold fruity colors on the walls, such as pumpkin orange or yellow. "The 'green' store served us well over the years, but the customer has become more sophisticated," said Joanne Calabrese, president of the Body Shop Americas region.

Breaking the mold with a new store concept, The Body Shop is brighter and more calming, featuring pale wood flooring and freestanding light fixtures. Products on glass wall shelving are backlit against a hemp screen and separated by bamboo dividers. Green is still used as an accent color, but it is no longer the theme of the store. Another change is the store's logo, featuring the retailer's pod symbol in the middle of its brand name.

According to David Gray, president of retail consultancy Sixth Line Solutions, "The change is long overdue. They were so far ahead of their time in terms of building a retail concept around a set of values, but once everyone else started doing it there wasn't really differentiation anymore. The retail assortment itself didn't really evolve over the last 10 years. A lot of people have gone into that space and Body Shop had lost its differentiation."

The strategy is all part of The Body Shop's effort to solidify its position in what Ms. Calabrese calls the "masstige" beauty segment—a combination of offering prestige brands like Chanel and Estee Lauder and mass channel cosmetics like Maybelline.

Source: The Body Shop Web site "About us," http://www.thebodyshopinternational.com/web/tbsgl/about.jsp, July 21, 2005. Hollie Shaw, "Body Shop dons a new coat: Bid to revive sales" *National Post* (July 13, 2005): FP.3.

Case Questions

1. Assume you are responsible for testing The Body Shop's new store concept in the United States. Your task is to find out how target consumers feel about the new store and whether the new store concept can boost sales. Which type of experimental design will you use? Why?

2. If a test market is to be conducted, which test market technique(s) will you use? Why?

Notes

1. Chris Barker, Nancy Pistrang, and Robert Elliot, *Research Methods in Clinical and Counseling Psychology* (New York: Wiley, 1994), 138.
2. Jerome L. Myers, *Fundamentals of Experimental Design* (Boston: Allyn & Bacon, 1979), 1.
3. CCH, Inc., "Laboratory studies," http://www.toolkit.cch.com/text/P03_3101.asp, June 25, 2005.
4. CCH, Inc., "Field studies," http://www.toolkit.cch.com/text/P03_3120.asp, June 25, 2005.
5. Klaus Hinkelmann and Oscar Kempthorne, *Design and Analysis of Experiments* (New York: Wiley, 1994), 317.
6. Irene Cherkassky, "Partners in profit," *Beverage World* 119, no. 1688 (March 15, 2000): 70–77.
7. Kevin J. Clancy, and Robert S. Shulman, "Test for success: How simulated test marketing can dramatically improve the forecasting of a new product's sales," *Sales & Marketing Management* 147, no. 10 (1995): 111–114.
8. CCH, Inc., "Laboratory studies," http://www.toolkit.cch.com/text/P03_3101.asp, June 20, 2005.
9. Kevin J. Clancy and Robert S. Shulman, "Test for success: How simulated test marketing can dramatically improve the forecasting of a new product's sales," *Sales & Marketing Management* 147, no. 10 (1995): 111–114.
10. Glen L. Urban and John R. Hauser, *Design and Marketing of New Products* (Upper Saddle River, NJ: Prentice-Hall, 1993).
11. Jon S. Armstrong, *Principles of Forecasting: A Handbook for Researchers and Practitioners,* (Norwell, MA: Kluwer Academic Publishers, 2001).

Fundamentals of Sampling

Chapter Ten

Source: © 2007 JupiterImages Corporation.

Key Terms

area sample (p. 243)

census (p. 237)

cluster sampling (p. 242)

confidence interval (p. 251)

confidence level (p. 251)

confidence limits (p. 251)

convenience sampling (p. 244)

finite population (p. 237)

infinite population (p. 237)

information-processing error (p. 259)

intentional interviewer bias (p. 259)

interviewer error (p. 259)

judgment sampling (p. 244)

measurement instrument error (p. 257)

nonprobability sampling (p. 238)

nonresponse error (p. 258)

normal curve (p. 248)

normal distribution (p. 248)

parameter (p. 237)

population (p. 237)

population definition error (p. 257)

probability sampling (p. 238)

procedure error (p. 257)

quota sampling (p. 244)

random error (p. 255)

response error (p. 258)

sample (p. 237)

sample selection error (p. 257)

sampling error (p. 246)

sampling frame (p. 237)

sample frame bias (p. 237)

simple random sampling (p. 239)

Learning Objectives

After studying this chapter, you will be able to:

- Explain why researchers use samples and why findings based on a sample can approximate the findings for the population.

- Explain the sampling process.

- Describe how to properly collect samples.

- Explain how to determine sample size and perform some calculations.

- Understand the potential errors in the data collection process and how to minimize them.

An Opinion about Opinion Polls

When researchers conduct scientific studies, it typically means that they are using unbiased, systematic, and well-thought-out techniques to arrive at conclusions. So what does it mean when researchers conduct unscientific studies? That they are using biased, unsystematic, and poorly thought out techniques to arrive at inconclusive findings?

In a local evening news program, the newscasters announced early in the broadcast that they were taking a nonscientific poll on the question, "Is the president doing a good job managing the economy?" Viewers were told to dial a specific telephone number if they thought "yes" and another number if they thought "no." The newscasters promised to reveal the results of the study toward the conclusion of the newscast. As a result, that specific poll showed 41% of the respondents answering affirmatively to the query.

Oftentimes these types of unscientific polls provide directional information that is more entertaining than conclusive. Some marketers refer to them as "infotainment," but researchers should ponder how both the general public and those who should know better perceive the results. What does "nonscientific" mean, anyway? These polls add to the perception that opinion research is not to be taken seriously, as in "Vote early; vote often."

If someone feels passionately about one of the topics used in these polls, they can call in several times—loading the dice, so to speak. Another shortcoming with these types of polls is that they violate sound sampling principles. This is why they are nonscientific.

The two aspects of sampling that scientific pollsters and marketing researchers are attentive to are quality and quantity. The quality of a sample indicates how well it represents the population. When capable researchers are attempting to determine how a population feels about an issue, or perhaps reacts to an advertisement or a concept, they work diligently to ensure that the sample is representative of that population. How representative it can be depends on the interviewing technique being used. If the technique is telephone or mail interviewing, the sample can be representative of the population of interest. If it is in-person interviewing or online, researchers use quota sampling to make certain that the sample appears representative and that it encompasses all types of people needed in the proper proportions.

When quantity is the key concern, the rule is simply more is better. Researchers can determine the number necessary to meet certain goals, but really it is typically budgetary constraints that set the sample size. It basically boils down to the question, "How many interviews can we afford?" The unscientific call-in poll does not attempt to be representative of the viewing populations, and—in the case of the local station that ran the unscientific survey about people's feelings about the president's performance—did not even report how many calls came in. (The station probably did not even know how many people called.)

The number of respondents is a random aspect of how many viewers call in, and the "quality" is based on those who self-select, which may or may not represent the attitudes of viewers. Respondents are not representative of people in a city or viewing area, rendering the poll results useless because they represent nothing.

There are clearly two possible dangers that can result from nonscientific surveys. First, when seeing these free-and-easy, entertainment-oriented, nonscientific polls, people will likely believe that the polls truly represent something, but in reality, they do not. A second danger is that after recognizing the entertainment purpose of these polls, people will think that no polls or surveys are accurate and reject all data of this type, even when it could be very useful. All in all, infotainment polls are a bad idea.

Source: Stephen J. Hellebusch, "Infotainment polls give MR a bad rap," *Marketing News* 38, no. 2 (February 1, 2004): 35.

Key Terms (*continued*)

snowball sampling   (p. 244)
standard deviation   (p. 246)
standard error of the mean   (p. 249)
standard error of the proportion   (p. 246)
standard error of the statistic   (p. 246)
statistic   (p. 246)
strata   (p. 241)
stratified sampling   (p. 241)
systematic error (or constant error)   (p. 255)
systematic sampling   (p. 240)
total error   (p. 255)
unintentional bias   (p. 259)
variance   (p. 246)

Now Ask Yourself

- Why are infotainment polls not scientific and just for entertainment?

- What are the two key aspects of sampling? How do they help researchers obtain accurate information from the target market?

The benefit of sampling is obvious. If a survey of 1,000 people can come close to representing a population of 200 million, then companies in need of reliable information can save a lot of money by surveying only 1,000 people instead of the total population. However, as illustrated in the "Get This" feature, while opinion polls can be informative, they can be misleading if conducted improperly. In this chapter, we discuss why companies sample, who they should include in their samples, how they draw samples, and how many they should include in their samples to represent target populations.

Companies often take a sample of elements to represent the target market because cost and time considerations make surveying an entire population in the market impractical. While this may seem like a flawed approach, in reality, people do this all the time. Consider the following examples:

- We dip our toes in a pool to feel the water temperature of the entire pool.

- We taste a few grapes to determine the ripeness of the entire vine of grapes.

- We taste a spoonful of soup to determine whether the whole bowlful needs more salt.

- We try on a pair of shoes to compare their comfort to that of other shoes.

- We read part of a book to determine whether it appears interesting enough to keep reading.

- We watch the beginning of a television program to decide whether to watch the whole show.

As these examples show, sampling is really nothing new to most people. However, scientific sampling follows certain methods and distributions to make sure that the sample represents the target population as accurately as possible. It is undeniable, to most statistical experts, that both small and large samples can be highly accurate—provided the sampling plan is sound. As shown in Exhibit 10-1, a five-step sampling process is recommended. The first step is to define the target population. This decision must be based on the marketing manager's research objectives. The second step is to

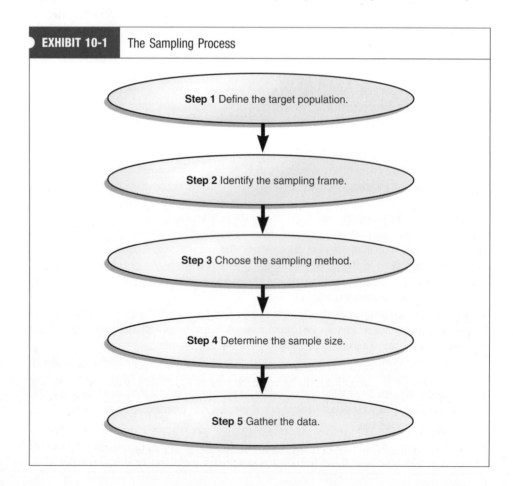

> **EXHIBIT 10-1**   The Sampling Process
>
> **Step 1** Define the target population.
>
> **Step 2** Identify the sampling frame.
>
> **Step 3** Choose the sampling method.
>
> **Step 4** Determine the sample size.
>
> **Step 5** Gather the data.

identify the sampling frame, followed by choosing the sampling method, determining the sample size, and finally, gathering the data from the proper sample.

10-1 Define the Target Population

A **population** is the entire group of people, markets, companies, or products that is being investigated by a researcher. The definition of the population is entirely determined by research objectives. For example, if we intend to understand the purchase patterns of the 25 students in a marketing class, the marketing class of 25 students is the population. If we want to study the lifestyles of college students in the United States, then the target population is the whole group of college students in all the places throughout the United States.

A population can be *finite* or *infinite*. A **finite population** has a limited or fixed number of individuals or objects, whereas an **infinite population** has an unlimited or non-fixed number. For example, a marketing class of 25 students is a finite population. The number of college students in the United States during the past, present, and future is unlimited; therefore, such students form an infinite population.

A **parameter** is a measurement used to describe some characteristic of a population, such as the arithmetic mean, median, or standard deviation of a population. Parameters are rarely known for the population, so statistics from samples are typically used to estimate them. If a population is sampled in its entirety, that sampling is by definition a **census.** A census will provide the researcher with the parameter. Otherwise, a statistic from a sample must be used as an estimate of the parameter.

The task of collecting a complete set of data (a census) from a small population is relatively simple. If we wish to obtain the ages of the 25 students in the marketing class, we may simply ask each student his or her age; thus, we have a complete set of data. However, collecting such data from a large population is sometimes impossible or impractical. It is possible to collect a complete set of data on the ages of all students from all schools throughout the United States on October 1, 2005, for example, but it would be impractical because of the time and the cost involved.

To avoid the impossible or impractical, researchers draw a **sample** consisting of a subset of representative units from the population. The sample is then used to represent the population for statistical study, and the findings from the sample are used as the basis for estimating or predicting the characteristics of the population. If the study's intent was to find consumer perceptions toward McDonald's hamburgers, then randomly sampling 1,000 people would have given us information similar to what we would have found had we surveyed all 200 million people—given a certain margin of error. If properly implemented, sampling can provide similar information about a population in less time and at a much lower cost than surveying the entire population. An important part of this plan is to use a correct sampling frame.

> **population** The entire group of people, markets, companies, or products that is being investigated by a researcher.

> **finite population** A limited or fixed number of individuals or objects in a population.

> **infinite population** An unlimited or non-fixed number of individuals or objects in a population.

> **parameter** A numerical measure used to describe some characteristic of a population.

> **census** A population sampled in its entirety.

> **sample** A subset of representative units from the population.

10-2 Identify the Sampling Frame

A **sampling frame** is the actual list of each element or member of the target population. It might be a list of any group, including consumers, businesses, subscribers, and financial supporters. For example, if we wanted to sample Cincinnati teenagers who have watched MTV during the past month, the target population would consist of the actual group of all teenagers in Cincinnati who have watched MTV during the past month. However, our sampling frame—the list of names we compile from available records—may not exactly match the actual population. Some of the people on the list may no longer be teenagers or perhaps have died or moved away. This difference between the sampling frame and the actual population creates a potential for bias in any sample, which is referred to as **sample frame bias.** Consider Example 10-1.

> **sampling frame** The actual list of each element of the target population from which a sample is drawn.

> **sample frame bias** The difference between the sampling frame and the actual population.

Example 10-1

Samples for surveying a firm's customers are often based on a list provided by a firm. This appears to be an ideal sampling frame. However, not every company has a complete list of its customers. For instance, it is impossible for supermarkets or restaurants to have a full list of their customers. If we draw a sample from such an incomplete list, we will miss customers who are not on the list and thereby create an unrepresentative sample. Alternatively, we may use the telephone directory as a sample frame to approach the customers of a supermarket. However, this creates the other type of error because not all the people on the telephone directory are the customers of the supermarket.

Unfortunately, an accurate sampling frame does not guarantee a representative sample. One main source of bias is inappropriate sampling methods. To minimize the chance of sampling bias, a random sample should be taken; that is, each element of the sampling frame must have an equal chance of being selected. If for some reason the chance is unequal, this may create a potential sample bias that must be taken into consideration in the analysis and interpretation of the results. In the 1992 general election in the United Kingdom, a non-random sampling was used, and it produced poor results (see Research Realities 10-1. In section 10-3 we will discuss how to select an appropriate sampling method.

10-3 Choose the Sampling Method

probability sampling A sampling method where every member of the target population has a known and nonzero chance of being included in the sample.

There are two major categories of sampling method: probability and nonprobability sampling. **Probability sampling** is a sampling method where every member of the target population has a known and nonzero chance of being included in the sample. **Nonprobability sampling** is a sampling method where sample selection is judgmental, and the probability of being chosen is unknown. Exhibit 10-2 shows the sampling methods used for drawing probability and nonprobability samples.

nonprobability sampling A sampling method where sample selection is judgmental, and the probability of being chosen is unknown.

10-3a Probability Sampling

In probability sampling, each sample element is chosen by chance, and the chance is known for each element being selected. Probability samples are generally preferred over nonprobability samples because sample selection is objective and sampling error

Research Realities 10-1 *Research Takes a Hit from Poor Choice of Sampling Technique*

Predictions are nothing more than educated guesses. When used in politics, their complexity can range from econometric models to simple public opinion polls. However the degree of difficulty, the findings seem to often be questionable. "The verdict is a damning indictment of the market research industry's practices." This quote came from a report about a study commissioned by the Market Research Society in the United Kingdom. The study sampled voters to try to predict the outcome of an upcoming general election, but the study results were four percentage points away from the actual election results. Three reasons were given for the miscue: (1) the sampling techniques did not accurately reflect the social profile of the electorate at the time, (2) the pollsters did not

compensate for Conservative supporters' reluctance to reveal party loyalty, and (3) the late swing to the Tories caught them all completely unaware.

To avoid future mistakes, the Market Research Society decided to change its sampling methods to ensure that the surveys would be as representative as possible. In a later study, secret-ballot and random-sampling techniques were used instead of quota sampling to produce an accurate poll of European election voting in London.

Source: Andrew Leigh and Justin Wolfers, "Competing Approaches to Forecasting Elections: Economic Models, Opinion Polling, and Prediction Markets," *Economic Record,* vol. 82, no. 258 (September 2006), pp. 325–340; Ruth Davis, "Research slams polls practices," *Marketing* (July 14, 1994): 14.

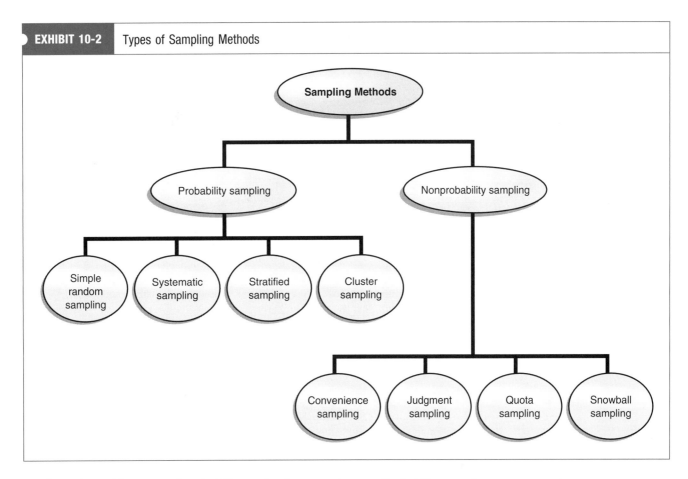

> **EXHIBIT 10-2** Types of Sampling Methods

can be estimated in terms of probability under the normal curve. Probability samples have also been found to be more accurate than nonprobability samples.[1] Common types of probability sampling are simple random sampling, systematic sampling, stratified sampling, and cluster sampling.

Simple Random Sampling

Simple random sampling is a sampling technique in which each element of the population or each possible sample of the same size from the population has an equal chance of being selected. Each possible sample has a known and equal chance of being selected. Simple random sampling is carried out by assigning each element of the sampling frame a number. Then a series of random numbers is generated, using either a computer or a random number table. The sample becomes the elements whose numbers appear on the list of random numbers.[2] Exhibit 10-3 shows a random number table.

> simple random sampling A sampling technique in which each element of the population or each possible sample of the same size from the population has an equal chance of being selected.

Using the random number table to identify a sample is rather simple. If we wish to select four students at random from a group of 30 students, we follow these steps:

1. Assign each student a number from 01 to 30.
2. Select a starting point in the table at random, such as by closing your eyes and letting your finger drop on the table.
3. Choose a direction to move from the starting point, such as down, up, right, left, or diagonally.
4. Select for the sample the student whose number corresponds to the starting point. Then move in the chosen direction on the table, selecting each qualified number as you come to it, until you have a total of four numbers (your sample size). Your sample consists of the students corresponding to these numbers.

Assume that the starting point for this example is the third column and eleventh row of Exhibit 10-3, and the moving direction is from the starting point down. Only

	(1)	(2)	(3)	(4)	(5)	(6)
EXHIBIT 10-3		A Random Number Table				
1	24571	23165	39407	60614	99692	53643
2	13670	32919	85543	04891	95940	36404
3	30051	56205	28399	57818	50250	64143
4	17977	66365	89867	29215	16767	78664
5	92178	52766	05531	89370	29936	73564
6	55136	12504	50905	63482	77089	16116
7	56292	65313	87697	77362	25261	41434
8	28852	23758	99995	89994	80072	16037
9	36575	00384	56044	71864	37692	93583
10	73548	41988	41754	77623	74789	47006
11	72077	60626	22039	28633	10540	56804
12	62212	73377	80482	52186	90008	51570
13	15835	56281	64703	21641	93937	02247
14	11418	68647	23526	89468	08261	30923
15	75712	08920	23339	55006	41144	12413
16	75596	87992	28897	85916	53472	84681
17	21980	74852	01770	82811	57641	19156

Source: Dr. Stephen P. Shao, Sr., *Statistics for Business and Economics,* 3d ed. (Columbus, Ohio: Charles E. Merrill, 1976). Used with permission.

the first two digits in each group of five digits on the table are needed for our purpose because our numbers are each two digits long (from 01 to 30). The numbers are ignored if they are larger than the largest number in the population (30) or are repetitions of numbers already chosen. Thus the numbers representing the four students are 22 (80 and 64 are ignored because they are larger than 30), 23 (the second 23 is ignored), 28, and 01.

Simple random sampling is commonly used in situations that use a computer to generate random numbers. For example, in telephone surveys, random digit dialing (RDD) is often used to generate random telephone numbers including area code, prefix, and suffix. This technique overcomes the problem of unlisted or new telephone numbers, and thus assures that households with telephone numbers have an equal opportunity of being included in the sample.

Simple random sampling is easy to understand and guarantees that the sample is representative of the population as each element in the population has an equal chance of being selected. However, to obtain a simple random sample is not an easy or practical undertaking under many circumstances. It may be time-consuming or costly and sometimes is theoretically impossible. For example, if we wish to take a simple random sample from a large population of 1 million families, although it is possible, it is not a simple task to assign a number to each of the families and then draw a sample at random from the numbers. When a sample frame is not available, numbering each element of the population is impossible. Therefore, simple random sampling is normally used in three cases: when there is a small population, when random digit dialing is feasible, and when sampling from a computerized database can occur. For other occasions, simple random sampling needs some modifications. The most common types of modified probability samples are systematic, stratified, and cluster samples.

Telephone marketing has been complicated by the establishment of the National Do Not Call Registry (NDNCR). Within the first two hours of the establishment of the service on June 28, 2003, 250,000 people registered their numbers with the NDNCR.[3]

Systematic Sampling
Systematic sampling is a sampling technique in which a sample is drawn by arbitrarily choosing a beginning point in a list and then sequentially selecting every *i*th element

systematic sampling A sampling technique in which a sample is drawn by arbitrarily choosing a beginning point in a list and then sequentially selecting every *i*th element from the list.

from the list. For a systematic sample, a list of the population is necessary. The selection procedure depends on the population size *(N)* and the sample size *(n)*. The frequency with which the elements are drawn—the skip interval *(i)*—is determined by dividing the population size *(N)* by the sample size *(n)*. That is, $i = N/n$.

In systematic sampling, the first item of the sample is selected at random. The rest of the sample is chosen by selecting every ith element from the ordered population list until the sample size is reached. For example, if we want to select 4 students from a class with 40 students, then the skip interval $= 40/4 = 10$. If the randomly selected starting point is 16, then the sample will consist of 16, 26, 36, and 6. Consider Example 10-2.

Example 10-2

A telephone company wants to understand their customers' satisfaction with its mobile phone service. It has a list of 25,000 customers, filed in alphabetical order. If a sample of 250 is desired, the sample can be selected from the list for every 100th customer $(25,000/250 = 100)$ with the first one selected at random. If the first item is 18th in the population, the second will be 118th $(= 18 + 100)$, the third will be 218th, the fourth will be 318th, and so on.

Systematic sampling is faster and less costly to implement than simple random sampling because random selection is only done once. It may yield the same precision as a simple random sample if the order of items in the population is unimportant to the study. Therefore, systematic sampling is widely used when a list of the population is available (e.g., a telephone directory). However, with the rapid development of computerized databases, its popularity has decreased recently. Systematic sampling can be also employed when a sample frame is not available. For example, in mall-intercept interviews, we can intercept every ith person leaving the shopping mall.

Stratified Sampling

Stratified sampling is a sampling technique in which the researcher first divides the population into natural subgroups that are more homogeneous than the population as a whole. Then items are selected for the sample at random or by a systematic method from each subgroup.

Stratified sampling is usually used when a *large variation* exists within a population and the researcher has some *prior knowledge* about natural subgroupings within the population. The first step is to divide the population into these natural subgroups, called **strata.** Strata are formed based on two conditions: (1) elements within strata must be homogeneous, and (2) elements between strata must be heterogeneous.

For example, the subgroups may be divided by age, income, gender, and so on. In Exhibit 10-4, they are divided by race. The elements in each stratum would then be more like each other (more homogeneous) than like the rest of the population. The items of the sample are then selected at random or by a systematic method from each stratum. Estimates of the population based on the stratified sample usually have greater precision (or smaller sampling error) than if the whole population was sampled by simple random sampling.

The number of items selected from each stratum may be proportionate or disproportionate to the size of the stratum in relation to the population. Under the proportionate method, for example, if the size of stratum A is 40% of the population, then 40% of the sample will come from stratum A. Thus if the sample size is 200 items, 40% of the sample size, or 80 items, are to be selected from stratum A. When the selection is disproportionate, it is relatively difficult to weigh the results from individual strata properly.

The major benefit from stratified sampling is that the sample will include items from each stratum and thus improve the accuracy of the sample results. The disadvantages of stratified sampling are that it is more costly and time-consuming, and

stratified sampling A sampling technique in which the researcher first divides the population into natural subgroups that are more homogeneous than the population as a whole. Then items are selected for the sample at random or by a systematic method from each subgroup.

strata Subgroups formed based on the criteria that (1) elements within strata must be homogeneous, and (2) elements between strata must be heterogeneous.

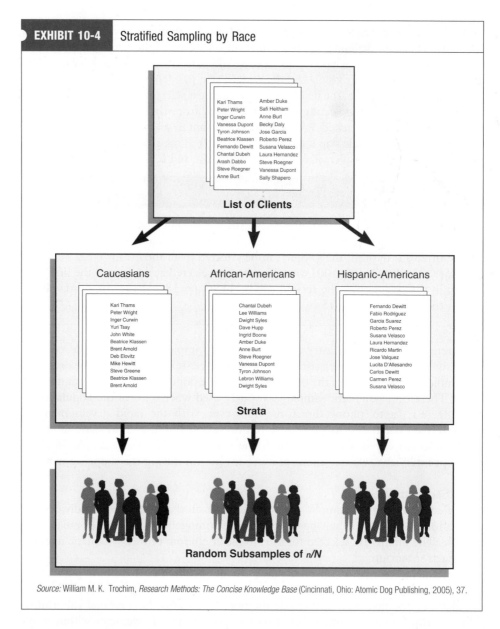

EXHIBIT 10-4   Stratified Sampling by Race

List of Clients

Kari Thams	Amber Duke
Peter Wright	Safi Heitham
Inger Curwin	Anne Burt
Vanessa Dupont	Becky Daly
Tyron Johnson	Jose Garcia
Beatrice Klassen	Roberto Perez
Fernando Dewitt	Susana Velasco
Chantal Dubeh	Laura Hernandez
Arash Dabbo	Steve Roegner
Steve Roegner	Vanessa Dupont
Anne Burt	Sally Shapero

Caucasians

Kari Thams
Peter Wright
Inger Curwin
Yuri Tsay
John White
Beatrice Klassen
Brent Arnold
Deb Elovitz
Mike Hewitt
Steve Greene
Beatrice Klassen
Brent Arnold

African-Americans

Chantal Dubeh
Lee Williams
Dwight Syles
Dave Hupp
Ingrid Boone
Amber Duke
Anne Burt
Steve Roegner
Vanessa Dupont
Tyron Johnson
Lebron Williams
Dwight Syles

Hispanic-Americans

Fernando Dewitt
Fabio Rodriguez
Garcia Suarez
Roberto Perez
Susana Velasco
Laura Hernandez
Ricardo Martin
Jose Valquez
Lucita D'Allesandro
Carlos Dewitt
Carmen Perez
Susana Velasco

Strata

Random Subsamples of n/N

Source: William M. K. Trochim, *Research Methods: The Concise Knowledge Base* (Cincinnati, Ohio: Atomic Dog Publishing, 2005), 37.

requires prior knowledge of the target population. Therefore, researchers must balance the accuracy with the cost when considering using stratified sampling.

Cluster Sampling

cluster sampling A sampling technique in which the target population is divided into mutually exclusive groups, or clusters, and then a random sample of clusters (subgroups) of sampling units is chosen.

In **cluster sampling,** the population is first divided into clusters (subgroups) that are convenient and economical for sampling; next, clusters (subgroups) are selected at random or by a systematic method; and finally, all or some of the items in the selected clusters are taken at random or by a systematic method to make up the sample. If all the members of the selected subgroups are sampled, it is a one-stage cluster sample. If a sample of the selected subgroups is randomly chosen, it is a two-stage cluster sample. In contrast to stratified samples, clusters are formed based on two conditions: (1) elements within a cluster must be heterogeneous, and (2) elements between clusters must be homogeneous.

One of the most popular ways of forming clusters is by geographic areas. It is impractical to take a simple random sample from a population of 1 million families in a city, so the city is divided into small areas according to a city map. A number is assigned to each area. Some of the areas are selected at random or by a systematic method from the numbers representing all areas. Families within the selected areas are

Source: © 2007 JupiterImages Corporation.

interviewed, either all of the families or families selected at random or by a systematic method. The previous example demonstrated a specific kind of cluster sample called an **area sample.**

The major advantages of cluster sampling are its low cost and ease of implementation. Under this method, although not all groups are sampled, every group does have an equal chance of being selected. Thus the sample is random. A cluster sample may represent the population as precisely as a simple random sample if the variation of individual items within each cluster is as great as that of the population. However, a cluster sample usually contains greater sampling error (and thus represents the population less precisely) than a simple random sample of the same size. Individual items within each cluster tend to be alike. For example, rich people may live in one neighborhood and poor people in another. Not all areas are sampled in area sampling. This problem may be reduced by increasing the size of the cluster, which is easily done in an area sample. The interviewers do not have to travel too far in a small area to interview more families. Thus a large cluster sample may be obtained within a short period of time and at a low cost.

area sample A cluster sample in which the clusters, or groups, are made up of geographic areas.

10-3b Nonprobability Sampling

Nonprobability sampling violates scientific principles, since the researcher's personal judgment dominates when selecting sample elements. Therefore, there is no way to determine the probability of selecting a specific element into the sample. As a result, the findings obtained from nonprobability sampling techniques are not projectable to the population. This does not mean, however, that the findings are of no use. The results may, in fact, do a good job in portraying the target population, but there is no way to determine how precise they really are. That is, the degree of sampling error cannot be assessed. So why use this type of sampling procedure? The most common reason is that nonprobability samples are easy and inexpensive to gather. A study looking at web users used different nonprobability methods and found "that nonprobability sampling methods allow the researcher to make useful inferences about web users' attitudes toward the new medium, but the sampling techniques do not seem appropriate for generating representative results concerning the demographics and webographics of the WWW user population."[4]

The major types of nonprobability sampling methods are convenience, judgment, quota, and snowball sampling.

Convenience Sampling

convenience sampling A type of nonprobability sampling in which sample elements are chosen primarily because of their convenience to the researcher.

Sometimes when researchers want to obtain information, there is little time or money available to perform an elaborate study. In these cases, researchers may do **convenience sampling**—selecting sample items that are close at hand or otherwise easy to obtain. In fact, there may be no other way to gather data in some cases than to sample a group of individuals who are available and easily accessible. Often, for example, college professors will use their students as a sample because students are a captive audience and are convenient for the study. The major problem here lies with the subjective selection of the sample and the lack of generalizability of the results.

Judgment Sampling

judgment sampling A type of nonprobabilistic sampling in which the sample items are selected by using a researcher's personal judgment.

Judgment sampling is a nonprobability sampling method in which the sample items are selected by using a researcher's personal judgment. It is usually inexpensive to implement and takes little time to administer. The person who selects the sample items feels sufficiently qualified to identify items that are characteristic of the population. Researchers using this type of sampling method are usually experienced in the area under study. Let's assume that we want to test-market a new shampoo. If we choose five cities to sample that we believe are representative of the target population, then it would be a judgment sample. While the gathered information will likely be valuable to us, there is no guarantee that it reflects the entire target population.

Quota Sampling

quota sampling A type of nonprobability sampling that involves determining the proportion of the population believed to possess certain characteristics that affect the research subject and choosing for the sample a specific number with these characteristics to reflect their proportion in the population.

Sometimes researchers want to make sure that their sample includes a sufficient number of individuals with particular characteristics that affect the study, such as age, income, race, gender, and so on. In these cases, the researchers determine the percentage of the target population that possesses the characteristics of interest and then specify the number of these individuals to be included in the sample to reflect their proportion in the population. This sampling method is called **quota sampling,** and it is done to ensure that the proportion of individuals with these characteristics in the sample is the same as their proportion in the population.

Suppose we want to sample 300 men and women who are residents of France, are between 35 and 40 years of age, and wear glasses. We first determine the percentage of French residents in this age range who wear glasses. If from the secondary data analysis this percentage comes out as one-third of males and two-thirds of females, then one-third of our sample (100 individuals) should be male and two-thirds (200 individuals) female to obtain a sample in proportion to our target population. Quota sampling is rather *subjective,* since the elements included in the sample are based on the researcher's judgment.

Snowball Sampling

snowball sampling A type of nonprobabilistic sampling in which respondents provide names of additional respondents to include in a sample; used when additional respondents are difficult to locate because they are a small part of the population.

Snowball sampling is a sampling procedure in which initial respondents provide names of additional respondents to include in a sample. Researchers use this referral method when potential respondents are difficult to locate because they are a tiny part of the entire population. Consider Example 10-3.

Example 10-3

A manufacturer of pet supplies is interested in developing a collar for iguanas. Sampling 1,000 pet owners about their desire for iguana collars would likely be a waste of resources because probably fewer than 20 of the respondents actually own iguanas or plan to own one in the near future. It makes more economic sense to initially sample perhaps 500 members of the target population, and ask respondents to identify by name and contact number (that is, telephone, fax, email, addresses) other people who either own iguanas or know of somebody who owns one.

The major advantage of snowball sampling is the reduction in costs due to the decrease in search effort and sample size. However, this technique can lead to a fair amount of sample bias, since the individuals providing referrals are likely to be quite similar to the people they refer. A summary of the strengths and weaknesses of snowball sampling, as well as other sampling methods, is provided in Exhibit 10-5.

EXHIBIT 10-5	Strengths and Weaknesses of Sampling Methods	
Probability Sampling	**Strengths**	**Weaknesses**
Simple random	Generalizability of results	Tends to be expensive; time consuming
Systematic	Ease of implementation	Items in the population must be in some type of order
Stratified	Takes into account sub-groups; relative precision	Difficult to determine proper strata
Cluster	Inexpensive; ease of implementation	Relatively low precision
Nonprobability Sampling		
Convenience	Convenient; inexpensive; little time to administer	Biased; lack of generalizability
Judgment	Inexpensive; little time to administer	Subjective; lack of generalizability
Quota	Can be used to examine groups with certain traits	Subjective
Snowball	Can be used to examine unusual groups	Takes a lot of time to administer

10-4 Determine the Sample Size

It seems strange that before 1940, whenever the Bureau of the Census wanted to know something about the U.S. population, it would ask every citizen. Researchers have come a long way since then, and sampling is the norm rather than the exception in most organizations. Read Research Realities 10-2 for a description of "rules of thumb" when it comes to determining sample size.

Consider some of the following samples by leading research companies to really appreciate the extent to which sampling is used:

- InterSurvey regularly samples a panel of 25,000 households throughout the United States, giving them free Internet access and hardware to participate in their studies.

- Westat performs in-person studies involving from 1,500 to more than 30,000 households. It performs telephone surveys to as many as 40,000 individuals and mail surveys to 90,000 respondents.

- NFO (National Family Opinion) has a panel of 600,000 U.S. households to provide consumer data to more than 450 leading corporations. It also has a

---

Research Realities 10-2   *MarketSearch "Rules of Thumb" When Sampling*

MarketSearch, a large marketing research firm, believes that balanced against the advantages of a large sample size are the limitations of time and cost, and often, there is a question of whether precision is even necessary. They have found that most often their clients choose to do studies with a sample of 300 to 500 respondents—which strikes a good balance between moderate cost and usefulness of detail. Based on their experiences, here are some of their "rules of thumb":

- The smaller the subgroup within the sample, the less likely it is that your information about the subgroup is reliable.
- The larger your sample size, the more seriously your conclusions will be taken by others.
- The simpler and more clear-cut the issues, the fewer respondents it takes to get the answers.

Source: Information from MarketSearch, "A MarketSearch brief: sample size and sampling error," http://www.msearch.com/filecabinet/BriefSampleSize.doc, June 20, 2005.

panel of 2,000 new mothers and 2,000 expectant mothers it calls the "Baby Panel."

- ACNielsen Worldwide Consumer Panel Services provide consumer insights in 18 countries from 125,000 households.
- Mediamark Research, Inc., has a sample size of 26,000 U.S. adults to provide audience research data for the magazine industry.

Clearly, there is a lot of sampling going on throughout the world. However, many researchers still do not know how large their samples should be. This section will cover this important concern. But before we discuss how to determine sample size, you need to review or learn some key terms.

- *Statistic.* As you already know, the term "statistics" has two meanings: one as a mathematical field and another as numerical data. In this section, we will be using the term in its numerical sense. More precisely, a **statistic** is a measure used to describe some characteristic of a sample, such as an arithmetic mean, a median, or a standard deviation.
- *Parameter.* As noted in section 10-1, a parameter is a measure used to describe some characteristic of a population, such as an arithmetic mean, a median, a standard deviation, or variance. The **standard deviation** is the square root of the arithmetic mean of the individual deviations squared; the most common measure of dispersion. **Variance,** a measure of dispersion, is the standard deviation squared. Notice that the difference between a statistic and a parameter is in what they describe—a sample or a population.
- *Standard error of the statistic.* The standard deviation of a sampling distribution of a statistic is the **standard error of the statistic.** For example, the standard deviation of the means of all possible samples of the same size drawn from a population is the *standard error of the mean.* Likewise, the standard deviation of the proportions of all possible samples of the same size drawn from a population is the **standard error of the proportion.** The difference between the terms "standard deviation" and "standard error" is that the former concerns original values, whereas the latter concerns computed values. A statistic is a computed value, computed from the items included in a sample.
- *Sampling error.* The difference between the result obtained from a sample (a statistic) and the result that would have been obtained from the population (the corresponding parameter) is called the **sampling error.** A sampling error usually occurs when the complete survey of the population is not carried out, but a sample is taken for estimating the characteristic of the population.

The determination of the correct sample size from a population is an important and practical problem in a sampling study. If the sample size is too large, more money and time will be spent than is really necessary to survey that sample, but the result obtained from the large sample may not be more accurate than that from a smaller sample. On the other hand, if the sample size is too small, the study may not reach a valid conclusion. It is important to realize that the more elements that are properly sampled from the population, the less the sampling error. This error exists because the whole population is not examined, ultimately leaving something out of the investigation. It is the researcher's job to make sure that enough elements are sampled from the population to provide sufficient information. (See Research Realities 10-3 for a description of all kinds of problems encountered by a firm known as Just the Facts.)

10-4a Basic Facts about Sample Size Determination

Before we get into actually determining sample size, here are a few basic principles:

1. *Determining sample size involves both managerial and financial considerations.* Whenever sample sizes are to be determined, researchers must consult with

statistic A measure used to describe some characteristic of a sample, such as an arithmetic mean, median, or standard deviation.

standard deviation The square root of the arithmetic mean of the individual deviations squared; the most common measure of dispersion.

variance The standard deviation squared; a measure of dispersion.

standard error of the statistic The standard deviation of a sampling distribution of a statistic.

standard error of the proportion The standard deviation of the proportions of all possible samples of the same size drawn from a population.

sampling error The difference between the result obtained from a sample and the result that would have been obtained from the population.

Just Bad Research

The following is a true story by Bruce Tincknell of Just the Facts, Inc., a marketing research firm in Arlington Hts., Illinois, explaining his company's experiences with poor sampling techniques:

> A client came to us asking that we replicate a survey procedure, which they had been conducting at various customer events in the United States. Basically, the procedure the client was using involved handing out follow-up cards at each event, retrieving them back before the respondents left the event, and then completing 20 satisfaction phone interviews per event. In total, the client conducted 40–50 events annually in various locations around the country. This meant the total sample ranged from 800 to 1,000 for all events. Typically, each event would draw several thousand attendees. The respondent cards asked for name, phone, address, and if they would participate in a follow-up survey. Anywhere from 50 to 100 respondent cards would be retrieved for each event.

Just the Facts recognized several problems with the methodology employed. First, there was no attempt to obtain a broad base of respondents at each event. The cards were handed out at the end of the event as attendees were all scrambling to leave. Further, the returned cards were all subject to a significant self-selection bias. Many attendees declined to fill out the cards, or did not turn them in, or

gave false information (e.g., wrong phone numbers). The client felt they were doing well if they got back even 25–30 cards per event. They were also satisfied with only 20 completed phone interviews from each event. As Tincknell noted:

> Major problems are inherent with the client's design and execution of this research. First, because they wanted to obtain a satisfaction reading from each event, a call completion rate on only 20 interviews per event is too small to make any reasonable conclusions about the respondents' satisfaction. Second, there was no attempt to gain a breadth of response from different audiences in attendance (e.g., age, gender, ethnicity, and other factors). Third, because the respondents were opting in or out, the self-selection bias is a huge problem. The client has no idea if the 20 respondents per event are reflective of the total audience or not. Fourth, even if the client were reading all 40–50 events combined, where respondents totaled 800–1,000, the responses would still be unrepresentative due to the sampling technique. Further, each of the events had different aspects to their program format and presentation, so measuring one event against another, or in total, could not be done effectively with the current methodology.

Source: Bruce Tincknell of Just the Facts, Inc.[®], a marketing research firm in Arlington Hts., Illinois.

---

management (or clients if performing research for an outside organization) to ensure they clearly understand the objectives of the sampling exercise as well as the financial constraints.

2. *There is no direct relationship between the size of the population and the size of the sample needed to estimate a certain population parameter.* The size of the population does not enter into the calculations of the sample size unless it is a finite population and the determined sample size exceeds 10% of the target population.

3. *Generally the sample size will not be more than 10% of the population.* This rule applies when large target populations are under examination. If the sample size exceeds 10% of the target population, then the researcher should use the finite population correction factor (fpc). We'll discuss this factor shortly.

4. *Typically the larger the sample size, the less the sampling error.* This indicates that we could eliminate sampling error by investigating every element in the entire population. MarketSearch states, "Simply put, the more people you talk to, the more likely you will produce a picture that accurately reflects the opinions of the larger population you are studying."[5] However, there is no need to consider every element because we can obtain a similar result with an acceptable level of precision with a much smaller sample of respondents.

5. *The costs of larger samples tend to increase on a linear basis; not so for sampling error.* If the sample size is quadrupled, the costs to gather the data will be quadrupled, but the level of sampling error will be reduced by only one-half.

10-4b Methods for Determining Sample Size

There are four major ways to determine sample size:

1. *Blind guessing.* This technique is the worst way to determine sample size. It is performed exactly the way it sounds. The researcher simply guesses how many elements should be sampled from the population. There is no scientific justification for choosing the particular sample size.

2. *Industry rules of thumb.* This technique is most often used when some industry standards have been established. That is, if 500 customers are typically sampled to examine customer satisfaction in the banking industry, then a particular company may follow suit. Although this technique is often developed from experience in a particular industry, it suffers from the same shortcoming as the "blind guessing" technique. There is no scientific explanation to support the sample size that will be used.

3. *Affordability method.* As the name indicates, a company may choose to sample as many elements of the target population as it can afford to sample. This method is often used when a company allocates a certain amount of money for the sampling project.

4. *Statistical method.* This is the best technique to determine sample size, since it is supported by scientific principles. Let's take a closer look at this technique.

10-4c Statistical Method of Computing Sample Size

Before we discuss how to compute sample size, let us go over some statistical concepts.

Normal Distribution

A **normal distribution** is a frequency distribution represented graphically by a bell-shaped curve that is symmetrical about the mean. This bell-shaped curve that depicts the normal distribution is called the **normal curve.** As shown in Exhibit 10-6, almost all (99.7%) of the normal curve's values are within ±3 standard deviations from its mean. Since the normal distribution is symmetrical, the midpoint under the curve is the mean of the distribution. The shape of the normal curve indicates that the

normal distribution A frequency distribution represented graphically by a bell-shaped curve that is symmetrical about the mean.

normal curve A symmetrical, bell-shaped curve that has almost all of its values within ±3 standard deviations from its mean.

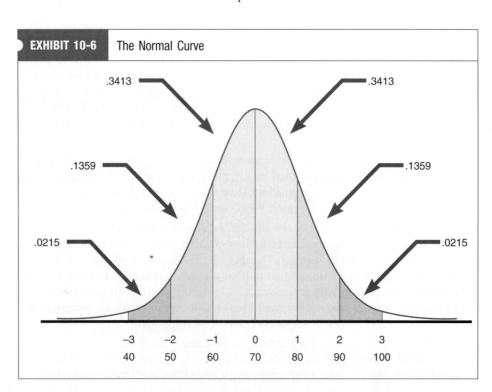

EXHIBIT 10-6 | The Normal Curve

frequencies in a normal distribution are concentrated in the center portion of the distribution and the values above and below the mean are equally distributed.

To demonstrate the normal curve, suppose a company asks consumers to indicate their satisfaction with the company's service using a scale from 1 (poor) to 100 (excellent). From the responses, 99.7% of the scores range from 40 to 100, with a mean of 70. Exhibit 10-6 shows that a standard deviation for consumers' rankings equaled 10 (70 to 60 or 70 to 80). Two standard deviations from the mean was 20 (70 to 50 or 70 to 90), and three standard deviations from the mean was 30 (70 to 40 or 70 to 100). Therefore, about two-thirds (actually 34.134% + 34.134%, or 68.27%) of the respondents gave the company a score of 60 to 80 points.

The normal curve is a continuous distribution, which means that it has an infinite number of events or occurrences. The probability of the occurrence of a certain event is therefore measured according to the area representing the event under the normal curve. The normal curve of a population may be approximated by using a sample. The approximated normal curve thus allows researchers to make statistical inferences concerning the population based on the sample.

While there are an infinite number of normal distribution curves, statisticians have simplified things for researchers by calculating areas under a special normal distribution curve that has a mean of 0 and a standard deviation of 1. This special curve, called the *standard normal distribution curve,* is useful to marketers, since it allows them to use a single table of probability values to solve problems rather than an infinite number of different tables, each representing one of the infinite possible normal distribution curves. An interesting property of the standard normal distribution curve is that its values represent standard deviation units. The random variable for the curve is represented by the symbol z. A z-value of ± 2.00 indicates 2 standard deviation units above the mean of the distribution, and a z-value of 0 corresponds to the mean.[6] The standard normal curve has the following properties:

1. The curve is symmetrical.
2. The curve approaches the X-axis more and more closely when z is greater than $+3$ or less than -3. However, the curve extends without ending in both directions.
3. The curve has a maximum height when $z = 0$.
4. The curve has points of inflection when $z = \pm 1$; that is, the curve is concave downward between $z = -1$ and $z = +1$, and it is concave upward to the right of $z = +1$ and to the left of $z = -1$.
5. The total area under the normal curve and above the X-axis is the total probability of the distribution, which is equal to 1.
6. The population may represent a finite population as well as an infinite population, or $N = 1 = 100\%$.

Confidence Intervals

Before we discuss confidence intervals, we need to define a few terms. First of all, we will be using the symbol $\sigma_{\bar{x}}$ (described as "sigma sub x-bar") to denote the **standard error of the mean,** which is the standard deviation of the means of all possible samples of the same size drawn from a population. It is calculated as follows:

$$\sigma_{\bar{x}} = \frac{\sigma}{\sqrt{n}}$$

The symbol μ (Greek letter "mu") is the population mean, and $\bar{X}_1$ is the sample mean of the first group.

As you learned in the previous section, we know that with any normal distribution:

- 68.27% of the sample means will be within $\pm 1\sigma_{\bar{x}}$ of the population mean
- 95.45% of the sample means will be within $\pm 2\sigma_{\bar{x}}$ of the population mean
- 99.73% of the sample means will be within $\pm 3\sigma_{\bar{x}}$ of the population mean

standard error of the mean
The standard deviation of the means of all possible samples of the same size drawn from a population.

EXHIBIT 10-7	Common Confidence Coefficients and Their z Values						
Confidence Coefficient	50%	68.27%	90%	95%	95.45%	99%	99.73%
z	0.6745	1.00	1.645	1.96	2.00	2.58	3.00

Where $z = \frac{\bar{X} - \mu}{\sigma_{\bar{x}}}$ for a sampling distribution of the mean, $\bar{X}$; or $z = \frac{p - P}{\sigma_p}$ for a sampling distribution of the proportion, p.

EXHIBIT 10-8	A 68% Confidence Interval for a Sampling Distribution of the Mean ($\bar{X}$)

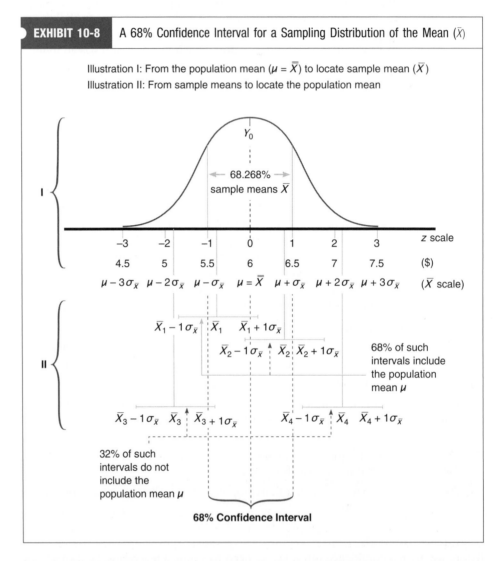

Illustration I: From the population mean ($\mu = \bar{\bar{X}}$) to locate sample mean ($\bar{X}$)

Illustration II: From sample means to locate the population mean

68% Confidence Interval

Exhibit 10-7 provides a list of confidence coefficients and their z values. The probability that the sample means lie within a range from $\mu + 1\sigma_{\bar{x}}$ to $\mu - 1\sigma_{\bar{x}}$ is represented by the area under the normal curve between Y_0 and $z = \pm 1$ and is $0.34134 + 0.34134 = 0.6827$ or 68.27%. The 68.27% probability indicates that about 68 out of every 100 sample means will lie within the range of $\mu \pm 1\sigma_{\bar{x}}$.

For example, let $\mu = \$6$, $\sigma_{\bar{x}} = \$0.50$, and the number of possible samples drawn from a given population = 100 million. Each sample, of course, has a mean. Then, 68.27 million sample means, out of the 100 million sample means, will have their values between $5.50 and $6.50, or *within* the range

$$\text{from } \mu - 1\sigma_{\bar{x}} = 6 - 0.50 = \$5.50 \text{ to } \mu + 1\sigma_{\bar{x}} = 6 + 0.50 = \$6.50.$$

This range is shown graphically in Illustration I of Exhibit 10-8. Conversely, if we select a sample mean within the range, such as $\bar{X}_1$ or $\bar{X}_2$ as shown in Illustration II of

Exhibit 10-8, the interval represented by the sample mean ± one standard error, such as

$$\bar{X}_1 \pm 1\sigma_{\bar{x}} = 5.62 \pm 0.50 = \$5.12 \text{ to } \$6.12$$

or

$$\bar{X}_2 \pm 1\sigma_{\bar{x}} = 6.38 \pm 0.50 = \$5.88 \text{ to } \$6.88$$

will include the population mean μ (= \$6). We have 68.27 million such intervals. Stated in a different way, we have 31.73 million (= 100 million − 68.27 million) sample means, such as $\bar{X}_3$ and $\bar{X}_4$ shown in Exhibit 10-8, having their values *outside* the range from \$5.50 to \$6.50. The intervals based on $\bar{X}_3$ and $\bar{X}_4$ values do not include the population mean μ. Thus, we have the *confidence* to make a statement that if we select a sample at random to estimate the population mean, we will have 68 out of 100 chances to have the true population mean within the interval of the sample mean ± one standard error of the mean.

Again, let $\mu = \$6$, and $\sigma_{\bar{x}} = \$0.50$, the range $\mu \pm 1\sigma_{\bar{x}}$ may be written in different forms as follows:

$$\mu \pm 1\sigma_{\bar{x}}, \text{ or } \$6 \pm \$0.50, \text{ or } \$5.50 \text{ to } \$6.50$$

The range of values that we are confident contains the population parameter and that is written in these three forms is called the **confidence interval;** the two values (\$5.50 and \$6.50) which specify the ranges are called the **confidence limits;** and the probability, 68.27%, is called the **confidence level.** Likewise, a 95% confidence interval may be expressed as:

$$\mu \pm 1.96\sigma_{\bar{x}}, \text{ where } z = \pm 1.96$$

The area under the normal curve between Υ_0 and $z = \pm 1.96$ is

$$0.47500 + 0.47500 = 0.95 \text{ or } 95\%$$

When trying to interpret a confidence interval, we can state that "the procedure is such that in the long run 95% of the intervals obtained will include the true (fixed) parameter." You should be careful not to assume that the particular interval you have obtained has any special property not possessed from comparable intervals that would be obtained from other samples. It is permissible to state that "we are 95% confident that the particular interval we have constructed contains the population parameter," as long as we mean that 95% of *all possible intervals* constructed in this way will include the parameter concerned. Thus, our particular interval has a 0.95 chance to be one of them.[7]

In summary, a confidence interval reflects a range of values that we are confident—but not certain—contains the population parameter. The wider the confidence interval, the more confident we can be that the particular interval will contain our parameter. Of course, the narrower the confidence interval, the less confident we can be that the particular interval will contain our parameter.

Information Needed to Compute Sample Size

Three pieces of information are necessary to compute the required sample size. They are as follows:

- *Desired precision* (± E). This basically asks the question, "How precise does the measurement need to be?" That is, the researcher must determine the largest acceptable difference between the sample mean and the population mean. It is specified by an acceptable degree of sampling error. In general, the smaller the acceptable degree of sampling error, the larger the sample size must be. The acceptable degree of sampling error will be based on the importance of the decision.

confidence interval A range of values that we are confident—but not certain—contains the population parameter.

confidence limits The two values that specify the ranges of a confidence interval.

confidence level The chance or probability that a confidence interval includes the population parameter.

As an example, we want to estimate the average weight of 50 students in a marketing class within ±5 pounds. The precision level is ±5 pounds.

- *Value associated with desired confidence level (Z).* This asks the question, "How confident do you want to be that the specified confidence interval takes in the population mean?" The greater the desired confidence, the larger the sample size must be.

  The most often used confidence levels are 95% ($Z = 1.96$) and 99% ($Z = 2.58$). The more serious the consequence of being wrong, the greater researchers want the confidence level to be.

  For example, if we want to estimate the average weight of the students in a marketing class with a precision of ±5 pounds and we want to be 95% confident that this estimate contains the true population value, then the confidence level is 95%.

- *Estimator of the standard deviation of the population (s).* This asks the question, "How heterogeneous are the members that are being investigated?" This variability is measured by estimating the population standard deviation. The more heterogeneous (variability of) the population, the larger the necessary sample size.

While the researcher must set the desired precision and desired confidence level, the standard deviation of the population is a bit more complicated. The researcher must estimate it. The following methods may be used to estimate the population standard deviation:

1. *Use information from an earlier study.* If the researchers already investigated a similar issue, they can use this information.

2. *Conduct a small-scale study of the population.* Using a relatively small number of target population members, the researchers may conduct a small study to better understand the group's degree of dispersion from the average regarding the variable under study.

3. *Use secondary data.* Researchers take advantage of the vast amounts of information available inside a company, on the Internet, and at the local library. This existing information may help them create an estimate of the population standard deviation. It may be obtained from a variety of sources, such as government documents, competitors' data, industry averages, and so on.

4. *Talk to informed people.* If nothing else is available, researchers use the judgment of people knowledgeable about the particular topic under investigation. Sometimes the judgment from a variety of experienced managers is sufficient.

Determining Sample Size: Means

Once we have all of the required pieces, we can calculate the sample size. To calculate the required sample size for problems that involve the estimation of a mean, we can use the following formula:

$$n = \frac{Z^2 s^2}{E^2}$$

where
Z = standardized value indicating the level of confidence
E = acceptable magnitude of sampling error (that is, precision)
s = estimator of the population standard deviation

Consider Example 10-4.

Example 10-4

Managers at the new Hard Body Health Club are wondering how often their new customers might use their facility. Therefore, they want to estimate the average number of times each week that people visit a health club. This can be determined by substituting the following pieces of information into the formula:

- After consulting with managers at the Hard Body Health Club, the marketing researchers determine that the goal of the study is to estimate the average number of times that individuals who exercise visit a health club each week. They further determine that the managers want a high degree of accuracy, which indicates that the estimate should be within ± 0.10 (one-tenth) of the true population mean. This value (0.10) should be substituted into the formula for the value of E, which is the maximum desired margin of error (that is, precision).

- The marketing researchers have decided that, all things considered, they need to be 95% confident that the amount of sampling error will not exceed 0.10, so 1.96 would be substituted into the equation for Z.

- Finally, the researchers need to determine what value to use for the standard deviation. Fortunately, the company had previously conducted a similar study at another health club, and in that study, the standard deviation for the variable was 1.39 times. This is the best estimate of the population standard deviation (σ) available. Therefore, a value of 1.39 would be substituted into the formula for the value of s.

The calculation is as follows:

$$n = \frac{Z^2 s^2}{E^2}$$
$$= \frac{(1.96)^2 (1.39)^2}{(0.10)^2}$$
$$= \frac{3.84(1.93)}{0.01}$$
$$= 741$$

Therefore, a sample of 741 people is necessary to meet the requirements outlined.

If the determined sample size is 10% or more of the population, the finite population correction factor (fpc) should be applied:

$$n_c = \frac{nN}{N + n - 1}$$

where
n = sample size without fpc
n_c = sample size with fpc
N = size of target population

If $n = 741$ and, say, $N = 7,000$, then

$$n_c = \frac{741(7000)}{7000 + 741 - 1} = 670.16 = 671$$

Out of a target population of 7,000 people, only 671 people need to be sampled rather than 741 as originally calculated. Therefore, using the fpc, this company saved resources that would have been spent unnecessarily sampling 70 additional individuals (741–671).

Determining Sample Size: Proportions

Sometime what we are interested in is a proportion. For example, we may want to know the percentage *(P)* of the individuals who are likely to join a health club. In this case, we calculate the required sample size in a similar manner as we did when we estimated a mean statistic, using the following formula:

$$n = \frac{P(1 - P)Z^2}{E^2}$$

where Z = standardized value indicating the level of confidence
         E = acceptable magnitude of sampling error (that is, precision)
         $P(1 - P)$ = estimator of the population standard deviation

In the proportion case, the population variance is given by P times $(1 - P)$. For example, if prior knowledge indicates 30% of the individuals in the target area belong to a health club, then variance is $30\% \times (1 - 30\%) = 30\% \times 70\% = .21$. This proportion may be estimated based on the results from an earlier study, the execution of a small-scale study, information gained from secondary sources, and/or information from knowledgeable people. However, if the researchers have no knowledge about the population proportion, then they use 0.5 as the estimate ($P = 0.5$). This is the most conservative estimate and will result in the largest possible sample for a given confidence level and precision. Consider Example 10-5.

Example 10-5

Suppose we are interested in estimating the proportion of individuals who may join a health club. In a study of the same issue conducted a year ago, it was found that 55% of the households in the target population belonged to a health club. Thus $P = 0.55$. Furthermore, the researchers want to estimate with 95% confidence that the amount of sampling error will not exceed 5%. The sample size would be determined as follows:

$$n = \frac{P(1 - P)Z^2}{E^2} = \frac{0.55(1 - 0.55)(1.96)^2}{(0.05)^2} = 381$$

If the resulting sample size represents 10% or more of the population, the finite population correction factor should be applied:

$$n_c = \frac{nN}{N + n - 1}$$

where n = sample size without fpc

n_c = sample size with fpc

If $n = 381$ and, say, $N = 3,500$, then

$$n_c = \frac{381(3500)}{3500 + 381 - 1} = 343.69 = 344$$

Therefore, 344 people should be sampled to determine the proportion of individuals who may join a health club.

10-5 Gather the Data: Minimizing Survey Errors

There is an old joke about three accountants applying for a job. When the first accountant entered the office, the boss asked, "How much is two plus two?" The candidate paused for a moment and replied "Four!" The boss frowned and immediately dismissed the candidate. The second candidate was also asked, "How much is two plus two?" She thought a minute and proudly responded "Five!" whereupon the boss thanked her and asked her to wait in the next room. The third candidate was then asked, "How much is two plus two?" He hesitated and then replied, "How much would you like it to be?" The boss hired him on the spot.[8] The point is that "truth" can be in the eye of the beholder. Problems inherent in the data collection process can cause responses to be less than accurate and lead to imperfect results. This phenomenon is called systematic error. Researchers must be aware of and try to minimize these errors.

10-5a Systematic Error

Marketing researchers want the truth from their respondents. However, absolute truth may not be possible. Consider the following statement appearing in the *Journal of the Market Research Society:*

> One of the biggest problems in market research from the very beginning has been in getting respondents to express the truth. It is often the case that people want to "impress" the interviewer, or are, for other reasons, ashamed to admit the facts because it lowers their self-esteem. Another important consideration is repression; where the respondent has hidden from himself, or herself, a "truth" which is too hurtful to reveal.[9]

The **total error** that exists in any study is the difference between the *true information* being sought (called the "true score") and the *collected information* resulting from the measurement process (called the "observed score"). For example, a bank's true degree of customer satisfaction (true score), using a 5-point scale, may be a 4.2; but when a sample of customers is surveyed (observed), the resulting score is 3.8. The total error is the difference between the true score and observed score: $4.2 - 3.8 = 0.4$.

The total error that exists in any study includes two types of error: *systematic error* and *random error.* **Systematic error** (sometimes called **constant error**) is error caused by a constant bias in the design or implementation of the measurement instrument. **Random error** is error caused by inconsistent differences in respondents or

total error Difference between the true information being sought and the information collected for the study.

systematic error (or constant error) An error caused by a constant bias in the design or implementation of the measurement instrument.

random error An error caused by inconsistencies in respondents or their circumstances.

circumstances. The relationship between these types of errors may be explained by the following mathematical model:

Collected information = True information + systematic error + random error

or simply,

Observed score = True score + systematic error + random error

If these errors could be eliminated, the observed score would equal the true score. However, random error is unavoidable. There will always be individual differences among respondents and variation in the circumstances surrounding the research. In this chapter, we concentrate on systematic error, which is controllable. Systematic error results from problems in the research design or from faulty implementation of the sample design. As illustrated in Exhibit 10-9, it can occur before sampling is implemented *(presampling error)*, during sampling implementation *(present-sampling error)*, or after the sample is taken *(postsampling error)*. Here we will focus on various types of systematic error.

EXHIBIT 10-9   Types of Systematic Error

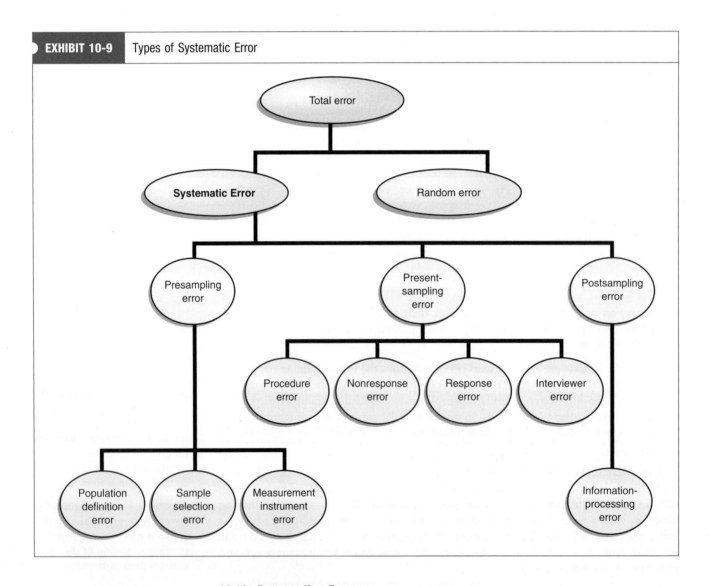

10-5b Presampling Errors

If researchers are not careful in planning the data collection process, faulty research findings can result. Three types of errors that occur in the planning stage, before data collection, are population definition error, sample selection error, and measurement instrument error.

Population Definition Error

A **population definition error** results when the population from which the sample is to be taken is wrongly defined. Let's say we define our population as all college students. However, after we draw our sample and collect the data, we determine that only undergraduates, not graduates should have been included in the population. If the graduate students differ significantly from undergraduate students regarding the research topic, then an error will result, biasing the findings.

Sample Selection Error

Suppose we have correctly defined the population for our study. Now we need to select our sample. The sample must be representative of the population from which it is drawn, so that the research results can be generalized to this target population. A **sample selection error** occurs if we select a sample that is not representative of the population. A nonrepresentative sample occurs when a sample size is too small or a sampling procedure is used that does not achieve the intended sample. Sampling procedures must be couched in accurate, easy-to-follow language for those doing the sampling. For example, if a group of consumers at a mall is to be sampled, the guidelines must clearly describe who should be selected and when, where, and how to choose them.

Measurement Instrument Error

A measurement instrument is the questionnaire or survey used to gather the information of interest. A **measurement instrument error** results if the survey contains questions or statements that bias respondents or make it difficult for the researcher to clearly understand intended responses. For example, individuals' responses will be biased if a supermarket's researchers asked them, "How often do you shop at our competitors' stores, which have higher prices and inferior service?" To minimize the chance of measurement instrument errors, surveys should be pretested before they are used.

10-5c Present-Sampling Errors

After the population and sample have been determined and the measurement instrument has been developed, it is time to collect data from the sample respondents. Once again, many things can go wrong.

Procedure Error

When errors in sample selection occur, problems snowball because the sample may not be representative of the population. A **procedure error** occurs when sample subjects are improperly selected, resulting in a nonrepresentative sample. For example, if the population consists of 100,000 consumers, and a novice researcher mistakenly determines that a sample size of 250 is statistically valid when the number should have been 2,500, the results will be invalid because they are nonrepresentative. Therefore, sampling procedures should be carefully followed.

Poorly formulated sampling procedures can also cause improper sampling. Loosely worded instructions, for example, can cause confusion and chaos in the data collection process. Interviewers may create their own directions or abandon the stated procedures altogether. Studies have found that, unless properly directed, interviewers will reword questions, answer the questions that interviewees don't want to answer, and even manufacture answers to entire surveys.[10]

Nonresponse Error

When a group is sampled, there are always individuals who do not participate. Refusal rates can range from zero in personal interviews to more than 90% for mail

population definition error
An error resulting from faulty definition of the population to be sampled.

sample selection error An error that occurs when the selected sample is not representative of the population.

measurement instrument error An error that results when the questionnaire or survey questions bias respondents or make it difficult for the researcher to clearly understand intended responses.

procedure error An error that occurs when sample subjects are improperly selected, resulting in a nonrepresentative sample.

surveys conducted in multiple global markets. People decline to respond for numerous reasons—lack of time, lack of interest in the topic, fear of reprisal, feeling their privacy will be invaded, the absence of financial compensation, lack of patience, and unfamiliarity with language used in the study. Sometimes people don't have a choice about participating. Perhaps they were vacationing during the time a mail survey was being administered or maybe the survey was lost in the mail. When a high percentage of respondents do not participate, **nonresponse error** (or *nonresponse bias*) exists.

nonresponse error An error that occurs when a high percentage of respondents do not participate in a study, and the nonrespondents differ significantly from the respondents on the topic under study.

This source of error becomes a problem only when there is a statistically significant difference between those who respond and those who don't. Put another way, nonresponse error is the difference between a true mean of the sample from the observed sample mean. Let's assume that a college textbook publisher wants to investigate the satisfaction levels of students using its marketing research book in a current course. The company mails out 200 surveys to a random sample of students currently using the textbook but receives only 50 completed surveys within the scheduled time period. If the students who respond to the survey represent a different level of satisfaction than those who don't respond, then nonresponse error exists. That is, if a reason exists that is consistent across those responding and those not responding, the absence of this response in the results biases the results. Say the students who didn't respond all have jobs and would prefer a shorter book compared to the responding students. Because the findings don't reflect this opinion, the results are biased toward students who don't mind a longer book.

Response Error

response error An error that occurs when respondents answer particular questions incorrectly, either intentionally or unintentionally.

Response error (also called *response bias*) exists when respondents answer particular questions or statements incorrectly. Such responses may be intentional or unintentional—this doesn't matter; distortions now exist.

False responses occur for numerous reasons. People knowingly distort their answers to avoid embarrassment, to conceal confidential information, or to influence the way people perceive them. Even people attempting to answer honestly and accurately sometimes give untrue responses. People forget details, they lack knowledge about a particular subject, or they misconstrue particular questions. People often guess.

Other factors that cause response bias include the following:

- *Habitual response bias.* Some respondents always respond the same way on a scale; they may always answer in extremes (say, "excellent" or "poor"), or always in a noncommittal (neutral) way.

- *Amenable bias.* Certain respondents find it difficult to disagree. They think it's confrontational to take a stance other than the one being stated.

- *Conductor bias.* Respondents can be biased because of the company or person conducting the study. For example, if a large conglomerate known for its tobacco products asks consumers questions about its food products, anti-smoking respondents may respond negatively, even though they have favorable attitudes toward the product.

- *Societal bias.* Respondents often give socially acceptable answers in order to create a positive impression. For example, if individuals are asked how often they go to church, they may respond "At least once a week" when actually they attend only once a month.

- *Self-perception bias.* Respondents answer questions according to their perceptions of themselves, whether or not these perceptions are accurate. For example, if an automobile company asks, "What kind of car do you drive?" certain respondents will answer "luxury" when in fact they drive economy cars because they perceive themselves as upper-class individuals.

- *Intention bias.* Respondents often refer to their intentions when they answer questions. If an automobile company asks, "Which company produced your automobile?'' respondents who presently own a Chevrolet but intend to purchase a Mercedes-Benz some time in the future may respond by naming the more upscale car.

- *Fabricator bias.* Not all respondents take surveys seriously. Certain individuals "have fun" with surveys by purposely fabricating their responses.

Interviewer Error

Whenever a person administers a survey, there is a chance that the interviewer will influence responses by providing additional information. This is called **interviewer error** (or *interviewer bias*). Such bias may be intentional or unintentional and can take such forms as rephrased questions, commentaries on particular topics, or body gestures such as smiling and frowning. **Intentional interviewer bias** results when interviewers knowingly provide information that will influence the respondent. For example, if a researcher asks a subject, "Have you recently tried any tobacco product?" and comments about his or her disgust toward smokers, he or she has intentionally attempted to bias the response. **Unintentional bias** results when interviewers inadvertently influence responses. For example, if an attractive woman asks a young male college student whether he has tried her company's new cologne, and she smiles brightly when the respondent smells the cologne, he may be more likely to respond in a positive manner.

10-5d Postsampling Errors

Once the data is collected, it must be processed. As in other stages, errors also creep in during this phase. Data must be keyed into the computer, opening up numerous opportunities for **information-processing error.** Operators may, for example, transpose numbers or misspell words. This topic is discussed further in Chapter 12.

> **interviewer error** An error that occurs when the interviewer influences responses by supplying additional information, either intentionally or unintentionally.
>
> **intentional interviewer bias** Bias caused by interviewers providing additional information purposely to influence respondents.
>
> **unintentional bias** Bias caused by interviewers providing additional information related to survey questions without realizing they are influencing respondents.
>
> **information-processing error** An error caused by mistakes in coding or inputting data into a computer for analysis.

Decision Time!

After reading this chapter, you can see that sampling has its cost advantages. However, it also has its problems, such as sampling biases. These biases are more likely with nonprobability sampling than with probability sampling because a researcher's judgment comes much more into play with the former method. As a marketing manager, you learn from your company's researchers that they can reduce sampling problems if they can increase the sample size. Let's say that your market consists of only 2,500 people. Would you tell them to go ahead and sample everybody in the population or use the sample size formula to calculate the number of people to sample, given a certain margin of error? What factors should you consider when making this important decision?

Net Impact

The Internet can be used to sample respondents from a broad population because it provides information from most parts of the world. Today, studies looking at Internet usage, shopping behavior, customer satisfaction, and a wide variety of other concerns are being performed through the Internet. However, many of these studies use nonprobability sampling techniques. This considerably limits the extent to which we can project the results to the general population.

The Internet can also be used in helping researchers estimate the population standard deviation, which is necessary when determining sample size. As we noted earlier in the chapter, this can be done by using data from an earlier study, conducting a small-scale study of the population, using secondary information, or communicating with individuals who are informed about the topic under investigation. Much of this information is available online.

On the Lighter Side—Does Statistics Lie?

According to Mark Twain, "There are three kinds of lies: lies, damned lies, and statistics." However, statistics does not lie, but the interpretation does. Paul Cox has a Web site that reports mathematical mistakes (http://members.cox.net/mathmistakes/). One that he reported in March 2004 dealt with the interpretation of a statistical result.

Cox asks the question, "How much influence does the President really have on the economy?" His answer is "very little" if we believe the majority of experts. But he contends that most voters believe that politics and the economy are closely linked and under the control of the residing president. Cox asks us to consider the following graph that has often appeared at various Internet sites:

Cox goes on the assumption that the graphs shown in Exhibit 10-10 are based on actual data and are accurate up to that point. He does not believe anyone would make up a graph that lies, especially when the actual figures are so easily found.

Cox advocates that there are some obvious math mistakes in the graph. First, it is a zoom graph that does not start at 0%, so the drastic changes displayed are not as drastic as they appear. Second, there is the instantaneous growth of unemployment in Bush's first year. The two biggest factors in unemployment that year were the dot com bust (which started while Clinton was still in office) and the 9/11 disaster and other terrorist acts which Bush had to react to. Cox believes the recent unemployment problem is more Clinton's legacy than Bush's fault.

Cox concluded that the fact the unemployment rate had not dropped over the past 3 years since 9/11 was going to be a major issue in the presidential campaign.

Source: Paul Cox, "Politics and economics don't mix," http://members.cox.net/mathmistakes/poly-econ.htm. June 22, 2005.

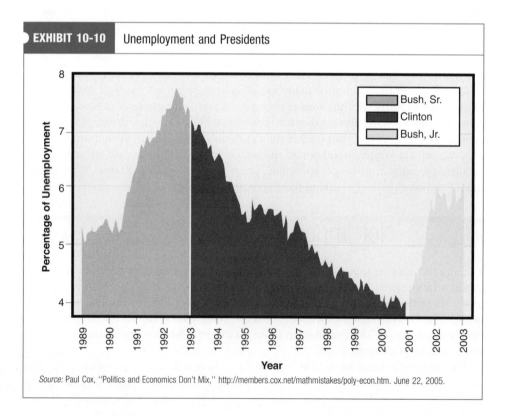

EXHIBIT 10-10   Unemployment and Presidents

Source: Paul Cox, "Politics and Economics Don't Mix," http://members.cox.net/mathmistakes/poly-econ.htm. June 22, 2005.

Chapter Summary

Due to cost and time considerations, research is usually done using a sample rather than the entire target population. To draw a representative sample, the sampling frame—the actual list of people or objects from which the sample is drawn—must be accurate. An accurate sampling frame, however, does not guarantee a representative sample. The sampling method is also critical for obtaining a representative sample.

All methods of sampling may be classified as either nonprobability sampling or probability sampling. Nonprobability sampling is based on researchers' subjective judgment rather than on scientific principles. However, this does not mean the results are useless. On the contrary, researchers may do a good job in portraying the target population, but without scientifically determined samples, there is no way to determine how precise the results are. But the ease in obtaining the sample and the low cost associated with drawing nonprobability samples often compensate for their lack of statistical support. Judgment sampling, convenience sampling, quota sampling, and snowball sampling are popular nonprobability sampling methods.

Probability sampling is any sampling plan in which the chance of being selected is known and nonzero for every sampling unit in the population. Statisticians prefer these methods, since sample selection is objective and the sampling error may be measured in terms of probability under the normal curve. Simple random sampling, systematic sampling, stratified sampling, and cluster sampling are types of probabilistic sampling methods.

For a sample to be statistically useful, it must be representative of the target population. While industry rules of thumb, affordability, and statistical methods can all be used to determine sample size, the statistical method is preferred because it is supported by scientific principles. Using this method, researchers need three pieces of information: desired precision, desired confidence level, and an estimation of the population standard deviation or parameter.

Unfortunately, there will always be some degree of error present in every study. The total error that exists in a study is the difference between the true information being sought and the collected information. If systematic error and random error could be eliminated, the observed score would equal the true score. Systematic error, the focus of this chapter, occurs when there is a constant bias or problem with the measurement instrument or process.

Systematic error can occur before, during, or after the sample is taken. Presampling errors include population definition error, sample selection error, and measurement instrument error. Errors during the measurement process include procedure error, nonresponse error, response error, and interviewer error. Finally, the most common postsampling error is information-processing error.

Review Questions

1. Why should a researcher sample only part of the target population? Why not just use the entire target population if errors are bound to occur when sampling?

2. What is a sampling frame? What biases may occur when sampling?

3. Explain the major types of probability and nonprobability sampling.

4. List three reasons to use nonprobability sampling instead of probability sampling.

5. What three pieces of information do researchers need to compute sample size? Briefly explain each one.

6. What is the difference between standard error and sampling error?

Practice Quiz

Note: You can find the correct answers to these questions by taking the quiz and then submitting your answers in the Online Edition. The program will automatically score your submission. If you miss a question, the program will provide the correct answer, a rationale for the answer, and the section number in the chapter where the topic is discussed.

1. A sampling frame is the actual list of each element or member of the target population from which a sample is drawn.
   a. True
   b. False

2. A sample frame bias (error) is the difference between the sample and sample frame.
   a. True
   b. False

3. A nonprobability sample is a subset of the population in which every member of the target population has a known and nonzero chance of being included in the sample.
   a. True
   b. False

4. Systematic sampling is a sampling technique in which a sample is drawn by randomly choosing a beginning point in a list and then sequentially selecting every *k*th element from the list.
   a. True
   b. False

5. Typically the larger the sample size, the larger the sampling error.
   a. True
   b. False

6. _____ sampling is when the researcher divides the population into natural subgroups that are more homogeneous than the population as a whole.
   a. Systematic
   b. Simple random
   c. Stratified
   d. Cluster
   e. Area

7. Which of the following is a type of probability sampling?
   a. Quota
   b. Cluster
   c. Convenient

   d. Snowball
   e. Judgment

8. _____ of values are within 2 standard deviations from the mean under a normal curve.
   a. 68.27%
   b. 75.80%
   c. 95.45%
   d. 97.70%
   e. 99.73%

9. Which of the following is a type of nonprobability sampling?
   a. Stratified
   b. Systematic
   c. Simple random
   d. Cluster
   e. Quota

10. Which sampling method is suitable when potential respondents are difficult to locate?
    a. Quota
    b. Snowball
    c. Judgment
    d. Convenience
    e. Cluster

Thinking Critically

1. In the chapter, we noted that people sample items all the time, such as by tasting grapes, tasting a spoonful of soup, trying on a pair of shoes, reading a part of a book, and watching the beginning of a television show. What other things do we do in our daily lives that require us to sample items? How do we determine the sample size for these actions?

2. Two middle school students are planning to begin a lawn-care business. A father of one of the boys informed them that they should concentrate their efforts on their neighborhood, which has 325 dwellings because neither of the boys has a driver's license. The boys are not sure how many services they should offer. Should they only mow lawns, or should they broaden their services to include trimming bushes and hedges; fertilizing soil; planting flowers, shrubs, and small trees; and digging up tree trunks? They decided to sample some of the neighbors to determine the average number of services to offer.

   a. Which type of sampling procedure do you recommend?
   b. Describe the population.
   c. Assuming a confidence level of 95%, a desired level of precision of 60.10 of the true population mean, and a standard deviation of 1, how many households should they sample?

Net Exercises

1. Maritz Marketing Research, Inc., specializes in large-scale, custom-designed research studies that provide critical marketing information to many of the world's largest and most successful companies. Maritz's National Data Collection Group is one of the largest data collection networks in the United States. Go on its virtual tour at http://www. maritzresearch.com/ to understand whom it samples and how it does the sampling.

2. Use the Internet to locate two studies that used convenience samples and two studies that used systematic sampling. Describe and evaluate each of these sampling methodologies.

Experiencing Marketing Research

1. Make a list of ten friends you can visit. Ask each of them the following questions: What is your height? How much do you weigh? Be sure to write down their responses. A very short time later, provided they agree, use an accurate measuring tape and scale to measure their heights and weights. How many of your friends accurately reported their sizes? Do you feel that they reported their sizes as truthfully as possible? For those who misrepresented their sizes, do you feel that they were being unethical? Why or why not?

2. A manufacturer of hair care products in the United States wants to determine how satisfied consumers are with the hair-coloring products they are presently using. The information is considered critical because the company wants to create a product that satisfies its customers' needs. Visit five retail stores that sell hair-coloring products and observe the hair color of people who purchase these items.
   a. Describe the population and sampling frame you feel the company should use.
   b. Which type of sampling technique should the company use? Why?

3. Assume that your marketing professor is working on an important research project that will ultimately help advertisers better understand the viewing habits of the television audience that regularly watches MTV. However, she is unsure how to define the population. She is also unsure about whether college students should be used to complete surveys about MTV programs. Gather enough primary and/or secondary data to help your professor with her research. What recommendations would you make?

Case 10-1

Chrysler and Dodge Out-Sample the Competition

Chrysler Corporation has been thwarted by Japanese automobile manufacturers for such a long time that it finally decided to do something about it, so it took the gloves off and went at them. In Chrysler's "Meet the Americans that beat the Honda" campaign, it claimed that the majority of owners who had driven both Chrysler cars and Honda's Accord or Civic preferred Chrysler to the imports. A similar study a short time later compared two Chrysler models against Toyota's Camry and Tercel. Once again, the Chrysler cars were declared the winners, hands down. Of the 100 consumers in the Toyota Camry comparison, the study indicated that 80 respondents selected Chrysler. Chrysler said that 83 people preferred its two models to the Accord. And the group that tested Chrysler cars against the Toyota Tercel Deluxe preferred the American automobile 91 to 9, according to Chrysler.

The Chrysler Corporation declared itself the outright champion in the automobile industry. However, there may be more to the story than Chrysler reported. Consider the methodology of the study. It went something like this:

Of the 100 people tested, all of them were living in California at the time of the study. Chrysler described the respondents as "import intenders," defined by Chrysler as domestic-brand car owners "who are thinking about buying an imported car." None of the respondents owned a foreign car.

Local Dodge dealers in the New York City area performed a similar study. Dodge found that the majority of owners of four models made by competitors (specifically Toyota, Honda, Ford, and Chevrolet) preferred the Dodge Shadow. Once again, 100 people were surveyed, and they all were owners of one of the competitors' cars. They were provided an opportunity to examine a new version of Dodge Shadow and a new version of their own car. But they were only allowed to drive the Dodge. The results showed that 70% preferred the Dodge to their own cars.

Of course, who asks the questions, where, and to whom makes a big difference in study outcomes. Consider another—possibly less-biased—study performed by Advertising Age. Many people can recall Jason Alexander's reprise of former Chrysler CEO's television claim, "If you can find a better car, buy it." In 2005, more than 1,000 adults were asked in an online survey whether they could indeed find a better vehicle than a Chrysler, Dodge, or Jeep, 80 percent of the respondents said yes.

Source: Cynthia Crossen, *Tainted truth: The Manipulation of Fact in America* (New York: Simon & Schuster, 1994), 76–77; Anonymous, "Be careful what you ask for," *Automotive News,* vol. 79, no. 6158 (July 25, 2005), p. 46.

Case Questions

1. Evaluate the sampling methods used in each study. What biases may have existed in the studies? Do you feel that any of the actions by Chrysler or Dodge were unethical?

2. Describe the population that should have been sampled in the Chrysler study.

3. Which type of method did Chrysler and Dodge use, probabilistic or nonprobabilistic sampling? Explain your answer.

Case 10-2

Suzuki Searches for Answers

A decade ago, Suzuki Machinery was the admiration of the metal-framing industry. It was clearly the market leader with 70% market share, offered quality products, and was growing by leaps and bounds. However, after numerous takeovers by German, French, and most recently a Japanese firm, Suzuki's market share has dwindled to barely 10%. The company is obviously concerned and realizes something must be done to draw back its former customers as well as attract some new ones.

Suzuki Machinery, Ltd., is located in Raleigh, North Carolina, but its headquarters is in Tokyo, Japan. The company currently has 100 employees who work long hours to manufacture only the highest quality metal-framing machines. The company knows that quality must not be compromised, especially since customers will spend up to $500,000 for one machine. The key to the high quality of Suzuki products lies in the Total Quality Control activities performed by the entire company. Technology, manufacturing, sales, and technical service sectors all integrate their efforts toward the creation of reliable products.

Suzuki is presently experiencing problems that are common to former market leaders in a saturated market like the metal-framing industry. There are about 3,000 metal-forming shops that are interested in purchasing expensive machines like the ones manufactured by Suzuki. However, these companies are spread throughout North America, and competition is intense. Although there are only five key competitors in the entire industry, their backgrounds and capabilities differ widely. They include Japanese-owned Amada, which has roughly 50% share of the market; Strippit, with about 20%; Finn-Power International and Suzuki, each with 10%; and German-owned Trumpf, with 5%. Several small companies have the remaining 5% share.

Management at Suzuki has decided that the key to recapturing market share leadership is to know their potential customers better. Therefore, they have hired a marketing research firm to help them answer the following questions:

- What is the customers' perception of Suzuki Machinery, Ltd.?
- What is the customers' perception of using direct selling versus agents?
- How important is the level of automation as a buying factor?
- Why don't potential customers buy from Suzuki Machinery, Ltd.?
- How important is price in customers' buying decision?

Note: The industry information in the case is accurate, but the name of the primary company (Suzuki) has been changed for confidentiality reasons.

Case Questions

To answer the following questions, pretend that you are part of the marketing research team hired by Suzuki.

1. Would you use probability or nonprobability sampling to communicate with the potential customers (i.e., metal-forming shops)? Why? What sampling method would you use, and why?

2. How would you determine the sample size?

3. What problems might you encounter while sampling the target population?

Notes

1. Barbara A. Bailar, "Does sampling work?" *Business Economics* 32, no. 1 (January 1997): 47(7).

2. Ann van Ackere, "Taking samples," *Financial Times,* no. 32829 (November 10, 1995): S2–S4.

3. Ernan Roman, and Scott Hornstein, *Opt-in Marketing,* (McGraw-Hill Professional, 2004), 28.

4. Niels Schillewaert, Fred Langerak, and Tim Duhamel, "Nonprobability sampling for WWW surveys: A comparison of methods," *Journal of the Market Research Society* 40, no. 4 (October 1998): 307–322.

5. MarketSearch, "A MarketSearch brief: choosing a sample size," http://www.msearch.com/, accessed August 20, 2000.

6. Donald H. Sanders, *Statistics: A First Course* (New York: McGraw Hill, 1995), 173.

7. Adamantios Diamantopoulos, and Bodo B. Schlegelmilch, *Taking the Fear Out of Data Analysis* (London: The Dryden Press, 1997), 120–121.

8. Richard A. Bowers, "The resource directory: Doing research on market research," *CD-ROM Professional* 8, no. 4 (April 1995): 111–116.

9. William Schlackman, "A discussion of the use of sensitivity panels in market research," *Journal of the Market Research Society* 39, no. 1 (January 1997): 145.

10. Pamela Kiecker, and James E. Nelson, "Do interviewers follow telephone survey instructions?" *Journal of the Market Research Society* 38, no. 2 (April 1996): 161–176.

Marketing Research Worldwide

Source: © 2007 JupiterImages Corporation.

Key Terms

acquiescence bias (p. 275)

back translation (p. 271)

qualitative group discussion (p. 273)

Learning Objectives

After studying this chapter, you will be able to:

- Explain the importance of international marketing research.

- Enlighten others about secondary data in markets abroad.

- Inform others about primary research in markets abroad and discuss various concerns when conducting international research.

- Describe the future of international marketing research.

GET THIS

McKetchup in Europe

McDonald's is the largest and best-known global foodservice retailer, with more than 30,000 restaurants serving nearly 50 million people in more than 119 countries each day. Yet on any day, even as the market leader, McDonald's serves less than 1% of the world's population. The McDonald's vision is "To be the world's best quick service restaurant experience. Being the best means providing outstanding quality, service, cleanliness and value, so that we make every customer in every restaurant smile." The company also operates other restaurant concepts including Aroma Café, Chipotle Mexican Grill, and Donatos Pizza.

The company seems to be doing quite well. It has produced high return to shareholders, with a compound annual total return of 21% over the past 10 years. But in some European markets, the numbers are not so rosy, so McDonald's is trying to make up for sluggish restaurant sales by introducing a strategic extension program, starting with the launch of its own brand of ketchup. It is a popular product worldwide. Consider the following examples:

- United States—Ketchup is a must with hamburgers and French fries, both American icons.

- Sweden—Swedes pour ketchup on plain pasta such as ziti. Sweden also buys the most ketchup on a per capita basis, followed by Australia, the United States, Canada, and Germany.

- Thailand—Teens in Thailand dip potato chips in ketchup for a snack.

- Asia—Asians like ketchup with seafood, especially when deep-fried or stir-fried.

- Canada—Canadians love ketchup on hot dogs, sausages, and brats.

- Eastern Europe—In Eastern Europe, ketchup is a favorite pizza topping.

- Great Britain—Brits like their fish and chips with ketchup, and they like it sweet.

- Spain and India—Both Spaniards and Indians pour ketchup on omelets and other egg dishes.

McDonald's is test marketing their ketchup in supermarkets in Germany, Austria, and Poland. It has also launched a range of branded children's clothing and shoes through Wal-Mart stores in the United States. Jack Greenberg, chief executive at the company, noted, "We have an obligation to explore ways to leverage our brand. This is an enormous opportunity to find new streams of income."

After only a few months on the market, McDonald's ketchup has captured 3% of the German ketchup market, lagging far behind Heinz with 22% market share. It fairs about the same in other markets.

Sources: Suzanne Martinson, "In the kitchen," *Post.Gazette.com Magazine* (June 29, 2000); http://www.post-gazette.com/food/20000629-ketchup2.asp, August 9, 2000; Paul Whitfield, "McDonald's diversifies brand in European trial," *Marketing* (April 20, 2000): 4; McDonald's corporate site, "About McDonald's," http://www.mcdonalds.com/corp/about.html, accessed July 9, 2005.

Now Ask Yourself

- Given the different use of ketchup in different countries, is it necessary to introduce ketchup with different flavor in various countries?

- Imagine you have been hired by McDonald's to test market its ketchup in European markets. Your goal is to find out how target consumers feel about the taste of ketchup. Which type of marketing research will you use? And why?

- Do you feel it is necessary to use a different technique to conduct the research in different countries? If so, why? If not, why not?

The "Get This" feature illustrates the challenge for marketing researchers to introduce a product in the global market. The diversity of the global market makes market research more complicated and resource consuming. Companies can't simply travel abroad and expect to use the same surveys or other research methods they used in their home markets. There are adjustments that must be made to collect accurate information from the global market. This chapter will introduce you to many of the concerns international marketing researchers face when practicing their craft.

11-1 The Global Marketing Research Industry

Marketing research is big business in the United States. It is also big business throughout most of the developed regions of the world. In 2003, the total world value for marketing research data in the top 10 markets was $15.4 billion. By region, Europe had the greatest world marketing research value of $8.3 billion, most of which came from the 15 European Union member nations. North America was not far behind at $7.1 billion, of which $6.7 billion came from the United States. Asia Pacific totaled $2.6 billion, with the value in Japan totaling $1.2 billion. Finally, Central and South America totaled $685 million together. Mexico had the greatest amount of marketing research expenditures in Latin America, totaling $267 million.[1] As shown in Exhibit 11-1, the largest country, in value of marketing research data, is clearly the United States at $6.67 billion. Five of the top 10 countries are in Europe. The second-largest country in terms of marketing research value is the United Kingdom at $2.0 billion.

11-1a Domestic versus International Marketing Research

Most marketing researchers would agree that the development of successful international marketing strategies depends on detailed market information. But to

EXHIBIT 11-1	Ten Largest Markets in Value of Marketing Research Data (in Millions of Dollars)	
Country	**2003**	**2002**
United States	$6,660	$6,307
United Kingdom	$1,997	$1,775
Germany	$1,805	$1,492
France	$1,580	$1,261
Japan	$1,164	$1,057
Italy	$ 581	$ 461
Canada	$ 477	$ 400
Spain	$ 395	$ 311
China	$ 387	$ 302
Australia	$ 383	$ 304

Source: Anonymous, "10 largest markets in value of marketing research data," *Marketing News,* (July 15, 2005). Reprinted with permission from the American Marketing Association.

obtain the appropriate market information, researchers must be familiar with the market in which it operates. The environment will dictate how much data collection is necessary and which marketing research tools and techniques to use for an organization to successfully gather important information.

Basically what differentiates a domestic market from markets abroad is the business environment in which it operates. As shown in Exhibit 11-2, when the marketing research company is operating in its domestic market, it must contend with the cultural-social, competitive, demographic, political-legal, technological, and economic environments. As its market expands abroad, it must contend with another set of environmental elements. If it expands into multiple foreign markets, it is faced with adjusting to multiple environmental elements.

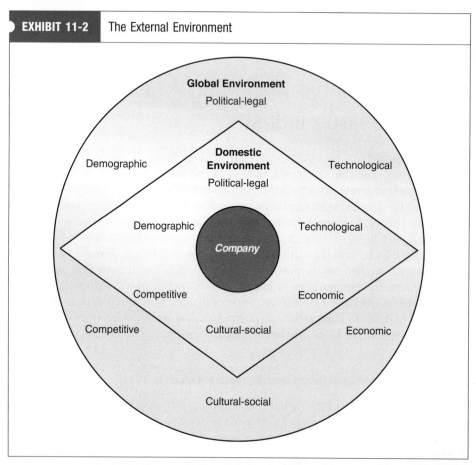

EXHIBIT 11-2 The External Environment

For the most part, these concerns are uncontrollable elements, but they certainly cannot be ignored, so whenever marketing research agencies—or virtually any business for that matter—expand their operations, they must adjust their practices to new sets of environmental elements. Think of it this way: If Coca-Cola hires A&S Research Company to measure customer satisfaction with a new beverage it has sold in the United States, it must concern itself with demographic, social, cultural, competitive, and economic environments, just to name a few. If Coca-Cola wants customer satisfaction measured in, say, France, it must concern itself with an entirely new set of environmental elements. If customer satisfaction in all of Western Europe is to be measured, then the task becomes increasingly complex.

11-1b Multicountry Research Comparisons

If a research company is operating in only one country, it will use many of the research methods we've discussed in previous chapters. If it is operating in multiple countries, it can use many of those same methods, but severe problems will likely arise. High levels of unfamiliarity with foreign markets combined with the cultural diversity across countries create a need for reliable marketing research data. Another complication is that, due to the same cultural differentiation creating this need, problems can easily arise when comparing research data across borders. Consider Example 11-1.

Example 11-1

- Cultural dissimilarity can cause respondents in different countries to respond differently to questions. Consider how respondents use rating scales. Some tend to use extreme scores, and some only assign high scores, while others tend to use the middle of the scale. Three respondents that are equally likely to buy a product may give different responses to a question based on their differing interpretation of the question and how the scale should be used.[2]

- The effect of cultural differences is also apparent in color schemes. International business-to-business advertisements have been heavily impacted by the colors that were used in their ads. A study that compared ad colors in France, the United States and Venezuela found that Venezuelan ads use much more red, orange, and green, while ads in France and the United States tend to use higher proportions of black and brown. The United States also uses significantly more black and white ads than do the other two countries.[3]

11-2 International Marketing Research Process

When analysts conduct research in familiar environments, they deal with numerous issues to generate reliable results, but these issues are at least known to them. When research is conducted in a less familiar environment such as a foreign country, there are many additional concerns. The problem is compounded when researchers accustomed to examining *developed* markets are faced with problems or opportunities in *developing* markets. (See Exhibit 11-3 for a comparison of developed and developing markets.) In Chapter 2, we discussed the seven steps of the marketing research process. Each step will be examined as it relates to international concerns.

11-2a Define the Problem or Opportunity

In the new millennium, technology is thrusting us into a global economy. Global marketing is the name of the new game. Companies in industrialized nations are

EXHIBIT 11-3	Factors Affecting Marketing Research in Developed and Developing Markets	
Developed Country	**Developing Country**	
Research focus on operational issues	Research focus on strategic issues	
Secondary data that is widely available, easy to gather, and reliable	Secondary data that is difficult and time-consuming to gather and not reliable	
Sophisticated research infrastructure	Unsophisticated research infrastructure	
Media that are advanced and available	Media that are undeveloped and poor in quality	
Lack of government interference	Government involved in business decisions	
Advanced communication systems	Inefficient communication systems	

Source: Philip R. Cateora and John L. Graham, *International Marketing*, 12th ed. © 2005 McGraw-Hill Companies, Inc.

experiencing minimal or negligible sales growth in their domestic markets, so more of them than ever are venturing abroad to ferret out new business opportunities. Products in the mature or declining stage in their home markets often experience a resurgence in sales abroad. The tobacco industry is a prime example. In the United States, smoking has become a social taboo as more people realize its hazards to health, and tobacco sales have declined dramatically. On the global scene, however, a very different scenario is unfolding. International sales have jumped by record numbers—and tobacco manufacturers are stepping up efforts to maintain the growth. Consider the following realities:

- In China, the world's biggest tobacco market, Philip Morris has become the biggest supporter of soccer, underwriting the Marlboro Soccer League, named for the company's flagship brand.

- In Prague, capital of the Czech Republic, R. J. Reynolds has paid for couples' "Camel weddings," and then shuttled them off in Camel-insignia taxis.

- In the Philippines, Asia's most Roman Catholic nation, promotional calendars display U.S. and local cigarette brands under a picture of the Virgin Mary.[4]

- In Eastern Europe, Philip Morris and R. J. Reynolds have stepped up their efforts to hook some new markets by entering 14 joint ventures with state tobacco companies.

There has been a lot of discussion in the U.S. regarding the ethical aspects of tobacco manufacturers targeting foreign markets. At the forefront of this concern is the reality that targeted consumers in many countries abroad are not as informed as U.S. citizens about the health problems associated with tobacco consumption. Unfortunately for tobacco manufacturers, the World Health Organization (WHO) has singled out tobacco as one of the greatest public health problems of the new century. There are over 1 billion smokers worldwide, four-fifths of them in developing countries and a third in China alone. Tobacco-related illnesses such as lung cancer and heart disease kill 4 million people a year.[5] Nonetheless, cigarette maker Philip Morris insists it wants to be regulated. The company wants an end to underage smoking, to post health warnings on all of its products, and to institute international campaigns teaching the dangers of smoking.[6]

Of course, not all companies research overseas markets to seek business opportunities. Many of them are already operating abroad and have particular problems to solve. Consider Example 11-2.

Example 11-2

Managers from General Motors went to Japan to find out why Japanese consumers were not interested in buying American cars. They found that their product didn't fit the market; the Japanese are more concerned with the interior and exterior of the car than its performance on the road. GM concluded that the auto's exterior must be flawless, with narrow, perfectly uniform sheet-metal seams and mirrorlike paint jobs. The Japanese also prefer plush pile carpeting, an additional floor mat to hide the rear-floor hump, side-view mirrors that fold in because streets are so narrow, and self-regulating air-conditioning systems.[7]

11-2b State the Research Objectives

Research objectives are statements that describe what it is management wants to learn from the research exercise. As pointed out in Chapter 2, these objectives should flow from, and be totally consistent with, the problem definition. To increase the likelihood that the results from the research will be useful, the statement of objectives should be approved by managers at the appropriate offices. In cases where a company has its home office in one country and its affiliate office in another country, which managers should approve the research objectives? It depends on who needs the information for decision-making purposes and who initially sought the information. All managers who intend to use the results should approve the objectives.

11-2c Develop a Research Design

Research design is the framework that directs marketing research efforts. It may be exploratory, descriptive, or causal. When designing the research project, there are several things to consider, such as:

- What can and cannot be standardized?
- Is it affordable?
- Is it actionable, and at what level?
- Will it be comparable?
- Should it be executed locally or centrally coordinated?

The fact is, designs differ dramatically when foreign markets are researched. Many additional environmental factors come into play, and researchers must ensure that the design is politically correct, legal, culturally sensitive, and within the company's limited resources. Cultural factors are particularly important, since research for the most part tends to be culture-bound. Take, for example, survey development. If the scaling and wording of the questionnaire are not culturally sensitive, meaningless responses will result. Poor translations can be inadvertently insulting or simply nonsensical.

Whenever possible, use the local language to conduct any study. Research agencies have found that they get better results using the local language, since respondents will open up and express themselves more clearly with their native tongue. If a written survey is going to be used, make sure that it is translated correctly. This can be accomplished through **back translation,** which means translating from one language to another, after which a second person translates it back into the original language. For example, let's say that our questionnaire was originally in English. We have it translated into French and then back into English. If the two English versions are not similar, there is likely an error in the French translation. If the original questionnaire and the second version differ, this is a warning that things can go awry, so take great care to make corrections.

Here are additional environmental factors that should be considered when developing research designs for global markets:

- Telephone interviewing is a familiar interviewing technique in most developed countries where telephones are the household norm; they are not the norm in many developing nations where far fewer households own telephones.
- Response rates on written questionnaires differ widely by country. Therefore, high literacy rates are prerequisites for successful written surveys.
- Inefficient postal systems can influence the effectiveness of mail surveys.
- Religious considerations influence response rates. People often provide answers to questions on buying behavior that do not reflect their actual behavior. These differences exist according to country and culture.
- In conservative societies, respondents are increasingly reluctant to participate in personal interviews because they feel the survey is a cultural intrusion.[8]

back translation The process that occurs when information is translated from one language to another, after which a second person translates it back into the original language.

11-2d Prepare for Data Collection

The researcher must decide whether to collect qualitative or quantitative data. This decision depends on the cultural, political, and religious environment of the target population. Collecting useful quantitative data by survey is usually costly, tedious, and time-consuming in any market, but gathering qualitative data can be just as challenging in global markets. Consider the following realities in overseas markets:

- Many countries do not have rooms with one-way mirrors (which facilitate group interviewing).
- Moderators often limit group interview sessions to one group a day.
- Slipping notes with spur-of-the-moment questions to the moderator during a group interview session can be a social mistake.
- Young Asians often defer to the opinions of older people.
- Mixed-gender sessions inhibit open discussion.
- In business-to-business groups, a mix of title levels can cause problems in open discussions.

Usually the best way to gather data in global markets is through personal interviews. This allows respondents to "speak their minds." Whenever data is gathered, researchers are always concerned about obtaining acceptable response rates. If the data is to come from overseas subsidiaries or affiliates, researchers should initially contact the parent company to obtain prior approval. Nothing frustrates parent companies more than having their busy subsidiaries or affiliates abroad bombarded by unapproved surveys. Prior approval can simplify data collection because overseas subsidiaries and affiliates are more likely to respond to surveys that have been approved by the home office.

11-2e Collect the Data

Collecting data in global markets is no task for the novice. There are specialists who have been researching global markets for decades. Research International, for example, has over 3,000 research executives operating in 130 countries. ACNielsen, a VNU company, is the leading research firm with more than 9,000 clients in over 100 countries measuring competitive marketplace dynamics, consumer attitudes, and behavior, and developing advanced analytical insights that generate increased sales and profits.[9]

11-2f Analyze the Data

The analyst must be familiar with the particular environment from which the data originates. It is often risky to take data collected in foreign countries at face value. Findings that contradict reason should be questioned. For example, Latin respondents tend to overstate their positions on questionnaires, while Asians are typically noncommittal. Only an individual familiar with the market of interest will be in a position to adjust for such culturally dependent differences.

11-2g Write and Present the Research Report

Often the research report must be translated for managers at overseas affiliates and subsidiaries. This can be difficult because English words and expressions don't always translate directly. The report writer must be especially careful to avoid jargon and idiomatic expressions. Making back translations can help avoid difficulties.

Source: © 2007 JupiterImages Corporation.

11-3 Secondary Data Collection

Using secondary data is a cost-effective means of evaluating foreign markets, so whenever reliable and valid secondary data is available, it should be used instead of more expensive primary data. As we exhibited in Chapters 3 and 4, there are numerous online and offline sources to use when researching markets abroad. It is widely known that insufficient knowledge is the main reason companies fail in the international marketplace. Of course, the availability of data in global markets depends heavily on the level of development of the country being researched. In general, the more developed a nation, the more likely it is that reliable information is available. Researchers have little trouble obtaining a variety of information in the United States, Canada, Western Europe, Japan, Australia, and other well-established markets. In emerging markets like China, Poland, Mexico, and Brazil, however, reliable and useful information occurs only sporadically—although this situation is improving.

In China, the government has improved the marketing research infrastructure by implementing the Law of Statistics. This law provides legal guidance for research activities in China. Many research organizations have improved data collection and tabulation methods and sampling techniques to alleviate the problem of inaccuracy and to improve the representation of the data.[10] Today most countries and organizations around the world realize the importance of data collection and storage.

11-4 Primary Data Collection

When secondary data is unavailable to aid decision makers to solve a particular international problem, it becomes necessary to gather primary data. We will discuss focus groups, in-depth interviews, projective techniques, and survey research—including questionnaire design—as they relate to foreign markets.

11-4a Focus Groups

The term *focus groups* can take on different meanings in different countries. In the United Kingdom, some companies use it to describe a semi-structured, prescribed question methodology resulting in information, while **qualitative group discussions**

qualitative group discussion
The type of discussion used to describe exploratory, open, non-directive groups leading to understanding.

are used to describe exploratory, open, nondirective groups leading to understanding. In some places in Europe, the analysis of focus groups through sociological and psychological models is widespread; in the United States the group moderator often is a different person from the qualitative researcher. In Australia, the moderator is usually the market researcher, permitting interaction and development of the research process as the group evolves. Focus groups are typically exploratory and look to understand rather than prescribe.

Although focus group research is increasing in popularity worldwide, it is unclear if its usage rate in other industrialized countries parallels use in the United States, since there have been few studies addressing this issue. One thing that is clear is the importance of using highly qualified moderators to run sessions abroad. A study that examined 248 moderators from the United States, Germany, and Japan found that regardless of where sessions are conducted, group moderators are crucial in achieving study objectives.[11]

In the United States, researchers are using focus groups more and more to learn about ethnic markets. A major trend is the growth of Asian-American focus groups. A company in California has recruited more than a dozen respondent groups who speak Chinese (both Mandarin and Cantonese), Korean, Vietnamese, and Japanese. Understanding of Hispanics is also increasing through focus group interviewing.[12]

Although focus group research is possible in Mexico, many of the major cities do not have the proper facilities, so most sessions are carried out in hotels or in a place where observers can watch on closed-circuit television. Careful screening of participants is especially important in Mexico because participants like to bring along friends and relatives who don't meet the study requirements.[13]

In the United Kingdom, the dramatic increase in the number of viewing facilities is indicative of the increased use of focus group research. Richard Barnes, qualitative research field director of Research Resources, stated, "Where there used to be only five or six viewing facilities in London, there are over 30 here now. One pops up every week." He believes the increased use of focus groups is due partly to a growth in business-to-business research.[14] In fact, it was reported a few years ago, "The Queen has approved the appointment of the first Royal focus group, following the death of Diana, Princess of Wales, to act as an instant sounding board to help her and top courtiers cope with any future family crisis."[15]

In Asia, focus groups seldom run smoothly. As noted earlier, young Asians often defer to the opinions of older people. Also, mixed-gender sessions inhibit open discussion. In business-to-business groups, a mix of authority levels often blocks interaction.

Here are some of the major differences in focus group research in the United States and abroad:

- *Time frame.* Lead times tend to be much longer abroad, with East Asia being the most troublesome. If it takes two weeks to set up groups in the United States, it will take almost twice that amount of time in most of Europe and even more in Asia.

- *Structure.* Groups of four to six people are most effective in foreign countries, compared to six to eight for U.S. focus groups, and session length tends to be longer than in the U.S.—up to four hours.

- *Recruiting and rescreening.* In general, market researchers in the United States are much more careful in recruiting and rescreening than are researchers in most foreign countries.

- *Approach.* Foreign moderators tend to be less structured and authoritative to make group members feel comfortable with each other and to build rapport.

- *Project length.* Projects can take much longer to execute abroad. In the United States, usually two to four sessions are undertaken in a day, but typically one group session per day is the limit abroad, due to the time they are scheduled, length of sessions, and demands on the moderators.

Source: © 2007 JupiterImages Corporation.

- *Facilities.* Facilities outside the United States and Canada are similar to U.S. facilities of 20 years ago. Video and audio equipment tends to be less sophisticated than what U.S. researchers are used to.

- *Costs.* Costs for sessions abroad vary tremendously; it is not unusual to pay almost twice as much per group for sessions conducted in Europe and three times as much in many Asian nations.[16]

11-4b Depth Interviews

Depth interviews are extremely useful in cultures that have idiosyncratic behavior. For example, if a Japanese executive is going to reveal something to someone, he or she must first have a relationship with the interviewer. In most cases, that dictates that the executive must be interviewed in person. Telephone interviews won't work until the relationship is firmly established after several in-person encounters.[17]

When conducting in-depth interviews, it is important for the interviewer to understand that response biases may occur. In some lesser-developed countries, there is a genuine desire to please the interviewer.[18] A study in Kazakhstan looked at **acquiescence bias**—tendencies of respondents to agree with statements presented to them rather than disagree.[19] Although this study was mainly concerned with international survey research, it is certainly a concern with personal interviews.

acquiescence bias The tendency of survey or focus group respondents to agree with statements presented to them rather than disagree.

11-4c Projective Techniques

Projective tests are universal in that unstructured stimuli serve as the basis for assessment and do not pose a language barrier. While these techniques have been widely used in the United States, they are just as relevant overseas. For example, one of the world's largest custom marketing research agencies, Research International's division, Research International Qualitatif, which is based in Paris, specializes in qualitative research, projective techniques in particular. Projective tests are used as the major method of personality assessment worldwide, mainly because of the lack of local norms and standardization of objective tests.[20]

11-4d Survey Research

It is important to realize in researching unfamiliar markets that cultural differences dramatically influence how consumers respond to surveys. Some research methods that are standard in one culture may be offensive or even illegal in other cultures. Failure to address the cultural issue can give companies a misleading impression of the potential market for their products. Consider the following in Example 11-3.

Example 11-3

- Telephone interviewing is an acceptable research tool in the United States, but it is considered inappropriate in many East Asian cultures. And in some countries it is just infeasible because the penetration of telephones is as low as 10%.[21]

- Interviewing sessions with facilities in "shopping malls" don't exist in most countries.

- In-person interviewing is done either in the home with interviewers going door-to-door, by street intercepts where the respondent is invited to a meeting room or hall, or by prerecruitment where the interviewer and respondent will meet at an agreed location.

- In Saudi Arabia, market researchers are not allowed to interview women at all; those who do face prosecution.

- "Basic products" such as mouthwash, which are taken for granted in the United States, are luxuries in parts of Africa. Mass telephone surveys for such products in those countries are a waste of company resources. And in some countries, questions about such products are perceived as too personal and offensive.

- In the United Kingdom and Germany, the postal system is reliable and fast. Not so in Nigeria and other emerging markets, where the mail system is unreliable and slow.

- Surveying consumers' purchase intention or price sensitivity should be complemented with observations of purchasing patterns and other behaviors in many developing countries, where consumer perceptions are difficult to survey directly.

Using qualified interviewers is important when conducting surveys abroad. However, the status of interviewers varies by country. In Kenya, for example, it is a job filled mostly by educated individuals. In other cultures, interviewers are often housewives. In Singapore, Malays and Chinese-speaking people will not interview each other. In South Africa, interviewers often speak four or five languages. In Egypt, interviewing is not acceptable on Fridays; in Israel, not on Saturdays; and in many other places, not on Sundays. In some countries, interviewers do not have their own transportation. In Africa, public transportation is frequently not available; researchers must arrange to have interviewers transported to their locations.

Interviewers must not only be qualified to carry out the interviews, they must also understand their respondents. For example, Brazilian and Italian consumers display what is called "the courtesy effect"—that is, they are likely to tell interviewers what they think the interviewers want to hear to avoid offending them with a negative response. The Japanese, on the other hand, feel that it is impolite to overreact to something, so they rarely respond with superlatives.

11-4e Questionnaire Design

As we discussed in Chapters 8, questionnaires are constructed in three phases. Each phase presents issues that must be resolved before researchers proceed to the next phase.

Source: © 2007 JupiterImages Corporation.

We will now examine these phases and see what researchers consider as they design and construct effective questionnaires in markets abroad.

Preconstruction

When researchers design questionnaires for foreign markets, they must consider cultural idiosyncrasies and social norms. They must also think about how unfamiliar infrastructures might impact their data collection method. Outside the United States and other industrialized nations, the personal interview is the most popular data collection method because of the problems in developing markets with telephone and mail infrastructures. Telephone availability is usually not a problem when surveying businesses, however, because companies in developing countries do have telephones. (See Research Realities 11-1 to learn about the strides that are being made in Asia and other world regions to improve telephone-interviewing capabilities.) In developed nations such as many European and North American countries, the preferred method of collecting data from individuals is the telephone interview because consumers in these countries are more and more reluctant to participate in personal interviews. They don't want to admit someone they don't know into their homes.

Construction

When constructing a questionnaire that will be used in a foreign country, several factors must be taken into consideration. The biggest hurdle is, of course, language. Differences in idioms and problems with exact translations abound. Some factors to consider when constructing questionnaires for international markets include the following:

- *What is the literacy rate of the target respondents?* If it is low, as is often the case in developing countries, questionnaires may need to be verbally administered, using open-ended questions. Open-ended questions are useful in cross-cultural research because they help identify respondents' frame of reference and sometimes permit respondents to set their own frames of reference. If closed-ended questions are used, the number of response categories should be limited to a manageable number.

Research Realities 11-1   *Telemarketers Beware in Asia!*

In March 2006, Merrill Lynch was fined $5 million for alleged violations stemming from their call centers. It was reported that their centers were poorly supervised, mutual fund trades weren't monitored properly, clients were periodically steered into unsuitable and costly funds, and most importantly violations occurred against giving non-cash sales incentives. Today 90 percent of Merrill's call center clients say they're "highly satisfied" with their service.

As businesses bring their "Western" models of data collection into Asia and other world regions, telephone research is becoming increasingly popular. Many local companies are expanding their telephone-interviewing capabilities to accommodate increased demand. Some companies are trying to develop regional calling centers, in which calls all over Asia, for example, are made from a centralized location using students or other locals who know the language. While this creates economies of scale and efficiently uses resources, a lack of cultural and linguistic understanding of a market can cause problems for naïve researchers.

When centralized or localized calling is done, there are some things for telemarketers to consider in Asia:

- *Manage local nuances in languages.* There are multiple languages that are spoken in Asia, so interviewers

must be careful to differentiate them. For example, "ji xuan ji" means "calculator" to Singaporean and Malaysian speakers of Mandarin Chinese but "computer" among many Chinese and Taiwanese speakers.

- *Manage translation issues.* Don't attempt to translate messages word-for-word. Translate locally with an eye toward content.
- *Consider the telecommunications infrastructure.* Telephone interviews make more sense in some markets than others. Familiarize yourself with telephone usage infrastructure before deciding on the interview technique.
- *Consider the length of the interview.* Throughout most of Asia, most telephone interviews will need to be less than 20 minutes long.
- *Consider cultural issues when setting the study's objectives.* Asians prefer face-to-face interaction when disseminating personal information. This concern and other cultural factors should be considered before examining any market.

Source: Tony Chapelle, "NASD Fines Merrill Lynch Over Call Center Problems," *On Wall Street*, vol. 16, no. 5 (May 2006): 22; Kevin Reagan, "In Asia, think globally, communicate locally," *Marketing News* 33, no. 15 (July 19, 1999): 12, 14.

EXHIBIT 11-4   Translation Faux Pas

- In the United States, Scandinavian vacuum manufacturer Electrolux used the following in its ad campaign: "Nothing sucks like an Electrolux."
- In Taiwan, the translation of the Pepsi slogan "Come alive with the Pepsi Generation" read as "Pepsi will bring your ancestors back from the dead."
- In China, the Kentucky Fried Chicken slogan "finger-lickin' good" came out as, "eat your fingers off."
- In Mexico, the translation of the NOVA car means "no go."
- In Spanish, North American beer brand Coors' direct translation of "turn it loose" read as "suffer from explosive diarrhea" for Spanish consumers.
- In a Mexican hotel, a sign read: "The manager has personally passed all the water here."
- In a Japanese hotel, a sign read: "You are invited to take advantage of the chambermaid."

Sources: Kristina Greene, "Translation—It's money well spent," *The Press* (New Zealand) (July 19, 2004): b6; Virginia, Division of International Trade Web site, "Translation mishaps," http://www.exportvirginia.org/12JAN2005.htm#FA2, July 25, 2005.

- *Does the translation closely match the intent and meaning of the original questionnaire?* The researcher should be comfortable with the wording of the questionnaire, first in the original language, and then in the translated version. Surveys for foreign markets should be translated into the respondents' native tongue. Faulty translations are all too common. Consider the examples in Exhibit 11-4.
- *Is the terminology familiar to the respondents?* Care should be taken to ensure that idioms and different usages are not misused or abused. Tragic and

laughable examples litter the bulletin boards of embarrassed marketing researchers. Even such a universal term as "family" has different meanings in different countries. In the United States, it typically means only parents and children. In Latin countries, it means parents, children, grandparents, cousins, uncles, aunts—what North Americans usually call the extended family.[22]

- *What is the respondents' frame of reference?* Products may be used quite differently abroad than they are at home. For example, people ride bicycles in the United States mainly for recreation. In China, bicycles are the basic mode of transportation. Therefore, questions about bicycle use in China should reflect knowledge of this difference.

Postconstruction

Several postconstruction concerns can cause problems when surveying foreign markets. These include pretesting, instrument translation, and costs associated with implementation.

When dealing with foreign markets, the pretest results must be carefully analyzed. Since two cultures are involved here—the culture of the researcher and the culture of the respondent—the pretest results should be analyzed by an individual who understands both cultures. Consider the following problems noted in *The Bulletin:*

> One respondent's mark on a scale indicating that he or she "strongly agrees" may not be exactly the same as another respondent's "strongly agrees." First, the respondent may not have interpreted the question in the same way. Second, even assuming a similar interpretation of the question, the same response may express a more or less strongly felt agreement. When survey responses are obtained from respondents in multiple cultures, the differences in possible meanings become even larger. A survey of the communication needs within one international business organization found a number of culturally based differences in expectations and understandings that affected the results. Questions such as "What is your job description?" elicited responses of very different lengths. U.S. responses to this question averaged 10 words; Puerto Rican responses averaged 20 words; and Asian responses from Taiwan, Hong Kong, and Singapore averaged 25 words—all written in English.[23]

11-4f Sampling

The initial step in any sampling effort is to decide who should be studied. This depends entirely on the objectives set forth by marketing managers at the beginning of the study. Then the sampling frame must be determined. It is not an easy task to obtain a list of populations for the sampling frame, nor is it entirely necessary. While marketing managers usually prefer probabilistic sampling on the home front, nonprobabilistic sampling is often the preferred method for data gathering abroad. Many countries have homogeneous populations and thus require less random sampling, and regional differences may affect results only marginally.

In sum, researchers must be very careful when conducting international marketing research. Exhibit 11-5 provides a checklist of concerns when conducting research abroad. This list is not meant to be exhaustive but is given to display the various concerns related to conducting international research.

11-5 Future of Marketing Research in Global Markets

Increasingly, the marketing research industry has become truly international in nature (see Exhibit 1-3 in Chapter 1). Of the $13.3 billion in revenues the top 25 research firms enjoyed in 2004, $8.94 billion—or 67%—came from operations outside their home country. This is truly a cosmopolitan group. And, in the case of the huge VNU

> **EXHIBIT 11-5** Checklist of Concerns When Conducting International Marketing Research

- *Are there cultural idiosyncrasies to be concerned about?* When a company used a five-point scale where five is "very satisfied" and one is "very dissatisfied," they found that it worked well in most countries, except in the Far East (e.g., Japan and China). Respondents there are very moderate in their philosophy, so their scores tend to cluster around three. Also, in China, the cultivation of personal relationships may mean the difference between an individual completing a survey and not responding to it at all.
- *How much will it cost to conduct research?* Research costs differ among markets. Costs tend to be considerably less in developing countries and high in larger cities of developed countries.
- *What is the research infrastructure like?* Consider the problems associated with communication vehicles. For example, in Venezuela the mail delivery system is highly unreliable. When conducting mail surveys, almost 40% never reach the destination. Telephone surveys often require numerous attempts, and personal interviews are nearly impossible since there is very little private time at homes and offices. And forget about mall intercept interviews—this is not an acceptable practice in Venezuela.
- *What is the country's literacy rate?* Most developed countries have literacy rates above 90% but many developing markets have much lower rates. Companies operating in countries with low literacy rates may have problems questioning consumers via written questionnaires.
- *What are the offerings of local research organizations?* Consider which services research organizations offer to companies in global markets.
- *Are there language differences?* Exhibit 11-4 demonstrates that translation mistakes can result in some embarrassing results.
- *What is the most popular data collection method?* Consider that in Europe roughly 60 to 70% of all quantitative research involves face-to-face studies.
- *How available is secondary data?* Secondary data can be scarce and unreliable in many developing countries.
- *How different are the populations?* The difference in populations will directly impact sample size determination. Highly different populations will require larger sample sizes. India, for example, has 14 official languages and numerous unofficial ones.
- *Should a financial incentive be offered for survey participation?* Consider this comment by a company that often conducts surveys in China: "We prefer to offer a gratuity worldwide, and this token of appreciation is very effective in China."
- *How available is the Internet?* Most of the leading research organizations regularly use Internet panels and other modes of online data collection. However, presently less than 10% of all marketing research is performed online. This will gradually change as more households and businesses worldwide use the Internet on a regular basis.

Sources: Carol Z. Shea and Carol LeBourveau, "Jumping the 'hurdles' of marketing research," *Marketing Research* 12, no. 3 (Fall 2000): 22–30; V. Kumar, *International Marketing Research* (Upper Saddle River, NJ: Prentice Hall, 2000); Paula Lyon Andruss, "1.3 billion potentially satisfied customers," *Marketing News* 34, no. 22 (October 23, 2000): 41–42.

operation, based in Haarlem, Netherlands, only 1.0% of its research revenues came from operations within its home country; the balance came from operations in 81 other countries around the world.

Of the 2004 top 25 research firms, 12 are U.S.-owned, and those account for 30.0% of top 25 revenues. Five are British, and they accounted for 28.9% of the total revenue of the top 25 firms. Just one, VNU, is based in the Netherlands, but it alone accounted for 25.7% of the total, due to ownership of ACNielsen, Nielsen Media Research, and several other firms in the United States and abroad. France is home to one firm, and that accounts for 5.7% of the total, and Japan, with four of the top 25, accounted for 4.1%. There is just one of the top 25 firms based in Germany, but it accounted for 6.3% of the total from operations and subsidiaries in 59 countries.[24]

There are many changes coming about in the marketing research industry worldwide. First of all, as the world becomes smaller due to advances in information technology, there is no doubt that the majority of marketing researchers—whether domestic or international—will continue to take advantage of it. Just look at the signs of technology moving rapidly forward. According to statistics updated on March 2005 by Internet World Stats, there were at that time an estimated 888.7 million Internet users worldwide (13.9% of the population worldwide), up from 497.7 million in 2001. In 1999, the world total of e-commerce was $145 billion. This number swelled to $6.7 *trillion* in 2004.[25]

Second, marketing research firms will continue to expand their operations into foreign markets. Since it is increasingly convenient to learn about and communicate with those markets, it makes sense to take advantage of opportunities that exist there.

Third, large marketing research firms will continue to acquire smaller firms. The top 25 firms in 2004 acquired 29 research firms around the world, and they had in total $360 million in revenue at the time of acquisition. Author Jack Honomichl noted that the "urge to merge" continued into 2005. In the first half of 2005, the top 25 firms have acquired 19 smaller firms with annual revenue of more than $510 million—led by the GfK Group's acquisition of NOP World.[26]

Fourth, the advantages already apparent on the Internet will become increasingly so to marketing research firms worldwide. Research firms will increasingly use online focus groups throughout the world as voice and audio technology continues to improve. Through chat rooms and bulletin boards there is already quite of bit of interaction between focus group members and moderators. More and more computer users will install software that permits them to hear and see the people they are communicating with, regardless of their locations. Research firms will also increasingly use online panel groups to include consumers throughout the world. The low cost of conducting online research will become even lower relative to traditional research methods. Consider these other likely improvements:

- More rapid turnaround of data
- Increasingly automated data collection
- Better graphics and video
- Improved data quality
- Seamless international coordination[27]

Decision Time!

Assume that you have developed a new back support system that relieves the everyday pains of the lower back. Before you attempt to commercialize the system, you want to know what the potential market is in the United States and throughout European Union member countries. How would you proceed with the research effort? Would you research it differently in the U.S. than in the EU?

Net Impact

The impact of the Internet on global marketing research is apparent throughout the chapter. From efficient gathering of secondary information to online focus groups and survey implementation, the Internet is changing the entire research industry. It will continue to advance on a daily basis, making information widely available and less expensive—much to the delight of marketing researchers.

On the Lighter Side—Now That's Funny!

In Britain, Dr. Richard Wiseman, a psychologist at the University of Hertfordshire, conducted an online survey to find the best joke. More than 40,000 jokes were submitted and almost two million people rated them. Respondents used a "Gigglemeter" that had a five-point scale ranging from "not very funny" to "very funny." And here's the winner:

> Two hunters are out in the woods when one of them collapses. He doesn't seem to be breathing, and his eyes are glazed. The other guy takes out his phone and calls the emergency services. He gasps, "My friend is dead! What can I do?" The operator says,

"Calm down, I can help. First, let's make sure he's dead." There is a silence; then a gunshot is heard. Back on the phone, the guy says: "OK, now what?"

Wiseman said that the joke was popular across many different countries and appealed to both genders and all ages. It was interesting that Germans, not known for their sense of humor, found almost all jokes funny. People in Ireland, the UK, Australia, and New Zealand preferred jokes using word plays. Many Europeans, such as the French and Danish, often preferred offbeat surreal humor, while Americans and Canadians preferred jokes where there was a strong sense of superiority—either because someone seemed stupid or looked that way. A final finding: Data analysis showed that jokes with 103 words were thought to be especially funny.

Source: Anonymous, "Official! World's funniest joke," *CNN.com/Science & Space*, http://archives.cnn.com/2002/TECH/science/10/03/joke.funniest/, Retrieved October 11, 2005.

Chapter Summary

Marketing research is popular worldwide, particularly in developed and emerging markets. What differentiates a domestic firm from markets abroad is the business environment in which it operates. Companies must contend with not only cultural and social differences; they must deal with competitive, demographic, political-legal, technological, and economic environments. If research expands into multiple countries, researchers must contend with additional uncontrollable environmental elements.

The seven-step marketing research process discussed in Chapter 2 is relevant in foreign markets, but there are new considerations in each step. Some of these concerns include scale and question interpretation, language differences, telephone interviewing idiosyncrasies, and response rate differences when using certain media vehicles. The personal interview is the best way to gather information in foreign markets because of the face-to-face interaction. When collecting data in global markets, there are numerous experienced specialists to help, such as ACNielsen, Research International, and Research Resources, to name just a few.

When researching foreign markets, secondary data is the sensible way to go, due to cost savings. But when reliable and valid secondary data is not available, primary data collection should be undertaken. While it can take many forms, some of the most popular data collection methods include focus groups, in-depth interviews, projective techniques, and survey research. Focus groups are increasingly used in markets abroad. Survey research, as well as all data-gathering methods, must take into consideration various kinds of cultural peculiarities. For example, telephone interviewing is difficult to implement in many Asian countries because of Asians' desire to cultivate relationships prior to responding to questions about themselves.

When companies have international marketing research needs, they can either hire a research organization or conduct their own research. They will need to consider culture, cost, research infrastructure, research service offerings, language differences, data collection method popularity, availability of secondary data, population similarities, Internet availability, and many other concerns.

The future of marketing research in foreign markets is certain to be besieged by technological advancements that will facilitate the research process. The Internet will be an increasingly important communication vehicle to gather both secondary and primary data. Other changes likely to occur include continued global expansion of research markets and continued acquisition of smaller research firms by larger research firms.

Review Questions

1. Which country had the greatest marketing research value in the same year?

2. What differentiates domestic research from research conducted in foreign markets?

3. Name four problems in the marketing research process that can arise when conducting marketing research abroad.

4. How might focus groups differ in Asian markets than those conducted in the United States?

5. Name five problems that can arise when conducting survey research in a foreign market.

6. What is the most popular data collection method outside of the United States?

7. What factors should be considered when constructing questionnaires for international markets?

8. What does the future of the marketing research industry look like?

Practice Quiz

Note: You can find the correct answers to these questions by taking the quiz and then submitting your answers in the Online Edition. The program will automatically score your submission. If you miss a question, the program will provide the correct answer, a rationale for the answer, and the section number in the chapter where the topic is discussed.

1. The initial stage of the international marketing research process is to define the problem or opportunity.
   a. True
   b. False

2. When conducting research in foreign markets, the statement of objectives should be approved by managers at the appropriate offices; this will increase the likelihood that the results from the research will be useful.
   a. True
   b. False

3. An example of back translation is to have Jane Smith translate a questionnaire that was originally in English into French and then have Jane translate it back to English.
   a. True
   b. False

4. Response bias is a tendency of respondents to agree with statements presented to them rather than disagree.
   a. True
   b. False

5. Probability sampling is the preferred method for data gathering abroad.
   a. True
   b. False

6. Which of the following is *not* true regarding marketing research in developing countries?
   a. Inefficient communication systems
   b. Unsophisticated research infrastructure
   c. Media that are undeveloped and poor in quality
   d. Research that focuses on strategic issues
   e. Little government interference

7. Which of the following is *true* about marketing research in developing countries?
   a. Research focuses on strategic issues.
   b. Secondary data is difficult and time-consuming to gather and not reliable.
   c. Media are undeveloped and poor in quality.
   d. Communication systems are inefficient.
   e. All of the above are correct.

8. Which of the following is a concern of conducting international marketing research?
   a. How much will it cost to conduct research?
   b. What is the research infrastructure like?
   c. What is the country's literacy rate?
   d. Are there language differences?
   e. All of the above are correct.

9. Which of the following is the definition of the "courtesy effect" present in Brazil and Italy?
   a. Retailers tell interviewers that they price products according to consumer demand to maximize profit.
   b. Consumers are likely to tell interviewers the opposite of what they think interviewers want to hear.
   c. Retailers tell interviewers that they price products at a discount price to increase sales volume.
   d. Consumers are likely to tell interviewers what they think the interviewers want to hear to avoid offending them with a negative response.
   e. None of the above

10. What is the sixth step of the international marketing research process?
    a. State research objectives.
    b. Analyze the data.
    c. Collect the data.
    d. Develop a research design.
    e. Write and present the research report.

Thinking Critically

1. You are a marketing researcher in the U.S. and have been asked by Kentucky Fried Chicken (KFC) to evaluate market opportunities in Eastern Europe. Since your business experiences have been solely in the U.S., what non-U.S. concerns should you consider to effectively evaluate Eastern European markets?

2. When implementing a survey, the literacy rate of target respondents can be a problem in developing countries. Assume that you are doing a study of toothpastes in Argentina. How would you overcome literacy problems in your sample?

Net Exercises

1. SIS International Research is a full-service market research supplier for qualitative and quantitative research. Its qualitative research studies include focus groups and in-depth executive interviews. Its quantitative studies include large-scale surveys that utilize telephone and face-to-face interviews. All of its fieldwork is supervised by its staff of skilled international project directors, who are fluent in the native languages. Visit the SIS Web site at http://www.sisinternational.com to learn more about its services. What is particular about the international marketing research?

2. According to the text discussion, focus groups are being used throughout the world. Search the web and locate two focus group research organizations in two countries that offer some entirely different services that are necessary for their home markets. How do they differ? Why do they differ?

Experiencing Marketing Research

Based on your knowledge of questionnaire design, create a five-question survey asking undergraduate college students about their attitudes toward Nike athletic shoes manufactured in Vietnam. Next, have someone translate the five questions into another language, and then have someone else translate the questions back into English. How closely did your original survey compare to the translated version?

Case 11-1

Market Research in the Land of the Rising Sun

Lee Iacocca, former CEO of Chrysler, appeared in his first of his 61 Chrysler commercials in 1979. He has been retired for more than two decades ago, yet more than 8 in 10 consumers who've seen his Chrysler ads say he is "believable" and a "relevant" pitchman, according to an Advertising Age survey. But Iacocca has problems identifying with young adults. While 79 percent of overall adults have heard of him, Just 36 percent of 18-to-24-year olds know who he is. Age is just one of many demographic concerns for researchers.

"The Japanese have always trusted executives' inspiration as much, or more, than pure data," says Tim Clark, president of TKAI, Inc., in Portland, Oregon, a firm that specializes in Internet research and working in the Japanese market. For decades, most Americans viewed Japan as a closed culture, with close relationships between companies and government officials; and an attitude of suspicion toward outsiders. The keiretsu (i.e., informal domestic Japanese strategic alliances) that operated in several industries never did much to dispel the image. Now that Japan is getting its economy back in order and some laws have changed to entice foreign investment, American attitudes are changing. Patrick Bray, director of business development in the San Francisco office of the Japan External Trade Organization—a government-financed clearinghouse for data and assistance—notes that "A decade ago, a U.S. company couldn't buy a company in Japan, so it didn't bother to develop information on the marketplace. Now that the economy is being restructured, there are lots of strategic opportunities." Some of this success can be attributed to better marketing research methods. More and more foreign companies are approaching Japan with important facts and data. In 2008, the Japanese market research industry is forecast to have a value of $1.31 billion, an increase of 12.7 percent from 2003.

The information that's needed cannot be extracted the same way as it's done in the United States, however. Japanese consumers and executives usually don't respond to phone sampling at all. When focus groups are attempted, younger employees will defer to their elders. Market research has been no better than a guessing game in the past. Popular products like Sony's Walkman were launched with no prior consumer testing.

Another challenge is that it is becoming more difficult to reach Japanese consumers. Postal rates are high, costing about 75 cents to mail a one-ounce letter. Nippon Telegraph and Telephone—a state-owned phone monopoly—is extremely expensive for toll-free numbers and protects its database of regular phone numbers. To obtain lists of residents, research companies often must go to local city halls to obtain voter rolls—a daunting task, since Tokyo alone has 23 ward offices, each with its own proprietary voter data.

The language is a constant hurdle for American companies looking to learn more about Japan. For example, "I agree with you" in Japan may be interpreted by a Japanese respondent to mean that he or she understands you, though he or she doesn't necessarily endorse what you have to say. Gale Wallmark, director of market research for DFS Group, Ltd., in San Francisco, which runs duty-free shops throughout Asia and regularly polls Japanese consumers' opinions says, "You can write a question that looks very plain and direct, but in Japanese it might be interpreted in several ways."

There are many kinds of marketing research being done today in Japan. According to *Nikkei Weekly,* an English-language newspaper, 5% of all polling in Japan is done by telephone. About 30% is done in respondents' offices, 20% is conducted by mail, 19% is done in surveyors' offices, 14% occurs in focus groups, and 2% happens on the street. The rest is done by other means.

Tim Clark of TKAI is helping to pioneer a new survey methodology in Japan. He has started to sample opinion over the Internet. He notes, "The Japanese tend to be very honest when they are speaking in private while maintaining complete anonymity. And on the Internet, you eliminate the dominant-personality bias that is common in focus groups."

Source: Bradley Johnson, "Survey says: Iacocca's still got it." *Advertising Age,* vol. 76, no. 29 (July 18, 2005), p. 33; Market Research in Japan, *Datamonitor,* Industry Profile, http://www.datamonitor.com, retrieved August 29, 2006; H. Lee Murphy, "Japanese keeping fewer secrets from U.S. firms," *Marketing News* 33, no. 13 (June 21, 1999): 4, 6.

Case Questions

1. Do you find the following statement believable: "For decades, most Americans viewed Japan as a closed culture, with close relationships between companies and government officials; and an attitude of suspicion toward outsiders." Why or why not?

2. When marketing research is conducted in Japan, should it use the same techniques employed in the United States? If not, what's different?

3. What can companies do to circumvent some of the high costs of conducting marketing research in Japan?

Case 11-2

How Will Demographic Surveys Be Received by International Members?

What's your race? How much money do you make? How much education have you obtained? Are these questions that make you uncomfortable? If so, you're not alone. In a posting on the American Society of Association Executives' (ASAE) International Section email list, an executive wanted some feedback on how demographic surveys would be received by international members of her association. She wanted suggestions on how to word questions regarding such issues as ethnicity, income, and education level. The responses below indicate that these surveys must be carefully worded and attention given to language.

- "Working for an association that has members in 75 countries, I can only say to be very careful when gathering information on income level, ethnicity, and so forth. Many of our members do not appreciate such questions."

- "We do an annual survey that goes to all our members worldwide. However, it is tailored so that only

U.S. and Canadian members are asked about salary. The only financial issue we ask our members outside of the United States and Canada about is the volume, within ranges, of their business. They have not had a problem answering that question."

- "In addition to the sensitive nature of such questions, to compare income levels between countries is to compare apples with potatoes. Income levels only make sense relative to the range of incomes within a country."

Source: Anonymous, "What shouldn't you ask in international surveys?" *Association Management* 51, no. 12 (November 1999): 131.

Case Questions

1. Do you agree with the recommendations that were given? Why or why not?

2. What recommendations would you give regarding how to word questions on demographic surveys?

3. Do you think that demographic questions are received differently in different countries? Why or why not?

Notes

1. ESOMAR, "World value for marketing research data," *Marketing News* (July 15, 2005): 25.
2. Neil Helgeson, "Research isn't linear when done globally," *Marketing News* 33, no. 15 (July 19, 1999): 13.
3. Irvine Clarke, III and Earl D. Honeycutt, Jr., "Color usage in international business-to-business print advertising," *Industrial Marketing Management* 29, no. 3 (May 2000): 255–261.

4. Marieke K. DeMooij, and Warren Keegan, *Advertising Worldwide* (Upper Saddle River, NJ: Prentice Hall, 1991), 311–312.

5. Anonymous, "The tobacco war goes global," *Economist* 357, no. 8192 (October 14, 2000): 97.

6. Francis Y. Capistrano, "Weekender: Marketing," *BusinessWorld, Manila* (March 18, 2005): 1.

7. Valerie Reitman, and Gabriella Stern, "Adapting a U.S. car to Japanese tastes," *Wall Street Journal* (June 26, 1995): B1.

8. Myron Levin, "Cigarette makers go overseas to ignite sales," *Chicago-Sun Times* (November 20, 1994): 41.

9. ACNielsen, web page, http://www.acnielsen.com/site/about, July 13, 2005.

10. Sherriff T.K. Luk, "The use of secondary information published by the PRC government," *Journal of the Market Research Society* 41, no. 3 (July 1999): 355–365. Anonymous, "Data accuracy requires independent collecting system," *Business Daily Update* (March 16, 2005): 16

11. Lucy L. Henke, "A longitudinal analysis of the ad agency-client relationship: Predictors of an agency switch," *Journal of Advertising Research,* vol. 35, no. 2 (March–April 1995): 24 (7).

12. Cyndee Miller, "Sampling program strikes out at moviegoers," *Marketing News* 29, no. 8 (April 10, 1995): 1–2.

13. Cyndee Miller, "Researcher reaches Xers with her focus groups on the road," *Marketing News* 29, no. 1 (January 2, 1995): 10.

14. Robert Barash, "The dying art of qualitative research," *Marketing News* 31, no. 12 (June 9, 1997): 17.

15. James C.P. Cowley, "Strategic qualitative focus group research—define and articulate our skills or we will be replaced by others," *International Journal of Market Research* 42, no. 1 (2000): 17–38.

16. V. Kumar, *International Marketing Research* (Upper Saddle River, NJ: Prentice Hall, 2000), 145.

17. H. Lee Murphy, "Japanese keeping fewer secrets from U.S. firms," *Marketing News* 33, no. 13 (June 21, 1999): 4, 6.

18. Brad Frevert, "Is global research different?" *Marketing Research* 12, no. 1 (Spring 2000): 49–51.

19. Thomas T. Semon, "No easy answers to acquiescence bias," *Marketing News* 34, no. 3 (January 31, 2000): 7.

20. Chris Piotrowski, and John W. Keller, "Projective techniques: An international perspective," *Psychological Reports* 72 (1993): 179–182.

21. Brad Frevert, "Is global research different?" *Marketing Research* 12, no. 1 (Spring 2000): 49–51.

22. Philip R. Cateora, and John L. Graham, *International Marketing,* 12th ed. (New York: McGraw-Hill, 2005).

23. Sherblom, John C., Claire F. Sullivan, and Elizabeth C. Sherblom. "The What, the Whom, and the Hows of Survey Research," *ABCA Bulletin* (1993): 61.

24. Jack Honomichl, "Acquisitions up, growth rate varies," *Marketing News* (August 15, 2005): H4

25. Anonymous, "New media review," http://www.etcnewmedia.com/review/default.asp?SectionID=10 (July 1, 2005); Forrester Research, "Total worldwide e-commerce revenues, 2004 (B2B & B2C)," http://www.epaynews.com/statistics/transactions.html (July 1, 2005).

26. Jack Honomichl, "Acquisitions up, growth rate varies," *Marketing News* (August 15, 2005): H3.

27. Carol Phillips, and Linda Stegeman, "Hybrid approach tends to yield more insight," *Marketing News* 39, no. 6 (April 1, 2005): 22.

Research Implementation

Preparation of Data for Analysis

Chapter Twelve

Key Terms

codebook   (p. 296)
coding   (p. 292)
computer editing   (p. 292)
cross-tabulation   (p. 300)
editing   (p. 289)
field editing   (p. 292)

frequency distribution   (p. 300)
office editing   (p. 292)
optical scanning device   (p. 299)
personal editing   (p. 291)
simple tabulation   (p. 299)
tabulation   (p. 299)

Learning Objectives

After studying this chapter, you will be able to:

- Prepare information for analysis.
- Edit and code data.
- Handle problems in the editing and coding processes.

- Review tabulations and use frequency distributions to check data entry.

GET THIS

Suffering from Data Overload?

"Let's see . . . when I go to Yahoo! and type in 'computers,' I get a list of over 50,000 sites to visit. When I type in 'marketing' I get over 5,000 sites. Do I really need this much information? Where do I start? Where do I finish?" Are these thoughts you've had when researching a topic? The Internet and other advances in technology have created data overload for many researchers: There is twice as much new information in the world today as there was just three years ago.

A team of researchers working for Microsoft, Intel, and other tech giants estimated that the amount of new information generated last year was roughly 23 exabytes. An exabyte is equal to one million megabytes, or roughly the content of one million books. According to these exabyte experts, such new information really is new and, what's more, the amount of it is increasing by 30% a year. The researchers came up with their estimate by analyzing 10,000 Web sites and reviewing "typical" hard drives, among other things. Their findings therefore are limited to digital information.

Data overload occurs in all industries, however. For example, according to the Private Label Manufacturers Association, the retail industry gathers 10 times more information than it did five years ago—and five years later it will be gathering 10 times more information than it does today. Companies are therefore struggling to find ways to convert all that data into actionable intelligence as mountains of information grow rapidly.

Sources: Cam Fuller, "Learn more about information overload," *The Star Phoenix* (March 12, 2005): E5; Anonymous, "More than we need to know; Suffering from information overload? There's a reason" *Sarasota Herald-Tribune* (December 30, 2003): A10, 317.

Now Ask Yourself

- Since the Internet and technology in general are increasing the amount of data available, how can the problem of information overload be remedied?

- For companies, what should be done to manage the mountains of information and transfer it into useful intelligence?

As evidenced in the "Get This" feature, researchers are becoming overwhelmed by the amount of data that is available to them, and the situation is not going to improve unless the data available is organized in some way. Companies must have a system in place to manage and filter the information. In this chapter, you will learn about the critical issues associated with organizing and preparing data for analysis. There are basically five steps in properly preparing information for examination, as outlined in Exhibit 12-1.

12-1 Editing

Whether information is being gathered by telephone, personal interview, mail, the Internet, or some other way, it must be checked to ensure that the data are as complete, consistent, readable, and free of mistakes as possible. Therefore, once the data begin arriving, researchers edit each piece of information received. **Editing** involves checking survey data for completeness, legibility, consistency, and accuracy. When necessary, researchers make minor adjustments to the data during editing, so that they can be properly coded and stored. Some companies refer to editing as "cleaning data."

editing Checking survey data for completeness, legibility, consistency, and accuracy.

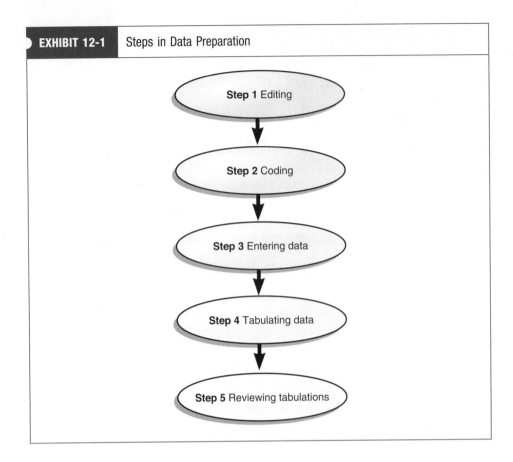

EXHIBIT 12-1 Steps in Data Preparation

Step 1 Editing

Step 2 Coding

Step 3 Entering data

Step 4 Tabulating data

Step 5 Reviewing tabulations

The most important purpose of editing is to eliminate or at least reduce the number of errors in the raw data. As discussed in Chapter 10, two forms of error can exist in raw survey data: *interviewer error* and *respondent error*. Interviewers sometimes mark incorrect response categories or wrongly record open-ended responses. Respondents sometimes provide inconsistent answers or make illegible or confusing marks on surveys.

12-1a Response Problems and Solutions

Let's say that we are using a mail questionnaire to collect data, and we have sent 1,000 surveys to people throughout the world. All kinds of problems can detract from the quality of information supplied on the questionnaire. If we obtain a 25% response rate, we receive 250 surveys. However, it is highly unlikely that all responses from the 250 respondents will be usable. Consider just a few of the potential problems:

- *Wrong informant.* The survey may have been completed by someone other than the intended respondent. If the researcher sent a survey to the vice president of international operations for her to complete but found out that her secretary filled it out instead, then the information should not be used. The main reason this problem exists is because executives stay so busy.

- *Return to sender.* Sometimes when conducting research, unopened envelopes with surveys will be returned to the researcher with the message "Retour," "Returned To Sender," "Moved, Not Forwardable," "Undeliverable As Addressed, Unable to Forward," or "Alremitente." These messages occur because the intended respondent no longer works at the company, the company changed addresses with no forwarding address, or the business is no longer in operation.

- *Illegible writing.* Sometimes the responses on surveys are so poorly written that the answers are not comprehensible.

- *Incomplete responses.* This is particularly a problem with longer surveys or those requesting confidential information. Sometimes respondents will only answer part of the survey because they either do not wish to share the requested information for confidentiality reasons or perhaps the survey was perceived as being too long.

- *Damaged measuring instrument.* Usually surveys have to travel for days, being tossed about from one postal employee to another. If a survey is returned with a portion of it missing or so damaged that responses cannot be obtained, the only choices are to return the survey to the respondent to complete again, use the remaining information that is useful, or omit the entire survey from analysis.

- *Apparently confused respondent.* If the responses demonstrate that the respondent did not understand the directions for particular questions, those responses may have to be ignored. For example, if a question uses a 1 (indicating "strongly agree") to 5 scale (indicating "strongly disagree") and the respondent replies for whatever reason with a few 7's and 8's, then the respondent was obviously confused.

- *Lack of variance among responses.* This problem exists when a respondent provides the same or nearly the same answers for all questions. Let's say a 7-point Likert scale was used to respond to 20 customer-satisfaction statements. If the respondent provided 4's (indicating "neither agree nor disagree") to all questions, then the researcher should question whether the respondent read each statement carefully, or at all.

- *Lack of consistency among responses.* It is possible for respondents to contradict themselves when filling out a questionnaire. For example, if an individual responds to questions about home ownership and in another part of the questionnaire he states that he has never owned a home, an obvious problem exists.

- *Late responses.* Unavoidable to the researcher, a few responses ultimately arrive after the predetermined time for the study to end.

The preceding problems may be handled a number of ways. Follow-up interviews may be conducted to solve any of these concerns. In cases where responses were incomplete or the form was incorrectly filled out, the researchers may send the respondent another form or re-interview the respondent, if time permits. However, this time the researchers will explain the problems that were encountered so that the same problems do not reoccur. This way, the respondent may provide more useful information. However, since time has elapsed and the respondent has already seen the questions, some response bias may exist.

If only a portion of the responses were not provided by a respondent and time or the situation does not allow for a second interview, the researchers may consider assigning values that indicate "no valid response." This would allow the researchers to use the responses that were provided. This remedy is particularly important when sample sizes are small.

If all else fails, the researchers may consider eliminating all unacceptable surveys. Unacceptable surveys may include those involving wrong informants; an abundance of illegible, incomplete, or inconsistent responses; a damaged measuring instrument; apparently confused respondents; and late responses. One major problem that may occur, however, is that if the responses from discarded surveys differ significantly from those not discarded, then the results may be biased.

12-1b Data Editing

Every response must be carefully examined during the editing process. Eliminating problems during editing makes the next step easier to perform. Editing is performed in two ways: *personal editing* and *computer editing*. **Personal editing** is performed manually; however, this method is slow and inefficient. It is also prone to random

personal editing Editing performed by a person.

computer editing Editing performed by a computer.

field editing Editing of personal-interview, mall-intercept, and telephone surveys as the data collection takes place.

office editing Editing performed at a central location by an office staff after all data collection is finished.

mistakes. **Computer editing** is, of course, performed by a computer and is the norm today. The computer editing process begins with data collection. If respondents or interviewers enter inconsistent responses, the computer will not allow them to continue until the problem is remedied. Most researchers use computers because they can instruct the computer on what response patterns are acceptable for each question in the sequence. The computer then knows what to do with all response scenarios, such as contingent questions, inconsistent responses, incorrect skip patterns (a "skip pattern" informs respondents to skip certain questions that do not pertain to them), and unanswered questions. It is also much less prone to random mistakes.

Based on where the editing takes place, editing can be classified as *field editing* and *office editing*. **Field editing** is editing done on personal-interview, mall-intercept, and telephone surveys as the data collection takes place. The editing must occur on the same day the data is collected because if any of the collected information is unclear, incomplete, or incorrectly done, the field supervisor can then go to the individual who gathered the data and attempt to remedy the problems. Time is of the essence, since the editor hopes that because the data was collected that day, then perhaps the interviewer will remember the responses and be able to correct the problem. For example, if an interviewer was assigned to have 100 people complete surveys in a shopping mall, the field supervisor may periodically throughout the day examine the already-completed surveys and inquire about questionable or omitted responses.

Whereas field editing is typically performed on the same day as the data were gathered, **office editing** is done at a central location by an office staff after all data collection is finished. Therefore, since considerable time elapses between receipt of the earliest and latest responses, the interviewer or data collector probably will not remember specific responses. This becomes a major problem, and usually an irreconcilable one, when interviewers perform their duties incorrectly throughout data collection. Since all responses have already been completed, interviewers cannot be given feedback that will improve the readability or accuracy of the responses. When returned responses are either unclear or incomplete, the office editor may choose to recontact the respondents to clarify the responses, but of course this is a problem if responses were from anonymous respondents.

12-2 Coding

coding The process of systematically and consistently assigning each survey response a numerical score or code.

Once the supplied data have been edited and are as free of mistakes as possible, the information must be put in a form that can be read by the computer. If the computer cannot properly read the information, it will not be able to analyze it. **Coding** is the process of systematically and consistently assigning each response a numerical score.

For surveys that use closed-ended questions, coding is a rather simple yet time-consuming process, especially if there are numerous respondents. There are hundreds of companies like United Marketing Research and PERT Survey Research that can assist organizations with their coding needs.

Exhibit 12-2 shows a questionnaire used by Embassy Suites hotels. Customers were asked to answer questions 1–3 by selecting A (Excellent), B (Good), C (Average), D (Fair), or F (Poor). These choices are coded in Exhibit 12-3 using 1 for A and 5 for F. The next question asks for a "yes" or "no" response. In this case, the "yes" may be coded as 1 and the "no" as 0. For the remaining questions, which are open-ended, response categories were created after all answers were received. Say the responses fall into ten categories; the responses are then coded 0–9.

Exhibit 12-3 shows how ten respondents' answers were coded and recorded. The first three columns are used to identify the respondents. For example, the first respondent was "001," the second respondent was "002," and so on. If there were 100 respondents, the one-hundredth respondent would have "100" coded in the first three columns. In Exhibit 12-3, nine columns are used: three for respondent identification and the remaining six for responses.

EXHIBIT 12-2 Survey from Embassy Suites

EMBASSY SUITES

WELCOME

Dear Embassy Suites Guest,

All of us at Embassy Suites have only one job to do . . . to provide you with the best hotel accommodations, service and value available today.

If you have any concerns during your stay, please let me or a member of the hotel staff know immediately. Every Embassy Suites team member is committed to ensuring your satisfaction. We promise that we will listen and respond to your needs and concerns in a friendly and efficient manner. If we are unable to resolve the situation to your satisfaction, your night's stay is free.

To help us continue to provide you with the best in service and accommodations, please take a minute to write your comments and suggestions on the back of this card and drop it off at the front desk.

Thank you for helping us to provide you with the best in service and accommodations. After all, we may run the hotels, but when it comes to staying in them, you're the expert.

Sincerely,

General Manager

Source: Embassy Suites Hotel. Reprinted with permission.

Please complete the information below and leave this card at the front desk. Thanks for your help.

How do you rate this Embassy Suite hotel on:

	A (Excellent)	B (Good)	C (Average)	D (Fair)	F (Poor)
1. An overall basis	❑	❑	❑	❑	❑
2. Physical condition of furnishings and cleanliness?	❑	❑	❑	❑	❑
3. Staff responsiveness and friendliness?	❑	❑	❑	❑	❑

Was everything in your suite in working order? Yes ❑ No ❑

If not, please comment: _____

_____
_____

If you were serviced by an outstanding hotel employee(s), please give us their name(s)/department(s): _____

_____
_____

What, if anything, could we do to improve your next stay at this Embassy Suites Hotel? _____

_____
_____
_____
_____
_____

Name: _____
Company: _____
Address: _____
City/State: _____ Zip _____
Phone: _____
Embassy Suite Location: _____
Date of Stay: _____
Suite Number: _____

The key to a good coding system is for the coding categories to be mutually exclusive and the entire system to be collectively exhaustive. To be mutually exclusive, every response must fit into only one category. To be collectively exhaustive, all possible responses must fit into one of the categories. For example, consider the following set of response categories:

12 years of age and younger

12–20 years of age

21–30 years of age

31–40 years of age

41–50 years of age

The first two choices are not mutually exclusive because both include the "12 years of age" selection. To remedy the situation, the first category should be "younger than 12 years of age." The set of categories is also not collectively exhaustive because there

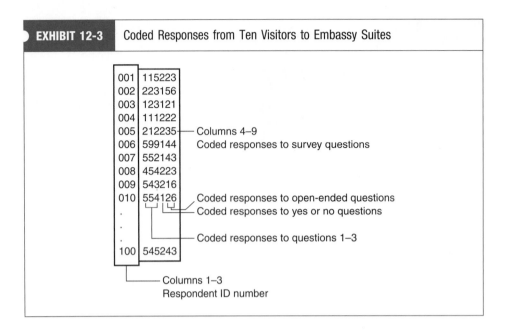

| EXHIBIT 12-3 | Coded Responses from Ten Visitors to Embassy Suites |

is no category for people who are over 50. To remedy this situation, a final category of "Over 50 years of age" should have been included.

12-2a Coding Missing Numbers

Inevitably, some respondents fail to complete portions of the survey. They may be tired or frustrated, or they may not want to reveal certain information. Whatever the reason for incomplete surveys, researchers must indicate to the computer that there was no response provided by the respondent.

There are two ways to deal with missing responses. First, we can simply leave it blank. The computer software will automatically treat it as missing response. Second, we can use a number to represent the missing responses. Any number can be used, although it cannot be a number that represents a valid response. Most researchers will use "9" or "99" to represent missing responses.

For example, a user of the computer program SPSS can input data using the Data Editor, then go to the "Variable View" tab. The user can click on the variable under "Missing" and indicate which number or numbers (e.g., 9) represent missing responses. The numbers should be used consistently throughout the coding process to avoid confusion. Exhibit 12-3 shows that respondent 006 did not provide answers to questions 2 and 3.

12-2b Coding Open-Ended Questions

Sometimes researchers will use open-ended questions during the interview process because (1) they did not know which choices to provide as responses, (2) there were too many potential responses to list, or (3) they did not want to limit the breadth of responses. If open-ended questions are used, researchers must create categories. When they receive the first several responses, perhaps 10 to 20 of them, the typical procedure is to examine the results to get a feel for the categories needed, and then specify the categories and apply them to the rest of the responses. An early pattern of responses is usually easy to identify. Other categories may need to be added as more responses arrive. Consider what RT Nelson Company says about its coding of open-ended data: "Our experienced coding team, who have a thorough understanding of the project and your information needs, carefully review the data and then develop clear and meaningful categories for organizing responses for each open-ended question. Then, all responses are carefully coded into the client-approved categories."[1] Consider Example 12-1.

Example 12-1

All responses must fit into a category, once all responses have been returned. Furthermore, similar responses should fall into the same category. Let's say we asked the following question: "Why don't you shop at our store?" The following responses may be provided:

- Checkout lines too long
- Poor fresh fruit selection
- Parking lot too small
- No on-duty butcher
- Store hours too short
- Too few meat choices
- Not enough frozen foods
- No seafood selection
- Not enough floral assistance
- Need more baggers to carry groceries for senior citizens

These responses can be reasonably grouped into three categories:

"Limited food selection," as indicated by "poor fresh fruit selection," "too few meat choices," "not enough frozen foods," "no seafood selection"

"Shoppers' inconvenience," as indicated by "checkout lines too long," "parking lot too small," "store hours too short"

"Not enough service," as indicated by "no on-duty butcher," "not enough floral assistance," "need more baggers to carry groceries for senior citizens"

Categorizing can be a tedious process, but it is necessary so that each response can be coded for analysis. The shortcoming of this process is the obvious subjectivity. The categories and assignment of responses to individual categories are based on the researcher's judgment. In our previous example, the response "checkout lines are too long" could have been placed in the "not enough service" category rather than the "shoppers' inconvenience" category. The strong point of open-ended questions, though, is that they do not limit responses, so that respondents are freer to say what is on their minds.

12-2c Precoded Questionnaires

Sometimes researchers place codes on the actual questionnaire, which simplifies data entry. The correct code number will appear on the same line as the response. This technique can only be used for closed-ended questions.

Typically, questions have two sets of codes. One set of codes is for individual responses. That is, a number is assigned to each potential response. In the first question (Q1) of the Harrah's Casino survey (a portion of which is shown in Exhibit 12-4), "A (excellent)" is coded as 1, "B" as 2, "C" as 3, "D" as 4, and "F (failure)" as 5.

The second set of codes is for individual questions. Although an item on the survey may be numbered as a single question, it may actually contain several questions. The survey must be coded so that each question within multiple-part items has its own code. For example, in Exhibit 12-4, the second question (Q2) actually has seven questions that deal with the service of the front desk.

As shown in the Harrah's Casino Survey in Exhibit 12-4, the precoded responses and coded question number are placed immediately beside the choices. Sometimes researchers prefer to place the precoded responses with each question and the coded question number at the far right of each potential response. But as long as they do not confuse respondents,

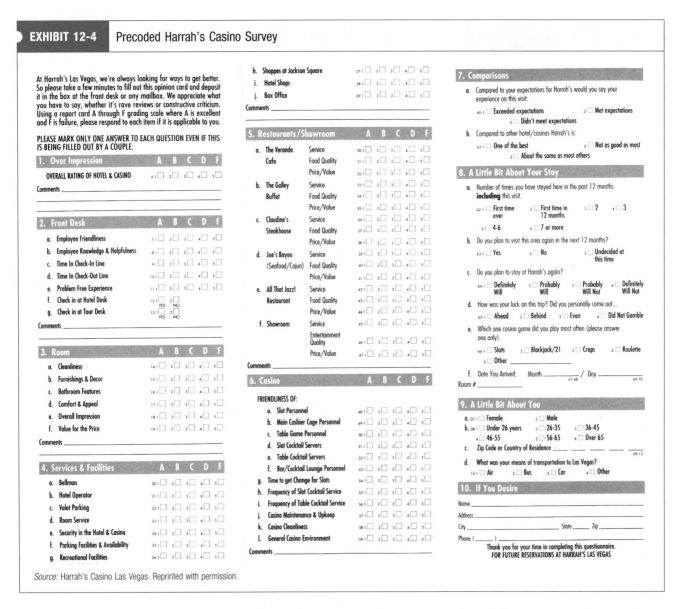

EXHIBIT 12-4 Precoded Harrah's Casino Survey

Source: Harrah's Casino Las Vegas. Reprinted with permission.

the codes can be positioned in any convenient place. Of course, respondent confusion should be detected and eliminated during the pretesting phase of questionnaire design.

12-2d Codebook

codebook A book that contains the instructions for the individuals who code survey data.

Whenever tasks must be carried out in a particular fashion, the people responsible for performing them must be carefully instructed. Companies often have procedures manuals for this reason. A **codebook** contains the instructions for the people who code survey data. It is the blueprint for proper data coding. As shown in Exhibit 12-5, and using questions 1–7 of the Harrah's survey (Exhibit 12-4), the codebook typically includes the following:

- *Column number*—indicates where to place the numeric codes
- *Variable number*—indicates the variable to be coded
- *Variable name*—indicates the name of the variable to be coded
- *Question number*—indicates the question number according to the survey or interview
- *Coding instructions*—provides instructions for the people responsible for coding

EXHIBIT 12-5		Example of a Codebook (Using Harrah's Survey from Exhibit 12-4)		
Column Number	**Variable Number**	**Variable Name**	**Question Number**	**Coding Instructions**
1–3	1	Respondent ID number		001–100
4	2	Record number		1 (all respondents)
5	3	Interviewer code		1 = John Doe 2 = Sally Roe 3 = Roger Rhodes 4 = other
6	4	Overall impression	1	1 = excellent 2 = very good 3 = good 4 = fair 5 = failure 9 = no response
7–11	5	Front desk	2	1 = excellent 2 = very good 3 = good 4 = fair 5 = failure 9 = no response
12–13	6	Front desk	2	1 = yes 2 = no 9 = no response
14–19	7	Room	3	1 = excellent 2 = very good 3 = good 4 = fair 5 = failure 9 = no response
20–29	8	Services and facilities	4	1 = excellent 2 = very good 3 = good 4 = fair 5 = failure 9 = no response
30–47	9	Restaurants/showroom	5	1 = excellent 2 = very good 3 = good 4 = fair 5 = failure 9 = no response
48–59	10	Casino	6	1 = excellent 2 = very good 3 = good 4 = fair 5 = failure 9 = no response
60	11	Comparison (to your expectations)	7a	1 = exceeded expectations 2 = met expectations 3 = didn't meet expectations 9 = no response
61	12	Comparison (to other hotels/ casinos)	7b	1 = one of the best 2 = not as good as most 3 = about the same as most others 9 = no response

Note: The ''variable number'' and ''question number'' do not match (for example, the ''overall impression'' [4 versus 1]) because the former is the fourth variable being studied but the first question on the survey.

12-3 Entering Data

If the survey respondents or the interviewers are entering the responses into a computer terminal during data collection, then data-entry operators are not needed. However, if data entry is not instantaneous, then once coding is completed, someone has to enter the data. This task is typically performed by data-entry operators, also known as *keyboard operators,* who input the coded data into the computer. The information is then ready for analysis. There are hundreds of companies like Le Sphinx Developpement (France), Data Entry Services, Inc., and Tab House that can assist companies with their data entry needs. Tab House, for example, gives this description of its services: "Programs are set in place to specify allowable input data on a column by column basis, to ensure accuracy. Data is then re-keyed (verified), again to ensure a greater degree of accuracy. Following 'verification,' the database is 'custom cleaned'... data can be entered in a multipunch column-binary format, or in a single-punch ASCII format. Once data is keyed, it can be converted into any type of format desired, for those requiring raw data files."[2] SPSS is another company that helps to facilitate the data entry process (see Research Realities 12-1).

Today, many researchers have their data entered into software programs that have statistical analysis capabilities, like SPSS, SAS, and Microsoft Excel. Each of these programs has the ability to perform many types of statistical tests, such as correlations, regressions, analysis of variance, and other tests we will discuss in

Research Realities 12-1   *SPSS Data Entry Network Server*

The SPSS Data Entry Network Server enables multiple people in an organization to simultaneously enter data directly to the same central file already structured for cleaning and analysis. It allows multiple people to enter data via networked Data Entry Builders or Data Entry Stations. The SPSS Data Entry Network Server automatically routes and merges the data into the correct, centrally stored file. Since there is no need to manually match and merge files, data entry staff can manage several projects simultaneously.

The SPSS Data Entry Network Server includes the SPSS Data Entry Builder for designing professional printed and onscreen data entry forms. As forms are created, the SPSS Data Entry Builder automatically incorporates metadata (data about the data). Additionally, Smart Navigation options such as skip-and-fill rules, which guide data entry staff through only relevant questions, speed up the data entry process. All of this makes collected data ready sooner for analysis in SPSS for Windows.

The SPSS Data Entry Network Server is comprised of data collection server software and the SPSS Data Entry Builder. The SPSS Data Entry Builder offers survey and forms design, keyboard data collection, and data cleaning. Users can format their questions any way they like, including check boxes, buttons, and lists for paper surveys, and drop-down lists and option buttons for online forms.

Other benefits of the Entry Network Server include its ability to:

- *Collect data quickly.* With smart options for form- and table-based entry in an intuitive Windows interface, data can be entered quickly. Users do not need to enter or memorize codes, meaning that they can start entering data within minutes.

- *Ensure reliable data.* The Rules Wizard makes it easy to add data checking and validation rules as well as skip-and-fill rules to forms, which provides for more accurate data.

- *Gain greater control and security.* The SPSS Data Entry Network Server ensures that the correct form is being used for data entry throughout every project, and the data reside on a secure, centralized network server.

- *Manage multiple projects with confidence.* The SPSS Data Entry Network Server matches and merges files automatically, giving users the ability to manage several projects simultaneously and without manual intervention. Users can be confident that the correct data are routed and merged into the appropriate file automatically.

Source: SPSS web page, "SPSS ships SPSS data entry network server," http://www.spss.com, accessed July 29, 2005.

Source: © 2007 JupiterImages Corporation.

subsequent chapters. Regardless of which program is used, data entry is a straightforward process, since it simply involves entering numbers into cells on a spreadsheet. Preparing entered data for analysis is more complex; this will be covered in subsequent chapters.

While data entry is a straightforward and repetitive process, problems can and do occur. One of the most common problems is the transposing of data. For example, instead of entering "15" the keyboard operator inputs "51." Another problem that often exists is inputting an infeasible code. If the codes for indicating gender are "1" for males and "2" for females, obviously "3" is incorrect. Some computers can be programmed to signal incorrect or inconsistent entries. Some problems can be avoided by having another individual check the data-entry operator's work for input errors. While this still does not guarantee total accuracy, it reduces the number of mistakes.

Instead of entering data manually, researchers often use **optical scanning devices.** These are data-processing machines that electronically read survey answers that are in a prescribed form, such as numbers, codes, or words. The devices then store the data. The first surveys that used these devices required respondents to indicate their answers by completely shading in boxes using a dark-leaded pencil, so that the optical-scanning device could read them. However, with advancements in technology, the scanning devices can now read responses completed in pencil, pen, marker, or any other writing device, and they can even read responses that appear as Xs, circled responses, shaded boxes, and other forms.

With rapidly advancing technologies, data entry will become ever more streamlined. Some experts believe that combining voice recognition with already existing technologies, such as keyboards and the pen or mouse, will play an important role in making the process of data entry more efficient. Handwriting recognition is not currently the best method for inputting data. This may be changing, though, as advancements in handwriting-recognition technology are becoming increasingly apparent in global markets, especially throughout East Asia.

optical scanning device A data processing machine that can electronically read survey answers that are in a prescribed form, such as numbers, codes, or words, and store the data.

12-4 Data Tabulation

Once the data is coded, edited, and entered into the computer, it is then necessary to tabulate the results. **Tabulation** consists of arranging the data in a tabular format that is easy for the researcher to read. Researchers tabulate data to count the number of responses to each question. This can be done through *simple tabulation* or *cross-tabulation*. **Simple tabulation** involves tabulating the results of only one variable, which informs the researcher how often each response was given. As shown in

tabulation A process that involves arranging the data in a table format that is easy for the researcher to read.

simple tabulation A process that involves tabulating the results of only one variable, which informs the researcher how often each response was given.

EXHIBIT 12-6	Frequencies Associated with Actual Ages of Affiliates	
Affiliate Age	**Frequency**	**Percentage of Total**
Less than 10 years	126	37.8
10–20 years	90	27.0
21–30 years	38	11.4
31–40 years	27	8.1
More than 40 years	49	14.7
No Response	3	0.9

EXHIBIT 12-7	Cross-Tabulation using Age and Income				
	Income				
Affiliate Age	**<$20,000**	**$20,001–$50,000**	**>$50,000**	**Frequency**	**Percentage**
Less Than 10 Years	20	40	66	126	37.8
10–20 Years	15	25	50	90	27.0
21–30 Years	5	10	23	38	11.4
31–40 Years	12	6	9	27	8.1
More Than 40 Years	14	15	20	49	14.7
No Response	0	1	2	3	0.9

cross-tabulation A process that involves examining the responses to two or more variables simultaneously and informing the researcher how often each response was given.

Exhibit 12-6, the only variable response that is summarized is affiliate age. **Cross-tabulation** involves tabulating the results of two or more variables simultaneously and informs the researcher how often each response was given. Exhibit 12-7 shows the cross-tabulation of two variables: affiliate age and income.

12-5 Reviewing Tabulations

Even when coding, editing, and data entry are carefully done, problems still creep in. Sometimes these problems can be quite severe. For marketing researchers, however, most problems associated with data preparation are caused by inaccurate data entry, so researchers need to review the study's tabulations to determine if the data contain any additional mistakes before they begin running statistical tests. This check can be partially accomplished by running frequency distributions. A **frequency distribution** shows values grouped into several classes based on quantity and indicates the frequency of the values within each class. A frequency distribution provides a breakdown of all groups in designated categories.

frequency distribution A chart showing values grouped into several classes based on quantity that indicates the frequency of the values within each class; a breakdown of all groups in designated categories.

A study of the ages of affiliates of U.S. multinational advertising agencies yielded the frequency distribution shown in Exhibit 12-8.[3] The distribution shows that the majority of affiliates had less than two decades of experience. In some cases, certain data-entry problems can be detected in frequency distributions. Let's say that we used the following codes to represent the categories: 1 = less than 10 years, 2 = 10–20 years, 3 = 21–30 years, 4 = 31–40 years, 5 = more than 40 years, and 9 = no response. If the data-entry operator inadvertently coded one of the responses a "6" and another a "7," which were not code choices, the frequency distribution would display these mistakes, as shown in Exhibit 12-8. Notice that no categories were provided for these mistakes. Therefore, the researcher would need to revisit

EXHIBIT 12-8	Frequencies Associated with Actual Ages of Affiliates (with Two Coded Mistakes)	
Affiliate Age	**Frequency**	**Percentage of Total**
Less than 10 years	125	37.54
10–20 years	89	26.7
21–30 years	38	11.4
31–40 years	27	8.1
More than 40 years	49	14.7
No response	3	0.9
	1	0.3
	1	0.3

the coding to locate the incorrect data entry. Although examining frequency distributions will not detect erroneous coding when a logical choice was selected (for example, coding a "1" for male when the respondent was a female, so that the wrong code was input but was not detected, since "1" was a choice), it does locate a number of mistakes.

Decision Time!

You are the marketing manager of an industrial firm that manufactures heavy machinery. Due to intense competition, you have your researcher regularly survey the target market to better understand what customers want in your machines. Your marketing researcher just handed you the frequency distributions to an important customer survey, but the responses are far different from what you expected. What would you do? Would you (1) accept the data; (2) tell the researcher to go back and check his or her work, even though time is critical; (3) tell the researcher to redo the study; (4) disregard the results and go with your instincts; or (5) other? Explain your decision.

Net Impact

Many of the surveys performed through the Internet are automatically edited and coded. As responses are input online into the computer, the server immediately examines the information and makes sure that respondents are providing acceptable responses. If problems occur, such as inconsistent responses or incomplete questionnaires, the server can be programmed to continue asking the problematic question until it is satisfied with the response.

Many Internet surveys provide respondents instant online access to the total tabulations. This may be done for a couple of reasons. One reason is to encourage the site visitor to respond to the survey. Total tabulations may not be available to the site visitor unless he or she completes the survey. They may also be encouraged to respond if they see the number of "hits" on the particular Web site, showing the popularity of the survey. Some sites publish the results online instantaneously to simply satisfy visitors' curiosity. In fact, the results of many studies about Internet usage are available online instantly to anyone interested in the findings.

On the Lighter Side—Parents Aren't So Bad After All, Say Teens

Those teenage years of kids are the times parents dread the most. It's a time when pimples, attitudes, and hormones rule ... or do they? A *USA Weekend* Teens & Parents survey found a generation of young people who actually like their parents and like the ways they are being raised. They felt that their parents understand them and that they can speak candidly to their parents about their problems. Here are some of the findings based on responses of more than 84,000 students in grades 6–12 (40% male, 60% female; 79% white, 8% black, 6% Hispanic, 3% multiracial, 2% Asian, 2% other; school type: 37% rural, 44% suburban, 19% urban):

- Four in five responded that their relationship with their parents has improved or remained the same over the past two years.
- Four in five indicated that one of their parents has told them he or she loves them in recent days.
- Three in four have told their parents they love them in recent days.
- Three in five eat dinner with their parents at least five nights a week.
- Four in five would confide in one or both parents if they had a serious problem.
- Four in five think their parents are similar to or cooler than their friends' parents.
- One in two felt that their parents were always supportive.
- Three in four believe that their parents understand the problems and situations they face as teens very or somewhat well.
- One in two give their parents a grade of A in raising them.

Sources: "Teens & parents USA WEEKEND survey results" and William Damon, "The gap generation," *USA Weekend* (April 29, 2001); http://www.usaweekend.com/01_issues/010429/010429teens.html, accessed October 10, 2005.

Chapter Summary

Preceding chapters focused on obtaining reliable data from individuals. In this chapter, you learned about preparing the data for analysis once it has been obtained.

A good data-preparation procedure follows five basic steps. The first step is editing. This involves checking survey data for completeness, legibility, consistency, and accuracy, and making minor adjustments to the data so that it can be properly coded and stored. Editing can be done on the same day the data are collected (field editing) or at a centralized location by an office staff once the data collection is completed (office editing).

For information to be useful, it must be accurate and in a format that users can understand. But many potential problems detract from the usefulness of the data. Some of these problems are (1) an unintended person completes the survey; (2) the survey is returned without being completed because the target respondent changed addresses, the respondent is no longer employed at the company, or the business is no longer in operation; (3) the handwriting on

the survey is illegible; (4) responses are incomplete; (5) the measuring instrument is damaged; (6) the respondent is confused by some of the questions; (7) the responses are the same for all questions, indicating that the respondent did not read the questions carefully; and (8) some responses were received after the cutoff date. Some of these problems can be handled by sending another wave of surveys, by coding nonresponses as "no valid response," or by eliminating unacceptable interview responses.

After the supplied data has been edited, it must be coded so that the computer can read and store it. Coding is the process of systematically and consistently assigning each response a numerical score. Data entry follows the coding process and is a vital part of data preparation. Today, all kinds of computer technologies can provide instant data entry. However, when computers are not used during data collection, the coded data must be keyed into a computer by data-entry operators or "keyboard operators" and stored on a diskette or CD.

Then the information is ready for analysis by a marketing researcher.

Following data entry, the data must be tabulated and the tabulations should be reviewed to ensure that all data is entered as correctly as possible. Frequency distributions help in this check by providing breakdowns of all groups in designated categories. Once tabulations have been checked, the researcher must determine the data analysis strategy.

Review Questions

1. What problems can occur during the editing process? How might they be handled?
2. What is the difference between office editing and field editing?
3. What is "coding"? How are unanswered questions coded?
4. How are open-ended questions coded?
5. What problems can result from precoded questionnaires?
6. What is a codebook used for?
7. How will data likely be entered into computers in the future?
8. Why use frequency distributions to review tabulations?

Practice Quiz

Note: You can find the correct answers to these questions by taking the quiz and then submitting your answers in the Online Edition. The program will automatically score your submission. If you miss a question, the program will provide the correct answer, a rationale for the answer, and the section number in the chapter where the topic is discussed.

1. Coding involves checking survey data for completeness, legibility, consistency, and accuracy.
   a. True
   b. False

2. Coding must follow editing.
   a. True
   b. False

3. A codebook provides instructions for coding survey data.
   a. True
   b. False

4. A useful coding system has coding categories that are mutually exclusive and the whole system is collectively exhaustive.
   a. True
   b. False

5. One of the least common data entry problems is the transposing of data such as entering "42" instead of "24."
   a. True
   b. False

6. When using a codebook, _____ indicates the variable to be coded.
   a. variable name
   b. variable code
   c. variable number
   d. variable question
   e. column number

7. When using a codebook, _____ indicates the name of the variable to be coded.
   a. variable code
   b. variable name
   c. variable question
   d. variable number
   e. column number

8. Which of the following data preparation steps comes first?
   a. Reviewing tabulations
   b. Entering data
   c. Editing
   d. Coding
   e. None of the above comes first.

9. _____ do not permit editing of the data to occur.
   a. Telephone interviews
   b. Personal interviews
   c. Internet surveys
   d. Mail surveys
   e. All of the above permit editing to occur.

10. Which of the following is *not* a potential characteristic of online surveys?
    a. The survey can be automatically edited and coded.
    b. There is instant online access to the total tabulations.
    c. There is access to the total tabulations only if the respondent answers the online questions.
    d. The number of "hits" can be shown at the survey Web site.
    e. All of the above are potential characteristics of online surveys.

EXHIBIT 12-9 | Survey of Customer Satisfaction

For statements 1–11, please use the following scale to rate your level of satisfaction with our restaurant.
Please circle the response that best describes your opinion.

1 = Totally agree	5 = Disagree
2 = Strongly agree	6 = Strongly disagree
3 = Agree	7 = Totally disagree
4 = Neither agree nor disagree	

1. The food tastes good.	1 2 3 4 5 6 7
2. The service is acceptable.	1 2 3 4 5 6 7
3. The prices are too high.	1 2 3 4 5 6 7
4. The restaurant's atmosphere is pleasant.	1 2 3 4 5 6 7
5. The restaurant's location is convenient for me.	1 2 3 4 5 6 7
6. The lighting is too bright.	1 2 3 4 5 6 7
7. The restaurant's temperature is comfortable.	1 2 3 4 5 6 7
8. I did not wait too long to get seated at a table.	1 2 3 4 5 6 7
9. The restaurant is not open enough hours each day.	1 2 3 4 5 6 7
10. My food was just the right temperature when it arrived at my table.	1 2 3 4 5 6 7
11. I will return for another visit to this restaurant.	1 2 3 4 5 6 7

Please provide the following background information.

12. Have you ever eaten at our restaurant before?	Yes	No
13. What is your gender?	Male	Female
14. Are you married?	Yes	No
15. Did you come to the restaurant alone?	Yes	No

Comments you would like to share:

_____

_____

Thinking Critically

1. You are responsible for manually entering data into a computer and your boss keeps asking you to work faster. You tell him that you are working as fast as you can, but he is not satisfied with your response. What suggestions can you give him to help speed up the work, besides hiring additional data-entry operators?

2. For the customer satisfaction survey shown in Exhibit 12.9, devise a codebook for the responses. Assume there will be 50 respondents.

3. Assume that the restaurant survey in question 2 gathered the following comments. Create appropriate response categories and then group comments by appropriate category.
   - I didn't like your menu selections.
   - Are you trying to cook us? The temperature was too hot in the restaurant!
   - The sun was shining directly in my eyes while I ate.
   - The tables are much too close to each other.
   - The food was soggy when I finally got it.
   - My compliments to the chef. The taste was scrumptious!
   - Great menu selection. Keep up the good work.
   - Why not offer some vegetarian selections on the menu?
   - I needed a high chair for my year-old son, and there was not one available.
   - My waitress was not nice. She must have had a bad day.
   - The price of my order was too high. I'll never come back until you drop your prices.
   - You need to offer more selections for children.
   - Why not offer senior citizen discounts?
   - You need to turn down the music. It was too loud in here.

Net Exercises

1. Several companies have powerful software to assist marketing researchers with data entry. Microtab Software can assist researchers with modules for data entry, manipulation, conversion, tabulation, and evaluation. Principia Products, Inc., is a leader in Windows-based Optical Mark Recognition, which provides complete data-entry solutions with its mix of office products. Pulse Train Technology, Ltd., is a British software company based in London that supplies the market research industry with data design, data collection, data manipulation, and data analysis. Visit these companies' Web sites and read about their data-entry capabilities. Principia Products and Pulse Train Technology allow you to try their product demos. Their Web site addresses are:
   - Microtab Software: http://www.microtab.com/software.html
   - Principia Products, Inc.: http://www.PrincipiaProducts.com/
   - Pulse Train Technology Ltd.: http://www.pulsetrain.com

2. Administer the questionnaire you created with Web-Surveyor (www.websurveyor.com), but this time to 10 people on the Internet. Then code the responses and tabulate the results. Discuss your experience or any problems you encountered.

Experiencing Marketing Research

Create a questionnaire inquiring about whether respondents believe using scare tactics in advertising to encourage people to buy home alarm systems is an acceptable practice. Make sure that your questionnaire contains at least five closed-ended questions and two open-ended questions, and then do the following:

1. Precode the questionnaire.
2. Create a codebook.
3. Administer the questionnaire to 20 friends.
4. Code the responses and create categories for the open-ended questions.
5. Discuss any problems you encountered with the responses.

Case 12-1

U.S. Census Leads the Way in Data Tabulation

The U.S. Census Bureau conducts a variety of censuses and surveys every month, quarter, and year. They gather important information on social and economic conditions in a country, including employment, housing, manufacturing, trade, and a variety of other topics from households and businesses. Today, researchers have the luxury of using super-quick and highly powerful computers to help them with data tabulations. No longer is it necessary to manually tabulate data, since computers can do it more efficiently. But think of the pains associated with data preparation in the 1800s, well before the advent of computer technology. A look at the early days of the U.S. Census Office can help you appreciate its struggles.

In 1790, the first U.S. census takers, called assistant U.S. marshals, visited each American household and asked the same questions: the name of the family head and the number of individuals living there who were free white males 16 years and older, free white males under the age of 16, free white females, slaves, and other persons. The answers were recorded on sheets of paper called schedules, on which a horizontal line represented a single household, and vertical columns represented the numbers of persons in each category. When the schedule was completed, the assistant marshals totaled each column and sent the form to the U.S. marshal, who consolidated the data for his district and forwarded that data to the Census Office in Washington, D.C. Three workers in the Census Office tabulated the enormous amount of statistics.

The task of data-gathering grew increasingly difficult as the population grew from about 4 million in 1790 to 40 million in 1870. The amount of data to be collected from each household grew as well. Census takers wanted to know the name, age, sex, race, occupation, value of real estate owned, value of personal estate, birthplace, whether parents were foreign-born, month of birth if born within the year, month of marriage if married within the year, and vast amounts of other personal data. A census taker, ridiculed in a cartoon that appeared in the *Saturday Evening Post* in 1860, says, "I jist want to know how many of yez is deaf, dumb, blind, insane, and idiotic—likewise how many convicts there is in the family—what all your ages are, especially the old woman and the young ladies—and how many dollars the old gentleman is worth!" In spite of people's feelings about census takers illustrated in this cartoon, their efforts resulted in vast amounts of information needing compilation and analysis. As the census tasks continued over the years, the population grew and the government sought increasingly more information. This presented an unprecedented challenge that required revolutionizing the data preparation and analysis processes.

It is not surprising that as the census became more difficult, the number of errors in data collection and tabulation increased. In fact, the American Statistical Association petitioned Congress for a revised and corrected edition of the 1840 census on the grounds that there were too many contradictions, and conclusions from the results would not be valid. To increase the efficiency of data tabulation, Charles W. Seaton, chief clerk of the census, invented the Seaton Device, consisting of a wood box into which were set two series of rollers: eight in a row at the top and seven in a row at the bottom. By threading a continuous roll of paper through the box, an operator could position eight lines adjacent to one another (for example, those that needed to be filled in with similar information, such as the age of the head of the household) and therefore could record data without having to spend time searching on the spreadsheet for the proper tally spot. Other tabulation devices followed suit, including an electrical tabulating machine and the punched-card tabulator. These inventions were all forerun-

ners of computer technology as we know it today, which has made data preparation a less intimidating process.

After all of its painful growth, the census data today are used by researchers to learn more about the target markets of their companies. The U.S. government uses it for two primary applications. First, census data may be used to determine eligibility for a particular federal aid program. Second, population data and its derivatives are used in formulas for distribution of many significant federal grant and other assistance programs.

Sources: "Are You in a Survey or Census," U.S. Census Bureau, retrieved from http://www.census.gov/epct/mso, August 29, 2006; Robert M. Lloyd, "Census 2000," *Business and Economic Review* 46, no. 4 (July–September 2000): 11–15; Keith S. Reid-Green, "The history of census tabulation," *Scientific American* (February 1989): 98–103.

Case Questions

1. Do you feel that it is the marketing manager's responsibility to ensure that data tabulation efforts are properly performed? Whose responsibility do you think it is at the Census Bureau?

2. How do you think the Internet has helped the U.S. government disseminate the information gathered by the Census Bureau?

Case 12-2

Offshore Data Entry

How hard can it be? A company receives a large amount of information and has an employee code it on a data sheet and enter the data into a spreadsheet—preparing it to be analyzed. It really doesn't take much training. This is why data entry is being performed throughout the world. It is big business, particularly in many less-developed countries (LDCs). But it comes at a cost. CareFirst BlueCross BlueShield of Owings Mills, Maryland, laid off 134 employees as it outsources claims data entry work. A positive result is that the outsourcing saves the company $7.6 million each year.

International subcontracting of data entry, referred to as "offshore data entry," is increasing. The data can be sent either online or through hard copy. Hardcopy in the form of paper documents, cards, diskettes, CDs, and audio recordings are sent overseas by air, ship, or courier. Hardcopy data are entered electronically onto diskettes or CDs, then shipped back to North America (in the case of Caribbean operations) for storage, printing on paper, or direct input into computers for analysis. Online data sent

to data-entry companies is often returned via online data transfer.

Offshore data entry began expanding in the 1980s with the development of personal computer systems and electronic links to mainframe systems. One major location of offshore U.S. data entry is in the Caribbean, mainly in Barbados, Jamaica, and the Dominican Republic. Other facilities are known to operate in China, India, Ireland, the Republic of Korea, the Philippines, and Singapore. In India, for example, System Support Services specializes in offshore data processing and data entry. The company employs more than 110 people and hosts a number of terminals and peripherals.

More recently, companies have begun using college students rather than outsourcing offshore firms for data entry. For example, DOCX, a company specializing in providing lien releases, assignments, and county recording information and solutions, launched a Students at Work program. This program is designed to use American college students to perform data entry services from their dormitory rooms. The company started using college students over a year ago to perform rudimentary data entry services from remote locations. DOCX also contracted with overseas resources from India and the Philippines. Lorraine O'Reilly Brown, president of DOCX, praised college students for their quality work and the value they provide her company. She further stated that "Security concerns, communications, and clients' desire to use domestic resources for their processing were all factors in establishing the program." According to DOCX, the Students at Work program provides data entry services to the lending community at rates comparable to the overseas market.

Sources: "CareFirst to Outsource Data-Entry Work," *Managed Care Outlook,* vol. 18 no. 3 (February 1, 2005), p. 12. Ruth Pearson and Swasti Mitter, "Employment and working conditions of low-skilled information-processing workers in less developed countries," *International Labour Review* 132, no 1 (January–February 1993): 49–

64; System Support Services, http://www. gatewaytoindia. com/sss/index.html, accessed July 29, 2005; Ted Cornwell, "An alternative to off-shoring helps servicers manage data entry," National Mortgage News 29, no. 7 (October 25, 2004): 29.

Case Questions

1. If offshore data entry is performed by individuals in developing nations, should clients be concerned about the quality of data entry? What problems might occur?

2. How may advances in computer technology affect the usage of offshore data-entry personnel?

3. Which method do you think can provide higher data quality—offshore data entry or using college students? And why?

Notes

1. RT Nelson Company, "Services," http://www.rtnielson.com/pages/services.shtml. Accessed July 24, 2005.

2. Tab House, web page, "Your complete survey tabulation resource," http://www.tabhouse.com/nfdentry.htm. Accessed July 29, 2005.

3. Alan T. Shao, *An Empirical Study of the Structures, Strategies, and Environments of U.S. Multinational Advertising Agency Affiliates* (Ann Arbor, MI: UMI Dissertation Information Service, 1989), 155.

Descriptive Analysis

Chapter Thirteen

Source: © 2007 JupiterImages Corporation.

Key Terms

arithmetic mean   (p. 312)

array   (p. 317)

average   (p. 312)

coefficient of skewness (S_k)   (p. 319)

coefficient of variation (V)   (p. 319)

correlation and regression analysis   (p. 311)

descriptive analysis   (p. 311)

difference analysis   (p. 311)

frequency   (p. 317)

frequency array   (p. 317)

frequency distribution   (p. 317)

inferential analysis   (p. 311)

kurtosis   (p. 319)

leptokurtic curve   (p. 321)

mean   (p. 312)

measures of central tendency   (p. 312)

median   (p. 313)

mode   (p. 315)

multivariate analysis   (p. 311)

normal curve   (p. 321)

platykurtic curve   (p. 321)

range   (p. 317)

raw data   (p. 317)

skewness   (p. 319)

standard deviation   (p. 318)

Learning Objectives

After studying this chapter, you will be able to:

- Explain the different types of statistical analysis techniques.
- Discuss the importance of descriptive statistics.
- Describe and calculate several measures of central tendency.

- Explain what a frequency distribution is and discuss several types of frequency distributions.
- Determine the proper descriptive statistic to use.

GET THIS

Web site Describes Religious Order Worldwide

The Adherents.com collection of religious adherent statistics has over 46,000 adherent statistic citations, for over 4,200 different faith groups, covering all countries of the world. One of the more intriguing statistics reported at the site is the percentage of major religions of the world. As shown in Exhibit 13-1 below, they have summarized their data to make it easily understandable. They are not interested in passing judgment about any particular religion. Nor do they attempt to make inferences from the data. They are simply describing the religious bodies worldwide.

> **EXHIBIT 13-1** | Percentage of Major Religions of the World

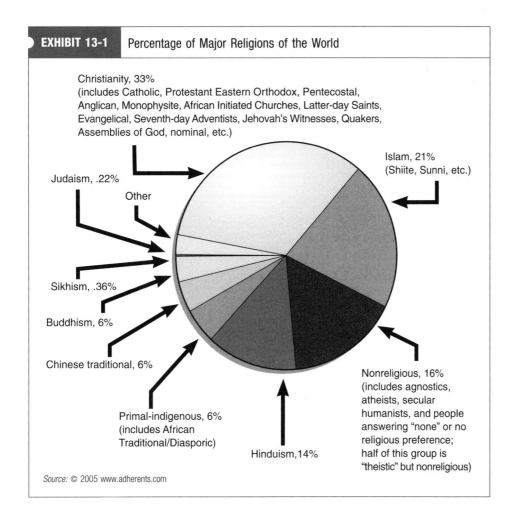

Christianity, 33%
(includes Catholic, Protestant Eastern Orthodox, Pentecostal, Anglican, Monophysite, African Initiated Churches, Latter-day Saints, Evangelical, Seventh-day Adventists, Jehovah's Witnesses, Quakers, Assemblies of God, nominal, etc.)

Islam, 21%
(Shiite, Sunni, etc.)

Judaism, .22%

Other

Sikhism, .36%

Buddhism, 6%

Chinese traditional, 6%

Nonreligious, 16%
(includes agnostics, atheists, secular humanists, and people answering "none" or no religious preference; half of this group is "theistic" but nonreligious)

Primal-indigenous, 6%
(includes African Traditional/Diasporic)

Hinduism, 14%

Source: © 2005 www.adherents.com

According to their estimates, Christianity comprises one-third of the world's religious sector. This group is followed by Islam, Hinduism, nonreligious, Buddhism, Chinese traditional religion, and primal-indigenous. The raw numbers for the top 10 religions break down this way:

1. Christianity: 2.1 billion

2. Islam: 1.3 billion

3. Secular/Nonreligious/Agnostic/Atheist: 1.1 billion

4. Hinduism: 900 million

5. Chinese traditional religion: 394 million

6. Buddhism: 376 million

7. Primal-indigenous: 300 million

8. African traditional and diasporic: 100 million

9. Sikhism: 23 million

10. Juche: 19 million

The adherent counts presented on the Web site are estimates of the number of people who have at least a minimal level of self-identification as adherents of the religion. Levels of participation vary within all groups. These numbers tend toward the high end of reasonable worldwide estimates. They state that valid arguments can be made for different figures, but if the same criteria are used for all groups, the relative order should be the same.

The numbers of adherents in a faith group that were used for this site were derived using five main methods:

- *Organizational reporting:* Religious bodies (such as churches or denominations) are asked how many adherents or members they have.

- *Census records:* Many countries periodically conduct a comprehensive household-by-household census. Religious preference is often a question included in these census counts.

- *Polls and surveys:* Statistical sampling using surveys and polls is used to determine affiliation based on religious self-identification.

- *Estimates based on indirect data:* Many adherent counts are only obtained by estimates based on indirect data rather than direct questioning or directly from membership roles.

- *Fieldwork:* To count some small groups, or to count the number of adherents a larger group has within a specific geographical area, researchers sometimes do ''fieldwork'' to count adherents. This is usually the only way to count members of small tribal groups or semi-secretive, publicity-shy sects.

Sources: Adherents Web site, ''Major religions of the world ranked by number of adherents,'' http://www.adherents.com/Religions_By_ Adherents. html, accessed August 1, 2005; Charles Bowen, ''Holy cow! Religion site hits a homer,'' *Editor & Publisher* 133, no. 33 (August 14, 2000): I18.

Now Ask Yourself

- What does this story have to do with ''descriptive statistics''—the essence of this chapter?

- Considering the data collection methods, are the statistics trustworthy?

- Who do you think Adherents.com is targeting their Web site to?

As the article in the ''Get This'' feature illustrates, statistics are used by all kinds of groups throughout the world— including the religious sector. There are easy-to-understand statistics, and then there are more complex statistics. The religious site Adherents.com chose to simplify the figures and make them as easy as possible to analyze and understand. In this chapter, we continue our progress toward effective data analysis by introducing you to some important statistical analysis techniques. We will focus on descriptive statistics—the most basic of analysis techniques. Subsequent chapters will concentrate on more advanced statistical techniques used by researchers.

13-1 Statistical Analysis Techniques

Researchers can use statistics to describe samples or make inferences about populations by using sample data. They can also use statistics by looking at one, two, or multiple variables at a time. The types of analyses used by marketing researchers include *descriptive, inferential, difference, correlation and regression,* and *multivariate*. Each of these statistics will be briefly discussed in this chapter. Chapters 14–17 will discuss each of them—except descriptive statistics—in more detail.

Descriptive analysis is statistics used by researchers to summarize sample data. The purpose of descriptive statistics is not to draw any conclusions or inferences about a population from the sample if the statistical study deals with sample data. The intent is not to make a prediction based on the data. Descriptive statistics are often portrayed by different shapes of frequency distributions (skewness and kurtosis, both discussed later in the chapter). Descriptive data also take the form of measures of central tendency and measures of dispersion.

descriptive analysis Statistics used by researchers to summarize sample data.

Inferential analysis (*hypothesis testing*) is statistics that permit researchers to draw inferences from sample data. To be specific, inferential statistics includes the methods of generalizing, estimating, or predicting the characteristics of a population or universe based on a sample. Hypothesis testing is a method of inferential statistics. Given sample data, researchers can draw conclusions about a population. If inferential statistics were not possible, it would be necessary to obtain information from the census—that is, the entire population. Inferential analysis involves hypothesis testing that estimates population values based on sample information. This will be the focus of Chapter 14.

inferential analysis Statistics that permit researchers to draw inferences from sample data.

Difference analysis assesses whether two groups or market segments are truly different from each other. Many times companies must segment the whole market into several segments. However, without knowing the differences between the segments, it would be difficult and meaningless for the companies to do the segmentation. For example, a company may attempt to introduce a new type of toothpaste especially developed for women. However, if women and men are not different with respect to their perceptions, use patterns, and needs for toothpaste, it would be meaningless to introduce a toothpaste just for women. Difference analysis enables us to test the differences between groups and therefore help managers to make the right decisions. Chapter 15 will cover this topic.

difference analysis Statistics assessing whether two groups or market segments are truly different from each other.

Correlation and regression analysis tests if and how variables are related to each other. Correlation analysis involves the test of relationships between two variables, and regression analysis can include more than two variables. This topic will be the focus of Chapter 16.

correlation and regression analysis Statistics that test if and how variables are related to each other.

Multivariate analysis has been used extensively in the physical, social, and medical sciences. In a broad sense, it refers to any simultaneous analysis of *more than two* variables. Many times, multivariate techniques are a means of performing in one analysis what used to take multiple analyses using univariate techniques (analysis of single-variable distributions). This topic will be discussed throughout Chapter 17.

multivariate analysis Statistics that refers to any simultaneous analysis of more than two variables.

13-2 Descriptive Analysis

The focus of this chapter is on descriptive statistics. As the name indicates, this type of statistics describes sample data and often leads to subsequent analyses. To better understand descriptive statistics, consider sample means and standard deviations. These types of descriptive statistics give researchers an indication of the norm and variability of a target population, but they do not give researchers the opportunity to draw conclusions about the population based on the drawn sample. Some questions that can be addressed through descriptive statistics include:

- What is the average income of the sample?
- How old is the average employee in Company X?
- How different are the ages in Company X?
- How spread out is the income data that has been drawn as a sample of the population?

Descriptive statistics can be categorized into three groups. The first group deals with the central tendency of the variable. This may be represented by the mean, median, or mode. The second group represents dispersion. This can be estimated by using the range, variation (or standard deviation), and the coefficient of variation. The third group represents the shape of the distribution and is measured using skewness or kurtosis. We will discuss each of these groups.

13-3 Measures of Central Tendency

average A single value that is typical or representative of a group of numbers.

An **average** is a single value that is typical or representative of a group of numbers. For example, the average U.S. male is 5 feet 9 inches tall and weighs 181 pounds. (See Research Realities 13-1 for more data about the average U.S. male.) The values included in a group of data usually vary in magnitude; some of them are small and some are large. A representative value for a group of numbers is normally neither the smallest nor the largest value, but is somewhere in the middle of the group. Thus an average is frequently referred to as a measure of central tendency. The most commonly known **measures of central tendency** in statistics are the *arithmetic mean,* the *median,* and the *mode.*

measures of central tendency Measures indicating the central tendency of a variable. The most common types are the arithmetic mean, the median, and the mode.

arithmetic mean The sum of values divided by the number of values.

mean An average calculated as the sum of the values in a data set divided by the number of values in the set; one measure of central tendency.

13-3a Arithmetic Mean

The **arithmetic mean,** or simply the **mean,** is the most commonly used measure of central tendency covered in this chapter. It is computed as follows:

$$\text{Mean} = \frac{\text{Sum of values}}{\text{Number of values}}$$

$$\bar{X} = \frac{\sum X}{n}$$

where

$X =$ the set of values, or X-variable

$n =$ the number of values in the set

$\sum =$ "the sum of " (Greek letter sigma)

$\bar{X} =$ mean of X-variable, called "X bar"

The bar on the top of a letter usually represents "the arithmetic mean of."

Research Realities 13-1 *Who Is Joe Average?*

When people describe a man as "an average guy," what do they mean? Some people would interpret it to mean that he is like all the other guys. But really the "average" man can be characterized much more specifically than that. The *Men's Health* magazine used reports, surveys, and reams of marketing data to compile the profile of the average guy. Joe Average . . .

- Is 5 feet 9.1 inches tall
- Weighs 181 pounds

- Can run 1.5 mile in 12.5 minutes
- Can bench press 93% of his body weight
- Has the biggest decade-to-decade jump in body fat from his 20s (16.6%) to 30s (19.7%)
- Makes $39,429 annually
- Has gulped 11 beers in the last seven days

Sources: "The shape you're in," *Men's Health* 19, no. 4 (May 2004): 162; "Are you fiscally fit?" *Men's Health* 20, no. 3 (April 2005): 158.

Consider Example 13-1.

Example 13-1

Suppose the miles traveled by five students going to Shelton Park Elementary School from their homes is 1, 4, 10, 8, and 10 miles, as shown in Exhibit 13-2.

EXHIBIT 13-2	Miles Traveled by Students to Shelton Park Elementary School	
	Students	**Miles Traveled (X)**
	A	1
	B	4
	C	10
	D	8
	E	10
	Total	33

The mean of the miles traveled by the five students would be calculated as follows:

Solution:

$$\sum X = 1 + 4 + 10 + 8 + 10 = 33$$
$$n = 5 \text{ (students)}$$
$$\bar{X} = \frac{33}{5} = 6.6 \text{ miles}$$

The major characteristic of the mean is that *the computation of the arithmetic mean is based on all values of a set of data.* The value of every item in the data thus affects the value of the mean. When some extreme values are included in the data, the mean may become less representative of the entire values. For example, the mean of values 1, 2, 4, and 93 is 25. The mean is not close to any one of the four values. The mean of values 24, 25, 25, and 26 is also 25. It is obvious that the mean 25 is less representative of the group of values 1, 2, 4, and 93 than of the latter group of values.

Because the mean is computed as sum of values/number of values, *if any two of the three terms in the expression (mean, sum of values, and number of values) are known, the third one can be determined.* For example, if the mean is 5 and the number of values is 8, the sum of the values in the data can be determined, or 5 × 8 = 40.

13-3b Median

The **median** is another measure of central tendency in statistics. It is the value of the middle item when the numbers are arranged in order of magnitude. To find the median,

median The value of the middle number in an array; one measure of central tendency.

the values are arranged in an array, either from the smallest to the largest or vice versa. Then the middle value is located; that is, the number of values above the median is the same as the number of values below the median. The methods used to locate the median differ slightly, depending on whether the array has an even or odd number of values.

For an Odd Number of Values

If the number of values in a data set is odd, the median is determined in the following manner:

• Arrange the raw data in an array.

• Locate the middle item as the median. It is at the position numbered $\left(\frac{n+1}{2}\right)$.

Consider Example 13-2.

Example 13-2

Find the median of the values 1, 4, 10, 8, and 10, representing the miles traveled by five students.

Solution: The values are first arranged in an array according to their magnitude, from the smallest to the largest, as follows:

Item	Miles Traveled
1st	1
2nd	4
3rd (middle)	8
4th	10
5th	10

The third item $\left(\frac{n+1}{2} = \frac{5+1}{2} = \frac{6}{2} = 3\right)$ is the middle item. Thus the median is equal to 8 miles. There are two items (1 and 4) below the median and the same number of items (10 and 10) above the median.

For an Even Number of Values

If the number of values in a data set is even, there is no true median, since no value in the array has an equal number of values above and below it. The median is thus assumed to be halfway between the two middle values in the array. It is the midpoint of the values at the positions numbered $\left(\frac{n}{2}\right)$ and $\left(\frac{n+2}{2}\right)$. Consider Example 13-3.

Example 13-3

Find the median of the values $9, $6, $2, $5, $18, and $12.

Solution: The given values are first arranged in an array.

Item	Values
1st	$2
2nd	5
3rd	6
Middle	7.5 (median)
4th	9
5th	12
6th	18

The median is the midpoint of the values of 6 and 9, or

$$\text{Median} = \frac{6+9}{2} = \$7.5$$

EXHIBIT 13-3	Deviation from the Median	
Value (Miles)	Deviation from the Median (8)	Deviation from Selected Value (6)
1	7 (= 1 − 8)	5 (= 1 − 6)
4	4	2
8	0	2
10	2	4
10	2	4
Total (disregarding signs)	15	17

Major Characteristics of the Median

The following are some important characteristics of the median:

- *The median is a positional average.* It is not affected by extreme values as is the mean, since the median is not computed from all values. For example, the median of values 4, 5, and 6 is 5, and the median of values 1, 5, and 1,000 is also 5.

- *The median is not defined algebraically as is the arithmetic mean.* For example, if the median is 8 and the number of values is 5, the sum of the five values is not necessarily 40 (8 × 5). Note that the sum of values in our earlier example (for an odd number of values) is 33 (or 1 + 4 + 10 + 8 + 10 = 33), and the median is 8.

- *The median, in some cases, cannot be computed exactly as can the mean.* When the number of items included in a series of data is even, the median is determined approximately as the mid-point of the two middle items.

- *The median is centrally located.* The absolute sum (disregarding positive and negative signs) of the deviations of the individual values from the median is minimum. In other words, the absolute sum of the deviations (or the sum of the distances) of the individual values from a value *other than the median* will exceed (or at least be equal to) the absolute sum of the deviations from the median. For example, as shown Exhibit 13-3, the absolute sum of the deviations from the median 8 in our earlier example is 15, whereas the absolute sum of the deviations from the arbitrarily selected value 6 is 17 as shown below. The difference between the two sums is 2 miles (= 17 − 15).

13-3c Mode

The **mode** of a set of values is the value that occurs most frequently in the set. If a value is selected at random from the set, a modal value is the most likely value to be selected. Thus the mode is regarded as the most typical value in a series of data. That is, it is the number that occurs most often in a group of numbers. When there are two or more modes in a set of data, the data is called *bimodal* or *multimodal*. The mode for a few values can be obtained by inspection, as illustrated in Example 13-4.

mode The value that occurs most frequently in a set of numbers; one measure of central tendency.

Example 13-4

Find the mode of the values 1, 4, 10, 8, and 10, representing the miles traveled by five students.

Solution: The mode of the five values is 10. The value 10 occurs twice, but each of the other values—1, 4, and 8—occurs only once.

Major Characteristics of the Mode

There are a few important characteristics of the mode.

- *The mode is the value with the highest frequency in the set of values.* It represents more items than any other value could represent in the set. The mode is not computed from all values and is not defined algebraically as is the mean. For example, if the mode is 10 and the number of values in the data is 5, the sum of the values is not necessarily 50 (or 10×5). Note that the sum of values 1, 4, 8, 10, and 10 is 33.

- *The mode, by definition, is not affected by extreme values.* For example, the mode of values 1, 5, 5, and 8 is 5, and the mode of values 1, 5, 5, and 800 is also 5.

- *The mode of a set of discrete data is easy to compute.* However, the true mode of a set of continuous data, strictly speaking, may never exist. The values of items included in continuous data are seldom exactly alike before rounding. For example, the heights of a group of persons may be measured as 5.601, 5.602, 5.608,…feet, and no two persons are exactly the same height. Thus, it is doubtful if there is a perfect method to compute the value of the mode for continuous data.

- *The value of the mode may be greatly affected by the method of designating the class intervals.* For example, there is no mode in the following group of 8 values, since each value occurs only once:

1, 2, 3, 5, 6, 7, 8, and 12

When the same values are grouped into the different types of class intervals, as given in distributions A, B, and C in Exhibit 13-4, the value of the mode for each distribution is different from the others.

A summary of the major characteristics of mean, median, and mode is shown in Exhibit 13-5.

EXHIBIT 13-4	Classification and Mode				
Distribution A		**Distribution B**		**Distribution C**	
Class Intervals	**Frequency**	**Class Intervals**	**Frequency**	**Class Intervals**	**Frequency**
1–2	2	1–4	3	1–5	4
3–4	1	5–8	4	6–10	3
5–6	2	9–12	1	11–15	1
7–8	2				
9–10	0				
11–12	1				
Total	8		8		8

EXHIBIT 13-5	Summary of the Key Characteristics of Three Measures of Central Tendency		
Characteristics	**Mean ($\bar{X}$)**	**Median (Md)**	**Mode (Mo)**
Computation based on	Every value	Middle value	Value with highest frequency
Affected by extreme values	Greatest	No (affected by middle items only)	No
Algebraic manipulation	Yes	No (position)	No (frequency)
Comparison of answers to same data	May be larger or smaller than M_d and M_o	Typically between $\bar{X}$ and M_o	May be larger or smaller than M_d and $\bar{X}$

13-4 Measures of Dispersion (Variability)

Whereas central tendency (i.e., mean, median, and mode) reflects the typical responses, dispersion (variability) describes the dissimilarity of the responses. Typical measures of variability include frequency distribution, range, and standard deviation and variance. Frequency distribution can be used for any type of scales, but range and standard deviation and variance are calculated based on interval and ratio scales.

13-4a Frequency Distribution

Generally, when a group of collected data consists of only a few items, there may be no need for organization. The collected data that has not been organized numerically is called **raw data.** However, a large group of numerical data should be organized to facilitate statistical analysis. The data may first be arranged according to ascending or descending order of magnitude, called an **array.** Thus the values 4, 6, 2, 9, 8, 4, 8, and 8 are raw data that can be arranged as an array: 2, 4, 4, 6, 8, 8, 8, 9. There are repeating values in the array. When repeating values are shown, the arrangement is then called a **frequency array.** The number of times a value is repeated is called the **frequency.**[1] A frequency array may be constructed by using tally marks, as shown in Exhibit 13-6.

By grouping the values into several classes based on quantity and showing the frequency of values for each class, a more compact tabular presentation will result. A table showing data grouped by quantity and the frequency for each group is called a **frequency distribution,** as shown in Exhibit 13-7.

raw data Collected data that have not been organized numerically.

array Data arranged in ascending or descending order of magnitude.

frequency array An array of values in which repeated values are shown.

frequency The number of times a value is repeated.

frequency distribution A table showing data grouped by quantity and the frequency for each group.

range The difference between the lowest and the highest values in a set of numbers.

13-4b Range

The **range** of a group of values is the difference between the lowest and the highest values, or

$$R = X_n - X_1$$

where R = range, X_n = the highest value, and X_1 = the lowest value.

EXHIBIT 13-6	Frequency Array	
Value	**Tally**	**Frequency**
2	/	1
4	//	2
6	/	1
8	///	3
9	/	1
		Total: 8 values

EXHIBIT 13-7	Frequency Distribution
Class Interval	**Frequency**
1–3	1
4–6	3
7–9	4
	Total: 8 values

Consider Example 13-5.

Example 13-5

Find the range of the values 1, 4, 8, 10, and 10.

Solution: The highest value is 10 and the lowest value is 1. Therefore, $R = 10 - 1 = 9$.

13-4c Standard Deviation and Variance

standard deviation Square root of the arithmetic mean of the individual deviations squared; the most common measure of dispersion.

The standard deviation and variance are the most popular measures of variability. They assess the spread (variance) in the data. The **standard deviation** of a set of values is the square root of the arithmetic mean of the individual deviations squared. The procedure for computing the standard deviation for ungrouped data is as follows:

1. Find the arithmetic mean of the given data, $\bar{X}$.
2. Find the deviation of each value from the arithmetic mean, or $X - \bar{X}$.
3. Square each deviation to make it positive, or $(X - \bar{X})^2$.
4. Find the sum of the deviations squared, or $\sum(X - \bar{X})^2$.
5. Find the variance (s^2) by dividing the sum by the number of values minus 1 or $(n - 1)$.

$$s^2 = \frac{\sum(X - \bar{X})^2}{n - 1}$$

6. Extract the square root of the variance to get the standard deviation (s).

$$s = \sqrt{\frac{\sum(X - \bar{X})^2}{n - 1}}$$

Consider Example 13-6.

Example 13-6

Find the standard deviation of the values 2, 3, 5, 7, and 10.

Solution: First calculate the deviations from the mean and square each of them, as shown in Exhibit 13-8.

EXHIBIT 13-8	Calculating Variance and Standard Deviation	
Values	**Deviations ($X - \bar{X}$)**	**Deviations Squared**
2	−3.4	11.56
3	−2.4	5.76
5	−0.4	0.16
7	1.6	2.56
10	4.6	21.16
$\bar{X} = \frac{27}{5} = 5.4$	$\sum(X - \bar{X}) = 0$	$\sum(X - \bar{X})^2 = 41.20$

Variance $s^2 = \dfrac{\sum(X - \bar{X})^2}{n - 1} = \dfrac{41.20}{5 - 1} = 10.30$

Standard deviation $s = \sqrt{10.30} = 3.21$

EXHIBIT 13-9	Mean and Standard Deviation	
Student Classification	**Average Weight ($\bar{X}$) (in Pounds)**	**Standard Deviation (s) (in Pounds)**
Elementary	50	13.2
College	200	40

The **coefficient of variation (V)** is a commonly used measure of dispersion expressed in a relative value. It is the standard deviation divided by the arithmetic mean, or simply

$$V = \frac{s}{\bar{X}}$$

Assume that the standard deviation and mean of college students and elementary students are as shown in Exhibit 13-9.

The coefficient of variation of the weights of the college students is

$$V = \frac{40}{200} = 0.20 \text{ or } 20\%$$

The coefficient of variation of the weights of the elementary students is

$$V = \frac{13.2}{50} = 0.264 \text{ or } 26.4\%$$

The relative dispersion of the weights of the elementary school students is larger than that of the weights of the college students, although the raw dispersion is much smaller for the elementary school students (i.e., 13.2 vs. 40 pounds).

13-5 Measures of Shapes of Distributions

In addition to the averages and dispersions, two other measures are used in describing the characteristics of a group of data. These measures are *skewness* and *kurtosis*. They are especially useful in describing the shapes of frequency distributions. A measure of **skewness** indicates the direction of an asymmetrical distribution, either leaning toward higher values or lower values. A measure of **kurtosis** indicates the relative peakedness or flatness of the curve according to the frequency distribution. The kurtosis of a normal distribution is zero. Distributions can have either sharp, high peaks, called "leptokurtic," or they can be non-peaked and relatively flat, called "platykurtic."

13-5a Measure of Skewness

In a symmetrical unimodal frequency distribution, the values of the mean ($\bar{X}$), median (M_d), and mode (M_o) will coincide under the frequency curve; that is, $\bar{X} = M_d = M_o$. When a frequency distribution is asymmetrical, the three values depart from each other. The more the mean departs from the mode, the greater the skewness. As shown in Exhibit 13-10, the frequency curve may skew either to the right side on the X-scale (positively skewed) or to the left side on the X-scale (negatively skewed). In either case, the median is between the mode and the mean. When the difference between the mean and the mode is multiplied by three and then divided by the standard deviation, the quotient is called a **coefficient of skewness (S_k)** and is used for measuring the degree of skewness, or

$$S_k = \frac{3(\bar{X} - M_o)}{s}$$

coefficient of variation (V) The most commonly used measure of dispersion expressed in a relative value. It is the standard deviation divided by the arithmetic mean.

skewness The direction of an asymmetrical distribution, either leaning toward higher values or lower values.

kurtosis The relative peakedness or flatness of the curve according to the frequency distribution.

coefficient of skewness (S_k) The quotient that results when the difference between the mean and the mode is multiplied by three and then is divided by the standard deviation.

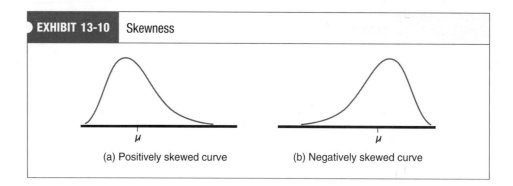

EXHIBIT 13-10 | Skewness

(a) Positively skewed curve   (b) Negatively skewed curve

It should be noted that this coefficient has extreme possible values of $+3$ and -3, where skewness is maximized. Values closer to 0 connote lower levels of skewness and a greater degree of symmetry.

Consider Example 13-7.

Example 13-7

Calculate the coefficient of skewness of the distribution of miles traveled by 20 students in coming to National University, shown in Exhibit 13-11.

EXHIBIT 13-11 | Calculating the Coefficient of Skewness

Miles Traveled (*X*)	Number of Students (*f*)	Total Miles Traveled (*fX*)	*X(fX)*
1	2	2	2
3	5	15	45
5	4	20	100
7	8	56	392
9	1	9	81
	$\sum f = n = 20$	$\sum(fX) = 102$	$\sum fX^2 = 620$

Solution:

$$\bar{X} = \frac{\sum(fX)}{n} = \frac{102}{20} = 5.1 \text{ miles}$$

$$M_o = 7$$

$$s = \sqrt{\frac{\sum fX^2}{n} - (\bar{X})^2} = \sqrt{\frac{620}{20} - \left(\frac{102}{20}\right)^2} = 2.23 \text{ miles}$$

$$S_k = \frac{3(\bar{X} - M_o)}{s} = \frac{3(5.1 - 7)}{2.23} = -2.56$$

Since the coefficient is a negative value, the distribution is skewed to the left, or toward smaller values on the X-scale. The negative value is close to an extreme value of -3, indicating a large degree of negative skewness.

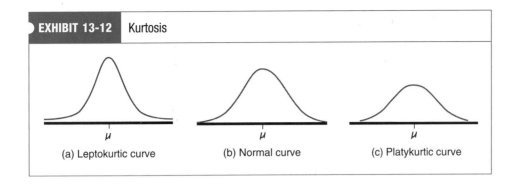

EXHIBIT 13-12	Kurtosis

(a) Leptokurtic curve   (b) Normal curve   (c) Platykurtic curve

13-5b Measure of Kurtosis

In describing a frequency distribution, a person can use (1) an average to show the typical value or the central tendency in the distribution; (2) a measure of dispersion to show the variation of values either within certain values (such as the range and the quartile deviation) or around an average of the distribution (that is, the average deviation and the standard deviation); and (3) a measure of skewness to show the direction of the distribution—either skewed to the higher values (the right side on the X-scale) or to the lower values (the left side on the X-scale). The fourth device in describing the frequency distribution is the measure of kurtosis, which indicates the relative peakedness or flatness of the curve.

A simple method of finding the size of the distribution's tails is to examine the shape of the frequency curve. Exhibit 13-12 shows three types of curves: (a) the **leptokurtic curve,** a high peak distribution, which has a fatter tail than the corresponding normal distribution; (b) the **normal curve;** and (c) the **platykurtic curve,** a relatively flat distribution, which has a thinner tail than the corresponding normal distribution. It is assumed that the three distributions represented by the curves are symmetrical and have the same means and the same dispersion as measured by the ranges.

leptokurtic curve A sharp, high-peaked curve according to the frequency distribution.

normal curve A symmetrical, bell-shaped curve that has almost all of its values within ±3 standard deviations from its mean.

platykurtic curve A nonpeaked, relatively flat curve according to the frequency distribution.

13-6 Choosing the Right Descriptive Statistic

Which descriptive statistic to use largely depends on the scales used in the measures. If nominal data—numbers employed to simply identify or label objects—is used, then the only feasible options are the mode and frequency distributions. When interval data is used, means and standard deviations make the most sense. And when ordinal data is used, the median is typically used. But oftentimes, researchers will run frequency distributions to take a broad look at the data. Exhibit 13-13 summarizes the appropriate descriptive analysis for each circumstance.

EXHIBIT 13-13	Measurement Scales and Descriptive Analysis		
	Nominal Scale	**Ordinal Scale**	**Interval/Ratio Scale**
Central Tendency	Mode	Median	Mean
Dispersion (Variability)	Frequency distribution	Frequency distribution	Standard deviation and variance

Decision Time!

You, the marketing manager at a large computer firm, have been under a lot of stress lately. You're not very comfortable reading numbers, but the decline in your company's bottom line is clear. A lapse in memory caused you to ask your marketing researcher to provide a summary of data to give you the latest customer satisfaction information. But your statistical shortcomings will become obvious if you tell your marketing researcher you don't understand the descriptive statistics presented to you. What are you going to do to overcome your problem?

Net Impact

The Internet is not going to be much help to researchers when calculating descriptive statistics, except when gathering data. We've noted in previous chapters that the Internet is cost- and time-efficient when collecting information, but its analytical ability is limited. If you are still unclear about any part of descriptive statistics, the Internet can be used to search for additional explanations of the concepts introduced in this chapter.

On the Lighter Side—Surprising Findings about Males

The question concerning "Who and what is the modern man?" was raised by AskMen.com on their Great Male Survey. They attempted to define modern men and get an idea of who they are. Their findings were less than predictable. They claimed that the typical perceptions of men that are often seen in the media were totally off base. Instead they found that most men are conservative and look for a balanced lifestyle between work and family. From their astounding 72,000 respondents and over 2 million answers, here are a few of their findings:

- To "Which of the following best describes your grooming approach?" 76% stated, "Just the basics: haircut, shower, and shave."
- To "Are moral standards in business and society on the decline?" 68% stated, "Yes, I wish we could go back to when a handshake meant something."
- To "How many times a month do you visit a strip club?" 87% responded "0 times," and 13% stated "1 to 5 times a month."
- To "Which statement best reflects your opinion on men's rights?" 69% of men responded that they get the short end of the stick when it comes to divorce, alimony, and child custody.
- To "What is the best topic to discuss on a first date?" 83% stated, "Her interests (not my interests), current events, or politics."
- To "If there was no chance your partner would find out, would you cheat on her?" 65% stated that they would not.
- To "Do you believe in the institution of marriage?" 70% stated strongly yes.
- To "What method of contraception do you use?" 18% stated, "None at all."
- To "How do you feel about your sex life overall?" 60% stated, "I wish I had more variety and more sex in general."
- To "If you had insider information on a stock, what would you do?" 57% stated, "Act on it."

Source: "Great Male Survey Results" AskMen.com Solutions. Reprinted with permission.

Chapter Summary

This chapter focuses on descriptive statistics—statistics used by researchers to summarize sample data—but other types of statistics are introduced. Inferential statistics—statistics that permit researchers to draw inferences from sample data—will be discussed in subsequent chapters. Descriptive statistics can be categorized into three groups. The first group is the most commonly known measures of central tendency in statistics—the arithmetic mean, median, and mode. The second group represents dispersion, which can be estimated by using the range, variance, standard deviation, and coefficient of variation.

The third group represents the shape of the distribution and is measured using skewness and kurtosis. Skewness indicates the direction of an asymmetric distribution, and kurtosis indicates the relative peakedness or flatness of the curve according to the frequency distribution. A high peak distribution is known as "leptokurtic," and a relatively flat distribution is known as "platykurtic." The normal distribution is a frequency distribution represented graphically by a bell-shaped curve that is symmetrical about the mean.

When trying to decide which descriptive statistic to use, researchers must consider whether the data is nominal, ordinal, interval, or ratio. Sometimes researchers use frequency distributions to take a broad look at the data.

Review Questions

1. Name and briefly explain the major statistical analysis techniques.

2. What are the differences between a mean, median, and mode?

3. What are the popular measures of variability?

4. What is a coefficient of variation, and how is it calculated?

5. What is the difference between skewness and kurtosis?

6. How can a researcher decide which descriptive statistic to use?

Practice Quiz

Note: You can find the correct answers to these questions by taking the quiz and then submitting your answers in the Online Edition. The program will automatically score your submission. If you miss a question, the program will provide the correct answer, a rationale for the answer, and the section number in the chapter where the topic is discussed.

1. Descriptive analysis is statistics that researchers use to summarize sample data.
   a. True
   b. False

2. Multivariate statistics are statistics used when a researcher investigates the relationship between one independent variable and one dependent variable.
   a. True
   b. False

3. Kurtosis specifies the direction of an asymmetrical distribution, either leaning toward higher values or lower values.
   a. True
   b. False

4. A platykurtic curve is a high-peaked curve.
   a. True
   b. False

5. The coefficient of skewness has extreme possible values of +3 and −3. Values closer to −2 connote the lowest level of skewness.
   a. True
   b. False

6. What is the median of the following numbers: 2, 3, 4, 4, 5, 6?
   a. 2
   b. 3
   c. 4
   d. 5
   e. 6

7. What is the mode of the following numbers: 2, 3, 4, 4, 5, 6?
   a. 2
   b. 3
   c. 4
   d. 5
   e. 6

8. The _____ of data summarizes the number of times a certain value of a variable occurs.
   a. dispersion
   b. frequency distribution
   c. variance
   d. coefficient
   e. None of the above

9. Which of the following coefficient of variations indicates the greatest dispersion?
   a. 0.05
   b. 0.10
   c. 0.50
   d. 0.80
   e. 0.90

10. If the standard deviation is 15 and the mean is 5, what is the coefficient of variation?
    a. 1/3
    b. 3
    c. 75
    d. 1/15
    e. None of the above

Thinking Critically

1. Using the following information about how many times a group of students studied for a marketing exam the previous week, compute the arithmetic mean, median, and mode.

Student	Number of Times Studied Last Week
Abdul	5
Bailey	6
Chico	7
Damara	7
Elinor	9
Fredrick	3
Gimbya	5
Total:	42

2. Using the distribution in question 1, what is the coefficient of variation of the set of values? What does the measure mean?

3. Using the distribution in question 1, calculate the coefficient of skewness. What does this measure mean?

4. The weights (in pounds) of the 11 players on each of the two college football teams are as follows. Compute the standard deviations.

Alpha University:	160, 180, 190, 200, 210, 170, 250, 220, 180, 200, 240
Beta University:	160, 190, 210, 230, 240, 220, 150, 190, 210, 160, 240

5. The following frequency distribution table shows the heights of 18 salespersons at Baylake Pines Company. Compute the coefficient of skewness.

Height (Inches)	Number of Salespersons
61	2
63	3
65	7
67	5
69	1

Net Exercises

1. The United Nations offers an easy-to-use database called InfoNation, with over 30 different fields of information—including important statistics—on 185 different countries. You can find anything from population to the level of carbon emission, from the average temperature to the gross domestic product (GDP). Visit its site at http://www.un.org/cyberschoolbus/index.html and find out the top ten nations with the highest GDP and the top ten nations with the highest GDP/capita.

2. Go to ESPN's Web site (http://sports.espn.go.com/mlb/statistics) and find the batting averages of the top 20 batters in each league (National and American) of major league baseball. Then calculate the mean and coefficient of variation for the top 20 batters in each league. Based on the top 20 batters' statistics, which league has better batters? Support your claim.

Experiencing Marketing Research

Since you are taking a marketing research course, you are likely either a junior or senior. Therefore, you've probably taken several courses thus far in your academic career. Go back to your most recent transcript and write down as a frequency distribution the number of A's, B's, C's, D's, and F's you've obtained while in college. Multiply the number of A's you've received by 4, B's by 3, C's by 2, D's by 1, and F's by 0.

1. Calculate the mean, median, and mode. Does the mean equal the reported grade point average on your transcript? If not, why not?

2. Calculate the coefficient of variation. What does it mean?

Case 13-1

Agreement between the U.S. and China: Will It Change the Balance of Trade?

In 2000, U.S. President Bill Clinton signed a bill granting China permanent normal trade relations with the United States. China became a member of the World Trade Organization (WTO) in 2002. The World Trade Organization, with its 148 member nations, is the only global organization dealing with the rules of trade between nations. At its heart are the WTO agreements, negotiated and signed by the majority of the world's trading nations and ratified in their parliaments. The goal is to help producers of goods and services, exporters, and importers conduct their business. The implications to China and the United States are huge. Based on the WTO agreements, China opens its doors wider, inviting U.S. companies to increase trade with them—at lower tariff rates—and the Unites States extends the same opportunity to China.

Although U.S. business proponents of trade with China point to the tremendous opportunities there, there are skeptics who believe China will "open the flood gates" and overwhelm the U.S. market with their products. The country's economic profile is enticing, but the U.S. trade deficit since the 1990s disturbs a lot of Americans (see Exhibits 13-14 and 13-15).

EXHIBIT 13-15	U.S. Trade Balance with China (Millions of U.S. Dollars)	
Year	Exports	Imports
2004	$34,744.1	$196,682.0
2003	28,367.9	152,436.1
2002	22,127.7	125,192.6
2001	19,182.3	102,278.4
2000	16,185.2	100,018.2
1999	13,111.0	81,788.2
1998	14,241.3	71,168.7
1997	12,862.3	62,557.6
1996	11,992.6	51,512.6
1995	11,753.6	45,543.2
1994	9,281.8	38,786.7
1993	8,762.8	31,539.9
1992	7,418.4	25,727.6
1991	6,278.3	18,969.0
1990	4,806.4	15,237.3

Sources: U.S. Department of State, "Background note: China," http://www.census.gov/foreign-trade/balance/c5700.html# 2005, accessed March 2005; U.S. Census Bureau, "Trade in goods (imports, exports and trade balance) with China," http://www.state.gov/r/pa/ei/bgn/18902.htm, accessed June 9, 2005.

EXHIBIT 13-14	Economic Profile of China in 2004

- Population—1.3 billion
- Gross domestic product (GDP) —$1.65 trillion (U.S. dollars; exchange rate based)
- GDP per capita—$1,200
- GDP real growth rate—9.5%
- Literacy rate—86%
- Global trade surplus—$32 billion
- Primary trading partners: Japan, the EU, the U.S., and South Korea

Case Questions

1. Using some of the descriptive statistical techniques discussed in the chapter and the data given in the case, describe the present trade relationship between the U.S. and China.

2. Using the data given in Exhibit 2, what is the coefficient of variation for exports? For imports? Interpret the numbers.

Case 13-2

The Integrated Case—Part 4

Cheerwine—In Need of Unique Research

After several painstaking weeks of getting individuals to complete surveys, Alan Young was glad that the data collection was finally finished. He decided that he would have one of his best students run the statistical analyses. He wanted to make sure that the chosen individual could handle such an important responsibility. Eventually he decided on hiring Eva Gonzalez, an "A" student in his marketing research class and an individual who had approached him several times about doing a directed study under his guidance. When Alan asked Eva about running the data analysis for him, she answered, "Absolutely. This will give me an opportunity to work with some real-world data and see what conclusions can be drawn. In addition, I drink Cheerwine all of the time and am curious what the results will reveal."

After a few days, Alan sent Eva the data. At the beginning she stared at it, not knowing what to do with it. She knew she had to run some statistical tests, but was unsure which tests made sense. Then she remembered that some descriptive statistics would help her summarize sample data and draw some preliminary conclusions.

Pretend that instead of Eva being given the responsibility to run the analysis, you must do it. You have been instructed to run a descriptive analysis using the dataset Cheerwine.sav.

Case Questions

Referring to the decision problems and research objectives identified in Case 2-3 and the Questionnaire in Case 8-2, complete the following tasks:

1. Identify survey questionnaire items for each research objective (RO).

2. Run the descriptive analysis, and report the key findings.

3. Draw recommendations for actions based on the findings.

You may use the following template to organize your answers:

	RO1
What Are the Questionnaire Items for This RO?	
Key Findings	
Recommendations for Actions	
	RO2
What Are the Questionnaire Items for This RO?	
Key Findings	
Recommendations for Actions	
Overall Recommendations	

Note

1. For an excellent discussion on frequency distributions and other basic statistics terms, see Donald H. Sanders, *Statistics: A First Course* (New York: McGraw-Hill, 1995).

Hypothesis Testing

Chapter Fourteen

Chapter Outline

Key Terms

alternative hypothesis   (p. 330)

biased estimator of the parameter   (p. 331)

chi-square distribution   (p. 342)

chi-square goodness-of-fit test   (p. 344)

chi-square statistic   (p. 342)

critical values   (p. 337)

decision rule   (p. 338)

degrees of freedom   (p. 332)

estimator   (p. 331)

hypothesis   (p. 328)

interval estimate   (p. 331)

level of significance   (p. 334)

null hypothesis   (p. 329)

one-tailed test   (p. 335)

point estimate   (p. 331)

power of a hypothesis test   (p. 334)

statistical significance   (p. 332)

t-distribution   (p. 341)

test statistic   (p. 333)

t-test   (p. 341)

two-tailed test   (p. 335)

type I error (α)   (p. 334)

type II error (β)   (p. 334)

unbiased estimator of the parameter   (p. 331)

z-test   (p. 338)

Learning Objectives

After studying this chapter, you will be able to:

- Discuss the concept of hypothesis testing.
- Show others how to run hypothesis tests.

- Conduct statistical tests for hypothesis testing.

GET THIS

Westernized Advertising Appeals Dominate in Taiwan

Today Asia comprises about two-fifths of the world's population and contains some of the most aggressive and promising markets throughout the world. Most nations view this region as a haven for business opportunity, as well as a strong competitive force because of its sheer size and potential economic strength.

One of the countries getting a lot of attention is Taiwan—a tiny island (about the size of West Virginia) with a small population (22.7 million). The country has evolved from an underdeveloped, agricultural island to an economic power that is a leading producer of high-technology goods. Its economy continues to expand at roughly 3–4% per year, with virtually full employment and low inflation. The U.S. Department of Commerce has classified the island as a "big emerging market," due to its tremendous market potential for American businesses to invest there.

Whenever success comes to a market, advertising will likely be well entrenched, and this certainly is the case in Taiwan. To better understand some of the characteristics of advertising there, a study sought to provide insight on how to advertise effectively in Taiwan given the constraints faced by advertisers. Advertising literature indicated that three advertising appeals—Eastern, Western, and Universal—exist throughout the world. "Eastern" appeals include those based on tradition, respect for elders, "soft-sell" appeals, group consensus appeals, and oneness-with-nature appeals. "Western" appeals include those based on individualism, independence, youth, or modernity, as well as "hard-sell" appeals and manipulation appeals. Appeals classified as "Universal" (neutral) were product-merit appeals and appeals to pride in a product's country of origin. Some earlier studies had indicated that contrary to Asian culture, "Western" appeals and themes tend to dominate in Taiwan. Therefore, the researchers proposed the following hypothesis:

H_0: Advertising appeals in Taiwan tend to be dominated more by "westernized" cultural values than by traditional Chinese values.

Sixty-one managing directors of advertising agencies were personally interviewed in Taipei, the capital city of Taiwan. The study results supported the proposed hypothesis. The researchers determined that Taiwan, with its modern advertising industry, tended to be dominated more by "westernized" cultural values than by Chinese traditional values.

Sources: Alan T. Shao, Mary Anne Raymond, and Charles R. Taylor, "Shifting advertising appeals in Taiwan," *Journal of Advertising Research* 39, no. 6 (November/December 1999) 61–69; Government Information Office, "Taiwan at a glance 2004–2005," http://www.gio.gov.tw/taiwan-website/5-gp/glance/ch1.htm, accessed July 10, 2005.

Now Ask Yourself

- What is a "hypothesis"?
- How did the researchers decide what the hypothesis would be?
- How did the researchers decide that the "study results supported the proposed hypothesis"?

In the "Get This" feature, researchers were interested in understanding advertising appeals in Taiwan. They developed a research hypothesis and then gathered data to determine whether the hypothesis was supported. This chapter will look closely at hypothesis testing. Hypothesis testing is one method of inferential analysis, which permits researchers to draw inferences from sample data.

14-1 An Overview of Hypothesis Testing

hypothesis An assumption made about a population characteristic.

A *statistical hypothesis,* or simply **hypothesis,** is an assumption or an informed guess made about a population characteristic. In more scientific terms, it can be defined as an unproven statement or proposition about something under investigation by a researcher. The hypothesis in the "Get This!" feature was the researchers' initial assumption that advertising appeals in Taiwan tend to be dominated more by "westernized" cultural values than by traditional Chinese values. It was simply an educated guess to be supported or refuted through statistical testing. With the heavy competition in most industries, managers cannot afford to act on hunches alone. They must test their hypotheses about their markets to find out what is really happening before taking action.

As you read the following typical business assumptions, think about the consequences if the companies were to act on these assumptions and the assumptions proved to be wrong.

- Managers at Computer Store believe that their sales coupons will be redeemed more often when they are in the Saturday rather than Sunday local newspapers.

- First Bank believes that its decrease in market share is attributable to a reduction in customer satisfaction over the last two years.

- Managers at Buy-It Store think that about three out of every ten shoppers come into their store without making a purchase.

- Managers at Hungry-Boy Restaurant assume that they have more males than females eating at their establishment.

- Managers at Brain Bookstore guess that the average intelligence quotient of customers at their store is approximately 125.

- At Excellent University, administrators are concerned that their students are eating too often at off-campus restaurants. They think that their students go off-campus for about 40% of their meals.

Before accepting or rejecting any hypothesis, marketing managers test it to determine the likelihood of it being true. A sure way to test a hypothesis would be to examine the entire population (i.e., conduct a census). However, testing an entire population is impractical, so researchers use a representative sample to approximate the parameter of interest. Using the sample data, they test hypotheses to determine whether to accept or reject them. Then marketing managers make their decisions, based on acceptance or rejection of the hypotheses. Consider Example 14-1.

Example 14-1

A French company is going to introduce a newly developed perfume, Flicia. The managers believe that they can sell this new perfume comfortably at a price of $68 per bottle. However, as this initial hypothesis is based on the managers' past experience, it may not be accurate today. To price Flicia appropriately, a market research project is conducted to assess the price that target consumers are willing to pay for Flicia.

To test the hypothesis, researchers randomly sample 400 consumers and test the hypothesis based on the sample mean. If the test using sample data shows a high probability that the population mean is not significantly different from $68, they can then state that the test results are not inconsistent with the hypothesis. They can therefore accept the hypothesis and set the price at $68. On the other hand, if the information from the sample data shows a low probability that the mean is $68, then the test results are inconsistent with the hypothesis and, thus, they must reject the initial hypothesis. In this case, managers would likely use an alternative price for Flicia.

The hypothesis to be tested for possible acceptance or rejection (nullification) is called the **null hypothesis.** It is the assertion about one or more population parameters that is believed to be true until enough statistical evidence is provided by a researcher to conclude otherwise. A null hypothesis is usually denoted by the symbol H_0.

null hypothesis A hypothesis to be tested for possible acceptance or rejection.

In the Flicia example, the null hypothesis is:

H_0: The average price that consumers are willing to pay for Flicia is $68.

Or symbolically,

H_0: μ = $68

Notice that the Greek letter μ (pronounced "mu") is used to represent the mean height of the population. Typically, Greek letters refer to population parameters, and we use population parameters in our hypotheses because we are attempting to make an inference about a population.

An **alternative hypothesis** is an assertion believed to be true if the null hypothesis is false. An alternative hypothesis is denoted by H_1. In a given test, there is usually only one null hypothesis, but there may be several alternative hypotheses. Consider Example 14-2.

alternative hypothesis An assertion believed to be true if the null hypothesis is false.

Example 14-2

Concerning the pricing of Flicia, we can state the null and alternative hypotheses as follows:

H_0: μ = $68

H_1: $\mu \neq$ $68 (or μ is "not equal to" $68)

In this example, if the null hypothesis is false, then one of several alternative hypotheses could be true:

H_1: $\mu \neq$ $68

H_1: $\mu >$ $68

H_1: $\mu <$ $68

Hypotheses are not always stated quantitatively as we have demonstrated thus far. As shown in Research Realities 14-1, they are often stated qualitatively. The statistical methods used to decide whether to accept or reject statistical hypotheses are called *tests of hypotheses* or *tests of significance*.

Another way of expressing a hypothesis is to state that there is no difference between two values, such as between the population mean and the sample mean. The phrase "no

Research Realities 14-1

Knowledge Sharing and Marketing Effectiveness

Is there a relationship between knowledge sharing and an organization's marketing effectiveness? There is little academic research available on the relationship. Two researchers offer interesting perspectives. M. Brannback proposes that in order to satisfy customers, the firm needs to understand customer needs and then organizes them into organizational knowledge; knowledge then should be transferred and blended into the marketing activities. Philip Kotler, on the other hand, advocates that the purpose of the marketing concept is to satisfy customer needs through integrated marketing activities. Kotler noted, "...when all the company's departments work together to serve the customer's interests, the result is integrated marketing."

Professor Li-Yueh Chen at Chungchou Institute of Technology in Taiwan sought to answer the initial query.

He proposed the following hypothesis:

Knowledge sharing is positively correlated with the organizational marketing effectiveness in the strategic alliance setting.

He surveyed 16 accounting firm branch offices in Taiwan and 135 branch offices in the U.S. and found that knowledge sharing is positively related to organizational marketing effectiveness in a strategic alliance setting. He concluded that knowledge-sharing activities must come before organizational marketing effectiveness can be enhanced.

Source: Li-Yueh Chen, "Effect of Knowledge Sharing to Organizational Marketing Effectiveness in Large Accounting Firms That Are Strategically Aligned," *The Journal of American Academy of Business,* vol. 9, no. 1 (March 2006), pp. 176–182.

difference" does not mean that the actual value of the difference is zero. Instead, it means that the difference is merely due to sampling fluctuation; therefore, the difference is considered to be "no difference" or "zero." For example, in the Flicia case, if the average price of the sample is found to be $67.5 and it is not significantly different from $68, we can accept the hypothesis that the mean is $68 because the difference, $68 − 67.5 = 0.5$, is *not significant* (that is, it is only due to sampling fluctuation).

14-2 Terminology

To understand hypothesis testing, you first need to understand a few key terms: estimates, estimators, degrees of freedom, and statistical significance.

14-2a Point Estimate and Interval Estimate

An estimate of a parameter may be expressed in two ways: as a point estimate or an interval estimate. A **point estimate** is a single number used to represent the estimate of the parameter. An **interval estimate** is a stated range of numbers within which we expect the parameter to lie. For example, if the estimate of the average hourly wage in a restaurant is expressed as $6.00, it is a point estimate; if it is expressed as between $5.00 and $7.00, it is an interval estimate.

14-2b Estimators

A statistic used for estimating a parameter is called an **estimator,** such as a sample mean used to estimate the population mean. An estimator is an **unbiased estimator of the parameter** when its expected value is equal to the value of the parameter. An estimator is a **biased estimator of the parameter** when its expected value is not equal to the value of the parameter. The expected value of the statistic (expressed symbolically as E) is the arithmetic mean of the sampling distribution of the statistic. Since the mean of the sampling distribution of the mean is equal to the population mean, a sample mean is an unbiased estimator; or stated in a different way,

$\bar{X}$ is an unbiased estimator of μ, since $E(\bar{X}) = \mu$

point estimate A single number used to represent the estimate of a parameter.

interval estimate The stated range within which a parameter is expected to lie.

estimator A statistic used for estimating a parameter.

unbiased estimator of the parameter A statistic with an expected value equal to the value of the parameter.

biased estimator of the parameter A statistic with an expected value not equal to the value of the parameter.

Source: © 2007 Jupiterimages Corporation.

Likewise, since the mean of the sampling distribution of the sample proportion is equal to the population proportion, a sample proportion is an unbiased estimator, or

p is an unbiased estimator of P, since $E(p) = P$.

However, the mean of the sampling distribution of the sample variance (s^2) is not equal to the population variance (σ^2), or

s^2 is a biased estimator of σ^2 since $E(s^2) \neq \sigma^2$.

14-2c Degrees of Freedom

degrees of freedom The number of observations in a statistical problem that can vary freely under certain conditions; in general, it is calculated as $(n - k)$, where n is the total number of observations and k is the number of parameters or constraints needed to calculate a sample statistic or test statistic.

The number of variables that can vary freely in a set of variables under certain conditions is referred to as the number of **degrees of freedom.** It is usually represented as $n - k$, where n is the total number of observations and k is the number of parameters or assumptions required to calculate the test statistic.

14-2d Statistical Significance

statistical significance Differences in findings that cannot be caused by chance or sampling error alone.

Throughout this chapter, we will be examining whether the difference between two or more samples is "statistically significant." **Statistical significance** refers to differences in findings that cannot be caused by chance or sampling error alone. The layperson would say that a difference exists whenever two numbers taken from samples are not exactly the same. But marketing researchers and statisticians know that just because two numbers are not the same does not mean that they are significantly different. However, if a difference between two numbers that come from samples exists and it cannot be attributed to chance or sampling error alone, the difference is statistically significant.

14-3 Procedure for Testing Hypotheses

Hypothesis testing begins with a hypothesis and ends with a decision to accept or reject the hypothesis. Let's take a look at each step in the procedure (see Exhibit 14-1).

14-3a Step 1: State the Null and Alternative Hypotheses

The null hypothesis indicates the initial assumption of the population mean. It also can be stated as having no difference between the two given values, or the difference is zero. In other words, the initial assumption is that any difference between the two given values is due to sampling fluctuation or chance; therefore, the difference is "not significant." Consider Example 14-3.

Example 14-3

In our earlier example, we stated the following hypotheses:

H_0: $\mu = \$68$

H_1: $\mu \neq \$68$

H_0 indicates that the average price that consumers are willing to pay is $68. The alternative hypothesis, H_1, indicates that the average price that consumers are willing to pay is not $68. We also could have stated one of the following set of hypotheses:

H_0: $\mu = \$68$

H_1: $\mu \neq \$68$

or

H_1: $\mu > \$68$

or

H_1: $\mu < \$68$

Notice that this set has three alternative hypotheses, indicating that the average price consumers are willing to pay is not equal to $68, is greater than $68, or is less than $68. The description of alternative hypotheses depends on the nature of the problem. For example, if a marketing researcher believes that the average price is less than $68 (that is, reject the null hypothesis), then H_1 should be stated as $\mu < \$68$.

14-3b Step 2: Select a Suitable Test Statistic and Its Distribution

Once the hypotheses have been stated, the researchers must select a suitable test statistic and its distribution. To decide on the appropriate test statistic, the researchers should consider the shape and characteristics of the sampling distribution. The **test statistic** is a statistic calculated from the sample data, whose sampling distribution is used to test whether we may reject the null hypothesis. A test statistic can assume many possible values, since it depends on the particular sample drawn. The test statistic plays the role of decision maker, since the decision to reject or not reject the null hypothesis depends on its magnitude. In the next section, we will discuss some methods to determine test statistics—z-distribution, t-distribution, and chi-square goodness-of-fit test.

test statistic A statistic, calculated from the sample data, whose sampling distribution is used to test the hypothesis.

14-3c Step 3: Select the Level of Significance and Critical Values

In our daily lives, we strive to accomplish numerous tasks. Unfortunately, the results are typically less than perfect. This is usually the case when we make deductions about populations. Two types of problems, or errors, can result: Type I and Type II errors.

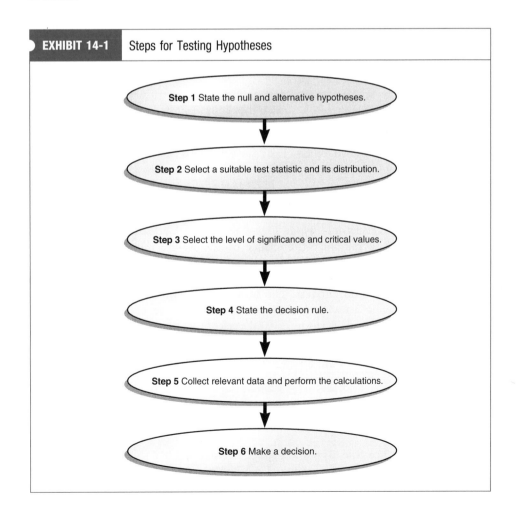

EXHIBIT 14-1 Steps for Testing Hypotheses

Step 1 State the null and alternative hypotheses.

Step 2 Select a suitable test statistic and its distribution.

Step 3 Select the level of significance and critical values.

Step 4 State the decision rule.

Step 5 Collect relevant data and perform the calculations.

Step 6 Make a decision.

Type I Error and Type II Error

There are always two possible errors to a given problem.

In the example concerning the price of Flicia, one possible reality is that the null hypothesis is true:

The average price consumers are willing to pay for Flicia is $68.

The other possible reality is that the null hypothesis is not true:

The average price consumers are willing to pay for Flicia is not $68.

When researchers decide to reject or not reject the null hypothesis, their decision may be correct or incorrect, depending on the true value of the parameter. In general, the results of making such decisions can be classified in the following manner:

1. Two types of correct decisions:
   The researcher *rejects* a null hypothesis when it is *not true*.
   The researcher *accepts* (that is, fails to reject) a null hypothesis when it is *true*.

2. Two types of incorrect decisions or errors:
   Type I error (α): The researcher *rejects* a null hypothesis that actually is *true*. This is sometimes referred to as a "false positive."
   Type II error (β): The researcher *accepts* a null hypothesis that is actually *not true*. This is sometimes referred to as a "false negative."

> **type I error (α)** Rejection of a null hypothesis that is true; probability is represented as alpha (α).

> **type II error (β)** Acceptance of (or failure to reject) a null hypothesis that is false; probability is represented as beta (β).

Thus, in the preceding example, if the hypothesis of $\mu = \$68$ is rejected according to the result of the test—but the average is actually $68—a Type I error has been made. On the other hand, if the hypothesis of $\mu = \$68$ is accepted according to the test result—but the average is actually $55 (or not $68)—a Type II error has been made.

The likelihood or probability of making a Type I error is usually denoted by α; it is the significance level the researcher must establish at the beginning of the analysis. The likelihood or probability of committing a Type II error is denoted by β; it is the probability of making the wrong decision. The possible decisions and the results from the decisions concerning our example are summarized in Exhibit 14-2.

EXHIBIT 14-2	Decision Results for Stated Hypotheses—Possible Realities	
Possible Decision	H_0 **is true ($68)**	H_0 **is not true ($55)**
Reject H_0	Incorrect decision—Type I error (α)	Correct decision
Accept H_0	Correct decision	Incorrect decision—Type II error (β)

Power of a Test (1 – β)

Researchers strive to reject null hypotheses whenever they are false. In other words, researchers attempt to minimize the chance of accepting a null hypothesis that is actually false—a Type II error or β. They prefer that β be as low as possible. When we subtract β from 1, the smaller β is, then the closer the result gets to 1.0 and the stronger or more powerful our test. The **power of a hypothesis test** indicates the probability of rejecting a null hypothesis that should be rejected. Simply stated, it indicates the extent a test is performing well.

> **power of a hypothesis test** The probability of rejecting a null hypothesis that should be rejected; it indicates the extent a test is performing well and is calculated as $1 - \beta$, where a high value indicates the test is working well.

There is a close association between α and β. In general, whenever α is low, β tends to be high. To deal with this relationship, most researchers will not set α at an extremely low level (for example, .001 or .005) to reduce the likelihood of a Type II error. Instead, a more conservative .05 level is often used. There is also a close relationship between β and n (sample size). The greater the sample size, the lower the likelihood of a Type II error. To make our test more powerful, then, we may increase the sample size.

Level of Significance Specifying a Type I Error (α)

> **level of significance** The maximum probability of making a Type I error specified in a hypothesis test.

The maximum probability of making a Type I error specified in a hypothesis test is called the **level of significance.** The level of significance is usually specified before a test is made. Otherwise, the result obtained from the test may influence the decision concerning the hypothesis. In practice, the value of 5% ($\alpha = .05$) or 1% ($\alpha = .01$) is frequently used to set the level of significance, although other values may also be used. Consider Example 14-4.

Example 14-4

In the illustration concerning the average price, if we select a .05 level of significance, we will expect that the probability of making the error of rejecting the hypothesis (assumed to be $68) when it is true (actually it is $68) is 5%. In other words, we are approximately 95% confident that we will make a correct decision, although we could be wrong with a probability of 5%, or about 5 chances out of 100 of being wrong when the null hypothesis is true.

Two-Tailed Tests and One-Tailed Tests

The level of significance may be represented by a portion of the area under the normal curve in two ways: (1) two "tails" or sides under the curve (Exhibit 14-3), and (2) one "tail" or side under the curve—either the right tail (Exhibit 14-4A) or the left tail (Exhibit 14-4B). The hypothesis tests based on the level of significance represented by both tails under the normal curve are called **two-tailed tests** or *two-sided tests*. This type of test is used when the alternative hypothesis contains the operator $\neq$. If the level of significance is represented by only one tail, the tests are called **one-tailed tests** or *one-sided tests*. This test is used when the alternative hypothesis contains either the operator $>$ (for a right-tailed test) or $<$ (for a left-tailed test).

The fundamental concepts of the two kinds of tests are illustrated by using the following information:

- Null hypothesis: The average monthly expenditure on grocery shopping of residents in an area (i.e., the mean of a certain population) is $500, or $H_0: \mu = \$500$.

- The standard error of the sampling distribution of the mean drawn from the population is $5, or $\sigma_{\bar{x}} = \$5$.

- The level of significance is 5%, or $\alpha = 0.05$.

Consider Example 14-5.

two-tailed test A test in which the alternative hypothesis is not expressed in one direction; it shows a population parameter is either larger or smaller than a specified value; the rejection region is in both tails of the distribution.

one-tailed test A test in which the alternative hypothesis is expressed in one direction; the rejection region is in one tail of the distribution.

EXHIBIT 14-3 Two-Tailed Test, Level of Significance, $\alpha = .05$

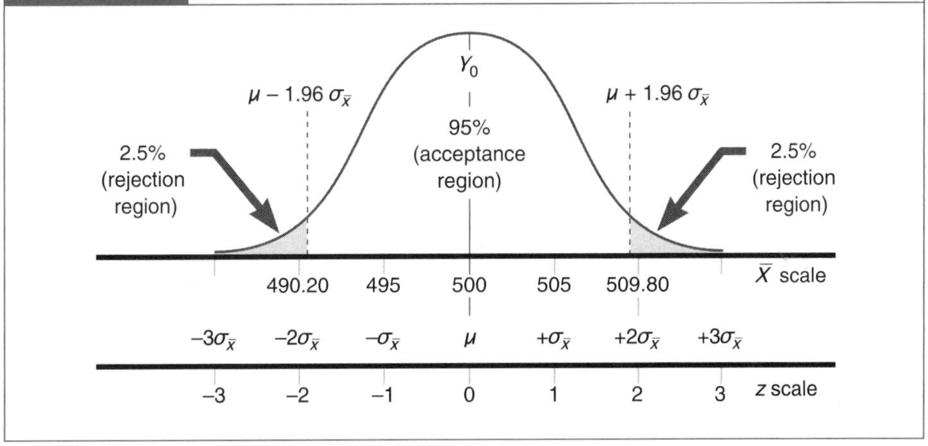

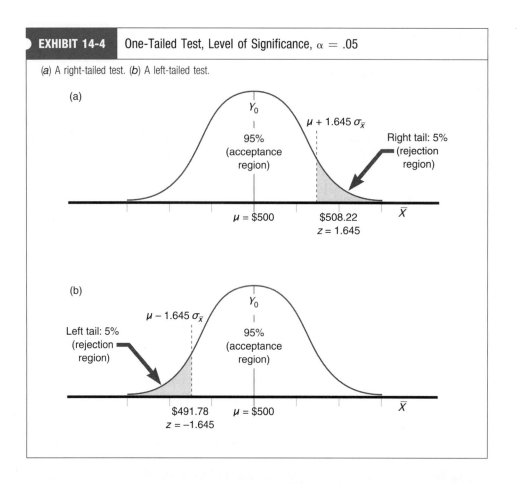

EXHIBIT 14-4 | One-Tailed Test, Level of Significance, $\alpha = .05$

(a) A right-tailed test. (b) A left-tailed test.

(a)

Y_0

$\mu + 1.645\,\sigma_{\bar{x}}$

95%
(acceptance region)

Right tail: 5%
(rejection region)

$\mu = \$500$

$\$508.22$
$z = 1.645$

$\bar{X}$

(b)

Y_0

$\mu - 1.645\,\sigma_{\bar{x}}$

Left tail: 5%
(rejection region)

95%
(acceptance region)

$\$491.78$
$z = -1.645$

$\mu = \$500$

$\bar{X}$

Example 14-5

A two-tailed test answers the question, "What sample mean, which may be below or above the hypothetical mean (\$500), will enable us to reject the null hypothesis?" We know that the mean of a sampling distribution of the mean (or the mean of the means of all possible samples of the same size drawn from the population) is equal to the population mean. Thus if the null hypothesis is true, the mean of a sampling distribution of the mean of a given sample size should also be \$500. Further, if the null hypothesis is true, 95% (or 100% − 5%) of the sample means of the distribution will fall within the range or the confidence interval:

$$\mu \pm z\sigma_{\bar{x}} = 500 \pm 1.96(5) = 500 \pm 9.80 = \$490.20 \text{ to } \$509.80$$

If we actually take a simple random sample and find that the sample mean is *less* than \$490.20 or *more* than \$509.80, we would have reason to conclude that the difference between the hypothetical population mean and the sample mean is statistically significant. If the null hypothesis is true, such a sample mean (an extreme value) could happen with a probability of only 5%. Since the sample gives better information (observed facts) than the null hypothesis, which may not be more than a rough guess, we thus reject the null hypothesis based on the sampling study. However, if the sample mean has a value within the range of \$490.20 to \$509.80, we accept the null hypothesis since a sample mean with such a value has a high probability of being selected if the null hypothesis is true.

The sampling distribution of the mean based on the hypothetical population mean is shown in Exhibit 14-3. The 5% level of significance ($\alpha = .05$) is represented by the shaded areas located on both tails of the normal curve in the chart. It is split into two equal areas: 2.5% on each tail of the normal curve. The z values that demarcate the two equal areas are called **critical values** and are ±1.96. The critical values may also be expressed in the actual units: $490.20 and $509.80. The shaded areas that are outside the range of $z = \pm 1.96$ are called the *region of rejection of the hypothesis,* or simply the *rejection region.* The area inside the range is then called the *region of acceptance of the hypothesis,* or the *acceptance region.* Therefore, the critical values of a test statistic separate the acceptance region from the rejection region. Consider Example 14-6.

critical values Cutoff limits or values that lie on the edges of the rejection region.

Example 14-6

This is a one-tailed test. The research hypothesis, the 5% level of significance, and the value of the standard error of the mean stated previously are again used in the illustration for the following two cases.

• *Test involving extreme high values (a right-tailed test):* This kind of test answers the question: What sample mean, which is higher than the hypothetical population mean ($500), will enable us to reject the null hypothesis? The hypothesis would be:

H_0: $\mu = 500$

H_1: $\mu > 500$

Exhibit 14-4a shows that the 5% of extremely high values far above the population mean of $500 are represented by the single shaded area located on the right tail of the normal curve. The critical value of z is precisely +1.645, which is obtained from Table 1, "Areas under the Normal Curve," in the Appendix at the end of the book. We look for .45 (.50 − .05) in the table. It separates the normal curve into two parts: the 5% rejection region and the 95% acceptance region. The critical value may also be expressed as a dollar value:

$$\mu + z\sigma_{\bar{x}} = \$500 + 1.645(\$5) = \$508.22$$

If we actually take a simple random sample and find that the sample mean is more than $508.22, we would conclude that the difference is significant and reject the hypothesis that the population mean is $500. We would then accept the hypothesis that it is greater than $500.

• *Test involving extreme low values (a left-tailed test):* This kind of test answers the question, What sample mean, which is smaller than the hypothetical population mean ($500), will enable us to reject the null hypothesis? The hypothesis would be:

H_0: $\mu = 500$

H_1: $\mu < 500$

Exhibit 14-4b shows that the 5% values far below the hypothetical population mean of $500 are represented by the single shaded area located on the left tail of the normal curve. The critical value of z is −1.645 standard error units, or expressed as a dollar value:

$$\mu - z\sigma_{\bar{x}} = \$500 - 1.645(\$5) = \$491.78$$

If we actually take a simple random sample and find that the sample mean is less than $491.78, we would conclude that the difference is significant and reject the hypothesis that the population mean is $500. We would then accept the hypothesis that it is less than $500.

14-3d Step 4: State the Decision Rule

decision rule A formal statement of the conditions under which the null hypothesis may be rejected, given the sample results.

A **decision rule** specifies the conditions under which the null hypothesis may be rejected, given the sample results. It is based on the level of significance—either for a two-tailed test or for a one-tailed test—and is stated prior to data collection. The general format is as follows:

Reject the null hypothesis if the difference between the sample mean and the hypothesized population mean falls into a rejection region. Otherwise, accept the null hypothesis.

14-3e Step 5: Collect Relevant Data and Perform the Calculations

We have stated the "rules of the game" in the previous steps, so we are now prepared to collect the relevant information and perform the calculations. This is a critical step, since poor data collection and analysis yield spurious results. Data collection was covered in detail in preceding chapters.

14-3f Step 6: Make a Decision

To make a proper decision, we must refer to our decision rule (step 4). We reject the null hypothesis when the computed value falls in the rejection region or accept it when the computed value falls in the acceptance region.

14-4 Selected Hypothesis Tests

There are several ways to test hypotheses statistically. The most commonly used methods are based on z (standard normal deviate), t (Student's), χ^2 (chi-square), and F (variance ratio) distributions. This chapter discusses specifically z- and t-tests, as well as chi-square tests.

14-4a z-Test and z-Distribution

Two popular test statistics for testing hypotheses are the z- and t-distributions. Both test statistics take the following form:

$$\text{Test statistic} = \frac{\text{Sample statistic } - \text{ Value of hypothesized or expected parameter}}{\text{Standard error of the statistic}}$$

z-test When a z-distribution is used to test a hypothesis when the sample is large and the population standard deviation is known.

To test a hypothesis about the population mean (μ) when the true population standard deviation (σ) is known, the z-distribution can be used. When a z-distribution is used to test a hypothesis, it is called a **z-test**. To use this test, however, the sample size must be large (that is, n is greater than 30). When the sample size does not exceed 30, the t-test is recommended. (This test will be discussed in Section 14-4b.)

The value of z for the difference between a sample mean and a population mean, as noted earlier, is expressed in units of the standard error of the mean as follows:

$$z = \frac{\bar{X} - \mu}{\sigma_{\bar{x}}} \quad \text{where} \quad \sigma_{\bar{x}} = \frac{\sigma}{\sqrt{n}} \times \sqrt{\frac{N - n}{N - 1}}$$

or

$$\sigma_{\bar{x}} = \frac{\sigma}{\sqrt{n}} \text{ (when } N \text{ is large)}$$

Thus

$$z = \frac{\bar{X} - \mu}{\frac{\sigma}{\sqrt{n}}}$$

where z = a test statistic

$\bar{X}$ = The sample mean

μ = The hypothetical population mean

$\sigma_{\bar{x}}$ = The standard error of the distribution of the sample means, or the values of $\bar{X}$

When the value of z is obtained, Table 1, "Areas under the Normal Curve," in the Appendix at the end of the book can be used in the test of hypotheses. The distribution of the z values is normal and is called the *standard normal distribution* with mean 0 and standard deviation 1. Consider Example 14-7.

Example 14-7

The Mega Company is preparing to market a new and improved type of thread they have been developing for the past 12 months, but before they introduce it, they asked a marketing research firm to test its strength. Previous production records indicate that the mean breaking strength of the thread is 12.46 ounces and the standard deviation is 1.80 ounces. The production manager took a random sample of 100 pieces of thread and found that the mean breaking strength of the sample was 12.82 ounces. Can it be concluded that the quality of the thread has changed? Let the level of significance be .05.

Solution: The statistical hypotheses are:

H_0: $\mu = 12.46$

H_1: $\mu \neq 12.46$

The mean breaking strength of the thread of the previous measure is the hypothetical population mean (μ). Thus

$$\bar{X} = 12.82 \text{ ounces}, \; n = 100, \text{ and } \; \mu = 12.46 \text{ ounces}$$

Next we must find z using the formula given previously. The true standard deviation is known: $\sigma = 1.80$ ounces (if the population has not been changed, or if H_0 is true). Substitute the given values in the formula:

$$\sigma_{\bar{x}} = \frac{\sigma}{\sqrt{n}} = \frac{1.80}{\sqrt{100}} = 0.18$$

$$z = \frac{\bar{X} - \mu}{\sigma_{\bar{x}}} = \frac{12.82 - 12.46}{0.18} = 2$$

Now we must make a decision based on the level of significance. Here we are interested in testing whether there has been any change in the mean breaking strength of the thread. Thus a two-tailed test is used in locating the critical value of z.

At .05 level of significance (Exhibit 14-5), the critical value of $z = \pm 1.96$. (The 1.96 came from Table 1 in the Appendix at the end of the book. You look up .475 [.50 − .025] for a two-tailed test and find it is located at 1.96.) The calculated value of $z = 2$ falls in the rejection region. Thus we reject the hypothesis that the average thread strength is equal to 12.46 in favor of the alternative that it is not equal to 12.46. Since the rejection occurred in the right side of the distribution, we can say that the average thread strength is likely more than 12.46 ounces. Furthermore, we can

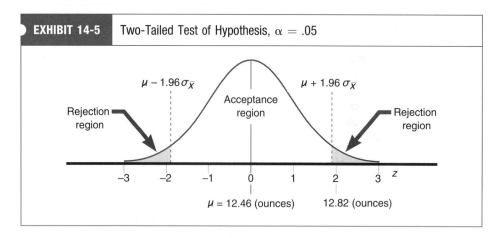

EXHIBIT 14-5 | Two-Tailed Test of Hypothesis, $\alpha = .05$

conclude that the difference between the average thread strength reported previously (12.46) and the average thread strength from the sample (12.82) is significant.

The null hypothesis (H_0: $\mu = 12.46$) can also be tested using the sampling distribution of the sample mean. The following formulas must be used:

Critical value (lower limit): $\mu - z\sigma_{\bar{x}}$

Critical value (upper limit): $\mu + z\sigma_{\bar{x}}$

or they can be written as follows:

Critical value (lower limit): $\bar{X} - z_{\alpha/2}\frac{s}{\sqrt{n}}$

Critical value (upper limit): $\bar{X} + z_{\alpha/2}\frac{s}{\sqrt{n}}$

Thus the calculations are as follows:

Critical value (lower limit): $12.46 - 1.96\left(\frac{1.80}{\sqrt{100}}\right) = 12.11$

Critical value (upper limit): $12.46 + 1.96\left(\frac{1.80}{\sqrt{100}}\right) = 12.81$

Therefore, the researcher may be 95% confident that the average breaking strength of the thread is anywhere from 12.11 to 12.81 ounces. Since we took a sample and found that the sample mean (12.82) is greater than the upper limit of 12.81, we have reason to conclude that the difference between the hypothetical population mean and the sample mean is significant. See Exhibit 14-6 for a labeled schema of the distribution.

14-4b *t*-Test and *t*-Distribution

The *t*-distribution is also called the *Student's distribution*. The name "Student" is the pseudonym used by William S. Gosset for the publication of his work on the *t*-distribution in 1908 because Gosset's employer did not permit him to use his real

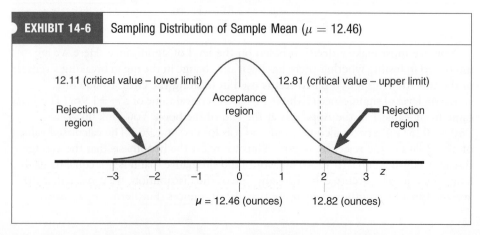

EXHIBIT 14-6 | Sampling Distribution of Sample Mean ($\mu = 12.46$)

name for the publication. The **t-distribution** is a bell-shaped and symmetric distribution that is used for testing small samples ($n \leq 30$).

The t-distribution is a statistic used to test a hypothesis about a sample mean when the population standard deviation (σ) is unknown and the sample size is considered small, usually less than or equal to 30. (When a t-distribution is used to test a hypothesis, then the test is called a **t-test.**) When the true population mean (μ) is unknown, the true population standard deviation (σ) is generally considered unknown. Thus, $s_{\bar{x}}$, the standard error of the mean, is substituted for $\sigma_{\bar{x}}$ and the formula becomes

$$t = \frac{\bar{X} - \mu}{s_{\bar{x}}} \qquad \text{where} \quad s_{\bar{x}} = \frac{s}{\sqrt{n}}$$

Thus,

$$t = \frac{\bar{X} - \mu}{s/\sqrt{n}}$$

As mentioned earlier, this formula is preferred when the sample size (n) is small, usually less than or equal to 30. When the sample size n is large, the formula may then be written

$$z = \frac{\bar{X} - \mu}{s/\sqrt{n}}$$

The value of z, instead of t, is used in the preceding formula because when n is large, s approaches σ. Therefore, the normal curve may be used to approximate the t-distribution when the sample size n becomes large, more than 30.

When the value of t is obtained, the t-distribution table, exemplified by a few critical values in Exhibit 14-7, can be used to test hypotheses. A complete list of values can be found in Table 2 in the Appendix at the end of the book.

The distribution of the values of t is not normal, but its use and the shape are somewhat analogous to those of the standard normal distribution of z. The t-distribution is also symmetrical about 0 on the t-scale. However, there is a series of t-distributions. The shape of each t-distribution is affected by the number of degrees of

t-distribution A bell-shaped and symmetric distribution that is used for testing small sample sizes (n less than or equal to 30).

t-test The test that occurs when a t-distribution is used to test a hypothesis about a sample mean when the standard deviation is unknown and the sample size is considered small, usually less than or equal to 30.

EXHIBIT 14-7	Comparison of Selected Values of t and z Representing the Same Probabilities for One-Tailed Tests		
	Probabilities (α) (or Areas under the t- and z-Distribution Curves)		
	.10	.05	.01
Number of Degrees of Freedom (D)		**Values of t**	
1	3.078	6.314	31.821
2	1.886	2.920	6.965
3	1.638	2.353	4.541
4	1.533	2.132	3.747
5	1.476	2.015	3.365
10	1.372	1.812	2.764
20	1.325	1.725	2.528
30	1.310	1.697	2.457
40	1.303	1.684	2.423
120	1.289	1.658	2.358
∞	1.282	1.645	
		Values of z	
	1.282	1.645	2.358

Source: Dr. Stephen P. Shao, Sr., *Statistics for Business and Economics,* 3d ed. (Columbus, Ohio: Charles E. Merrill, 1976). Used with permission.

freedom, D, which is computed from the sample size n. As explained earlier, the value $n - 1$ represents the number of degrees of freedom. If $n = 3$, $D = n - 1 = 3 - 1 = 2$.

Just as we can construct a table showing the areas under the standard normal curve, we can also construct a table showing the areas under a t-distribution curve between the maximum ordinate Υ_0 and the ordinate at t for every number of degrees of freedom that may possibly occur; that is, $D = 1, 2, 3, \ldots$. However, in practice, only the most frequently used values of t are tabulated in a compact form. Exhibit 14-7 (and Table 2 in the Appendix at the end of the book) gives the selected values of t.

Just as we did for a z-distribution, a confidence interval for μ can also be constructed for a t-distribution. The formula to use is:

$$\bar{X} \pm t_{\alpha/2} \frac{s}{\sqrt{n}}$$

where $df = n - 1$, and $t_{\alpha/2} =$ value of the t-distribution,
or it can be stated as follows:

Critical value (lower limit): $\bar{X} - t_{\alpha/2} \frac{s}{\sqrt{n}}$
Critical value (upper limit): $\bar{X} + t_{\alpha/2} \frac{s}{\sqrt{n}}$

Consider Example 14-8.

Example 14-8

A retail store wants to estimate the average amount of sales of a new toy. A sample (n) of 20 days yields an average amount of sales $(\bar{X})$ of 11 and a standard deviation (s) of 1.5. A 95% confidence interval will be used.

Solution: Since the sample size (n) is 20, when we use the t-distribution, the degrees of freedom will be 19 $(n - 1 = 20 - 1)$. In Table 2, in the row corresponding to 19 degrees of freedom and the column used for a right-tail region of .025 (which is $\alpha/2$), we find $t = 2.093$. We must then construct the confidence interval as follows:

$$\bar{X} - t_{\alpha/2} \frac{s}{\sqrt{n}} = 11 - 2.093\left(\frac{1.5}{\sqrt{20}}\right) = 10.298$$

$$\bar{X} + t_{\alpha/2} \frac{s}{\sqrt{n}} = 11 + 2.093\left(\frac{1.5}{\sqrt{20}}\right) = 11.702$$

Therefore, the researcher can be 95% confident that the average amount of sales of a new toy is between 10.298 and 11.702.

14-4c Chi-Square Distribution

chi-square statistic A sample statistic used to measure the degree of association among nominally scaled variables.

A **chi-square statistic,** denoted χ^2, can be used to test the significance between observed sample frequencies and expected frequencies. The **chi-square distribution** is a frequency distribution used to test how well a set of *observed* sample frequencies corresponds to or "fits" a set of *expected* or theoretical frequencies. The chi-square statistic is computed as follows:

chi-square distribution A frequency distribution used to test how well a set of observed sample frequencies corresponds to or "fits" a set of expected or theoretical frequencies.

$$\chi^2 = \sum_{i=1}^{k} \frac{(O_i - E_i)^2}{E_i} \qquad \text{[Formula 14-1]}$$

where $O_i =$ the observed frequency in cell i
$E_i =$ the expected or theoretical frequency in cell i
$k =$ the number of mutually exclusive categories

To demonstrate the concept behind a chi-square distribution, we will use probability theory.

Consider Example 14-9.

Example 14-9

Let's say we throw 8 coins and get 6 heads and 2 tails in the throw—these are the observed frequencies. However, the expected frequency of heads in the single throw is 4 ($8 \times 0.5 = 4$ heads, 0.5 being the probability of having a head in a single throw of a coin). The expected number of tails in the single throw is also 4. The value of χ^2 in this single experiment is computed as follows (see Exhibit 14-8):

$$\chi^2 = \frac{(6-4)^2}{4} + \frac{(2-4)^2}{4} = 1 + 1 = 2$$

Likewise, if we get 1 head and 7 tails in the throw, the value of χ^2 is 4.5:

$$\chi^2 = \frac{(1-4)^2}{4} + \frac{(7-4)^2}{4} = 4.5$$

There are 9 possible outcomes in throwing 8 coins at a time, as shown in the first two columns of Exhibit 14-9. The values of χ^2 of other possible outcomes in the exhibit are computed in a similar manner. We may consider each outcome as a sample drawn from an infinite population. Exhibit 14-9 shows the coin-toss experiment's sampling distribution of χ^2 for all possible samples. In general, the χ^2 distribution is used to approximate the sampling distribution of chi-square when the expected frequency in each case is at least 5.

| **EXHIBIT 14-8** | Computation of Chi-Square Value | | | | |

	Frequency				
Observed	*Expected*				
(O)	*(E)*	*O – E*	*(O – E)²*	*(O – E)²/E*
6 (heads)	4 (heads)	2	4	$4/4 = 1$
2 (tails)	4 (tails)	–2	4	$4/4 = 1$
8 (sides)	8 (sides)	0		$\chi^2 = 2$

| **EXHIBIT 14-9** | Sampling Distribution of χ^2 for Throwing Eight Coins (Degrees of Freedom = 1) |

	Possible Outcomes		
	Heads	**Tails**	χ^2
	0	8	8.0
	1	7	4.5
	2	6	2.0
	3	5	0.5
	4	4	0.0
	5	3	0.5
	6	2	2.0
	7	1	4.5
	8	0	8.0
Total	9	9	

Chi-Square Tests and Interpretations

We test a hypothesis using the χ^2 distribution to determine whether the differences between the two sets of frequencies are significant, that is, whether the differences are too great to be attributed to sampling fluctuation. Observe the χ^2 values in Exhibit 14-9. If $\chi^2 = 0$, the observed frequencies will agree exactly with the expected or theoretical frequencies. The larger the value of χ^2, the greater the difference between observed and expected or theoretical frequencies.

You can apply the χ^2 test whenever you have a set of observed frequencies (or sample data), and you can derive a set of corresponding expected or theoretical frequencies. As a rule, to use χ^2 tests, no more than 20% of the cells can have expected frequencies less than 5.

Note that the values in the chi-square distribution table, Table 3 in the Appendix at the end of the book, are limited to the distributions with degrees of freedom from 1 to 100. The use of the chi-square distribution table is analogous to that of the t-distribution table, except that the chi-square distribution table is primarily designed for one-tailed tests.

Tests for Goodness-of-Fit

chi-square goodness-of-fit test A test used to determine whether a set of theoretical or expected frequencies fit a corresponding set of observed sample frequencies.

The **chi-square goodness-of-fit test** can be used to determine whether a set of theoretical or expected frequencies fit a corresponding set of observed sample frequencies. The degrees of freedom (D) for this type of test can be obtained as follows:

$$D = k - 1$$

where $k =$ the number of mutually exclusive categories.

Consider Example 14-10.

Example 14-10

A television station claims that 70% of the television sets in New York City that were on at the time of the broadcast were tuned to the season premiere of *Monday Night Football*. A competitor wants to challenge this claim. The competitor thus took a random sample of 200 families who were watching television during that time, and found that 130 sets were tuned to the program. Can the competitor conclude that the claim was not valid, using a 0.05 level of significance?

To apply this test, follow these steps:

1. *Specify the null and alternative hypotheses:*

    H_0: From the population of television sets operating at the time, the proportion tuned to *Monday Night Football* was 70%.

    H_1: From the population of television sets operating at the time, the proportion tuned in to *Monday Night Football* was not 70%.

2. *Determine the proportion of television sets expected to be tuned to* Monday Night Football *if the null hypotheses were correct*. If the hypothesis is true, the expected number of families whose television sets were tuned to the program is $200 \times 70\% = 140$. The expected number of televisions turned on but not tuned to *Monday Night Football* is $200 \times (100\% - 70\%) = 60$.

3. *Set the level of significance*. In this example, we will use .05 as our level of significance.

4. *Determine the degrees of freedom*.

    $k = 2$,   there are two groups with data in a column or row

    $$D = 2 - 1 = 1$$

5. *Calculate the* χ^2 *value*.

    Use formula 14-1. Exhibit 14-10 shows the calculations.

$$\chi^2 = \sum_{i=1}^{k} \frac{(O_i - E_i)^2}{E_i}$$

EXHIBIT 14-10	Computation of χ^2 Statistic for Example of Televisions Tuned to *Monday Night Football*				
	Televisions Tuned to Program				
Groups	**Observed or Actual (O)**	**Expected (E)**	$O - E$	$(O - E)^2$	$(O - E)^2/E$
Tuned to the program	130	140	−10	100	0.714
Not tuned to the program	70	60	10	100	1.667
Total	200	200	0		$\chi^2 = 2.381$

6. *Make a decision.* At a .05 level, the difference is significant if χ^2 with 1 degree of freedom is above 3.841 or falls in the rejection region. This value (3.841) can be found in Table 3 in the Appendix at the end of the book. The computed value of $\chi^2 = 2.381$ is less than the critical value 3.841; that is, it falls in the acceptance region. We thus accept the hypothesis that 70% of the television sets operating at the time were tuned to *Monday Night Football.*

Remember, though, that the chi-square value means virtually nothing by itself. It is basically a means to an end. What we are really interested in is whether we can reject the hypothesis based on the number of degrees of freedom. In this case, we cannot reject the hypothesis relating to *Monday Night Football* viewership.

Since fast and efficient software is available to perform the statistical calculations, you should take advantage of these programs whenever possible (see Research Realities 14-2).

14-4d Considerations When Selecting a Test Technique

In this chapter, you were introduced to three techniques: the z-test, t-test, and chi-square test. It is one thing knowing how to use the methods; it is another thing knowing which method to use. When making this important decision, there are a few major considerations.

Source: © 2007 Jupiterimages Corporation.

Calculating Chi-Square Goodness-of-Fit Tests Using Computers

The *Monday Night Football* example can also be calculated using SPSS and Microsoft's Excel software. In most cases, SPSS will be able to run almost any test. Excel cannot perform as many direct statistical tests, but it is a valuable tool in many cases since most people use Windows-based software.

To calculate the chi-square goodness-of-fit test using SPSS, follow these steps:

1. Open a new spreadsheet.
2. Type the observed values in the appropriate cells of the first column. That is, type "1" (representing operating TVs that were tuned to the program) in cells 1–130 and "2" (representing operating TVs not tuned to the program) in cells 131–200.
3. Using the headings on the page, click "Analyze."
4. Using the subheadings under "Analyze," click on "Nonparametric Tests" and then "Chi-Square."
5. Shift "var00001" over to "Test Variable List."
6. Under the heading "Expected Values," locate "Values" and type "140," and then click "add." Do the same for "60."
7. Click on "ok." The output shown in Exhibit 1 will appear.

EXHIBIT 1 SPSS Table for Chi-Square Goodness-of-Fit Test

VAR00001			
	Observed *N*	Expected *N*	Residual
1.00	130	140.0	−10.0
2.00	70	60.0	10.0
Total	200		

Test Statistics

	VAR00001
Chi-Square[a]	2.381
df	1
Asymp. Sig.	.123

[a]0 cells (.0%) have expected frequencies less than 5. The minimum expected cell frequency is 60.0.

To run the goodness-of-fit test using Excel, follow these steps:

1. Open a new spreadsheet.
2. Enter the data in appropriate columns. Using our example, the observed data (130 and 70) should go in the first two cells in the first column, and the expected data (140 and 60) should go in the first two cells in the second column.
3. Once all of the data has been entered into the spreadsheet, click on any empty cell and type the following command:

   =CHITEST(A1:A2,B1:B2)

(The A1:A2 indicates the range where the observed data can be found. The B1:B2 indicates the range where the expected data can be found.)

4. The output is rather simple. The only data to appear is the value .122823, the level of significance.

We achieved the same results with Excel as we obtained using SPSS. The level of significance was .123, indicating that there is support for the hypothesis that the population proportion of operating television sets tuned to *Monday Night Football* was 70%. The same conclusions may be drawn here as we explained earlier when the more laborious manual calculations were used.

You need to remember a couple of rules to properly interpret the data. Assume that the level of significance is .05 and we are testing for a difference between two values. Therefore, the null hypothesis would state that there is no difference between the two values. The rules are:

- When the calculated level of significance is equal to or less than .05 ($p \leq .05$), then we reject the null hypothesis and conclude that the difference between the values cannot be attributed to sampling variation alone. That is, there is a statistically significant difference between the two values.

- When the calculated level of significance is greater than .05 ($p > .05$), then we do not reject the null hypothesis, and we conclude that the difference between the values is due to sampling variation. Therefore, there is no difference between the two values.

The first concern is our research objectives. That is, what is it that we want to know? For example, if we want to test the difference between a sample mean and a population mean, then a z-test or t-test can be used. Which one to use depends on knowledge of the population standard deviation and sample size.

A second concern is the type of scale (nominal, ordinal, interval, or ratio) used for data collection. When interval scales are used, and only one sample is considered, then *z*-tests and *t*-tests make the most sense. Of course, the sample size and population standard deviation must again be considered when deciding which of these two methods to use. When nominal scales are used for a single sample, and a comparison between a set of observed and expected outcomes is to be performed, the chi-square goodness-of-fit test should be used.

In subsequent chapters, other statistical tests will be introduced. For example, chi-square will be discussed again but to resolve a somewhat different type of problem. We will explain the appropriate tests in the chapter in which they are being discussed.

Decision Time!

There seems to be a lot to learn about hypothesis testing. As a marketing manager, you are responsible for making strategic decisions that impact the success of your organization. To what extent, if any, do you (as a marketing manager) believe you need to understand hypothesis testing? Should you have a detailed or basic understanding of the concepts, or is it entirely the marketing researcher's responsibility to understand this type of testing and report the results to you only in qualitative summary form?

Net Impact

To develop effective hypotheses, researchers must clearly understand the situation under consideration. The Internet aids the hypothesis testing effort by providing researchers with a wide range of information. The Internet can also assist novice researchers in understanding hypothesis testing because many academicians and consultants post their hypothesis testing lecture notes and presentations on the web. Furthermore, the Internet serves as a promotional tool for companies prepared to perform hypothesis testing for individuals and businesses on a fee basis.

On the Lighter Side—The Not-So-Lighter Side

You've heard the warnings about obesity. There are numerous claims about its negative impact on the body, including heart disease, diabetes, high blood pressure, joint stress, and other health problems. A recent study of more than 150 college students found that one-fourth were overweight; 6% were prediabetic, and 10% either had high total cholesterol or low HDL (good) cholesterol. However, Laurie Demeritt, a trend tracker who is president and COO of the Hartman Group, says that many people still aren't overly concerned about their own risks and therefore aren't motivated to lose weight. She surveyed 5,000 adults across the U.S. and revealed some surprising findings. First, she uncovered that while most people say they want to lose weight and attempt to do so for a short time, dieting isn't a priority in their lives. She found that the strongest motivation to lose weight comes from a social network. If a friend is on a diet and successfully loses weight, then you're more likely to try it, but if everyone around you is overweight then you're much less likely to attempt to drop the excess pounds. It seems that younger people are becoming overweight, too. Teen obesity has doubled in the last 30 years. According to another recent study, certain weight-control techniques may even contribute to weight problems. A study of 500 adolescent girls found that those who used radical weight control, or were depressed or had obese parents, were more likely to become obese.

Source: Bev Bennett, "Research on dieting yields a few surprising results," *The Detroit News*, May 13, 2005. http://www.detnews.com/2005/health/0505/13/D08-180045.htm. Retrieved October 10, 2005.

Chapter Summary

Using assumptions or educated guesses about some characteristic of a population may be sufficient in some situations, but when companies are competing, they need more reliable information. Businesses must know for sure that they are basing their decisions on the most accurate information they can get. Therefore, hypotheses—which are unproven statements or propositions about something under investigation by a researcher—are formulated and put to the test. Hypotheses to be tested for possible acceptance or rejection (nullification) are called null hypotheses. An alternative hypothesis is a hypothesis that would be true if the null hypothesis is false.

Hypothesis testing follows these steps:

1. State the null and alternative hypotheses.
2. Select a suitable test statistic and its distribution.
3. Select the level of significance and critical values.
4. State the decision rule.
5. Collect relevant data and perform the calculations.
6. Make a decision.

When testing hypotheses, two correct decisions exist. Researchers can either reject the null hypothesis when it is not true or accept (that is, fail to reject) the null hypothesis when it is true. There are also two incorrect decisions, or errors, that may result. A Type I error means that the researchers reject the null hypothesis when it is actually true. A Type II error occurs when researchers accept the null hypothesis when it is not true. The maximum probability of making a Type I error specified in a hypothesis test is called the level of significance. It may be represented by a portion of the area under the normal curve, described as either one tail or single side under the curve or two tail, which involves both sides under the curve. We can examine how well our test is performing by looking at the power of our test.

There are several univariate techniques to statistically test hypotheses. The most commonly used methods are based on the distributions of z, t, and χ^2 (chi-square) goodness-of-fit. The z-test is used to test a hypothesis about a population mean when the true population standard deviation is known and the sample size is considered large. When the sample size does not exceed 30, the t-test is used.

When a researcher is attempting to decide which statistical method to use, knowledge of the population standard deviation, sample size, and type of scale used for data collection should be considered.

Review Questions

1. State the difference between (a) a null hypothesis and an alternative hypothesis, and (b) a Type I error and a Type II error.

2. Explain the following:
   a. Level of significance
   b. Critical value
   c. Region of rejection
   d. Region of acceptance
   e. Degrees of freedom
   f. Power of a test

3. Explain the difference between (a) a two-tailed test and a one-tailed test, and (b) a left-tailed test and a right-tailed test.

4. When a Type I error probability is specified, such as 1%, can we reduce Type II error probability under a given alternative hypothesis? If we can, what is the minimum value of Type II error probability?

5. What is the difference between a z-test and a t-test?

6. When would a researcher use a chi-square goodness-of-fit test?

7. When a researcher is attempting to decide which statistical method to use, what should be considered?

Practice Quiz

Note: You can find the correct answers to these questions by taking the quiz and then submitting your answers in the Online Edition. The program will automatically score your submission. If you miss a question, the program will provide the correct answer, a rationale for the answer, and the section number in the chapter where the topic is discussed.

1. An alternative hypothesis is an assertion believed to be true if the null hypothesis is false.
   a. True
   b. False

2. The number of variables that cannot vary freely in a set of variables under certain conditions is referred to as the number of degrees of freedom.
   a. True
   b. False

3. A Type II error occurs when the researcher accepts a null hypothesis that is actually not true.
   a. True
   b. False

4. If a critical value is greater than the computed value, the researcher should reject the null hypothesis.
   a. True
   b. False

5. Statistical significance is the difference in findings that cannot be attributed to chance or sampling error alone.
   a. True
   b. False

6. What is the first step when testing a hypothesis?
   a. Collect relevant data and perform the calculations.
   b. State the null and alternative hypotheses.
   c. Select a suitable test statistic and its distribution.
   d. State the decision rules.
   e. Select the level of significance and critical values.

7. A Type II error occurs when a researcher

   a. rejects a null hypothesis that is actually true.
   b. rejects a null hypothesis that is actually false.
   c. accepts a null hypothesis that is actually not true.
   d. None of the above

8. _____ represents the power of a test.
   a. β
   b. α
   c. $1 - \alpha$
   d. $1 - \beta$
   e. None of the above

9. _____ denotes a Type I error.
   a. α
   b. β
   c. $1 - \alpha$
   d. $1 - \beta$
   e. None of the above

10. Which of the following computed values would force you to accept the null hypothesis when the critical value is 4.987 and you are running a chi-square goodness-of-fit test?
    a. 4.90
    b. 5.00
    c. 5.50
    d. 6.00
    e. None of the above

Thinking Critically

1. Give the reasons and the conditions, if any, to support the following statements:
   a. $\bar{X}$ is an unbiased estimator of μ.
   b. s^2 is a biased estimator of σ^2.
   c. $\hat{s}^2$ is an unbiased estimator of σ^2.
   d. s^2 is an unbiased estimator of σ^2.

2. A company claims that the mean lifetime of all the car batteries it produces is 40 months. However, you have found that the mean lifetime of a sample of 100 of the company's batteries is only 38.5 months with a standard deviation of 5 months. Determine whether the company's claim is overstated; use a level of significance of .05.

3. Refer to Problem 2. Now suppose you have found the mean lifetime of a sample of 26 batteries produced by the company to be 38.5 months with a standard deviation of 5 months. Determine whether the company's claim is overstated; use a .05 level of significance.

4. A medicine manufacturer claims that its product, All-Right Now, is 95% effective in relieving hay fever misery within a period of 5 hours. A sample of 150 persons who used the product showed that it provided such relief for 138 persons. Do you believe that the claim made by the manufacturer is valid at a .10 level of significance?

5. In previous years, the sales record of Johnson's Automobile Company showed that the cars sold in districts A, B, C, and D were 20, 10, 30, and 40%, respectively, of the total cars sold by the company. In the current year, the cars sold in the same districts were, respectively, 85, 60, 175, and 180 cars. Does the sales distribution in previous years differ significantly from that of the current year at a .05 level of significance?

Net Exercises

1. The Web site http://www.statistics.com has all kinds of statistical links in which students should be interested. For example, it has a "Courses" section, offering instruction in basic and applied statistics, sampling, and data mining. Briefly summarize what you find on hypothesis testing.

2. The Internet Glossary of Statistical Terms provides definitions and explanations to many of the terms used in this chapter, including null hypothesis, *t*-test, statistical significance, beta, power, and statistical test. Visit its Web site at http://www.animatedsoftware.com/statglos/statglos.htm and see its unique style of illustrations.

Experiencing Marketing Research

Your campus bookstore wants you to estimate the average number of newspapers it can expect to sell each day. Visit the bookstore for 5 days at the beginning and end of the day to determine the average number of sales and the standard deviation. Assuming a normal population of sales, give a 95% confidence interval for the average number of newspapers sold each day.

Case 14-1

Something Smells in Here!

Walk into a bakery, and the aroma of fresh-baked bread entices you to purchase a loaf or two. Enter a coffee shop, and the scent of freshly brewed coffee motivates you to order a cup. Other retail establishments, such as tobacco shops and popcorn and nut shops, also rely on the smell of their products to attract customers. Recently, though, retailers that carry diverse product lines or products without distinctive scents have used their own concoctions to draw customers. This "ambient scent," one that is not emanating from a particular object but is present in the environment, appears to affect consumer perceptions of the store, its atmosphere, and its products. For example, the Marriott Hotel chain scents its lobbies to relieve stress, and slot machine usage has increased 45% in scented casinos. But it is unclear how accurate claims of cause and effect are, since many studies are conducted in uncontrolled environments.

A supermarket chain is interested in using scents to boost sales. It hopes to increase its sales by 2% by introducing a system that emits a fresh smell and adjust the emission level automatically based on the density of clients. After one month of testing in 25 of its supermarkets, the sales change (in %) were as follows:

0.5,	1.2,	2.5,	3.5,	2.0,
2.5,	0.6,	3.4,	−0.8,	3.8,
0.5,	2.1,	2.2,	1.5,	1.0,
0.2,	2.8,	3.3,	2.5,	4.1,
2.1,	0.6,	0.4,	2.3,	2.5,

Note that for the 25 supermarkets in the control group, there is no change in their average sales.

Case Questions

1. What are the null hypothesis and alternative hypothesis for this case?

2. What test should be used to run the hypothesis testing? What is the result of the hypothesis testing?

3. Based on the result, what is your recommendation to the supermarket chain as to whether to adopt the scent system?

Group Difference Tests

Source: © 2007 JupiterImages Corporation.

Chapter Fifteen

Key Terms

Learning Objectives

After studying this chapter, you will be able to:

- Describe the difference between tests of differences and tests of associations.
- Explain how to use *z*- and *t*-tests to compare two groups.
- Talk about and calculate the *F*-test.

- Discuss the meaning and use of analysis of variance.
- Compute one-way analysis of variance manually and by computer.

GET THIS

My Name Is Important to Me

The most popular boys' names are Jack, Joshua, Thomas, James, Daniel, and Samuel. These names suggest conservatism and have biblical references—perhaps a reflection of the terrorist acts that occurred on 9/11. What does your name mean to you? Would you be offended if someone you thought was your friend forgot your name? Do you feel good when someone you do not know well remembers your name? In the book *How to Win Friends and Influence People,* Dale Carnegie wrote, "Remember that a person's name is to that person the sweetest and most important sound in any language." A marketing study ran an experiment to determine whether name remembrance is perceived as a compliment by the person remembered and increases the likelihood that the person will comply with a request.

At a university, a professor used his classroom as the research setting. On the first day of class, he asked students to publicly introduce themselves and to briefly describe their background or interests. All students provided their names as part of their introduction. After the first day of class, the professor talked to students individually to determine their level of preparation for the course. When the students arrived at the office, the professor would say:

> Don't tell me your name. Let me see if I can remember. I'm terrible at names and I'm trying to train myself to be better at it. . . . I haven't looked at the appointment sheet, so don't tell me. . . . I remember you introducing yourself in class.

Students were classified into three groups: *names* (those whose names he could remember), *no-names* (those he couldn't remember), and *neutral-names* (those whose names he never made reference to during the conversations). At the end of each meeting, the professor would state:

> Oh, I have to ask you something else. My wife is selling some cookies for the church. If you want any, they're only 25 cents.

This offer was made to examine if remembrance of a student's name made a difference regarding whether or not he or she would comply with a request (that is, purchase the cookies).

The results were analyzed using several different statistical techniques, one being analysis of variance. The professor decided to use this method because it tests whether there are statistically significant differences among the means of each of the student groups. The findings were enlightening to say the least. He found the following:

- Not being able to remember a student's name produced compliance results (that is, purchasing cookies) no different from those of a condition in which the issue of the student's name was never raised.

- The higher purchasing rate for those students whose names were remembered indicates that name remembrance facilitates compliance.

Source: Andrew Martin, "Class Conscious," *New Statesman,* vol. 135, no. 4726 (February 7, 2005), p. 63; Daniel J. Howard, Charles Gengler, and Ambuj Jain, "What's in a name? A complimentary means of persuasion,"*Journal of Consumer Research,* vol. 22 (September,1995): 200–211. Reprinted with permission from The University of Chicago Press.

Now Ask Yourself

- How many groups were involved in the analysis? Why couldn't we tell the difference between groups based on their mean responses?

- What was meant by, "The professor decided to use this method (analysis of variance) because it tests whether there are statistically significant differences among the means of each of the student groups"?
- Were the results surprising to you? If so, what did you expect? If not, why not?

As shown in the "Get This" feature, group difference tests enable us to examine whether the differences between groups are truly significant. **Difference tests** can be used whenever a researcher is interested in comparing some characteristic of one group with a characteristic of another and determining whether a significant difference exists between the two groups. Hypothesis tests often examine differences between males and females, college students and non-college students, lower income and higher income individuals, and young versus old citizens. More specifically, researchers may be interested in comparing how often any of these groups watch a particular television program. This chapter covers the most popular group difference analyses available to researchers: z-tests, t-tests, and analysis of variance. These tests are all **parametric tests** of differences, which assume that the dependent variables under investigation are measured using either *interval* or *ratio* scales.

In the following discussions, the first population and its samples are identified by the subscript 1, and the second population and its samples are identified by the subscript 2. Thus $\bar{X}_1$ represents the mean of the sample drawn from population 1, and $\bar{X}_2$ represents the mean of the sample drawn from population 2.

difference tests Tests that compare some characteristic of one group with a characteristic of another and determine whether or not a statistically significant difference exists between the two groups.

parametric tests Hypothesis tests that assume that variables under investigation are measured using either interval or ratio scales.

15-1 The z-Test: Difference between Means

Sometimes researchers want to determine whether a significant difference exists between two means. Here they would want to know whether the two population means differ from one another. This can be determined by using either the z- or t-test, depending on the sample size and whether or not the population standard deviation is known for either group. If the sample size is at least 30 and the population standard deviations are known, the z-test should be used.

To test whether the two population means are equal, the following formula is necessary:

$$z = \frac{(\bar{X}_1 - \bar{X}_2) - (\mu_1 - \mu_2)}{\sigma_{(\bar{x}_1 - \bar{x}_2)}} \quad \text{where } \sigma_{(\bar{x}_1 - \bar{x}_2)} = \sqrt{\frac{\sigma_1^2}{n_1} + \frac{\sigma_2^2}{n_2}} \qquad \text{[Formula 15-1]}$$

where $(\bar{X}_1 - \bar{X}_2)$ = the difference between sample means
$(\mu_1 - \mu_2)$ = the difference between population means
$\bar{X}_1$ and $\bar{X}_2$ = sample means for the two variables
$\sigma_{\bar{x}_1 - \bar{x}_2}$ = standard error of the difference between the means

Consider Example 15-1.

Example 15-1

A marketing researcher gave a customer satisfaction test to two groups of customers— new and loyal. The best possible score on the test is 100 points. There were 300 new customers, but a sample of 48 customers was taken. The mean score of this group was 72 points with a standard deviation of 12 points. From 400 loyal customers, a sample of 36 customers produced a mean score of 75 points with a standard deviation of 6 points. Is there a significant difference between the mean performances of the two groups of customers based on this information? Use a level of significance of .05.

Solution: Let μ_1 be the mean of the first population from which the new customer sample was drawn, and μ_2 be the mean of the second population from which the loyal customer sample was drawn.

H_0: $\mu_1 = \mu_2$ or $\mu_1 - \mu_2 = 0$
H_1: $\mu_1 \neq \mu_2$ or $\mu_1 - \mu_2 \neq 0$

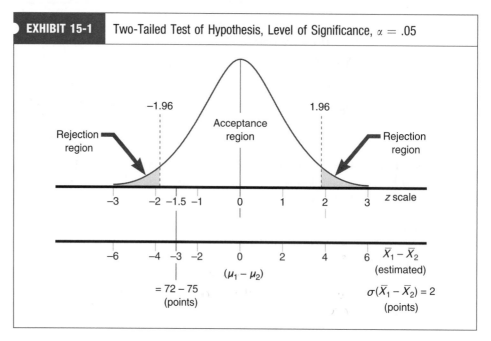

EXHIBIT 15-1 Two-Tailed Test of Hypothesis, Level of Significance, $\alpha = .05$

Now we must find the z value by using formula 15-1. Since we do not know the true population standard deviations, we must use the sample standard deviation as estimates of σ_1 and σ_2. If necessary, when N and n are large, we can use the sample variances s_1^2 and s_2^2 as estimates of σ_1^2 and σ_2^2. Then the formula is written as follows:

$$z = \frac{(\bar{X}_1 - \bar{X}_2) - (\mu_1 - \mu_2)}{s_{(\bar{x}_1 - \bar{x}_2)}}$$ [Formula 15-2]

$$s_{(\bar{x}_1 - \bar{x}_2)} = \sqrt{\frac{s_1^2}{n_1} + \frac{s_2^2}{n_2}} = \sqrt{\frac{12^2}{48} + \frac{6^2}{36}} = 2$$

$$z = \frac{(\bar{X}_1 - \bar{X}_2) - (\mu_1 - \mu_2)}{s_{(\bar{x}_1 - \bar{x}_2)}} = \frac{(72 - 75) - 0}{2} = -1.5$$

At the .05 level, the difference is significant for a two-tailed test if z falls outside the range ± 1.96 (We obtain 1.96 by using $1.0 - .05 = .95$; for a two-tailed test use $.95/2 = .475$). This value can be seen in Exhibit 15-1. The computed value of z is -1.5, which is inside the acceptance region. Thus, we conclude that the two population means are the same. In other words, the two groups have the same mean.

15-2 The *t*-Test: Difference between Means

When the sample size is less than 30 and the population standard deviations are unknown, we can determine whether a significant difference exists between two means (or whether the two population means are equal) using the *t*-test and formula 15-3.

To test whether the two population means differ, the following formula should be used:

$$t = \frac{(\bar{X}_1 - \bar{X}_2) - (\mu_1 - \mu_2)}{s_{(\bar{x}_1 - \bar{x}_2)}}$$ [Formula 15-3]

where

$$s_{(\bar{x}_1 - \bar{x}_2)} = \sqrt{\left(\frac{n_1 s_1^2 + n_2 s_2^2}{n_1 + n_2 - 2}\right)\left(\frac{n_1 + n_2}{n_1 n_2}\right)}$$

and

$$\text{degrees of freedom} = n_1 + n_2 - 2$$

Consider Example 15-2.

Example 15-2

Two samples were taken at a computer company to determine whether the mean monthly sales levels of men differ significantly from the mean monthly sales levels of women. The two samples of a given month and computations of the mean and the sum of the squared deviations for each gender are shown in Exhibit 15-2. Assume that the sales levels of each gender are normally distributed and use a level of significance of .05.

Solution: Let μ_1 and μ_2 be the means of the periodical sales levels of all men and women at the computer company, respectively.

$H_0: \mu_1 = \mu_2$ or $\mu_1 - \mu_2 = 0$

$H_1: \mu_1 - \mu_2 \neq 0$

Because the two samples are small, we find t using formula 15-3. To do this, we assume that the two samples are drawn from two populations with the same variance. Substitute the given values in the formula:

$$s_{\bar{x}_1 - \bar{x}_2} = \sqrt{\left(\frac{n_1 s_1^2 + n_2 s_2^2}{n_1 + n_2 - 2}\right)\left(\frac{n_1 + n_2}{n_1 n_2}\right)} = \sqrt{\left(\frac{46 + 20}{4 + 5 - 2}\right)\left(\frac{5 + 4}{20}\right)} = 2.06$$

$$t = \frac{(\bar{X}_1 - \bar{X}_2) - (\mu_1 - \mu_2)}{s_{(\bar{x}_1 - \bar{x}_2)}} = \frac{(70 - 75) - 0}{2.06} = -2.427$$

At the .05 level, the difference is significant for a two-tailed test if t, with 7 degrees of freedom $(n_1 + n_2 - 2 = 4 + 5 - 2 = 7)$, falls outside the range ± 2.365. (The value of 2.365 can be found in Table 2 in the Appendix at the end of the book.) The computed t value is -2.427, which falls outside the range in the rejection region. We thus reject the hypothesis that the two population means are the same. In other words, the difference between the two population means is significant. The mean of women sales levels is higher than that of men sales levels at the computer company.

EXHIBIT 15-2 | Average Monthly Sales Levels by Gender

Men	Monthly Sales Levels X_1	x_1	x_1^2	Women	Monthly Sales Levels X_2	x_2	x_2^2
Adam	74	4	16	Logan	75	0	0
Bahar	65	−5	25	Machiko	78	3	9
Carter	72	2	4	Nida	74	−1	1
Dmitri	69	−1	1	Orin	76	1	1
				Palmer	72	−3	9
$n_1 = 4$				$n_2 = 5$			
Total	280	0	46	Total	375	0	20
$\bar{X}_1 = \frac{280}{4} = 70$				$\bar{X}_2 = \frac{375}{5} = 75$			
$n_1 s_1^2 = \sum x_1^2 = 46$				$n_2 s_2^2 = \sum x_2^2 = 20$			

Source: © 2007 JupiterImages Corporation.

15-3 Calculating the *t*-Test Using Computers

Thus far, many of our calculations have been tedious because we did them manually. Many statistical software packages such as SPSS and SAS permit researchers to shift the tedious computations to the computer. Most students have access to Microsoft Excel and possibly one of the other statistical analysis software packages previously listed. Use the software to follow along as we solve the preceding problem using Microsoft's Excel and SPSS for Windows. Although we explained earlier that the *z*-test is the appropriate test to use when $n > 30$, SPSS and SAS use the *t*-test for all sample sizes.

15-3a Using Excel to Run the *t*-Test

To do the analysis, follow these steps:

1. Open a new spreadsheet.
2. Enter all of the men's monthly sales levels in the first column. Then enter all of the women's monthly sales levels in the second column.
3. At the top of the spreadsheet, open up the "Tools" menu. Then click on "Data Analysis."
4. Highlight "t-test: Two-Sample Assuming Equal Variances," then click on "ok."
5. Specify the Variable 1 Range and Variable 2 Range. For the numbers in the first group, in cells A1 through A4, type in "A1:A4" for Variable 1 Range. For the numbers in the second group, in cells B1 through B5, type in "B1:B5" in Variable 2 Range.
6. Click on "ok."

The spreadsheet shown in Exhibit 15-3 will appear on the screen.

15-3b Using SPSS to Run the *t*-Test

To do the analysis, follow these steps:

1. Open a new spreadsheet. Enter all of the men's and women's monthly sales levels into the first column. For consistency, first enter the men's sales levels in the first four cells and then enter the women's sales levels in the next five cells.

EXHIBIT 15-3	The *t*-Test: Two-Sample Assuming Equal Variances

	Variable 1	Variable 2
Mean	70	75
Variance	15.33333	5
Observations	4	5
Pooled Variance	9.428571	
Hypothesized Mean Difference	0	
Df	7	
t Stat	−2.4274	
P(T<=t) one-tail	0.022797	
t Critical one-tail	1.894578	
P(T<=t) two-tail	0.045594	
t Critical two-tail	2.364623	

EXHIBIT 15-4	SPSS Tables for Group Statistics and Independent Samples Test

Group Statistics

	VAR00002	N	Mean	Std. Deviation	Std. Error Mean
VAR00001	1.00	4	70.0000	3.9158	1.9579
	2.00	5	75.0000	2.2361	1.0000

Independent Samples Test

		Levene's Test for Equality of Variances		*t*-test for Equality of Means					95% Confidence Interval of the Difference	
		F	Sig.	t	df	Sig. (2-tailed)	Mean Difference	Std. Error Difference	Lower	Upper
VAR00001	Equal variances assumed	1.773	.225	−2.427	7	.046	−5.0000	2.0598	−9.8707	−.1293
	Equal variances not assumed			−2.274	4.538	.077	−5.0000	2.1985	−10.8290	.8290

2. In the second column, type a "1" next to each monthly sales level for the men. Still in the second column, type a "2" next to each monthly sales level for the women.

3. Highlight the heading "Analyze" and go to "Compare Means." Then click on "Independent-Samples T Test."

4. Highlight "var00001." Then using the large arrow, shift "var00001" over to the side that says "Test Variable."

5. Highlight "var00002." Then using the second large arrow, shift "var00002" over to the side that says "Grouping Variable."

6. Under "Grouping Variable," click "Define Groups." For "Group 1," type "1" and for "Group 2," type "2." This will indicate the groups (i.e., women and men) of monthly sales levels that will be compared.

7. Click on "Continue" and "ok."

The output shown in Exhibit 15-4 will appear on the screen.

Both spreadsheets in Exhibit 15-4 display results similar to those obtained manually. There are, however, a few differences, the major one being that SPSS displays Levene's test for equality of variances. Since SPSS displays the most data, we will discuss this output, although much of the discussion will also pertain to the Excel output.

Levene's test for equality of variances is used to examine whether the spread of the groups differs (the variance indicates the dispersion or spread of data). The null hypothesis is that the two population variances are the same. Here the F-statistic is 1.773 with a significance level (or p-value) of 0.225, which indicates that the hypothesis of equal variances cannot be rejected. Thus it is appropriate to use the "Equal variances assumed" test to compare means. Since the variances are assumed to be equal, we can use the first t-test, which is the "pooled-variance t-test." If the variances were assumed not to be equal, we would have used the second t-test, which is the "separate-variance t-test." Using the "Equal variances assumed" t-test, we can determine that the sample means of 70 and 75 do not come from populations with equal means. The means differ significantly. The t statistic is -2.427 with 7 degrees of freedom and has an associated probability (or significance) of 0.046. Based on the size of the means, we can conclude that women's sales levels are significantly higher than men's sales levels.

> **Levene's test for equality of variances** A test used to examine whether the spread of two groups differ.

15-4 Difference between Two Proportions of Independent Samples

Let p_1 and p_2 be the proportions of two samples drawn from respective populations with proportions P_1 and P_2. The null hypothesis is that there is no difference between the two population proportions; that is, $P_1 = P_2$, or stated another way, $P_1 - P_2 = 0$. If the null hypothesis is true, $P_1 = P_2$, the two populations are really the same population.

The basic concept concerning the difference between two sample proportions is analogous to that concerning the difference between two sample means.

1. The mean of the sampling distribution $(p_1 - p_2)$ is equal to the difference between the two population proportions, P_1 and P_2, or $p_1 - p_2 = P_1 - P_2$.

2. The variance of the difference between two sample proportions is the sum of variances of the two sample proportions,

$$\sigma^2_{(p_1-p_2)} = \sigma^2_{p_1} + \sigma^2_{p_2} = \frac{P_1 Q_1}{n_1} + \frac{P_2 Q_2}{n_2}$$

where $Q_1 = 1 - P_1$
$Q_2 = 1 - P_2$

When the sampling distributions of p_1 and p_2 are normal, the distribution of the differences between p_1 and p_2 is also normal. Since the mean of the sampling distribution of $(p_1 - p_2)$ is equal to the difference between the two population proportions, the distribution that follows is normal.

$$z = \frac{(p_1 - p_2) - (P_1 - P_2)}{\sigma_{(p_1-p_2)}}$$

$p_1 = $ sample proportion successes in first group

$p_2 = $ sample proportion successes in second group

$P_1 = $ population proportion of first group

$P_2 = $ population proportion of second group

$\sigma_{(p_1-p_2)} = $ variance of the difference between two sample proportions

When $P_1 = P_2$, $P_1 - P_2 = 0$ and $P_1 Q_1 = P_2 Q_2 = PQ$ where $Q = 1 - P$. Thus

$$z = \frac{p_1 - p_2}{\sigma_{(p_1 - p_2)}}$$

where

$$\sigma_{(p_1 - p_2)} = \sqrt{\frac{P_1 Q_1}{n_1} + \frac{P_2 Q_2}{n_2}} = \sqrt{PQ \left(\frac{1}{n_1} + \frac{1}{n_2} \right)}$$

When the value of P is to be estimated by using the two sample proportions and when the sample sizes of the two samples are large, z becomes an approximated value and is when

$$z = \frac{(p_1 - p_2)(P_1 - P_2)}{s_{(p_1 - p_2)}}$$

where $s_{(p_1 - p_2)} = \sqrt{pq \left(\frac{1}{n_1} + \frac{1}{n_2} \right)}$ and $p = \frac{n_1 p_1 + n_2 p_2}{n_1 + n_2}$ [Formula 15-5]

The best estimate of the population proportion P is p and $q = 1 - p$. That is, p is the weighted mean of the two sample proportions, p_1 and p_2. The weights are based on sample sizes n_1 and n_2. Consider Example 15-3.

Example 15-3

A sample of 500 consumers taken from New York City shows that 59.6% of the customers favor a new buffalo burger, and a sample of 300 customers taken from Atlanta shows that 50% of the customers favor the buffalo burger. The burger was test-marketed for a longer time period in New York City. Is there a significant difference between the opinions of the two cities concerning the new burger? Use a level of significance of .05.

Solution: Let P_1 and P_2 denote the population (city) proportions of the customers in favor of the buffalo burger.

H_0: $P_1 - P_2 = 0$ (There is no difference between the two population proportions.)
H_0: $P_1 - P_2 \neq 0$

Find z by using formula 15-5.

$n_1 = 500$, $p_1 = 59.6\% = .596$
$n_2 = 300$, $p_2 = 50\% = .50$

$$p = \frac{500(.596) + 300(.5)}{500 + 300} = .56 \quad \text{and} \quad q = 1 - .56 = .44$$

$$s_{(p_1 - p_2)} = \sqrt{(.56)(.44) \left(\frac{1}{500} + \frac{1}{300} \right)} = .036$$

$$z = \frac{(.596 - .5) - 0}{.036} = \frac{.096}{.036} = 2.67$$

We are interested in finding the critical values that form the boundaries of the regions of the area $.05/2 = .025$ in each tail. A two-tailed test is used because the alternative hypothesis contains the operator $\neq$. At the .05 level, the difference is significant for a two-tailed test if z is outside the range ± 1.96. The computed value of z falls outside the range or in the rejection region. Thus we reject the null hypothesis. There is a significant difference in the opinions between the two cities about the buffalo burger.

15-5 Analysis of Variance (ANOVA)

The two tests (z-tests and t-tests) we discussed earlier were useful when testing a null hypothesis when only two samples are involved, but when more than two samples are involved, it doesn't make sense to test differences between the means two at a time. Think about it: six samples would warrant 15 t-tests to test all pairs of means. Furthermore, the likelihood of a Type I error is dramatically increased as z- and t-tests are used to test for differences among three or more means.

analysis of variance (ANOVA) A technique for testing whether there is a significant difference among the means of two or more independent samples.

Analysis of variance (ANOVA) is often the preferred method to test whether there is a significant difference among means of two or more independent samples. It is applicable whenever a study involves an interval- or ratio-scaled dependent variable. Although its roots are from the agricultural sector, ANOVA is a powerful tool in analyzing different types of scientific problems as well as problems in marketing research. (See Research Realities 15-1.)

one-way analysis of variance A technique for comparing the means of more than two samples or populations when there is only one independent variable.

In this chapter, we will concentrate on **one-way analysis of variance,** since it is a bivariate statistical technique that involves only one independent variable, although there may be multiple levels of that variable.

The null hypothesis for ANOVA is that the means of normally distributed populations, such as three populations a, b, and c, are equal, or $\mu_a = \mu_b = \mu_c$. The alternative hypothesis is that at least one of the means is significantly different from the other means. If we further assume that the variances of the populations are equal, we will have three equal populations. When the three populations are combined into a single large population, it is reasonable to expect that the mean and the variance of the large population (μ_a and σ^2) will be equal to those of the original populations, or

$$\mu = \mu_a = \mu_b = \mu_c \quad \text{and} \quad \sigma^2 = \sigma_a^2 = \sigma_b^2 = \sigma_c^2$$

If we take a random sample from each of the three original populations, we may consider the three samples of subsets of a single large sample drawn from the single

Research Realities 15-1

ANOVA in Product Development Research

In today's intensified competitive markets, companies frequently introduce new products to gain a competitive edge. Improving existing attributes (an enhancing strategy), adding new features (a unique strategy), and pure imitation are three common strategies for companies to introduce their products. To test which strategy is more effective in enabling a firm to achieve superior performance, a series of experiments were run that demonstrated the use of ANOVA in comparing the effectiveness of these three strategies.

The results show that both enhancing and unique strategies are superior to the pure imitation strategy. However, the effectiveness of enhancing vs. unique strategies depends on the maturity of the market. If the market is mature, a unique strategy works better; for the premature market, however, an enhancing strategy is more effective.

Source: Kevin Zheng Zhou, "Achieving Late-Mover Advantage: The Effects of Enhancing and Distinctive Strategies," *Virginia Polytechnic Institute and State University Dissertation* (May 2002).

EXHIBIT 15-5	Sample Data Presentation in Columns

Observations in Each Sample	Sample		
	(a)	(b)	(c)
1	X_a	X_b	X_c
2	X_a	X_b	X_c
3	X_a	X_b	X_c
4	X_a	X_b	X_c
5	—	X_b	—
Total	$\sum X_a$	$\sum X_b$	$\sum X_c$
Sample mean	$\bar{X}_a$	$\bar{X}_b$	$\bar{X}_c$

EXHIBIT 15-6	Sample Data Presentation in Rows

	Observations in Each Sample					Sample	
Sample	1	2	3	4	5	Total	Mean
(a)	X_a	X_a	X_a	X_a	—	$\sum X_a$	$\bar{X}_a$
(b)	X_b	X_b	X_b	X_b	X_b	$\sum X_b$	$\bar{X}_b$
(c)	X_c	X_c	X_c	X_c	—	$\sum X_c$	$\bar{X}_c$

large population. The sample data may be arranged in columns (Exhibit 15-5) or rows (Exhibit 15-6).

$$\bar{\bar{X}} = \text{Grand mean} = \frac{\sum X_a + \sum X_b + \sum X_c}{4 + 5 + 4} = \frac{\sum X}{13}$$

The unbiased estimate of the large population variance (σ^2) based on the preceding samples may be obtained by calculating the variance between groups [MSA ($\hat{s}_1^2$)] and the variance within groups [MSE ($\hat{s}_2^2$)].

15-5a Variance between Groups

The variance between groups (or between samples) is also referred to as the "mean sum of squares between (among) groups." It is sometimes denoted as MSA or $\hat{s}_1^2$. It is calculated as follows:

$$\hat{s}_1^2 = \frac{\text{Sum of variations of group means from grand mean}}{\text{Degrees of freedom between groups}}$$

$$= \frac{n_a(\bar{X}_a - \bar{\bar{X}})^2 + n_b(\bar{X}_b - \bar{\bar{X}})^2 + n_c(\bar{X}_c - \bar{\bar{X}})^2}{r - 1}$$

$$= \frac{\text{Sum of squares}_\text{between}}{\text{Degrees of freedom}}$$

Or, it can be written in a general form, as follows:

$$\hat{s}_1^2 = MSA = \frac{SS_\text{between}}{df} = \frac{\sum n_i(\bar{X}_i - \bar{\bar{X}})^2}{r - 1}$$

where

i = individual groups or samples a, b, c, ...

n_i = size of group i, or size of sample drawn from population i, such as $n_a = 4$, $n_b = 5$, $n_c = 4$ in the preceding illustration

$\bar{X}_i$ = mean of the items in group or sample i

$\bar{\bar{X}}$ = grand mean, or mean of all items in the single large sample

$\bar{X}_i - \bar{\bar{X}}$ = deviation of group mean from grand mean

$(\bar{X}_i - \bar{\bar{X}})^2$ = variation, or squared deviation (The term "variation" has been used loosely in previous discussions. Here, the term is limited to represent the squared deviation.)

r = number of groups or samples, such as 3 groups in the above illustration

treatment Different levels of a factor.

Note that the deviation $(\bar{X}_i - \bar{\bar{X}})$ is called the *effect* and the nature of the sample i is called the **treatment**. Furthermore, whenever ANOVA is used, the independent variables are called **factors**, so the different levels (or categories) of a factor are the treatments. An effect is due to a particular type of treatment, just as applying different types of fertilizers (treatments) to different sections of a tract of land will produce different grades of corn (effects) in an agricultural experiment.

factors The independent variables whenever ANOVA is used.

15-5b Variance within Groups

mean square error (MSE) An estimate of the random error existing in the data.

The variance within groups (or within individual samples) is also referred to as the **mean square error (MSE)** or $\hat{s}_2^2$, since it is an estimate of the random error existing in the data. It is calculated as follows:

$$\hat{s}_2^2 = \frac{\text{Sum of variations of group items from group means}}{\text{Degrees of freedom within groups}}$$

$$= \frac{\text{Sum of squares}_{\text{within}}}{\text{Degrees of freedom}}$$

$$= \frac{\sum(X_a - \bar{X}_a)^2 + \sum(X_b - \bar{X}_b)^2 + \sum(X_c - \bar{X}_c)^2}{n_a + n_b + n_c - r}$$

Or, it can be written in a general form as follows:

$$\hat{s}_2^2 = MSE = \frac{SS_{\text{within}}}{df} = \frac{\sum[\sum(X_i - \bar{X}_i)^2]}{n - r}$$

where X_i = individual items in group i

$n = n_a + n_b + n_c$ = number of items in the single large sample

15-5c The *F*-Test

The letter F, used in honor of the founder of this test, R. A. Fisher, represents the variance ratio showing the relationship between the two independently estimated population variances we showed how to compute in section 15-5a:

$$F = \frac{\hat{s}_1^2}{\hat{s}_2^2}$$

where the subscripts 1 (in the numerator) and 2 (in the denominator) indicate the sample numbers and each represents the estimate of the population variance based on the sample.

F-statistic A measure of the variance between groups divided by the variance within groups, calculated by dividing one sample variance by another sample variance.

The **F-statistic** is the variance between groups divided by the variance within groups. It is used to test for group differences and compares one sample variance with another sample variance. It can be presented this way:

$$F = \frac{\text{Variance between groups}}{\text{Variance within groups}} = \frac{MSA}{MSE}$$

There are specific reasons for selecting the two terms:

1. If the hypothesis is true (or $\mu = \mu_a = \mu_b = \mu_c$) and the assumption regarding the same variance is valid (or $\sigma^2 = \sigma_a^2 = \sigma_b^2 = \sigma_c^2$), the two independent estimates of the large population variance should not be greatly different; that is, $\hat{s}_1^2$ should be close to $\hat{s}_2^2$. The value of the F-statistic, therefore, should be close to unity, or 1.

2. If the hypothesis is true, the means of the samples drawn from the populations a, b, and c should not vary significantly from each other or from the grand mean (except for variation attributed to chance). That is $\bar{X}_a, \bar{X}_b, \bar{X}_c$ and $\bar{\bar{X}}$ should be close to each other. Thus the variance between groups should be small. In fact, the variance is zero if the sample means and the grand mean are the same. Therefore, the value of the F-statistic should be small or close to zero if the hypothesis is true.

3. If the hypothesis is not true, the sample means will differ from each other and also the grand mean by more than the extent attributed to chance. Thus the variance between groups becomes large. On the other hand, the variance within groups is not affected by the differences in the sample means, since it is obtained from the deviations within individual groups. Therefore, the value of the F-statistic is large if the hypothesis is not true.

How large should the F-statistic be in order to reject the hypothesis? This decision is usually based on the *right-tail test* according to the F-distribution. For this reason, the values given in the F tables cover only the upper probability points in the F distribution, since

(Variations between groups) + (Variations within groups) = (Variations of all items)

Also,

$$\text{Degrees of freedom between groups} + \text{Degrees of freedom within groups} = \text{Degrees of freedom of all items}$$

Consider Example 15-4.

Example 15-4

A marketing researcher took a sample of the number of sales calls made by 13 employees in Boston during a given period. She classified the sales calls into three groups according to occupations: electricians, carpenters, and painters, as shown in Exhibit 15-7. She wants to determine whether the means of the number of sales calls classified by the three different occupations are significantly different. Use a level of significance of .05.

EXHIBIT 15-7	Sales Calls of Employees by Occupation					
	Number of Sales Calls during the Given Period					
Occupation	**Sample Item (Employee)**					**Total**
	1	2	3	4	5	
Electricians	74	65	72	69	—	280
Carpenters	75	78	74	76	72	375
Painters	56	55	53	52	—	216
Grand total						871

Solution: H_0: The means of the number of sales calls of the three different occupations in Boston are equal, or $\mu_a = \mu_b = \mu_c$, where group a represents the number of sales calls made to electricians, group b represents the number of sales calls made to carpenters, and group c represents the number of sales calls made to painters.

H_1: At least one of the means is different from the other means. We will assume that the three populations (or number of sales calls of the occupations) are normally distributed. The F-statistic calculations are shown in Exhibit 15-8.

The calculation to determine the variance *between* groups is

$$\hat{s}_1^2 = \frac{4(70-67)^2 + 5(75-67)^2 + 4(54-67)^2}{3-1} = \frac{1{,}032}{2} = 516$$

The calculation to determine the variance *within* groups is

$$\hat{s}_2^2 = \frac{46 + 20 + 10}{(4+5+4)-3} = \frac{76}{13-3} = 7.6$$

EXHIBIT 15-8   Computation of the ANOVA

Items in Each Group	Number of Sales Calls X_i or X	Between Groups		Within Groups		Total	
		$\bar{X}_i - \bar{\bar{X}}$	$n_i(\bar{X}_i - \bar{\bar{X}})^2$	$X_i - \bar{X}_i$	$(X_i - \bar{X}_i)^2$	$X - \bar{\bar{X}}$	$(X - \bar{\bar{X}})^2$
			i = a, or Group a (electricians); n_a = 4				
1	74			4	16	7	49
2	65			−5	25	−2	4
3	72			2	4	5	25
4	69			−1	1	2	4
Total	280			0	46	12	82

$\bar{X}_a = \frac{280}{4} = 70$ $70 - 67 = 3$ $4(3)^2 = 36$

			i = b, or Group b (carpenters); n_b = 5				
1	75			0	0	8	64
2	78			3	9	11	121
3	74			−1	1	7	49
4	76			1	1	9	81
5	72			−3	9	5	25
Total	375			0	20	40	340

$\bar{X}_b = \frac{375}{5} = 75$ $75 - 67 = 8$ $5(8)^2 = 320$

			i = c, or Group c (painters); n_c = 4				
1	56			2	4	−11	121
2	55			1	1	−12	144
3	53			−1	1	−14	196
4	52			−2	4	−15	225
Total	216			0	10	−52	686

$\bar{X}_c = \frac{216}{4} = 54$ $54 - 67 = -13$ $4(-13)^2 = 676$

Grand total	871		1,032	0	76	0	1108

$n = 13$ $D_1 = 3 - 1 = 2$ $D_2 = 13 - 3 = 10$ $D = 13 - 1 = 12$

$\bar{\bar{X}} = \frac{871}{13} = 67$ $\hat{s}_1^2 = \frac{1032}{2} = 516$ $\hat{s}_2^2 = \frac{76}{10} = 7.6$ $\hat{s}^2 = \frac{1108}{12} = 92.33$

$$F = \frac{\hat{s}_1^2}{\hat{s}_2^2} = \frac{516}{7.6} = 67.89$$

Therefore, the *F*-statistic is determined as follows:

$$F = \frac{516}{7.6} = 67.89$$

Check the variations:

1,032 (between groups) + 76 (within groups) = 1,108 (total)

Check the degrees of freedom:

$(r - 1) + (n - r) = (3 - 1)$ for between groups $+ (13 - 3)$ for within groups $= 12$

The total variation and the total degrees of freedom are shown in the last column of Exhibit 15-8.

With $D_1 = 3 - 1 = 2$ and $D_2 = 13 - 3 = 10$, the *F*-statistic is significantly large if based on the right-tailed test:

The *F* value is above 4.10 at the .05 level of significance.

The 4.10 was obtained by using Table 4 in the Appendix at the end of the book and referring to the .05 probability table, $D_1 = 2$ and $D_2 = 10$. Since the computed *F*-statistic, 67.89, is far above 4.10, we may reject the hypothesis and state that at least one of the means of the number of sales calls made from the three different occupations in the city is not equal to the other means. At least one of the means of the three populations, sales calls of electricians, carpenters, and painters, is different. The entire procedure for testing the hypothesis for the example is summarized in the analysis of variance table in Exhibit 15-9.

EXHIBIT 15-9	Summary of ANOVA Example				

Source of Variation	Variation (Sum of Squares)	Degrees of Freedom	Variance (Mean Square)	F-Statistic Computed	at 5%
Between groups	$\sum n_i(\bar{X}_i - \bar{\bar{X}})^2 = 1,032$	$3 - 1 = 2$	$\frac{1032}{2} = 516$	$\frac{516}{7.6} = 67.89$	4.10
Within groups	$\sum[\sum(X_i - \bar{X}_i)^2] = 76$	$n - 3 = 10$	$\frac{76}{10} = 7.6$		
Total	$\sum(X - \bar{\bar{X}})^2 = 1,108$	$n - 1 = 12$		Test result: Reject H_0	

15-5d Calculating ANOVA Using Computers

Whenever computer software, such as SPSS, SAS, or Excel, is available to calculate the ANOVA statistics, you should use it, since it considerably simplifies the effort. In this section, we will calculate ANOVA using SPSS for Windows and then Microsoft's Excel, since most of you have access to at least one of these software packages.

Running ANOVA with SPSS

If you have SPSS, follow these steps to calculate the ANOVA statistics for our previous example:

1. Open a new spreadsheet.

2. Enter successively all of the data in the first column, grouped according to occupation. That is, enter 74, 65, 72, 69, 75, 78, and so on until all 13 numbers are in the first 13 cells. Then in the second column, enter a "1" next to all sales calls made by electricians. Enter a "2" next to all sales calls made by carpenters. Finally, enter a "3" next to all sales calls made by painters. This tells the computer which numbers belong in designated groups. That is, the 1's next to the cells containing 74, 65, 72, and 69 indicate that all of these numbers belong to the first group (which in this case is electricians). The same logic applies for 2's and 3's.

3. At the top of the first column, double click on "var00001." Under "Name" type "sales" in place of "var00001." Then click on "var00002" and type "occupat." (The cell is limited to only eight letters.) Then at the bottom of the spreadsheet, click on the "Data View" tab. This optional exercise simply names the categories.

4. At the top of the spreadsheet, click on "Analyze." Then click on "Compare Means" and "One-Way ANOVA." These commands designate the statistical test to be run.

5. Using the arrows, shift "sales" over to "Dependent List" and shift "occupat" over to "Factor." This shows that "sales" is the dependent variable and "occupation" is the independent variable to be examined.

6. Click "ok." The SPSS output shown in Exhibit 15-10 will appear:

EXHIBIT 15-10	SPSS Anova Table				
Sales			**Anova**		
	Sum of Squares	df	Mean Square	F	Sig.
Between Groups	1032.000	2	516.000	67.895	.000
Within Groups	76.000	10	7.600		
Total	1108.000	12			

Running ANOVA with Excel

To make the same calculations using Microsoft's Excel, follow these steps:

1. Open a new spreadsheet.

2. Input the data into the first three columns of the spreadsheet (ranging from cells A1 to C5). The first column should be the number of sales calls of the four electricians. The second column should be the number of sales calls of the

five carpenters. Finally, the third column should be the number of sales calls of the four painters. The data should be inputted as follows:

74	75	56
65	78	55
72	74	53
69	76	52
	72	

3. At the top of the spreadsheet, select "Tools" and "Data Analysis." Then click on "ANOVA."

4. Under the command "Input Range:" enter "A1:C5" to indicate that the data is in the cells from A1 to C5.

5. The default alpha level is .05. For our example, leave the alpha level at .05.

6. Click "ok." The Excel output shown in Exhibit 15-11 will appear:

EXHIBIT 15-11 **Excel ANOVA Table**

Anova: Single Factor

SUMMARY

Groups	Count	Sum	Average	Variance
Column 1	4	280	70	15.33333
Column 2	5	375	75	5
Column 3	4	216	54	3.333333

ANOVA

Source of Variation	SS	df	MS	F	P-value	F crit
Between Groups	1032	2	516	67.89474	1.52E-06	4.102816
Within Groups	76	10	7.6			
Total	1108	12				

Notice that with both the SPSS and Excel runs, the output closely resembles the ANOVA table we constructed manually. As discussed earlier, these tables should be interpreted the same way. Of particular importance is the large F values and the small p-value (which is below .05), which indicate that one or more of the three population means is different. In fact, the smaller the p-value, the less likely the result can be attributed to chance alone (that is, sampling error).

Decision Time!

This chapter covers the statistical techniques of group difference analysis, which can be used to do segmentation study. As a marketing manager of a perfume company, you want to know how to segment the market based on demographic variables such as gender, age, and income. But how can you make sure the proposed segmentation (e.g., by age) is meaningful? What kind of analysis can you run to show whether or not such segmentation makes sense?

Net Impact

The Internet can be a valuable tool to learn about the statistical techniques we discussed in this chapter. Using almost any search engine, you can find a variety of discussions about the topic. These discussions may be available on the Internet as part of a company's promotion of its statistical services, a university professor's statistical course notes, or PowerPoint slides that were used in a seminar presentation.

On the Lighter Side—Are Boys and Girls from the Same Planet? Consider Their Attitudes

John Gray, author of *Men Are from Mars, Women Are from Venus,* commented that a USA Weekend survey of teenagers confirmed his premise that they are entirely different species. The results don't totally bear this notion. Consider the following findings:

- The majority of teens believe that a person's physical appearance is what initially catches the attention of the opposite gender. While looks plays a role in the game of attraction, boys usually admit it more than girls. Many girls stated that personality is just as important as looks.

- Half of the girls and 34% of the guys solicit advice on the opposite sex from their friends. Almost one-fourth of the guys keep their thoughts on this issue. They don't want to open up their thoughts to others.

- More than 90% of teens are gender blind and admit that it's okay to have close friends of the opposite sex. However, 53% of guys and 50% of girls find it more difficult to relate to friends of the opposite sex.

- On Saturday nights, almost half of boys and 64% of girls prefer to hang out with friends of both sexes.

- More than 80% of teens feel that it's fine for a girl to ask a boy out on a date.

- Many teens think less of girls who have had sex than of boys who have had sex.

Source: Originally appeared in the April 18–20, 2003 issue of USA WEEKEND. Reprinted with permission.

Chapter Summary

There are several ways to statistically test group differences. Some of the most commonly used methods are the z-test, t-test, and analysis of variance. This chapter concentrated on bivariate statistics that uses these parametric tests, which involve an interval- or ratio-scaled dependent variable. The z-test, t-test, and analysis of variance are tests used to compare some characteristic of one group with a characteristic of another and to determine whether or not a significant difference exists between the two groups. While z- and t-tests are useful when testing a null hypothesis when only two samples are involved, analysis of variance is the appropriate test when looking for significant differences among the means of two or more independent samples. When running an analysis of variance test, the F-test is used, which represents the variance ratio, showing the relationship between two independently estimated population variances. It can be used to test the equality of two population variances.

Review Questions

1. When should a z-test be used instead of a t-test?

2. When should an analysis of variance test be used instead of a z- or t-test?

3. What are the assumptions that have been made for the analysis of variance?

4. Why should we select the variance between groups and the variance within groups as the two terms of the F-statistic in the one-way analysis of variance?

5. What is the relationship between an "effect" and a "treatment"?

Practice Quiz

Note: You can find the correct answers to these questions by taking the quiz and then submitting your answers in the Online Edition. The program will automatically score your submission. If you miss a question, the program will provide the correct answer, a rationale for the answer, and the section number in the chapter where the topic is discussed.

1. Parametric tests assume that variables under investigation are measured using either nominal or ordinal scales.
   a. True
   b. False

2. Analysis of variance is a statistical tool that tests whether there is a significant difference among the means of two or more independent samples.
   a. True
   b. False

3. The *F*-statistic is the variance between groups divided by the variance within groups.
   a. True
   b. False

4. If a researcher uses analysis of variance to conduct a statistical test, the independent variables are called "treatments."
   a. True
   b. False

5. A *t*-test is used to compare the difference between two means when the population standard deviations are known.
   a. True
   b. False

6. If the estimate of the population variance of the first group is 16 and the estimate of the population variance of the second group is 4, what would be the *F*-value?
   a. 64
   b. 4

   c. 0.25
   d. 0
   e. None of the above

7. If the mean sum of squares between groups is 100 and the mean sum of squares among groups is 10, what would be the *F*-statistic?
   a. 1,000
   b. 100
   c. 10
   d. 10
   e. None of the above

8. Which test should be used to test the difference between two proportions of independent samples?
   a. *t*-test
   b. *z*-test
   c. *F*-test
   d. ANOVA
   e. None of the above

9. Which test should be used to test the mean differences of four independent samples?
   a. *t*-test
   b. *z*-test
   c. *F*-test
   d. ANOVA
   e. None of the above

10. The *t*-test is used to _____.
    a. compare two means when the population standard deviations are unknown
    b. compare two means when the population standard deviations are known
    c. compare two proportions
    d. compare two proportions when the population standard deviations are known
    e. None of the above

Thinking Critically

1. Assume the following information: $\sum x_1 = 64$, $n_1 = 5$, $\sum x_2^2 = 12$, $n_2 = 7$. Compute the *F*-statistic. Test the hypothesis that the two variances are the same at the (a) .05 and (b) .01 level of significance.

2. Assume the following information: $s_1 = 21$, $n_1 = 8$, $s_2 = 15$, $n_2 = 31$. Compute the *F*-statistic. Test the hypothesis that the two variances are the same at the (a) .05 and (b) .01 level of significance.

3. Assume the following information: $\hat{s}_1^2 = 30$, $n_1 = 6$, $\hat{s}_2^2 = 10$, $n_2 = 21$. Compute the *F*-statistic. Test the

hypothesis that the two variances are the same at the (a) .05 and (b) .01 level of significance.

4. A marketing manager sampled 15 convenience store customers and examined the number of items that were purchased by each customer. She classified the results into four groups according to years of college education of the customers. Test the hypothesis that the means of the number of items purchased of the four groups are the same. Use a level of significance of .05.

Customer Number (in Each Group)	Years of College (Group)			
	1	2	3	4
	Number of Items Purchased			
1	2	4	10	7
2	3	5	7	8
3	3	3	10	9
4	4	6	9	

5. A marketing manager took a sample of training class grades of 15 students. He classified the grades on the basis of teaching style (lecture, case studies, and role playing) as shown in the following table. Test the hypothesis that the means of the grades of the three classes are the same. Use a level of significance of .05.

Teaching Style	Student Number				
	1	2	3	4	5
	Grade				
Lecture	2	3	6	10	4
Case studies	3	7	3	10	7
Role playing	4	5	9	8	9

Net Exercise

The United Nations Statistics Division provides all kinds of statistical outputs and services for producers and users of statistics worldwide. It reports economic statistics, environment statistics, demographic and social statistics, and statistical databases online. Visit its site at http://unstats.un.org/unsd/default.htm and look at the types of data and publications it provides online.

Experiencing Marketing Research

You are responsible for determining whether the number of hours per week that supermarkets, department stores, and gasoline stations are open for business is significantly different. Randomly select ten stores in your area for each retail classification and make the decision. Use a level of significance of .01. Report your findings.

Case 15-1

Single Moms or Two-Parent Families: Who Spends More at Restaurants?

Eat-Out, Incorporated, is a conglomerate that owns both fast-food and full-service restaurants throughout the United States. Its sales have been decreasing, and management worries have been on the rise. They know that the composition of American families has been changing but are unsure how these demographic changes affect expenditures at both types of restaurants. They found from the U.S. Bureau of the Census that the average annual income for single-parent females with children was $34,354 in 2003 compared with $78,275 for dual-parent households with children. Furthermore, they realize that a two-parent family has the potential for two incomes, with over half of all such families having both spouses employed. They believe that time pressures on a working single mother probably cause her to patronize restaurants at a higher frequency than a two-parent family might. However, her comparatively limited financial resources would mean she spends less.

Eat-Out management has decided to hire a marketing researcher so that they can better understand the spending patterns of female-headed single-parent and dual-parent families. The marketing researcher decided to use a sampling frame consisting of single-mother households and married-mother households, taken from the national membership list of the Market Facts Incorporated Consumer Mail Panel (CMP). A total of 818 surveys were mailed out, 348 to mothers heading families alone and 470 to mothers who have a spouse in the household. A total of 520 surveys were returned—210 from the single mothers and 310 from the married mothers. The analysis of variance statistical procedure was used to determine whether there were significant differences in expenditures between the two family types that can be related to (a) family type, (b) the employment status of the mother, (c) the number of children, and (d) the household income level (i.e., four factors). The ANOVA summaries are shown in the Exhibits 15-C1 and 15-C2 (for fast-food and full-service restaurants).

Republished with permission, Emerald Group Publishing Limited.

| EXHIBIT 15-C1 | Analysis of Variance Summary: Expenditures in Fast-Food Restaurants |

Source of Variation	Mean Dollars Spent Typical Week	n	F-value	p-value
Family type				
Single parent	11.04	210	0.29	.59
Two parent	13.57	309		
Employment of mother				
Employed	13.32	317	5.57	.02
Unemployed	11.33	202		
Number of children				
One	10.32	177	5.95	.00
Two or three	13.37	309		
Four to six	16.85	33		
Household income				
Less than $10,000	10.19	108	1.76	.15
$10,000–19,999	11.44	126		
$20,000–29,999	12.09	115		
$30,000 or more	15.18	170		

| EXHIBIT 15-C2 | Analysis of Variance Summary: Expenditures in Full-Service Restaurants |

Source of Variation	Mean Dollars Spent Typical Week	n	F-value	p-value
Family type				
Single parent	7.25	210	1.56	.21
Two parent	13.50	309		
Employment of mother				
Employed	11.53	317	0.12	.91
Unemployed	10.09	202		
Number of children				
One	10.84	177	0.70	.50
Two or three	11.10	309		
Four to six	10.45	33		
Household income				
Less than $10,000	5.38	108	9.19	.00
$10,000–19,999	8.06	126		
$20,000–29,999	9.79	115		
$30,000 or more	17.47	170		

Sources: Roshan D. Ahuja and Mary Walker, "Female-headed single parent families," *Journal of Consumer Marketing* 11 (Fall 1994): 41–54; U.S. Census Bureau, "Family income table of contents," http://pubdb3.census.gov/macro/032004/faminc/new01_001.htm (March 2004), accessed June 26, 2005.

Case Questions

1. According to family type, is there a significant difference regarding expenditures in fast-food restaurants? Regarding expenditures in full-service restaurants?

2. What other conclusions can you draw from the two exhibits?

Nonparametric Methods for Difference Tests—Rank-Sum Tests

Nonparametric methods
Distribution-free methods, used when the required assumptions about the shape of population distribution cannot be made, and used when nominal- or ordinal-scaled data must be analyzed.

The difference analysis statistics such as the z-test, t-test, and ANOVA are all **parametric tests,** which assume that variables under investigation are measured using either interval or ratio scales. Furthermore, parametric tests make some additional assumptions: (1) the sample data should be randomly drawn from a normally distributed population; (2) the sample data drawn must be independent of each another; and (3) when examining central tendency for which two or more samples are drawn, the populations should have equal variances. However, in some situations, we cannot make these specific assumptions about the shape of the population distribution. In these cases we will turn to nonparametric methods.

Nonparametric methods of testing hypotheses are not concerned with particular population parameters. The advantage of these methods is that we do not have to know the shape of the population (whether it is distributed normally or is skewed) or make specific assumptions about the population for the purpose of testing hypotheses. Another advantage of nonparametric techniques is their relative ease of computation and understanding. Further, they can be used with ranked information and for tests involving small samples. However, their applications are limited to certain types of information, and they tend to be less precise and efficient than parametric methods.

So when do we use nonparametric methods? We use them when (1) the population distribution from which the sample is drawn cannot be assumed to be normal, (2) the sampling distribution is known not to be normal, or (3) nonmetric (nominal- or ordinal-scaled) data are used.

rank-sum tests Tests that use some sort of ranking totals in their calculations.

Rank-sum tests, a nonparametric method for difference tests, have become more popular in recent years. Rank-sum tests use some sort of ranking totals in their calculations. There are several ways to perform rank-sum tests. The most basic three techniques are: (1) the Wilcoxon test for matched pairs, (2) the Mann-Whitney (U) test, and (3) the Kruskal-Wallis (H) test.

Wilcoxon Test for Matched Pairs

Wilcoxon test Rank-sum test that analyzes ordinal data for differences between two related samples by using plus and minus signs and considers the magnitudes of the differences and ranks of the differences between the paired values.

The **Wilcoxon test,** also called the *signed-rank test,* compares two populations in which we have paired observations. This test makes sense when there is a natural way to pair data, such as two members from the same family reporting their attitudes toward certain advertisements. Also, it works well for before and after data to test for a median difference of zero. This test considers both the magnitudes of the differences and ranks of the differences between the paired values. It can take the place of a one-sample *t*-test when we cannot assume a normal distribution.

Let *n* be the number of paired values and *d* the difference of each pair of values. First, rank the *n* differences according to their absolute values ($|d|$, disregarding the + and − signs of *d*) from the smallest (ranked number 1) to the largest (ranked number *n*). If two or more differences are tied in ranks, give each difference the mean of the ranks. Thus if two differences are tied in the third and fourth ranks, each difference is ranked as $3.5 = (3 + 4) \div 2$. Next, give each rank the original sign of the difference it represents. Then compute the sum of all positive ranks and the sum of all negative ranks.

The null hypothesis assumes that the two populations, from which the two samples (or two sets of values) to be analyzed are drawn, are the same. Thus the expected rank sums for the positive and negative differences should be equal, or

(Sum of positive ranks) = (Sum of negative ranks) = (Sum of all ranks ÷ 2)

The sum of all ranks, 1, 2, 3, ... *n* can be obtained by the formula

$$\frac{n}{2}(1 + n)$$

If $n = 18$, the sum of all ranks 1−18 is

$$\frac{18}{2}(1 + 18) = 171$$

and the expected sum of either positive ranks or negative ranks is

$$\frac{171}{2} = 85.5$$

The purpose of the Wilcoxon test is to decide whether the difference between a *computed* signed-rank sum and the *expected* rank sum of the same sign is large enough to be significant. Let $T =$ the computed total of either the positive ranks or the negative ranks, whichever is smaller. The expected value of *T* is 1/2 of the sum of all ranks, or

$$E(T) = \frac{n(1 + n)}{4}$$

When the sample size is large, preferably 10 or more, the sampling distribution of *T* is approximately normal. The standard error of the statistic *T* is

$$\sigma_T = \sqrt{\frac{n(n + 1)(2n + 1)}{24}}$$

and the standard normal deviate *z* is

$$z = \frac{T - E(T)}{\sigma_T}$$

Consider Example A-1.

Example A-1

We are interested in determining whether there is a significant difference between the mileage yields for Easy-Go Gasoline's brand of premium unleaded gasoline and its closest competitor's premium unleaded gasoline.

Solution: H_0: There is no difference between the two kinds of gasoline in mileage yields.

   H_1: The mileage yields are different.

> **EXHIBIT 15-A1** | Results from the Two Grades of Gasoline Using Signed Ranks

Car Number	Miles per Gallon by Easy-Go Brand (1)	Miles per Gallon by Competitor's Brand (2)	D(1) − (2)	Rank of $|d|$	Signed Rank Positive Rank	Signed Rank Negative Rank
1	15	18	−3	3.5		−3.5
2	13	12	+1	1	+1	
3	14	16	−2	2		−2
4	18	22	−4	5		−5
5	19	24	−5	6.5		−6.5
6	12	18	−6	8		−8
7	20	13	+7	9	+9	
8	16	13	+3	3.5	+3.5	
9	15	23	−8	10		−10
10	21	21	0	excluded		
11	18	27	−9	11		−11
12	25	15	+10	12	+12	
13	23	11	+12	14	+14	
14	11	24	−13	15		−15
15	12	27	−15	17		−17
16	12	26	−14	16		−16
17	20	20	0	excluded		
18	16	11	+5	6.5	+6.5	
19	28	12	+16	18	+18	
20	13	24	−11	13		−13
Total	7 + signs 11 − signs 18 signs = sample size n			171	+64 = T, smaller total	−107

To find z, we must first of all determine σ_T. See the calculations in Exhibit 15-A1. Based on Exhibit 15-A1, the following calculations are performed:

$$T = +64$$

$$E(T) = \frac{n(1 + n)}{4} = \frac{18(1 + 18)}{4} = \frac{171}{2} = 85.5$$

$$\sigma_T = \sqrt{\frac{n(n + 1)(2n + 1)}{24}} = \sqrt{\frac{18(18 + 1)(2 \times 18 + 1)}{24}} = 22.96$$

$$z = \frac{64 - 85.5}{22.96} = -.94$$

Using a level of significance of .05 for a one-tailed test, the critical value of $z = -1.645$. The computed value of $z = -0.94$ falls in the acceptance region. Thus we accept the hypothesis, as we did in the previous example. The findings indicate that there is no difference between the two kinds of gasoline in mileage yields.

Mann-Whitney test Rank-sum test that analyzes ordinal data by determining whether exactly two independent samples are drawn from identical populations or from two populations with the same median; also called the U test.

Mann-Whitney (U) Test

The **Mann-Whitney test,** also called the U test, is another type of rank-sum test. This test can be used to determine whether two independent samples are drawn from identical populations or from two populations with the same median. This test can take the place of the two-sample t-test when the researcher is unsure about the normality assumption.

$$\text{Let } n_1 = \text{ the number of items in sample A}$$
$$n_2 = \text{ the number of items in sample B}$$

Next, arrange all $(n_1 + n_2)$ items into one group according to their magnitudes and rank them. If two or more items of different samples are tied in rank, give each item the mean of the ranks.

Then, the sum of cumulative items of first sample A, denoted by the letter U, can be obtained by two methods:

Method 1: Count the number of A items that precede each B item. The sum of the numbers counted is the value of U.

Method 2: Use the following formula:

$$U = n_1 + n_2 + \frac{n_1(n_1 + 1)}{2} - R_1 \quad \text{where} \quad R_1 = \text{ total of ranks of } A \text{ items}$$

Thus if sample A has 4 items (60, 64, 72, and 78) and sample B has 5 items (62, 67, 69, 72, and 74), or $n_1 = 4$ and $n_2 = 5$, the value of U for the combined sample of 9 items is 10.5 by Method (1), as shown in Exhibit 15-A2.

The value of U is computed using Method 2 as follows: Substituting $n_1 = 4$, $n_2 = 5$, and $R_1 = 19.5$ into the formula,

$$U = (4)(5) + \frac{4(4 + 1)}{2} - 19.5 = 10.5$$

Method 1 explains the meaning of the U value, while method 2 gives a simpler way to compute U. In the following discussion, method 2 is used.

When the sample sizes are large, preferably both n_1 and n_2 larger than 10, the sampling distribution of the U is approximately normal. The expected value of U is

$$E(U) = \frac{n_1 n_2}{2}$$

the standard error of the statistic U is

$$\sigma_U = \sqrt{\frac{n_1 n_2 (n_1 + n_2 + 1)}{12}}$$

▶ EXHIBIT 15-A2	Computed Values Using the Mann-Whitney Test		
Items Arranged	Rank	Method 1: Number of A Items Precedes Each B*	Method 2: Rank of A Items
60A	1		1
62B	2	1	
64A	3		3
67B	4	2*	
69B	5	2	
72A	6.5		6.5
72B	6.5	2.5*	
74B	8	3	
78A	9		9
Total		10.5 = U	19.5 = R_1

*For example, the 2 A items before 67B are 60A and 64A. The 2.5 items before 72B are 60A, 64A, and 72A (72A is counted as 1/2 of an item since it ties with 72B).

and the standard normal deviate is

$$z = \frac{U - E(U)}{\sigma_U}$$

Consider Example A-2

Example A-2

A marketing research firm has asked two panels of consumers to rate a new dishwashing detergent using a scale from 1 (poor) to 100 (excellent). The first panel has 12 consumers, and the second panel has 10 consumers. The consumer responses are ranked and listed in Exhibit 15-A3. The group moderator wants to know whether there is a significant difference between the median scores of the two panels. Use a level of significance of .05.

EXHIBIT 15-A3	Scores of Two Consumer Panels Rating New Detergent				
	Group A			**Group B**	
Consumer Number	**Score**	**Rank**		**Score**	**Rank**
1	60	1		62	2
2	64	3		67	4
3	72	6.5		69	5
4	78	9		72	6.5
5	80	10		74	8
6	88	14.5		82	11
7	88	14.5		84	12
8	91	17		86	13
9	93	18		90	16
10	96	20		95	19
11	97	21			
12	100	22			
Total	1,007	$R_1 = 156.5$		781	
Median	88			78	

Solution: H_0: The two population medians are the same; there is no difference between the two class medians.

H_1: The two population medians are different.

Calculate the z value.

Based on Exhibit 15-A3, the following calculations are performed:

$$U = n_1 n_2 + \frac{n_1(n_1 + 1)}{2} - R_1 = 12(10) + \frac{12(12 + 1)}{2} - 156.5 = 41.5$$

$$E(U) = \frac{n_1 n_2}{2} = \frac{12(10)}{2} = 60$$

$$\sigma_U = \sqrt{\frac{n_1 n_2(n_1 + n_2 + 1)}{12}} = \sqrt{\frac{(12)(10)(12 + 10 + 1)}{12}} = \sqrt{230} = 15.16$$

$$z = \frac{U - E(U)}{\sigma_U} = \frac{41.5 - 60}{15.16} = -1.22$$

Here we are interested in testing whether the sum U obtained from the ranks of the items of sample A is significantly larger or smaller than the expected sum $E(U)$. Thus a two-tailed test is used in locating the critical value of z. At a .05 level, the difference is significant if z falls outside the range of ± 1.96. The computed z value is -1.22, which is inside the range of the acceptance region. Thus we accept the hypothesis.

Kruskal-Wallis (*H*) Test

The **Kruskal-Wallis test** is also a type of rank-sum test. This test can be used to determine whether k independent samples are drawn from identical populations or from k populations with the same median. The nonparametric test may be used to substitute for the method of one-way analysis of variance.

Let

$$n_1 = 5 \text{ (the number of items in the } i\text{th sample)}$$
$$i = 1, 2, 3, \cdots, \text{k}$$
$$n = \text{the number of all items in the combined large sample}$$
$$= n_1 + n_2 + n_3 + \cdots n_k$$

R_i = the total of ranks of n_1 items in the ith sample after the k samples are combined into one large sample and all items are ranked according to their magnitudes. The method of computing R_i is similar to that of computing R_i in the Mann-Whitney test.

Therefore, the statistic H can be used in the test:

$$H = \frac{12}{n(n+1)} \sum \left[\frac{R_i^2}{n_i} \right] - 3(n+1)$$

The Kruskal-Wallis test thus is also called the *H test*. If the null hypothesis that k samples are drawn from identical populations is true and each sample size is 5 or more, the sampling distribution of the statistic H can be approximated by the χ^2 distribution with D (degrees of freedom) $= k - 1$. Thus the χ^2 distribution Table 3 in the Appendix at the end of the book can be used in the H test process.

Consider Example A-3

> **Kruskal-Wallis test** Rank-sum test that analyzes ordinal data by determining whether two or more independent samples are drawn from identical populations or from two or more populations with the same median; also called the *H* test.

Example A-3

Assume that a marketing research firm took a sample of the daily summertime wages of 13 high school students in Los Angeles, California. The wages were classified into three groups, according to type of employment: construction workers, restaurant waiters/waitresses, and lifeguards, as shown in Exhibit 15-A4. Use the H test to determine whether the medians of the wages classified by the three different types of employment are significantly different. Let the level of significance be .05.

Solution: H_0: The population medians of the wages of the three occupations are the same.

                 H_1: The population medians of the wages of the three occupations are not the same.

To determine H, we use the following values from Exhibit 15-A4:

$n_1 = 4$, $n_2 = 5$, $n_3 = 4$, $n = 4 + 5 + 4 = 13$, $R_1 = 28$, $R_2 = 53$, and $R_3 = 10$

Substitute the values into the formula:

$$H = \frac{12}{n(n+1)} \sum \left[\frac{R_i^2}{n_i} \right] - 3(n-1)$$

$$H = \frac{12}{13(13+1)} \left(\frac{28^2}{4} + \frac{53^2}{5} + \frac{10^2}{4} \right) - 3(13+1) = 9.61$$

| EXHIBIT 15-A4 | Wages of Three Groups of Students | | | | | |

Sample	SAMPLE 1		SAMPLE 2		SAMPLE 3	
Item	(construction workers)		(waiters/waitresses)		(lifeguards)	
	Sample 1		Sample 2		Sample 3	
	(Construction Workers)		(Restaurant Servers)		(Lifeguards)	
Sample Item (Student)	Wages	Rank	Wages	Rank	Wages	Rank
1	$65	5	$72	7.5	$52	1
2	69	6	74	9.5	53	2
3	72	7.5	75	11	55	3
4	74	9.5	76	12	56	4
5			78	13		
Total	$280	$28.0 = R_1$	$375	$53.0 = R_2$	$216	$10 = R_3$
Median	$70.5		$75		$54	

Note: The sum of all ranks 1–13 is $R_1 + R_2 + R_3 = 28 + 53 + 10 = 91$, which can be checked by using the formula

$$\frac{n}{2}(1 + n) = \frac{13}{2}(1 + 13) = 91$$

At a .05 level of significance, the difference is significant if χ^2 with $D = k - 1 = 3 - 1 = 2$ degrees of freedom is above 5.991. The computed $H = 9.61$ is larger than the critical value of 5.991. Thus we reject the hypothesis. We may state that the medians of the wages of three occupations in the populations are not equal. The three populations are different.

Calculating Rank-Sum Tests Using Computers

To calculate the Wilcoxon test for matched pairs using SPSS, follow these steps:

1. Open a new spreadsheet.
2. Refer to the data in Exhibit 15-A1. Type the first group of numbers in the first column and the second group of numbers in the second column.
3. Using the headings of the page, click "Analyze."
4. Click on "Nonparametric Tests" and then click on "2 Related Samples Test."
5. Under "Test Type," click on "Wilcoxon."
6. Shift "var00001" and "var00002" over to "Test Pair(s) List."
7. Click on "OK."

The printout in Exhibit 15-A5 will appear:

Notice that the level of significance is .349, which indicates that we cannot reject the null hypothesis and must conclude that there is no difference between the two types of gasoline in mileage yields.

To use SPSS to calculate the Mann-Whitney test, follow the same steps as for the Wilcoxon test, except in step 4, after selecting "Nonparametric Tests," click on "2 Independent Samples Test." To calculate the Kruskal-Wallis test, also follow the same

EXHIBIT 15-A5	SPSS Tables for Wilcoxon Test for Matched Pairs

Ranks

		N	Mean Rank	Sum of Ranks
VAR00002 - VAR00001	**Negative Ranks**	7	9.14	64.00
	Positive Ranks	11	9.73	107.00
	Ties	2		
	Total	20		

a VAR00002 < VAR00001
b VAR00002 > VAR00001
c VAR00001 = VAR00002

Test Statistics

	VAR00002 - VAR00001
Z	−.937
Asymp. Sig. (2-tailed)	.349

a Based on negative ranks.
b Wilcoxon Signed Ranks Test

steps, except this time click on "*k* Independent Samples." Excel offers a variety of statistical tests under its "Data Analysis" command. However, it does not offer options for any of the rank-sum tests, so other software packages should be used for these particular tests.

Correlation and Regression

Chapter Sixteen

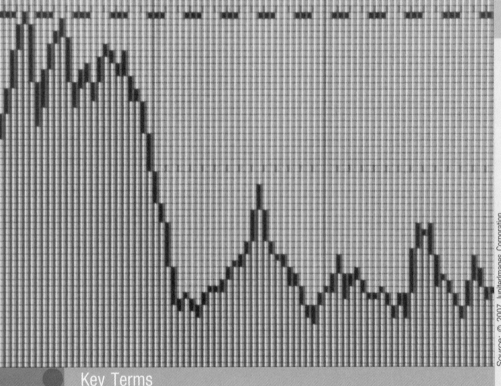

Source: © 2007 Jupiterimages Corporation.

Key Terms

Learning Objectives

After studying this chapter, you will be able to:

- Describe correlation and regression analyses.
- Calculate and interpret correlation and regression statistics.
- Perform regression analysis by computer.
- Understand nonparametric methods.
- Calculate and interpret the chi-square test of independence.

GET THIS

Important Ingredients of Brand Names: Relevance, Connotation, Pronunciation

When a company decides on a brand name for a new product or service, it establishes the foundation of the brand's image. The selection of the right brand name is one of the most important marketing decisions an organization will make, since it is typically the centerpiece of introductory marketing programs. While there is little doubt the brand name is an integral piece of an organization, its precise contribution to the organization is difficult to quantify. Indeed, organizations are often befuddled when attempting to understand the value added to a product by its brand name.

Brand names are often systematically researched before being chosen. Creating a brand name is typically a daunting task. Some of the challenges include keeping it simple, making it easy to pronounce, making it memorable, gaining legal clearance, making sure that there are no negative connotations (in any language), and being distinctive.

A recent study examined the effects of brand relevance, connotation, and pronunciation on consumers' preferences for new brand names. Relevance was defined as the degree to which a brand name suggests descriptive information of the product/service category. It varies along a continuum from high to low. For example, Burger King holds high relevance while Vincent's holds low relevance when used as a brand name for a fast food restaurant. Connotation relates to but also differs from relevance. The latter is more of a descriptive nature, while the former is more of a persuasive nature. Consider that consumers may evaluate poorly a brand name with negative connotation. The classic "Nova" (meaning "no go" in Spanish) automobile case is a good example for the latter scenario. Another important dimension of this component is the pronunciation of the word. When a brand is easy to pronounce, it likely facilitates a sense of familiarity with the word and increases consumers' intention to further process/retrieve the information related to the word in memory. On the contrary, a word that is difficult to pronounce may demand extra efforts to process or retrieve in an individual's mind.

Three researchers tested the following relevant hypotheses:

- H_1: Relevance of new brand name to product category contributes to brand preference.

- H_2: Positive connotation of new brand name contributes to brand preference.

- H_3: Easy pronunciation of a new brand name contributes to brand preference.

Two studies were conducted to test the research hypotheses. The first study looked at consumers' preferences of various brand names for a long-term healthcare organization that owns nursing homes and intensive care hospitals. Respondents were asked to pronounce the word, provide thoughts that came to mind, classify whether the thought was positive, indicate preference for the brand name, and tell whether the name reminded them of any other names in the marketplace. The second study examined the same concerns but used soft drink names instead of healthcare organization names.

Through a series of statistical tests, including correlation and regression analysis, the researchers found that higher relevance, positive connotation, and easy pronunciation lead to greater brand preference. Thus, the three hypotheses were supported.

Source: Yeqing Bao, Alan T. Shao, and Drew Rivers, "Creating new brand names: Effects of relevance, connotation, and pronunciation," unpublished working paper 2005.

Now Ask Yourself

● Do you think the positive connotation of a new brand name will lead to consumer preference for the brand? How would you test this relationship?

● Do you think easy pronunciation of a new brand name will lead to a more positive evaluation of the brand? How would you test this relationship?

As illustrated in the "Get This" feature, this chapter will examine associations between two or more variables. In our daily lives, we associate one thing with another and draw conclusions about these relationships all the time. For example, most people associate studying with grades, and conclude that more time spent studying can lead to better grades. You probably also associate a good education with higher future wages or with getting the job you want. In marketing, some of the more apparent relationships include associations between advertising and sales, company size and advertising budget, supply and demand for products, and customer satisfaction and customer loyalty.

predictor variable The independent variable in tests of associations.

criterion variable The dependent variable in tests of associations.

When two groups are studied, there will always be a variable that predicts the actions of another variable. The **predictor variable** is the independent variable and the **criterion variable** is the dependent variable. If we are attempting to predict the impact of advertising on sales levels, advertising would be the predictor (independent) variable and sales would be the criterion (dependent) variable.

Two important techniques used to measure the statistical relationship between variables are correlation analysis and regression analysis. You will learn about these topics, but first let's use scatter diagrams to visualize how data is related.

16-1 Scatter Diagrams

bivariate data Two related variables.

scatter diagram When two related variables are plotted as points on a graph.

When two related variables, called **bivariate data,** are plotted as points on a graph, the graph is called a **scatter diagram.** Exhibit 16-1 shows four scatter diagrams. Each point on the diagrams represents a pair of values, one based on values of the X scale (independent variable) and the other based on values of the Y scale (dependent variable). Making a scatter diagram usually is the initial step in investigating the

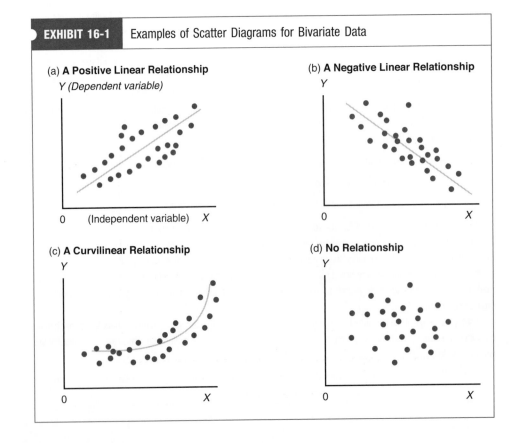

EXHIBIT 16-1 Examples of Scatter Diagrams for Bivariate Data

(a) **A Positive Linear Relationship**

(b) **A Negative Linear Relationship**

(c) **A Curvilinear Relationship**

(d) **No Relationship**

relationship between two variables because the diagram shows visually the shape and degree of closeness of the relationship between the X and Y variables.

The points in diagrams (a) and (b) in Exhibit 16-1 suggest straight-line relationships. The points in diagram (c) suggest a curvilinear relationship. There is obviously a strong relationship between the two variables, but it is not a straight line or linear one. Diagrams (a) and (b) also show a high degree of closeness of the relationships. However, diagram (c) shows a relationship that is not very close, compared to diagrams (a) and (b). Notice that in diagrams (a) and (b) many of the points fall on the straight line, whereas none of the points fall on the curvilinear line in diagram (c). The points in diagram (d) seem to form no discernible linear or curvilinear pattern, suggesting no relationship between the two variables.

A scatter diagram also indicates whether the relationship between the two variables is *positive* or *negative*. When large X values are paired with large Y values and small X values are paired with small Y values as shown in diagram A, the relationship between the X and Y variables is positive or upward sloping. On the other hand, when large X values are paired with small Y values and small X values are paired with large Y values as shown in diagram B, the relationship is negative or downward sloping. Correlation analysis provides the researcher with an understanding of the relationship between variables.

Exhibit 16-2 shows the amount of sales (Y) made by a group of eight salespeople in a company during a given period and the years of sales experience (X) of each salesperson plotted in scatter diagrams.

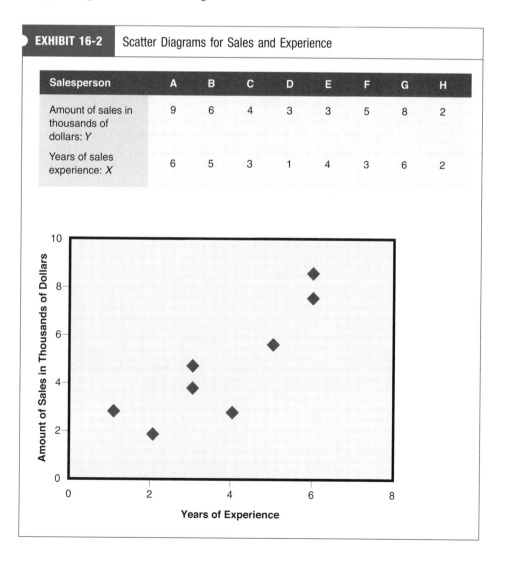

EXHIBIT 16-2 Scatter Diagrams for Sales and Experience

Salesperson	A	B	C	D	E	F	G	H
Amount of sales in thousands of dollars: Y	9	6	4	3	3	5	8	2
Years of sales experience: X	6	5	3	1	4	3	6	2

16-2 Correlation Analysis

Correlation analysis refers to the statistical techniques for measuring the closeness of the relationship between two metric (interval or ratio scaled) variables. It measures the degree to which changes in one variable are associated with changes in another. The computation concerning the degree of closeness is based on regression statistics. However, it is possible to perform correlation analysis without actually having a regression equation.

Note that a high degree of correlation does not indicate a *cause-and-effect* relationship between variables. Two variables can be highly correlated, yet the relationship has no meaning. For example, when both the number of hamburgers sold at McDonald's in Atlanta and the divorce rate in Rome are rising, we cannot conclude that one is the cause of the other. The high degree of correlation indicates only a mathematical result called a "statistical artifact." Conclusions must be based on logical reasoning and intelligent investigation, not just on mathematical results. Therefore, correlation analysis can indicate only the degree of association or *covariance* between variables. *Covariance* is a measure of the extent to which two variables are related or vary together. Thus the covariance between dependent and independent variables may be either positive or negative. Assessing covariance answers the question, "As the values observed for one variable rise (or fall), what tends to happen to the values observed in another variable?"[1]

16-2a Total Deviation, Coefficient of Determination, and Correlation Coefficient

In Exhibit 16-1, different diagrams of bivariate data were presented, but little detail could be given about the data besides the fact that some degree of covariance existed. Ideally, we would like to be able to quantify the strength of the relationship between the variables and indicate the amount of variance in the dependent variable that is explained by the independent variable, or vice versa. This can be done by using the following measures: (1) the coefficient of determination, denoted by r^2, or (2) the correlation coefficient, denoted by r (which is the square root of r^2). Before we discuss these measures, let's begin with an illustration of the concept of total deviation.

Total Deviation $(Y - \bar{Y})$

Assume there are two variables, X and Y. The arithmetic mean of Y values $= (\Sigma Y)/n$, $\bar{Y}$, is obtained without referring to X values. The Y_c, representing the regression line of Y values $= a + bx$, is obtained with the influence of X values. If Y values are related to X values to some degree, the deviations of Y values from $\bar{Y}$ must be reduced somewhat by the introduction of X values in computing Y_c values. The extent of the reduction of the deviations is diagramed in Exhibit 16-3. (Data from Exhibits 16-2 is used in the example.) The diagram shows that at a given X value, denoted by X_g, the total deviation of Y from the mean $\bar{Y}$ is divided into two parts:

$$\text{Total deviation} = \text{Unexplained deviation} + \text{Explained deviation}$$
$$Y - \bar{Y} = Y - Y_c + Y_c - \bar{Y}$$

Total deviation is equal to the sum of the unexplained deviation and the explained deviation. The terms "explained" and "unexplained" are used here to indicate whether or not a portion of the total deviation $(Y - \bar{Y})$ is reduced by the introduction of the X values in computing Y_c, values. When these values are summed and squared individually, they estimate the explained and unexplained variation of Y. The explained variation $\sum(Y_c - \bar{Y})^2$ may also be referred to as the *regression sum of*

> **EXHIBIT 16-3** | Diagram of Total Deviation

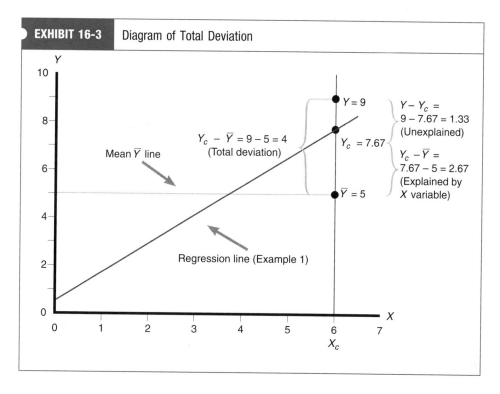

squares (RSS). On the other hand, the unexplained variation $\sum(Y - Y_c)^2$ is called the *error sum of squares* (ESS). This relationship may be expressed as

$$\text{Total variation} = \text{Unexplained variation} + \text{Explained variation}$$
$$\text{TSS} = \text{ESS} + \text{RSS}$$
$$\sum(Y - \bar{Y})^2 = \sum(Y - Y_c)^2 + \sum(Y_c - \bar{Y})^2$$

As shown here, the total variation may also be referred to as the *total sum of squares* (TSS).

Coefficient of Determination (r^2)

The **coefficient of determination** (r^2) is the strength of association or degree of closeness of the relationship between two variables measured by a relative value. It demonstrates how well the regression line fits the scattered points. It does not matter which variable is the dependent one and which is the independent one. That is, the coefficient of determination can indicate the amount of variation in the dependent variable that is explained by the variation in the independent variable, and vice versa. It may be defined as the ratio of the explained variation to the total variation:

coefficient of determination (r^2) The strength of association or degree of closeness of the relationship between two variables measured by a relative value.

$$\text{Coefficient of determination} = \frac{\text{Explained variation}}{\text{Total variation}} = \frac{\text{RSS}}{\text{TSS}}$$

or symbolically,

$$r^2 = \frac{\sum(Y_c - \bar{Y})^2}{\sum(Y - \bar{Y})^2}$$

Note that when all Y points fall on the regression line, that is, $Y_c = Y$ or $\sum(Y_c - \bar{Y})^2 = \sum(Y - \bar{Y})^2$, the value of $r^2 = 1$, which indicates a perfect correlation. On the other hand, when the Y points are scattered far away from the regression line Y_c, then $\sum(Y - Y_c)^2$ becomes very large. Since the total variation $\sum(Y - \bar{Y})^2$ is fixed, the ratio of $\sum(Y_c - \bar{Y})^2$ to $\sum(Y - \bar{Y})^2$ becomes very small. The value of r^2 will approach 0, which indicates that there is no correlation based on the regression line. The range of the r^2 value is therefore from 0 to 1. Stated in a different way, *when r^2 is close to 1, the Y values are very close to the regression line. When r^2 is close to 0, the Y values are not close to the regression line.* Thus, the total variation of Y values is more explained by the line, and the Y variable is closely related to the X variable. When r^2 is close to 0, the Y values are not close to the regression line. Thus the total variation of Y values is mostly unexplained by the regression line and the Y variable is not very related to the X variable.

Note that r^2 is always a positive number. It does not indicate whether the relationship between the two variables is positive or negative.

Correlation Coefficient

correlation coefficient A number that indicates the direction of a relationship and the degree of that relationship; an indication of the correlation between the observed and predicted values of the dependent variable.

The **correlation coefficient,** the square root of r^2 or $\sqrt{r^2} = \pm r$, is frequently computed to indicate the direction of the relationship in addition to indicating the degree of the relationship. It is the correlation between the observed and predicted values of the dependent variable. Since the range of r^2 is from 0 to 1, the coefficient of correlation r will vary within the range of $\sqrt{0}$ to $\sqrt{1}$, or from 0 to ± 1. The $+$ sign of r will indicate a positive correlation, whereas the $-$ sign will mean a negative correlation. The sign of r is the same as the sign of b (the slope) in the regression equation. Consider Example 16-1.

Example 16-1

Compute the coefficient of determination r^2 and the correlation coefficient r for the data given in Exhibit 16-2.

Solution: By applying the formula to calculate r^2, first arrange the data as shown in Exhibit 16-4 to obtain the required value of the denominator; that is, $\sum(Y - \bar{Y})^2 = 44$.

The numerator is computed as follows:

$$\sum(Y_c - \bar{Y})^2 = \sum(Y - \bar{Y})^2 - \sum(Y - \bar{Y}_c)^2$$

$$\begin{aligned} RSS &= TSS - ESS \\ &= 44 - 10.64 \text{ (value explained in section 16-3c)} \\ &= 33.36 \end{aligned}$$

$$r^2 = \frac{\sum(Y_c - \bar{Y})^2}{\sum(Y - \bar{Y})^2} = \frac{RSS}{TSS} = \frac{33.36}{44} = .7582$$

EXHIBIT 16-4	Calculations for Coefficient of Determination			
(1) Salesperson	(2) X	(3) Y	(4) $Y - \bar{Y}$	(5) $(Y - \bar{Y})^2$
A	6	9	4	16
B	5	6	1	1
C	3	4	−1	1
D	1	3	−2	4
E	4	3	−2	4
F	3	5	0	0
G	6	8	3	9
H	2	2	−3	9
Total ($\sum$)	30	40	0	44

16-3 Regression Analysis

The term *regression* used to be interpreted as "the return to a mean or average value." Francis Galton originated the term in his work "Regression toward Mediocrity in Hereditary Stature," published in the *Journal of the Anthropological Institute* in 1885. He analyzed the relationship between the average height of the two parents in a family and the average height of their adult children. He constructed a scatter diagram for the bivariate data, each point representing the heights of one family. The diagram resembled Exhibit 16-1(a). As expected, in general, tall parents tended to have tall children and short parents tended to have short children. However, he also found that the heights of the children deviated less from the average height of all children than the heights of their parents from the average height of all parents. That is, on average, tall parents have tall children, but the children are not quite as tall compared to their peers as are their parents compared to their peers. Similarly, short parents have short children, but the children are not quite as short as are their parents, compared to their respective peers. The tall or short parents have children more "mediocre" than themselves. The heights of the children tended to go back or to regress toward the average height of the population. Galton termed the line describing the average relationship between the two variables as the *line of regression.*

Today, **regression analysis** refers to statistical techniques for measuring the linear or curvilinear relationship between a dependent variable and one or more independent variables. The relationship between two variables is characterized by how they vary together. Given pairs of X and Y variables, regression analysis measures the direction (positive or negative) and rate of change (slope) in Y as X changes, or vice versa. Using the values of the independent variable, regression analysis attempts to predict the values of an interval- or ratio-scaled dependent variable.

> **regression analysis** Statistical techniques that measure the linear or curvilinear relationship between a dependent variable and one or more independent variables.

Regression analysis requires two operations: (1) Derive an equation, called the *regression equation,* and a line representing the equation to describe the shape of the relationship between the variables. The **regression line** is the line drawn through a scatter diagram that "best fits" the data points and most accurately describes the relationship between the two variables. The equation and its line may be linear or curvilinear, as shown in Exhibit 16-1. (2) Estimate the dependent variable (Y) from the independent variable (X), based on the relationship described by the regression equation.

> **regression line** A line drawn through a scatter diagram that "best fits" the data points and most accurately describes the relationship between the two variables.

16-3a Regression Equation and Line

Earlier it was noted that the shape of a line drawn through data points can indicate how two variables are related. While all shapes are informative, a straight line is especially useful because it is the easiest to deal with in regression analysis to describe the shape of the average relationship between two variables. The straight line can be expressed by the following linear equation:

$$Y_c = a + bX$$

where Y_c = the computed value of the dependent variable

a = the Y-intercept where X equals zero

b = the slope of the regression line, which is the increase or decrease in Y for each change of one unit of X

X = a given value of the independent variable

To create a regression model, researchers estimate the regression line using the following equation:

$$Y = \beta_0 + \beta_1 X_1 + \varepsilon_i$$

where β_0 = the Y-intercept where X equals zero

β_1 = the slope of the regression line, which is the increase or decrease in Y for each change of one unit of X

X_1 = a given value of the independent variable

i = the observation number

ε_i = the error term associated with the ith observation

This model involves parameters that are unknown (β_0 and β_1) that can be estimated from sample data. The error term, ε_i, is also unobservable, but it can be estimated from sample data. This unobservable error is the cause of the inexact relationship. The lack of precision can be attributed to a number of reasons, as follows:[2]

1. Due to the complexity of most marketing and other business problems, complex relationships exist between variables. Therefore, it is unrealistic to expect a perfect linear relation between two variables. When developing a model, we tend to use only those independent variables that we believe can account for the majority of the variation in the dependent variable. Thus the error term accounts for any variables that were omitted from the model.

2. Even when all relevant variables are included in a model, the functional form of the relationship between the dependent and independent variables may differ from the one selected. Of course, the model will not be of much use if the correct form of the relationship differs significantly from the one chosen. If the selected form is a good approximation of the actual relationship, the model can be useful for prediction and understanding.

3. The measurement of the dependent and independent variables may be imperfect. For example, the dependent or independent variable may not be measured accurately because of an imprecise measuring instrument. If such measurements in the dependent variable are unrelated to the independent variables, then they cannot be explained. Thus the greater such measurement errors, the greater the error term in the model.

4. Data is typically available only at an aggregate level. If the relationship differs between individuals or if it changes over time, then we should try to accommodate these differences in the modeling effort. But if these differences are minor or nonsystematic, we may assume a fixed relationship, indicating that the error term in the model may reflect differences between individuals or changes in the relationship over time.

5. Since the data we use is based on human behavior, the error term in the model may account for a "random" component in behavior.

16-3b The Least-Squares Method

A straight regression line can be obtained in different ways. For example, it can be obtained by simply drawing a line through the scatter diagram that visually seems to fit the data points most closely. However, the most precise and most common procedure to obtain the linear equation is the least-squares method. The **least-squares method** is a statistical technique that fits a straight line to a scatter diagram by finding the smallest sum of the vertical distances squared (i.e., $\sum e_i^2$) of all the points from the straight line. The equation derived by this method will yield a regression line that best fits the data.

As you saw from the scatter diagrams in Exhibit 16-1, a straight line usually does not go through every point in the diagram. When a straight line cannot fit the points perfectly, the individual values (Y) deviate from the computed values on the line (Y_c), where c stands for computed value. The least-squares method uses formulas that minimize the sum of the squares of these errors. Once again, it determines the line that best fits the data by minimizing the vertical distances squared of all data points

least-squares method A statistical technique that fits a straight line to a scatter diagram by finding the smallest sum of the vertical distances squared of all the points from the straight line.

from the line. The properties of the regression line based on the least-squares method are similar to those of an arithmetic mean. The properties are as follows:

1. The algebraic sum of the deviations of individual values (Y) from above and below the line (Y_c) is zero (except for rounding error). That is, the average value of the error term = 0, or

$$\sum(Y - Y_c) = \sum e_i = 0$$

2. The sum of the squared deviations from the line is the least possible sum, or $\sum(Y - Y_c)^2$ or $\sum e_i^2$ is smaller than $\sum (Y - $ a corresponding value on any other straight line$)^2$

3. The error term is normally distributed.

To calculate the straight line by the least-squares method, the equation $Y_c = a + bX$ is used. We must first determine the constants, a and b, which are called regression coefficients. **Regression coefficients** are the values that represent the effect of the individual independent variables on the dependent variable. We calculate the straight line as follows:

$$b = \frac{n(\sum XY) - \sum X \cdot \sum Y}{n(\sum X^2) - (\sum X)^2}$$

$$a = \frac{\sum Y}{n} - b\frac{\sum X}{n}$$

or

$$a = \bar{Y} - b\bar{X}$$

regression coefficients The values that represent the effect of the individual independent variables on the dependent variable.

Obtaining a regression equation and fitting a regression line with these formulas is illustrated in the following problem. It shows the method of estimating values of the dependent variable from values of the independent variable based on the least-squares equation. Consider Example 16-2.

Example 16-2

The first three columns of Exhibit 16-5 show the amount of sales (Y) made by a group of eight salespeople in a company during a given period and the years of sales experience (X) of each salesperson. We will perform the following tasks:

EXHIBIT 16-5 Sales and Years of Experience

(1)	(2)	(3)	(4)	(5)	(6)
	Amount of Sales ($1,000)	Years of Sales Experience			
Salesperson	Y	X	XY	X²	Y²
A	9	6	54	36	81
B	6	5	30	25	36
C	4	3	12	9	16
D	3	1	3	1	9
E	3	4	12	16	9
F	5	3	15	9	25
G	8	6	48	36	64
H	2	2	4	4	4
Total ($\sum$)	40	30	178	136	244

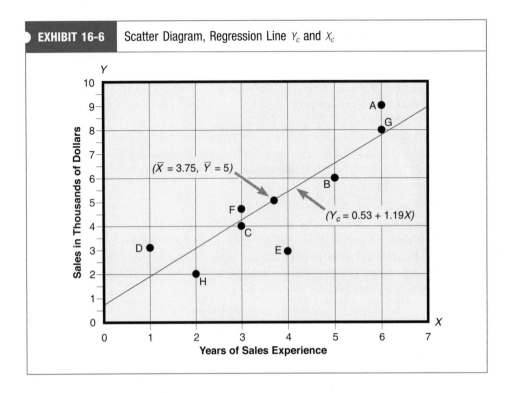

EXHIBIT 16-6 Scatter Diagram, Regression Line Y_c and X_c

1. Plot a scatter diagram.
2. Compute the linear regression equation by the least-squares method.
3. Draw the regression line based on the equation on the scatter diagram.
4. Estimate the amount of sales to expect from a salesperson with four years of experience.

Solution:

1. The scatter diagram is plotted in Exhibit 16-6. Each point ($n = 8$ points) represents the amount of sales and the number of years of sales experience of a salesperson.
2. Columns 4 and 5 of Exhibit 16-5 are used to obtain the required values $\sum(XY)$ and $\sum X^2$ for computing the linear regression equation based on the least-squares method. (Column 6 is added for use in subsequent examples and the X_c value to be presented later in the chapter.) Using the previous formulas, we can calculate b and a to determine the regression line:

$$b = \frac{8(178) - 30(40)}{8(136) - 30^2} = \frac{224}{188} = \frac{56}{47} = 1.19$$

$$a = \frac{\sum Y}{n} - b\frac{\sum X}{n} = \frac{40}{8} - \frac{56}{47}\left(\frac{30}{8}\right) = \frac{25}{47} = 0.53$$

Thus the linear regression equation $Y_c = a + bX$ can be written:

$$Y_c = 0.53 + 1.19X$$

3. The line representing equation $Y_c = 0.53 + 1.19X$ is drawn on Exhibit 16-6. The line can be determined by any two points representing the coordinates of Y_c and X values. However, a third point is usually computed for checking the answers. The three points must be obtained as follows:

when $X = 1$, $Y_c = 0.53 + 1.19(1) = 1.72$
$X = 4$, $Y_c = 0.53 + 1.19(4) = 5.29$
$X = 6$, $Y_c = 0.53 + 1.19(6) = 7.67$

4. The estimation of the amount of sales to expect from a salesperson with 4 years of sales experience can be made from the regression equation by letting $X = 4$. Thus $Y_c = 5.29$, which is computed in (3). The estimated amount of sales based on the average relationship is $5,290 (= 5.29 \times \$1,000$, the unit of Y value).

16-3c Standard Deviation of Regression

The standard deviation of the Y values from the regression line (Y_c) is called the **standard deviation of regression.** It is also popularly called the *standard of error of estimate,* since it can be used to measure the error of the estimates of individual Y values based on the regression line. Thus

s_y = the standard deviation of Y values from the mean $\bar{Y}$

s_x = the standard deviation of X values from the mean $\bar{X}$

s_{yx} = the standard deviation of regression of Y values from Y_c

s_{xy} = the standard deviation of regression of X values from X_c

The standard deviation of Y values from the regression line Y_c can be computed in a manner similar to the standard deviation of Y values from the arithmetic mean $\bar{Y}$. However, it is based on the points representing Y values scattered around the least-squares line. The closer the points are to the line, the smaller the value of the standard deviation of regression. Thus, the estimates of Y values based on the line are more reliable. On the other hand, the wider the points are scattered around the least-squares line, the larger the standard deviation of regression and the smaller the reliability of the estimates based on the line or the regression equation. The general formula for the standard deviation of regression of Y values on X is

$$s_{yx} = \sqrt{\frac{\sum (Y - Y_c)^2}{n - k}}$$

where k = the number of total (dependent and independent) variables. However, a simpler method of computing s_{yx} is to use the following formula:

$$s_{yx} = \sqrt{\frac{\sum Y^2 - a \sum Y - b \sum XY}{n - k}}$$

When the latter formula is used, the values provided for obtaining the regression equation can be used. The only addition to the provided values is $\sum Y^2$, which can easily be obtained by adding a Y^2 column to Exhibit 16-6, as shown in the first example. Thus the tedious work of computing Y_c and $(Y - Y_c)^2$ values can be avoided. Consider Example 16-3.

standard deviation of regression The standard deviation of the Y values from the regression line; the standard error of estimate.

Example 16-3

Compute the standard deviation of regression of Y values for the data given in the first example.

Solution: To apply the preceding general formula, to calculate s_{yx}, the data should be arranged for the computations as shown in Exhibit 16-7.

EXHIBIT 16-7	Computations to Determine the Standard Deviation of Regression				
(1) Salesperson	(2) Y	(3) X	(4) $Y_c = 0.53 + 1.19\,X$	(5) $Y - Y_c$	(6) $(Y - Y_c)^2$
A	9	6	7.67	1.33	1.77
B	6	5	6.48	−0.48	0.23
C	4	3	4.10	−0.10	0.01
D	3	1	1.72	1.28	1.64
E	3	4	5.29	−2.29	5.24
F	5	3	4.10	0.90	0.81
G	8	6	7.67	0.33	0.11
H	2	2	2.91	−0.91	0.83
Total ($\sum$)	40	30	39.94	0.06	10.64

By using the values obtained from Exhibit 16-7, the standard deviation of regression is

$$s_{yx} = \sqrt{\frac{\sum (Y - Y_c)^2}{n - k}} = \sqrt{\frac{10.64}{8 - 2}} = 1.33$$

The value of s_{yx} indicates the error range of the estimates of individual Y values. The interpretation of s_{yx} with respect to the line Y_c is similar to that of s_y with respect to the mean $\bar{Y}$. If Y values are normally distributed, 68.3% of the values will lie within a distance of 1 standard deviation of regression, or $1 s_{yx}$, from (above and below) the line, approximately 95.5% for 2 standard deviations from the line, and approximately 99.7% for 3 standard deviations from the line. The 68.3% area for the example is plotted on Exhibit 16-8 by the two dashed lines. The dotted lines representing $Y_c \pm 1 s_{yx}$ can be determined by computing any two points on each line.

For the line representing $Y_c \pm 1 s_{yx}$:

when $X = 1$, $Y_c + 1 s_{yx} = 1.72 + 1.33 = 3.05$
when $X = 4$, $Y_c + 1 s_{yx} = 5.29 + 1.33 = 6.62$

For the line representing $Y_c - 1 s_{yx}$:

when $X = 1$, $Y_c - 1 s_{yx} = 1.72 - 1.33 = 0.39$
when $X = 4$, $Y_c - 1 s_{yx} = 5.29 - 1.33 = 3.96$

Note that there are actually 5 (B, C, F, G, H) out of 8 points or $5/8 = 62.5\%$ within the range of $Y_c + 1 s_{yx}$. The actual occurrence, 62.5%, is fairly close to the theoretical occurrence, 68% in this case. If the number of points is increased, the percent of the actual occurrence can be expected to approach the theoretical occurrence for a normal distribution.

The standard deviation of regression is computed from the points representing Y values scattered around the regression line. Thus, the value of s_{yx} can be used as a measure of the degree of closeness of the relationship between two variables. For example, the larger the standard deviation of regression, the wider the scatter of the individual points from the line and the smaller the degree of closeness of the relationship. However, the use of the standard deviation of regression in measuring the degree of relationship is rather difficult, since it is expressed in original units, such as dollars and miles. A more convenient way to measure the degree of relationship is to use a relative value, as developed in the next section.

> **EXHIBIT 16-8**   Scatter Diagram and Regression Line

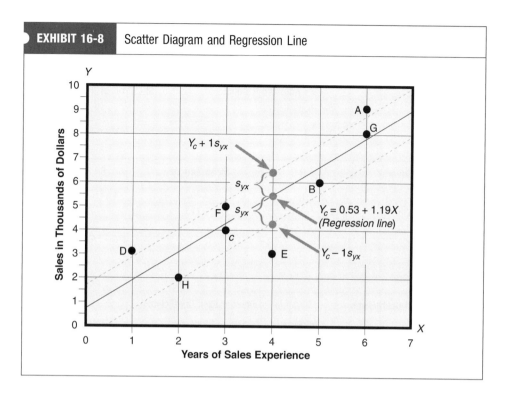

16-3d Calculating Regressions Using Computers

When calculating regressions by hand, the task is both time-consuming and error-prone due to the vast number of computations. With the computer technology now available, there is little reason to calculate any regressions by hand. We will first describe how to perform the calculations using SPSS for Windows, followed by a description of how to carry out the calculations using Microsoft's Excel software.

Run Regression with SPSS
To run the calculations using SPSS, follow these steps:

1. Open a new spreadsheet.

2. Enter successively all of the sales amount data in the first column labeled "var00001." That is, enter 9, 6, 4, 3, and so on until all eight numbers are in the first eight cells of the first column. Then enter successively all of the years-of-experience data in the second column labeled "var00002."

3. At the top of the spreadsheet, click on "Analyze." Then click on "Regression" and "Linear." These commands designate the statistical test to be run.

4. Using the arrows, shift "var00001" (which represents sales amounts) over to the box labeled "Dependent:" and shift "var00002" (which represents sales experience) over to the box labeled "Independent(s):".

5. Click "ok."

The SPSS printouts shown in Exhibit 16-9 will appear:

Run Regression with Excel
Follow these steps to run the calculations using Excel:

1. Open a new spreadsheet.

2. As we did in the SPSS steps, enter successively all of the sales amount data in the first column. Then enter successively all of the years-of-experience data in the second column.

EXHIBIT 16-9	SPSS Tables for Regression

Model Summary

Model	R	R Square	Adjusted R Square	Std. Error of the Estimate
1	.871[a]	.758	.718	1.3316

[a] Predictors: (Constant), VAR00002

ANOVA[b]

Model		Sum of Squares	df	Mean Square	F	Sig.
1	Regression	33.362	1	33.362	18.816	.005[a]
	Residual	10.638	6	1.773		
	Total	44.000	7			

[a] Predictors: (Constant), VAR00002
[b] Dependent Variable: VAR00001

Coefficients[a]

Model		Unstandardized Coefficients		Standardized Coefficients	t	Sig.
		B	Std. Error	Beta		
1	(Constant)	.532	1.133		.470	.655
	VAR00002	1.191	.275	.871	4.338	.005

[a] Dependent Variable: VAR00001

EXHIBIT 16-10	Excel Table for Regression

SUMMARY OUTPUT

Regression Statistics

Multiple R	0.870759
R Square	0.758221
Adjusted R Square	0.717924
Standard Error	1.331559
Observations	8

AVONA

	df	SS	MS	F	Significance F
Regression	1	33.3617	33.3617	18.816	0.004887
Residual	6	10.6383	1.77305		
Total	7	44			

	Coefficients	Standard Error	t Stat	P-value	Lower 95%	Upper 95%	Lower 95.0%	Upper 95.0%
Intercept	0.531915	1.132533	0.469668	0.655175	−2.2393	3.303126	−2.2393	3.303126
X Variable 1	1.191489	0.27468	4.337741	0.004887	0.519372	1.863607	0.519372	1.863607

3. At the top of the spreadsheet, click on "Tools" and "Data Analysis." Then click on "Regression."

4. Where it asks for "Input Y Range:" enter "A1:A8" to indicate the location of the dependent variables. Where it asks for "Input × Range:" enter "B1:B8" to indicate the location of the independent variables. Leave the confidence level at 95%.

The output shown in Exhibit 16-10 will appear:

The SPSS and Excel printouts are quite similar in appearance and data. Note that the *R square* is the same as the r^2 we discussed earlier. The following points will help you interpret the data:

- The *multiple R* or simply *R* value (.87) is the simple correlation between sales amount and sales experience.

- The *R square* shows how well the straight line fits the scattered points (which are the Y values). As a general rule, the closer the R^2 value is to 1, the better the straight (regression) line fits the scattered points. In our example, $R^2 = .758$, which says that sales experience explains 75.8% of the variation in sales amount.

- The *adjusted R square* (.7179) shrinks the *R* square, since it considers the sample size and number of parameters estimated in the analysis.

- The *standard error of the estimate* or s_{yx} (1.3316) is the square root of the residual mean square in the ANOVA table and measures the spread of the errors (also called "residuals") about the fitted line.

- The *F-statistic* (18.816) is used to test the hypothesis that the slope is 0. Note that *F* is large when the independent variable helps to explain the variation in the dependent variable. In our example, the linear equation is highly significant (.005). This indicates that we should reject the null hypothesis that the regression model does not fit the analyzed data. If the significance *F* value had been greater than .05, we would have not rejected the null hypothesis and concluded that the model did not fit the analyzed data.

- The estimates of our model coefficients β_0 (intercept) and β_1 (slope) are, respectively, 0.53 and 1.19. So the estimated model is

  Sales amount $= 0.53 + 1.19X$ (where $X =$ sales experience)

- The *t statistics* (each coefficient divided by its standard error) are of some interest to researchers. The first *t* (0.4697) tests the significance of the difference of the constant from 0 and rarely is of interest to researchers. However, the second *t* statistic (4.338) tests the significance of the slope, which is equivalent to testing the significance of the correlation between sales amount and sales experience.

- The *p-values* (.6551 and .0049) are the probabilities associated with the *t* statistics.

16-4 Nonparametric Methods for Association Analysis

The analysis statistics such as z-test, t-test, ANOVA, correlation, and regression are all **parametric tests,** which assume that variables under investigation are measured using either interval or ratio scales. Furthermore, parametric tests make some additional assumptions: (1) the sample data should be randomly drawn from a normally distributed population; (2) the sample data drawn must be independent of each another; and (3) when examining central tendency for which two or more samples are drawn, the populations should have equal variances. However, in some situations, we cannot make these specific assumptions about the shape of the population distribution. In those cases we will turn to nonparametric methods.

Nonparametric methods of testing hypotheses are not concerned with particular population parameters. The advantage of these methods is that we do not have to know the shape of the population (whether it is distributed normally or is skewed) or make specific assumptions about the population for the purpose of testing hypotheses. Another advantage of nonparametric techniques is their relative ease of computation and understanding. Further, they can be used with ranked information and for tests

parametric tests Tests used when variables under investigation are measured using either interval or ratio scales.

nonparametric methods Methods used when the specific assumptions about the shape of a population distribution cannot be made, and used when nominal- or ordinal-scaled data must be analyzed.

involving small samples. However, their applications are limited to certain types of information, and they tend to be less precise and efficient than parametric methods.

So when do we use nonparametric methods? We use them in any of the following situations:

1. When the population distribution from which the sample is drawn cannot be assumed to be normal

2. When the sampling distribution is known not to be normal

3. When nonmetric (nominal- or ordinal-scaled) data is used

Remember to use parametric tests whenever possible, since they are more powerful, more sensitive, and less likely to have Type II errors. This is not always possible, however, so in this chapter you will learn about nonparametric methods. In Chapter 14, we discussed a chi-square test, a nonparametric statistical technique. In this section, we will move beyond the goodness-of-fit test and look at the chi-square (χ^2) test of independence.

16-4a Contingency Tables—The Chi-Square Test of Independence

contingency (or crosstabulation) table A table in which row entries classify data according to one variable and column entries classify the data according to another variable.

cell frequencies The frequencies in contingency table cells.

marginal frequency The total of the frequencies in each row or each column of a contingency table.

A **contingency or cross-tabulation table** is a statistical table in which row entries classify data according to one variable and column entries classify data according to another variable. When there are r rows and c columns in the table, it is called an $r \times c$ contingency table. For example, a 2×2 contingency table has two rows and two columns. There are four cells in a 2×2 table. The frequencies in the cells are called **cell frequencies.** The total of the frequencies in each row or each column is called the **marginal frequency.**

The same formula we used in Chapter 14 to explain the goodness-of-fit test can be used here to compute the value of χ^2. You should recall that the formula was:

$$\chi^2 = \sum_{i=1}^{k} \frac{(O_i - E_i)^2}{E_i}$$

where $O_i =$ the observed frequency in cell i
$E_i =$ the expected or theoretical frequency in cell i
$k =$ the number of mutually exclusive categories

The χ^2 distribution table is used in the usual manner, provided each expected cell frequency is not too small—preferably 5 or more. The number of degrees of freedom of an $r \times c$ contingency table is $(r-1)(c-1)$. There are r values in each column of the table. When any $(r-1)$ of the r values are assigned, the remaining 1 value is automatically determined. Similarly, there are c values in each row of the table. When any $(c-1)$ of the c values are assigned, the remaining 1 value is automatically determined. Thus, for a 2×2 contingency table, there is $(2-1)(2-1) = 1$ degree of freedom. When the expected frequency in any one of the four cells is known, the frequencies in the other three cells are automatically determined by the known row and column totals (the marginal frequencies). Likewise, for a 3×4 contingency table, there are $(3-1)(4-1) = 2 \times 3 = 6$ degrees of freedom, and so on.

Contingency tables may be constructed in various ways. Sometimes they simply show the *numbers of elements* in each cell, as shown in Exhibit 16-11. Other times, *raw percentages* are provided in each cell, where the number of elements in each cell is divided by the total number of elements in the table. The total percentages in all cells combined must equal 100%. Finally, cross-tabulation tables may display *percentages* by *row* or *column*. Researchers must designate which format they want displayed from the statistical analysis software they are using.

Contingency tables are frequently used in tests of independence. This type of test tells us whether or not the two bases of classification used in rows and columns of a contingency table are independent (not related). Consider Example 16-4.

Example 16-4

We are interested in the relationship between adults in a given city who enjoy grocery shopping and their educational levels. One hundred adults are surveyed. The results are shown in Exhibit 16-11. Find whether the relationship exists when the level of significance is at .05.

Solution: H_0: There is no relationship between enjoying grocery shopping and educational levels of the adults in the city; that is, enjoying grocery shopping and educational levels are independent.

H_1: Enjoying grocery shopping and educational level are dependent.

EXHIBIT 16-11	Sample of 100 Adults Regarding Educational Level and Shopping Enjoyment		
Educational Level	**Adults Enjoying Grocery Shopping**	**Adults Not Enjoying Grocery Shopping**	**Total (Marginal Frequency)**
Elementary	7	3	10
High school	14	16	30
College	39	21	60
Total (marginal frequency)	60	40	100

To find the value of χ^2, we first must compute the expected cell frequencies. The expected cell frequencies are computed on the basis of the hypothesis. If the hypothesis that educational levels have nothing to do with whether someone enjoys grocery shopping is true, then the same ratio of educational levels to total population should apply to both types of adults, those who like and those who dislike grocery shopping. Thus, 10 out of every 100 adults in the city should have had an elementary school education, 30 out of every 100 should have had a high school education, and 60 out of 100 adults should have had a college education. The computation of the expected cell frequencies is shown in Exhibit 16-12.

Source: © 2007 JupiterImages Corporation.

> **EXHIBIT 16-12** Computation of the Expected Cell Frequencies

Educational Level	Expected Number of Adults Who		Total
	Enjoy Grocery Shopping	Do Not Enjoying Grocery Shopping	
Elementary	$60 \times (10/100) = 6$	$40 \times (10/100) = 4$	10
High school	$60 \times (30/100) = 18$	$40 \times (30/100) = 12$	30
College	$60 \times (60/100) = 36$	$40 \times (60/100) = 24$	60
Totals	60	40	100

> **EXHIBIT 16-13** Computation of the Value of χ^2

Types of Adults	Number of Adults				
	Observed (O)	Expected (E)	$O - E$	$(O - E)^2$	$(O - E)^2/E$
Elementary, E[*]	7	6	1	1	0.1667
Elementary, NE[†]	3	4	−1	1	0.2500
High school, E	14	18	−4	16	0.8889
High school, NE	16	12	4	16	1.3333
College, E	39	36	3	9	0.2500
College, NE	21	24	−3	9	0.3750
Totals	100	100	0	0	$\chi^2 = 3.2639$

[*] E = Enjoy grocery shopping
[†] NE = Do not enjoy grocery shopping
Degrees of freedom = $(3 - 1)(2 - 1) = 2$

Next, arrange the corresponding observed and theoretical frequencies in an orderly form. Then compute the χ^2 value as shown in Exhibit 16-13.

If the expected frequencies in 2 [$= 2$ (3 − 1 values in a column) × 1 (or 2 − 1 values in a row)] of the 6 ($= 3 \times 2$) cells are filled, the frequencies of the remaining 4 cells are automatically determined from the known totals (marginal frequencies). At a .05 level, the difference is significant if χ^2 with 2 degrees of freedom is above 5.991. This value (5.991) can be found in Table 3 in the Appendix at the end of the book. The computed value of $\chi^2 = 3.2639$ is smaller than the critical value, or it falls in the acceptance region. Thus we *fail to reject* the hypothesis and conclude that there is no relationship between grocery shopping enjoyment and educational levels of the adults in the city.

16-4b Calculating the Chi-Square Test of Independence Using Computers

Once the expected cell frequencies are computed, the chi-square test of independence can be calculated by computer using the same steps as we used to calculate the chi-square goodness-of-fit tests. Calculating the chi-square test with Excel is not straightforward. Therefore, we focus on how to run the chi-square test of independence with SPSS:

1. Open a new spreadsheet.
2. In the first column containing the Education data, type "1" (representing those with only elementary school education) in cells 1–10, "2" (representing those with a high school education) in cells 11–40, and "3" (representing those with a college education) in cells 41–100.
3. In the second column containing the Shopping Enjoyment data, type "1" to represent those who enjoy grocery shopping and "2" to represent those who do not enjoy grocery shopping. Therefore, a "1" should be typed in cells 1–7, 11–24, and 41–79. A "2" should be typed in cells 8–10, 25–40, and 80–100.
4. At this point, you need to define the variable labels in the first column. You'll notice at the bottom of the spreadsheet there are two tabs: "Data View" and "Variable View."

Click on the "Variable View" tab. Then click on "var00001" under "Name" and type "educat" and on "var00002" type "enjoy." Under the "Label" column, type "education" in the first row and "enjoyment" in the second row to label the data.

5. Under the "Values" label, click on the first row. You'll notice a shaded area in the cell with three dots. Click on the three dots. This will allow you to give values to the data. Once you click on the dots, it will take you to a box titled "Value Labels." In the "Value" box, type "1" and under "Variable Label" type "elementary". Click on "Add." We do the same for our second value. So under "Value," type "2" and under "Variable Label" type "high school". Click on "Add." Finally, we must do the same for our third value. So under "Value," type "3" and under "Variable Label" type "college". Click on "Add" and then "OK."

6. Now define the value labels for the "enjoyment" data. Under the "Values" label, click on the second row. Once again you'll notice a shaded area in the cell with three dots. Click on the three dots. This will allow you to give values to the data. Once you click on the dots, it will take you to a box called "Value Labels." In the "Value" box, type "1" and under "Variable Label" type "enjoys grocery shopping". Click on "Add." Now we do the same for our second value. So under "Value," type "2" and under "Variable Label" type "does not enjoy grocery shopping". Click on "Add." Now click on "OK."

7. Click on the "Data View" tab at the bottom of the page.

8. At this point, we are ready to run our tests. So using the headings of the page, click "Analyze."

9. Using the subheadings under "Analyze," click on "Descriptive Statistics" and then "Crosstabs." At the bottom, click on "Statistics" and then click on the box labeled "Chi-square." Then click on "Continue."

10. Shift "education" in the left column to "Row(s):" and shift "enjoyment" over to "Column(s):".

11. Click on "OK."

The printouts shown in Exhibit 16-14 will appear on the screen:

EXHIBIT 16-14 | SPSS Tables for the Chi-Square Test of Independence

Case Processing Summary

	Cases					
	Valid		Missing		Total	
	N	Percent	N	Percent	N	Percent
education • enjoyment	100	100.0%	0	.0%	100	100.0%

education • enjoyment Crosstabulation Count

		Enjoyment		Total
		enjoys grocery shopping	does not enjoy grocery shopping	
education	elementary	7	3	10
	high school	14	16	30
	college	39	21	60
Total		60	40	100

Chi-Square Tests

	Value	df	Asymp. Sig. (2-sided)
Pearson Chi-Square	3.264	2	.196
Likelihood Ratio	3.236	2	.198
Linear-by-Linear Association	.367	1	.545
N of Valid Cases	100		

[a] 1 cells (16.7%) have expected count less than 5. The minimum expected count is 4.00.

The SPSS run and manual calculations came to the same conclusion. That is, we do not reject the hypothesis and thus conclude that there is no relationship between grocery shopping enjoyment and the educational levels of adults in the city.

The information on the SPSS printout in Exhibit 16-14 requires interpretation. The first table simply summarizes the number of cases that were processed. In the second table, the cross-tabulation or contingency table is provided. In the third table, the Pearson chi-square test is the only statistic we are interested in at this point. It tested the null hypothesis that the row and column variables are independent of each other. The last table provides the same statistics as we manually calculated earlier. We can conclude, once again, that there is statistical support for the hypothesis that there is no relationship between enjoying grocery shopping and educational levels of the adults in the city. (We cannot reject the null hypothesis because the value of .196 was greater than our .05 level of significance.)

Decision Time!

Correlation analysis is a method that many researchers feel comfortable with, since it shows the strength of association between two or more variables and is relatively easy to compute. As a marketing manager, you want information from marketing researchers that can enhance your decision-making abilities. If correlation analysis is a popular and informative statistical method, why should researchers bother using the somewhat intimidating multivariate statistical techniques? Do you feel that there is really that much to gain from these methods? Why or why not?

Net Impact

The Internet does not help much in correlation and regression analysis. Statistical software is the best tool for this. The Internet does help, however, explain why certain events occur. That is, it can contribute information that helps researchers better understand the relationships that the tests reveal. For example, if researchers find that TV advertising expenses are not strongly related to firm performance, the Internet may qualitatively explain why this phenomenon is present. Perhaps articles found on the Internet show that a greater percentage of consumers indicate they are sick of TV commercials.

Source: © 2007 JupiterImages Corporation.

On the Lighter Side—Is Correlation Causation?

The light-hearted headline read: "New Poll Shows Correlation Is Causation." A University of Michigan Web site posted an article that explained: "The results of a new survey conducted by pollsters suggest that, contrary to common scientific wisdom, correlation does in fact imply causation. The highly reputable source, Gallup Polls, Inc., surveyed 1,009 Americans during the month of October and asked them, 'Do you believe correlation implies causation?' An overwhelming 64% of Americans answered 'YES,' while only 38% replied 'NO.' Another 8% were undecided. This result threatens to shake the foundations of both the scientific and mainstream community. "It is really a mandate from the people," commented one pundit who wished to remain anonymous. "It says that the American people are sick and tired of the scientific mumbo-jumbo that they keep trying to shove down our throats, and want some clear rules about what to believe. Now that correlation implies causation, not only is everything easier to understand, it also shows that even science must answer to the will of John and Jane Q. Public."

Source: "New poll shows correlation is causation," http://www.obereed.net/hh/correlation.html. Accessed August 23, 2005.

Chapter Summary

To examine associations between two or more variables, one can use correlation and regression analysis. Correlation analysis measures the closeness of the relationship between two metric variables. It measures the degree to which changes in one variable are associated with changes in another. The correlation of determination is the strength of association or degree of closeness of the relationship between two variables measured by a relative value. It shows how well the regression line fits the scattered points. Regression analysis refers to statistical techniques for measuring the linear or curvilinear relationship between a dependent variable and one or more independent variables. The least-squares method is a statistical technique that fits a straight line to

a scatter diagram by finding the smallest sum of the vertical distances square of all the points from the straight line.

Correlation and regression analyses assume that the population is normally distributed and the population parameters, such as the population mean and population variance, are used in the tests. However, in cases when (1) the population distribution from which the sample is drawn cannot be assumed to be normal, (2) the sampling distribution is known not to be normal, and (3) ordinal- or nominal-scaled data is involved, nonparametric methods should be used. The chi-square statistic is one nonparametric test often used to assess association among two or more nominally scaled variables.

Review Questions

1. What is the association between an "effect" and a "treatment"?

2. Briefly explain each term:
   • Scatter diagram
   • Standard deviation of regression
   • Coefficient of determination
   • Correlation coefficient

3. What is the difference between regression and correlation analysis?

4. What is meant by TSS, RSS, and ESS? How are they related? How do they relate to the coefficient of determination?

5. What is the difference between a parametric and a nonparametric test?

6. What is a contingency table used for?

7. When would a researcher use the chi-square test of independence?

Practice Quiz

Note: You can find the correct answers to these questions by taking the quiz and then submitting your answers in the Online Edition. The program will automatically score your

submission. If you miss a question, the program will provide the correct answer, a rationale for the answer, and the section number in the chapter where the topic is discussed.

1. The least-squares method of regression is a statistical technique that fits a straight line to a scatter diagram by finding the smallest sum of the vertical distances squared of all the points from the straight line.
   a. True
   b. False

2. The chi-square test of independence shows whether the two bases of classification used in rows and columns of a contingency table are independent (not related).
   a. True
   b. False

3. The criterion variable is called as independent variable.
   a. True
   b. False

4. A scatter diagram can indicate whether the relationship between the two variables is positive or negative.
   a. True
   b. False

5. A high degree of correlation implies a causal relationship between variables.
   a. True
   b. False

6. What does the Y stand for in the straight-line formula $Y = a + bx$?
   a. slope of the regression line
   b. computed value of the dependent variable
   c. a given value of the independent variable
   d. Y-intercept when X equals zero
   e. None of the above

7. In the formula $Y - \bar{Y} = (Y - Y_c) + (Y_c - \bar{Y})$, _____ is the unexplained deviation.
   a. $Y - \bar{Y}$
   b. $Y_c - \bar{Y}$
   c. $Y - Y_c$
   d. None of the above

8. Which of the following R square values indicates the best straight line fit of the scattered points when interpreting a regression printout?
   a. 10%
   b. 40%
   c. 70%
   d. 80%
   e. 90%

9. The correlation coefficient ranges from
   a. −1 to 1.
   b. −99 to .99.
   c. −.5 to .5.
   d. 1−100.
   e. None of the above

10. R square ranges from
    a. −1 to 1.
    b. −.99 to .99.
    c. 0 to 1.
    d. 1 to 100.
    e. None of the above

Thinking Critically

1. The following table shows the number of hours (X) interviewers spent soliciting shoppers for personal interviews at a shopping mall and the number of interviews obtained (Y) by each of the five interviewers in a research firm.

   - Plot a scatter diagram.
   - Computer the linear regression equation by the least-squares method manually and using SPSS.
   - Draw the regression line based on the least-squares equation.
   - Estimate the number of interviews obtained by an interviewer who has spent three hours at the mall.

   - Compute the standard deviation of regression.
   - Compute the coefficient of determination and correlation coefficient. Interpret the values.

2. In 2004, the sales record of Johnson's Automobile Company showed that the cars sold in districts A, B, C, and D were 20%, 10%, 30%, and 40%, respectively, of the total cars sold by the company. In 2005, the cars sold in the same districts were, respectively, 85, 60, 175, and 180 cars. Does the sales distribution in 2005 differ significantly from that of 2004 at a .05 level?

Interviewer	X, Hours Soliciting Interviews	Y, Number of Interviews Obtained
Albert	1	2
Bertha	2	10
Christina	6	20
Denzel	7	14
Edward	5	11

2004		2005	
Evaluation Score	Percent Distribution	Evaluation Score	Number of Instructors
A	15%	A	120
B	18%	B	190
C	30%	C	330
D	25%	D	270
F	12%	F	90
Total	100%	**Total**	1,000

3. Several physical education instructors evaluated a new exercise machine over a two-year period to determine its effectiveness. The scores are summarized as follows:

Use the chi-square test to determine whether the evaluation distribution of 2004 differs significantly from that of 2005 at a .01 level of significance.

4. The sales records of Fox Company indicated that Mr. Rodriguez sold 652 times out of 1,000 calls and Ms. Solomon sold 1,048 times out of 1,500 calls. Does Rodriguez's sales performance differ significantly from Solomon's performance? Use the chi-square test at a .05 level of significance.

Net Exercise

Regression is a powerful tool for predictive analysis. In addition to the commonly used linear regression, the types of regression also include multinomial logistic regression, binary logistic regression, nonlinear regression, constrained nonlinear regression, weighted least squares, two-stage least squares, and others. Visit http://www.spss.com/regression/data_analysis.htm for more information of different types of regression analysis.

Experiencing Marketing Research

You are responsible for examining whether the income level of females is positively associated with their purchase of perfume. Randomly interview 20 females and run the analysis with a level of significance of .01. Report your findings.

Case 16-1

Research Organizations Are Going Global

The world is a big place. There are hundreds of countries spanning thousands of miles. There are billions of people and thousands of businesses residing in that vast space. So where in the world are research organizations concentrating their efforts? In Chapter 11 it was reported that the marketing research industry has indeed become extremely global. You may recall that of the $ 13.3 billion in revenues the top 25 businesses enjoyed in 2004, 67% came from operations outside their home country. In the case of VNU, based in the Netherlands, we saw an extreme case where only 1.0% of its research revenues came from operations within its home country; the balance came from operations in 81 other countries around the world.

Of the top 25 companies, 12 were U.S.-owned firms, accounting for 30.0% of their revenues. Five were British firms, and they accounted for 28.9% of the top 25's total revenue. Just one company was based in the Netherlands, but it accounted for more than one-quarter of the top 25 total—due to ownership of ACNielsen, Nielsen Media Research, and several other firms in the United States and abroad. France was home to one firm on the top 25 list, and that accounted for 5.7% of the total. Japan, with four of the top 25 firms, accounted for 4.1%. There was just one of the top 25 firms based in Germany, but it made up 6.3% of the total from operations and subsidiaries in 59 countries.

The author of the study, Jack Honomichl, claimed in his report that "Generally, the smaller the organization, the higher the growth rate." He further added that most of the large conglomerates in his study have been built by a load of acquisitions. The top 25 organizations acquired 29 other research firms, which had annual revenue of more than $360 million.

Source: Jack Honomichl, "Honomichl global top 25: Acquisitions up, growth rate varies," *Marketing News* (August 15, 2005): H3–H4.

Case Questions

1. Do you agree with Honomichl's claim that smaller organizations had higher growth rates? Why do you believe this is or is not the case?

2. Using the information in Exhibit 1-3, what other relationships are noteworthy?

3. Can you find any regional associations among the data presented in the table? If so, what do you find?

4. Is regression a useful statistical tool to examine relationships among the column categories below? If so, what would you look at in your analysis?

Notes

1. William E. Becker, *Statistics for Business and Economics* (Cincinnati, OH: South-Western College Publishing, 1995), 502.

2. Dick R. Wittink, *The Application of Regression Analysis* (Boston: Allyn & Bacon, 1988), 30–31.

Multivariate Statistics

Chapter Seventeen

Source: © 2007 JupiterImages Corporation.

Key Terms

Learning Objectives

After studying this chapter, you will be able to:

- Discuss the basics of multivariate statistical analysis.
- Explain which technique is appropriate given the type of variables involved.
- Describe the usefulness of multivariate statistics.

Fore! Golfers Benefit from Conjoint Analysis

Thanks to Arnold Palmer, Jack Nicklaus, and Tiger Woods, golf has evolved into an extremely popular sport. The majority of golfers are recreational players with high handicaps and wicked slices. But every golfer has two things in common. They're all looking to drive the ball further and to hit it with more accuracy. This is not a revelation to golf ball manufacturers like Pinnacle and Top Flite. But are accuracy and distance the most important concerns to golfers when choosing golf balls?

Sawtooth Technologies knows how to find the answer. The company provides software for research data collection and analysis. Its customers include marketing research firms, marketing and management consulting firms, research departments of Fortune 500 companies, academic and not-for-profit institutions, political pollsters, government agencies, and many research organizations. Joseph Curry, the President of Sawtooth Technologies, explains how conjoint analysis, a popular multivariate statistical analysis technique, can help a company market a new golf ball:

> Suppose we want to market a new golf ball. We know from experience and from talking with golfers that there are three important product features: average driving distance, average ball life, and price. We further know that there is a range of feasible alternatives for each of these features. Obviously, the market's "ideal" ball would be the one that drives the farthest, lasts the longest, and is the least expensive. The manufacturing company's ideal ball would be the one with the least driving distance, lasts the least amount of time, and is the most expensive. The basic marketing issue is: The company would lose their shirts selling the first ball and the market wouldn't buy the second. The most viable product is somewhere in between, but where? Conjoint analysis helps managers make that decision.

> Conjoint analysis encompasses three critical steps—collecting trade-offs, estimating buyer value systems, and making choice predictions. The *trade-offs* might deal with paying a little extra for a ball that travels further. A golfer might *value* a long drive more than a highly durable ball. And a *choice prediction* might be that a golfer prefers the long-life ball to the distance ball, since it has the larger total value. All of these findings would be based on computations from conjoint analysis.

Source: Jeo Curry, "Understanding conjoint analysis in 15 minutes," Sawtooth Technologies web page, http://www.sawtooth.com/news/library/articles/15min.htm. Accessed August 22, 2005.

Now Ask Yourself

- Does conjoint analysis make intuitive sense to you? If so, why is it needed?
- What other multivariate techniques are available to researchers?
- Does one need to be a statistical expert to understand multivariate statistical analysis?

The "Get This" feature explains how conjoint analysis can help a manufacturer of golf balls decide which attributes are important to golfers. This information can be helpful when promoting its new golf balls. In previous chapters, the statistical techniques we learned allow us to investigate either one variable at a time (univariate statistics) or two variables at a time (bivariate statistics). In this chapter, we will look at **multivariate statistics**—statistics that investigate more than two variables at a time. Multivariate statistical analyses have been used extensively in the physical, social, and medical sciences.

multivariate statistics Any simultaneous analysis of more than two variables.

405

The intention of this chapter is not to offer an exhaustive explanation of these techniques. Rather, it is to introduce you to these common multivariate techniques: multiple regression, multiple discriminate analysis, factor analysis, cluster analysis multidimensional scaling, and conjoint analysis.[1]

17-1 Multiple Regression Analysis

The premise behind multiple regression analysis is consistent with that of simple regression analysis: to determine the association or relationship between dependent and independent variables. However, in simple regression analysis, only two variables were included; the dependent variable was represented by Y and the independent variable by X. In multiple regression analysis, however, more than two variables are included in the examination. The dependent and independent variables must be interval- or ratio-scaled to use this technique. While the dependent variables are still represented by Y, the independent variables are represented by $X_1, X_2, X_3, \ldots$. Based on these symbols, the general form of the multiple regression model is as follows:

$$Y = \beta_0 + \beta_1 X_1 + \beta_2 X_2 + \cdots + \beta_n X_n$$

where $\beta_0 =$ the Y intercept of the regression model

$\beta_1, \beta_2 \ldots \beta_n =$ the slope of the regression model

or the computed multiple regression model is

$$Y_c = a + b_1 X_1 + b_2 X_2 + \cdots + b_n X_n$$

where
Y_c = the computed value of the dependent variable
a = the y intercept when x equals zero
b_1 and $b_2 \ldots b_n$ = partial regression coefficients
$X_1, X_2, \ldots, X_n$ = independent variables

Exhibit 17-1 shows a few examples of three or more related variables.

partial regression coefficient
A coefficient that shows the change in the computed dependent variable per unit change in one independent variable when all other independent variables are held constant.

Notice that b_1 is termed a **partial regression coefficient.** This denotes the change in the computed value, Y_c, per one unit change in X_1 when all other independent variables are held constant. Furthermore, b_2 represents the expected change in Y when X_2 changes by one unit but X_1 and all other independent variables remain constant. Hence, b_1 and b_2 are both partial regression coefficients. Since X_1 and X_2 are usually related, the partial regression coefficient, b_1, differs from the simple linear regression coefficient, b, brought about by regressing Y on X_1 alone. This illustrates that the magnitude of the partial regression coefficient of an independent variable differs, in general, from that of its bivariate regression coefficient.

In Chapter 16 when we looked at bivariate data, the coefficient of determination, r^2, was the strength of association or degree of closeness of the relationship between two variables. It indicated how much variation in the dependent variable was

EXHIBIT 17-1	Examples of Three or More Related Variables
Dependent Variable (Y)	**Related Independent Variable ($X_1, X_2, \ldots$)**
Amount of sales by each salesperson in a company (Y)	Years of sales experience (X_1) and intelligence test score (X_2) of each salesperson
Monthly sales at a restaurant (Y)	Number of cars passing by the restaurant (X_1), number of competitors (X_2), seating availability (X_3), and advertising budget (X_4)
Annual sales of new apparel line (Y) distribution	Annual advertising budget (X_1), product appeal (X_2), and effectiveness of channels (X_3)

explained by the variation in the independent variable. Since with multiple regression we are dealing with more than one independent variable, we refer to the association between the dependent and independent variables as the **coefficient of multiple determination,** denoted by R^2. It can be interpreted in a similar manner as we did when we referred to bivariate data. Consider Example 17-1.

coefficient of multiple determination The coefficient that indicates the association between the dependent and independent variables.

Example 17-1

The first four columns of Exhibit 17-2 show the amount of sales (Y) made by a group of eight salespeople during a given period, the years of sales experience (X_1), and the intelligence test scores (X_2) of each salesperson.

The following calculations will be made:

(a) The multiple regression equation

(b) The standard deviation of regression

(c) The coefficient of multiple determination

Solution: (a) Substitute the totals obtained in Exhibit 17-2 in the three normal equations of the following formulas:

I. $\qquad \sum Y = na + b_1 \sum X_1 + b_2 \sum X_2$

II. $\qquad \sum (YX_1) = a \sum X_1 + b_1 \sum X_1^2 + b_2 \sum (X_1 X_2)$

III. $\qquad \sum YX_2 = a \sum X_2 + b_1 \sum (X_1 X_2) + b_2 \sum (X_2^2)$

Therefore,

I. $\qquad 8a + 30b_1 + 16b_2 = 40$

II. $\qquad 30a + 136b_1 + 68b_2 = 178$

III. $\qquad 16a + 68b_1 + 38b_2 = 94$

By using either matrix algebra or the method of elimination, the solutions are

$$a = -0.4545, \quad b_1 = 0.7273, \quad b_2 = 1.3636$$

Therefore, the multiple regression equation is as follows:

$$Y_c = -0.4545 + 0.7273X_1 + 1.3636X_2$$

	(1)	(2)	(3)	(4)	(5)	(6)	(7)	(8)	(9)	(10)
EXHIBIT 17-2		Calculation for the Multiple Regression Equation by the Least-Squares Method								
Sales Person	Amount of Sales (in $1,000)	Years of Sales Experience	Intelligence Test Score						
	Y	X_1	X_2	Y^2	X_1^2	X_2^2	YX_1	YX_2	$X_1 X_2$
A	9	6	3	81	36	9	54	27	18
B	6	5	2	36	25	4	30	12	10
C	4	3	2	16	9	4	12	8	6
D	3	1	1	9	1	1	3	3	1
E	3	4	1	9	16	1	12	3	4
F	5	3	3	25	9	9	15	15	9
G	8	6	3	64	36	9	48	24	18
H	2	2	1	4	4	1	4	2	2
Total	40	30	16	244	136	38	178	94	68

| EXHIBIT 17-3 | Calculation for Y_c and the Standard Deviation of Regression s |

(1)	(2)	(3)	(4)	(5)	(6)	(7)
Salesperson	Y	X_1	X_2	$Y_c = -0.4545 + 0.7273X_1 + 1.3636X_2$	$Y - Y_c$	$(Y - Y_c)^2$
A	9	6	3	8.00	1.00	1.00
B	6	5	2	5.91	0.09	0.01
C	4	3	2	4.45	−0.45	0.20
D	3	1	1	1.64	1.36	1.85
E	3	4	1	3.82	−0.82	0.67
F	5	3	3	5.82	−0.82	0.67
G	8	6	3	8.00	0.00	0.00
H	2	2	1	2.36	−0.36	0.13
Total	40	30	16	40.00	0.00	4.53

(b) To calculate the standard deviation of regression, the values of Y_c must be computed first by the multiple regression equation:

For salesperson A: $X_1 = 6$ and $X_2 = 3$

$$Y_c = -0.4545 + 0.7273(6) + 1.3636(3)$$
$$Y_c = -0.4545 + 4.3638 + 4.0908$$
$$Y_c = 8.0001$$

In a similar manner, the Y_c values for other salespeople are computed and listed in column (5) of Exhibit 17-3. The standard deviation of regression is computed from the variation shown in column (7) of Exhibit 17-3 as follows:

$$s_y = \sqrt{\frac{\sum(Y - Y_c)^2}{n - k}} = \sqrt{\frac{4.53}{8 - 3}} = 0.952 \text{(in units of } \$1,000)$$

To compute the standard deviation of the Y values without computing the $(Y - Y_c)^2$ values, use the following formula:

$$s_y = \sqrt{\frac{\sum Y^2 - a \sum Y - b_1 \sum(YX_1) - b_2 \sum(YX_2)}{n - k}}$$

$$s_y = \sqrt{\frac{244 - (-0.4545)(40) - 0.7273(178) - 1.3636(94)}{8 - 3}}$$

Therefore,

$$s_y = \sqrt{\frac{4.5422}{8 - 3}} = \sqrt{0.9084} = 0.953 \text{(same as above except for rounding)}$$

This measure of dispersion is based on the linear relationship between sales and the two independent variables, years of sales experience and intelligence test scores. Its values ($s_y = 0.95$) are smaller than that based on the linear relationship between sales and only one variable, years of sales experience ($s_{yx} = 1.33$). In general, therefore, the multiple regression equation gives better estimates than does the simple regression equation.

Next, compare individually the squared deviation $(Y - Y_c)^2$ based on the multiple regression (4.53) in Exhibit 17-3 with the squared deviation $(Y - Y_c)^2$ based on the simple regression (10.64) calculated in Chapter 16 (Exhibit 16-7). The estimates of the simple regression by Y_c for salespeople C and D are closer to the actual sales (Y) than the multiple regression estimates by Y_c. However, the multiple regression estimates by Y_c for the other six salespeople are closer to the actual sales than those by Y_c from the simple regression equation. For example, the estimated amount of sales for salesperson E, who has 4 years of sales experience ($X_1 = 4$) and an intelligence test score of 1 point ($X_2 = 1$), is \$3,820 ($Y_c = 3.82 \times \$1,000$, the Y_c unit). This estimate is closer to the actual sales of salesperson E ($Y = \$3,000$) than the simple regression estimate made earlier ($Y_c = 5.29 \times \$1,000 = \$5,290$) without taking the intelligence test score into consideration.

(c) The coefficient of multiple determination, R^2, is computed as follows:

$$R^2 = \frac{RSS}{TSS} = 1 - \frac{ESS}{TSS} = 1 - \frac{4.53}{44} = .8970$$

(TSS = 44, as given earlier in Chapter 16, Exhibit 16-4; ESS = 4.53, given in Exhibit 17-3)

where   TSS = the total sum of squares $= \sum(Y - \bar{Y})^2$

RSS = the regression sum of squares $= \sum(Y_c - \bar{Y})^2$

ESS = the error sum of squares $= \sum(Y - Y_c)^2$

The value of R^2 can be interpreted in the same manner as r^2 for bivariate linear regression. Thus 89.7% of the variation in sales (Y) is related to, or explained by, the variation in the years of sales experience (X_1) and the intelligence test scores (X_2) of the salespeople, based on the multiple regression equation.

17-1a Calculating Multiple Regression Using Computers

Regression Analysis with SPSS

1. Open a new spreadsheet.
2. Label the first column "sales," and enter successively all of the sales data in the first column labeled "sales." That is, enter 9, 6, 4, 3, and so on until all eight numbers are in the first eight cells of the first column. Then, label the second column "years," and enter successively all of the years-of-experience data in the second column. Finally, label the third column "IQ," and enter successively all of the intelligence test scores in the third column.
3. At the top of the spreadsheet, click on "Analyze." Then click on "Regression" and "Linear." These commands designate the statistical test to be run.
4. Using the arrows, shift "sales" (which represents sales amounts) over to "Dependent:" and shift "years" (which represents sales experience) and "IQ" (which represents intelligence scores) over to "Independent(s):".
5. Click "OK."

The SPSS printouts shown in Exhibit 17-4 will appear:

Regression Analysis with Excel

1. Open a new spreadsheet.
2. As we did in the SPSS steps, enter successively all of the sales data in the first column. Then enter successively all of the years-of-experience data in the second column. Finally, enter successively all of the intelligence test scores in the third column.

EXHIBIT 17-4 | SPSS Tables for Regression Analysis

Model Summary

Model	R	R Square	Adjusted R Square	Std. Error of the Estimate
1	.947	.897	.855	.9535

[a]Predictors: (Constant), IQ, years

ANOVA

Model		Sum of Squares	df	Mean Square	F	Sig.
1	Regression	39.455	2	19.727	21.700	.003
	Residual	4.545	5	.909		
	Total	44.000	7			

[a]Predictors: (Constant), IQ, years
[b]Dependent Variable: sales

Coefficients

Model		Unstandardized Coefficients		Standardized Coefficients	t	Sig.
		B	Std. Error	Beta		
1	(Constant)	−455	.896		−.507	.634
	Years	.727	.266	.532	2.733	.041
	IQ	1.364	.527	.504	2.589	.049

[a]Dependent Variable: Sales

EXHIBIT 17-5 | Excel Table for Regression Analysis

SUMMARY OUTPUT

Regression Statistics

Multiple R	0.946939
R Square	0.896694
Adjusted R Square	0.855372
Standard Error	0.953463
Observations	8

ANOVA

	df	SS	MS	F	Significance F
Regression	2	39.45455	19.72727	21.7	0.00343
Residual	5	4.545455	0.909091		
Total	7	44			

	Coefficients	Standard Error	t Stat	P-value	Lower 95%	Upper 95%	Lower 95.0%	Upper 95.0%
Intercept	−0.45455	0.89601	−0.5073	0.633522	−2.75781	1.848717	−2.75781	1.848717
X Variable 1	0.727273	0.266155	2.73252	0.041157	0.043102	1.411444	0.043102	1.411444
X Variable 2	1.363636	0.526735	2.588847	0.048905	0.009623	2.71765	0.009623	2.71765

---

3. At the top of the spreadsheet, click on "Tools" and "Data Analysis." Then click on "Regression."

4. Where it asks for "Input Y Range:" enter "A1:A8" to indicate the location of the dependent variables. Where it asks for "Input X Range:" enter "B1:C8" to indicate the location of the independent variables. Leave the confidence level at 95%.

The output shown in Exhibit 17-5 will appear:

Interpretation of the Output

Each of the preceding printouts can be interpreted the same way as with the simple linear regression results. Some of the major concerns are as follows:

1. The *multiple R* or simply R value (.9469) is the correlation between the observed and predicted values of the dependent variable (that is, the correlation between sales and values of sales predicted by the model).

2. The *R square* shows how well the line fits the actual data (which are the Y values). As a general rule, the higher the R^2 value, the better the straight (regression) line fits the data. In our example, $R^2 = .897$, which says that knowing sales experience and intelligence test score explains almost 90% of the variation in sales.

3. The *adjusted R square* (.8554) shrinks the R square, since it considers the sample size and number of parameters estimated in the analysis.

4. The *standard error of the estimate* (0.9535) is the square root of the residual mean square in the ANOVA table and measures the spread of the errors (or residuals) about the fitted line.

5. The *F-statistic* (21.7) is used to test the hypothesis that the multiple regression model adequately fits the observed data. F is large when the independent variables help to explain the variation in the dependent variable. In our example, the linear equation is highly significant (.003). This indicates that we should reject the null hypothesis that the regression model does not fit the analyzed data. If the significance F value had been greater than .05, we would have failed to reject the null hypothesis and concluded that the model did not fit the analyzed data.

6. The estimates of our model coefficients a, b_1, and b_2, are, respectively, -0.4545, 0.7273, and 1.36, so the estimated model is

$$\text{Sales amount} = -0.4545 + 0.7273 \, X_1 \text{ (sales experience)} + 1.36 \, X_2 \text{ (intelligence test score)}$$

7. The *t statistics* (each coefficient divided by its standard error) are of some interest to researchers. They provide some idea regarding the relative importance of each variable in the model.

8. The *p-values* (.6335, .0412, and .0489) are the probabilities associated with the *t* statistics. They should not be used as a formal test regarding the importance of each variable.

17-2 Multiple Discriminant Analysis

Multiple discriminant analysis (MDA) is the appropriate tool for predicting the membership of observations in two or more groups. It is actually similar to multiple regression analysis except that different types of variables are involved. MDA is used if the dependent variable is *nominal* or *categorical* (either dichotomous, for example, young-old, male-female, user-nonuser, or multichotomous, for example, small-medium-large) and the independent variables are interval data. When two classifications are being examined, it is referred to as a *two-group discriminant analysis*. When three or more classifications are identified, then the term multiple discriminant analysis is used.

MDA is useful in situations where the total sample can be divided into groups, based on a dependent variable characterizing several known classes. The intent of this technique is two-fold: (1) to understand group differences, and (2) to predict the likelihood that a variable will belong to a particular group, based on several independent variables. The linear combination is known as the **discriminant function** and is derived from the following equation:[1]

$$Z = b_1 X_1 + b_2 X_2 + b_3 X_3 + \cdots + b_n X_n$$

multiple discriminant analysis (MDA) A statistical technique for predicting the membership of observations in two or more groups; used if the dependent variable is categorical and the independent variables are either interval or ratio data.

discriminant function The linear combination of the independent variables created by discriminant analysis to discriminate between the categories of the dependent variable.

where Z = discriminant score

b_i = discriminant weight for variable i

X_i = independent variable i

Discriminant analysis multiplies each independent variable by its corresponding weight and obtains a sum of these products, resulting in a single composite discriminant score for each individual in the analysis. By averaging the discriminant scores for all the individuals within a certain group, we create a group mean, also referred to as a **centroid.** If the analysis involves two groups, there are two centroids; three groups would have three centroids, and so on. The centroids suggest the most typical location of any particular group, and a comparison of the centroids shows how dispersed the groups are along the dimension being studied. Individual observations are assigned to the group with the closest centroid to the value of the individual observation.

centroid The group mean created by averaging the discriminant scores for all the individuals within a certain group.

An important function of discriminant analysis is to create a **classification matrix,** which shows the number of correctly and incorrectly classified cases. The numbers on the diagonal of the matrix represent the properly classified cases, since the predicted and actual groups are identical. All numbers off the diagonal of the matrix represent incorrect classifications. The total number of properly classified cases divided by the total number of cases is used to determine the **hit ratio**—the percentage of properly classified cases. Consider Example 17-2.

classification matrix A matrix that contains the number of properly and improperly classified cases.

hit ratio The percentage of properly classified cases in the classification matrix.

Example 17-2

A team of researchers sought to identify the behavioral correlates of frequent-flier members and nonmembers in the United States. The independent variables that provided the greatest group separation were regarded as significant descriptor variables associated with each market segment. Behavioral characteristics were measured by asking respondents to rate (on a 5-point scale; 1 = very important and 5 = not at all important) the following variables in choosing an airline:

X_1 = convenience of schedules
X_2 = overall service by attendants
X_3 = food and beverage quality
X_4 = on-time departures and arrivals
X_5 = frequent-flier program
X_6 = low or discount fares
X_7 = recommendation of travel agent
X_8 = recommendation of corporate travel planner

The variables found to discriminate between members and nonmembers were frequent-flier programs (X_5), recommendation of travel agent (X_7), convenience of schedules (X_1), overall service by attendants (X_2), and on-time departures and arrivals (X_4). Using our earlier equation, the relationships can be stated as follows:

$$Z = b_1 X_1 + b_2 X_2 + b_3 X_3 + \cdots + b_n X_n$$

$$= 1.0545 X_5 + (-0.3827 X_7) + 0.2998 X_1 + (-0.2600 X_2) + 0.1775 X_4$$

where Z = an individual's discriminant score

b_n = the discriminant coefficient for the nth variable

X_n = an individual's value on the nth independent variable

Source: © 2007 JupiterImages Corporation.

This indicates that an airline's frequent-flier program is the most important discriminating factor, followed by recommendation of travel agent, convenience of schedules, and so on. The hit ratio (which measures the proportion of members and nonmembers correctly classified) was 73%.[2]

17-3 Factor Analysis

Whereas MDA identifies groups of attributes on which individual objects differ, factor analysis groups attributes that are alike. **Factor analysis** can be used to examine interrelationships among many variables and to explain these variables in terms of their common underlying and unobservable dimensions (called "factors"). Marketing researchers use factor analysis to reduce the information contained in several original variables into a smaller, more manageable set of variables while losing as little information as possible. While there is no distinction between dependent and independent variables when using this analysis technique, data must be gathered from interval scales. Consider Example 17-3.

factor analysis A statistical technique used to examine interrelationships among many variables and to explain these variables in terms of their common underlying and unobservable dimensions (called "factors").

Example 17-3

A contractor is planning to build an apartment complex near a university and has hired a marketing research firm to determine the main concerns of college students regarding where they live. The firm surveyed 100 randomly selected students, using interval scales to determine which attributes they wanted in an apartment. The results of the study are shown in Exhibit 17-6.

Exhibit 17-6 shows the variables with similar underlying dimensions grouped or "loaded" together, as shown by the high correlations, on each of the four factors. As the data shows, the four factors (paranoids, studiers, exercisers, and partiers) explained 75% of the overall variance in all of the data. These factors can help the building contractor decide which segment of the market he or she wants to appeal to.

The factor model that is used for calculations is:

$$F_i = W_i X_1 + W_i X_2 + W_i X_3 + \cdots + W_i X_k$$

where
F_i = the estimate of the ith factor
W_i = the weight or factor score coefficient
k = the number of variables

> **EXHIBIT 17-6** | Factor Analysis of Students' Perceptions of Apartment Needs

	Survey Topics	Paranoids	Studiers	Exercisers	Partiers
(1)	I want a safe place to live	.75	.25	.20	.05
(2)	I want a full-time security guard on premises	.92	.30	.14	.09
(3)	I want to be near the library	.15	.94	.30	.29
(4)	I want to be near the bookstore	.05	.75	.27	.10
(5)	I want to be near a pool	.07	.20	.88	.05
(6)	I want to be near the gymnasium	.09	.17	.78	.23
(7)	I want to be near a running track	.10	.33	.69	.33
(8)	I want exercise facilities	.12	.14	.89	.28
(9)	I want to be where the parties are	.09	.15	.21	.78
(10)	I want to be near a liquor store	.02	.07	.17	.67
(11)	I want to be near fraternity row	.05	.10	.29	.79

17-4 Cluster Analysis

cluster analysis A statistical technique in which groups are formed in such a way that elements in the same group are similar to each other, and elements in different groups are as different as possible.

Cluster analysis involves grouping data into "clusters" such that elements in the same group are similar to each other, and elements in different groups are as different as possible. It is a statistical method that classifies or segments a sample into homogeneous classes. Marketers often use cluster analysis to identify market segments—groups of consumers with relatively similar needs. They also use the technique to design products and establish brands, target direct mail, make decisions about customer conversion and retention, and decide on marketing cost levels. Unlike factor analysis, which seeks to identify constructs that underlie several variables, cluster analysis seeks to identify constructs that underlie objects. Like factor analysis, though, in order to use clustering analysis, interval scales must be used during data gathering.

While cluster analysis is similar to factor analysis in that it is often used to reduce complexity in a data set, factor analysis is concerned with reducing the number of variables; cluster analysis tries to reduce the number of objects (e.g., individuals, products, advertisements).[3] Cluster analysis differs from discriminant analysis in that cluster analysis actually creates groups of like items, whereas discriminant analysis assigns elements to groups that were defined beforehand. That is, discriminant analysis requires previous knowledge of the group membership for each item included, whereas cluster analysis assumes no prior knowledge about the group and so groups or clusters are identified by the data. Consider Example 17-4.

Example 17-4

A marketing researcher wants to determine market segments in a large retail store. A random sample of shoppers is taken and is examined using two different criteria: income and age. Then the respondents are plotted on Exhibit 17-7.

Exhibit 17-7 shows that two distinct clusters exist. Apparently in this retail store, one group of customers is relatively young and financially more sound than the other segment, which is considerably older with less annual income.

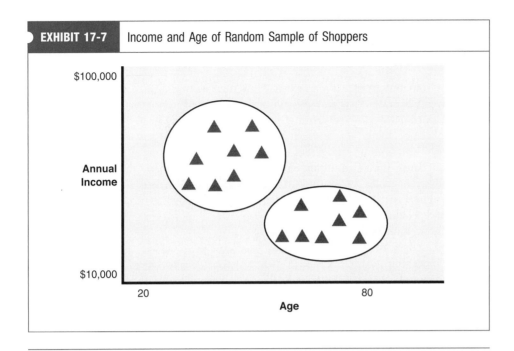

EXHIBIT 17-7 Income and Age of Random Sample of Shoppers

17-5 Multidimensional Scaling

Multidimensional scaling, also referred to as *perceptual mapping,* is a technique used to identify important dimensions underlying respondents' evaluations of test objects. The objective is to convert judgments of similarity or preference into distances represented in multidimensional space. That is, if respondents perceive items A and B to be the most similar of all possible pairs of test items, then multidimensional scaling should position items A and B so that the distance between them in multidimensional space is smaller than the distance between any other item pairs. It basically allows the researcher to illustrate relationships within data using pictures (a spatial representation of data) rather than only numbers. Just like we noted in factor analysis, there is no distinction between dependent and independent variables.

Marketing researchers tend to use multidimensional scaling techniques to identify important dimensions underlying customer evaluations of products, services, or companies. (See Research Realities 17-1.) Consider Example 17-5.

multidimensional scaling The technique used to identify important dimensions underlying respondents' evaluations of test objects by representing these evaluations as distances in multidimensional space; also referred to as "perceptual mapping."

Example 17-5

A researcher used multidimensional scaling to examine perceptions of various sources of medical information and to gain insight for a health care organization that was designing a new medical information service. The research focused on the following questions:

1. What are the most relevant characteristics of medical information sources?
2. How important are those characteristics to consumers when seeking medical information?
3. How do consumers rate the currently available medical information sources?
4. What are the major perceptual dimensions of medical information sources?
5. How are existing medical information sources perceived relative to one another?

Research Realities 17-1   *The Many Dimensions of Beauty*

You've heard the old saying, "Beauty is skin deep, but ugly is down to the bone!" Maybe that's why even China is ushering in a new era with its first-ever crowned Miss Plastic Surgery. Whatever the reason, people enjoy being beautiful, regardless how deep it may go. More and more companies such as Hugo Boss, Clinique and American Eagle are stepping up their promotions in different media.

Multidimensional scaling was used to examine the correspondence between types of beauty and product images in advertising. Six distinct types of good looks and the prototypical fashion models who embodied these types were identified from the data. The beauty types were differentially associated with a set of perfumes and

women's magazines representing diverse images. The study's significance was related to product imagery in advertising, particularly for beauty-related products. It found that there is more to beauty than a simple good/bad judgment of attractiveness. It proposed that beauty is multidimensional. A beautiful woman can be a "classic beauty," "cute," "sex kitten," "sensual," "girl-next-door," "exotic," "feminine," or "trendy."

Source: Anonymous, "Hugo Boss Adds Femme Perfume," *Marketing,* July 26, 2006, p. 4; Anonymous, "Saving Face," *Cosmetic Surgery Times,* September 2006, p. 20. M. R. Solomon, R. D. Ashmore, and L. C. Longo, "The beauty match-up hypothesis: Congruence between types of beauty and product images in advertising," *Journal of Advertising* 21, no. 4 (December 1992): 23–34.

Based on previous research and focus group discussions, seven sources of medical information were included in the questionnaire: (1) health publications, (2) prerecorded health messages, (3) television, newspapers, radio, and magazines, (4) doctors, (5) other medical professionals, (6) libraries, and (7) disease foundations and associations. Exhibit 17-8 shows a perceptual map. It shows that libraries and disease foundations and associations were both high in quality and readily accessible. While neither of these sources was perceived to have the high quality of information that might be obtained by doctors, they were more accessible. Media sources that provide medical news and advice were found to be low on quality but high on accessibility. Prerecorded health messages were perceived as being low on both quality and accessibility. Finally, the information received from doctors and other medical professionals were perceived as being of high quality but low on accessibility.

EXHIBIT 17-8   Perceptual Map of Medical Information Sources

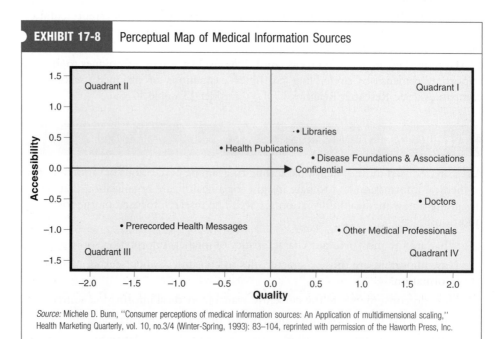

Source: Michele D. Bunn, "Consumer perceptions of medical information sources: An Application of multidimensional scaling," Health Marketing Quarterly, vol. 10, no.3/4 (Winter-Spring, 1993): 83–104, reprinted with permission of the Haworth Press, Inc.

17-6 Conjoint Analysis

One of the most popular analysis techniques in marketing research today, particularly for analysis of consumer behavior, is conjoint analysis.[4] **Conjoint analysis** provides information about the relative importance respondents place on individual attributes when choosing from multiple products or brands. It is an appropriate tool for nominal independent variables and an ordinal dependent variable. Marketing researchers have used conjoint analysis to answer a variety of questions, including:

1. Will changes in product design influence consumer preference for the product?

2. Will changes in design affect product sales?

3. Which new products will succeed in the marketplace?

4. What product attributes influence whether someone will purchase a product?

5. Are there certain market segments that exist for a product?

The interesting part of conjoint analysis is that if respondents are directly asked about their preferences, they may have a difficult time indicating the attributes they were using or how they were using them to create their overall judgments. Conjoint analysis takes care of this problem by estimating the value of each attribute based on the choices respondents make among product concepts that are systematically differed. Respondents' preferences regarding the attributes are inferred from their choices rather than from self reporting. Consider Example 17-6.

> conjoint analysis A statistical technique that provides information about the relative importance respondents place on individual attributes when choosing from multiple products or brands.

Example 17-6

To help you understand the concept behind conjoint analysis, think about the choices consumers make when choosing airline flights. If you are interested in flying from New York to Los Angeles and it costs either $300 or $600, you would choose the $300 flight if cost is the only consideration. Suppose you could choose between a 15-inch seat and a 20-inch seat; you'd likely choose the 20-inch seat if seat size is the only consideration. And what if you have the choice between a direct four-hour flight and a six-hour flight with a short stop in Chicago? The selection would be obvious if time is the only consideration. But these decisions are not entirely realistic because rarely do consumers make decisions based on only one product attribute. The conjoint analysis technique is built on the assumption that consumers make complex decisions based not on one factor at a time but on several factors "jointly" (hence the term *conjoint*). Consumers make trade-offs in their decisions that will create the most satisfaction. Conjoint analysis predicts what products and services consumers will select and evaluates the weight people give to various factors that underlie their decisions.

Let's further consider our example. The decisions are summarized in Exhibit 17-9.

To collect the information using conjoint analysis, a sample of consumers might be shown a series of cards, each containing a written description of the product. If a consumer product is being tested, a picture of the product might accompany the written description. The number of cards used in the study would be limited by using statistical manipulations. Typical conjoint studies have respondents rating only 10 to 20 cards.

Referring to Exhibit 17-9, based on the eight choices, the fourth choice (20-inch seat, $300, 4 hours) is the most desirable and the fifth choice (15-inch seat, $600,

EXHIBIT 17-9	Airline Choices Using Conjoint Analysis		
Choice	Seat Size (in inches)	Price	Duration (in hours)
1	20	$600	6
2	20	$600	4
3	20	$300	6
4	20	$300	4
5	15	$600	6
6	15	$600	4
7	15	$300	6
8	15	$300	4

EXHIBIT 17-10	Hypothetical List of a Consumer's Utilities				
Seat Size	Utility	Price	Utility	Duration	Utility
20	15	600	5	6	22
15	12	300	61	4	42

6 hours) is the least desirable. Conjoint analysis can determine the relative importance of each attribute, attribute level, and combinations of attributes. Perhaps the airline cannot offer the fourth choice. If this is the case, conjoint analysis can identify the second-most desirable choice.

Different segments of travelers may have different preferences. For example, business travelers may not care about price, so the second choice (20-inch seat, $600, 4 hours) may be their optimal selection. In this case, cost is of low utility value. If cost is important to the traveler, then it would have high utility value. **Utility** is the number that represents the value consumers place on an attribute. Conjoint analysis creates a **part-worth function** that describes the utility respondents give to the levels of each attribute. Consider the hypothetical list of utilities for a consumer in Exhibit 17-10.

Based on the consumer's utilities, the following conclusions can be reached:

1. The value placed on seat size is minimal (15 versus 12).
2. The value placed on a $300 flight is much higher than the value placed on a $600 flight (61 versus 5).
3. The value placed on a 4-hour flight is much higher than the value placed on a 6-hour flight (42 versus 22).

The relative importance of each of the three attributes can be calculated:

Duration:	Range = 20 (42 − 22)	
Seat size:	Range = 3 (15 − 12)	*Least important factor*
Cost:	Range = 56 (61 − 5)	*Most important factor*

Finally, conjoint analysis can be a part of computer choice simulations. These simulations show consumer preference for particular products created by the researcher. They can inform researchers about "what if" scenarios regarding the company's products and competitor's products. Researchers can simulate market situations by changing product features and adding or eliminating products in the market. For example, consider the three flights designed by the researcher in Exhibit 17-11.

This simulation indicates the proportion of consumers that prefer each flight. Perhaps it shows that consumers will travel longer if they can pay less for the ticket and

utility The number that represents the value consumers place on an attribute when using conjoint analysis.

part-worth function The function that describes the utility respondents give to the levels of each attribute when using conjoint analysis.

EXHIBIT 17-11	Computer Choice Simulations			
Flight Number	Cost	Duration	Number of Connections	Meal
1	$400	6 hours	2	Full meal
2	$600	5 hours	1	Snack
3	$800	4 hours	direct	None

EXHIBIT 17-12	Multivariate Tests According to Scaled Data	
Multivariate Test	Independent Variable	Dependent Variable
Multiple regression	Interval	Interval
Multiple discriminant analysis	Interval	Nominal
Factor analysis[*]	Interval	Interval
Cluster analysis[*]	Interval	Interval
Multidimensional scaling[*]	Any type of data	Any type of data
Conjoint analysis	Nominal	Ordinal

*Note: No distinction is made between independent and dependent variables.

get a full meal. Simulations permit researchers to estimate preference, sales, and share for new flights before they are actually offered on the market.[5]

17-7 Choosing the Appropriate Test

It is difficult deciding which multivariate test to use. As noted in each section, there are several issues to be concerned with, but the type of scale that was used during data collection is the major concern. Exhibit 17-12 shows which test to use according to the scaled data.

Decision Time!

This chapter covers a few challenging statistical analysis techniques. It takes some understanding of intermediate statistics to fully comprehend each method. You are a marketing manager of a mid-sized company, and your marketing researcher has recently returned from a two-day seminar on multivariate statistics. He starts using at the company some of the techniques he learned, but you feel that the research results he presents you with contradict your knowledge of the market. What are you going to do? Confront him and admit that you do not know anything about multivariate statistics but you are uncomfortable with the research results? Or educate yourself before confronting him? Is it your responsibility to learn statistical techniques?

Net Impact

As we noted in other chapters on statistics, the Internet will not directly help researchers with statistical analyses. It can, however, lend qualitative support for the research findings obtained from the quantitative analyses. It can also inform researchers about advancements made in statistical analyses through published manuscripts, clipboards, and chat groups. Finally, it can clarify researchers' understanding of multivariate concepts by offering pertinent articles and demonstrations online. (See the "Net Exercise" in this chapter for an online demonstration of conjoint analysis.)

On the Lighter Side—Statistics for Wildlife and Ecology

Sometimes marketing researchers believe that certain statistical procedures were invented just for their purposes, but actually statistics are used in all walks of life. Kevin McGarigal, S. Cushman, and S. Stafford wrote a book entitled *Multivariate Statistics for Wildlife and Ecology Research*. While this book may sound like the ideal business student text—especially the "wildlife" part—it actually gives the reader a solid conceptual understanding of the role of multivariate statistics in ecological applications. The detailed examples using real wildlife data sets are also helpful for readers to learn how to apply the techniques in practice.

Source: Barnes & Noble.com web page, http://search.barnesandnoble.com/booksearch/isbnInquiry. asp?userid=YG2Owu3CYl&isbn=0387986421&TXT=Y&itm=1, accessed August 25, 2005.

Chapter Summary

Multivariate statistics allows researchers to investigate more than two variables at a time. It has been used extensively in the physical, social, and medical sciences. Some of the most popular multivariate methods include multiple regression, multiple discriminate analysis, factor analysis, cluster analysis, multidimensional scaling, and conjoint analysis.

Multiple regression analysis determines the association or relationship between the dependent variable and two or more independent variables. The coefficient of multiple determination (R^2) is a measure of association between the dependent and independent variables taken together. It can be interpreted in a similar manner as we did when we referred to bivariate data.

Multiple discriminant analysis is used to predict the membership of observations in two or more groups. It is like multiple regression, but different types of variables are involved. It is used if the dependent variable is nominal scaled, categorical, or multichotomous and the independent variables are interval scaled. Factor analysis is used to examine interrelationships among many variables and to explain these variables in terms of their common underlying and unobservable dimensions. Marketing researchers use factor analysis to reduce the information contained in several original variables into a smaller, more manageable set of variables.

Cluster analysis groups data so that elements in the same group are similar to each other, and elements in different groups are as different as possible. Multidimensional scaling is a technique used to identify important dimensions underlying respondents' evaluations of test objects. The purpose is to convert judgments of similarity or preference into distances represented in multidimensional space. Finally, conjoint analysis, a highly popular tool among researchers, provides information about the relative importance respondents place on individual attributes when choosing from multiple products or brands. It is appropriate when working with nominal independent variables and an ordinal dependent variable.

Review Questions

1. In general, what is multivariate statistical analysis? When would a researcher use it?

2. What does the coefficient of multiple determination indicate to a researcher?

3. What is a centroid?

4. How do multiple discriminant analysis, multidimensional scaling, factor analysis, conjoint analysis, and cluster analysis differ? How are they alike?

5. What types of scales do multiple discriminant analysis, multidimensional scaling, factor analysis, conjoint analysis, and cluster analysis require?

6. What is cluster analysis, and how does it benefit marketing researchers?

7. What is meant by "utility"?

8. What is a "part-worth function"?

Practice Quiz

Note: You can find the correct answers to these questions by taking the quiz and then submitting your answers in the Online Edition. The program will automatically score your submission. If you miss a question, the program will provide the correct answer, a rationale for the answer, and the section number in the chapter where the topic is discussed.

1. When using multiple regression analysis, the relationship between the dependent and independent variables is referred to as the partial regression coefficient.
   a. True
   b. False

2. When a researcher interprets a computer printout and reads the coefficient of multiple determination, he or she examines the multiple R—the correlation between the observed and predicted values of the dependent variable.
   a. True
   b. False

3. When a researcher interprets a computer printout and reads the coefficient of multiple determination, he or she examines the F-statistic to test the hypothesis that the multiple regression model adequately fits the observed data.
   a. True
   b. False

4. When a researcher uses multiple discriminant analysis, a classification matrix is created that exclusively shows the number of incorrectly classified cases.
   a. True
   b. False

5. Conjoint analysis is an appropriate tool for ratio-scaled independent variables and interval-scaled dependent variables.
   a. True
   b. False

6. Which of the following tests is used to identify important dimensions underlying respondents' evaluations of test objects?
   a. Cluster analysis
   b. Multidimensional scaling
   c. Multiple discriminant analysis
   d. Factor analysis
   e. Conjoint analysis

7. Which of the following provides information about the relative importance respondents place on individual attributes when choosing from multiple products or brands?
   a. Cluster analysis
   b. Conjoint analysis
   c. Multiple discriminant analysis
   d. Multidimensional scaling
   e. Factor analysis

8. Which of the following is used to group data so that elements in the same group are similar to each other and elements in different groups are as different as possible? It partitions a sample into homogeneous classes.
   a. Conjoint analysis
   b. Factor analysis
   c. Multiple discriminant analysis
   d. Multidimensional scaling
   e. Cluster analysis

9. _____ is a multivariate technique that uses the model $Y = \beta_0 + \beta_1 X_1 + \beta_2 X_2 + \cdots + \beta_n X_n$.
   a. Cluster analysis
   b. Multiple regression analysis
   c. Multiple discriminant analysis
   d. Multidimensional scaling
   e. Factor analysis

10. _____ is a multivariate technique that uses the model $Z = b_1 X_1 + b_2 X_2 + b_3 X_3 + \cdots + b_n X_n$.
    a. Cluster analysis
    b. Factor analysis
    c. Multidimensional scaling
    d. Multiple discriminant analysis
    e. Multiple regression analysis

Thinking Critically

1. Use the following table containing each interviewer's years (X_2) of college education to compute:
   a. The regression equation of Y on X_1 and X_2 by the least-squares method
   b. The standard deviation of regression s
   c. The coefficient of multiple determination R^2

Employee	Y, Number of Interviews Obtained	X₁, Hours Soliciting Interviews	X₂, Years of College Education
Albert	2	1	1
Bertha	10	2	1
Christina	20	6	4
Denzel	14	7	2
Edward	11	5	2

2. You were introduced to several different multivariate statistical techniques in this chapter. To demonstrate that you have a basic understanding of each method, write an example using the following techniques:

a. Multiple discriminant analysis
b. Conjoint analysis
c. Factor analysis
d. Multidimensional scaling
e. Cluster analysis

Net Exercise

SurveySite conducts research for a wide range of organizations in both the private and public sector. One of its most often used statistical techniques is conjoint analysis. Visit its Web site at http://www.surveysite.com/ and try its excellent online conjoint analysis demo.

Experiencing Marketing Research

In the chapter, when we discussed factor analysis, we used an example about a contractor building an apartment complex near a university. Students provided several statements regarding the attributes they wanted in an apartment. Revisit the example and talk to a sample of students who live in apartments. Then add at least ten more attributes to the list. Decide which factor (paranoids, studiers, exercisers, or partiers) they load on.

Case 17-1

Avon's Calling for Help

David McConnell and his wife Lucy started Avon back in 1886 in a small room in New York City. McConnell began his career as a door-to-door seller of books but soon changed to selling perfume when he found that many women enjoyed the perfume he gave as a gift to his book customers. Today, Avon Products, Inc., has grown into the world's largest direct-selling company in the world, offering one of the world's most widely known cosmetics and fragrance brands. Avon is also one of the largest manufacturers of fashion jewelry and markets lines of apparel, gifts, and home decorative products. Avon's success is nothing short of staggering. It has current annual sales of $7.7 billion, conducts more than one billion customer transactions annually, has operations in over 60 countries, is marketed in more than 100 countries, and employs 4.9 million independent sales representatives worldwide.

Much of Avon's success hinges on the success of its sales representatives. While a small percentage of representatives enjoy six-figure annual incomes from their efforts, the majority take in a much more modest income. Their incomes vary widely, depending on the amount of time they devote to their business. Some prefer to do it only part-time to supplement their primary income. Others work at least 40 hours each week selling their products. There is some concern within the organization that management does not fully understand which variables are most important to their sales representatives so that they can successfully sell Avon products. In other words, they are unsure what factors lead to sales by their representatives. Is it strictly the sales pitch, or do location, years of experience, age, education, and other factors come into play?

Source: The historical data was taken from Avon's home page, http://www.avon.com/about.html, accessed August 23, 2005.

Case Questions

1. You have been hired to determine which factors lead to sales by Avon's sales representatives. Describe how you will find this information and which multivariate technique is appropriate to analyze the data.

2. What factors were involved in your decisions?

Case 17-2

Nike in Morocco

Nike, Inc., is a huge manufacturer of athletic footwear. Its name has become well known worldwide, and it consistently tallies an annual revenue approaching $14 billion and a net income around $1.1 billion. Phil Knight, CEO of Nike, stated, "I envision the company to become a globally dominant brand rivaling the likes of Coca-Cola and McDonald's." One market Nike has recently become interested in is Morocco.

Morocco is a link between Europe and Africa. It is a country in northwest Africa with approximately 29.9 million people. It is truly a beautiful country with modern cities and lots of desert land. In fact, the largest desert in the world, the Sahara, is located there. Many movies have been filmed there, including Humphrey Bogart's *Casablanca* and Orson Wells' *Othello*. The native language in Morocco is Arabic, but French and Spanish are widely spoken.

Nike knows that its success in this market hinges on the receptiveness of Moroccans to its shoes and the level of competition in the country. It has found that its major competition will come from already-established firms there, including the BATA, BOUTAJ, and JMC corporations. It also discovered from a local government report that most Moroccans anticipate purchasing at least three pairs of sneakers within the next five years, because Moroccans do a lot of walking.

To determine the perception of Nike products in Morocco, assume a marketing research firm surveyed 20 target consumers and revealed the data shown in Exhibit 1.

EXHIBIT 17-A1	Predicting Moroccans' Perceptions of Nike Products		
Respondent	Perception of Nike Products (10-point scale; 10 = highest rating) (Y)	Years of Athletic Competition (X_1)	Number of Subscriptions to American Sports Magazines (X_2)
1	9	8	4
2	7	4	2
3	6	4	5
4	5	6	7
5	8	5	1
6	4	8	1
7	3	9	3
8	7	12	2
9	3	14	4
10	4	6	3
11	2	7	6
12	6	4	2
13	7	8	3
14	6	7	2
15	9	9	1
16	3	3	1
17	4	6	4
18	6	4	3
19	8	5	2
20	7	8	4

Source: Nike home page, "Fiscal year 2005 annual report," http://www.nike.com/nikebiz/nikebiz.jhtml?page=17, accessed August 25, 2005; the figures in the table used in the case and the Moroccan scenario are fictitious.

Case Questions

1. Compute the multiple regression equation of Y, X_1, and X_2.

2. What is the coefficient of multiple determination? What does it indicate?

3. According to the fictitious table, what is the general perception of Nike products among Moroccans?

Notes

1. For an in-depth discussion of multivariate statistics, read *Multivariate Data Analysis,* 2nd ed., by Joseph Hair, Rolph Anderson, Ronald Tatham, and William Black (Upper Saddle River, NJ: Prentice-Hall, 1998).

2. Rex S. Toh and Michael Y. Hu, "A multiple discriminant approach to identifying frequent fliers in airline travel: Some implications for market segmentation, target marketing, and product differentiation," *Logistics and Transportation Review* 26, no. 2 (June 1990): 179(19).

3. Adamantios Diamantopoulos and Bodo B. Schlegelmilch, *Taking the Fear Out of Data Analysis* (London: The Dryden Press, 1997), 217.

4. For an alternative approach to the traditional conjoint analysis, see V. Srinivasan, and Chan Su Park, "Surprising robustness of the self-explicated approach to customer preference structure measurement," *Journal of Marketing Research* 34, no. 2 (May 1997), 286(6).

5. Part of the discussion and the entire example on conjoint analysis was taken from Professor Marshall Rice and Survey-Site's "Conjoint analysis tutorial," which is available at http://dev.survey-poll.com/newsite/docs/conjointtutor.html. Accessed August 30, 2005.

Communicating the Research Findings

Source: © 2007 JupiterImages Corporation.

Learning Objectives

After studying this chapter, you will be able to:

- Explain the importance of effective communication.
- Describe the communication process.
- Educate others about the barriers to communication.
- Identify and explain the keys to an effective written report.

- Identify and explain the keys to an effective oral presentation.
- Discuss the technology available to create effective oral and written presentations.

GET THIS

Better Written Communication Is a Global Concern

Some people say the world is getting smaller, since they can travel across the globe in less than a day, talk instantly on the telephone to someone who is thousands of miles away, send messages worldwide through electronic mail and facsimile machines in a matter of seconds, and be informed of world events by the mass media and the Internet as they happen. It seems that communication is becoming less of a problem for businesses operating in foreign markets. In fact, global networks have enabled companies to conveniently communicate with their overseas branches.

Because rapid and convenient communication capability plays a vital role in international communication, there is a growing need to communicate clearly, accurately, and effectively. The accrediting body of many colleges and universities, the American Assembly of Collegiate Schools of Business International (AACSB International), identifies the importance of written and oral communication abilities and the global aspects of communication. Furthermore, companies are offering communication training to meet management development needs and to enhance the productivity of employees. But does international written communication require different skills from those needed in domestic situations? Companies realize that their success abroad depends on developing cross-cultural appreciation and strengthening fundamental communication skills among their employees for national as well as international business activities. But in spite of their desire to hire employees with strong communication skills, employers find that most applicants have serious grammatical deficiencies, as well as a lack of practical business writing skills.

To determine whether there are differences between the written communication skills required of employees involved in international operations and those of employees involved in domestic operations, a survey of 120 international companies located in the United States was conducted. The sampling frame was identified as all companies listed in the AT&T toll-free 800 directory whose company names began with "international." The research revealed the following results:

- The major types of documents produced (from most to least) were letters/form letters, memorandums, reports, and grants/proposals; 51% of the companies listed reports as being among the most frequent types of documents produced.

- Documents originally created in longhand or at the computer were revised by support personnel in 58% of the companies. Originators prepared their own final copy in 27% of the companies. In 15% of the companies, both approaches are used, depending on the situation.

- The most often cited writing deficiency was "mechanics" (that is, spelling, grammar, punctuation, proofreading, and format) followed by "content" and "style and tone."

- Despite the call for strong written communication skills, 38% of the respondents reported that no screening techniques were used to assess the writing abilities of new hires. Most of them assumed that "All employees with major writing responsibilities are college graduates; therefore, they all write well." Many also felt like they could tell how well prospective employees could write during the interview process since "Good speakers are/will be good writers."

- The most frequently named countries with which international companies communicate were the United States, Great Britain, Canada, Japan, Australia, and Germany, respectively.

The majority of representatives from the companies reported no significant problems in communications when compared to domestic operations, since most business is conducted in English. However, all respondents in the sample made the following recommendations for ensuring successful international written communication:

1. Involve skills of bilingual employees or use translators or interpreters for critical or sensitive messages.

2. Keep messages short and simple, with clear wording.

3. Avoid slang.

4. Use the facsimile machine to transmit information, enabling information to be exchanged quickly, while allowing for equally speedy clarification of confusing or misunderstood terms before the exchange is finalized.

No doubt companies will increasingly use electronic mail to communicate both within and outside of the company. A recent study predicts that email volume in the U.S. will rise from over 2 trillion messages in 2005 to nearly 2.7 trillion by 2007.

Sources: William J. Wardrope and Marsha L. Bayless, "Content of the business communication course: An analysis of coverage," *Business Communication Quarterly* 62, no. 4 (December 1999): 33–40; Mona Casady and Lynn Wasson, "Written communication skills of international business persons," *Bulletin of the Association for Business Communication* 57, no. 4 (December 1994): 36–40; David Hallerman, "Email: Turning up the volume," http://www.imediaconnection.com/content/5630.asp, accessed April 29, 2005.

Now Ask Yourself

- Why is it necessary for marketers to learn how to write correctly, since most word processors can correct grammar and spelling mistakes?

- Do you agree with the comment that "All employees with major writing responsibilities are college graduates; therefore, they all write well"?

- Do you feel that the Internet has helped or hindered oral and written communication between individuals in companies? Explain your answer.

As you can see from the "Get This" feature, no matter where in the world a company conducts its business, effective written communication is extremely important. Unfortunately, though, most employers in the study found most applicants to have serious grammatical deficiencies as well as a lack of practical business writing skills. But written communication is just one way of exchanging information. Another important business skill is oral communication. In this chapter, you will gain some important communication skills and learn how to effectively communicate research findings to marketing managers. We will begin with a brief discussion about the importance of communication and the communication process. You will also learn how to prepare effective written reports and oral presentations.

18-1 The Role of Communication

The glue that binds people in companies and other organizations is communication. The absence of communication creates organizations that are run by individuals rather than teammates. Marketing researchers are dependent on effective communication to learn about problems that need to be resolved. Then they need to communicate to gather data and accurately convey research findings to managers. Imagine what it would be like for a marketing researcher to survey a company's target market and then not have the ability to communicate the results. The fact is that good communication is a vital part of success—whether we're talking about individuals or companies. A study of 354 managers found that the top three requirements of new college and university graduates are oral communication, problem-solving, and self-motivation abilities.[1] Another study of 229 responses from members of the Association for Business Communication rated 30 business communication concepts. The five most important concepts centered on written communication and were ranked as follows: use correct grammar and sentence structure, write memoranda, write persuasive news, write good new/positive message letters, and write reports.[2]

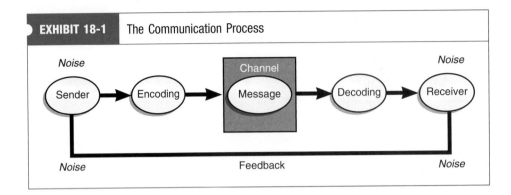

EXHIBIT 18-1   The Communication Process

18-1a The Communication Process

The importance of effective communication cannot be overstated. American businesses alone generate an estimated 30 billion pieces of writing each year. Workers on average spend one-third of their time on the job writing letters, memorandums, and reports.[3] Communication creates relationships between senders and receivers. In fact, communication has significantly advanced most aspects of business and technology, since it allows individuals to share their knowledge with others.

The success of your entire marketing research effort will depend on how well you communicate the information to management. The accuracy, content, and style of presentation of the data will play a critical role in management's evaluation of the research.

The communication process involves several interrelated parts, as illustrated in Exhibit 18-1.

To understand these components, let's assume that Mr. S recently finished analyzing the data that examines the satisfaction of Coca-Cola customers. He must report his findings to Ms. R, a senior marketing manager at Coca-Cola. The components in the interaction are as follows:

- *Sender*—the person or group conveying the information. In this case, Mr. S is the sender.

- *Receiver*—the person or group receiving the information. In this case, Ms. R (and other managers reading/listening to the report/presentation) is the receiver.

- *Message*—the information that the sender conveys. In our hypothetical example, Coca-Cola customers are extremely satisfied with the product but unhappy with its high sugar content.

- *Encoding*—involves putting the information to be conveyed in a form that can be understood by both the sender and receiver. For example, Mr. S creates words and presentations to get the intended points across about the high regard for Coca-Cola's taste but the dissatisfaction regarding the sugar content of the drink.

- *Decoding*—involves the receiver putting the information conveyed by the sender into his or her own thoughts. That is, it is the receiver's interpretation of the message. Ideally, the receiver's decoding of the message will match the sender's encoding of the message; however, meaning often gets distorted in the encoding-decoding process. In our example, Ms. R correctly interprets Mr. S as saying that Coca-Cola customers are highly satisfied with the product but are dissatisfied with the amount of sugar in the beverage.

- *Channel*—links the sender with the receiver. The researcher's communication channel with management is usually through either oral presentations or written reports. Various communication vehicles, such as computers, television, videotapes, and telephones, can be used to convey oral or written communication. In our example, Mr. S presents the findings in person, using a multimedia format that includes both audio and video technology to effectively communicate with Ms. R.

- *Noise*—any unplanned interference during the communication process. Noise can take the form of people talking in the audience, telephones ringing, babies crying, automobile horns blowing, equipment problems, and so on. In our example, as Mr. S is presenting his findings to Ms. R, an ambulance goes by with its horns loudly blowing and disrupts the presentation, since the audience momentarily cannot hear well.

- *Feedback*—a check on how effective the communication was between the sender and receiver. Communication is effective if the decoded message matches the encoded message, that is, if the receiver interprets the message as the sender intended. Feedback also indicates to the sender how the message affected the receiver. In our example, after the presentation, Ms. R comments to Mr. S that she will move forward with some of his recommendations regarding how to lessen customer concerns about the sugar content of the soft drink.

18-1b Barriers to Effective Communication

The communication process is most effective when the receiver understands the message from the sender the way it was intended to be understood. But this does not always happen. Earlier we touched on "noise"—unplanned interference with the communication process. Let's look a bit deeper into communication intrusion. Several problems can evolve during conversation that can inhibit effective communication:

1. The first problem is "bypassing," which occurs when people do not properly interpret each other's intended meaning. For example, a marketing manager of a bank wants the researcher to study the level of customer satisfaction with automatic teller machines, but the researcher believes that the manager wants to learn about their customers' satisfaction with human tellers.

2. A second problem is an individual's frame of reference. This exists because everyone has different backgrounds and life experiences that cause them to look at things somewhat differently.

3. A third problem deals with language skills. It is important for the sender and receiver of information to have a good grasp of their language—whether it's oral or written.

4. A fourth communication problem is inferior listening skills. Far too often people do not listen closely enough to what others are conveying to them. This can cause the receiver to sometimes have less than enough knowledge about a topic to make a proper decision.

5. A fifth problem during communication is attributable to emotions. Feelings of happiness, depression, eagerness, and anger can muddle the mind.

6. A sixth problem is physical distractions such as a lousy Internet connection, static in a telephone line, passing automobiles, and sloppy penmanship, all of which can detract from effective communication between two or more individuals.[4]

18-2 Written Communication

Written communication is usually a one-shot deal. That is, you may only have one opportunity to get your message across to your audience. Since there is often no immediate feedback to help you reach your readers like you can get from oral communication, it becomes extremely important to do your best job from the beginning. Employees typically spend a large part of their time communicating in writing. In fact, employees in many companies spend 20 to 40 percent of their time writing.[5] A French manager of the Citroen auto manufacturer once stated that unless something is written down, and thus documented, it has no reality.[6] At Procter & Gamble, effective writing is a requirement of all employees. P&G even has its own

Research Realities 18-1   *Reports in 3D*

Experienced writers know that people are more likely to read a report if they find it interesting and easy to understand. Visual aids can help accomplish both of these goals. Marketing researchers use diagrams, charts, maps, pictures, and other visual images to illustrate the relationships and structural patterns in the data. However, traditional visual displays are restricted to the two-dimensional printed page. To overcome this restriction and add unique appeal, researchers are experimenting with visual techniques not often used in report writing: stereographic construction of three-dimensional representations. These representations not only add to visual attractiveness of the report but can also display the data in ways that make it easier to understand and interpret. Figures in three dimensions can even be viewed without the aid of a device, like 3D glasses. However, special lenses can widen the viewing area for a more impressive effect.

Consider AstraZeneca, a major pharmaceutical company that spends over $15 million each year on research and development of new medicines. Their scientists create high-resolution, 3D presentations to show the complex molecular structures used in the creation of drugs such as Armidex, Casodex, and Nexium. Their company built a 3D projection room that has a "3D multiplexer" that splits and renders images to create a pop-off-the-screen effect when used with a pair of projectors.

Source: Morris B. Holbrook, "Stereographic visual displays and the three-dimensional communication of findings in marketing research," *Journal of Marketing Research* 34, no. 4 (November 1997): 526–536; Steven Regenoid, "Astrazeneca's 3D Projection Experiment," *Presentations*, vol. 19, no. 12 (December 2005), p. 10.

"colleges" to train everyone in all aspects of company business—especially effective writing. However, an overabundance of written communication, especially if it is too wordy or unimportant to the receiver, is not effective communication.

The written research report is an organized record of the entire study. It provides a tangible record of the information that can be carefully prepared and directed to a particular audience, and then stored for later reference. However, written communication is only effective if the receiver reads and understands it. As you will see in Research Realities 18-1, marketing researchers are trying out innovative ways to present their written information to make their reports more appealing and easier to understand.

18-2a Keys to an Effective Written Report

A few simple guidelines can help you write reports that effectively convey your message. Following these guidelines will help you write any report, not just research reports:

1. *Carefully consider what information you want to convey.* Research produces a vast amount of information, yet seldom does the audience need or want all of this information. Researchers must decide what information is important to the audience, and leave out the rest. Often, for example, managers do not care about the details of the research methodology. They may want to know that the information was gathered and analyzed expertly, but they will concentrate on the information that will help them make better decisions. Whenever researchers perform a major study, they are tempted to show managers the prodigious effort they put into it by producing a thick report. In report writing, more is not necessarily better. Managers do not want to sort through mounds of words to find the information they need for decision making. Good reports tell managers what they want to know, and then move on.

2. *Know your audience.* To determine what information is important to your audience, you must know your audience. A report intended for lower-level employees will likely differ from one targeted to upper management.

   When researchers present the findings from their customer satisfaction study for First Bank, branch employees will read a different report from the one intended for vice presidents and the CEO at the main office. Since branch employees make decisions related only to their branch, the content of their report will focus on information specific to the branch. However, upper management makes decisions that affect the entire corporation, so the report for the main office will contain broader information. To better know your audience, here are some basic questions to ask yourself:

- Who is my reader?
- What does my reader know about this subject?
- What does the reader need to know?
- How will the reader respond?
- Will he or she be receptive to the information I will present?
- Will he or she object to the information I will present?
- Will he or she be hostile toward me?
- Will he or she be indifferent toward me or the information I will present?[7]

3. *Use a clear, logical progression.* Write down the main points, or parts, of your communication in the most logical order. As this is being done, consider the points in terms of occurrence or chronology. This will organize your ideas.

4. *Use familiar terminology.* Use language, words, and phrases familiar to the audience, so they can easily understand. Particular industries have their own vocabulary, so use their terminology. Obviously, a message in French requires a receiver who understands French. Just as obviously, a message in technical or professional jargon requires a recipient who understands that jargon.

5. *Use tables and exhibits to present large quantities of data.* Large amounts of statistical data can be organized and conveyed most effectively through tables and exhibits. Word pictures may be sufficient for a few simple items, but for large quantities of data, words are cumbersome. Tables and exhibits summarize information and present it in an easy-to-understand form.

6. *Avoid unnecessary words and phrases.* Mark Twain once wrote, "I never write 'metropolis' for seven cents because I get the same price for 'city.'"[8] Don't try to impress your readers with big words and flowery phrases. Tell them what they want to know understandably and concisely. Don't make them work for it.

7. *Document all assumptions.* Sometimes in written reports, researchers must make assumptions about consumers, the economy, budgets, work force size, and so on. Assumptions are permissible, as long as they are expressed in the written report. Typically, assumptions are stated in the appendix of the report.

8. *Proofread everything in the report.* Read your report several times, and then have other people read it. Since they are not as close to it as you are, they may see problems that eluded you. A research report often requires several drafts to make it as accurate, concise, and easy to understand as possible. Researchers usually have at least two other people in the industry read the report and make recommendations before they revise it into final form.

18-2b Format of the Written Report

The best report structure is the one that conveys your message as accurately and understandably as possible. Although there is no single right way to design a written report (see Exhibit 18-2), most research reports contain the following components:

1. Title page
2. Executive summary
   a. Objectives
   b. Findings
   c. Costs
   d. Conclusions
   e. Recommendations
3. Table of contents

> **EXHIBIT 18-2** | Alternative Report Formats

Generic Academic Report	Generic Company Report
1. Title page	1. Title page
2. Table of contents	2. Table of contents
3. Summary	3. Executive summary
4. Introduction	4. Introduction
5. Literature review	5. Body (results)
6. Methodology	6. Conclusions and recommendations
7. Findings	7. Appendices (including methodology)
8. Conclusions and recommendations	
9. Limitations and future research	
10. Bibliography	
11. Appendices	

Source: Adamantios Diamantopoulos and Bodo Schlegelmilch, *Taking the Fear Out of Data Analysis* (New York: The Dryden Press, 1997), 222.

4. Introduction
   a. Brief overview of industry and purpose of study
   b. Statement of objectives
5. Research methodology
6. Analysis of results
7. Research limitations
8. Conclusions and recommendations
9. Appendix
   a. Forms used to gather information
   b. Calculations to support quantitative information conveyed in the study
   c. References cited in the body of the paper
   d. Tables to support information conveyed in the study
   e. Miscellaneous information conveyed in the study, such as drawings of products and plant layouts

Title Page

The title page should include the title of the study, the date when the study was completed, the name(s) of the targeted audience, and the names and affiliations of the researchers.

Executive Summary

The executive summary is a brief overview—usually one or two pages—of the major contents of the report. It is intended to be sympathetic to the time limitations of management. It should include the key objectives, findings, costs, conclusions, and recommendations made in the report.

Table of Contents

The table of contents is a "road map" of the major sections and subsections included in the report, with page numbers to help readers quickly find the information important to them.

Introduction

The introduction sometimes provides a brief overview of the industry but should always discuss the purpose and objectives of the research effort.

Research Methodology

This section reviews the study's methodology. It should include the research design, sampling group(s), data-gathering procedures, and statistical tools used in the study.

Analysis of Results

This section will consume the majority of the research report. It should carefully address each research objective and detail how the objectives were either satisfied or not satisfied. Although much of this section is narrative, it usually includes pertinent tables and exhibits to support findings. The flow of information must be logical and consistent with the purpose of the research stated at the beginning of the report.

Research Limitations

This section should clearly specify any assumptions that were made in the study. Studies that depend on such things as the state of the economy, a particular size of budget, or certain market growth rates often require some assumptions that must be stated in this section. Besides assumptions, other limitations such as time allocated to complete the study and budget earmarked to perform the study should be included in this section of the report.

Conclusions and Recommendations

In a concise and well-organized fashion, this section should convey the study's conclusions and recommendations. Since managers are likely to use this information in strategic planning, it should be both precise and lucid.

Appendix

The appendix is often used to store all support information referred to in the study but not actually placed in any of the previous sections. For example, if a survey was used and discussed in one of the previous sections, the questionnaire should be included in this section. Other pieces of information that may be included here are mathematical calculations, references, and certain support tables and exhibits.

18-3 Oral Communication

Oral communication is second nature to all of us—we've been doing it all our lives. We use it to convince, cajole, complain, or just converse. As with written communication, oral communication is effective only if it successfully conveys our intended message to

Source: © 2007 JupiterImages Corporation.

the receiver. For researchers, the oral presentation is the opportunity to explain the findings and "sell" their recommendations directly to management. To be effective, an oral presentation must be interesting enough to hold the audience's attention as it presents its message in a clear, well-organized flow of information.

18-3a Keys to an Effective Oral Presentation

Making an oral presentation can be an intimidating experience, especially if you must address high-level managers. However, these guidelines can make the task a bit easier.

1. *Consider the composition of the audience.* As is the case with written communication, you will present differently to top-level executives than to mid- and lower-level managers. Top executives will not command as much detail in most cases.

2. *Display an outline at the beginning of your presentation.* Show an outline of your presentation at the outset, to let the audience know where you are headed. This will give the audience some idea of what you will cover and help them ask questions at appropriate times. The outline should be skeletal, showing only headings and subheadings.

3. *Consider using some humor periodically.* Although it should not be forced into a presentation, sometimes a presentation can lend itself to the use of humorous anecdotes and illustrations. These can be used to make an important point and at the same time lighten up the atmosphere in the room.[9]

4. *Follow the format of the written report.* Your presentation should highly correlate with the written report. The written report should be more comprehensive than the oral presentation, so there is seldom a need to present information not covered in the written report. The majority of the presentation time should be spent on the Analysis of Results and Recommendations sections, with very little time spent on Research Methodology. Some sections in the written report, such as the Executive Summary and Table of Contents, should not be included in the oral presentation at all.

5. *Know the material well and avoid reading.* The better you know the material, the less you will need to read from note cards. Listening to a presenter read a presentation can be exceedingly boring. Good presenters entertain the audience with an energetic and enlightening presentation while looking at them, not at notes.

6. *Use plenty of visual aids.* People enjoy a presentation more and get more out of it if they can look at something relevant while they are listening. Graphs, exhibits, tables, or any other type of visual aid dramatically improve presentations. Historically, visual aids have been displayed using overhead transparencies and flip charts, but in today's era of technology, computerized screen projections are among the most effective and impressive modes of presentation. Many Macintosh and Windows presentation software packages allow users to generate electronic slides that include text, a color background, clip art, photographs, or other graphic enhancements.

7. *Rehearse the presentation prior to the real thing.* Practice the presentation several times before making the formal presentation. Practice can provide two important benefits. First, you can assess how long the presentation will take. Second, you can make adjustments during practice to hone the message and delivery to smooth-flowing perfection.

8. *Allow ample time for questions from the audience.* Since oral presentations offer the important advantage of direct interaction between presenter and audience, allot ample time for questions. Listeners may need clarification or may want to challenge something you've said, giving you the opportunity to repair any miscommunication.

9. *Conclude the presentation on a positive note.* At the end of the presentation, review the key points in the findings and recommendations to reinforce your message. Outline the study's benefits to the company and what the company will gain from implementing the recommendations. Then thank the audience for their patience and attentiveness during the presentation.

18-3b Multimedia Presentations

Bells and whistles are the name of the game in today's presentations. The use of computerized multimedia is the conduit to maximize your presentation. Recent advancements in technology have made it relatively easy to create presentation pages or "slides" on the computer and develop these slides into presentations that can incorporate both animation and sound. Programs such as PowerPoint, Charisma, or Persuasion allow presenters to produce highly sophisticated visual aids. The most popular presentation software is Microsoft Office's PowerPoint. We'll take a brief look at this powerful tool to highlight some of its most appealing features available on presentation software.

As you may already know, PowerPoint allows you to create slides that can be printed on plain paper, printed on acetate transparencies for overhead projection, reproduced as 35-mm color slides, or projected directly from the computer screen. You can also print notes to yourself on the slide pages as well as a complete outline of the presentation. You can produce a straightforward text-based presentation or incorporate a huge range of sound and pictures, from simple clip art to full-motion video. PowerPoint presentations can include the following features:

- A variety of colors
- Timed slide transitions
- Clip art (predrawn pictures that can be inserted into slides)
- Various types of charts (organizational charts, bar charts, pie charts, and so on)
- An equation editor
- Multimedia enhancements

PowerPoint offers a few multimedia enhancements to add flash to presentations. If you are going to make your presentation on a computer with a sound card, you can insert a variety of sounds. These sounds can come from the program itself, kind of like sound "clip art," or you can record your own sounds. PowerPoint also offers users with Windows Media Player the opportunity to add video clips to presentations. Media Player permits the user to both see and hear a video file.

Almost everyone would agree that the Internet is a rich source of information. One such item exists at http://www.beyondbullets.com/2006/05/seminar_recordi.html where author Cliff Atkinson makes available a 45 minute recording of his seminar on how to create more interesting PowerPoint presentations. Atkinson uses techniques borrowed from Hollywood where movie makers have been communicating well without text on the screen for many years.[10]

18-4 Types of Graphic Aids

Most people have five senses, all of which can be used in communicating. In general, the more senses that a presenter or writer can activate in the audience, the more effective the communication will be. Obviously, the hearing sense will be used throughout oral presentations, but if you can engage the sense of sight as well, your presentations will be more effective. In fact, what we see and hear can account for better than 90% of what we learn.[11] A study conducted at the Wharton Business School's Applied Research Center found that presenters using visual aids were perceived as better prepared, more persuasive, and more interesting, and got their points across 67% of the time. Those who did not use graphics were only able to make their points 33% of the time.[12]

By providing effective visual aids with oral or written reports, you give the audience the opportunity to see what they are hearing or reading. The visual element serves as the link between you and the audience by immediately seizing and holding their attention. Graphics communicate with more impact, direct the audience's attention, save time, display complex relationships, and clarify abstract concepts. Tables and charts are pictorial devices that can graphically aid most oral presentations and written reports.

18-4a Tables

The format of tables may vary. In general, most tables should include the following parts: (1) table number, (2) title, (3) captions, (4) stub, (5) body, (6) headnote, (7) footnote, and (8) source of data. The first five parts are basic and should be included in any table. The remaining three parts are used only when needed.

All parts should be presented in a clear and simple, yet attractive and complete manner, so that the reader can get the most information from the table in the least amount of time. Table creators should use rules, spacing, and special type styles, such as boldface, italics, roman capitals, and lowercase letters, to improve the appearance and clarity of a table. Exhibit 18-3 serves as an example.

1. *Table number:* When more than one table is presented in a report, each table should be numbered. The table number is especially important, as it is easier to refer to a table number than to the entire title of the table. The tables and figures in this book are called "exhibits," so "Exhibit 18-3" is the table number in our example.

2. *Title:* The title is a description of the contents of the table. It should be compact yet provide a good overview of what is in the table.

3. *Captions:* The caption, also called the boxhead or column head, is the heading at the top of each column. The simplest table may consist of only two columns and two captions: one for stubs and one for data. However, many tables have more than two captions and sometimes have many captions and subcaptions.

4. *Stub:* The row descriptions are called stubs. Stubs are placed at the left side of the table. They usually classify the numbers in the table body. The caption over the column of stubs describes stub classifications.

> **EXHIBIT 18-3** Example of a Table

Title { **Headnote** {

U.S. International Trade in Goods and Services: 2002—2004
In millions of dollars. Details may not equal totals due to seasonal adjustment and rounding.

	Balance			Exports			Imports		
Year	*Total*	*Goods (1)*	*Services*	*Total*	*Goods (1)*	*Services*	*Total*	*Goods (1)*	*Services*
2002	(421,180)	(482,297)	61,117	977,276	682,422	294,854	1,398,457	1,164,720	233,737
2003	(494,814)	(547,296)	52,482	1,022,567	713,421	309,146	1,517,381	1,260,717	256,664
2004	(617,583)	(665,390)	47,807	1,151,448	807,536	343,912	1,769,031	1,472,926	296,105

Captions — header row with Year, Total, Goods (1), Services

Stubs — 2002, 2003, 2004

Footnote { *Note:* (1) Data presented on a Balance of Payments (BOP) basis. For information on data sources and methodology, see the information section on page 26 of the FT-900 release, or at http://www.census.gov/ft900 or http://www.bea.gov/bea/di/home/trade/htm.

Source { *Source:* U.S. Census Bureau, "U.S. international trade in goods and services," http://www.census.gov, accessed on September 9, 2005.

5. *Body:* The body is the content of the data. Data presented in the body is arranged according to the descriptions or classifications of the captions and stubs. Thus, effective presentation of the data in a table depends on the arrangement of the columns and rows. If the purpose of the table is to compare, the numbers in a table should be arranged for easy comparison.

   In general, numbers can be compared more easily when they are placed in a column rather than a row. When two or more sets of numbers are to be compared, they should be placed in adjacent columns or as close as possible. Furthermore, important numbers should be placed in the most noticeable positions in the table. Since Americans read from left to right and from top to bottom, the column nearest to the stubs and the row immediately below the captions are in the most noticeable positions for American readers.

6. *Headnote:* Headnotes are usually written just above the captions and below the title. They are used to explain certain points relating to the whole table that have not been included in the title, captions, or stubs. For example, the unit of the data is frequently written as a headnote, such as "Numbers in Millions of Dollars."

7. *Footnote:* Footnotes are usually placed below the stubs. They clarify unexplained elements in the table.

8. *Source:* The source of data is usually written below the footnotes. If the data is collected and presented by the same person, it is customary not to state the source in the table. Details concerning the collection are noted in the discussion along with the tabular presentation. However, if the data is taken from other sources, such as secondary sources of published data, these sources should be stated in the table. The statement will enable the viewer or reader to evaluate the data or to obtain additional information from the original source, if needed, and will give proper credit to the original collector of the data.

18-4b Charts

Charts (sometimes called "figures" or "graphs") are graphical or pictorial representations of data. Charts contain many of the same elements as tables: figure number, title, body, and sometimes a footnote and/or source note. In addition, some charts have a legend, which is a "key" that defines some elements in the chart. For example, the legend in Exhibit 18-5 defines the lines representing data about electricians, carpenters, and painters. It is important to match the chart type with your objectives. See Exhibit 18-4 for a summary of matches between visual aid and objectives.

Charts can take several graphic forms. The most common types of charts are (1) line charts, (2) pie charts, (3) bar charts, and (4) pictograms.

EXHIBIT 18-4	Matching Visual Aid with Objectives
Visual Aid	**Objective**
Table	To show exact figures and values
Bar chart	To compare one item with others
Line chart	To demonstrate changes in quantitative data over time
Pie chart	To visualize a whole unit and the proportions of its components
Flow chart	To display a process or procedure
Organization chart	To define a hierarchy of elements
Photograph, map, illustration	To create authenticity, to spotlight a location, and to show an item in use

Source: Mary Ellen Guffey, *Business Communication: Process & Product,* 2nd ed. (Cincinnati, OH: South-Western College Publishing, 1997), 385.

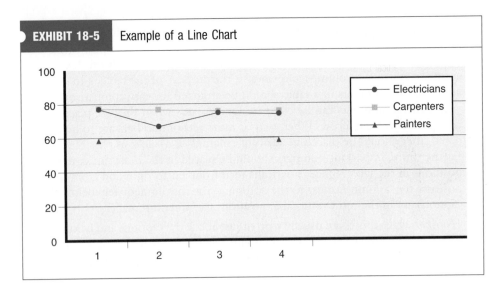

EXHIBIT 18-5 Example of a Line Chart

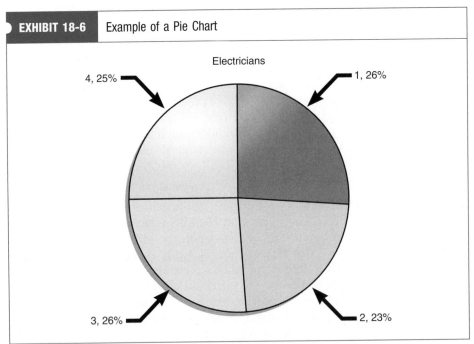

EXHIBIT 18-6 Example of a Pie Chart

Line Chart

A chart that consists of lines or broken lines for representing data is referred to as a line chart (see Exhibit 18-5). To construct a line chart, first plot the data by points according to the scales on the two reference lines. Then connect the points by straight lines. The scales used on the two reference lines are usually quantitative and are continuously labeled. They may or may not be equal. Line charts are used mostly to show data classified by quantity or time.

Pie Chart

One of the easiest charts to interpret is the pie or ''circle'' chart, since each slice of the pie is proportional to the percentage of the whole. Pie charts are often used for demonstrating percentages. For example, Exhibit 18-6 shows that when all electricians are considered from the sample, 26% belonged to group 1, 23% to group 2, 26% to group 3, and 25% to group 4. Pie charts are useful as long as they are clearly labeled and limited to an easily readable number of slices. Many times companies use them to show a variety of demographic information, such as the percentage of males

> **EXHIBIT 18-7** | Bar Charts

(a) Example of a vertical bar chart. (b) Example of a horizontal bar chart.

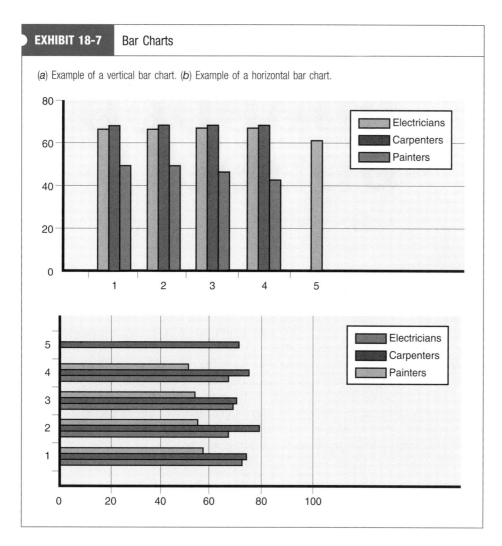

versus females, income levels in an organization, religious affiliation, age categories, and education levels of employees.

Bar Chart

A bar chart displays data as rectangular bars, extending vertically or horizontally, as shown in Exhibit 18-7a and 18b. The bars in the same chart are usually of equal width. The length of each bar represents the data. Bar charts emphasize the differences among individual items, but line charts emphasize the continuous changes or general trend among the items. Bar charts are used in presenting data classified by any basis (time, place, quantity, or quality).

Pictogram

A chart that uses pictures to represent numerical data is called a **pictogram** or *pictograph* (see Exhibit 18-8). The symbols are usually of the same size, and each of them represents the same kind of information with a fixed value. A pictogram is essentially a modified type of bar chart. In a bar chart, the length of each bar represents the magnitude of the data it represents. In a pictogram, the number of pictures in the row or column shows the magnitude of the data. Statistical presentation by pictogram is particularly useful in stimulating the reader's interest or in showing the data to an individual with little knowledge of a particular industry, because it is readily self-explanatory and user-friendly. Pictograms can sometimes be confusing and must be carefully depicted, since in some cases partial pictures are used, such as half a money bag.

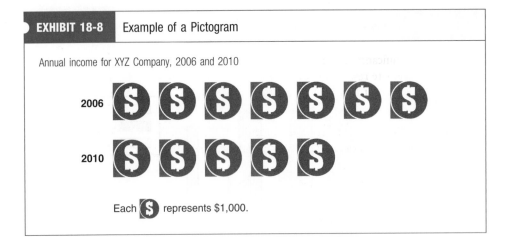

EXHIBIT 18-8   Example of a Pictogram

Annual income for XYZ Company, 2006 and 2010

2006 $ $ $ $ $ $ $

2010 $ $ $ $ $

Each $ represents $1,000.

18-5 Report Follow-Up

Once the written report and oral presentation are completed, researchers allow some time to pass for managers or other users of the information to absorb all that has been presented to them. Then, a short time later, the researchers contact the key users of the study findings to ask if they need clarification or additional information. This follow-up step is beneficial in three ways: (1) It lets the key people at the client company know that the researchers are willing to address any additional questions, (2) it provides clients an opportunity to ask specific questions after they have read the report, and (3) it allows adjustments to be made to the study if necessary and if company resources permit.

Source: © 2007 JupiterImages Corporation.

Decision Time!

Exhibit 18-2, which listed alternative report formats, made the point that the format of academic reports often differs from company reports. If your company did some marketing research for a university, what would you recommend the written report look like?

Net Impact

The Internet significantly impacts the communication process, since it provides another avenue to disseminate research findings. Here is a brief list of some Internet communication tools in use today that will likely continue to evolve and influence communications in the future:[13]

- *Email* allows individuals to send partial and complete reports to others throughout the world. This is typically achieved by attaching a file to the document.
- *Web pages* allow companies to post a variety of information on the World Wide Web. Companies often post past reports on their web page.
- *Conferencing software* (e.g., Microsoft NetMeeting) allows users to hold text, audio, or video conferences over the Internet. Users can simultaneously work on shared whiteboards.
- *Webcam* is the hardware device that transmits a real-time video image over the web.
- *Streamlining audio* delivers either live audio or stored audio on demand over the Internet.
- *CD-quality audio* is growing in popularity because Internet users can obtain high-quality sound on the web.
- *Streamlining video* delivers live and quality video over the Internet.

On the Lighter Side—Communicate with Your Senses

San Jose, California-based Immersion Corporation has developed a mouse that uses a small internal motor to simulate the sense of touch as you move your cursor across the computer screen. It's as if the contents of your screen have been turned into a Braille version of themselves. Move your screen cursor over a "feedback enabled" icon, and you can feel a bump as you ride over its edge. A variety of sensations can be selected: crisp, rubbery, metallic. "There's an infinite variety of sensations, and users can modify them at will," says Immersion's CTO Bruce Schena. DigiScents is doing a similar thing, but for your nose instead of your fingers. The Oakland-based company has created a PC peripheral that looks like an audio speaker but emits a gentle poof of scent—patchouli, grape, freshly cut grass—instead of sound. The company's system, appropriately called iSmell, consists of cartridges that contain 128 organic scent compounds that can be mixed in varying ratios to create thousands of more complex odors. When a scent-enabled web link is clicked on, iSmell processes the digital recipe for a scent, the cartridge squirts it out in the proper ratio, and a small fan blows an aromatic cloud toward your nose.

Source: Jennifer Tanaka, "Touch me, feel me," *Newsweek* 136, no. 9 (August 28, 2000): 61–62.

Chapter Summary

After collecting and analyzing the research data, researchers must effectively communicate the results to the managers who need the information for decision making. The accuracy, organization, and style of presentation of the data all play a critical role in management's evaluation of the research project.

The role of communication is to bring together people in companies and organizations. This is accomplished by creating relationships between sender and receivers. The key elements in the communication process are the sender, receiver, message, encoding, decoding, channel, noise, and feedback. Communication is effective if the receiver interprets the message as the sender intended. There can be a variety of barriers to communication, including bypassing, frame of reference, language skills, listening skills, emotions, and physical distractions.

Research findings are generally communicated through written reports and oral presentations. A written report provides a tangible record of the information that can be carefully prepared and directed to a particular audience, and then stored for later reference. Following these guidelines can help you prepare an effective report of any kind: (1) Carefully consider what information you want to convey, (2) know your audience, (3) use a clear, logical progression, (4) use familiar terminology, (5) use tables and exhibits to present large quantities of data, (6) avoid unnecessary words and phrases, (7) document all assumptions, and (8) proofread everything in the report. Although research reports can be organized in a number of ways, they generally follow this format: title page, executive summary, table of contents, introduction, research methodology, analysis of results, research limitations, conclusions and recommendations, and appendix.

For effective oral presentations, follow these guidelines: (1) Consider the composition of the audience, (2) display an outline at the beginning of your presentation,

(3) consider using some humor periodically, (4) follow the format of the written report, (5) know the material well and avoid reading, (4) use plenty of visual aids, (5) rehearse the presentation prior to the real thing, (6) allow ample time for questions from the audience, and (7) conclude the presentation on a positive note.

The use of visual aids and multimedia can make any report more interesting and easier to understand. Tables organize large amounts of data. Tables have some or all the following components: table number, title, caption, stub, body, headnote, footnote, and source of data. Charts are graphical representations of data. Common types are line charts, pie charts, bar charts, and pictograms.

Shortly after communicating research results, researchers should contact the clients to answer questions and make adjustments, if necessary.

Review Questions

1. What is the role of communication, and why study it if we have been doing it all our lives?

2. What are some barriers to effective communication?

3. What is the difference between encoding and decoding? As a sender, do you want encoding and decoding to be the same or different? As a receiver, will you know if they differ?

4. When creating a written research report, is it acceptable to make assumptions? If so, why? If not, why not?

5. What is the purpose of an appendix in a written report?

6. When making an oral presentation, why is it important to conclude on a positive note?

7. What is a legend, and where is it used?

8. After completing the oral presentation and written report, what should the researcher do next? Why?

9. What is multimedia?

10. How can the Internet enhance the communication process?

Practice Quiz

Note: You can find the correct answers to these questions by taking the quiz and then submitting your answers in the Online Edition. The program will automatically score your submission. If you miss a question, the program will provide the correct answer, a rationale for the answer, and the section number in the chapter where the topic is discussed.

1. All of the following are components of the title page: the title of the study, the date when the study was completed, the name(s) of the target audience, and the names and affiliations of the researchers.
   a. True
   b. False

2. All support information referred to in the study but not actually placed in any of the previous sections should be put in the "appendix" section.
   a. True
   b. False

3. During an oral presentation, a presenter should use no more than six visual aids, since he or she doesn't want to bore the audience.
   a. True
   b. False

4. If there is nothing positive about your findings, don't attempt to conclude an oral presentation on a positive note.
   a. True
   b. False

5. Bar charts emphasize the differences among individual items, but line charts emphasize the continuous changes or general trend among items.
   a. True
   b. False

6. Which of the following is *not* a key to an effective oral presentation?
   a. Use plenty of visual aids.
   b. Allow ample time for questions.

c. Rehearse the presentation prior to the real thing.

d. Be sure to carefully read the report to the audience.

e. Follow the format of the written report.

7. The _____ section(s) follow the research methodology of the written academic report.

a. conclusions and recommendations

b. research limitations

c. appendix

d. analysis of results

e. findings

8. Which of the following is in the correct order of the communication process?

a. Sender, decoding, encoding, channel, receiver

b. Sender, encoding, channel, decoding, receiver

c. Sender, encoding, decoding, channel, receiver

d. Sender, encoding, channel, receiver, decoding

e. Sender, decoding, channel, encoding, receiver

9. What we see and hear can account for _____ of what we learn.

a. 20%

b. 40%

c. 50%

d. 70%

e. 90%

10. The _____ section(s) follow the title page of the written report.

a. introduction

b. executive summary

c. table of contents

d. research methodology

e. summary of findings

Thinking Critically

1. From the following table, construct a bar chart, line chart, pie chart, and pictogram. Which type of chart seems most appropriate for the given data? Which seems to be the least appropriate? Why?

Units Sold in Two Department Stores, 2000–2006

Year	Poor-Person's Department Store	Rich-Person's Department Store
2000	2,400	8,500
2001	3,200	8,700
2002	4,300	9,200
2003	5,700	9,700
2004	6,900	10,200
2005	8,200	12,600
2006	9,500	13,800

2. Besides the keys to an effective written report that were listed in the chapter, what additional considerations can help you write an effective report?

3. Besides the keys to an effective oral presentation that were listed in the chapter, what additional considerations can help you present an effective oral report?

4. You are an employee of Excellence Marketing Research Firm, and your manager has asked you to explain the difference between conclusions and recommendations in your written report. What would you tell him? Are they similar in any way?

Net Exercises

1. Booher Consultants offers a variety of online writing courses that help individuals write emails, letters, reports, proposals, manuals and other forms of documentation. Visit their site at http://www.booherconsultants.com and click on "Written Communication." You can also read about their "Oral Presentations" and "Interpersonal Communications" seminars.

2. Strategic Communications is a Connecticut-based firm that consults with U.S. and multi-national companies and government agencies in all areas of written and oral communication skills. Many of its clients are large financial institutions, Fortune 100 companies, and major consulting firms. The Strategic Communications World Wide Web site offers information and support for professionals and companies interested in all aspects of business communication. Along with information on Strategic Communications and the services it offers, the firm's resource library gives you access to various articles on successful communication. Visit the Web site and read about the company, its services, and its markets, and see what communication articles you can find at the resource library. The address is http://www.strategiccomm.com.

Experiencing Marketing Research

1. You are a researcher for a large company in the United States. You are to interview five foreign students who use English as their second language and determine whether they find it more difficult to write or speak the English language. What problems have they encountered in writing English? What problems have they encountered in speaking English? How have these problems impeded their communication with others?

2. Go to a professor who is currently teaching a business communications course and ask him or her if you can observe some of the class presentations.

Based on these presentations, answer the following questions:

a. Were the presenters effective communicators? If so, why? If not, how can they improve?

b. Did the communicators do anything that you found distracting?

c. Did the presenters seem to know their message content well?

d. Did the presenters use any visual aids or multimedia technology?

e. Did the presenters allow ample time for questions at the end of the presentation?

Case 18-1

It's Not Easy Making a Quality Presentation!

Sun Microsystems refers to the next generation of computing as "the Participation Age," when "sharing innovation and building communities comes to the forefront." Sun has committed resources to provide high-quality, instructor-led training experience in real time over the Web. This strategy may be the wave of the future, but regardless of how the message is presented to management today, it is oftentimes done poorly. All too often, managers have to sit through discussions that are too long and jammed with too much information that is either misleading or even wrong. Furthermore, too many presenters are less-than-compelling as speakers, and too many managers expect the presentations alone to tell them all they need to know about the research. One company recognized these problems and wanted to do something to improve the communication process, so they established a "Corrective Action Team" made up of the general counsel, the director of the quality process, and the head of the company's public and government affairs planning and programs section.

The team's initial assignment was to recommend procedures and policies for improving the quality of presentations. They created a questionnaire and asked 12 employees from a cross section of departments who routinely made committee presentations to complete them. Then they personally interviewed each respondent. The following key problems that affect the quality of presentations were revealed:

- Presenters said they were interrupted with questions so often that their presentations lost focus and impact.

- Managers said that they had to interrupt when presentations were too narrowly focused or failed to consider particular issues.

- Presenters said their presentation assignments were usually unclear.

- Managers often received an outline or written presentation summary only a few days before the presentation. Members said the material usually was not thorough enough or they didn't have enough time to read it.

- Presenters often failed to view the managers as an audience. They didn't always establish common ground or sufficiently understand the kind of information managers required to make a decision.

- Slides were a persistent problem. They often were not well integrated with the text. Individual slides often contained too many variables. Presenters spent too much time explaining their slides.

Source: Anonymous, "Virtual Class Delivers Worldwide,"- *Communications News,* vol. 42, no. 9 (September 2005), pp. 40–43; George P. Miga, "Quality presentations boost decision-making power," *Public Relations Journal* 50, no. 2 (February 1994): 24–25.

Case Questions

1. You have been hired as a consultant to resolve these problems. What recommendations would you make to management to deal with each of the problems stated?

2. Who is more to blame for these communication problems, management or presenters? Support your stance.

Notes

1. J.D. Maes, I.G. Weldy, and M.L. Icenogle, "A managerial perspective: Oral communication competency is most important for business students in the workplace," *The Journal of Business Communication* 34, no. 1: 67–80.

2. William J. Wardrope, and Marsha L. Bayless, "Content of the business communication course: An analysis of coverage," *Business Communication Quarterly* 62, no. 4 (December 1999): 33–40.

3. Anonymous, "Write on! Tips for effective communication," *HR Focus* 70, no. 8 (August 1993): 54.

4. Mary Ellen Guffey, *Business Communication: Process & Product*, 2nd ed. (Cincinnati, OH: South-Western College Publishing, 1997), 13–15.

5. Richard E. Neff, "CEOs want information, not just words: So . . . write smart, simple and short," *Communication World* 14, no. 5 (April–May 1997): 22(4).

6. Jean-Louis Barsoux, and Peter Lawrence, "The making of a French manager," *Harvard Business Review* (July–August 1991): 58–67.

7. Sandra E. Lamb, "How to write it," *Business and Economic Review* 46, no. 1 (October–December 1999): 14–23.

8. John Leach, "Seven steps to better writing: Advice from a journalist-turned planner," *Planning* 59, no. 6 (June 1993): 26–27.

9. Charles R. McConnell, "Speak up: The manager's guide to oral presentations," *The Health Care Manager* 18, no. 3 (March 2000): 70–77.

10. Clarie Hoffman, "Making a (Power)Point of Not Being Tiresome; Cliff Atkinson turns ordinary slides into a more engaging tool using a three-act storytelling structure," *Los Angeles Times*, BUSINESS; Business Desk; Part C; (April 19, 2006): 1.

11. Dona Z. Meilach, *Dynamics of Presentation Graphics* (Homewood, IL: Dow Jones-Irwin, 1986).

12. Marguerite Foxon, "I know you can't see this but . . ." *Training* 29, no. 11 (November 1992): 47–50.

13. Judy Strauss, and Raymond Frost, *E-Marketing* (Upper Saddle River, NJ: Prentice Hall, 2001).

Glossary

acquiescence bias The tendency of survey or focus group respondents to agree with statements presented to them rather than disagree.

alternative hypothesis An assertion believed to be true if the null hypothesis is false.

alternative-forms reliability Ability of two equivalent scales (scales that respondents perceive to be different but that measure the same content) to obtain consistent results.

analysis of variance (ANOVA) A technique for testing whether there is a significant difference among the means of two or more independent samples.

applied research Research undertaken to provide information about specific problems to help managers improve their decision making.

area sample A cluster sample in which the clusters, or groups, are made up of geographic areas.

arithmetic mean The sum of values divided by the number of values.

array Data arranged in ascending or descending order of magnitude.

attitude A learned tendency to respond in a consistently favorable or unfavorable manner toward something.

audit A method in which information is gathered by examining pertinent records or inventorying items under investigation.

average A single value that is typical or representative of a group of numbers.

back translation The process that occurs when information is translated from one language to another, after which a second person translates it back into the original language.

balanced scale A scale with the same number of favorable and unfavorable choices.

Basic research Research undertaken to provide information about a phenomenon or to test a theory or hypothesis; it is not intended to solve a specific marketing problem.

biased estimator of the parameter A statistic with an expected value not equal to the value of the parameter.

bibliographic databases Collections of complete citation information from published sources, such as marketing research studies, newspaper articles, magazine articles, journal articles, government reports, store audit reports, dissertations, and books.

bivariate data Two related variables.

business ethics Moral principles and standards that guide behavior in business.

cartoon technique A projective technique similar to third-person projection in which cartoon characters are the third party. Characters are shown in a particular situation, and respondents are asked to describe what the characters are doing and explain the situation depicted.

causal research Research that provides evidence that a cause-and-effect relationship exists or does not exist.

cell frequencies The frequencies in contingency table cells.

census A population sampled in its entirety.

centroid The group mean created by averaging the discriminant scores for all the individuals within a certain group.

chi-square distribution A frequency distribution used to test how well a set of observed sample frequencies corresponds to or "fits" a set of expected or theoretical frequencies.

chi-square goodness-of-fit test A test used to determine whether a set of theoretical or expected frequencies fit a corresponding set of observed sample frequencies.

chi-square statistic A sample statistic used to measure the degree of association among nominally scaled variables.

classification matrix A matrix that contains the number of properly and improperly classified cases.

closed-ended questions Questions that provide response choices from which respondents are expected to choose.

cluster analysis A statistical technique in which groups are formed in such a way that elements in the same group are similar to each other, and elements in different groups are as different as possible.

cluster sampling A sampling technique in which the target population is divided into mutually exclusive groups, or clusters, and then a random sample of clusters (subgroups) of sampling units is chosen.

codebook A book that contains the instructions for the individuals who code survey data.

coding The process of systematically and consistently assigning each survey response a numbered score or code.

coefficient alpha A technique for judging internal consistency of a measurement instrument by averaging all possible ways of splitting test items and examining their degree of correlation; the greater the correlation is to a score of 1, the higher the internal consistency.

coefficient of determination (r^2) The strength of association or degree of closeness of the relationship between two variables measured by a relative value.

coefficient of multiple determination The coefficient that indicates the association between the dependent and independent variables.

coefficient of skewness (S_k) The quotient that results when the difference between the mean and the mode is multiplied by three and then is divided by the standard deviation.

coefficient of variation (V) The most commonly used measure of dispersion expressed in a relative value. It is the standard deviation divided by the arithmetic mean.

comparative rating scale A scale on which respondents compare one characteristic or attribute against a specified standard, according to some predetermined criterion.

computer editing Editing performed by a computer.

computer-assisted personal interview (CAPI) A personal interview in which the interviewer inputs responses directly into a computer terminal during the interview.

computer-assisted self-interview (CASI) An interview in which a researcher locates potential respondents and leads them to nearby computer terminals, where the respondents read and respond to questions directly on the computer.

computer-assisted telephone interview (CATI) A telephone interview in which the questions are displayed in front of the interviewer on the computer screen and the interviewer inputs responses into the computer during the interview.

conclusive research Research that provides specific information that aids the decision maker in evaluating different courses of action.

concomitant variation Extent to which the cause (independent variable) and effect (dependent variable) vary together as hypothesized.

confidence interval A range of values that we are confident—but not certain—contains the population parameter.

confidence level The chance or probability that a confidence interval includes the population parameter.

confidence limits The two values that specify the ranges of a confidence interval.

conjoint analysis A statistical technique that provides information about the relative importance respondents place on individual attributes when choosing from multiple products or brands.

constant-sum scale A scale on which respondents allocate a predetermined number of rating points among several items, according to a predetermined criterion, to indicate relative preference or importance of each item compared to all others.

content analysis A research technique in which the content of a communication vehicle is examined to determine whether a study inference is valid.

content or face validity The ability of test scale items to measure the topic of interest, as judged subjectively by professionals or experts on the topic.

contingency (or cross-tabulation) table A table in which row entries classify data according to one variable and column entries classify the data according to another variable.

control group A group that has no treatments imposed on it so that it can be used for comparison against the experimental group.

controlled test marketing A test-marketing method in which the company hires an outside research firm to conduct the study.

convenience sampling A type of nonprobability sampling in which sample elements are chosen primarily because of their convenience to the researcher.

copyright A right granted by statute to the authors or originators of literary works, artistic productions, and computer programs.

correlation analysis A statistical technique that measures the closeness of the relationship between two metric variables.

correlation and regression analysis Statistics that test if and how variables are related to each other.

correlation coefficient A number that indicates the direction of a relationship and the degree of that relationship; an indication of the correlation between the observed and predicted values of the dependent variable.

Council of American Survey Research Organizations (CASRO) National trade association for commercial research firms in the United States.

criterion variable The dependent variable in tests of associations.

criterion-related validity The ability of a scale to perform as predicted in relation to a specified criterion.

critical values Cutoff limits or values that lie on the edges of the rejection region.

cross-sectional study A sample that looks at what is occurring at one moment in time; can be thought of as a still photograph, since it is a one-time study.

cross-tabulation A process that involves examining the responses to two or more variables simultaneously and informing the researcher how often each response was given.

data mart A subject-specific data warehouse.

data mining Involves extracting hidden predictive information in large databases through statistical analysis.

data warehouse A repository for an organization's existing and ongoing data; it collects data from multiple sources and stores it in a way that allows end users to have fast, easy, and flexible access to important information.

data warehousing A system that involves the entire information delivery process—from access and transformation of data from different operational stores, through the organization process that makes it available for decision making, to surfacing the data for exploitation via a range of decision support tools.

database A large collection of related data, organized for rapid search and retrieval.

database marketing The process of gathering relevant information about potential and existing customers to learn about their needs and to use this information to provide the right product, at the right price, at the right time.

debriefing An interview conducted after respondents have completed a questionnaire, in which they are informed that the exercise was a pretest and are asked to share with the researcher their thoughts about the questions, their answers, and any shortcomings of the survey.

decision rule A formal statement of the conditions under which the null hypothesis may be rejected, given the sample results.

decision-making process A series of steps that leads to a final judgment.

decision-support system (DSS) Any system that supports the decision-making process; it is an interactive, user-controlled information system that helps managers predict the results of various alternatives before making a decision.

degrees of freedom The number of observations in a statistical problem that can vary freely under certain conditions; in general, it is calculated as $(n - k)$, where n is the total number of observations and k is the number of parameters or constraints needed to calculate a sample statistic or test statistic.

Delphi technique A technique that uses a group of experts to determine the appropriate content of the survey. Group members first make concealed individual judgments. Then they are exposed to other members' judgments and can revise their judgments if they wish. After multiple iterations of revising judgments, the group reaches a conclusion.

dependent data mart A data mart that receives its data from a data warehouse.

dependent variable Variable to be affected or predicted through marketing research.

depth interviews Unstructured, one-on-one conversations between a highly skilled interviewer and a member of a target population.

descriptive analysis Statistics used by researchers to summarize sample data.

descriptive research Research that describes attitudes, perceptions, characteristics, activities, and situations.

dichotomous questions Closed-ended questions that provide two response choices.

difference analysis Statistics assessing whether two groups or market segments are truly different from each other.

difference tests Tests that compare some characteristic of one group with a characteristic of another and determine whether or not a statistically significant difference exists between the two groups.

direct observation A data-collection method in which researchers watch a behavior as it occurs and report what they see.

directory databases Directories and indexes that offer information on people, organizations, and services.

discriminant function The linear combination of the independent variables created by discriminant analysis to discriminate between the categories of the dependent variable.

disguised observation The same as unobtrusive observation; it exists when subjects do not realize they are being observed.

door-to-door interview A personal interview that takes place at respondents' homes.

double-barreled questions A single question that asks for two responses.

editing Carefully checking survey data for completeness, legibility, consistency, and accuracy.

electronic test marketing A method that uses scanner-based systems in supermarkets and highly sophisticated broadcasting systems to examine the relationship between what consumers purchase and different advertising messages they watch on television.

electronic white pages (EWP) A telephone dialing system that permits a researcher to draw a random sample from the directory listing in the white pages of the telephone book, which is available on compact disk.

estimator A statistic used for estimating a parameter.

ethics The study of the general nature of morals and of specific moral choices; the rules or standards governing the conduct of the members of a profession.

ethnographic research A research method that involves observation techniques, depth interviewing, and using videotape to record people in their natural settings.

European Society for Opinion and Marketing Research (ESOMAR) International trade association based in Europe and composed of more than 4,000 individual members.

experiment A research process designed to determine what factors influence a particular behavior, and the extent and direction of the influence.

experimental design A plan for running an experiment, in which the researcher has control over and will manipulate at least one independent variable.

experimental group A group of respondents that is exposed to the experimental treatment.

experimental research Research in which the researcher controls and manipulates elements of the research environment to measure the impact of each variable and to test a hypothesis.

exploratory research Research that identifies problems, generates hypotheses, and gains insights into particular subjects.

external data Information obtained from outside the organization for which the research is conducted.

external validity The degree to which the results of an experiment can be generalized beyond the experimental situation to other populations.

extraneous variables Variables other than the manipulated independent variable that affect the study and hence confound its results.

factor analysis A statistical technique used to examine interrelationships among many variables and to explain these variables in terms of their common underlying and unobservable dimensions (called "factors").

factors The independent variables whenever ANOVA is used.

field editing Editing of personal-interview, mall-intercept, and telephone surveys as the data collection takes place.

field setting A real-world or natural setting where numerous uncontrollable variables may exist.

field studies Studies performed in select "real-world" locations.

finite population A limited or fixed number of individuals or objects in a population.

focus group A qualitative research technique in which a skilled moderator leads a small group of participants in an unstructured discussion about a topic.

frequency The number of times a value is repeated.

frequency array An array of values in which repeated values are shown.

frequency distribution A chart showing values grouped into several classes based on quantity that indicates the frequency of the values within each class; a breakdown of all groups in designated categories.

F-statistic A measure of the variance between groups divided by the variance within groups, calculated by dividing one sample variance by another sample variance.

full-text databases Databases that contain the entire text of the source documents.

fully automated telephone interview (FATI) An interview in which an automated voice asks questions over the telephone and respondents enter their replies using keys on their touch-tone telephones.

funny-faces scale An ordinal scale in which the choices are smiling and frowning faces ranging from wide smiles to deep frowns.

graphic rating scale A scale in which respondents indicate their responses to questions on a continuum with two extreme points.

halo effect An overall evaluation of an object biases a respondent's answers on its specifics.

history External incidents that occur between the beginning and end of an experiment that are beyond the researcher's control but may influence results.

hit ratio The percentage of properly classified cases in the classification matrix.

human observation Observation performed by an individual designated to observe behavior.

hypothesis An assumption made about a population characteristic.

independent data mart A data mart that gets its data directly from transaction systems that don't rely on other data warehouses.

independent variable Variable believed to cause or explain variations in the dependent variable.

indirect observation Observation made by researchers who observe the results of a behavior rather than the behavior itself.

inferential analysis Statistics that permit researchers to draw inferences from sample data.

infinite population An unlimited or non-fixed number of individuals or objects in a population.

information system a system that collects, processes, stores, analyzes, and disseminates information for a specific purpose.

information-processing error An error caused by mistakes in coding or inputting data into a computer for analysis.

infringement When a copyrighted work is used without the appropriate permission.

input Raw data captured from inside or outside the organization.

instrumentation effect What occurs when the outcome of an experiment is influenced by a change of any of the following: how questions are asked, who asks the questions, problems with the surveys, and other procedures used to assess the dependent variable.

intentional interviewer bias Bias caused by interviewers providing additional information purposely to influence respondents.

interaction effect The extent to which the combination or interaction of independent variables influences the dependent variable.

internal data Information obtained from within the organization for which the research is conducted.

internal validity The degree to which an experiment can clearly show that the change in the dependent variable is caused by changes in the independent variables rather than by other outside factors.

internal-consistency reliability Assesses reliability by taking two or more measurements of the same theoretical concept at the same time and determining the extent to which the measurements agree.

interval estimate The stated range within which a parameter is expected to lie.

interval scale A scale that ranks characteristics using equal increments between ranking points to show relative amounts and has no fixed zero point.

interviewer error An error that occurs when the interviewer influences responses by supplying additional information, either intentionally or unintentionally.

item nonresponse When a respondent who agrees to participate in a study refuses to respond to certain questions.

itemized rating scale A scale on which respondents answer questions by selecting from a finite number of choices.

judgment sampling A type of nonprobabilistic sampling in which the sample items are selected by using a researcher's personal judgment.

Kruskal-Wallis test Rank-sum test that analyzes ordinal data by determining whether two or more independent samples are drawn from identical populations or from two or more populations with the same median; also called the H test.

kurtosis The relative peakedness or flatness of the curve according to the frequency distribution.

laboratory An artificial setting where researchers can run experiments and have considerable control over the research environment.

laboratory studies Studies performed in a highly controlled environment.

leading questions A question that influences respondents toward a particular answer.

least-squares method A statistical technique that fits a straight line to a scatter diagram by finding the smallest sum of the vertical distances squared of all the points from the straight line.

leptokurtic curve A sharp, high-peaked curve according to the frequency distribution.

level of significance The maximum probability of making a Type I error specified in a hypothesis test.

Levene's test for equality of variances A test used to examine whether the spread of two groups differ.

licensing Obtaining permission to use creative material by getting consent from a copyright owner.

Likert scale An itemized rating scale on which respondents select from choices ranging from "strongly agree" to "strongly disagree" to indicate their attitudes toward the statements presented to them.

longitudinal study A sample in which the same respondents are questioned or observed during predetermined time intervals over a span of time; can be thought of as a videotape of a market, since information is accumulated from a series of pictures taken at different time periods.

mail panel A consistent set of respondents who are questioned from time to time about marketing-related issues.

main effect The impact that each independent variable has on the dependent variable.

mall-intercept ("man-on-the-street") interview A personal interview that takes place at a shopping mall or similar shopping location.

Mann-Whitney test Rank-sum test that analyzes ordinal data by determining whether exactly two independent samples are drawn from identical populations or from two populations with the same median; also called the U test.

marginal frequency The total of the frequencies in each row or each column of a contingency table.

marketing The process of planning and executing the conception, pricing, promotion, and distribution of ideas, goods, and services to create exchanges that satisfy individual and organizational objectives.

Marketing concept Management philosophy in which the wants and needs of target markets are determined before the product is created.

marketing information system (MkIS) A system that facilitates information collection, storage, manipulation, and dissemination in marketing, including customer service and contacts.

Marketing management The analysis, planning, implementation, and control of programs designed to create, build, and maintain beneficial exchanges with target buyers for the purpose of achieving organizational objectives.

Marketing research Systematic and objective planning, gathering, recording, and analyzing of information to enhance the decision making of marketing managers.

maturation Changes in test subjects that occur during an experiment that are unrelated to the experiment but may influence the results.

mean An average calculated as the sum of the values in a data set divided by the number of values in the set; one measure of central tendency.

mean square error (MSE) An estimate of the random error existing in the data.

measurement Assigning numbers to characteristics according to specified rules to reflect the quantity of the characteristics that test products possess.

measurement error The difference between the information sought and the information obtained through the research process.

measurement instrument error An error that results when the questionnaire or survey questions bias respondents or make it difficult for the researcher to clearly understand intended responses.

measures of central tendency Measures indicating the central tendency of a variable. The most common types are the arithmetic mean, the median, and the mode.

mechanical observation Studies that use mechanical devices, such as scanners or television meters, to record observations.

median The value of the middle number in an array; one measure of central tendency.

mode The value that occurs most frequently in a set of numbers; one measure of central tendency.

moderator A skilled focus group leader.

mortality effect The effect on experimental results of the loss of test subjects while the experiment is taking place. Significant differences between subjects that leave and those that stay can bias results.

multidimensional scaling The technique used to identify important dimensions underlying respondents' evaluations of test objects by representing these evaluations as distances in multidimensional space; also referred to as "perceptual mapping."

multiple discriminant analysis (MDA) A statistical technique for predicting the membership of observations in two or more groups; used if the dependent variable is categorical and the independent variables are either interval or ratio data.

multiple-choice questions Closed-ended questions that provide more than two response choices.

multivariate analysis Statistics that refers to any simultaneous analysis of more than two variables.

multivariate statistics Any simultaneous analysis of more than two variables.

nominal scale A scale that uses names or numbers to label test topics or characteristics for identification, with no rank ordering implied.

noncomparative rating scale A scale on which respondents compare one characteristic or attribute against a standard of their own choosing, according to some predetermined criterion.

nonparametric methods Distribution-free methods, used when the required assumptions about the shape of population distribution cannot be made, and used when nominal- or ordinal-scaled data must be analyzed.

nonprobability sample Any subset of a population in which the probability of obtaining the sample cannot be computed.

nonprobability sampling A sampling method where sample selection is judgmental, and the probability of being chosen is unknown.

nonresponse error An error that occurs when a high percentage of respondents do not participate in a study, and the nonrespondents differ significantly from the respondents on the topic under study.

normal curve A symmetrical, bell-shaped curve that has almost all of its values within ±3 standard deviations from its mean.

normal distribution A frequency distribution represented graphically by a bell-shaped curve that is symmetrical about the mean.

North American Industry Classification System (NAICS) A six-digit code used to perform industry searches; improves on the Standard Industrial Classification (SIC) code by using a production-based framework.

null hypothesis A hypothesis to be tested for possible acceptance or rejection.

numeric databases Databases that contain numeric and statistical information from original surveys.

observation Data-collection methods in which researchers watch test subjects without interacting with them.

obtrusive observation Observation research in which the subjects realize they are being observed.

office editing Editing performed at a central location by an office staff after all data collection is finished.

office interview A personal interview that takes place at the respondent's place of business.

offline databases Collections of information that are electronically stored and managed but are not accessible from the Internet.

omnibus survey Regularly scheduled face-to-face interviews with a consistent set of respondents, using questions from multiple clients.

one-tailed test A test in which the alternative hypothesis is expressed in one direction; the rejection region is in one tail of the distribution.

one-time mail survey Mail surveys sent to respondents only once because the research issue doesn't require continuous information gathering.

one-way analysis of variance A technique for comparing the means of more than two samples or populations when there is only one independent variable.

online databases Collections of information, stored and managed electronically, that can be searched using the Internet.

online survey A survey placed directly on a website; respondents are invited to complete the entire form online.

open-ended questions Questions that do not supply response choices, that respondents can answer any way they want.

optical scanning device A data processing machine that can electronically read survey answers that are in a prescribed form, such as numbers, codes, or words, and store the data.

ordinal scale A scale with an implicit rank ordering, such as greater or smaller, higher or lower.

output Processed data that is transferred to the people who need it.

paired comparison scale A scale that asks respondents to select their preferences from among sets of two items, according to a predetermined criterion.

pantry audit An inventory of items in an individual's household.

parameter A numerical measure used to describe some characteristic of a population.

parametric tests Hypothesis tests that assume that variables under investigation are measured using either interval or ratio scales.

partial regression coefficient A coefficient that shows the change in the computed dependent variable per unit change in one independent variable when all other independent variables are held constant.

part-worth function The function that describes the utility respondents give to the levels of each attribute when using conjoint analysis.

personal editing Editing performed by a person.

personal interview Data collection through face-to-face communication between an interviewer and a respondent.

physical-trace analysis A research technique that examines evidence or "traces" of individuals that were left behind to understand their past behaviors.

picture interpretation A projective technique depicting abstract visual stimuli to help respondents describe thoughts and feelings that would not emerge otherwise.

plagiarism Using someone's work without giving credit or without obtaining permission when it is necessary.

platykurtic curve A nonpeaked, relatively flat curve according to the frequency distribution.

point estimate A single number used to represent the estimate of a parameter.

population The entire group of people, markets, companies, or products that is being investigated by a researcher.

population definition error An error resulting from faulty definition of the population to be sampled.

power of a hypothesis test The probability of rejecting a null hypothesis that should be rejected; it indicates the extent a test is performing well and is calculated as $1 - \beta$, where a high value indicates the test is working well.

predictor variable The independent variable in tests of associations.

pre-experimental designs Experimental designs that do not randomly assign test units to experimental and control groups.

pretesting A trial run of a questionnaire using a small sample from the target population to detect problems with the questionnaire.

primary data Original (new) data gathered to satisfy the purpose of the current study.

probability sample Subset of a population in which the probability of obtaining the sample can be computed and that is non-zero for every sampling unit in the population.

probability sampling A sampling method where every member of the target population has a known and nonzero chance of being included in the sample.

problem definition A statement of the specific decision problems for the marketing research project.

procedure error An error that occurs when sample subjects are improperly selected, resulting in a nonrepresentative sample.

processing The transformation of raw data into usable form.

projective techniques Research techniques that use verbal or visual stimuli to reveal respondents' unconscious feelings and attitudes.

protocol analysis An interviewing technique in which respondents think aloud while responding to each question.

Q-sort scale A scale on which respondents rank a group of items into sets, according to some criterion.

qualitative data Information gathered from a small sample of the target population that is used to understand a group's feelings and insights but cannot predict with absolute certainty and is not projectable to the target population.

qualitative group discussion The type of discussion used to describe exploratory, open, non-directive groups leading to understanding.

qualitative research Research that is exploratory in nature and involves a small sample with aims to provide insights and understanding of the question being researched.

quantitative data Information gathered from many members of the target population that can be quantified and projected to represent the entire target population.

quantitative research Research that is conclusive in nature and uses mathematical measures and statistical techniques to determine relationships and differences among large samples of target populations.

quasi-experimental designs Experimental designs in which the researcher controls the *when* and *to whom* aspects of data collection but does not totally control the scheduling of treatments and cannot subject test units to treatments randomly.

questionnaire A formal set of questions or statements designed to gather information from respondents that will accomplish the goals of the research project.

quota sampling A type of nonprobability sampling that involves determining the proportion of the population believed to possess certain characteristics that affect the research subject and choosing for the sample a specific number with these characteristics to reflect their proportion in the population.

random error Error that results from randomly occurring differences in respondents or circumstances.

random-digit dialing (RDD) A telephone dialing system that randomly generates telephone numbers of sample respondents.

range The difference between the lowest and the highest values in a set of numbers.

rank-order scale A scale on which respondents rank items, according to a predetermined criterion.

rank-sum tests Tests that use some sort of ranking totals in their calculations.

ratio scale An interval scale that has a true zero point and assumes equal intervals throughout.

raw data Collected data that have not been organized numerically.

regression analysis Statistical techniques that measure the linear or curvilinear relationship between a dependent variable and one or more independent variables.

regression coefficients The values that represent the effect of the individual independent variables on the dependent variable.

regression line A line drawn through a scatter diagram that "best fits" the data points and most accurately describes the relationship between the two variables.

regression toward the mean The tendency of participant responses to migrate (or regress) toward the average score as the experiment progresses.

reliability The ability of a scale to produce consistent results if repeated measurements are taken; the extent to which scales are free of random error and thus produce consistent results.

research Systematic and objective investigation of a subject or problem to discover relevant information or principles.

research design Framework that directs the marketing research efforts.

research objectives A statement of what information is needed to solve the decision problems.

response error An error that occurs when respondents answer particular questions incorrectly, either intentionally or unintentionally.

role-playing A projective technique in which participants play the role of someone else in a particular scenario; this allows participants to reveal their feelings in a less personal way.

sample A subset of representative units from the population.

sample Individuals or objects from a target population that are selected to represent the population of interest.

sample frame bias The difference between the sampling frame and the actual population.

sample selection error An error that occurs when the selected sample is not representative of the population.

sampling error The difference between the result obtained from a sample and the result that would have been obtained from the population.

sampling frame The actual list of each element of the target population from which a sample is drawn.

scale A measuring instrument designed to quantify and record the extent to which test products possess a characteristic.

scatter diagram When two related variables are plotted as points on a graph.

secondary data Data previously collected for a purpose other than the current study.

selection effect The bias that results when the experimental group differs significantly from the target population or from the control group.

semantic differential scale A five- or seven-point itemized ordinal scale with dichotomous pairs of descriptive words or phrases representing the two extremes and a neutral midpoint.

sentence completion A projective technique in which respondents complete a series of incomplete sentences.

simple random sampling A sampling technique in which each element of the population or each possible sample of the same size from the population has an equal chance of being selected.

simple tabulation A process that involves tabulating the results of only one variable, which informs the researcher how often each response was given.

simulated test marketing Test marketing done in a laboratory by exposing prospective customers to new products, competitive products, and marketing stimuli, and giving them money to make purchase decisions.

skewness The direction of an asymmetrical distribution, either leaning toward higher values or lower values.

snowball sampling A type of nonprobabilistic sampling in which respondents provide names of additional respondents to include in a sample; used when additional respondents are difficult to locate because they are a small part of the population.

social responsibility Business's obligation to maximize positive effects and minimize negative effects of its operations on society.

split-half technique A method of judging internal consistency of a measurement instrument by randomly splitting the total test items into two equal groups and examining their degree of correlation; the greater the correlation, the higher the internal consistency.

standard deviation Square root of the arithmetic mean of the individual deviations squared; the most common measure of dispersion.

standard deviation of regression The standard deviation of the Y values from the regression line; the standard error of estimate.

standard error of the mean The standard deviation of the means of all possible samples of the same size drawn from a population.

standard error of the proportion The standard deviation of the proportions of all possible samples of the same size drawn from a population.

standard error of the statistic The standard deviation of a sampling distribution of a statistic.

standard test marketing A test marketing method in which the company uses its normal distribution channels to distribute a product to a small segment of the market.

Stapel scale A scale that resembles a semantic differential scale but uses an even number of positive and negative points, usually +3 and −3, with a single descriptive word or phrase positioned in the middle of the ordinal scale to indicate the direction and intensity of attitudes.

statistic A measure used to describe some characteristic of a sample, such as an arithmetic mean, median, or standard deviation.

statistical experimental designs Experimental designs that are conducted simultaneously and allow the researcher to measure the effects of multiple independent variables.

statistical significance Differences in findings that cannot be caused by chance or sampling error alone.

strata Subgroups formed based on the criteria that (1) elements within strata must be homogeneous, and (2) elements between strata must be heterogeneous.

stratified sampling A sampling technique in which the researcher first divides the population into natural subgroups that are more homogeneous than the population as a whole.

Then items are selected for the sample at random or by a systematic method from each subgroup.

structured interviews Interviews that follow checklists to cover narrowly focused topics.

structured observation Observation research in which observers record only certain well-defined behaviors, typically on a checklist or standardized form.

survey research Research that obtains information through a structured questionnaire from a large, usually representative sample. It describes the characteristics, attitudes, and/or behaviors of the target population and intends to identify their relationships.

systematic error (or constant error) An error caused by a constant bias in the design or implementation of the measurement instrument.

systematic random-digit dialing (SRDD) A telephone dialing system that allows the researcher to specify particular geographic regions or area codes from which to randomly contact individuals.

systematic sampling A sampling technique in which a sample is drawn by arbitrarily choosing a beginning point in a list and then sequentially selecting every *i*th element from the list.

tabulation A process that involves arranging the data in a table format that is easy for the researcher to read.

***t*-distribution** A bell-shaped and symmetric distribution that is used for testing small sample sizes (*n* less than or equal to 30).

telephone survey A form of data collection in which the researcher communicates by telephone with respondents either directly, by voice, or indirectly, by fax, voice mail, or computer assistance.

test marketing Testing market acceptance of a new or altered existing product on a small scale before investing in a full-scale product launch.

test statistic A statistic, calculated from the sample data, whose sampling distribution is used to test the hypothesis.

testing effect The effect that occurs depending on the extent an initial test sensitizes respondents to the process of experimentation, causing respondents to react differently to a second test than they would if no initial test had been conducted.

test-retest reliability The ability of the same scale to produce consistent results when used more than once under similar conditions.

thematic apperception test (TAT) A picture interpretation technique that has respondents describe what is going on in pictures and predict what will happen as a result of the situation.

third-person technique A projective technique in which respondents answer questions for a third person, such as a neighbor or an acquaintance, instead of for themselves.

total error Difference between the true information being sought and the information collected for the study.

treatment Different levels of a factor.

treatment variable An independent or manipulated variable in an experiment.

true experimental designs Experimental designs that randomly assign test units to experimental and control groups.

***t*-test** The test that occurs when a *t*-distribution is used to test a hypothesis about a sample mean when the standard deviation is unknown and the sample size is considered small, usually less than or equal to 30.

two-tailed test A test in which the alternative hypothesis is not expressed in one direction; it shows a population parameter is either larger or smaller than a specified value; the rejection region is in both tails of the distribution.

type I error (α) Rejection of a null hypothesis that is true; probability is represented as alpha (α).

type II error (β) Acceptance of (or failure to reject) a null hypothesis that is false; probability is represented as beta (β).

unbalanced scale A scale with an uneven number of favorable and unfavorable choices and thus skewed in one direction.

unbiased estimator of the parameter A statistic with an expected value equal to the value of the parameter.

undisguised observation The same as obtrusive observation; observation that exists when subjects realize they are being observed.

unintentional bias Bias caused by interviewers providing additional information related to survey questions without realizing they are influencing respondents.

unobtrusive observation Observation research in which the subjects do not realize they are being observed.

unstructured interviews Interviews in which the subjects discussed are free-floating from one issue to the next.

unstructured observation Observation research in which the observers judge whether or not observed behaviors are important enough to record.

utility The number that represents the value consumers place on an attribute when using conjoint analysis.

validity The degree to which a test measures what it is supposed to measure.

variance The standard deviation squared; a measure of dispersion.

Wilcoxon test Rank-sum test that analyzes ordinal data for differences between two related samples by using plus and minus signs and considers the magnitudes of the differences and ranks of the differences between the paired values.

word association A projective technique in which respondents are given a word and they respond with the first word that comes to mind.

***z*-test** When a *z*-distribution is used to test a hypothesis when the sample is large and the population standard deviation is known.

Index